THORNTON WILDER

A Life

PENELOPE NIVEN

WITH A FOREWORD BY EDWARD ALBEE

HARPER ● PERENNIAL

NEW YORK ● LONDON ● TORONTO ● SYDNEY ● NEW DELHI ● AUCKLAND

HARPER ● PERENNIAL

The author and the publisher gratefully acknowledge the consent of the Wilder Family LLC, courtesy of The Barbara Hogenson Agency, to print the published and unpublished writings of Thornton Wilder and the Wilder family, as well as the photographs of Thornton Wilder and the Wilder family.
Permissions begin on page 811.

A hardcover edition of this book was published in 2012 by HarperCollins Publishers.

HarperCollins books may be purchased for educational, business, or sales promotional use. For information please e-mail the Special Markets Department at SPsales@harpercollins.com.

FIRST HARPER PERENNIAL EDITION PUBLISHED 2013.

Designed by Fritz Metsch

Library of Congress Cataloging-in-Publication Data has been applied for.

ISBN 978-0-06-083137-0 (pbk.)

13 14 15 16 17   OV/RRD   10 9 8 7 6 5 4 3 2 1

To Jennifer, my daughter,
who shares the journey and lights the way

Art is confession; art is the secret told. . . . But art is not only the desire to tell one's secret; it is the desire to tell it and hide it at the same time. And the secret is nothing more than the whole drama of the inner life.

—THORNTON WILDER,
"On Reading the Great Letter Writers"

"How does one live?" he asked the bright sky. "What does one do first?"

—THORNTON WILDER,
The Woman of Andros

CONTENTS

FOREWORD

Whenever I'm in a theater group and the discussion turns to the essential American playwrights—the ones whose accomplishments define our culture—I'm always startled and confused that Thornton Wilder's name comes to the fore so infrequently.

Eugene O'Neill is there, of course, in spite of his frequent tin ear. *Long Day's Journey into Night* is a great play, perhaps the only one of his in which everything comes together fully—the mind and the ear—in a way the other best ones only occasionally approach.

Tennessee Williams is there, naturally, for the poetry of his language, the intensity of his dramatic structure, and the three-dimensionality of his characterizations.

Arthur Miller is included as well, as much as anything for the sociological and political importance of his dramatic concerns.

But why is Thornton Wilder so infrequently placed up there where he belongs?

If I were asked to name what I consider to be the finest serious American play, I would immediately say *Our Town*—not for its giant Americanness but because it is a superbly written, gloriously observed, tough, and breathtaking statement of what it is to be alive, the wonder and hopeless loss of the space between birth and the grave.

While I prefer *The Skin of Our Teeth*—another first-rate play—to most of Wilder's novels, he was no slouch there either.

This new biography of Wilder, comprehensive and wisely fashioned, gives us sufficient view of his methods, his public and private life, and the reaches of his mind to begin to understand with what intellectual and creative sourcings he was able to write so persuasively about things that greatly matter.

This book is a splendid and long-needed work.

A side note: I was a twenty-two-year-old very mediocre poet when I met Thornton Wilder at the MacDowell Colony. I forced my poetry on him. He read it and took me to a small lake where he plied me with bourbon and told me to stop writing poetry, that it was no good. He suggested perhaps I start writing plays instead.

I wonder if he knew that one day I'd write forewords as well.

Edward Albee
New York City, 2011

"THE HISTORY OF A WRITER"

The history of a writer is his search for his own subject, his myth-theme,
hidden from him, but prepared for him in every hour of his life, his
Gulliver's Travels, *his* Robinson Crusoe.

—THORNTON WILDER,
"James Joyce, 1882–1941"

When he was in his seventies, Thornton Niven Wilder wrote a story about an American teenager running alone through the countryside near the school in Chefoo, China, where he had been sent to live and study. The boy had sought special permission to run long distances by himself outside the China Inland Mission School boundaries, near the Bohai Sea. Awkward at the competitive team sports the other boys enjoyed, he was an outsider, a misfit in a crowd. He was most at home in books and his imagination, and these solitary runs freed him to think and to daydream.

This unfinished, unpublished self-portrait was a fusion of memory and imagination, fiction and fact. "Already at that age I had the notion I would be a writer," Wilder reflected many years later, after he had written books and plays that resonated for countless people in the United States and around the world.[1]

His history as a writer spans three-quarters of the twentieth century, and he left behind a tantalizing trail of evidence—thousands of letters, journal entries, manuscript drafts, and documents that reveal his evolution as a person and an artist. "Art is confession; art is the secret told . . . ," he said when he was thirty-one and suddenly famous around the world as a novelist. "But art is not only the desire to tell one's secret; it is the desire to tell it and hide it at the same time. And the secret is nothing more than the whole drama of the inner life."[2] It is challenging enough for a biographer to attempt to do justice to the visible, exterior life—but where to turn for revelation of the "whole drama of the inner life"?

Because of the magnitude of his surviving papers—from childhood until his death in 1975—we can witness close-up Wilder's search for his own subject, his own myth-theme, his own true self. He left a richly detailed record of his lifelong education, much of it self-propelled. He left revealing portraits of his pivotal friendships and of his extraordinary family. This biography concentrates on his history as a writer and the drama of his inner life, but it is also a family saga, starring Thornton Wilder, with strong supporting roles played by his father, mother, and siblings.

He was a multifaceted man—son, brother, student, teacher, scholar, novelist, playwright, actor, musician, soldier, man of letters, international public figure. He was also enigmatic, intensely private. A twinless twin, he was schooled in solitude, accustomed from boyhood to living in self-doubt and shadows. He belonged to a close-knit, complicated family—two brilliant parents, five gifted children, and, for him, the specter of the twin brother lost at birth. From the year when he was nine until he was twenty-two, his family lived scattered around the globe, bound together by letters. Providentially most of those letters were saved after making the rounds from one parent or child on one continent to another parent or child oceans away.

The compelling evidence of Wilder's life, public and private, is contained in thousands of his papers housed in the Yale Collection of American Literature at the Beinecke Rare Book and Manuscript Library at Yale University, as well as in countless other papers and documents released or discovered in the years since his death. His sister Isabel, the keeper of the flame, died in 1995 at the age of ninety-five. Until the end of her life she was working on her own book about her brother and their family, and so had withheld crucial papers, records, and photographs—enough to fill nearly ninety banker's boxes. After her death, these resources went to the Beinecke Library as well. This uncataloged trove includes artifacts that ignite the imagination—the mother's fading album of memories and dreams, kept when she was a teenager; the father's worn brown leather diaries written in China; the family's passports stamped with ports of call around the world; and their intimate letters and papers.

When Tappan Wilder became the manager of his uncle's literary estate, he opened additional resources to Wilder scholars and students, and on his watch many more papers have been discovered, released, and collected. There are papers and documents enough to keep a throng of biographers, scholars, and critics busy for at least the next few decades. This biography, the first to emerge from that vast archive, narrates Wilder's life, private and public, and provides the history and context of his creative work, published and unpublished. This is *not*, however, a volume of literary criticism. The exhaustive documentation in the endnotes is a guide for readers, and may also be a compass for future students, scholars, and critics.

Just as Wilder took liberties with form and style in drama and fiction, he played with the mechanics of writing, especially punctuation. His letters and manuscripts were often animated with bold underscores in ink or colored pencil; with paragraph symbols; and with the equal sign—more emphatic, he thought, than the ordinary colon. But because Wilder the writer was far more attentive to substance than to mechanics, and because he could be cavalier about spelling and punctuation, occasional silent corrections have been made. Otherwise, you will encounter Wilder's words on the page exctly as he put them there. Thanks to the profusion of his letters and journals, and the generosity of his literary executor, much of Wilder's story is told here in his own voice.

In addition to the voluminous record of his later life—the celebrity years—extraordinary records document the first four decades of Wilder's life and work, the years that are the foundation for all that follows. I have examined those pivotal years with a virtual microscope. I have put a telescope to the nearly four decades that come afterward, a period of flourishing art and life illuminated by the seminal years.

Among Wilder's unpublished papers are handwritten reflections on biography, and I have taken them to heart. He wrote, "To BIOGRAPHIZE = means TO WRITE A LIFE = . . . TO BIOGRAPHIZE IN THE HIGHEST SENSE OF THE WORD: TO REVIVIFY. . . ." He went on to say,

> The most intimate feeling of living
> is the perpetual alternation
> of hope and dejection
> of Plans and Defeat
> of Aspiration and Rebuff.[3]

How to revivify such a life? How to understand the "hope and dejection," the "Aspiration and Rebuff"? Much of the drama took place in Wilder's mind and spirit—"the inward life," he called it. Fortunately he left deeply private revelations of that life in his journals, letters, and manuscripts. Other facets of his life are embedded in his published novels and plays. All told, he left behind countless "signposts, footprints, clues" that can lead us deep within his extraordinary mind and spirit.[4]

He was a refined gypsy, wandering the world, writing, he said, for and about "Everybody"—a fact his audiences around the globe have embraced. Within the circumference of his creative work there stands the person, his private, inward self, sometimes hidden and sometimes revealed in his art and in his papers.

Thornton Wilder became a man, like the boy in China, running alone, transcending the boundaries, searching for his Gulliver, for his Robinson Crusoe, for himself.

"GODLY FOLK"

Maine, Connecticut, New York, and Wisconsin (1862–1906)

Thornton Niven Wilder and his twin brother were delivered into the world prematurely on April 17, 1897, in an apartment at 14 West Gilman Street in Madison, Wisconsin, to Amos Parker Wilder, a loving, domineering father, and Isabella Thornton Niven Wilder, an equally strong, devoted mother.[1] The other Wilder twin was stillborn, leaving his brother Thornton a haunting legacy of loss and incompletion as well as a survivor's instinctive guilt. According to family memory, Amos Parker Wilder had planned to name the lost child Theophilus, after his own Wilder grandfather (a second son), and other ancestors given that name. Thornton was a frail infant, carried carefully on a small pillow for the first months of his life. As he grew older and stronger, the energetic, curious boy played with his brother, Amos Niven Wilder (who was born on September 18, 1895). They were joined on August 28, 1898, by a sister, Charlotte Elizabeth, and then on January 13, 1900, by another sister, Isabel. The youngest sister, Janet Frances, would not come along until June 3, 1910.

"We bring from childhood the passionate expectation that life will be colorful, but life is seldom ever as exciting as it was when we were five and six and seven years old," Thornton Wilder wrote when he was in his thirties.[2] During the early years of his life, he was shaped and molded in Madison, Wisconsin. He described himself as "a bookish, musing, sleep-walking kind of boy" who appreciated his Midwestern beginnings.[3]

The four older Wilder children grew up spending idyllic summers in the village of Maple Bluff on Lake Mendota's northeastern shore on the outskirts of Madison. The Wilders built a modest summer cottage there in 1901. Isabella designed it, and they called it Wilderness.[4] The Winnebago Indians had once staged their summer encampments in the dense woods lining McBride's Point, the beach where the Wilder children played, and an occasional Indian mound or artifact could still be discovered there.[5]

During the long, bitter Wisconsin winters, the children spent quiet days at home in Madison with their mother, who loved poetry, drama, music, and philosophy. Their robust, outspoken father kept a frenetic schedule, editing his newspaper, the *Wisconsin State Journal*, and traveling to make speeches about politics, municipal government, and current events. Amos Parker Wilder was born February 15, 1862, in Calais, Maine, the son of Charlotte Topliff Porter and Amos Lincoln Wilder, a dentist. His paternal grandfather, Theophilus Wilder, ran a grocery store in Milltown, Maine.[6] Amos Parker Wilder, called Parker by his family, described his Wilder relatives as "Baptists,—plain, stern, godly folk." They were descended from the Wilders who came from England's Thames Valley to settle in Hingham, Massachusetts, in about 1636.[7] Parker Wilder's religious heritage was an amalgam of Baptist and Puritan principles, Congregationalist philosophy, and the "Hebrew strain" he said he inherited from his mother's family. His great-grandmother, Betsy Marks Porter, was the daughter of Capt. Nehemiah Marks of Derby, Connecticut, son of a Jewish family who converted to Christianity.[8]

Young Parker Wilder especially revered his grandfather Porter, who lived to be ninety and was "strong, kind, religious, one of the best of men," Parker wrote proudly, noting as well that his grandfather was "a ship owner and lumberman of importance in the St. Croix Valley" on the border of Maine and Canada.[9] The Porter family also held shipping and lumber interests in New Brunswick, Canada. Parker's father worked and saved his money to finance dental school. He practiced dentistry first in Calais, and then in Augusta, where he invested in an oilcloth factory, which became his principal—and prosperous— business until his death at the age of seventy ("Sole Manufacturer of

Wilder's patent 'Drum-Made Floor Oil Cloths,' " his 1888 letterhead proclaimed).[10]

Young Parker Wilder inherited his father's drive and ambition, along with his ancestors' "plain, stern, godly" traits. When he was seven, he pledged himself to a life of total abstinence from alcohol. As a teenager, he learned the skills of telegraphy from Frank A. Munsey (1854–1925), the young man who managed the Western Union office in Augusta, a bustling shipping and publishing center as well as the capital of Maine. Parker Wilder mastered the craft well enough to earn money during his college years as a part-time telegrapher.[11] He made the most of his public school education and a year at Highland Military Academy in Worcester, Massachusetts, and then, largely through his mother's encouragement, went off to Yale in the fall of 1880. He adored his mother, and savored childhood memories of the family's summer vacations at Squirrel Island or Mouse Island, Maine: "We dug clams and caught young mackerel, sometimes from the net of big fishers in the Bay," he remembered. "In the more important years I went to Squirrel or Mouse with my Mother and we had quiet, rich days together. She was a tender, restful, heaven-associating soul, yet all sense and balance."[12]

He described her effusively in an autobiographical sketch he wrote for his own children: "Strong in body, possessed of great sense, having had many advantages in her youth, of a hopeful, serene nature, always able to see a bend in the road ahead, and wont to relate all the ordering of life to prayer, Mother has been and is one of the most normal and best women I have known."[13] Deliberately or not, Amos Parker Wilder implied a contrast between his mother and his wife, who was not always physically strong, or hopeful and serene, or optimistic about "the road ahead," or prayerful, or, for that matter, "normal," in the sense of the conventional, traditional nineteenth-century wife and mother.

Isabella Thornton Niven Wilder was, as much as she possibly could manage to be, her own person. A minister's daughter from Dobbs Ferry, New York, she was refined, cultured, and extraordinarily intelligent. Despite her independent spirit, her father thwarted her hopes of going to college to study medicine, as well as her plans to teach or otherwise establish an independent career.[14] He was proud of his

daughter's brilliance, but he still held firmly to his conventional opinions about a lady's proper place in polite society.[15] She was educated
at the Misses Masters Boarding and Day School for Young Ladies and
Children in Dobbs Ferry. Her father had helped the Misses Masters
lease the Dobbs Ferry residence that housed their school for the first
six years.[16] Not simply a finishing school for young women, the school
offered a strong liberal arts curriculum—literature, history, Latin,
psychology, astronomy, mathematics. Isabella wrote poetry, translated
the poems of others from French and Italian, played the piano skill-
fully, knew and enjoyed the literature of the theater, and competed in
local tennis tournaments.[17]

She was born in February 1873 to Elizabeth Lewis Niven and Dr.
Thornton MacNess Niven, Jr., a highly respected Presbyterian clergyman who was the son of the noted engineer, builder, architect, and
businessman Thornton MacNess Niven of Newburgh, New York.
T. M. Niven, Sr., who had started out as a stonemason, was described
as "a man of wealth, a vigorous writer, and a fine public speaker."[18]
In 1839 he had designed and built a house for his family at 201 Montgomery Street in Newburgh, a sturdy, spacious edifice still in use in
the twenty-first century, along with other buildings he designed, such
as the Newburgh courthouse. In 1841 the navy commissioned him to
supervise a ten-year-long, three-million-dollar project—the construction of its first dry dock. Dry Dock Number One in the Brooklyn Navy
Yard was also the first dry dock to be built in New York. T. M. Niven
arranged for massive blocks of prime granite to be floated down on
barges from Maine to be installed in tiers in what was hailed as "one of
the greatest structural achievements of its day."[19] He went blind in his
eighties, after failed cataract surgery, but the loss of vision did not keep
him from other pursuits, such as composing hymns and poems, including "Meditations of an Old Blind Man on His Eighty-eighth Birthday,"
written on February 3, 1894, the year before he died.

The Niven ancestors had immigrated to the northeastern United
States from Bowmere, a small village on the island of Islay off the west
coast of Scotland, now known for producing uncommonly good Scotch,
and in the New World they became engineers, masons, architects,

merchants, and ministers. Isabella's father, an 1855 graduate of Williams College, prepared for the ministry from 1856 until 1858 at the Newburgh, New York, Theological Seminary of the Associated Reform Church, for which his father had drawn the architectural plans in 1837. When the seminary closed in 1858, his father, who opposed abolition, dispatched him to complete his studies at Union Theological Seminary of Virginia, a Presbyterian school.[20] After graduating from the seminary in the middle of the Civil War, Thornton M. Niven, Jr., was ordained by the West Hanover, Virginia, Presbytery, preached in various churches in Virginia, and served as a chaplain under Gen. Stonewall Jackson.[21] After the Civil War, Niven became pastor of the Greenburgh Presbyterian Church in Dobbs Ferry, New York.

Isabella Thornton Niven was the Nivens' second child. Her older brother, Archibald Campbell Niven, died of tuberculosis in 1891 at the age of twenty, leaving a heartbroken family behind.[22] His letters indicate that he was a patient in 1889 in the famous Adirondack Cottage Sanitarium at Saranac Lake, New York, founded by Edward Livingston Trudeau in 1884—one of the foremost tuberculosis treatment centers in the country.[23] Archie Niven's parents later sent him to Pasadena, California, where the climate was touted as ideal for treating tuberculosis. They hoped in vain that he could recover from what he called his "terrible disease" in a letter written from Pasadena May 15, 1891, shortly before his death.[24] His mother and sister Charlotte were with him when he died.

Isabella's mother, Elizabeth, was much indulged by her husband because she was often ill, most likely with gynecological problems, leaving to Isabella many of the daily duties that usually fall to a minister's wife. Isabella's dynamic younger sister, Charlotte, was freer to go her own way. She was a gifted pianist who hoped to become a concert performer. Instead she would build a globally useful and visible career for herself as an officer of the international Young Women's Christian Association. Dr. Niven needed one of his daughters to stay in the home and help him in his ministry in ways his wife was not always able or willing to do. This seemed to be Isabella's destiny, not only as the older daughter but as the eldest surviving child.

Parker Wilder met Isabella Niven at a vacation house party in Dobbs Ferry, and from the first he was drawn to the lovely young woman— her gentility, her elegant good looks, her accomplishments—and her pedigree.[25] Her father's people had been successful in business and the ministry—but her mother's people had helped to shape history. Not only were Isabella's father and paternal grandfather prominent figures in their own right, but her maternal great-grandfather was Arthur Tappan, a wealthy merchant and a leading abolitionist, who had been elected first president of the American Anti-Slavery Society in 1833 and, after his break with abolitionist William Lloyd Garrison (and the society's decline), was voted first president of the American and Foreign Anti-Slavery Society in 1840. The Tappans had money, and used it for important causes. In 1835 Arthur Tappan began to make significant financial contributions to support the development of fledgling Oberlin College, the first coeducational college in the United States, and the first to have a race-blind admissions policy.[26] His generous patronage of Oberlin was conditional; he specified that "students should be ad- mitted irrespective of color, that entire freedom should be allowed on the anti-slavery question, and that a high order of religious instruction should be given, especially in favor of revivals of religion." He also supported the idea of the coeducation of males and females—an idea, unfortunately, which was not shared by some on the Niven branch of Isabella's family tree.[27] Arthur Tappan's brother, Lewis, had arranged for and helped to finance the defense of the slaves in the *Amistad* slave ship mutiny case, and chose John Quincy Adams to assist in presenting the case successfully to the Supreme Court.[28]

Isabella Niven possessed "rare good looks and personal charm," as well as a fine intellect and a courageous, independent spirit.[29] From 1892 through 1894 she kept a scrapbook recording her interests in her late teens and early twenties. She was a strong student at the Misses Masters School in Dobbs Ferry, earning 90s or above in all eleven of her courses, including first honors in six. After graduation she studied at the Dobbs Ferry University Extension Center, established in 1893, passing her course in the masterpieces of English literature with honors.

In her scrapbook she saved invitations to dances and parties, along with programs of tennis tournaments she played in and concerts she attended—including John Philip Sousa's Grand Concert at the Manhattan Beach Hotel on Coney Island, July 20, 1893. She traveled to Chicago to see the great World's Columbian Exposition of 1893—an enterprise that had, coincidentally, moved journalist Parker Wilder so profoundly that he composed an oration that was published in its entirety—filling a full newspaper page—on April 28, 1893, just before the official opening of the exposition on May 1.[30]

Also tucked between the leaves in Isabella's album were pressed flowers, and evidence of an evolving courtship: An undated news clipping reports that Mr. A. P. Wilder participated in a discussion at the "Splendid Gathering" at the Quill Club's monthly dinner. Another undated clipping, headlined "Patria Club Election: Prominent People Attend the Annual Meeting of the Organization Last Night," noted that the evening's topic was "The Industrial Emancipation of Woman," and that Amos Parker Wilder was elected recording secretary of the club, which was founded on the "cardinal principle" of the "inculcation of patriotic sentiment," and admitted both men and women to membership.[31] Saved also was an invitation to a dinner party in New York, with a note from her hostess: "When I hear from you I will write to Dr. Wilder inviting him."[32]

Several of Isabella's friends were getting married during those years, often with her father officiating and Isabella serving as a bridesmaid. She kept the invitation to the Michigan wedding of family friend William Lyon Phelps to Annabel Hubbard on December 21, 1892. Although there were suitors in her very active social life, none of them captured her attention for long. On their first meeting she found Amos Parker Wilder interesting but was not strongly attracted to him, and declined his wish to exchange letters. At their second meeting a year or so later, however, she changed her mind, and by spring of 1894, Amos Parker Wilder had declared his hopes and intentions to Dr. Niven.

Once they were engaged, Isabella was given to believe by the tall, charismatic Parker Wilder that she was not his first choice of wife. He had been engaged twice before, only to have the women break off the commitment. He was especially haunted by the memory of a young woman named Edith, who had the "same comfortable build and dominating personality" that his beloved mother possessed.[33] Nevertheless the engagement moved forward through letters flying back and forth between Amos on the road and in Madison, Wisconsin, and Isabella in Dobbs Ferry. A wedding was planned for spring of 1895, but Amos Lincoln Wilder fell ill and died of heart trouble at the age of seventy years and six months—"one of the leading men of the city," according to the November 1, 1894, *Daily Kennebec Journal*, a "dentist by profession" but for twenty-four years a "manufacturer of oil cloth." Incorrigibly practical, Parker Wilder suggested to the Nivens that they reschedule the wedding for December, since he had to travel east anyway for his father's funeral. His budget would not permit two long trips away from Madison just months apart, he said, and the marriage date was changed accordingly. Isabella was twenty-one and Amos Parker Wilder was thirty-two when her father presided over their wedding in Dobbs Ferry on December 3, 1894.

Years later, when she was forty-four and her son Amos was twenty-two, Isabella wrote to him about the circumstances of her marriage. Three days before the wedding, she confided, when it was "too late to turn back from it since eight hundred people were invited and my father and mother would have been horrified," Amos Parker told his bride-to-be that he was "a widower at heart, that he had no 'tenderness' left in him from a long seven-years courting that came to nothing."[34]

"Of course I was stunned," Isabella wrote to her son, "but with the courage of youth reviving next day, told myself he would forget all that, etc. But he never did. Never has."[35]

.   ———————

AMOS PARKER WILDER had built quite a résumé in the decade between his graduation from Yale and his marriage. "I matured late and so missed much at New Haven," he wrote later. "I trifled much of my time away."[36] During his college years, he wrote letters to his father that foreshadowed some of the letters his own son would send him from Yale years later—admitting his academic shortcomings, trying to justify the disappointment he knew his father would feel when he did not excel, and accounting penny by penny for every dollar his father gave to support him. Parker did not study as much as he should, he acknowledged, and he found that mathematics in particular came hard. He had written to his father on December 6, 1880, to prepare him for an academic-warning letter that was on its way from Yale. He was in the bottom third of his class, he confessed, and while he knew he should study harder, he defended himself on the grounds that he was not as well prepared as the boys from Andover and Exeter.[37] His academic performance was still disappointing in 1883, the year before he graduated, and he defended himself vigorously in a letter to his father: He was confident that he would pass his courses, and he would have done better had he "not been compelled to do so much telegraphing last term."

If his father would just understand how much money he needed and provide it, he wouldn't have to work so hard to earn money in New Haven. "I think if you would trust me a little more on money matters and let me exercise what little judgement I may have on expending a certain sum enough to pay all reasonable expenses things would move a little smoother and I *know* you would not receive anymore such letters," he complained.[38]

In fact he made quite a name for himself at Yale—writing for the college newspaper; winning election as "fence orator" in his freshman and sophomore years, and class historian in his senior year; and being chosen for membership in the Pundits, a group organized in 1884 and made up of men noted for their wit and gifts of satire. He was also elected to Skull and Bones, Yale's most prestigious secret society, founded in 1832 in the mode of the secret societies of university students in Germany. He was a popular, highly visible Yale man, noted for his ebullience and for his talents in singing, oratory, and mimicry.

After graduation Parker Wilder threw himself into a series of jobs, some of them obtained through the Yale network. He taught for a year in a Connecticut boarding school and another year in Faribault, Minnesota, at Shattuck Military Academy, considered one of the best schools for boys in the Northwest. He spent two summers working at the Albany, New York, *Journal*; was hired in 1886 as a reporter for the *Philadelphia Press*; and soon returned to the Albany paper, where he was assigned to cover the state legislature. When he was twenty-six he became editor of the New Haven, Connecticut, *Palladium,* the leading Republican newspaper in New Haven, where he stayed for three and a half years. He traveled to Europe during the summer of 1891, but otherwise, he remembered, he "worked all the time for many years."[39]

From the beginning of this peripatetic decade, his avocation was public speaking, and the demand grew for Amos Parker Wilder's entertaining, provocative speeches. Large and small newspapers of the 1890s carried reports of his political stump speeches, his Chautauqua lectures, his after-dinner discourses for civic and cultural groups, and his forward-looking commentary on issues facing American cities. While he was working on the newspaper in New Haven he had earned a doctoral degree at Yale, granted in 1892 in the Division of Economics, Sociology, and Government. He produced a thesis titled "The Government of Cities," which was later printed in pamphlet form by the New Haven Chamber of Commerce. A political dispute led to his departure from the New Haven newspaper, and he wound up in New York for two years, moving from one paper to another. "I have 'lost my job' a number of times," he wrote later, "and suffered great depression. One who has failed in business, or who is utterly cast down from any cause will often do well to begin life under a new environment—to move to another place."[40] He decided to do just that. He was engaged to be married. He needed to support his wife and a family. He wanted to buy a newspaper and be his own boss. It was on June 19, 1894, with his modest savings augmented by borrowed money, that Amos Parker Wilder bought a half interest in the *Wisconsin State Journal* and moved to Madison. According to the Madison journalist Edward S. Jordan, Wilder was a "scholarly young man, imbued with ideals" and a "brilliant, sensitive man, almost painfully honest, but with a subterranean fire of enthusiasm, and belief in MEN."[41]

———

BY MID-DECEMBER 1894, the Wilders were settling into married life in an apartment near his Madison newspaper office. By the sixth year of their marriage, despite her doctor's ongoing concern about the impact on her health, Isabella had given birth to five children, one still-born. (According to family memory, she had refused her husband's request that their first daughter be named Edith, after his lost love.)[42] Their son Amos was born September 18, 1895, a little more than nine months after his parents' marriage. The twins were born when Amos was nineteen months old. Charlotte was born when Thornton was sixteen months old and Amos was not quite three. Charlotte would be eighteen months old when Isabel was born January 13, 1900. Thus, of the first seventy-two months, or six years, of her marriage, Isabella had spent about fifty-two months, or four years and nearly four months, being pregnant.

Her deliveries were relatively easy, but her pregnancies could be difficult, and her doctor did not think Isabella should be caring for two small boys and a baby girl in the last months of her fourth pregnancy, even with the occasional help of nurse Margaret Donoghue, who had assisted at the births of her previous children.[43] Worried about Isabella's health and stamina, as well as the health and development of the unborn child, the doctor recommended sending baby Charlotte away during the last three months of Isabella's pregnancy, to be cared for by the nuns in a Catholic hospital for babies and children. The Wilders were instructed not to visit for the first month so that Charlotte would get used to her new "home." When Isabella returned a month later, the baby allowed her to hold and kiss her, but was so stiff and unresponsive that Isabella feared she had "lost Charlotte forever."[44]

Now with four small children to care for, Isabella could be seen walking up and down the street in her Madison neighborhood, pushing three little children in a large wicker baby carriage, with young Amos walking along beside. Sometimes neighbors saw Isabella herding her children with one hand and holding a book in the other. When she could find time to herself, she was active in French and Italian literary circles at the University of Wisconsin. One of her frequent pleasures was traveling to Chicago with Madison friends to go to the opera. In the spring of 1902 she spent three months in Europe, leaving the children in the care of their father and capable Nurse Donoghue while she traveled abroad in the company of three of her Madison friends.[45]

Amos Parker Wilder, all the while, was an earnestly busy man. In addition to his growing administrative as well as editorial responsibilities at the newspaper, he avidly followed local, state, and national politics, writing and speaking about important issues. Madison was home to a lively, contentious mix of political opinions, and he often found himself and his newspaper caught in the cross fire. To foster open civil dialogue, he helped organize the "Six O-Clock Club," inviting the town's leading citizens, regardless of political viewpoint, to meet for conversation. He served as club secretary for seven years.[46]

In 1902 he angered some of his fellow citizens when he "tried editorially to ride both a La Follette and a Spooner horse going in opposite ways."[47] Both men were Republicans running for reelection—Robert La Follette for governor and John Spooner for U.S. senator. They were rivals, if not political enemies, and Wilder used his editorial podium in June 1902 to criticize La Follette's political tactics, warning that "Mr. La Follette's political future lies not in rough riding, but in tact, fairness, in open, hearty co-operation with these elements of the party that seeks the just thing and will play fair." He went so far as to suggest that if La Follette's political attempts to humiliate Spooner continued, there might be "a great number of those who supported the Governor [who] would be most eager for his overthrow."[48] This was an insinuation that La Follette would not forget.

Dr. Wilder was a strong proponent of the suffrage movement, writing and speaking in favor of "equal suffrage" for the "modern woman." He carried his message far and wide in speeches, arguing that the "competency of the modern woman" was a strong imperative for granting women the right to vote. While women may once have been "mentally inferior," Wilder said, the ground had shifted, and the intelligence of the modern American woman was demonstrated in her growing participation in the professions. Now that women were "no longer dependent on men," and "no longer generically domestic," he contended, all arguments that justified the rights of men to vote at last applied as well to women, who needed the ballot to protect themselves, to enrich their lives, and to exert their influence for the good of the society. "Women have quick intuitions," asserted Dr. Wilder, son of one strong woman and husband of another. "The mother instinct would still be aggressive, and it is one to trust. It is a man's government now, and shows the absence of woman's conscience and devotion to simplicity and truth. Organized womanhood thrown into the disposal of problems, local and national, would be a power for good."[49]

When he was not stirring up controversy with his editorials or captivating audiences with his speeches, he was busy at Madison's First Congregational Church, the second-oldest church in the city. Amos and Isabella had joined the church on May 3, 1895, when he transferred his membership from the South Congregational Church in Augusta, Maine, and she hers from her father's church in Dobbs Ferry, New York.[50] Even so the Wilders had traveled back to Dobbs Ferry so that baby Amos could be baptized by Isabella's father in his church, but Thornton was baptized in Madison.[51] Dr. Wilder was a church deacon for seven years, beginning in 1902, and also served "long and exceptionally well" as superintendent of the Sunday school.[52] According to a story Thornton told many years later, his father would sit between his two boys for the Sunday services. During Dr. Eugene Grover Updike's sermon, Dr. Wilder would let his boys draw pictures on the starched white cuffs of his shirtsleeves.

One of their neighbors recalled in later years that Dr. Wilder insisted that his newspaper must be "clean enough" for his children to read it, for he was "alive to the needs of growing families."[53] Even then Thornton was known beyond the family for his curiosity, and he had already fallen in love with libraries. The children's librarian at the public library more than once found him "contentedly wandering the aisles of bookstacks open to staff only." She would lead the boy back to a small table laden with books from the children's section and encourage him to read there.[54] The Wilder home was full of books, and the children grew up reading and being read to—Sir Walter Scott, Dickens, Thackeray, and many more. Sunday readings dipped into the Bible and the works of John Bunyan, George Fox, and Henry David Thoreau.

Often on Sunday afternoons Dr. Wilder took his brood for a walk around Madison. The children enjoyed "the exciting and noisy city Water Works" and "the steps of the towering State House" and "the promenade along Lake Mendota." Isabel remembered that Thornton loved going with their father to the *Wisconsin State Journal* offices to see the printing presses spouting out the newspaper, and with his own hands to "push the keys on Father's typewriter to see words come out on paper."[55] His father introduced him to the thrill of words on paper, and his mother took him to see his first play, a production of Shakespeare's *As You Like It* in a Milwaukee theater, where they had balcony seats.[56] His brother recalled that Thornton was "addicted to clowning and striking poses, and took part early in the costuming and tableaux of Christmas events in the Sunday School."[57] These were the wonders of Thornton's life as a small boy—ordinary days full of familiar pleasures, interspersed with extraordinary events that seemed to him immensely exciting and colorful.

His father especially treasured the memories of those years. He wrote to his children in 1910:

> *When your Papa is "gone before" remember that in our little cottage with [his] wife and children were the happiest years of his life. He had heavy burdens in the city but when he walked along the lake shore in the early evening and saw the "lights of home," the cares slipped off like a harness—sweet children awaited him at the gate, or ran down to meet him—the mother with supper spread on the verandah; the pleasant converse, the reverent quiet, worship, each one joining in—the "all still and quiet"—Papa's few moments alone under the stars, with the wind murmuring through the forest in the rear—the restful sleep—those were the precious years.*[58]

"Did you have a happy childhood?" an interviewer asked Thornton Wilder in 1957 when he was famous around the world.

"I think I did, but I also think that that's a thing about which people tend to deceive themselves . . . ," he replied. "Yet I am convinced that, except in a few extraordinary cases, one form or another of an unhappy childhood is essential to the formation of exceptional gifts. Perhaps I should have been a better man if I had had an unequivocally unhappy childhood."[59]

2

"A FORETASTE OF HEAVEN"

*It used to be said that to have lived in China during those years between the
Boxer Rebellion and the 1911 Revolution was to have enjoyed
a foretaste of Heaven.*

—THORNTON WILDER,
"Chefoo, China," unpublished manuscript

China and California (1906–1909)

Just ten days before his ninth birthday, Thornton Niven Wilder set
out on one of the greatest adventures of his life. His ambitious father
and his harried mother had decided to move their family from the
tranquil streets of Madison, Wisconsin, to the British Crown Colony
of Hong Kong, China, where Amos Parker Wilder would become U.S.
consul general. He was appointed to the post in 1906 by President Theodore Roosevelt after months of political wrangling.

At the time Dr. Wilder, father of four, editor and owner of the *State
Journal*, and president of the State Journal Printing Company in Madison, Wisconsin, was still trying to repay the loans that had made it possible for him to buy a half interest and then the full interest in the paper.
His "coaching of talented young reporters and his editorials became
quasi-legendary," and stories abounded about his "unconventional assignments and irascible fiats in the editor's sanctum," his son Amos remembered, noting that his father "took pride in the fact that his was the
first daily paper which refused to accept liquor advertisements."[1]

His newspaper was a visible podium, and Dr. Wilder used it aggressively. While he had earlier supported Governor Robert La Follette's
"progressive" political movement, he grew wary of La Follette's increasing power, and by 1904 had turned his support to the "Stalwart"
branch of the Republican Party—the older, wealthier, conservative
movement represented by Senator John Coit Spooner. Year by year

Dr. Wilder took an increasingly confident, independent stance in his editorials and in his speeches. He frequently gave rousing motivational speeches. A perennially popular Chautauqua lecturer and speaker to civic and cultural groups throughout the United States, he often relied on humor to capture and hold an audience's attention. At a dinner meeting of the National Municipal League in New York in April 1905, for instance, he had the audience "roaring" with laughter, the *New York Times* reported.[2] Wilder was praised for his "brilliant style and his independent opinions," and hailed as "one of the country's greatest authorities" on the issue of better municipal governance.[3]

By the spring of 1905 he had begun to consider other career options, tentatively exploring the possibility of foreign service and actively lobbying for a diplomatic appointment. He solicited the help of Secretary of War William Howard Taft, whom he had known at Yale. "I know the President is anxious to do something, but that is indefinite. [Senator] Spooner, too, is anxious, but the question is 'How,'" Taft wrote April 14, 1905, in response to Wilder's persistent inquiries. In 1905 there were rumors in the press that he was going to receive a diplomatic appointment to Venezuela, but instead he was offered the position of American consul general in Hong Kong.[4] He traveled to Washington on January 24, 1906, to take the State Department examinations to qualify. The *Racine Daily Journal* reported that Amos P. Wilder had "recently been appointed United States consul general to Hongkong, China, one of the most important diplomatic posts at Uncle Sam's disposal," but that La Follette, newly elected to the senate from Wisconsin, had opposed his confirmation, "and the final result is still in doubt."[5]

"Thus far the principal senatorial service of Robert Marion La Follette has been to hold up the consular appointment of his distinguished fellow townsman, Amos Parker Wilder, of the Madison State Journal," the *New York World* reported, adding that Wilder was a friend of Wisconsin senator Spooner, who supported the diplomatic appointment that La Follette sought to block. The *World* noted that "some people think the United States government lucky to get men like Mr. Wilder to accept consular appointments."[6] Senator La Follette, with whom Wilder had clashed politically since the 1902 election in Wisconsin, opposed the appointment on the grounds that Amos Parker Wilder was "personally offensive to him," but Wilder's supporters prevailed and, with President Theodore Roosevelt's blessing, Wilder set out in March of 1906 to assume "one of the top consular positions at that time."[7]

It meant uprooting his wife and children from their comfortable life in Madison and transplanting them to the Far East, but he believed he could make money and an international reputation in China. In March 1906 Parker and Isabella and their four children traveled by train from Wisconsin to California, where on April 7, 1906—just ten days before Thornton's birthday, and eleven days before the devastation of the April 18 earthquake—they boarded the SS *Siberia* for the monthlong voyage from San Francisco to Hong Kong.[8]

The journey was the most exciting adventure that had ever befallen the Wilder children—Amos, now ten and a half; Thornton, almost nine; Charlotte Elizabeth, seven and a half; and Isabel, recently turned six. First there was the thrilling experience of riding the Atchison, Topeka & Santa Fe train through the vast American landscape, from Madison to San Francisco. The children roamed the train by day, and at night, knelt obediently by their Pullman car berths as their father led them through the hymn singing, scripture reading, and prayers that made up their bedtime ritual at home.

Then there was the fascination—sometimes terrifying, sometimes enchanting—of eating, sleeping, and living aboard the huge steamship, a world of its own, traversing the immense open sea. "Our trip was delightful—no sea sickness—on many days there were not even white-caps on the water," Dr. Wilder wrote to his mother. He and Isabella were seated at the captain's table. Father and children mingled with the passengers, including a group of missionaries en route to China, while Isabella rested from the exhaustion of the move and her anxiety about its outcome. After a few days at sea, however, she "resumed her health," her husband reported, and then "of course made friends with all."[9] The ship stopped in Hawaii for a few days, and put in for two days at a time at three Japanese ports, opening exotic new vistas to the Wilder children.[10] Thornton had looked forward to celebrating his birthday—April 17—on the voyage, unaware that when the ship crossed the international date line on April 16, the seventeenth would disappear entirely, but it was celebrated anyway.[11]

He was a thin, effervescent boy, with shaggy dark hair and vivid blue eyes alight with curiosity. He could be shy with other children, and gregarious with adults. One of his shipboard friends kept a diary—lined pages bound in green leather, with a gold-colored metal lock and key. Thornton was so impressed that he began his own makeshift journal on the blank side of the heavy paper on which dinner menus were printed each evening. Yung Kwai, the head steward of the children's table, handed out the leftover menus as souvenirs, and Thornton put them to immediate use, filling them with words, and then, with the steward's help, hiding the pages under the cover of an empty table in the corner of the dining salon. At the end of the voyage Thornton and his little sister, Isabel, went to collect the hidden journal pages, only to find that they had disappeared.[12] Sadly, Thornton's first journal, begun in April 1906, did not survive his first ocean voyage, but there would be journals, letters, and manuscript pages in the future, many of them composed at sea.

THE WILDERS arrived in Hong Kong May 7, 1906, and temporarily moved into the King Edward Hotel, one of the two largest in the city. At night, from the veranda of their rooms, they looked out at a city sparkling with lights like a "fairy-land."[13] Because there was no permanent residence for the consul general in Hong Kong, Dr. Wilder was expected to pay rent for appropriate quarters from his salary of $8,000 per year. Beginning on June 1, he leased a large furnished house for $112.50 in gold per month. The house was located on Victoria Peak, known as the Peak, a mountain overlooking the city and harbor. "It is a fitting place for a great man," Dr. Wilder teased in a letter to his mother.[14]

Colonial officials sought residences on the Peak not so much for the views as for escape from the oppressive humidity of the city. The Wilders' rented house and sprawling lawns had previously been occupied by a succession of high-ranking Western officials and their families, and came equipped with Chinese servants. Thus the Wilders inherited Wong, the "number one boy," who had worked for American consuls for many years, and so spoke fluent English. For a salary of ten dollars a month, Wong ran the household, hiring and supervising a staff composed, Dr. Wilder reported, of "a cook, a cook's helper, a house coolie, a gardener" among others, including a tailor, a laundryman, and, for nine dollars a month, an amah for the children—an "oldish woman" who was kind but, like most amahs, did not have "any control over children."[15] The house was reached by "a steam tram pulled by a wire rope which runs up 1400 feet like this," Dr. Wilder wrote, adding, "it is the steepest thing in the world."[16]

Such were the wonders of the new city surrounding Thornton and his siblings. In addition to thrilling rides up and down the Peak, they rode about the city in the standard conveyance—sedan chairs, each carried by at least two coolies, garbed only in breechcloths. Their father took the children on the streetcar line that ran for about four miles along the shore. Their amah took them for walks and watched over them while their mother was busy with her official duties—teas, tiffins (luncheons), and afternoon social calls. They tasted strange new foods, and, carefully supervised by their elders, went on swimming parties and explored the city, transfixed by the constant swirl of people and traffic. They attended the German school their parents had deemed the best option for their education in Hong Kong, riding in sedan chairs for tutoring every day after tea. They went to church weekly to hear the "grim language" of the ministers—"English and Scotchmen [who] quite outdo even me in theology," their father observed.[17]

The Wilders settled into a comfortable domestic routine at the Peak, surrounded by servants to see to their every need. The family ate breakfast and lunch together, but the children had an earlier dinner than their parents—"a jolly meal together with Wong, our 'No 1 Boy' and generalissimo in charge of house, and his assistant 'Ah Fie'—a boy of 17—to wait on them," their father wrote. "But, of course, I skirt about and quiet their quarrels. After their meal, they romp on the croquet ground, perhaps playing tag with Wong; and then they undress— and then we read all except the baby from little copies of Luke—each child taking turns."[18] He predicted that he and his wife and children would be content in Hong Kong "for a period of years."[19]

———

AMONG HIS papers Thornton Wilder left a twenty-page manuscript of semiautobiographical reflections titled "Chefoo, China"—as noted earlier, a fusion of memory, imagination, fact, and fiction, written in the late 1960s and embroidered here and there with strands of drama. Decades after his time in China, with an accuracy of detail confirmed in his father's letters of the period, Wilder described the luxurious life afforded to "foreign devils," such as his own family, who came to China from the "barely civilized powers of Europe and America." In his view diplomats, businessmen, and even missionaries enjoyed a life-style that many of them could never have afforded at home. "It used to be said that to have lived in China during those years between the Boxer Rebellion and the 1911 Revolution was to have enjoyed a fore-taste of Heaven," Wilder wrote in his manuscript draft. He recalled the "skilled and tireless servants who worked for a six-to-ten dollar monthly wage"; the "superb cooks and spirited gardeners"; the tailors who could reproduce the latest styles from Paris and London; the trav-eling from place to place in sedan chairs borne on men's shoulders, and the more modern rickshaw once rubber tires were available in China.[20]

Wilder remembered more than sixty years later that " 'Old China hands' still referred to those days as sheer Heaven," despite the fact that Americans and Europeans in China were surrounded by the social and economic problems facing the Chinese people.[21]

And, he wrote, perhaps with some dramatic license, "My own fa-ther—a rugged individualist from the state of Maine—returning to America after fifteen years was unable to tie his own shoes without a spasm of annoyance."[22]

———

IN THE summer of 1906 Consul General Wilder was enjoying his new life and his new salary—especially "after 12 years of nose on the grind-stone."[23] By July 15 he had sent home a thousand dollars to apply to his debts. He confided in his mother that after years of "standing off" creditors, "you cannot imagine the sweetness of wiping out these obligations beginning with the small ones."[24]

He was completely caught up in his official duties, "ratifying contracts and facilitating international commerce" and representing his "native land's character" as a "congenial and even convivial" good fellow.[25] The Hong Kong consul general carried heavy commercial and social responsibilities, although politically and industrially the post was not as important as other missions in China, especially in Shanghai and Peking. But Hong Kong—"the gate way of South China"—was one of the world's busiest ports, especially for United States business interests.[26] Hong Kong was "essentially a freight transit point" but the consul general was expected to be on the lookout for trade opportunities and to report on trade and industrial issues from his gateway perspective. While the U.S. consulate in Hong Kong was not heavily involved with Chinese officials and the keeping of public order, as was the case in Peking and Shanghai, Hong Kong was a strategic port city always on the lookout for international unrest.

Socially Dr. Wilder was directed to "take his place in the official life of the Colony with dignity, and if he be congenial to the prominent families outside the strictly official circle, mainly military and naval in a British Colony, it facilitates business at the consulate, and enhances American prestige."[27] Consul General Wilder and his wife and family were expected to do their part to support this mission.[28] In their rented house atop the Peak, the Wilders entertained often—on special holidays, on the occasion of visits from special guests, and at a weekly open house, among other times.[29] According to official reports, the Wilders were "very popular" in Hong Kong, performing their social duties with "grace and social tact." Furthermore, one government report noted, Isabella and the children "certainly" contributed to Amos Parker Wilder's official and social success in Hong Kong.[30]

But behind the scenes there were growing headaches. Isabella (whom her husband usually called Isabel) was increasingly exhausted by the daily social demands and the daily care of four rambunctious children, even though there were servants to help. Both parents worried over the limited opportunities for educating their bright youngsters. Dr. Wilder was continually appalled at the cost of living in Hong Kong. What had seemed like a comfortable salary was instead becoming sorely strained to pay the high costs of rent, food, entertaining, clothing, and dues for the clubs he was expected to join, as well as the personal costs of helping stranded Americans, hosting American tourists, and giving to charities to help the poor. Furthermore, back home, debts for the newspaper still had to be paid, along with the rent on their Madison apartment. The financial strain was wearing for Amos and Isabella, and stresses in their marriage intensified accordingly.

Both parents began to worry about how life in Hong Kong affected their children. At an early age most Western boys were sent back to their home countries for schooling, and girls were sent back to boarding schools in their early or midteens. In Hong Kong at that time there was only one reputable school for foreign children, and it was run by the local German Lutheran church, staffed by two German women, with no English spoken. Dr. Wilder hired a German tutor to work with Amos, Thornton, Charlotte, and Isabel after school, for none of the children knew a word of German. This was unsatisfactory even as a short-term arrangement for educating their brood—especially since Dr. Wilder was already thinking of preparing his sons to go to Yale and his daughters to go to Mount Holyoke.[31]

Isabella did not settle happily into life in Hong Kong, although she was recognized as a gracious hostess, especially at her weekly afternoon "at homes" and her dinner parties. Before their first dinner party, Isabella and her husband wrestled over the protocol of the "awful wine question," as he termed it—and he eventually won.[32] He was irrevocably a teetotaler; he had sworn that pledge as a boy, after all, and it was a matter of deep moral conviction. Furthermore, his own brother, Julian, was an alcoholic, so he had witnessed firsthand the harm excessive drinking could do. Dr. Wilder was not about to further corrupt the morals of his guests, who in his opinion would just have to survive his dinner parties without wine. Nevertheless he recognized the hardship his position would work on Isabella and their guests. He reported to his mother that he understood that it was

almost impossible to conceive a dinner without all kinds of wines etc. We
shall be adjudged cads, pharisees, bumpkins and stingy Americans . . .
Isabel wanted to do things "right" and put it on all sorts of grounds
of propriety, but I told her that I could not even consider it. She was
in great distress for weeks, tears and the like. . . . I had laid in a stock
of grape juice! And with Apollinaris water and the like and with no
apologies, the dinner went off swimmingly. Isabel had accepted the
inevitable some hours in advance & sparkled in conversation, and [the
guests] went home at 10:30 *reporting a happy evening.*[33]

The American consulate in Hong Kong traditionally hosted a Fourth
of July party for Americans, Chinese officials, and the international
community, always with "an abundance of all kinds of drinks." Consul
General Wilder was determined to change that practice. For the first
Fourth of July celebration he held, he saw to it that the consulate was
"handsomely decorated with flags and flowers," and that the guests
were lavishly served grape juice and bottled waters. He pronounced his
party a great success.[34]

EXCEPT FOR school, the Wilder children enjoyed their new life in
China—kite flying, pony rides, new games to play. With pride Dr.
Wilder described his children in a letter to his mother:

The fact is that Isabel is such a winsome little favorite that Charlotte is
overshadowed—but the latter is a strong, forceful self reliant girl and
will do us all proud. They have finished [reading] "Robinson Crusoe"
and now they are at work on Lamb's version of the Shakespeare plays.
They read to each other for Isabel[la] has no strength left for that and
what time I have is devoted to pounding the Bible into their little heads
and hearts.[35]

Committed as they were to the importance of education, both
Wilders grew increasingly unhappy with the schooling available to their
children in Hong Kong.[36] While Amos was already a good student, Dr.

Wilder worried that Thornton was "too much of a dreamer & without application to be a scholar," although he was "quick mentally" and was making friends. Charlotte was a "constant reader," her father said, and liked to read aloud to her siblings. He could tell she was nearsighted, but there was not a good doctor in Hong Kong to examine her eyes. "Isabel is everyone's pet," he wrote, "yet does not seem spoiled."[37]

Dr. Wilder wrote to his mother-in-law at length about his hopes for his sons and daughters:

> The education of the children is one of my dearest interests. I want the girls as well as the boys to have a college course. . . . Thornton is a very sweet boy but a dreamer. He does the things he wants to do but lacks application. He promises to be an impracticable, dependent little fellow and I must consult some wise educator, for the type must be a common one.[38]

His son Amos was a different matter, however. Dr. Wilder wished for Amos to have an experience with farm life to "bolster him up," but he told his mother-in-law that Isabella threw up her hands "in horror" at the idea. Amos was, his father wrote, "affectionate, makes friends with all and scatters sunshine with his perennial gladness."[39]

———

BY SEPTEMBER 1906 troubling events confronted the Wilders in Hong Kong: the visible economic and physical suffering of many of the Chinese people; the perennial rumors of political unrest; and the overpowering force of a natural disaster. On young Amos's eleventh birthday, September 18, a typhoon swept through Hong Kong without warning, followed by a tsunami, killing an estimated ten thousand people. Amos never forgot the specter of bodies floating in the sea.[40] As Consul General Wilder reported in graphic accounts dispatched to newspapers in the United States, thousands of disfigured and decomposing bodies washed ashore in Hong Kong. Isabella remembered that "the British soldiers had to turn out and bury them because the Chinese were superstitious and refused."[41]

The storm's hundred-mile-per-hour winds tossed and overturned rickshaws, streetcars, and huge steamers alike, wreaking massive damage throughout the city. It was disastrous for the Chinese economy, as well as for foreign businesses, and Dr. Wilder turned his attention to the practical urgency of helping to rebuild the port and the business ventures that depended on it.

At home, meanwhile, he was deeply concerned about the toll their demanding Hong Kong life was taking on his wife and children. Truth be known, the husband and wife were seldom completely happy in each other's company, and his letters reveal his anxiety not only about schools for their children but about his wife's well-being. Isabella was "economical as always," he wrote to his mother.

> It is rarely a consul has a wife who can so help him socially. . . . Isabel gets pretty well tired by the eternal making of senseless calls and other functions where it is necessary to keep up a flow of small talk—but she does it very successfully and is in great favor. She thinks later she would like to go to Italy or Switzerland and as the women come and go home (England) a good deal here to escape the climate, I may let her go with some or all of the children. It would be as cheap as keeping up an establishment.[42]

Isabella kept insisting that she should take the children to live in Switzerland or Italy, but her husband ultimately balked at that plan. If she had to leave, he thought she should go back to the United States and live on the West Coast. He insisted that his sons should stay with him in China, but Isabella wanted to keep all the children with her. Finally, after five and a half months in Hong Kong, the couple decided to live separately, with the children's education as the stated motivation. Consul General Wilder would, of course, remain in Hong Kong, and would move to a room at the nearby Peak Hotel. Isabella and the children would return to the United States to rent a house in Berkeley, California, where there were good schools, a university, and some old Madison friends.[43]

On October, 30, 1906, Isabella, Amos, Thornton, Charlotte, and

Isabel once again boarded the SS *Siberia* for a monthlong voyage, this time bound for San Francisco. Typhoon flags were flying at the harbor, and departure preparations were accelerated because of a looming storm. "It seemed best for Isabel & the children to go," Dr. Wilder wrote sadly to his mother, "though it was a hard decision to make."[44] He worried especially about Thornton, the one of his children who "dreads leaving his 'Papa' the most," he told her in another letter. Such family separations were "like pulling teeth—they break relationships, and it will not be so hard the next time to leave Papa—but God knows I am doing my duty as I see it. I have been clouded by debt and a lack of money so long that it has changed me."[45]

He took comfort that in California the children would have more playmates, more opportunity for healthy play outdoors, and, most of all, access to much better schools—and that he could save more money living on his own. He wrote to his mother in December, "I am happy enough in my lonely life."[46]

THE YEAR 1906 marked a turning point for the Wilder family. For the first time they did not live together under one roof. The children now inhabited a home with an absent father and a mother who had to manage the household, the budget, and the child rearing as best she could, almost entirely on her own. Now deprived of their father's daily presence, they had to rely on slow-moving letters to and from Hong Kong to sustain their relationship with him. This was also the time when the family's financial stress began to filter into their daily awareness. Amos Parker Wilder, lonely in China for his family in California, was now essentially responsible for maintaining and supporting three households—his own in Hong Kong, the rental house and the needs of his wife and four children in Berkeley, and the apartment he still leased in Madison. He had hoped that the family could live on half his salary, with the other half devoted to paying his debts. The budget was stretched tight, however, and the Wilder children began to learn the challenges, discomforts, and insecurities of genteel poverty. Young Amos remembered that the years in Berkeley "were sometimes desperately difficult for our mother, who had four young children to care for with very limited funds."[47]

Isabella created as much comfort in their Berkeley home life as her energy and resources would permit. Her children remembered that she had a great gift for making something out of nothing, and her "wonderful high spirits" came in part from the support she drew from music, art, and poetry.[48] The school-age children attended Emerson Grammar School in Berkeley. Just as Isabella had taken advantage of university resources in Madison, she explored the University of California community, making friends with faculty members, especially in the French and Italian circles. She wrote poetry and translated poems by Émile Verhaeren (1855–1916), a Belgian poet and critic who wrote in French, and Giosuè Carducci (1835–1907), one of Italy's greatest poets. She reconnected with her Dobbs Ferry Sunday school teacher, William Lyon Phelps, now famous as a writer, lecturer, and teacher of literature and the humanities. Phelps, a member of the English faculty at Yale, his alma mater, was a guest lecturer during the 1908 summer session at the university in Berkeley.[49]

As Isabella and her children adjusted to their new life in California, they filled their days with school and church activities and the rich cultural events of the university community. The children took music lessons, practicing on a rented piano in the parlor. They heard the Chicago Symphony Orchestra play, and saw the Ben Greet Players perform Shakespeare in the William Randolph Hearst Greek Theatre. The walled amphitheater, inspired by ancient Greek architecture, opened on the Berkeley campus of the University of California in 1903, a gift from Hearst. As often as her budget permitted, Isabella indulged her love for theater, taking one or more of the children with her—most often Thornton, who loved the spectacle and the magic of plays so much that he began making up his own dramas and staging them in the backyard, casting and directing his brother and sisters and any of the neighborhood children who would cooperate, costuming them in cheesecloth and filling their mouths with "grandiloquent speeches."[50] The Wilders lived just ten or twelve minutes away from the Berkeley hills that enfolded the Greek Theatre, where Isabella volunteered her skills as a seamstress. Her children were cast in mob scenes in plays there, as well as in Nativity pageants at their church. Thornton would often climb a tree or sneak into the theater to watch rehearsals in the Greek Theatre. Sometimes he got caught, but when he didn't, he sat enthralled. Those moments in the shadows, with his eyes and ears fixed on the stage, helped to launch his lifelong love affair with drama, including the fascinating collaborative rehearsal process.

The family often attended Sunday afternoon performances at the Greek Theatre—concerts, plays, dance recitals. There Thornton saw dramas by Shakespeare, Sophocles, Euripides, Aeschylus, and others. There were two theaters in Oakland, and in one of them Thornton saw the well-known actress Viola Allen in *Twelfth Night*, as well as popular comedies and melodramas.[51] Steeped in drama, his already robust imagination expanding, he began to get up early in the morning before school so he could write down his own plays. Thornton's love for books led him regularly to the university library as well as the public library. At his father's request, Thornton mailed letters to China about what he was reading. "Dear Papa, Books I have read this month:" he began one letter, listing Shakespeare's *Othello*, part of Washington Irving's *Sketch Book*, and Wilbur Fisk Crafts's *Successful Men of Today*, as well as John S. White's translation of Plutarch's *Lives* and Sarah Knowles Bolton's *Poor Boys Who Became Famous*. Thornton concluded his letter to his father with a brief evaluation: "None of the books were unsatisfactory."[52]

Isabella read to and with her children, experiences deeply imprinted in her son's imagination and memory. "Do you remember how we read 'Ulyssees [*sic*] together," he wrote to her when he was a teenager. "Since then I have learnt some of him by heart"[53] His passion for books, reading, and making up plays and stories marked him early on as a verbally gifted child, and as he began to write down his plays and stories, his attentive mother was "his confidante and stimulus."[54]

He could be glib as well, as in this fourth-grade English assignment when he was asked to write about Vulcan: "Vulcan was the god of goldsmiths, ironsmiths, leadsmiths, silversmiths, and Mrs. Smiths—there, now I'm out of breath."[55]

AMOS PARKER WILDER and his family were tethered by the letters that made their slow way from Hong Kong to Berkeley and back again. In China and in California, a part of each Sunday afternoon was devoted to sharing the news of the week in letters—long ones from Dr. Wilder, shorter ones from the children and Isabella. Dr. Wilder reported that he was giving literary and cultural lectures in Hong Kong, focusing in the fall of 1906 on Thoreau in a literary course at the Union Church.[56] He sent his wife an affectionate letter on December 3, 1906, their twelfth wedding anniversary. Isabella had often told her husband that their wedding day was "the worst day that ever befell either of us." Dr. Wilder wrote to his mother, adding,

> I *always* tell her that despite the long, weary way if I had it to do over,
> I would choose no other companion, and as I think of my dear children
> and the many happinesses, God knows I spread the truth. Had the dear
> girl married some more pliable fellow, some well-to-do man of the world,
> she might have been happier—but I am not sure. I am a patient old
> fool and in some of her moods perhaps I have been more successful than
> a higher-strung companion would have been. I never forget what a
> devoted, intelligent Mother she was in the early hard years. . . . I hope
> the coming years will be easier for [Isabella].[57]

Consul General Wilder was an active, visible, sometimes controversial force in Hong Kong business and government circles. In addition to befriending Western missionaries to China, he took a great interest in trying to prepare young Chinese for the future. His diplomatic and business territory encompassed Canton and parts of the mainland as well as Hong Kong, and he traveled widely over the country, recording his travels and observations in great detail in his diaries. As his son Amos later wrote, his father's "Hong Kong journal shows him reflecting on brutalities and suicides among the Western military and social circles on the island, and on the gulf between diplomatic formalism and the teeming humanity of the Far East."[58] Dr. Wilder adapted some details from his diaries for an article entitled "A Consul's Busy Day," illustrated with photographs, and published in *Hearst's International: The World Today* in 1908.[59]

He confronted an especially thorny problem in January 1908 when he received a letter from the American Brewing Company of St. Louis, Missouri, seeking to introduce its beers to the Chinese market.[60] He wrote to the State Department, making it emphatically clear that his personal "convictions of long standing" prevented his cooperation with the brewer's request.[61] Directed by Washington to "furnish the desired information," to the brewing company Consul General Wilder wrote another letter that was part sermon, part ultimatum:

> *The studied effort to force alcoholic drink on the Chinese people,*
> *the one cheerful phase of whose misery-laden existence is freedom from*
> *this evil, is a task in which I must decline to share even the most casual*
> *participation.*
>
> *I infer from the Department's dispatch that such views as I hold*
> *are irreconcilable with continued service as a consul. If this inference is*
> *correct I have the honor to tender with great regret my resignation as*
> *Consul General for appropriate action.*[62]

While the State Department regretted Wilder's stand, Acting Secretary of State Alvey A. Adee replied, "it sees no reason for you to tender your resignation in the premises."[63]

Much of Wilder's work was ceremonial and mundane, but he diligently studied Chinese culture and language, and attempted to apply to Hong Kong some of the progressive precepts he had espoused for American cities.[64] He was terribly lonely without his family, however, and he began to face grave doubts about the choices he had made. In April 1909 he was granted a leave of absence for a trip home to see his wife and children. He was aboard the SS *Nippon*, due to arrive in San Francisco on May 21, when he received a cablegram from the State Department instructing him to assume the role of American consul general in Shanghai.[65]

Shanghai. A change of scenery. A new challenge. Although the salary was the same, a more prestigious diplomatic post. An environment perhaps more conducive to family life. His new orders allowed him to make an abbreviated visit home, where he and Isabella decided that he should go to Shanghai alone and see for himself how congenial it might be for the family—especially for the education of the children.

Before he left the United States, Dr. Wilder gave the commencement address at the University of Minnesota in Minneapolis. One newspaper noted that he was a "powerful public speaker," and that he might be offered the presidency of the university, but nothing came of that.[66] He returned to China to wind up affairs in Hong Kong, where he was given several farewell receptions and tributes, and praised for his success in the city that was viewed by the State Department as "one of the social centers of the east." He was evaluated in official reports as an excellent officer. He left the Hong Kong consulate in better shape than he found it, and made many friends in the process. Now he would see what he could do for Shanghai.

3

"BEING LEFT"

I have no cause to complain of being left here because Amos has been left
alone in the continent with no other members of the Family.
—THORNTON WILDER TO AMOS PARKER WILDER,
March 3, 1912

China and California (1909–1911)

Amos Parker Wilder kept careful, attentive watch over his family from afar, this time from his new post in Shanghai. The Wilders had planned to be reunited in Shanghai in the fall of 1909, but that journey was postponed when Isabella discovered she was pregnant. Those were "hard confusing busy days for both Mamma and Papa," Dr. Wilder wrote to his children in Berkeley in March 1910, "and I shall be disappointed if each child does not make it a matter of earnest thought with himself and herself 'How can I help these parents of mine?' . . . So while Papa is working in Shanghai, with trying problems of office and newspaper and money affairs and separation from home—and Mamma is sick and troubled and lonely, my children should do their part *now*."[1] He lectured from more than six thousand miles away, "It is your part to love Mamma and tell her so; to avoid contradiction and quarreling among yourselves, to be helpful about the house and keep back un-charitable words and looks; to get each lesson well; to obey promptly, to attend to your teeth, and the other things in which you have been instructed."[2]

Despite his intimidating list of admonitions, Dr. Wilder encouraged his children to come to him, even in absentia, with any problem:

When you write Papa—tell him all things in your life: the things that perplex and trouble you: and if you want me to write to you privately I will send the answer in a sealed letter to you. So many things crowd into

the heart and brain of a child that sometimes they need someone they
love to hug them and talk it over. Keep back nothing from Papa—and
learn to take it to the Heavenly Father in prayer.[3]

Each Sunday afternoon Consul General Wilder sat down to type
long missives to his children, sometimes with praise and sometimes
with reproof, emphasizing the rules they were to follow, giving them
details of his comings and goings, offering lavish advice about books
they should read (the Bible, *The Imitation of Christ* by Thomas à Kempis,
Pilgrim's Progress, the novels of Charles Dickens and James Fenimore
Cooper, the poems of John Greenleaf Whittier), and reassuring them
continually that he loved them. There was whimsy in the letters as
well—funny drawings in bright colors, and an array of the silly jokes
that children understand and enjoy. Told that Thornton had taken a
twelve-mile walk, Papa Wilder teased, "Thornton complains of sore
feet: he will find it a help on a long walk to use one foot for, say, a mile,
then the other. This gives each foot a rest, and the wear on the shoe
leather is just one half."[4]

He reviewed the school report cards they mailed to him—compli-
menting them on good grades, chiding them to improve their marks
in arithmetic and penmanship—and deportment, in Thornton's case.
To his father's pride, Amos was already a tennis "sharp," and he hoped
Thornton would learn to play the game well, just as he hoped Amos
would continue his musical training.[5] Thornton, meanwhile, was busy
writing stories and plays (Dr. Wilder complained to his wife, "I wish
you would teach Thornton to spell 'writing'"). He was also collecting
stamps as a hobby, and playing the piano and the violin in recitals,
even though he occasionally suffered from stage fright. "He has played
in public so much that I expect an audience looks to him like a pile of
cord-wood," his father wrote. "I don't think the Wilders suffer much
from stage-fright."[6] Dr. Wilder remembered with pleasure the concerts
his children gave for him when he was on home leave. "Music is a fine
incidental to life: to brighten and refine it," he wrote to them. "Someone of you may give your life to it but I rather hope that you all will
have more earnest missions. However, let the Wilders have abundant

music."[7] He encouraged Charlotte's enthusiasm for studying flowers and insects. "There are many bug books for Charlotte in the library," he wrote, sending her his "hand-glass—very powerful" so she could "look at bugs through it, and flowers especially."[8]

Under their mother's influence, Amos, Thornton, and Charlotte were writing poetry, and Dr. Wilder praised the poems Amos and Charlotte sent, but usually teased Thornton about his. "Thornton's poetry reminds me of Tennyson's," Dr. Wilder wrote; "that is, it is in the English language. It is a little obscure like Browning's and shows a contempt for mere mechanical rhyme, like Walt Whitman. . . . It is lovely to have a genius in the family and I am very fond of my black-haired Thornton."[9]

Poetry written in one's spare time was one thing, but drama was something entirely different, and Dr. Wilder responded with alarm when news wafted his way from Berkeley that the children were involved in plays at the Greek Theatre—and that Thornton in particular was excited about this new activity. "As for Greek plays, you know Papa has only a limited admiration for 'art,'" he lectured them in a letter:

> Some of it—pictures, drama, music—is good as an incidental and diversion in life—but character is the thing in life to strive for. There are people who know all about pictures and Greek tragedy and the latest opera who are not interested in the poor and know little about kindness. . . . I want you to appreciate all good wholesome things of every age, but don't get side-tracked by dramatic art or Wagner music or postage-stamp collecting from present day living, throbbing problems and needs.[10]

His family—especially Isabella and Thornton—seemed to ignore his opinions about dramatic art. "I hope Thornton will not lay too much stress on Greek or any other plays," Dr. Wilder warned in a subsequent letter. "'Things that are pure and wholesome and of good report' we will encourage—but there is such a mass of poor, silly men and women rushing to see plays of all kinds to get a thrill of excitement, that I beg you to regard it as an incidental of life."[11] He wrote later in August to say that he hoped the Greek play had closed. He emphatically communicated his disapproval of "play-acting" and urged his children to embrace instead "the homely wholesome things of to-day."[12]

Dr. Wilder was continually dreaming big dreams for his children, and contemplating practical ways to fulfill them. He wrote that he was "exceedingly proud" of Amos's "excellence in tennis—I am glad he is a manly lad; not only a good mind but a strenuous body."[13] He was pleased that Charlotte and Isabel were captains of their respective baseball teams.[14] Thornton was the child he worried about most, and he outlined a recipe for his second son's personal success: "I hope Thornton is making a boy of sense and steadiness. If he can add these qualities to his temperament, he will make a good deal of a man. Let him play tennis, and concentrate on his books and 'study to be quiet,' and perhaps we'll make a 'State Journal' editor out of him!"[15]

Dr. Wilder steadfastly believed that the spiritual life was the compass for enduring success, and that education was the pathway—good schools, great books. He wanted his children to know a variety of people, a cross section of American society. He wanted the boys to learn about farm life, since in 1910, "half of the 90,000,000 Americans" were farmers, he told the children.[16] "It is my daily prayer," he wrote in one letter, "that my children may grow up to be leaders—loving their fellows, free from the little weaknesses that bind men down—fearless total abstinence men and women—college-educated,—trained in the languages and travel; in touch with the poor and simple."[17]

Amos Wilder received a cablegram June 6, 1910, informing him that his third daughter was born on June 3. "How glad I am and how I love the little thing already, without seeing her and I wonder what shall we name her. One might suppose that loving my big four I would have no love left for no. 5—but love is a funny thing,—the more you put out, the more you have." He affixed to this letter a jaunty signature:

Papa
Consul General for the United States of America
Father of Five Children

Husband of the Lady who lives on Dwight Way
Owner of 2 collar buttons
Author of "Do Horses Have Head-aches, or Life Among the Speedy"[18]

They named the baby Janet Frances Wilder, and it would be months before Isabella felt strong enough in body or spirit to take her brood back to China.

———

IN 1910 Amos Parker Wilder began signing letters and documents with his first name and middle initial, gradually moving from A. Parker Wilder to Amos P. Wilder. On July 4, 1910, he gave his Independence Day reception at the consulate in Shanghai, attended by four hundred people. There were flag decorations, a band—"and not a smell of wine on the place!" he reported proudly to his family.[19] Consul General Wilder distinguished himself in at least two significant ways from the other U.S. consuls to China: He advocated abstinence, and he tried to be of service to missionaries—the "noble Christian men and women" who spread out across the vast country preaching the gospel and trying to convert the "heathens" to their point of view. According to Thornton's recollection in later years, his father was "the only American (or even European) consul within memory who admired, who venerated missionaries," and when that became known, "there was great rejoicing" among the missionary populations scattered up and down the Yangtze River.[20]

Foreign diplomats and missionaries in China often clashed over politics and principles. The missionaries believed that the consuls should do more to protect the Chinese from "drought, flood, and famine," and desist from "smoking, drinking, card-playing . . . and otherwise misrepresenting before the Chinese people the great countries from which they came." The consuls believed the missionaries should refrain from the seeming arrogance of imposing their religious views on the Chinese, and from continually getting themselves into such dangerous predicaments that they had to be "rescued by river gunboats, literally dragged from their besieged churches and compounds."[21] Looking back on those years, Thornton recalled that his father in Shanghai "fell over himself in order to be serviceable in any possible way" to the missionaries.[22]

———

BY DECEMBER 1910 Isabella and the children were ready to leave their home in Berkeley and return to China. They would make the journey this time without young Amos, however. In January 1911 he entered the Thacher School in Ojai, California, a residential school founded and operated by Dr. Wilder's Yale friend Sherman Thacher, who had visited Isabella and the children in Berkeley to interview Amos for possible enrollment in his school.[23] Thacher wrote to Wilder afterward, giving an account of the five Wilder children:

> *I am immensely pleased with Amos's manliness and balance and charm: with Thornton's "soul," or whatever it is that seems to stick out of him, with plenty of sense mixed in at the same time. Charlotte looks like the picture of some distinguished character of history . . . and Isabella [sic] is the finest kind of a kid;—I have not been shown the baby, but she hollers in a way to suggest that she will be as fine an after-dinner speaker as her father, moving her audience to weep or smile, as she does already.*[24]

Thornton longed to have his family living all together in one place again. He believed they had been separated from their father far too long. Now they were temporarily regaining the father, but losing the brother who was, for thirteen-year-old Thornton, both role model and best friend. The family now included Margaret Donoghue, who had come from Wisconsin to be with Isabella when Janet was born in June, and stayed on to care for the baby and her mother. It was decided that Nurse Donoghue would accompany the family back to China.[25]

In Shanghai, Dr. Wilder eagerly prepared for his family's arrival. There was a spacious house where he believed they would live comfortably and happily. There were dogs and a cat, doves and a place for chickens, a couple of ponies for the children to ride. He arranged riding lessons. He found a violin teacher for Thornton, and even installed a cuckoo clock in the house, in memory of the one the children had grown up with in the Wisconsin cottage.[26] All these preparations greeted Isabella and the children when they arrived in Shanghai on February 2, 1911.[27]

Once again Isabella took up her social duties as the consul general's wife. Thornton, nearly fourteen, and Charlotte, twelve and a half, left the house each morning at 7:15 to ride the tram to school, and even their Sundays were carefully structured by their vigilant father. Church services were followed by tiffin and perhaps a nap, and on a typical Sunday afternoon, Dr. Wilder gathered his children together to read aloud from *Pilgrim's Progress* or other edifying literature. Then they had a "good talk"—most of the talking done by the father—about clippings and memorandums he had gathered to illustrate "the progress of Christian civilization."[28]

Shanghai presented Consul General Wilder and his family with an even more difficult set of circumstances than Hong Kong, however. The city was bigger, far more commercial, far more political, and even more social. Dr. Wilder had a much larger staff to oversee, significantly more paperwork to do, many more fires to put out, much more to learn. His additional expenses and workload were staggering. Early in his tenure in Shanghai, he once again felt compelled to confront the State Department and certain American and Chinese commercial interests on behalf of his own personal stance on prohibition. In February 1910 he had received a letter from a New York firm requesting his help in approaching "the leading wholesale drug and liquor dealers in Shanghai" to promote the sale of "a certain brand of bitters." He forwarded the letter to the State Department, asking "to be relieved of participating in the development of markets for alcoholic drinks."[29] Consul General Wilder was not a man to relinquish a principle, even in the face of the United States government.

President William Howard Taft was sympathetic. "I appreciate the difficulty of your situation, and I don't want you to worry yourself over it," the president wrote Dr. Wilder from the White House on April 14.[30] "This time my father was dealing with an old Yale friend [Taft] and a companion in 'Bones' where they take vows in blood for purity and clean cut lives," Thornton wrote a quarter of a century later. Furthermore, he added, his father's position had obvious roots in his own family experience, for Amos Parker Wilder's father "was intemperate and his brother was and still is the town-drunkard of Augusta, Maine."[31] Consul General Wilder replied to President Taft:

> *While recognizing the force of the Department's argument as a working rule of administration, as regards myself, it is more important that I be true to the light I have on this question than that I should fall in with the conventions of government. The conventions of government always lag behind the convictions of the few, and if the few who think they have new light accepted as unchanging the policies of the day, civilization would have no advances to record.*[32]

Once again he offered to resign, and once again he was permitted to stay on. In later years Thornton wrote to his brother, Amos: "It's not hard to imagine Taft's enormous bulk shaking with laughter as he remembers 'Amos' of the Skull and Bones days going through an agony of spirit on the matter, and answering with affectionate indulgence."[33]

Wilder and Taft had enjoyed a brief reunion in Hong Kong in October 1907 when Taft visited China as secretary of war. The two old friends were photographed in silk hats and frock coats. Wilder had ordered a reinforced sedan chair for Taft, who was portly, to say the least, and under whose weight, on a previous visit to China, a sedan chair had collapsed. The Chinese merchant who built the ornate red chair at Consul Wilder's behest invoiced: "Special sedan chair for great American giant."[34]

In Dr. Wilder's new post the grueling social schedule very quickly exhausted Isabella. There were dinners, luncheons, parties given by others, and a procession of hundreds of Chinese and foreigners—residents and tourists—into and out of the Wilders' home. In addition Isabella received a dozen to sixty guests on her "day at home" each Saturday.[35] Try as she might, she was not adjusting any more readily to Shanghai than she had adjusted to Hong Kong. She had not regained her full health, energy, and spirit after the last pregnancy.

Both she and her husband were unhappy with the German school in Shanghai, the only local option for their older children. With help from Nurse Donoghue and the Chinese staff, Isabella could manage the three girls at home awhile longer, but precocious Thornton, now nearly fourteen and missing his brother's companionship, needed more education, more supervision, and more stimulation. While Dr. Wilder was "much pleased with Thornton's cheery temperament and innocence," he worried about his son's strong artistic tendencies. When his head was not in a book, Thornton was dreaming up stories or playing music.[36]

Thornton's parents decided that he must go away to boarding school. Some thought was given to sending him to join Amos at the Thacher School in California, but an alternative lay 450 miles north of Shanghai, in Chefoo (today Yantai, in Shandong Province). The China Inland Mission School at Chefoo was a well-established English-style boarding school for children of missionaries and other foreigners, founded in 1881 for "the education of the children and the recuperation of missionaries suffering from ill-health."[37] Western missionaries braved the hazards of travel to get to the school compound for sanctuary and renewal, many of them leaving their children there to be educated and, it was hoped, stirred to become missionaries themselves. The curriculum was rigorous, the environment was safe, and the tuition was reasonable. Amos and Isabella decided that this would be the best place for Thornton, and plans were set in motion to enroll him for the spring term of 1911.

"I have just got permission to admit Thornton to the Chefoo School," Dr. Wilder wrote to Amos in late March, adding that the school was "on the sea, the physical line is strong, the influences good. . . . There is a hearty, out-door, wholesome flavor to an English school that I think will build Thornton up—make a man of him. He has some strong sides—much good sense and is not a weak fellow, as some might infer."[38]

The school sat on the shore of the bustling treaty port and resort town of Chefoo, overlooking the Bohai Sea as it flowed into the Yellow Sea. The climate and the inviting convergence of hills and sea drew travelers and tourists from all over China for rest and recreation. Native Chinese intermingled with a growing population of foreigners engaged in commerce, missionary work, and occasional warfare. Chefoo was a thriving business center, at any given time exporting exquisite embroidery and other Chinese crafts, along with such crops as peanuts, apples, and opium.[39]

Just as Thornton was preparing for his first sea voyage from Shanghai to Chefoo to enroll in the school, word reached his father that the port of Chefoo was quarantined because of the epidemic of severe pneumonic plague then sweeping through Chinese cities. It was Consul General Wilder's duty to monitor the tragedy in Shanghai and telegraph detailed reports to Washington and to the International Red Cross. "Hundreds a Day Dying of Plague," ran an Associated Press news story based on accounts from Dr. Wilder and other diplomats in China. In Wilder, the diplomat and the journalist now merged to give a graphic account of the ordeal: *"Dread Disease Is Spreading in Many Parts of China Very Rapidly. 65,000 Have Died. Thousands of Bodies Are Being Burned and Many Homes Destroyed."*[40] In some places frozen ground made it impossible to bury the victims, and "half a mile of coffins are visible. The people have finally consented to cremating of 4,000." Officials feared that the number of casualties would double before the crisis was over.[41]

By late April the danger of plague had subsided enough to permit the port to reopen, and soon afterward, fourteen-year-old Thornton joined a shipload of students bound for Chefoo and the tightly structured school experience that would influence him profoundly.

After two rough days and nights plowing northward through the East China Sea to the Yellow Sea, Thornton's ship—an old coastal steamer he described as "crowded, begrimed, smelly"—reached Chefoo.[42] Students traveled under the care of a schoolmaster and schoolmistress sent down from Chefoo to chaperone the journey. The ship put in at several ports along the way, dropping off mail and supplies and picking up passengers, including more students—from homesick eleven-year-olds to cocky teenagers who were "old boys" or "old girls" at the school. Most of the students were children of missionaries and had already traveled hundreds of miles from missionary outposts in the interior, some as far away as the border of Tibet, many knowing that because the journey was so long and expensive, it might be two years or more before they saw their parents again.[43]

While about 50 percent of the children enrolled at the Chefoo school came from China Inland Mission families, another 25 percent came from other Christian mission programs in China, and the remaining 25 percent were children of Western diplomats such as Amos Parker Wilder, or American, British, or European businessmen in China. Dr. Frank McCarthy was headmaster from 1895 until 1930, and "directed the school through many crises—the Japanese war of 1895, the Boxer Rising of 1900, the plague year of 1911, the uncertainties of 1912 when China ended the rule of emperors who had held sway for more than 2,000 years and became a republic"—and on through World War I and the 1920s.[44] The China Inland Mission School did an excellent job of educating boys and girls, and a remarkable job of protecting them. Amos Parker Wilder knew he could entrust his son's safety as well as his education to the Chefoo staff.

"Thornton is at a big English missionary school at Chefoo,—two days north," his father wrote to a friend in June 1911 from Shanghai. "It is a very economical place and the out-door life, sports, etc., are doing him good. He needs a little virility to keep him on the ground. He was soaking himself in medieval drama and like nonsense and I am delighted to have him playing cricket and swimming in the sea which lies in front of the school."[45] While he was at Chefoo, Thornton was required to write at least one weekly letter to his family, and his many surviving letters, penned often under duress each Sunday afternoon, provide vivid snapshots of his Chefoo experience. He wrote about his boyhood in China in detail decades later in "Chefoo, China," the unpublished manuscript that blended history, memory, and imagination, and in another unfinished manuscript entitled "Chinese Story," a fragment of a projected fictionalized version of his life in China. When those later manuscripts are juxtaposed with letters, diaries, and other documents actually written during the time, there is proof that his memory was remarkably reliable. Whether rooted in literal fact or in emotional truth, what survives in the patchwork of these two manuscripts is an

impressionistic story about a pivotal time in Thornton Wilder's boyhood—a time he felt compelled to revisit late in his life.

As his letters confirm, Thornton was terribly homesick at Chefoo at
first, even though the Wilders' fractured family life was by then habitual. Most of his classmates were the children of missionaries, including
young Henry Luce, born in 1898 to American Presbyterian missionary parents, and enrolled at the China Inland Mission School from the
time he was ten until he was fourteen. Compared with the frontier
mission homes many of the students had grown up in, the school was
luxurious. Most of the neo-Gothic buildings had been constructed in
1896. The Boys' School building with its archway and tower, complete
with weathercock, overlooked the shore of the bay, dotted with boat-
houses and bathhouses, and stood adjacent to well-groomed playing
fields. School terms were organized with "clockwork regularity," but
during the summer months children could "ramble at will" on school
playgrounds or go to the beach.[46] With supervision, they could climb
the nearby mountains overlooking the school grounds.

It was the intent of parents and school officials alike to "shield"
the boys and girls at Chefoo school from the "harmful" influences of
the Chinese "heathen" whom their parents risked health and life and
family solidarity to convert, but the children were still served by them.
Chinese boatmen looked after the school boathouse on the beach, and
carried the boats into the water. Chinese servants cooked the meals,
cleaned the buildings, and maintained the cricket pitch on the school
grounds. Chinese groundskeepers "dug, prepared, rolled, and marked"
the tennis courts, and Chinese workers quarried local stone and labored to construct school buildings.[47]

Students were safe and sheltered inside the school compound every
day but Sunday, when they marched into Chefoo "two by two" to attend
Church of England services. "Sunday is not a day of rest for the Chinese," Thornton remembered. "The long procession was often held up in
the narrow streets by a blockage of one kind or another. There we saw
on either side: the goitres, the tumors, the abscesses, the flaking white
stumps of a leper's arms and legs, the blind, the skeletal children."[48]

According to the picture he painted in his manuscripts years later,

Thornton was bristling with concern and curiosity, longing to explore Chefoo and its narrow streets crowded with foot traffic and rickshaws, its colorful markets and shadowed alleys with the omnipresent beggars. He wanted to talk to the Chinese inhabitants of nearby high-walled villages or the small farms spread neatly throughout the countryside. He was not as comfortable as most of his peers with the school's emphasis on sports—not only soccer and cricket but tennis, swimming, and boating—or on religion, the "constant 'barrage of prayer'" as one former Chefoo student described it. Thornton wanted instead to try to see and understand "the human multitude in China."[49] While the Western missionaries worked among that multitude, the European and American expatriates, the diplomats and the businessmen, were more insulated. Yet even they, Thornton wrote years later, "could not long remain entirely unaware of the ocean of suffering around them."[50]

As his letters reveal, Thornton soon discovered that at the China Inland Mission School, the boys were regularly expected to play cricket and soccer, two sports he did not play well and therefore did not enjoy. He tried, however: "The other day I played but they play a different game," he wrote in a letter to his family. "In this one they touch it only with their feet, backs and heads. And I play the little that I know of Rugby and take it in my hands and make a foul. It is something to unlearn."[51] He soon sought and received special permission to enjoy cross-country runs "through fields of monumental Chinese graves." As he remembered it, Thornton "contrived too—though less ambitiously—to leave the bounds" of the school compound and, as he put it, to "go to China."[52]

Most weekdays the boys were required to play cricket or soccer, but on Wednesdays they were allowed to choose their exercise, and that is why Thornton could run cross-country alone in the alluring landscape beyond the school and the city. "This privilege was open only to older boys of proven reliability," he wrote, "but it was accorded to me, probably because of my father's position. I gave my solemn promise not to linger in the villages, not to fall into conversation with the 'natives,' not to touch the offerings on the graves—simply to complete the three-mile course and return to the school."[53] As he relived them in memory years later, he delighted in those solitary treks, running out of the Boys' School grounds past the tennis courts and the walls enfolding the Girls' School, onto the country road that wound through lush farm fields, past farmhouses and tombs. "These were upright inscribed slabs, graceful *stelae*," he wrote. "At the base of many of them were small altars or thrones, some of them in the shape of primitive houses surrounded by offerings in bright colored paper and festooned with streamers invoking the dead."[54] It was at the midway point in his run that he entered the "Grove of the Ancestors," where ancient sycamores and gingko trees encircled a group of "noble tombs."[55]

He loved the "solitary and ruminative" experience of the Wednesday afternoon runs. He had already decided that he was going to be a writer. "It is well known that writers require long stretches of time alone—to think," he reflected in his manuscript decades afterward. "I thought throughout the entire course, but I thought best in the Grove."[56] His habit was to sit in the grove, leaning comfortably against a tree, and to think or, sometimes, to sleep before he ran down the hill back toward the school. He took advantage of any opportunity to try to talk with Chinese people he encountered on the way.

There was no escaping the strict academic regimen of the school, or the "great deal of corporal punishment, from the teachers on the students, and from the students on one another," Thornton wrote in 1929. As he recalled it, he quickly learned from painful experience that the three students with the lowest grades on any class quiz "received three sharp blows on the hand with a ruler and could watch for hours the rising blue welts."[57] "I had many occasions to compare my rising welts with those of my fellow-students," he wrote in his Chefoo manuscript.[58] This was a practice of which his parents disapproved. His father had written to his children that "in the English schools children are punished a good deal; while boys sometimes need a little thumping, I believe that plenty of love will do much the same. At all events, we are bringing you four up on that basis—though now I am absent, the responsibility is great on you all."[59]

The rigorous curriculum, designed in part to prepare students to take the Oxford entrance examinations and in part to produce a new generation of Protestant missionaries in China, included classes in biblical scripture, British history, world geography, English composition and literature, mathematics (including Euclid), science, Latin, music, and drawing, as well as courses in bookkeeping and shorthand. Thornton quickly realized that American boys, himself included, had certain obstacles to surmount. The English boys were far better educated. Furthermore the American boys "gave the impression of being stupid, ill-educated and uncouth," Thornton wrote, looking back. "There was little possibility of our ever, ever growing up to be gentlemen."[60]

He informed his father that he had been placed in a class "much higher than I ever expected and there is some doubt of how long I will stay. Im [sic] already tackling the six major declentions [sic] in a Latin grammar and the rudiments of Algebra." He issued a warning: "My marks will be awfull [sic] (just a little over half the Max, most of them) 65s and 68s." He begged his father not to show the grades to Amos, who was a very good student. "Wait another term. I am getting into the hang of it."[61] Even music, which Thornton loved, presented new complications. "The boys all learn by the Sol-Fa System," Thornton reported in a letter, "and the music-books look like Hiroglyphics [sic]."[62] He enjoyed the religion class taught by "the young and bounding Mr. Taylor," who managed to make it fun to memorize passages from the New Testament.[63]

Although one of his nicknames at home was Todger, Thornton was called Towser at Chefoo—or, more formally, Wilder Minor, since there were other Wilders (unrelated) in the student population. He wrote later, "Wilder Major and Wilder Tertius were to be my best friends among my fellow students, as well as five years later at Oberlin College."[64] These two were sons of Dr. George Wilder, a medical missionary in Peking.

In June 1911 Thornton was elated to learn that his sister Charlotte would soon be coming to Chefoo. His father wrote to a friend on June 10, 1911: "Let me add confidentially, that Mrs. Wilder may go to Europe soon, leaving Charlotte at Thornton's school in the hope that with the minimum cares she [Isabella] may pick up her strength and fire."[65] Isabella's doctor recommended the change of scenery, and once again plans were under way to split the family. She was "run-down and depleted," her husband knew, and she needed *"change—change, newness"* as well as "freedom *from care.*"[66] Dr. Wilder, of course, had to remain in Shanghai. Young Amos would stay at the Thacher School in the United States. Isabella would travel to Europe, as she had longed to do for years, first to Switzerland, and then to join her sister, Charlotte Niven, and her now-widowed mother in Florence, Italy, where Charlotte worked as one of the national secretaries of the YWCA in Europe. Isabella would take the two little girls with her—Isabel, now ten; and Janet, just a year old. And that left Amos in California, and Thornton at his boarding school in Chefoo.

But what to do with Charlotte? It was decided that she would join Thornton in Chefoo. The school was good for him, his parents believed, and they hoped it would be so for Charlotte. "She's a girl full of power," her father wrote to Amos, "if she can get it under control."[67] He had other concerns about Thornton, which he shared in July in a letter to Amos: "Thornton will go through life radiating good nature, I hope, but unless he gets more 'practical' I guess you have to support him!—tho these dreamers sometimes surprise one."[68]

Over their protest, and to their dismay, the decision was made for Thornton and Charlotte to be left to live at the China Inland Mission School. At least they would be together. Thornton waited eagerly for his sister's arrival, and finally, on a July morning, was summoned to the school gate to meet her. He was happy to have her nearby in the Girls' School, even though they were allowed only an hour and a half of "Brothers and Sisters" time each Saturday.[69] Just a year apart in age, they walked together, their dark heads bent toward each other, as Charlotte confided her worries and troubles to her older brother. "She is being made to take french [*sic*] instead of German," he reported in a letter to their father. "All communications about her should be addressed to Mrs. Hayward, Girls C. I. M. School, Chefoo."[70] Soon he wrote with pride that Charlotte was "doing sensational things up at the girls school."[71] A smart, shy, sometimes moody child, Charlotte nevertheless seemed to adjust to the school routine quickly.

Thornton and Charlotte stayed in Chefoo during the school's

summer vacation, while their mother finished preparations for her journey to Europe and their father carried on his work at the American consulate in Shanghai. Chefoo's fresh sea breezes and mild, sun-filled days attracted hundreds of visitors during July and August, and students from the China Inland Mission School had their own private beach for swimming and diving. Sometimes, Thornton reported, they were allowed to go swimming twice a day, and he was learning to dive off the pier a half mile from the school.[72] On her thirteenth birthday, August 28, 1911, Charlotte wrote proudly to her brother Amos that she could swim two hundred strokes, and that she was "getting on pretty well" in Latin, English, French, and geometry. "Can you come up to my height?" she asked her studious older brother. "Latin, French, German, Chinese, English, Eng. Money problems, etc., algebra, geometry at 13 years of age. I'll be a phenomenem [sic] before I finish!"[73]

Charlotte was disappointed that the school offered no courses in Chinese and that only upper-form students were allowed to study German. She asked her father to write to the head of the Girls' School to see if something could be done about that in her case. Many Chefoo students spoke Chinese fluently, having grown up surrounded by Chinese servants and raised by amahs. While it would seem sensible to teach Chinese language, history, and culture, especially to children who might grow up to be missionaries or diplomats like their parents, the teaching of anything Chinese at Chefoo was forbidden until sometime in the 1930s because school officials did not want students to be able to communicate in Chinese with servants or other townspeople.[74]

Harried as he was in Shanghai, Amos Parker Wilder always found time to write letters to his children, especially about their spiritual lives, regularly directing them to read the Bible. Charlotte reciprocated in a letter to her father in July 1911: "You look up I Timothy 2nd chapter 11 and 12 verse and you will find something about women's sufferage [sic]," she wrote. "You may wonder how I penetrated so deep into the Bible. Every morning and evening we have prayers and have quarter of an hour, called, 'silent time,' which we spend reading the Bible. I am beginning with Genesis and going right through."[75]

"My sister Charlotte and I were sent to the China Inland Mission

Boys' and Girls' Schools at Chefoo in Shantung Province, on the coast some 450 miles north of Shanghai," Thornton wrote years later in one passage of his Chefoo manuscript. "I suspect my father selected Charlotte and myself as the two of his children most in need of the edifying influences we would find there."[76]

BY LATE August 1911 the Wilder family was once again separated by oceans and continents, and Thornton thought this was the worst of all the separations he had so far endured. His mother and two sisters, accompanied by Nurse Donoghue, would live in Europe with his aunt and grandmother.[77] His brother, now fifteen, would live in the United States. His father would live in Shanghai. And he and Charlotte would live in Chefoo, 450 miles away from Papa and thousands of miles away from Amos and their mother and the two little sisters who, he despaired, would probably forget him before he saw them again.

Because Thornton and Charlotte dreaded the separation from their mother, Dr. Wilder traveled to Chefoo in late August to visit them to ease the departure. Heedless of the pressures of his father's official duties, his mother's health and desires, and the family's finances, Thornton came to believe that his father, "like a chess-player," moved "his wife and five children about the world, sending some to Europe, some to America, and some to north China—always in the interest of the young people's education."[78]

4

FOREIGN DEVILS

*All those hundreds of thousands of eyes rest on you for a moment, really see
you (you are the "foreign devil") and in those glances is neither antagonism
nor admiration nor even indifference,—there is a touch of curiosity
and some amusement.*

—THORNTON WILDER,
"*Chefoo, China*"

Chefoo, China (1911–1912)

On August 24, 1911, militant Chinese university students
from Szechuan (now Sichaun) in southwest China swarmed
the streets of Shanghai in angry protest against the nationalization of the railway. U.S. Consul General Amos Parker Wilder took
solace in the fact that his family was out of harm's way. His wife and
two youngest children were safely in Europe, his eldest son was with
family friends in the United States awaiting the new academic year at
the Thacher School, and Thornton and Charlotte were tucked away in
the China Inland Mission School compound in Chefoo, surrounded by
teachers and staff who were experienced in protecting their charges
from pestilence, battle, and other dangers.

Dr. Wilder poured his energy into the consular mission of protecting
American citizens and American interests from revolutionary forces in
and around Shanghai. "Safe-guarding the Americans in China" ran the
heading of a story with a Madison, Wisconsin, dateline in the *Waterloo
(Iowa) Times-Tribune* on November 23, 1911, complete with a picture of
the consul general, lauding Dr. Wilder for protecting American lives
and property in the "midst of the present epochal upheaval in the Chinese empire."[1]

In his private hours Dr. Wilder longed for his family. As if courting
his wife, he wrote to Isabella, who was in Lausanne, Switzerland: "My

sweet Isabel—I shall forever call you this in honor of dear days. . . . A fellow in absence must have some beautiful thing to cling to. Tell me if your heart warms a bit."[2] He wanted her to be well and serene again. He passed along the news that at last a buyer had been found for his newspaper. He regretted that he had been so "hampered" with financial worries for so long. He would do better, he promised. "If you have any new resolves in your sweet breast and are willing to be hugged and kissed," he wrote, "come back to me after you have had a winter of rejuvenation, and we will do the Shanghai life normally, as other people do and then go 'on leave.' But if you do not feel any conversion and know no sense of cooperation and dislike Shanghai, I will come and see you all later."[3]

Isabella wrote to assure her husband that she and the children were well and comfortable in Switzerland, although missing Nurse Donoghue, who had accompanied them to Lausanne, helped them get settled, and then returned to the United States. "If only you will get your nerves and serenity & wholesome view of life again," he answered, "*I care not where you go to find it.*"[4]

Dr. Wilder urged his wife to enroll Isabel in a good school and find an evangelical church to attend. He assured her that Charlotte, Thornton, and Amos were "doing nicely" in their respective schools, and seemed to be "very content and *doing good work.*"[5] He could report that Thornton's letters revealed him to be "happy & progressing: *playing tennis* now." He was satisfied that it had been "a great idea" to send Thornton and Charlotte to school in Chefoo, believing that the experience would give them "strong bodies, good English sense & directness, and, I hope, earnest character."[6] He missed Isabella and the children keenly, but, he said, "I am getting on all right; feel well & seem to be doing good work–tho' one never can tell the Washington end." He asked her to send him "a word of *affection.*"[7] He hoped she would come home to him with renewed "bodily health & soul calmness."[8] He reassured her that while the revolution in China was a serious matter, he was not in danger, for the "rebels make foreign friends by scrupulously keeping hands off foreign interests."[9]

DURING THE revolution life went on as usual in Chefoo, removed as it was from the Chinese cities where normal life was riven by bomb explosions, terrorism, bloody massacres, and fierce fighting by revolutionary societies opposed to the existing imperial government, the power of the military, the threatened nationalization of the railroads, and the long-standing "encroachments" of "foreign devils." That brutal autumn of 1911 led to the collapse of the Qing dynasty, the emergence of the fledgling Republic of China, and the ascent to power of Sun Yat-sen.[10]

Safe within the comfortable confines of the China Inland Mission School, Charlotte excelled in her studies, and Thornton began to improve in his, although he remained afraid that he could not achieve enough academically or athletically to please his father. This time, however, Dr. Wilder tried to cheer him up, and wrote to Amos, who was excelling in all ways at the Thacher School, that he didn't care about Thornton's shortcomings "so long as he has the kind and pure heart. He is an unconventional lad and I do not marvel that he does not do as others do." Dr. Wilder was pleased that Thornton had "lots of *sense* in him—for poet natures are sometimes abnormal."[11] He worried about Charlotte, however. Her letters were marked by "an extravagant, uncontrolled swing like her impatient conversations," even when they were full of joy. He wrote to Isabella, "I am troubled of all the children lest she prove unmanageable later—So strong, able and full of fire."[12]

As Thornton felt more at home at Chefoo, his performance on the athletic field also seemed to improve. He hoped to impress his father with reports of his athletic prowess. Most of all he enjoyed his solitary hours running and the hours swimming in the bay.[13] While he was "not a good enough rower to get in the boat-club," Thornton wrote, he did make the tennis club, and he made three runs on one cricket day. He was also learning to drill with Indian clubs, another required activity—although he found that sport perilous: Once, in his daily gym class, a fellow student lost control of a club and it flew across the room "at tremendous velocity," whacking Thornton in the forehead. He was "carried to the infirmary more dead than alive," he recalled years later (with some deliberate exaggeration), and the medical staff looked on in alarm as "the swelling rose to the size of an Easter egg."

Should they telegraph Consul General Wilder in Shanghai about his son's injury? A very concerned nurse reported to Dr. McCarthy, the school's headmaster, that Thornton was "talking very strangely. Very strangely indeed." She was afraid that they must "fear the worst."

"And from that moment," Thornton remembered, Dr. McCarthy knew "that all was well." He said to Thornton later, "If you had begun talking sense, I would have been obliged to telegraph your father."[14]

According to one Chefoo legend, while Thornton played cricket reluctantly, he gave it his best, even managing to make the school team. "He used to play as goalkeeper," schoolmates remembered, "and when the ball was safely at the farther end of the field, he would pull out a copy of Horace's Odes and read that—an admirable act and prophetic of his future greatness."[15] Thornton studied violin for two and a half hours weekly, sang in the glee club, and played the violin in two trios.[16] He respected his violin teacher, the Scotsman Ebenezer Murray, who was noted for "strict discipline" and his "passion for good music and all forms of beauty."[17] Decades later, when he heard that Murray was living in Canada in straitened circumstances, Wilder notified his former classmate, Henry Luce, and they joined other former schoolmates in a fund-raising effort to help their teacher.

In addition to his academic courses, Thornton was taking the required religion courses, including one in Old Testament texts, where he was "studying up Isaiah" and needing the "big Bible" his father had promised to send up from Shanghai.[18] One result of attending the required Sunday church services was that "we were all falling in and out of religious conversions a good deal of the time," Thornton recalled.[19] There was no doubt that this was a school with emphasis on religion, but Thornton had not yet encountered the " 'hell-fire' " evangelism that he would occasionally witness during his college years at Oberlin and Yale.[20] He believed that the majority of American missionaries in China preached a religion that "turned largely on *SIN*." In fact, he wrote years later, "The early translators of the Bible into Chinese found difficulty in translating that word. The Chinese knew all about wickedness and injustice, but when these 'foreign devils' harangued them from street corners, beseeching them to confess their sins to God and be saved, they could only listen with blank wonder. . . . Only an occasional missionary was able to render Christianity *attractive* to his native listeners, to himself, or to his family."[21]

Fascinated as he was by the Chinese people in every corner of the city, Thornton was aware that they in turn were intrigued by the presence of "foreign devils." He reflected six decades later,

> All those hundreds of thousands of eyes rest on you for a moment, really see you . . . and in those glances is neither antagonism nor admiration nor even indifference,—there is a touch of curiosity and some amusement. There is something that is more chilling for an occidental. The Chinese have lived in this density of population for tens of centuries (even the villages convey a shoulder-to-shoulder density); their customs are fashioned by it; their religion has been moulded by it. Those glances reflect also the reason for the omnipresent untended misery: they devaluate the importance of *any one individual life.*[22]

Here were the seeds of one of Thornton Wilder's recurring fundamental themes—the unique value of each individual life among the multiplicity and diversity of souls. As he reflected in later years, "Even small boys are affected by these confrontations."[23]

———

POLITICS RATHER than plague threatened to disrupt the 1911–12 school year at the China Inland Mission School, and many of the missionary parents stationed closer to the violence of the revolution fled to Chefoo for safety. Consequently, Thornton and Charlotte were surrounded by a large crowd of youngsters and adults during the Christmas holidays of 1911 at Chefoo, and they also enjoyed a visit to their father in Shanghai. "There was a great pillow fighting," their father wrote to Amos, and they hung the traditional Christmas stockings.[24] The family exchanged transoceanic gifts and letters as Papa, Thornton, and Charlotte celebrated Christmas in Shanghai; Amos in California; and Mama, Isabel, and Janet in Florence with Isabella's sister and mother.

To inaugurate the New Year, Dr. Wilder led Thornton, nearly fifteen, and Charlotte, thirteen, in a ritual that was dear to his heart—the signing of a temperance pledge. He wrote out the intimidating text by hand, and witnessed the two signatures: Thornton Wilder's first, followed by Charlotte Elizabeth Wilder's, inscribed January 7, 1912, at Shanghai. "My father has instructed me from my earliest years as to the evils of drink," the pledge began,

> and he has shown me that until drinking as a social custom abates, the terrible harvest of violence, misery, insanity, cruelty to children and death will continue, for habit will thus be engendered in the new generation forever coming on. As a Christian, knowing these things, I should count it a duty to refrain from doing anything that shall continue this dreadful waste & loss of human lives and souls; and with heartiness I should join in the efforts of earnest men and women of every race and every religion to bring in the glad day when there shall no longer be a drunkard. . . . I therefore promise solemnly, God keeping me, to abstain from all distilled, fermented and malt liquors as a beverage. . . .[25]

During this time the parents were debating their future plans by mail. Should Isabella and the children return to Berkeley, and if so, when, and should Amos Parker join them there? If so, how would he support them? "We will all be house-keeping in America soon enough—I fear," Dr. Wilder wrote,

> *for I would like to stay here indefinitely to get the income & keep [the] children at Chefoo & Amos at Thacher School for a couple of years. I may be able to do it—I will try; but with the Rebellion & Consular*

intensity, I know not. I think I shall take a room in this Consulate Jan.
I for economy until the early summer when I will ask for leave—if my
ship floats so long.[26]

He assured Isabella that her part, for the time being, was "to live
quietly & to get strong and serene."[27]

AGAINST A backdrop of profound political change in China, Dr. Wilder
tried to cope with his expanding duties in Shanghai. Now he was in
charge not only of oversight of the robust trade enterprises centered
in Shanghai, but of preparing a yearly commercial review of the entire
Chinese empire, based on annual reports forwarded from all the American consulates in China. He had to monitor international business
trends affecting China, Japan, the United States, and the Philippines.
He oversaw the consular court and endless customs, immigration, and
shipping matters. Quite simply, he found himself in charge of one of
the busiest, most important consular posts in the world—and he was
overwhelmed. He was also exhausted, with lackluster energy, but all
the while he did his best to care for his far-flung family, wishing they
were still at home together in Madison or even Berkeley.

No detail involving his children escaped his attention, and he posted
letters to two continents tending to arrangements for them: "Get little
Isabel's nose down to school," he instructed his wife in Florence. "She
is very immature as her dear letters indicate. But she is full of affection & goodness."[28] Get Amos a horse, he told his Yale friend Sherman Thacher. "Amos indicates that a horse is very desirable, not only
through his own wishes but perhaps for efficiency. Will you please get
him a suitable animal of economic cost. I will increase my November
remittance."[29] The Thacher School, which Amos was attending at reduced cost, emphasized the outdoor life, taking full advantage of the
surrounding mountains, canyons, and trails to give the boys experience camping, ranching, and horseback riding.

The elder Wilder wrote to Thacher in haste January 17, 1912: "I
enclose money order for $150.00. Pls. apply to Amos' account. . . . At

the end of this school—in the summer—I hope to clean you up in full. My newspaper is sold but being paid for in installments. Amos' letters are calculated to gladden the parental heart."[30] Dr. Wilder was greatly relieved to have finally found a buyer for his newspaper after struggling to meet the expenses of part of his family in Europe, part in China, and part in California, not to mention his own ever-growing expenses in Shanghai. By then he was "jaded with the Revolution." For the three most turbulent months of the conflict he had worked every day until midnight. "China will be upset for a long time," he predicted.[31] He hoped to get away in the summer for a rest in Japan, and, if possible, to travel to Europe to see his wife and daughters.

Thornton and Charlotte longed for their family to be reunited—and experienced firsthand one of the repercussions of the revolution. On February 10, 1912, Thornton wrote to his mother in Italy that the Chinese servants at the school were on strike because the revolutionary headquarters in Chefoo offered Chinese men eighteen dollars a month to join the army—ten dollars a month more than they were paid to work at the school. As a result, students at the Boys' School had to pitch in and do the work. Like his classmates, Thornton was washing dishes, serving meals, and carrying water.[32] He regretted that he was kept above the fray, inside the walls, not allowed to know the Chinese and their struggles, or to learn their language.

"You can't think how really close the life is here," he wrote to his mother.

> *It makes me lonely every night. No "Kindred spirits" (as Anne of Green Gables says) to converse with. I see I must hurry. I have written you an extra long letter because I am lonely. Won't we ever get together, Mother, Amos and all of us. . . . Try and arrange me away from prison.*[33]

By February 1912 the family faced a more urgent problem, for Dr. Wilder, heretofore endowed with almost superhuman stamina and good health, was very ill. He was suffering chronic digestive problems that sapped his energy and his customary zest for life and work. His illness was serious enough to lead him to take home leave, in hopes that doctors in the United States could come up with a diagnosis and cure. His leave was granted February 17, 1912, and would last until October 21, 1912. "Suffered much of many physicians. Tarried in four hospitals and sanitariums," Dr. Wilder wrote in his brown leather journal in October 1912.[34]

Leaving Charlotte and Thornton at Chefoo—with trusted friends standing by in case of emergency—he set out on the long voyage to San Francisco, where he would seek medical attention. He made a quick trip to Ojai to visit Amos at the Thacher School and came away so impressed that he began to think seriously of enrolling Thornton there as well, if he could afford it. He wrote to Sherman Thacher about Thornton: "I want for him the manliness and wholesome quality, physical and otherwise, that your school confers on boys."[35] Just as he had offered a flexible pay arrangement for Amos's tuition, Thacher extended such a provision for Thornton's.

In Berkeley doctors determined that Dr. Wilder had contracted Asian (or tropical) sprue, a chronic illness of the digestive system that would plague him for years to come.[36] His physician hospitalized him in Adler Sanitorium in San Francisco for a few days, but the illness persisted well into the summer, and he continued to lose weight and energy.

"This is my first letter since you have been ill," Thornton wrote from Chefoo in March. "Oh, my father, of course I am very sorry that you have gone but if you needed it, may there be no complaint from here." He would not gripe about being left behind with Charlotte in China, "because Amos has been left alone in the continent with no other members of the Family." Thornton did complain, however, about his mother's absence: "Oh, but Father, I wish I could see Mother. It seems many years since I saw her last. I want to see her very much. When you make your plans try and let me be near her and—Amos. And of course, father dear, I want you too; my—dear Papa." He asked his father to remember him to President Taft, and to "ask him when he's going to give me my papa for good and all. . . ."[37] He signed his letter "Lovingly Thornton Wilder."[38]

With their father now in the United States and their mother still in Europe, Thornton and Charlotte spent the spring and most of the summer at Chefoo. Thornton's grades were average to low: He received his highest score (80) in scripture, and his lowest (46) in algebra. He ranked fifth in Latin in a form of twenty-two students, and eighth in a form of twenty-three in English. His lowest rank—a twenty-second—came in penmanship. But a note from the form master affirmed that "his conduct during the time he has been at the school has been exemplary," his work "has been faithfully performed," and his music teacher pronounced his work excellent.[39]

He was caught up in what he called "self-educating"—reading Horace, learning to play Beethoven sonatas, learning a "flashy" Chopin prelude by heart "for those people who ask & Papa will not allow me to refuse."[40] Most of all, he was elated to learn that plans were under way—at last—for him and Charlotte to return to the United States. "Here we are again," he wrote to his mother. "Sunday Night. 8:15 PM. Charlie [his nickname for Charlotte] going to bed up in her nunnery and I still in prison with promise of release in a month."[41]

They were to sail on the SS *Nile* for San Francisco, with a family friend supervising their departure, since their father was still in the United States. Papa had instructed Thornton to write an account of the long homeward voyage, and he did so in at least one sixteen-page letter to his mother, illustrated with rough sketches. "Save it," Thornton asked, "so I can show him that I made some semblance of obeying." He wrote to his mother, "It seems years since I saw you and I can only imagine you in a dim, wistful way as being something like I'd like to be."[42]

THE YEARS of separation from family, and the boarding school discipline of weekly letters home, turned the young Thornton Wilder into an inveterate letter writer, and by the time he was a teenager the habit was entrenched. Even in his compulsory letters, he was adept at conveying the weekly news in dramatic form—avid criticism of activities he disliked; colorful accounts of swimming or eating or being seasick; a long list of "old letter debts to pay," as he put it, listing in one brief note eight adults back in Berkeley to whom he owed letters.[43] He devoted one entire compulsory letter to his father to a rant against cricket, laying out the rules that "surprised" him, and saying, in closing, "hoping you are not an enemy of raillery, I am still, Lovingly, Thornton Wilder."[44]

Following the orders of the prefect who read each boy's weekly letter, Thornton often had to write every misspelled word correctly several times: "Contents. Opinion. Surprise."[45] Once he had to re-write a compulsory letter three times because the supervising teacher "did not like the writing or paragraphing!"[46] This was his disciplined apprenticeship in letter writing. His letters gave his father sporadic satisfaction, some dismay, occasional pride, and a strong measure of paternal apprehension. Dr. Wilder forwarded one letter to his sister, Helen, with a headnote: "Here are sidelights on this dear & unusual lad, whose unfolding between Isabel's & my own diverging influences I watch with prayerful solicitude."[47]

Now and then there was a flash of precocious understanding of others. "Write me if there is anything but gladness in Mother's letters," Thornton had asked in a letter to his father on September 30, 1911, when his mother had reached Italy. "She has had bad hours, self-made it seemed to me then, in Berkeley and Florida. I hope she has none in her Utopia."[48] While Dr. Wilder wished his wife were "serene and enjoyed things more," he understood that "the long strain of raising a family has given her 'nerves'"—but according to Isabella's letters, she was still not "composed enough to make a home for you children yet."[49]

As the family letters wove their way from Chefoo to Shanghai to the United States to Europe and back, Thornton found companionship on paper with his mother in Italy or Switzerland and his father in China. With his mother he discussed poetry, plays, and music, and confessed his loneliness and his affection. To his father he gave practical reports of his activities, and glimpses of his worries and disappointments. Once his father was upset to discover that Thornton had written a private letter to his mother, and wrote to chastise his son. Thornton replied in self-defense: "First, it was very lush and sentimental, the mood that Mother can accept, if she is ready in her mood of a letter from the son. . . . Mother's letter held no words that I would not have you see. There was that part of my self that Mother shares with me: the expression of Sentimentality." His father, he knew, would have found it "silly" and "too weak and light for big, powerful people."[50]

CONSUL GENERAL WILDER had left a host of problems behind in Shanghai, and most of them awaited his return from his eight-month-long home leave. Whether because of his flagging health, or prolonged overwork, or his inability, despite his best intentions, to deal with the unremitting demands of his duties, he was not functioning well in his diplomatic post in Shanghai, as his official evaluations made painfully clear. He was liked and admired in Shanghai, as he had been in Hong Kong, and much in demand as a public speaker, wrote Consul-General-at-Large Fleming Cheshire, who had so enthusiastically praised Amos's accomplishments in Hong Kong. But Shanghai was a different story. While Dr. Wilder appeared to endeavor to "maintain a high standard of efficiency as Consul General," his 1911 inspection report had noted, he lacked "one very essential qualification . . . commercial instinct." He was criticized by some American merchants in Shanghai as being "political rather than mercantile." Instead of the "excellent" ratings he had attained in Hong Kong, Dr. Wilder had been demoted to "good" in 1911 in Shanghai.[51] By June 1913, that would drop to "poor," this time in the inspection conducted by Consul-General-at-Large George Murphy. Dr. Wilder was a fine man, but "exceedingly weak" in "administrative ability." Furthermore, as Wilder himself acknowledged, he had "no commercial training and had no aptitude for details." Despite these considerable failings, Murphy wrote, he considered Consul General Wilder to be "personally a most excellent man and, in some other respects, a useful and creditable Consular officer"—a man of "the highest personal standards" who was "popular and respected," "unobtrusively and generously charitable," and an influence for "peace and good will."[52]

THORNTON WILDER was nine years old the first time he saw China, and he lived there for six months before moving back to the United States to Berkeley, California. He was nearly fourteen the second time he saw China; this time he lived there for a year and eight months before returning to California. Decades later he revisited China in his memory and imagination and began to write about the Chinese experience in fiction and nonfiction. He started *Doremus*, a novel about Dr. Alexander Fuller Buckland, a Methodist missionary in China, and his wife, Mildred, and their children. (Dr. Wilder had a good friend, Doremus Scudder, who was a minister in Hawaii.) "The life of a missionary's children in China near the beginning of the present century would have [been] perfect joy except for one thing," Thornton wrote decades later. "Anything that was really adventurous or fascinating was forbidden."[53] The partial draft of the novel not only offered biting commentary on the missionary movement, but comedy verging on farce, including the spectacle of the Buckland children running wild, with their amah chasing them on bound feet. Then there was the graphic drama of the children witnessing a public execution.

Like the father of one of Thornton's roommates at Chefoo, the Reverend Doctor Buckland was a native of Tennessee. He was an "almost total failure" as a missionary. For him "Christianity turned largely on the Christian's conviction of sin." Thornton wrote in the manuscript draft, "Religion was presented under two guises, the ecstatic and the terrifying." Dr. Buckland believed "that every man and woman born into the world stood in dire need of salvation," and each had to be "frightened, bullied, or somehow lugged into Heaven."[54]

The unfinished, handwritten draft is testimony that the boy who went to China came home with the experience deeply etched in his memory and imagination. His years in China, especially in the Inland Mission School, left him with a firmly embedded skepticism about organized religion. The China experience awoke in him a fascination with the relationship between the multitude and the individual, the masses and the one, and he began as a teenager to try to decipher what it meant—a search that would last a lifetime.

The China experience also intensified the young Wilder's sense of being an outsider, a stranger. He was an American looked down on by many of his peers from England, cut off from his peers in China, separated from the family who loved him even if they did not always fully understand him. In those formative years Thornton grew resigned to the prolonged separations from his parents and siblings. How was he to know where he belonged, and with whom? How was he to function without kindred spirits—especially his mother and his brother? He idolized his brother. He adored his sometimes emotionally exhausted, frequently geographically distant mother. He loved, revered, and sometimes feared his dynamic father. He longed to have the family reunited.

Not only was Thornton separated from his parents and his brother and sisters; he was separated from his national identity, living surrounded by an exotically different culture but literally walled off from it, attending the rigorous English boarding school in the middle of China, where he studied German, French, and Latin but where there were no classes in Chinese, the language and the key to the culture he longed to explore. He was innately curious about the Chinese people, their customs, their daily lives. He was surrounded by the enigmas of the ancient, richly complex culture of China, yet denied the tools and the vocabulary that could help him know and understand it. Language, he thought, was the key to the mystery, and he began to discover the far-reaching power of the word.

5

"PARENTAL EXPECTATION"

For the man, a telling reflection: "Parental love is proportionate to the
intensity of parental expectation of a child's contribution to life."
—THORNTON WILDER,
"Chinese Story"

California and China (1912–1913)

W hat on earth shall I do at Thatcher [*sic*]—'I haven't a rag
to put on—not one!'" Thornton, now fifteen, wrote to
his mother from the SS *Nile* en route from Shanghai to San
Francisco in late summer 1912. He had two old suits, he complained,
but they were in "rags and tatters." He might begin wearing "long
trousers," he wrote. "I am as big as some boys @ school who wore
them. I wouldn't like to though."[1]

He was being sent to live and study at the Thacher School in Ojai,
California, where his brother Amos had already distinguished himself
as a top student, star athlete, and popular member of his class, and
Charlotte would go to school in Claremont, California. The heady freedom of the long sea voyage took Thornton's mind away, at least temporarily, from his anxiety. His long-held dream of returning to California
came closer to reality day by day during the monthlong voyage, and
although his father's friends had tipped a stewardess to watch over
Thornton and Charlotte, they were traveling virtually unencumbered
by any supervision—"two *lone Babes on the Sea*," Thornton joked in a
long letter to his mother.[2]

He slept on deck, along with many other passengers, and joined in
one evening's entertainment—a vaudeville performance, wherein, he
reported, "I recited an affair I made up impersonating 4 people." At
the shipboard fancy-dress evening, when passengers wore costumes, a
young woman lent him an evening dress, and Thornton dressed up as a

duchess, with yellow rope for hair. "Puritanical Charlotte expected to be shocked," he wrote, "but as it wasn't so very decoletée [*sic*] (how on earth does it go) she let it pass."[3] Meanwhile, young Amos was working hard during his summer vacation as a laborer on the farm of L. B. Husted near Saratoga, California, honoring his father's unorthodox vision of how his sons should spend their time between school terms. Years later, looking back, Amos interpreted his father's motivations:

> My father thought there was no experience for a growing boy more valuable than working in a country store or on a farm. . . . All this was part of what our parent called "broadening experience." . . . The long-range health factor weighed large, but most important was diversity of experience and initiation into varied aspects of the world's work and the common life.[4]

Over the years Dr. Wilder found summer employment for his sons on farms from coast to coast—in California, Wisconsin, Kentucky, Ohio, Massachusetts, and Vermont—and he dispatched his daughters to summer programs in Michigan, Pennsylvania, and Massachusetts.

Amos had greatly pleased his father by writing that he would "be glad to be a missionary or minister. . . . If I cannot be a great man in the world, I will be a great man in myself."[5] Sherman Thacher had recommended him to Farmer Husted with superlatives: Amos was "the finest kind of a boy, of the very highest moral character and of very careful religious training." Thacher went on to praise Amos as an excellent student, and "a boy that it is always a pleasure to have about, who can be relied upon to work faithfully, intelligently, one whom you may trust absolutely with any financial responsibility." Furthermore, Thacher wrote, Amos was "a boy who is contented anywhere, working, or playing, or reading a book, day after day."[6]

All the while Dr. Wilder was coping with his ongoing health problems, and he was mightily discouraged and depressed. Struggling to regain his health and eager to consult with American physicians, Dr. Wilder traveled to New York and New Haven in late summer 1912, far away from his duties in China and from his scattered. family—his

wife and two youngest children still in Europe, and his three older
children in California. His political and diplomatic worries intensified
in this presidential election year, for China was an issue. Democrats,
led by Woodrow Wilson, were advocating full diplomatic recognition
of China, a position opposed by the Republicans and incumbent Republican president William Howard Taft, Wilder's friend and patron.[7]

Despite the obstacles of illness and geography, Dr. Wilder worked
hard to make the best possible arrangements for Amos, Thornton, and
Charlotte, ultimately deciding that both the boys would go to Thacher
School. Charlotte would be sent to board with the Maynard family, his
friends in Claremont, California, but strangers to Charlotte, and she
would attend public school there. Getting Thornton to Thacher School
had been Dr. Wilder's goal since 1911, but Isabella—who held her own
very strong opinions about how the children should be brought up—
had overruled him then, insisting that Thornton and Charlotte accompany her back to China.[8]

Dr. Wilder felt that Thornton needed "the virile atmosphere" of
Thacher.[9] He was forthright as he filled out the required questionnaire
for Thornton's admission: Was his son quick tempered? He was "inclined that way." Did he get on well with other boys? "Not a good
'mixer'—has a few congenials." Did he have any difficulties in school?
"None." Yet, the father added, "Some teachers find him hard to clas-
sify." Was he accustomed to seeing people play cards or other games for
money? "On shipboard—and aware of it [in] Shanghai society." What
was his most serious fault or weakness? "He is 'the boy that is different'—Sensitive—Self conscious—radiantly happy when with those he
likes who understand him—May develop 'moods.'" Thornton was not
good at sports, the father reported, but he loved music, art, drama,
literature. He got low marks in many subjects because of "Lack of concentration." Thornton was "not a good drudge." He could be nervous,
even "terrorized" by certain pressures and routines that were "easy
to others." He had a "delicate, fine nature." He knew nothing about
guns or rifles, and his father would be "delighted" for him to learn. In
the matter of buying a horse for Thornton, "great economy" would be
necessary. Unless he was sick Thornton would be expected to attend

the Presbyterian church five miles from the school, where seats were reserved for Thacher boys.[10]

Fortunately Thornton was not privy to the portrait his father drew for Sherman Thacher, but he lived in continual awareness of his father's high expectations and his own shortcomings. "What you are now you will be later," Dr. Wilder had written to his son from Shanghai. "I know what a happy nature you are; and now to hold it. I much wish you might have more farm life—outdoor grandeur and practicality—that you might learn to work with your hands and depend on yourself."[11]

For his father Thornton's acceptance at Thacher was a goal achieved. For Thornton, it was one more move in his father's chess game. Bristling with resentment at another separation from family members, Thornton prepared reluctantly to go to one more strange place, one more new school. "How hard and callous the Wilder family will get through all the bi-monthly and even weekly leave-takings," he wrote to his mother.[12]

It had also been a sad leave-taking for Dr. Wilder. Not only would he live alone in China once more, but he was still grappling with his illness. His health had improved from the months of treatment and relative rest in the United States, but the disease would be chronically debilitating from that time on. He would never fully recapture the robust physical and intellectual energy that had defined him before he was felled by the Asian sprue. He found himself fifty years old and frail, and overwhelmed by his complicated responsibilities in Shanghai.

As a teenager Thornton did not understand the professional burdens his father carried. He was also unaware of how deeply his father suffered the consequences of separation from the family. For Thornton the overriding reality was that for nearly two years he had been living away from both his parents and one or another of his siblings, communicating with them primarily through letters. Bound for one more new "home," he hoped to hang on to some of his Chefoo friendships by correspondence. He had already learned, chameleonlike, to assume a definite persona for each recipient of a letter, changing colors as need be when he finished a letter to one person and began one to another, tailoring his voice and subject to the needs and interests of his correspondents. There seemed to be as many Thorntons as there were friends and relatives.

In his fifteenth year, embarking for California to live in his older brother's shadow at Thacher, Thornton slowly gave up trying to be the son he thought his father wanted him to be. He summoned the audacity and temerity to begin expressing his honest, sometimes obstreperous, true self. More and more often, as he stood on the bridge between boyhood and manhood, he struck a note of rebellion and defiance in letters to his father, despite his ongoing concern for the elder Wilder's health problems. In letters uncannily like the letters young Amos Parker Wilder had written to his own father, Thornton fired off complaints—attacking the school, his peers, and most of all, his father's edicts and decisions. By contrast, he still confided his hopes and dreams to his absent mother, and shared candidly with her the realities of his daily life and his intellectual and artistic pursuits.

He had been led to hope that his mother would return to California by midyear 1913, and he counted on that reunion. "I don't know to what degree I'll like school," he confessed to her. "But oh lady, you'll be back (with the eternal Wilder question-mark) in June."[13]

IN MID-SEPTEMBER of 1912, Thornton found himself in the Ojai Valley, near Nordhoff, California, living in a rustic, ranch-style school surrounded by high mountains and rough terrain, tamed here and there into avocado and citrus orchards, with the nearby Sespe River twisting through rugged crags and canyons. It took him several weeks to adjust to life at the Thacher School, where the boys often slept outdoors in the canyons, rode horses along the river, and worked on trail building or other ranch projects after their school day was done.

Two schools could hardly have been more different than Thacher and the China Inland Mission School. In Ojai, Thornton was transplanted into an environment where the school's founder believed that insofar as possible, school life should mirror real life, with a daily emphasis on self-reliance, practical as well as analytical thinking, good manners, kindness, tolerance for others, and appreciation and respect for the natural world. Sherman Thacher, a graduate of Yale, class of 1883, had founded his school in 1889. From his father, a Latin professor at Yale from 1842 until 1886, Thacher inherited "an aversion to people of wealth," and this often influenced his decision about whether to admit a young man to Thacher.[14] He would sometimes turn away a prospective pupil whose parents were ostentatiously wealthy, while he made every effort to admit worthy students whose parents lacked the financial resources to send them to Thacher, especially if he perceived the boys to be of sterling character. Such was the case for his Yale friend and fellow Skull and Bones member, Amos Parker Wilder, who wanted to entrust his sons to Sherman Thacher and the school, which was already building a reputation as an effective Yale feeder establishment.

Thacher's letters to Dr. Wilder were accommodating to a fault: Wilder was offered a reduced rate, to be paid monthly at his convenience, or any other plan that "may prove to be in accordance with what you can satisfactorily arrange."[15] Once Thacher wrote, "I enclose our school bill, as a matter of form, the understanding always being that you shall treat it as may be convenient to you."[16] Without this largesse, Amos and Thornton Wilder would never have been able to go to Thacher.

He hoped that his school would produce young men with independent minds. He set high standards in the classroom (hiring many teachers fresh out of his alma mater), but he also encouraged the arts and sports, especially horseback riding. He wanted each student to have a horse, and to learn how to care for the horse as well as to ride it. (Thacher believed there was "something about the outside of a horse" that was "good for the inside of a boy.") Once they were ready, students were free to ride all over the inviting, sometimes intimidating terrain of the Ojai Valley, and to explore the rugged, often desolate mountains and wilderness.

At Chefoo, Thornton had been confined by language, boundaries, and structure, cut off from home and denied access to the exotic country that surrounded him. At Thacher he was free. Nature was his classroom. His brother was already deeply at home at Thacher, with accomplishments greater than Thornton could even aspire to equal. He wouldn't excel, as Amos did, in the classroom, on the tennis court, in the student government, or on the baseball field. Thornton's interests lay beyond sports, and at Thacher he could indulge them freely. He could play in the orchestra and study piano and violin. ("Beethoven's Sonatas have been called the musician's Shakespeare, and if ever you live in the same house as I do you'll get to know them," he nagged his father.)[17] He spent hours in the library reading and writing. Best of all, not only could Thornton write plays; he could even see one of them produced. The school boasted a Greek-style amphitheater, located in a steep ravine surrounded by barns and pastures, an "Arcadian spot unmarred by artificial scenery, with a stream bed separating the audience and the actors."[18] It was the site of many remarkable performances, Thornton wrote his father. One of them was Thornton's *The Russian Princess: An Extravaganza in Two Acts*. The play was produced in the Outdoor Theatre on May 21, 1913, with Thornton directing and appearing as the villain, Grand Duke Alexis of Russia. He wore a heavy fur coat and, his classmate Lefty Lewis remembered, went "darting about the stage while his fellow-actors looked on helplessly."[19] The play was "Thornton's big moment at the Thacher School."[20] Written by Thornton and another student, Jack Drummond, the drama was set in Paris, in an apple-vendor's shop and in a cabaret. Others who witnessed the production believed that Thornton "furnished the plot, and Jack Drummond the spelling and punctuation" and one of the teachers thought that the drama owed its inspiration "to Thornton's fur coat."[21]

Although the Wilder children coped, each in his or her own way, with the prolonged parental absences, it was Amos who seemed to adjust most easily. He was quiet, self-effacing to the point of shyness, but popular, and his athletic prowess and academic achievement earned him the respect of teachers and fellow students. Isabel and Janet were happy and content with their mother, aunt, and grandmother. Janet knew no other way of life than to live in Europe far away from her father and brothers and sister Charlotte. The fractured family life was hardest on Thornton and Charlotte, both shy like Amos, but less stoic, more high-strung, and less equipped to acclimate to new surroundings.

The family separation was a special agony for Charlotte, as the middle child, for she had been sent away from the family before—as a baby, before the birth of Isabel; and as a schoolgirl in Chefoo, allowed only an hour and a half each week to see her brother. Now she was being sent to live with total strangers in a new place—the Maynard family in Claremont. Isabella later came to believe that Charlotte's displacements as a child caused serious problems for her as an adult.[22] Now in California, Charlotte was once again the Wilders' "sent-away" child.

Thornton's boyhood letters dramatically reveal the scope of his loneliness, and his longing for a normal family life. As he parted from his father and entered Thacher, not only was he homesick—for wherever home was—but he fell physically ill enough to be quarantined in the school sickroom. "This is the old situation of being sick after I leave you," he wrote forlornly to his father in a letter headed "Thatcher[*sic*]. Sick room. Broken Heart. Sunday P.M." Confined to bed and to his own company, he read and slept and played chess with himself "because no one else was allowed in the room for fear of catching appendicitis or gout."[23]

Dr. Wilder delivered Charlotte to Claremont that autumn of 1912 into the care of the Maynards, his friends who would board her and supervise her daily life, including her schoolwork and activities. Years later Isabel remembered that from their youth, her older sister was "handsome, very intelligent" and an eager student with "a mind full of curiosity" and an "intense" awareness of nature. Isabel added, "She was also highly sensitive and easily upset"—a "very private person" with a tendency to brood.[24] Charlotte had been happy at Chefoo, but she found much to brood about in her life in Claremont. Under Mrs. Maynard's strict supervision, Charlotte felt that she was being used as a household servant—washing dishes, cleaning, sweeping, with steady reproof and little praise from Mrs. Maynard.[25] Apparently at Dr. Wilder's instruction, Mrs. Maynard tried to teach Charlotte domestic skills, including sewing—a difficult task for Charlotte because she was left-handed. "In short," Charlotte wrote to her father, "I'm taken in as a member of the family without the privileges of a member of the family."[26] She recognized that some of Mrs. Maynard's discipline was good for her, but she dreaded the frequent scoldings, and even though she often enjoyed the company of the Maynard children, she begged her father not to send her back to Claremont for another year.

DURING HIS year at Thacher, Thornton applied himself industriously to the task of learning to ride a horse. He had not ridden since his Shanghai days, and then, more often than not, he had been astride a pony, but he soon reported to his father that he could ride pretty well. By March 1913, he was riding out into the valley regularly, often making the ten-mile round-trip to Nordhoff, the nearest town. "I like riding all right but the only thing is it hurts," he wrote to his father. "It made some huge blisters on me. I'll probably get used to it some day."[27] His horse was well into its teens, a white horse and "the nicest old thing ever bridled," Thornton wrote.[28]

Far more at home with music, books, and plays, Thornton worked hard at the piano and the violin, occasionally performing in concerts at Thacher. He played second violin in a quintet, and gave a solo concert one night to an audience of Thacher's Chinese staff members—a special "treat," Thornton wrote facetiously, "to keep them on the second day of their new year from going to some pagan festival."[29] Early in 1913 he wrote to his mother in disappointment about losing a part in the school play because of his father. The big Thacher event of the spring was a schoolwide festival that included a tennis tournament—in which young Amos, the California high school doubles champion, would no doubt be a star. Parents would be coming "from far and near," Thornton wistfully reported to his mother. There would be a big crowd for the gymkhana, the shooting matches, the tennis tournament, a dance, and then the play in the Outdoor Theatre—a performance of Oscar Wilde's *The Importance of Being Earnest*. Eager for a part in Wilde's "funny, frivolous farce," Thornton tried out for the play.

In a boys' school, of course, boys played all the roles, male and female. Thornton was thrilled when he won the part of one of the leads—"Lady Bracknell, a very sharp, lorgnette-carrying old Lady," he told his mother. "I began learning my part right off and fell to work trying not to laugh at the clever epigrams I had to say."[30] He was already something of a ham, not nearly so shy onstage as off, and especially fond of comedy and farce. Thornton was happily absorbed in preparations for the play until one evening when Sherman Thacher interrupted him as he sat reading by the fire in the parlor. Thornton described the ensuing scene in the letter to his mother:

> *"Oh Thornton," [Mr. Thacher] said, "your Father said in a letter*
> *that he would rather not have you in the plays taking female parts, so,*
> *altho' he didn't absolutely order you, I think we had better do as he*
> *says." I was terribly disappointed. Now another boy has the part. It'll*
> *be very un-funny to watch the part I might be taking. The worst part of*
> *all comes in the explaining to other boys all about how my puritanical*
> *pater disapproves, etc.*[31]

AS MUCH as he admired Sherman Thacher and his school, Dr. Wilder decided to move his "chess pieces" once again—to send Amos to Oberlin College and to withdraw Thornton from the school the coming year. When he heard of the plans, Sherman Thacher wrote Consul General Wilder a stern reprimand. He demonstrated "peculiar vacillations" with his sons, Thacher charged, moving them every few months. He told Dr. Wilder that he had received a letter from Mrs. Wilder saying that the only point on which she and her husband agreed in the children's education was that it was best for Thornton to return to Thacher. Furthermore, Thacher told Wilder, Amos was disappointed to be heading for Oberlin rather than Yale, although he accepted the decision "loyally and bravely." It was hard for Amos to see his friends go off to great universities while he "for some reason he can hardly appreciate is sent to a college that is hardly heard of far from its own locality and special friends."[32]

Dr. Wilder would later write Thacher to thank him for his influence on Amos and Thornton. "They are more manly in consequence and I believe lovers of truth," their father reflected. "Amos is a serious young man and introspective; without the tennis, horse back riding, the love of nature bred of the mountains, I suspect his development would have been feverish—as it is, he sadly mixes up God and Nature for which I am glad. Surely to love one is to love the other." As for Thornton, Dr. Wilder wrote, before he went to the Thacher School

> *he was the last word in high browism, a delicate, girl-playing, aesthetic lad in the early teens; this kind of boy making a one-sided, often unhappy, inadaptible [sic] man is familiar. By wise contact with outdoor life, wholesome farm work, physical weariness and honest country people, Thornton is really quite a man; has a fair chest, a firm handshake and mixes well with all classes. What was done with him can be done with many another "difficult" boy. But it requires wisdom.*[33]

BY JUNE 1913, Thornton was eager to travel to Berkeley, where his mother and little sisters were now recovering from the long journey from Europe and settling into a rented house at Third and Townsend streets.[34] He could hardly wait for the reunion, and he promised to take good care of his mother. The house creaked, she told him, and while she was happy there during the day, she was uneasy at night. He pledged that he would be her companion and protector, even her servant. "When I get there I will expect to wash dishes," he wrote, adding that he would willingly be her slave. "We will have a lovely time this summer."[35]

Thornton longed to spend the summer in Berkeley with his mother and sisters, and wanted "*very* much" to take a summer school course. He was determined to persuade his father that he should not, as Dr. Wilder wished, spend the summer working on a farm. Thornton couldn't bear the prospect of another separation from his mother so soon after her two-year absence. Besides, he complained to her, it was his father's "Dementia"—the idea that Thornton and Amos should spend the summer working on a Wisconsin farm. Rather than that "Wisconsin Agricultural idea," Thornton proposed, let him work in the garden at home in Berkeley. "Mother, you can make me dig up your garden for 15 minutes (or if necessary more) a day. We will send to Huyk and Von Style Brothers, Amsterdam, for some rare and costly bulbs over which one must work hourly. We can also get some inexpensive Portland cement and I will make you an Italian garden."[36]

Perhaps because he was outnumbered, or perhaps because he was sick and overworked, Amos Parker Wilder gave in to the family's wishes. Thornton stayed at home, did some volunteer work with children "in a poor part of town," he reported to his father in a letter, and found the children "as interesting as they were ragged." He read to them and played dominoes with them. And he was gardening after all: "I have already weeded extensively in our side gardens and back," he wrote, "with many plans for the future."[37]

MEANWHILE, IN Shanghai, Consul General Wilder generated another summer imbroglio over the annual Independence Day reception. He decided to hold the reception at his own expense, at his home rather than at the consulate, and to serve only grape juice and water. The American community, however, "decided to relieve Mr. Wilder of embarrassment by holding its reception in the Palace Hotel."[38] Afterward, an official State Department report condemned the "friction" created by Dr. Wilder's handling—or mishandling—of the 1913 celebration of the Fourth of July.[39]

Even in the throes of controversy in Shanghai, Dr. Wilder completed arrangements for the ongoing education of his children. He gave in to Isabella's demand to keep her younger children at home, but overruled Amos's desire to go to Yale, believing that Amos needed more maturity. To that end Dr. Wilder went forward with plans to send Amos first to Oberlin College. Thornton and Charlotte would enter the junior class at Berkeley High School. "I am again prepared to perhaps fall in with another school," Thornton wrote to his father in September 1913. "The beauty of the school is that so far it has left me entirely alone. I confess that I never expected that. I got a little of that at Chefoo, but never a drop at Thacher. I like it on that account, very much."[40]

Alone in Shanghai, Consul General Wilder struggled under the weight of incessant official details, reports, protocol, and procedures to the point that his superiors and many American citizens in Shanghai were displeased with his performance. Consul-General-at-Large George Murphy wrote in his official 1913 report that Wilder lacked "Consular training and official energy. He is a man of most respectable and creditable life. He is an eloquent speaker. He is a strong advocate of total abstinence. He is a man of good appearance,—quiet, gentlemanly, and amiable. BUT he is not by disposition competent to well and thoroughly conduct the affairs of this office."[41] He noted that Dr. Wilder's health had been bad, that he had been on extended home leave, but "He says that it is now improving."[42] In sum, Murphy reported that Amos Parker Wilder was a good man but a "poor consular officer."[43]

As of June 1913 Amos Parker Wilder was officially a failure in Shanghai, as well as the focus of considerable controversy. There were calls for the State Department to replace him. He was proud, stubborn, and ambitious—but he was no longer young or vigorously healthy. Separated from his wife and children, he left the daunting disorganization of his office at night and returned to the Shanghai Club and the room where he now lived, facing his doubts and problems in solitude, no doubt wondering how long he would keep his post in Shanghai and what he would do, at his age, if he lost it.

6

"ALL ASPIRATION"

It is a discouraging business to be an author at sixteen years of age.
Such an author is all aspiration and no fulfillment.

—THORNTON WILDER,
Foreword, The Angel That Troubled the Waters

California, Vermont, and China (1913–1915)

By the fall of 1913 five of the Wilders were consolidated under one roof in Berkeley, California—all but Amos Parker Wilder, in Shanghai; and young Amos, beginning his freshman year at Oberlin. At Berkeley High School, Thornton was enrolled in classes in English, German, geometry, beginning Greek, and Virgil. He quickly became an "impresario," he wrote his father, when his one-act farce, *The Advertisement League*, was chosen for a vaudeville entertainment at the school on September 26, 1913, to benefit the new gymnasium. "The Vaudeville Show has come to be one of the most enjoyable features of the school term," and Thornton's skit was "a truly original conception," according to the staff writers of *Olla Podrida*, the high school yearbook.[1]

In a letter to his father Thornton described his play facetiously as "a magnificent treatment of all the problems that ever ruined the worrying-powers of man. Its dynamic force in way of social uplift is almost as tremendous as it is negligible."[2] He was directing a cast of four girls and two other boys, and finding rehearsals "perfect nightmares" when there were no teachers on hand. In deference to his father, Thornton cast himself as Mr.—not Mrs.—Lydia Pinkham (the nineteenth-century Massachusetts woman whose famous vegetable compound could supposedly cure every malady known to womankind).[3] "Of course I have adhered to your demand that I remain in masculine clothes," he told Dr. Wilder. "When you have changed your mind as to it please notify."[4]

Thornton's letters to his father grew increasingly contentious, setting off an occasional transoceanic tug-of-war between father and son. Thornton questioned the decision to send Amos off to Oberlin. He had accompanied his brother to the train station for his departure. "I think that if you had been there you would have wondered how such a thing ever came into your head," Thornton scolded his father, attacking not only the decision but the college to which, in his view, his older brother had been dispatched unfairly. He wrote sarcastically that he had heard that "Oberlin is well spoken of in that portion of Ohio."[5] Despite Thornton's concerns, his brother seemed to thrive at Oberlin, and Thornton did not dread going to classes at Berkeley High School, as he had at Thacher. His grades were decent, and the pleasure of being at home with his mother and sisters offset most of the shortcomings of the school. Besides, he wrote to his father, a public school was better than a private one "because a public school is see-what-you-can find and a private is take-what-you've got."[6]

BACK IN Shanghai, Consul General Wilder had stepped from one controversy into another. On July 20, 1913, revolutionaries had taken up arms in Shanghai in a rebellion that was called the "Second Revolution," aimed at Yüan Shih-k'ai's government. On into August, sporadic fighting and bombardment endangered foreign enclaves in the city. With the help of the Shanghai Volunteer Corps and foreign naval forces, Shanghai's municipal police were finally able to quell the insurgency, but only after intense fighting. "We have just been reading the newspaper account of your Revolution-Excitement. What a night you must have had when the arsenal was thrice stormed and a 1000 soldiers killed and bombs falling into the French quarter and entrances to Foreign Settlements barricaded," Thornton wrote to his father. "Does business go on much as usual on a day like that [?]"[7]

Dr. Wilder tried to maintain business as usual, but official and unofficial criticism of his work mounted, and his health declined again.

Because he was losing weight and his energy was dissipating, he found it increasingly difficult to maintain his frenetic schedule. Whether or not the professional challenges and the physical stress were related, it became clear to him that it was time to leave Shanghai. He hoped for another, more congenial diplomatic appointment, perhaps in England or Canada. He wrote his official letter of resignation September 27, 1913, citing as the reason his physician's opinion that he could not continue to live in China or anywhere in Asia because of the Asian sprue, whose cure could be managed only, if at all, with a permanent change of climate. This time his resignation was accepted, with an official resignation date of December 18, 1913.[8]

It was a somber Christmas. To the family's disappointment, the tight budget would not permit Amos to come home from college for the holidays, nor was there much money for Christmas shopping. Most of the Wilders traditionally dreaded Christmas, not only because they were never all together for the holiday season, but also because there never seemed to be enough money to buy gifts. Charlotte and Isabel were making batches of candy to send to Amos in Ohio. Thornton had seventy-five cents to buy gifts for six or eight people. "I feel in the position of paupers who are driven to theft. How justified they are!" he wrote to his father.[9] Dr. Wilder wrote his family a nostalgic letter reminiscing about past Christmases, recalling tramping through the snow in Madison one Christmas Eve to find more apples because Thornton's stocking was not completely full.

"Oh Father," Thornton replied. "Imagine Mother overcome by a scarcity of apples."[10] There might be a paucity of other gifts that Christmas in Berkeley, but Thornton predicted that, as customary, aunts and cousins would "pelt" the children with handkerchiefs.[11]

IN JANUARY 1914 Consul General Wilder wrapped up his work in Shanghai and, because no further diplomatic appointment was offered, prepared to go back to the United States and pick up the threads of his life there. He had gone to China with great hopes and ambition. He left China with broken health, broken confidence, broken idealism, broken hopes. He had his adversaries and critics in Shanghai, but he also had many loyal friends, and they gave him farewell parties shortly before his scheduled departure in February 1914, with much press coverage. In January he bade his staff farewell, and a crowd of friends, Chinese, Americans, and Europeans, gathered to honor him.[12] They praised his service to China and expressed their regret that he was departing. They gave him a silver bowl, which, he assured the audience, would always remain in his home and would be passed down through the generations of his family as one of "the most treasured gifts he had ever received." His audience laughed when he told them that the silver cup would be filled only with "harmless" beverages. He left them with a heartfelt speech about his vision for the future of China and its place in the world.[13]

He arrived in Berkeley in late March of 1914, too late to see the February 13 vaudeville show at the high school, featuring another original playlet—*A Successful Failure*—by Thornton and his collaborator, fellow student Violette Still Wilson. It was recorded in the yearbook that Thornton gave a performance of the courtier, M. LeBeaux, that "will never be forgotten."[14] Dr. Wilder wrote to Amos that spring from 2350 Prospect Street in Berkeley that he was "much pleased" with the status of the family. "Mamma is well & normal," he wrote; "the children are dutiful (thus far certainly) with no obvious frictions—all are doing well in school. We are a bit crowded but are very happy together."[15]

"The days go pleasantly," Dr. Wilder wrote to Amos in April. He joined Thornton for a weekly walk to Oakland and back, and he "tramped the hills" with Charlotte. The family went to the Congregational church on Sunday morning, and Thornton attended Saint Mark's Episcopal Church, where he sang in the choir. Dr. Wilder had no plans at present, he told Amos. He would stay in Berkeley "indefinitely."[16] The longer he stayed, however, the more concerned he grew about his older children. Charlotte was clever, he thought, but tended to be cold. Thornton was a "high-brow" who needed "some virile currents in his life."[17] Dr. Wilder was working on summer plans for his sons, hoping to send Amos to Madison, Wisconsin, to take some agricultural courses and labor as a farmhand to "get a working knowledge of a farm." Now, with his own impaired health and the resulting uncertainties, he wrote Amos, one could never tell when this experience might pay off.[18] He was hoping to place Thornton at a farm and agricultural school at San Luis Obispo, California. The knowledge his sons could gain might come in handy to help support the family, their father observed, revealing to them a surprising new, far-fetched dream: "We might later own a ranch & work it [as] an investment and vacation home."[19]

Meanwhile he was convinced that the farm experience would do wonders for Thornton. "Of course it is a drastic thing to send a 'fine edition' to feeding pigs and milking cows and haying . . . but it is a wholesome business," Dr. Wilder wrote his elder son. "He will learn some things, get physical energy, and most important, get lifted for a time from this artificial life of book criticism and drama talk." Dr. Wilder would "keenly support" Thornton's literature and art, he promised, "when he gets laid a foundation of strong body and good sense."[20]

Thornton was a comical misfit as a first-time farmhand. "I've had two lessons in milking now. About two hours in all. Am still getting up at four-o'clock alarm altho' I don't have to," Thornton wrote to his family from the Ellwood Varney, Jr., farm in San Luis Obispo in June.[21] Ellwood Varney, Sr., was a member of a Maine Quaker family, friends of Dr. Wilder's, who left Maine years earlier and began farming in verdant San Luis Obispo County, known for its farms and vineyards as well as the scenic beauty along the rugged Pacific coastline. But Thornton had little time for anything but his labors on the farm, spending his rare free moments wrestling with the typewriter he had rented because he wanted to write. Except for Sunday evening church services, when he wore a suit, Thornton lived in overalls, doing his best with the farm chores, and struggling in vain to please Varney and, by extension, Amos Parker Wilder. "The great crises of life resolve themselves into milking-times and pig-feeding hours," he mused.[22]

While Thornton was trying to get the hang of farming and typing in California that summer, his brother, on completion of his first year at Oberlin, headed off to work on Tarpleywick Farm, the hundred-acre experimental farm owned by Professor H. C. Taylor five miles outside Madison, Wisconsin. Amos also studied animal husbandry, dairy husbandry, and agronomy at the University of Wisconsin summer school. He spent a grueling summer doing "man's not boy's work" from 5:00 a.m. until breakfast, and then from supper until dark, trekking five miles into Madison for his classes in between, and then five miles back to the farm. At least he was in congenial company: Of the half dozen or so farmworkers, there were several men with master's degrees and one with a Ph.D. Amos's boss told him he had "the makings of a farmer."[23]

Once his sons were off on their summer farming adventures, Dr. Wilder set out on a monthlong Sierra Club trip with Charlotte. He hoped to "instill love of 'the Wild,' and the Friendly Road" in his children.[24] Earlier he and Charlotte had taken a short trip to Yosemite, but he became so ill that he had to interrupt the journey. This time his health permitted him to enjoy thirty "notable days in the Mountains," he wrote to Amos, adding an aphorism: "While searching after stars, don't neglect gems at your feet."[25]

Dr. Wilder's first objective after his resignation and his reunion with the family was to attend to his health, and that required a journey to see specialists in New York. He planned to go on to New Haven from there, in pursuit of his second objective. He had to find a job, and he turned to the Yale network that had served him so well over the past twenty years.[26] He was soon offered a part-time appointment as secretary and treasurer of the Yale-in-China Association, a private, nondenominational organization founded in 1901 by a group of Yale graduates. First known as the Yale Foreign Missionary Society, the organization was called Yale-in-China by 1913. Although not an official arm of the university, Yale-in-China had its office on the campus in White Hall. Its mission was to work in the United States and in China to promote cross-cultural education, understanding, and communication, and to facilitate or establish school, college, medical, and cultural programs in China.[27] Former consul general Wilder, with his ties to China and to New Haven, seemed a perfect match for this endeavor.

He would move to New Haven right away, and wanted to move the whole family east, but after some debate he and Isabella decided that she would stay on in Berkeley with the children so that Thornton and Charlotte could graduate from Berkeley High School in 1915. After graduation, Dr. Wilder insisted, they would set up housekeeping together in Connecticut because it was "bad for a family to learn to live apart; it is better to keep together despite the disadvantages."[28]

LIFE DURING those years in Berkeley moved smoothly, despite the constant financial worry. From the outset Isabella seemed deeply refreshed and reinvigorated by her time abroad. She picked up the reins of family and community life with zest and energy—cooking, cleaning, mending, tending to the children and their activities at school and church, and joining her friends in various community activities, all the while operating on a frugal budget. Amos was doing well at Oberlin, and Thornton and Charlotte were settled into their routines at Berkeley High School. Isabel was making up ground at McKinley Grammar School, after those transient years in Europe, and four-year-old Janet spent her days at home with her mother. The family had been joined by a new member—a Chinese orphan named Kwong Ling, whom Amos Wilder sponsored to travel and study in the United States. Kwong Ling helped Isabella around the house, studied geography with Charlotte and English and arithmetic with Thornton, and attended church with the family. He would go on to become a minister and to adopt an Americanized name, John K. L. Yong.

Thornton wrote to his father that he "felt more and more" that he would like to teach for a while in the Yale-in-China program, but he doubted they would accept him, or if he would even be suited to teaching. He wondered if you could be a good teacher if you were not a good pupil. "I might like to learn Chinese and try to build a literature around the passing old schools—and around the village life," he told his father.[29] Dr. Wilder must have been pleased to hear that his son would even consider such a practical ambition as teaching.

IN AUGUST 1914, Amos was with some friends near the Wilders' old cottage on Lake Mendota at Maple Bluff, Wisconsin, when he heard the news that would soon reshape his life, along with the lives of so many others: War had broken out in Europe. Back in Berkeley that fall, Isabella Niven Wilder, like many other American citizens, was trying to do her part. She was "head over heels on the Red Cross Society of which she is secretary," Thornton wrote to his father, who was off on his prolonged quest for some sort of cure or at least palliative treatment for his chronic debilitating illness.[30] He had tried doctors and hospitals on the West Coast and the East Coast, and now, in September 1914, set his hopes on the Battle Creek Sanitarium in Michigan.

Concerned as he was about his father's health problems, Thornton did not let up on the continuous debate about his own college plans. Amos would be transferring to Yale, and Dr. Wilder seemed determined to send Thornton there as well. "You seem to be pretty eager for my entering Yale," he wrote to his father in the fall of 1914; "—it might be worse!—I've been reading Yale and Harvard etc. papers and mags. up at the U. C. Library and there's not much choice, but I might prefer the cloisters of Cambridge to the Bleachers of Yale, but there's not enough inclination either way to give me Splittering Colic if I'm crossed in the matter, so alright." At least if he went to Yale, he would be allowed to room on campus with his brother rather than live at home after the family moved to New Haven. Thornton was glad about that, believing that "Dorm. Life is college life while going home for meals is like from Kindergarten to High School."[31]

In the meantime he was the man of the house in Berkeley, reporting on family events regularly to his father and his brother. At his father's urging Thornton was working on athletics, trying to gain some skill in some sport, this time rowing. He was doing well enough with Indian clubs to be one of twenty boys chosen to do an exhibition at the house-warming of the new school gym.[32] Isabel reported to her father that Thornton's play was a hit at the high school, Charlotte had written a poem, and baby Janet was fine, "So Mother has something to talk & boast about."[33]

Thornton filled letters with extended details about his sisters, describing Isabel as a "very self-conscious, fluffy headed person, getting a little slangy, a little loungy-about, and a little vain, but all smiles when the sun shines." He admired her capacity for a "companionable good heartedness."[34] Charlotte was more complicated. By the time she was fourteen she had lived away from the family for more than three years of her life, and the years had left scars. She was a sensitive girl, sometimes volatile and unpredictable, but for a time in Berkeley, she was "unusually pacific and amiable," Thornton was happy to say.[35] Charlotte seemed to have inherited a double dose of Wilder/Niven stubbornness, however. She was, Thornton wrote,

> *a red cheeked, so-so plump girl in glasses; everything she says would be described as "stoutly" or "emphatically" put. She has a habit of talking protestingly which is the lighter side of her infallibility. You may not realize it but it's positively serious, the way Charlotte can't be corrected. . . . It's all based on great underlying consciousness of being perfect that often shows up curiously.*[36]

Yet she possessed an "unconscious charm," Thornton added, "a kind of tantalizing childishness." As the family member to whom Charlotte was closest, Thornton worried about his sister and felt responsible for her. The two of them took a long walk one spring day in 1915, searching the nearby hills for new flower specimens for their botany class. "Charlotte's always threatening to go to all the lonesomest and most distant mountain-tops alone, and because of her perverseness she probably will some day," he worried to his father; "but until then I have to act as guardian and 'take' her everywhere."[37]

BY THE end of March 1915, in his senior year, Thornton was ready for a dramatic change. Public school had its shortcomings, so Thornton turned to all of Berkeley, Oakland, and San Francisco for "classroom" space and experience, and gravitated to the theater world. When he wasn't writing his own plays or lurking around the Greek Theatre at the University of California nearby, he was reading European newspapers in the university library, avid for theatrical news, especially from Germany and Austria. He knew the names of prominent directors, producers, and playwrights at home and abroad, collecting information about them as other boys of his time fixed their attention on sports heroes or stamp collections. Before the move to Shanghai, Thornton had once mustered the courage to approach the famous playwright Percy MacKaye during rehearsals for one of his productions at the Greek Theatre. He told MacKaye that he, too, was writing plays, and had given MacKaye his address. When MacKaye had actually written to Thornton, he was "too shy" to write back, although he was "always dreaming of scenarios for Percy MacKaye."[38] Thornton attended every possible play, concert, and lecture, and seized every chance to participate in the arts. He auditioned for the Berkeley Oratorio Society, and was accepted.

He was fascinated by the ongoing construction along San Francisco Bay for the Panama-Pacific International Exposition—wonders to be unveiled in 1915 when the exposition opened its bejeweled grounds to more than eighteen million visitors. Before the exposition officially opened, Alexander Graham Bell himself had made the first transcontinental telephone call to officials in San Francisco, and one exciting highlight of the exposition was a daily cross-country telephone call. The exposition's Palace of Transportation featured a Ford assembly line that, during three hours every afternoon, Monday through Saturday, produced and polished one automobile every ten minutes—a total of 4,400 cars during the run of the exposition. There was also danger, and tragedy: The aviation idol Lincoln Beachy had perished March 14 when his specially built plane crashed into San Francisco Bay while he was demonstrating to a crowd of some fifty thousand that he could fly it upside down.

———

THORNTON DISCOVERED that he could go to the exposition as many times as he could afford to buy a ticket, and each time he could see different "wonders of the world"—the actual Liberty Bell; the first ukulele to be played in the United States; a beautiful three-acre Japanese garden; lavish "palaces"—buildings full of art and inventions and technology. One of the largest was the Palace of Machinery, the world's biggest steel-and-wood structure, fashioned after the Roman Baths of Caracalla, nearly a thousand feet long, with two intertwining miles of aisles crammed with exhibits. Best of all, Thornton thought, you could see plays, concerts, and works of art, as well as famous people—Thomas Edison himself; Amos Parker Wilder's friend and patron, President William Howard Taft; Buffalo Bill Cody and Charlie Chaplin and Helen Keller. The opulent centerpiece of the exposition was the Tower of Jewels, an Italianate tower encrusted with more than one hundred thousand "Novagems," glistening glass pieces that shimmered and shone in sunlight, or in the magical, manufactured light of evening. The 635 acres of exposition land also included the Zone, a wonderfully garish, flamboyant amusement park. Thornton loved wandering through the courts and lagoons and the waterfront. "It's most wonderful," he told Amos.[39] And, best of all, he got to perform there when the Berkeley Oratorio Society (with several other local choral societies) sang composer Gioacchino Antonio Rossini's setting of the *Stabat Mater Dolorosa*, first in Berkeley's Greek Theatre, and then at the Panama-Pacific International Exposition's Festival Hall. They also performed Brahms's *A German Requiem*. In exchange for singing they received free admission to the exposition for a whole day—"which means an awful lot," Thornton wrote, "at 50 cents admission."[40]

One of the Wilders' neighbors, Frederick Cheever Torrey, invited various members of the Wilder family to be his guests at concerts in Festival Hall. Thornton was thrilled to hear the Boston Symphony Orchestra give a series of twelve concerts. "It's a wonderful organization and plays like one brain," Thornton wrote to his father.[41] Isabella and Thornton sometimes bought the cheaper standing-room tickets to concerts at the exposition, and he planned to buy his mother a full ticket for her birthday.

The Wilders enjoyed an interesting circle of friends in Berkeley, largely because of Isabella's gifts for friendship and her wide-ranging cultural interests. Mr. Torrey, who took them to exposition concerts and gave Thornton the run of his excellent home library, was the nationally known San Francisco art and antiques dealer who had recently demonstrated the artistic foresight to purchase Marcel Duchamp's controversial *Nude Descending a Staircase, No. 2*, which had scandalized most viewers at the landmark 1913 Armory Show in New York. Thornton would have seen the painting, which was hung in the stairwell of Torrey's home during that time.[42]

Thornton frequently visited Mrs. Virgil Williams, widow of the painter who had been the founder and then director of San Francisco's School of Design from 1874 until 1886, the year of his death. Dora Norton Williams was also a painter of some note. However, to Thornton in 1915—the year of her death—she was an elderly invalid who lived in the neighborhood, knew and admired Amos Parker Wilder, and had known Robert Louis Stevenson and claimed that he had "dedicated his 'Silverado Squatters' to her—a thousand years ago," Thornton wrote to his father.[43] (Actually Stevenson dedicated the 1879 edition of his book to his cousin, Robert Alan Mowbray Stevenson.) Thornton frequently read aloud to Mrs. Williams and listened to her stories of the past. The Williamses were, indeed, close friends of Robert Louis Stevenson, and Dora Norton Williams was one of only two witnesses at his wedding to Fanny Osbourne on May 19, 1880, as well as Fanny Stevenson's lifelong friend and confidante.

Across the street from the Wilders lived a former English teacher at the Thacher School, Talcott Williamson, who tutored Thornton in the mechanics of English—spelling, punctuation, capitalization, and paragraphing—none of which, Williamson remembered, interested the teenager very much. Williamson "sweated blood" trying to teach Thornton, who, when chastised, would respond hopefully that perhaps, when he became a writer, he would always have a stenographer.[44]

FOR SEVERAL months during his senior year at Berkeley High School, Thornton and his father engaged in what Thornton, with his ongoing fondness for German, termed a "wortwechsel": an exchange of words (or a dispute) about where he would go to college. Since the Thacher School days, Dr. Wilder had hoped to send Thornton to Yale. He wanted to go to Harvard, however, because he thought it offered a more serious-minded academic atmosphere than Yale, his father's alma mater, and he no doubt knew how this opinion would rankle. He most definitely did not want to go to Oberlin. After two years there Amos was transferring to Yale, and Thornton longed to be able to join his brother at Yale for his freshman year, if he couldn't go to Harvard. "I sure hope we can keep a room at Yale," he wrote Amos, although he doubted he would ever get there.[45]

Thornton lobbied his father aggressively not to send him to Oberlin—"Oberlin with its compulsory chapels and prescribed Scripture-class-work and its suggested Christian endeavors, Bible-class, YMCAs and Temperance Society." He recognized that it might "seem awful" of him to complain about such an atmosphere. After all, he wrote, he was "the ridiculous ever-present of my own Sunday-school boy's division. The only one of my class of 12 to be present often; the official organist; the performer of official odd-jobs; moving tables and passing messages."[46]

But in the end Papa Wilder prevailed in his plan to send Thornton to Oberlin, and to transfer Amos to Yale for his junior and senior years. He believed strongly—and no doubt rightly—that Thornton needed the "congenial circle, the music, the quiet, the unaffected atmosphere of the old college town," and that this atmosphere would "ripen our boy and protect him for a year until he is older when he can resist the shocks of a place like [Yale]."[47] Dr. Wilder thought it would be easier for Thornton at Yale if he transferred there as an older, more mature, and experienced student.[48]

Thornton, just turned eighteen, resented the fact that his father was not only requiring him to go to Oberlin but denying him the freedom he had given Amos when he enrolled there. Amos had received a lump sum to set up his own living arrangements, whereas, Thornton protested, he was going to be "entrusted to two 'sweet-faced' old ladies" who ran Dascomb Cottage, the boardinghouse where he would live, and who would supervise him and his limited funds.[49] "He needs supervision, that is someone to look after his clothes etc.," Dr. Wilder wrote Amos. "He is a most helpless kid."[50]

"I feel I don't want to go to College at all," Thornton finally wrote to his father. "College is just a broader, more roaring brighter world for a bounded High School Boy anyway."[51] If he could really do what he wanted, he told his grandmother, he wouldn't go to college. He would just "travel and write, and live in ordinary, city boarding-houses and in the second class and steerage of boats, and in European attics and among the people of China. And 'accidentally' brush myself up against writers etc whom I admire, and get out of feeling that I'm always being hurt by father and always hurting him."[52]

DURING HIS senior year in Berkeley Thornton was dejected about the tight family budget, and feeling trapped in what he saw as the night-mare of high school. He wanted his father to understand his unhappi-ness, particularly as symbolized by his "old deformed clothes." Once, in his first-period class, in a long, dramatic letter marked "Private," Thornton poured out his misery. Some of his friends didn't want to be seen with him in the daytime, he wrote. They would take walks with him only in the evening. Thornton complained that he was wearing suits, hats, and even underwear handed down by his brother, his father, and some of his father's friends. "I have an awful revulsion against anyone else's underwear," he wrote,

> but when some of mine from Thacher becomes too torn and ragged, Mother takes it away and leaves nothing but Mr. O'Connor's for instance, and [that] old blue suit of his. It makes me sick all over but I have to be down at this hate [sic] school by 9:, so I have to. Mr. Thacher two Easters ago (Three that is) gave Amos a check and told him to take me to a store and fit me out in long trousers. And Amos got me two pairs of the wide trousers style that was just then on the wane. And now two years later, I have to wear them up and down the back streets of Berkeley, without any confidence and walking alone. I'm enough of a by-word here at school as it is. My unconscious periodic sentences and hunting-for-the-right-word and my mannerisms make that. A person can only be himself with ladies of 85 and with real art-ists of some kind.[53]

He had saved $14.50, $10.00 of it from his work at the Varney farm the previous summer, and he was tempted to take it out of the bank and buy some decent clothes. He felt that unless he was writing "a story or piece or something," he didn't have "any right to breathe." He was discouraged that when he wrote a story and showed it to his teacher and classmates "to vindicate" his existence, his writing was spurned. "I don't mean to acquire anything—just to vindicate and so live."[54]

Writing had already become a refuge and an absorption for him, as well as a means of vindication. He wrote at odd times, in odd places, and one favorite venue was any class in which he was bored or uninterested. In the spring of 1915, in the flyleaves of his first-year algebra textbook, he set up a table of contents for miniature plays he had begun to write, or planned to write.[55] He called them *Three-Minute Plays for Three Persons.* They were distinguished by exotic settings and characters and, of course, the economy of action and character development mandated by the three-minute framework. Sitting in algebra class in his worn, outdated, second- or thirdhand clothes, Thornton transported himself into another world, vividly populated by characters he imagined and invented, or characters he had read about. He also planned to create full-length dramas, which would, he daydreamed, be staged in theaters where they would "alternate with *The Wild Duck* and *Measure for Measure.*" He had grand visions of having his plays produced, and even cast them "with such a roll of great names as neither money nor loyalty could assemble."[56]

The world he imagined could, at least for a time, supersede the real world he inhabited. "Authors of fifteen and sixteen years of age spend their time drawing up title-pages and adjusting the tables of contents of works they have neither the perseverance nor the ability to execute," he wrote in 1928, when he was thirty-one. But the perseverance and execution could eventually grow out of the dreaming imagination, and the hunger to express it.

———

THAT SPRING Thornton began asking his brother for advice about how to organize his life at Oberlin. "I want to take College very mildly," he wrote, "and be able to keep all my irons and waffle-*pans* in the fire. I'd like to take choral work and harmony of music, but I dread piano or violin lessons. I've such a rough-and-tumble preparation."[57] But he couldn't let go of his disappointment that once again Wilder family life would be fractured, in yet another configuration. He managed to joke about it in a letter to his father: "Mother got a telegram last week. She thought it was from you saying possibly, 'Isabel go to school in Rhiems [*sic*]; Janet learn Fiji immediately—official—,' but it was from the Red Cross."[58]

"There will be a change of happiness for the coming year, won't there?" he wrote to his father.[59] Thornton would be at Oberlin; Amos would be at Yale; Charlotte would be at Mount Holyoke in South Hadley, Massachusetts. The first of the so-called Seven Sisters colleges, it traditionally offered a serious, rigorous education for women. With three family members in college, Isabella, Isabel, and Janet would move to New Haven to join Dr. Wilder, although Isabella had tried to persuade her husband to let her move with the younger daughters to Claremont, where her husband owned a rental house, now vacant.[60] "It will apparently convulse her to come to New Haven against her will," he wrote to Amos.[61] In the end, however, he convinced his wife that the move east had to be made.

Thornton wrote his father, "And you with your sheaf of plans won," and he began to worry about how his mother would fare in New Haven in a rented house, on a very limited budget.[62] Life was hard enough in Berkeley, he said, and his mother's daily duties were "beyond an ordinary woman as it is, but Mother has the energy for mopping floors and brushing corners in the mornings and organizing Red Cross chapters and meeting for speakers from European hospitals—and bazaars and teas and performances and sewing-circles and hospital kits all afternoon and darning our stockings in the evenings."[63]

Thornton had many more interests outside school than in school that term, he confessed to his father. "I've been doing worse and worse in School but better and better out," he wrote as his high school graduation ceremony approached. He was very glad that the final months of school had brought him "more friends [than] the previous twelve."[64] He was ashamed of himself that he could not seem to sustain friendships the way his brother could. Amos was "so much the real thing with the testimonial from everyone," Thornton reflected. "I don't seem to know anyone or to hold anyone long."[65]

Amos Parker Wilder's victorious "sheaf of plans" called for Thornton to give in to one more assignment: He had arranged for Thornton and Amos to spend part of the summer working on a farm near Dummerston Station in Vermont. Thornton bristled at their paltry compensation for unremitting, seemingly unappreciated hard work. "It's kind of cheap to work for money," he grumbled to his father, "but it's worse to work for board—it means that they don't regard your services as up to much and [you] can never tell which part of the board they are grudging you as unearned."[66] Imperviously, Dr. Wilder encouraged his boys to "keep speculating as to how you would manage your own farm to make it go; we may have one sometime." They could not have been happy to learn that their father was thinking that the three of them might buy or lease a farm someday and actually "make it pay," as Dr. Wilder wrote to them.[67] While Thornton was the most unlikely farmer of the trio, not one of the Wilder men was in any way suited for farming as a profession.

For Thornton life on the Vermont farm was a source of incessant misery. One week he was almost unable to write the obligatory letter to his father, he complained, for he was exhausted and the palms of his hands were covered with "a little gallery of blisters."[68] He was cutting hay, cleaning horse stalls, washing milk pails, doing dishes, sweeping, mopping, feeding chickens, emptying swill pails, bundling oats, gathering blackberries "from the wilderness of wolves and foxes to the south of us," picking currants for a pie, and hoeing beans. Try as he might, he did not do well enough at cow milking to be called on to do it again, but he worked industriously at the other chores. All in all, he complained, "I almost walked to my grave."[69]

7

"LITERARY DEVELOPMENT"

If I show any signs of expressing real feeling sentimentally please tell me because it's very important I should know before I go any farther in my literary development.

—THORNTON WILDER TO HIS MOTHER
[1915?]

Oberlin, Ohio (1915–1916)

A mos Parker Wilder firmly believed that "the earnest reverent life of Oberlin" would provide "a fitting environment" wherein his sons would inevitably mature. He had written to the president of Oberlin from Shanghai in 1913 to tell him that Amos would be coming to Oberlin in the fall, and to express his hopes that the president and the dean of the college would "help me to build this boy up perhaps to large things. I want him first to be a man of firm Christian character; to this I would add sense, a wholesome cheer and all possible attainments."[1] He had the same aspirations for Thornton—heightened by his anxiety about Thornton's academic readiness, his maturity, and his affection for theater and other seemingly extravagant, impractical interests. Before his sons entered the more sophisticated and more expensive world of Yale, his alma mater, Dr. Wilder wanted them to have this grounding in the sheltered, structured academic and social life at Oberlin. He greatly admired the Oberlin tradition of social service, coupled with a rigorous liberal education grounded in Christian idealism.

Thornton's maternal great-grandfather, with his brother, Lewis Tappan, had helped to found and endow the historic liberal arts college in 1833 as Oberlin Collegiate Institute, to train Christian teachers, missionaries, and other professionals. The town—or "colony"—of Oberlin was established at the same time, named for John Frederic Oberlin

(1740–1826), a minister and social reformer who believed in universal education. From the first, Arthur and Lewis Tappan had insisted that "the broad ground of moral reform, in all its departments, should characterize the instruction in Oberlin."[2] The institution was renamed Oberlin College in 1850, and in the 1890s was the site of the establishment of the Anti-Saloon League, solidifying a long tradition of temperance—another one of Amos Parker Wilder's fundamental causes.

Thornton had wanted to go to Harvard, and if not Harvard, Yale, and in the end, he gave in to his father—but not without demanding and receiving a written promise that after only one year at Oberlin he could transfer to Yale. He was one of 151 men in the freshman class of 1915, joined by 181 women, to make up what was then the largest freshman class in the college's history. As Thornton had anticipated, the student body was more provincial than cosmopolitan, with most students coming from Ohio. Dr. Wilder was optimistic that Thornton would conscientiously apply himself to absorbing all that Oberlin College could offer, and believed he would be safe there from the distracting influences of alcohol, theater, plays, and actors. Dr. Wilder was about to be disappointed, however, for Thornton quickly discovered to his great delight that Oberlin was rife with opportunities for writing and acting, and he lost no time in taking advantage of these pleasures.

Thornton arrived at Oberlin bent on majoring in English, but quickly grew disenchanted with the course content and requirements of the department. He spoke to his professor and to the department chairman about choosing psychology as a major instead. "They see very much why I don't want to take their English major highroad," he announced to his father. "It's not made for me. It's made for people who have to be talked to for two whole years before they know what to look for in Elizabethan poetry or Ruskin etc."[3] Dr. Wilder was determined that Thornton would come out of college equipped to earn a living— and he did not believe that a psychology major would prepare his son to do that. But there were possibilities of teaching the subject in a college, Thornton countered, adding with a college freshman's overconfidence and authority that his friends at Oberlin did not think he would have any problem earning a living with his writing. Besides, he pointed out, Oberlin considered psychology such an important subject that all juniors were required to take a yearlong psychology course.

But was Thornton suited to study psychology? his father wondered. "I don't know," Thornton wrote. "I know that I'm interested as I can be in all the points of it that come my way, and that I'm speculating on sides of it in my own mind all the time." He acknowledged that there would be "drudgery" in studying the physiology of the brain and taking the required zoology course. But he insisted that he could not major in English "as it's taught at Oberlin College, and that I believe myself suited to the study of Psych."[4]

Unlike Thornton, Amos had quietly accepted the fact that his father sent him to Oberlin to ensure that he would receive a "sound biblical and religious formation," and to study with trusted professors such as Charles H. A. Wager, the English Department chair and classics professor, who listened, no doubt with forbearance and amusement, to Thornton's assessment of the fitness of the department to facilitate his education.[5] But Thornton found opportunities all around him— and created others—for the development of his literary aspirations. At Oberlin he was a prolific writer, turning out plays, short stories, essays, and even an occasional poem, and sharing them widely with family, friends, and professors—anyone who would read or listen. Especially trusting his mother's advice, he wrote to her, "If I show any signs of expressing real feeling sentimentally please tell me because it's very important I should know before I go any farther in my literary development."[6]

As a college freshman, Thornton did not confine himself to his "literary development," however. He took English composition and the required course in the Bible, and studied Latin and classical literature, as well as German language, history, and literature. He struggled with geometry. He was required to take a gym class, and participated half-heartedly in the annual Sophomore-Freshman Tie-up—a boisterous ritual in which the two classes lined up on the designated evening on either side of a bonfire on the college athletic field and, at the sound of a pistol shot, rushed together to "try to tie hand and foot as many of the opp. class as possible and carry them to their goal." On the way home, "tired as a sack of old bottles," Thornton made up a short story about the experience.[7]

He auditioned for the choirs at two Oberlin churches, and was accepted in both. He auditioned for the college's Musical Union chorus, and was chosen—no small accomplishment in a school with a fine conservatory. But Thornton was a gifted musician, at home in the literature of classical music. He loved to sing in choirs and chorales, as he had done since his Berkeley days, when he was excused from the Congregational Sunday school five minutes early so he could run a couple of blocks over to Saint Mark's Episcopal Church, don a white surplice, and join the processional, "singing joyously," Isabel remembered.[8] He played piano, organ, and violin skillfully, and was particularly fond of the organ, having volunteered as a boy in Berkeley to pump the organ at the Congregational church while the organist practiced.

Thornton was also enthusiastic about Oberlin's growing art collection, which, he marveled, he could see and "get as used to as I like." And there was theater: He'd have given anything, he said, to audition for the Dramatic Association's production of Shaw's *Candida*, writing home, "I'd rather play the Poet in Candide [*sic*] than the Harp in Heaven! But with rage and horror I see the paper says that Freshmen are excluded."[9] He was frequently organizing and often writing and staging after-dinner entertainments at Dascomb Cottage, where he lived.[10] For fun he composed a one-act melodrama titled *The Primrose Path: The Wicked World Viewed from an Oberlin Cloister*, which enjoyed its debut performance in Dascomb on Thanksgiving Day, 1915. He submitted some of his manuscripts to the *Oberlin Literary Magazine*. One was, he said, "a story of the Suddenly Spiritual in the Mundanely Modern, like my others, but it was about the Campus and so vitally autobiographic that I had to send it in confessedly anonymous."[11]

It may have been music more than theology that drew Thornton to Oberlin church services and vespers, but he went, reporting in letters to his family on lectures and sermons but most of all on music. At vespers one Sunday, he "almost expired" because the music was so beautiful—a passage from Brahms's *Requiem*, followed by a cappella choral responses "pulled right out of the Russian Church Service and so noble and dignified" that he held his breath. Then he listened to the church organist's postlude, a skillful performance of a motet by Orlando di Lasso that, Thornton wrote, "I've been trying to make sound right on our Berkeley piano since ever so long."[12]

Thornton was now the Wilder living farthest away from the family. In New Haven, Dr. Wilder was overseeing the work of the Yale-in-China Association. Coincidentally, from his office in White Hall, he could keep a vigilant eye on Amos, now a junior. Dr. Wilder traveled often to speak on behalf of the program, fund-raising along the way. Occasionally he took time off to check in to the sanatorium at Battle Creek on his perennial quest to restore and maintain good health.

Isabella Wilder cared for her husband and two younger daughters in a drafty old colonial house on Whitney Avenue in Mount Carmel, Connecticut, six miles on the streetcar route from the heart of New Haven. Months before her arrival, without consulting his wife, Dr. Wilder had rented the house from New Haven friends. It had steam heat, he told her in a letter, and a bathroom (which, he did not tell her, he was installing at his own expense). There were "open fireplaces of the grand New England type," he wrote, and six acres and a storage shed. The streetcar ran right past the door and it was only a thirty-minute jaunt into New Haven. If she wanted to move closer to the Yale campus after a year, they could "finance a city home."[13] Isabella made the house as charming and comfortable as possible, and began to form friendships in the community, as well as within the Yale circle, as she had done at the universities in Madison and Berkeley. Isabel, fifteen, and Janet, five, attended local public schools, and Charlotte was happily engrossed in her freshman studies at Mount Holyoke, despite her anxiety that she was not fully prepared. She feared that her "whole education" was in danger of "toppling on a foundation of scrappy instruction," and did not want to be pushed to get her college degree.[14] Her father had tried but failed to arrange for her to study in Italy before beginning college. He wrote to Amos that Charlotte was "full of power and will get it harnessed in time."[15] She quickly found her footing at Mount Holyoke, where she would thrive and excel.

Letters flew back and forth from Connecticut to Ohio to Massachusetts, with Papa conducting his patriarchal oversight of his older children by mail. As young Amos later recalled, "There was a running fire of letters to every one of us [children] for years and years, with admonitions and inquisitions and affection and suggestions and warnings, all sorts of things." Their father was "a very intensive parental planner for his children," Amos said. "Father's democratic sympathies and his belief in the common people made him afraid we would become eggheads. Of course all of us did. Thornton and I and my sisters!"[16]

———

AT OBERLIN, Thornton was making friends more readily than he ever had before. He already knew Theodore Wilder, a Chefoo classmate, and because Amos had left his mark as scholar and Ohio collegiate tennis champion, Thornton was introduced to "scores and scores" of Oberlin juniors and seniors.[17] While he was making new friends, he also kept track of old ones. In Berkeley he and his family had met the young ballet dancer Hubert Jay Stowitts, who studied at the University of California from 1911 to 1915, and was discovered by the great Russian dancer Anna Pavlova when he danced at the Greek Theatre. A handsome gay man who lettered in track at the university, Stowitts also excelled in painting and design. "I certainly am living in a dream," he wrote to Thornton in November 1915, reporting that Pavlova had invited him to do a solo performance with her troupe. Stowitts was also designing costumes and sets for the Russian Ballet.[18] He urged Thornton, who was five years his junior, to write to him.[19] Stowitts's letters suggest an overt interest in the Thornton of the vivid blue eyes; the brilliant, seeking mind; the witty, sometimes sarcastic speech; the great zest for life. If so, Thornton appeared to be innocently unaware.

He was paying a good deal more attention to the young ladies at Oberlin, who eagerly read or listened to his plays, wanted to look after him when he was sick, and invited him to parties. He was making his own mark at the college, and he was studying, he informed his parents—"hours at a time about every other day."[20] He told his parents that "except for worries about you people and occasional fears about my German preparation, I'm as happy as the day is long."[21]

Once more the family budget prohibited the train trip home to Connecticut for Christmas, and his father suggested that Thornton spend the Christmas holidays working on a nearby farm. "Oh, let me stay where I am," he begged his father. "Quite a few other boys are staying here for me to get to know; and Mrs. Duncan [one of the proprietors of Dascomb] has offered me to earn my room-rent if I tend to the furnace . . . I don't want to go away; I'll be good; I'll be good."[22] His father relented, and Thornton spent Christmas of his freshman year at Oberlin.

CHARLOTTE SENT her brother a pocket diary for Christmas, and he used it, he told her, to record "memorandums of the original work I do." The second semester of his freshman year was a fertile time for him. He discovered that he could "think out" scenes for his plays and plots for his stories on long walks, and he established what would become a lifelong habit of walking for miles at a time, clearing his head, wrestling with ideas, composing passages of plays and stories—and sometimes, the musician taking over, even creating lyrics and melodies. The pocket diary went with him everywhere that winter of 1916, and documented the writing he began, the pieces he finished, the ideas he dreamed up and then discarded. There was a note about the rehearsal for his experimental play, *The Last Word About Burglars*, which would be performed by "The Strollers" for "The Dascomb Family and Friends" on May 9, 1916, at the Men's Building at 6:45.[23] Oberlin gave Thornton the stimulation and at least some of the free time he needed to write, and the diary documented his literary endeavors.[24]

Despite his extracurricular activities, Thornton passed all his first-semester courses, even solid geometry—most likely, he joked to his father, because the professor was "too well-bred" to flunk him.[25] On the other hand, Thornton reported, his English professor knew "the very pocket of my soul" because of the themes he was writing.[26] He was writing in earnest, far more drama than fiction, essays, or poetry, and he knew day in and day out the "great depressions and wild exhilarations" that visit young writers. The young author, Thornton reflected years later,

> is drunk on an imaginary kinship with the writers he most admires, and yet his poor overblotted notebooks show nothing to prove to others, or to himself, that the claim is justified. The shortest walk in the country is sufficient to start in his mind the theme, the plan and the title, especially the title, of a long book; and the shortest hour when he has returned to his desk is sufficient to deflate his ambition. Such fragments as he is finally able to commit to paper are a mass of echoes, awkward relative clauses and conflicting styles.[27]

As always, Thornton was reading insatiably, and he recognized that the pages he wrote were "full of allusions" to the pages he read.[28] His curiosity propelled his reading and his writing, and in his freshman year, his byline appeared frequently in the best venue then at his disposal: the *Oberlin Literary Magazine*. His *St. Francis Lake: A Comedy* appeared in December 1915, followed in January 1916 by *Flamingo Red: A Comedy in Cages* (a play his mother disliked). His prizewinning essay, "The Language of Emotion in Shakespeare," appeared in March 1916, followed in April by "Sealing-Wax," a short story, and in May by one of his three-minute plays, *Brother Fire: A Comedy for Saints*.

On February 18, Thornton wrote in his diary, he worked until one in the morning writing and polishing the essay to enter in the Shakespeare essay contest, and he was gratified to win, especially since the ten-dollar prize meant a significant addition to his pocketbook. He confessed to his brother that he was ashamed of the work, but "The Language of Emotion in Shakespeare" was remarkably thoughtful, fluid, and polished for an essay from the pen of a college freshman.[29] "We have lost a living, expressive speech," argued the fledgling playwright, who would later help transform the speech of modern drama. "Great plays need great, but natural language."[30]

ABSORBED AS he was in keeping up with his classes and indulging his love of reading, writing, and music, Thornton seemed unaware during his Oberlin days that he was attractive to women, young and old. At a dinner party he met an elderly lady he considered a "most remarkable" person, and planned to read aloud to her, as he had read to the late Dora Williams in Berkeley. "I'm going to be an expert in Old Lady psychology," he wrote to his family. "It's a little tiresome tho—when they start talking about Dickens—They were all about sixteen when Dickens was at his zenith."[31]

Young Oberlin coeds also sought Thornton's friendship and company, a welcome experience for him after the all-male environment at the Boys' School at Chefoo and at Thacher, and his casual friendships with a few girls at Berkeley High School. In the spring of his Oberlin freshman year, he wrote two long letters to his mother about Ruth Keller, a senior Latin major who was not "pleasing and beautiful" to boys, but whose "delightful, colored personality" made her one of his favorite companions. They took long walks, studied together, laughed a lot, and read aloud *Joseph Vance*, a bestselling novel by William Frend De Morgan. Thornton advised her about her future life, warning her not to "just live at home in her flat with her mother talking and sewing and gossiping" after she graduated.[32] (After Oberlin, she went on to marry, have six children, give one son Thornton as a middle name, and manage an interesting career.)

In letters, Thornton playfully passed along romantic advice and counsel to his sister Charlotte, almost, as a family member later observed, as if he were making up a drawing room comedy in his head.[33] "Do you see anything of boys up there?" he wrote to her at Mount Holyoke. "You must get them to call on you, too, remember. I can't have a sister who scares the boys away." He even proposed sending a picture of himself to Charlotte, signed "Yours, Herbert" or "Love, Chauncy"—or maybe she could get Amos to send a picture of himself in his tennis flannels. Then Charlotte could pretend they were her boyfriends. "It would give you a 'new dignity' and 'added prestige,'" Thornton urged his sister, "and, Lord [it's] what you need!"[34]

His own dignity and prestige were bound up in his writing, which brought him increasing visibility among Oberlin professors and students, and such regular publication in the college literary magazine that he reported to his family in May 1916 that he "had sworn off sending anything more" because it was "atrociously bad taste to have so many things in succession—a Freshman, too."[35] He had been working all spring on the May production of *The Last Word About Burglars*, subtitled *A Disordered Fancy in One Act*, which he called "the first honest 'artistic' thing of mine to be given."[36] There are three characters in the play, but the script runs to eight handwritten pages, longer than his typical three-minute playlets. As the play opens, a husband and wife come home from the theater and discuss the unnerving fact that the wife has been hearing someone in the house at night. Later that night the wife confronts the burglar—a young boy with a tragic story to tell. The husband rushes on the scene to rescue his wife—but he cannot see the burglar. "You are ill again," he tells his wife. "There was no one here. You have been brooding over burglars until you have nightmares of them. What was he like?"[37] While the fledgling psychology major was at work here, there are also signs of the fledgling playwright in the dramatic tension built through dialogue, through the symbolism—the interplay of darkness and light, illusion and reality, self-negation and affirmation—and through the final irony that the burglar actually restores rather than steals the heroine's sense of self.

Thornton was also writing a longer play, motivated by a competition sponsored by Grace George, whom he described as a "prominent and distinguished New York actress-manager."[38] A successful stage actress, director, translator, and adapter, George was offering a large monetary prize for the best American play by an American college undergraduate. Thornton decided "without much audacity" that he should enter the contest because, he said, "I'm such an undergraduate and I write plays as I eat."[39] The play's title morphed from *Ventures Joyous* to *The Belinda (Ventures Joyous)* to its ultimate title, *The Rocket: An American Comedy in Four Acts*. He completed one draft at Oberlin, and would continue to work on it at Yale. He summarized it for his father: "The story briefly concerns a young lady of a quiet, old wealthy family in Chicago who suddenly disturbs her family with an attack of ideals she has had."[40] Her idealism propels her to act in a "tuberculosis-propaganda moving-picture play" and to make "sincere and good little speeches to working girl leagues and to school-children in Central Park." When her sincerity is questioned and she is condemned for acting in a movie, the "misunderstood" heroine retires to a "small farmhouse in Illinois." His play was intended to be "a kind of High Comedy," Thornton explained to his father, and not a cynical commentary on "the folly of youthful idealism and enthusiasm."[41]

Finally he wrote to his mother that he was ready to mail *The Rocket* to Grace George, along with a "nice letter and a certificate" from Professor Wager.[42] Off to New York went Thornton Wilder's first full-length play to compete for a prize he would not win. But this advance from the three-minute playlet to the four-act, full-length drama was a significant leap for an aspiring playwright.

The encouragement he was hearing from his new mentor, Charles Wager, contrasted with the frequent criticism Thornton received from his father. "My heart stopped still when you said that I seemed only prepared to use the lighter forms of literature," Thornton wrote to his father in May. "I probably have even more respect for them than you; but please offer me encouragement toward (even) tragedy." He went on to report that "Even Prof. Wager thinks I ought to win the big prize—there is only one of course—with my play, as do naturally the lesser critics that are privileged to hear parts of it." Nevertheless Thornton expected *The Rocket* to come back to him, and then, he said, "I shall put it by and touch it up again when I am older. I am proud of the parts that I will never be able to touch up—but when I put myself in a professional reader's place and read it, I know too well that it is food for smiles." There were, he said, "realistic farm-interior domestic touches in the last Act. They're at first hand." He hoped his father might be proud of those.[43]

———————

AS USUAL, the elder Wilder was designing practical summer activities for his children. Isabel and Charlotte would attend a course of lectures at Chautauqua, and then go (against their wills, Isabel said) to a horticultural school for women in Ambler, Pennsylvania, where their father would pay for a month's stay—which turned into two months when the girls were quarantined at the school during that summer's polio epidemic.[44] Just as Thornton had tried to take Charlotte in hand, he wrote Isabel some detailed advice about how to be more grown up that summer, and to become a "real modern storming young woman."[45]

Amos, who had now completed his junior year at Yale, spent the summer playing tennis and working on the staff of a YMCA center that served Camp Washington, a military training camp populated by a thousand high school boys, located near Fort Terry, on Plum Island, off Orient Point, New York.[46] To his dismay, Thornton was destined for another farming summer, this time at the Mount Hermon School in Gill, Massachusetts. He was not happy about it. "The majestic contract for my valuable labor I return signed," he wrote to his father in May 1916. "Did you know," he continued, half in jest, "that you were doing what the psychologists call 'infringing on my personality' when you ask me to sign a blank agreement in which you fill in the details."[47]

Thornton dreaded ten summer weeks of nine-hour workdays on yet another farm. He bargained to be allowed to attend the Oberlin commencement ceremony before he went to Mount Hermon, and to have a few days in Mount Carmel with the family. By July 12, 1916, he was working like a Trojan, he complained, "under the hottest sun!"[48] It was easier to adjust physically than it was to accept the work "with resignation mentally," he confided in a letter to his mother, adding, "my fatalism increases with my blisters."[49]

8

"THE ART OF WRITING"

As I read my manuscript, I began to miss some of my cherished phrases; every now and then I saw that someone had inserted perfunctory bridges over which the timid mind might step—with petticoat lifted = when the art of writing is a matter of alpine climbing—peak to peak, and let the chasms snatch the fearful.

—THORNTON WILDER TO HIS SISTER CHARLOTTE, *October 16, 1916*

Mount Hermon and Oberlin (1916)

The evangelist Dwight L. Moody's Mount Hermon School for Boys was—like the China Inland Mission School, Thacher, and Oberlin—Amos Parker Wilder's kind of school. According to the Mount Hermon School catalog, the boys' school educated "young men of sound bodies, good minds, and high aims. It is designed for those who have already conceived a serious purpose in life; for those who are in earnest to secure a useful education; for those who desire to know more of the Bible."[1] To carry out his goals, Moody intended to "help young men of very limited means to get an education such as would have done me good when I was their age. I want to help them into lives that will count the most for the cause of Christ."[2] A "certain amount of manual labor daily" was required of all students. The school did not accept "vicious or idle boys," boys with "delicate physical constitutions," or "those who are drifting."[3] Dr. Wilder himself could not have created a better school environment.

Thornton was one of many boys who went to Mount Hermon to work on the farm for the summer. (At least one of them was sent there by parents who mistakenly thought it was a reform school.) The boys carried out their strenuous duties in the verdant fields surrounding the handsome school buildings, and lived in a dormitory on campus. "I won't be too enthusiastic about this place yet because I haven't started work, but so far it's great," Thornton wrote to his family in July 1916 from Mount Hermon.[4]

Once the work began, however, his opinion of the place shifted rapidly. He quickly discovered that summer farmhands were allowed to eat in the school dining hall, but not to sit with regular students—and he thought the food was awful. He complained to his father that even after "an incredibly hard day's work" when he was "hungry as a boar," the food made him "shudder." "Sometimes it's perfectly disgusting," he wrote. This rankled because he was informed after he arrived that there would be major deductions from his salary, which was only fifteen cents an hour for ten hours of work a day, six days a week: Of his weekly nine-dollar paycheck, four dollars would be deducted for room, board, electricity, and laundry.[5]

The work was "terrible," Thornton griped. "Half the time I can barely stagger up and down the rows."[6] To make matters worse, he was afflicted with mosquito bites, bedbugs, and sunburn. At least he had a private room in the workers' dormitory, where, tired as he was, he could read for an hour and a half each evening—currently Ibsen's plays, Boswell's *Life of Johnson*, and the worn copy of Thomas Browne's *Religio Medici* his father had lent him, with passages underlined throughout. When he wasn't reading he was writing in snatches of time—letters, stories, playlets in which there is evidence of his wide, deep reading in the after hours, before he fell asleep from a surfeit of exercise. (One compensation: He was gaining weight despite the bad food, growing husky, he could report, and developing a chest.)

Sunburned and exhausted after the day's labor in the fields, Thornton lost himself in the evening in *Religio Medici* (*A Doctor's Faith*), the spiritual testimony of the seventeenth-century physician and metaphysician Sir Thomas Browne (1605–82). Browne's often luminescent prose shed light for nineteen-year-old Thornton in his own spiritual ruminations. Dr. Wilder might have been surprised to know the depth of his son's fascination with the ideas and the language in *Religio Medici*. Thornton promised to send this "'devotional' book" to his brother, telling him it was written "in the most exquisite style." And, Thornton said, "The discussions of the supernatural especially are written in the most stirring eloquence I ever read."[7]

Powerful religious forces vied for Thornton's allegiance during his boyhood: his father's staunch moral and philosophical convictions, first of all; his mother's gentler, more open-minded idealism, and her wide reading, especially of William James; Thornton's own chorister's love for the liturgy and religious music of various faiths, especially the Catholic Church; his instinctive curiosity and stubborn need to question authority; his alternating interest in and resistance to the religious principles of the schools he attended at Chefoo and Oberlin, and his resulting skepticism about missionaries and evangelical movements; the ongoing tension between his sense of duty, bred from years immured in the rituals of church and Sunday school and Bible classes, and his innate need to question, to study, to read, to come to terms with his own spiritual identity in his own way.

"I am becoming more and more removed in any religious directions—mystical," he confided in his brother. "Beauty and spiritual occurrence and pities and permeations are my sure spots, and the Gospel of John vibrates of them;—but of course I don't know what I do think yet."[8] He occasionally tried to reassure his worried father: "I wish you wouldn't sound so harassed and pathetic about whether I read my Bible and pray or not," Thornton wrote. "Of course I do. If I didn't force of habit and superstition and a hundred and one other things would torment me all night."[9]

He could most likely identify with Sir Thomas Browne's assertion that he was religious despite the "several circumstances that might persuade the world" that he had no religion at all, in part, as Browne wrote, because of "the indifferency of my behavior and discourse in matters of religion, neither violently defending one, nor with that common ardor and contention opposing another."[10] As Browne said of himself, Thornton "could never hear the Ave-Maria bell without an elevation."[11] His rich imagination and aesthetic sensibility responded instinctively, often fervently to the music and liturgy of certain religious services—Protestant, Catholic, and Jewish. Thornton was often captivated by what Browne described as the "wingy mysteries in divinity and airy subtleties in religion."[12] One of Browne's ideas in particular seems to have resonated, at least subliminally, and made its way into Thornton's later fiction and drama: "Every man is not only himself; there have been many Diogenes and as many Timons, though but few of that name," Browne wrote. "Men are lived over again; the world is now as it was in ages past. There was none then but there hath been someone since that parallels him, and is as it were his revived self."[13]

Instinctively Thornton knew at nineteen what Browne had written in 1635, at thirty: He did not have to travel over "the flux and reflux of the sea" to explore the mysteries of world and of life itself. He could accomplish that travel, Browne wrote, "in the cosmography of myself. We carry with us the wonders we seek without us: there is all Africa and her prodigies in us."[14] And then there was Browne's compelling image: "Life is a pure flame, and we live by an invisible sun within us."[15]

Deliberately or not, his father had set Thornton on the path to two catalytic spiritual encounters during his first two years of college. The first came with the loan of Dr. Wilder's own marked-up copy of *Religio Medici*, which stirred Thornton's instinctive love for language and elegant literary style as well as his spiritual belief. The second came with Thornton's deepening regard for Oberlin professor Charles Wager, and through him, a host of influences, including Sophocles, Homer, Dante, Cervantes, Saint Francis of Assisi, and Cardinal John Henry Newman. Wager was "one of the greatest living authorities on St. Francis" and was writing a book on him, Thornton told his mother.[16] Not surprisingly, Saint Francis showed up in one of Thornton's playlets—*Brother Fire*—and when Professor Wager read it, he had announced in the company of Theodore Wilder that Thornton "had captured the exact spirit of the whole matter!"[17] ("Bring me not logic, sister. She is the least of the handmaids of Love," says Thornton's Brother Francis to the peasant woman Annunziata in her hut in the mountains of northern Italy.)[18]

In the midst of his summer misery, Thornton was reading Ibsen and J. M. Barrie, and declaiming "to the cows in the stanchions the judge's speech from Barrie's *The Legend of Leonora*."[19] Thornton the playwright was also dealing with the recent news that Miss Grace George did not find his play *The Rocket* "suitable for her purpose." He took it philosophically, however, planning to "put the thing bye [*sic*] for a year or two and then I daresay I'll see what she means."[20]

Dr. Wilder visited Thornton at Mount Hermon one Sunday in July, and found him "looking like a young athlete," and learning to get along with people. The outdoor life was doing him good, Dr. Wilder wrote to Amos, but he still wondered how his second son would support himself after college. He needed a profession that would enable him to earn a living, no matter how modest. Dr. Wilder had no faith that Thornton could ever support himself as a writer. "But for Thornton simply to be a good writer or to be clever in knowing music won't do; it won't pay the landlady," he told Amos. Perhaps Thornton could teach English literature, or learn typing and shorthand and "earn a living at least."[21] Dr. Wilder pronounced his son a "fine lad," and was confident that farm life and college "physical culture and life" were "ridding him of his peculiar gait and certain effeminate ways." Yet he was afraid, he wrote Amos, that Thornton might wake up at the age of thirty and find himself "an interesting derelict."[22]

Thornton confronted and challenged his father far more than any of his siblings did, including Amos, the first son. More so than his father, Thornton comforted and even counseled his mother when she was despondent because she felt she had done so little with her life. "Pray, take heart," he wrote to her in mid-July 1916. "I don't know what I can do for you . . . please do not fall into melancholy prowling around the ruins of your life. Five children and an acceptable calling-card are not so common. Don't call your life a ruin until one of us has wrecked it."[23]

Thornton was doing more that summer than declaiming to cows and haying under the blazing sun. He was experimenting with his literary voice and style, turning, as always, to books for inspiration. He was simultaneously reading *The Odyssey*, James Boswell on Samuel Johnson, and Thomas Babington Macaulay's *Life of Johnson*. He wrote a new three-minute playlet—his sixth, *The Greek Woman*, set in Venice during the Renaissance. He copied the script on the backs of several penny postcards and mailed them to Professor Wager, who wrote back with extravagant praise, and encouraged him: "Trust your prophetic soul, Thornton dearest; trust always your prophetic soul."[24]

Thornton was also at work on playlet number 7, *Mr. Bozzy*, about Dr. Johnson, Boswell, and Mrs. Henry Thrale—Hester Lynch Salusbury Thrale—along with her husband, Johnson's closest friends over two decades. Because Thornton believed that his father had unjustly blamed Mrs. Thrale for being jealous of Boswell, he was writing the play to set his father straight. But Boswell's influence was making his writing stiff, Thornton thought. "I see myself writing down an archaism, or Latin construction and I have to howl at myself," he wrote to Amos, "but *I cannot help it*. My style will either come out from this ordeal saved or ruined."[25]

AS HIS Mount Hermon summer wound to a close, Thornton looked forward to a real vacation. Their father saw to it that after Thornton and Amos worked hard each summer, they also had free time to enjoy the seashore or the mountains, to rest and play, episodes that Dr. Wilder called "flings."[26] The extent and location of the flings were usually determined by the dividends, if any, that he had received on his investments that year. Thornton was counting the days till freedom when he received the news that his father wanted to send him to Maine to visit relatives. He protested vigorously: "I don't want to go among anybody's relatives in Maine. Visiting relatives is the worst strain I know. I want to be mummified and laid away for an aeon or two."[27] His father insisted, however, and the visit was not as grim as Thornton had feared. He and Amos traveled by boat through a storm to Squirrel Island, Maine, to visit their uncle, George Hobson; his wife, Helen; and their son, Wilder, at Hobson's Choice, the Hobsons' rustic cabin on the island. Thornton and Amos boarded at an inn, while their mother and Janet vacationed in a rented cottage across the channel. Having dispatched his wife and three of his children to vacation and visit his relatives, Amos Parker Wilder set off on a five-day hike in Massachusetts.

"Your Squirrel Island is a wonderful place," Thornton wrote to his father. "I know every path of it, however hidden beneath berry-vines, and every ledge and shelf of it."[28] He rowed the circumference of the island, savoring the exercise of his "hard-earned muscle" as well as the misty views. One day he decided to row across the channel to visit his mother and sister, and amused a local "salt" with his questions ("Am I facing the right direction?") and his "antics" as he sought to steer the row-boat safely across the water. It was a "blister-raising ride," but he made it. His little sister was given to "disgusting" fits of temper, he reported to his father, but his mother seemed well and "full of humor." She was indulging her enthusiasms over her writing and reading, but seemed "no-tably less feverish" about it than she sometimes was.[29] As the summer waned Dr. Wilder urged Isabella to keep Janet in Maine because of the polio epidemic in metropolitan areas that had quarantined multitudes of people, including Isabel and Charlotte in Pennsylvania.[30]

While Amos won several tennis tournaments in Massachusetts and Maine that August, Thornton traveled alone to Monhegan Island, Maine, about ten miles out to sea, where he enjoyed a blissful vacation all on his own. By late August he was a guest at Monhegan House, the historic inn built in 1870 in the center of the island. A mile and a half long and only a half mile wide, Monhegan is bounded by steep cliffs overlooking the ocean on the eastern shore, and the more serene harbor and shoreline to the west. Thornton wrote to his father that it was "the most glorious place" he ever saw.[31]

A traditional sanctuary for migrating birds, the island was also a refuge for artists. "It's not just an Artists' Island," Thornton wrote to his mother after he had explored the island; "it's an artist's own hearth and home."[32] He saw the studios of painters Arthur B. Davies and Robert Henri, and the scenery moved Thornton to extravagant descriptions. "The sights are tremendous," he exulted. "I've climbed chasms and crept to the edge of edges all day," He found himself on "a high eminence and saw the great ocean kneeling at the base of a great cliff of grey rain-washed rock." He hiked and swam, attended a lecture on "Aspects of German Life," and met fascinating people, including a Hungarian who knew novelist George Moore personally.[33]

Thornton carried on brief flirtations with some of the hotel maids. "There are the prettiest maids in this Hotel you ever saw," he wrote his mother. "Did I get this common streak from you?—I *always* notice the servant girls, but forget to look into Limousines."[34] There were several interesting German academics in residence at the inn that week, some affiliated with German universities and some with American (and a few of them, unbeknownst to Thornton and the others, actually engaged in espionage). He was enthralled with their conversation, part in English, part in German. He also enjoyed meeting a "sweet-faced, motherly German lady" who was the mother of twins, one a painter and the other a golf champion. Thornton, the twinless twin, was intrigued to learn that they were "strangely lonesome" when they were separated.[35]

But the highlight of his luxuriously indolent stay on Monhegan was meeting the Austrian drama critic, translator, and impresario Rudolf Kommer, who, Thornton heard, "knew personally almost all the principal novelists and dramatists in Europe and England."[36] Thornton introduced himself to Kommer, who also represented the great Austrian producer Max Reinhardt's theatrical interests in the United States. Reinhardt had long been one of Thornton's theatrical idols. Since high school days he had avidly read (and collected records of) German-language theatrical performances. He kept track of productions in the great theaters of Germany and Austria, and of the playwrights, directors, and actors involved in them, Reinhardt foremost among them. Thornton often daydreamed about mounting his own plays on the great stages of the world, directed by legends such as Reinhardt, and starring the finest actors of his era. Now, after his stultifying summer in the fields of Mount Hermon, he found himself magically transplanted to a seaswept Maine island and savoring the company of Rudolf Kommer, the next best thing to the great Max Reinhardt himself. Kommer was "very much struck" with the young man's knowledge of modern German drama, which he found "creditably detailed," he told Thornton, "even for a cultured German."[37]

Thornton poured out his hopes to Kommer, who generously read and commented on Thornton's playlets, and listened to his disappointment over the rejection of his full-length play. He would heed Kommer's advice about revising his Johnson-Boswell playlet. "I'm bound to you for much encouragement and many new ideas—difficult to assimilate!—" Thornton wrote in appreciation.[38]

From Monhegan, Thornton traveled to Augusta, Maine, to join his brother in a visit to their father's brother, Julian, and his family. There they saw their father's old home place, near the Maine State House and next door to the home of Senator James G. Blaine, whose children had been Amos Parker Wilder's boyhood playmates. They found their uncle Julian Wilder "big and unconventional, affectionate, a little wild-looking." He was a dentist, an alcoholic, and something of an inventor, whose house and motorboat were full of laborsaving devices he had created.[39] Thornton and Amos then returned to Connecticut to spend some time with their father in early September, and enjoyed a "fine Sunday together" climbing nearby Mount Carmel.[40] Back at Oberlin, Thornton settled into a challenging academic schedule—required courses in chemistry, economics, exposition and essay writing, and English history; organ lessons in the Conservatory of Music; and—at long last—Dr. Wager's famous Classics in Translation.

Dr. Wilder, meanwhile, was giving Thornton detailed notes on *The Rocket*—"making marginal comments on it that it'll take me a week to erase," Thornton complained. His father's opinions, Thornton wrote to Kommer, were " 'antipodal' to yours."[41] He rejected his father's idea that the play was "remote from popular tastes because of etherealized shading" but then launched into self-criticism about the weakness of certain characters and his opinion that his own last act "was heavy with too-plain moralization, and dull to extinction."[42]

Thornton could take criticism in stride, but he was half amused, half irritated to discover that his sister Charlotte had actually rewritten some of his work. "As I read my manuscript," he wrote to her at Mount Holyoke, "I began to miss some of my cherished phrases; every now and then I saw that someone had inserted perfunctory bridges over which the timid mind might step—with petticoat lifted = when the art of writing is a matter of alpine climbing—peak to peak, and let the chasms snatch the fearful."[43]

DURING THE summer of 1916, while Thornton was coping with mindless drudgery and constant sunburn to bring in the hay and the strawberries at Mount Hermon, and Amos was honing his championship

tennis game and trying to ward off the tedium at the military training camp on Plum Island, the war in Europe was moving ever closer
to the consciousness of citizens of the United States. Reaching out to
young men, Theodore Roosevelt sought to advance the cause in a rousing speech to the teenagers at the Plum Island training camp on the
"disgrace" of America's delay in joining the war.[44]

Beginning with the first battle of the Marne in 1914–15, Americans,
led by the American colony in Paris, had begun to help open convalescent centers in Paris for wounded soldiers, and to organize an ambulance corps to help the French transport war casualties. The Paris
Service, as the volunteer ambulance service was coming to be known,
was staffed largely by Americans, mostly young men from American
colleges and universities, who were volunteering in great numbers. Dr.
Wilder, following these events closely, began to mention the Ambulance Service to Amos, who turned twenty-one on September 18, 1916,
and was about to begin his senior year at Yale.

"On my twenty-first birthday Papa threw out another hint concerning the American Ambulance," young Amos wrote in his diary October 6. "I said nothing about it until the next day, though I thought
much. I then took him up on it and said I wanted to go. The best thing
in these dilemmas is to do the extraordinary thing." Amos recognized
that the volunteer ambulance drivers came to their service from a variety of motives: "The main idea, as with the aviators of the Lafayette
Escadrille, was to be where the action was, and with this was mixed
the romance of adventure."[45] There were different, far more personal
reasons underlying the decision for Amos, as he wrote privately in his
journal:

> *I have no definite convictions about my life work. I am not powerfully*
> *impelled by religious convictions. My certain aim is to make people*
> *happy—in an ultimate and lasting way of course. . . . But I am as*
> *yet no zealot. I am interested in the social movements of the day. . . .*
> *It would delight me to be a country pastor, a worker in the schools of*
> *China, a farmer, a writer. I would like to study more after college. I*
> *would like to travel in Europe. . . . I wish to be a good speaker.*[46]

His motive in going to the American Ambulance Field Service in France, Amos said, "was that of education, development, experience." He would miss his senior year at Yale, but he thought he would later enjoy it "all the more for an interim." He would be meeting a demanding need in wartime—and, at the same time, seizing an opportunity to get off on his own and test his self-reliance.[47]

By September 26 Amos Niven Wilder had been accepted to begin work as a volunteer in the ambulance service in Paris. Like many young men at that time, he was an inexperienced driver, so he immediately enrolled in a driving and maintenance course at Tom O'Connor's Depot Garage in New Haven.[48] On October 21, Amos sailed from New York for Liverpool. In London, he paid a visit to that tennis mecca, Wimbledon, finding it deserted, with faded old posters clinging to the stands. "It was as though everybody had gone off to war and left it exactly as it was on August 1, 1914," he wrote in his journal, not then imagining that he would play doubles at Wimbeldon in 1922.[49] On November 6 Amos arrived in Paris to join hundreds of other American student volunteers who would serve as ambulance drivers in France.

———

DR. WILDER, still running Yale-in-China in New Haven, was very busy in the fall of 1916—as always, the "chess master" moving his children from one place to another on a global chessboard. If the war continued, he thought, Thornton and Charlotte should go to Europe to be part of it. "You know I regard [the war] *the* great University at this time and want you *all* in it (but done judiciously and at the right time)," he wrote Amos.[50] With Amos in France, Thornton at Oberlin, and Charlotte at Mount Holyoke, he turned his attention to Isabel. (Seven-year-old Janet was much too young yet to warrant one of his grand designs—although it was an ominous sign that she loved play-acting, usually casting herself as a queen.) Satisfied with Thornton's experience at Mount Hermon, Amos decided that Isabel must be enrolled at the companion school for girls, Northfield Seminary in Northfield, Massachusetts. Isabel was sixteen years and eight months old, pretty and petite—just a half inch over five feet tall—and a freshman at New

Haven High School, where she was a good student and "a young lady of fine qualities and great promise," according to school officials.[51] The Northfield enrollment was at capacity, however, so Isabel stayed at home in Mount Carmel, helping her mother with Janet and the house-keeping chores, and attending New Haven High. Her grades were good, and she was popular with students and teachers alike.

Her father went ahead with the official application for her admission to Northfield in the fall of 1917, listing the patchwork of schools she had attended, from Shanghai to Berkeley to Florence, Italy, to Vevey, Switzerland, back to Berkeley, and now to New Haven. He thought his daughter was interested in arts and crafts and sewing and possibly drawing. She was a "practical type" without any particular life goals as yet, he wrote. She was "quiet, efficient, domestic rather than intellectual," although her grades were good. He wanted her to attend Northfield because he wanted his daughter in a community that stressed Christian character.[52] Isabel was accepted for the fall of 1917, and would spend two years at Northfield. On June 30, 1919, Amos Parker Wilder would write to inform the Northfield administration that he deeply appreciated their care of Isabel, and that she had "improved in all ways." But Miss Masters of the Misses Masters Boarding and Day School for Young Ladies and Children in Dobbs Ferry, New York—Isabella's alma mater—was "good enough to propose that our Isabel go there this Fall." After the "steadying of two years at Northfield," he wrote, he "dared to believe that the girl can have comradeship with the wealthy without being impaired."[53]

———

"AMOS'S GOING away has intoxicated you and Papa so with swelling emotions that letters from Oberlin will surprise you by their thinness," Thornton wrote to his mother. "Soon letters will be coming to you from Red Cross hospitals with censor-stamps on the back and Papa will feel that at last he has a son in the foreign field. How relentlessly I am shown up by it all—a minor who doesn't study hard and who needs money from time to time."[54] He urged his brother to write him all the details of his war work—"the knots, under the rug"—instead of the "grand skeleton letters" he wrote to spare the family worry.[55]

Dr. Wilder was soon encouraging Thornton to volunteer as a hospital aide in France and join his brother in the cause. "Please look into the matter," Thornton wrote to Amos, "and tell me if I could ever harden myself to terrible sights and sounds."[56]

Meanwhile, as an Oberlin sophomore, Thornton found himself, for the "only time" in his life, truly interested in his studies.[57] He respected most of his professors—but the finest, in Thornton's grateful opinion, was Charles Henry Adams Wager. Dr. Wager, who had earned his Ph.D. in English at Yale in 1896, was a meticulous scholar, a dynamic teacher, and a sympathetic mentor. He and his wife, Annie, regularly entertained students in their comfortable home near the campus. In a sense the students were the children of this childless couple, and teaching at Oberlin was Dr. Wager's life. He wrote scholarly articles, including occasional reviews for the *Dial*, but he concentrated on teaching. His challenging, often inspiring courses usually had waiting lists, especially his Classics in Translation.

Dr. Wager's intellectual interests and expertise encompassed the classical world, the Italian Renaissance, and Elizabethan and Victorian England. In the Oberlin College Archives may be found his course notes for many of the classes he offered over his thirty-five-year career at the college: Classics in Translation, first of all—the course that would so captivate and inspire Thornton Wilder. Wager was also a specialist in the Franciscan order, and traveled to Italy many times to deepen his knowledge, along the way collecting a comprehensive Franciscan library. All of his life Thornton would pay homage to this teacher. "Prof. Wager here is one of the greatest living authorities on St. Francis," Thornton wrote to his mother in one of many letters praising his professor.[58] Wager was, Thornton thought then and later, "the greatest class lecturer I have ever heard."[59] He wrote to his mother, "Prof. Wager is my great friend. Every time he opens his mouth I'm 'influenced' to the depths of my being. He's looking after my reading—irreproachable."[60]

Thornton was learning "the complete art of Starched Prose" in his Exposition and Essay-Writing course. His class elected him one of two assistant editors of the school newspaper, and he joined the college library committee. Not only was he prospering academically, but with some of his summer earnings he bought himself a new suit. He was measured for it on a trip to New York. "It is dark grey," he told Amos. "The vest is of that careless opulent cut. The collar is English rolled and fits carelessly well. I have [not?] tried the trousers but I know they won't drag on the ground."[61] But he needed a new winter overcoat and hated to ask for one. Even his father noticed that his old one was a "weird" garment, Thornton said; he had been wearing the same one since Chefoo days, and dreaded discussing the need with his father. He told his mother about it first, adding that he "could recall St. Francis' vow of Poverty and wear it another year if necessary." He asked his mother to write to him privately about his father's "money state and tell me whether it would be adding the last straw to an impossible load if I presented the question to him."[62] Thornton finally broached the matter and got the money for an overcoat, but not without conflict, and he wrote a passionate letter to his father in rebuke:

> *You have a way of not being open about money matters that is perfectly harrowing for us. . . . You ask me to get a coat between sixteen and eighteen dollars [Thornton got it on sale for seventeen] but in your heart of heart you expect it will be twenty-two. Just because Amos and I have been so minutely brought up we comply to the letter when our whole life and thought would be happier if we could feel proud of working out our own economies on our own money. Money and money-matters will be the last end of our family anyway. Poor mother has almost been robbed of her mind by worry over money; she can get so wrought up over the price of a pair of shoes that she is intellectually nil for a week. You are secretive and furtive about it; you may sometime become suspicious and injured. I hate to ask for money or talk about it and so I drag on for weeks without soap or equally absurd details because I feel that money is such an oppressive difficult thing.*

Thornton went on to remind his father dramatically that when Saint Francis of Assisi changed from his old life to his new life of poverty, "he ran naked out of his father's house."[63]

THORNTON WAS soon hopelessly behind in all his sophomore courses, even organ, but at least his writing was yielding pleasure: His playlet *A Fable for Those Who Plague* was performed in Finney Chapel "as an item on the Vaudeville of Society Night" at Oberlin. Although the play was "too slight and sub-tile [*sic*] for the hall or for the carnival mood" of the event, "the great audience laughed and applauded," Thornton reported.[64] He was also having fun as an actor—and getting a good review in the school paper. He performed in the Latin Department drama as Peniculus, "the Sponge, the Parasite," in a metrical translation of Plautus's *Menaechmi*, the source for Shakespeare's *Comedy of Errors*. "I had a light beard the color of fried apples and a red nose," he wrote to his mother. "We acted in front of a picturesque Roman street and the play was happily over-flowing with the customs and manners of Ancient Roman Bourgouisie [*sic*]."[65]

All in all, he told his mother, "I'm having a great time this year. Probably because I'm better dressed."[66] He was socializing and writing with zest. One Monday morning he took a vigorous four-mile walk and came home with an idea that he converted into a new three-minute playlet "about the mixture of Classical and Christian mythology in the Renaissance." He named it *Proserpina and the Devil: A Comedy for Marionettes*, and it would show up in the college literary magazine in December 1916.[67] While he wasn't studying as much as he should, he was doing

> *a good deal of original writing. . . . The best has been the Saint Story in the Magazine and a 3-minute playlet called "Proserpina and the Devil" for Marionettes. And a "Masque of the Bright Haired" for the Red Headed Club = "Order of the Golden Fleece" they call themselves. I shall send this Masque to Percy MacKaye since it is his*

line—reminding him of the ridiculous urchin during the rehearsals of Antigone.[68]

Thornton also collaborated on some writing projects with Marion Tyler, describing her as "the brightest and most charming girl in College (slim and great dark eyes with quaint embroidered things on her dark dresses; shy but vivid)." They were writing two essays and a one-act play, set on the China coast, "*for the market*," he wrote proudly. He was supplying the "purple patches and general ideas" while Marion added ideas and structure.[69]

He often visited the Wagers, and wrote to his mother, "They sit me down and start laughing before I speak, and all of me is suddenly released and I talk and talk like an old crow. I get the horrible thought that he likes me better than what I write."[70] Professor Wager had taken his often socially awkward student under his wing, tactfully coaching him to "bring out the idealler strains" of his "inherited personality." Since boyhood Thornton had been more comfortable in the company of adults than with people his own age. By his own admission, he could be "a kind of Breakfast-table Kaiser," dominating conversations, becoming "educative," criticizing his peers when they uttered "bromides," asking their opinions only to "disagree with them noisily." He told his father, "To put it short—I see you in myself and laugh, and then go on exaggerating what I saw."[71]

As a result of Dr. Wager's gentle criticism, advice, and encouragement, Thornton found himself acquiring new friends. "I always thot [thought] that I was constitutionally disgusting to all men," Thornton wrote to his father. "But now I know I have four friends among the Philistines where before I had one. And I *do* like them more and more . . . I will always say that Prof. Wager did half but my new coat did the other half."[72]

Thornton would have to stay at Oberlin for the holidays, for, as usual, there was no money for a trip home at Thanksgiving or Christmas. Dr. Wilder was off on a Yale-in-China speaking and fund-raising tour of the Midwest, which would take him to Battle Creek, among other places. Grandmother Niven joined her daughter and granddaughters for Thanksgiving, and they missed Thornton and Amos "awfully," Isabella wrote.[73] She also sent Thornton a copy of a poem she had written on hearing of the tragic death of one of her favorite poets, Émile Verhaeren, the famous Belgian Symbolist whose poems she had translated from French into English. She planned to send her poem to the *New Republic*.[74] In their letters to each other, Isabella and Thornton enjoyed an ongoing dialogue about music and literature they loved, and prose or poetry they had written, freely exchanging criticism and advice writer to writer, more than mother to son. "I am very happy in getting letters with poems [in] them . . . ," Thornton wrote to his mother after he had dissected some of her poetry. "And such good ones too."

He was becoming a mystic, he told her, sometimes even cutting classes under the pretext of an earache or some other malady so he could work on an essay on "mysticism and its literature." Professor Wager's courses were opening Thornton's mind and imagination to the world of the ancient and classical mystics, and to the more recent work of Cardinal Newman and other Catholic theologians. "Perhaps we can enter the Catholic Church together and be out of the old American stupidity," he wrote to his mother.[75] Thornton later told his brother that he knew that his "Roman Catholic tendency" pained his "dear Papa so, and Mama too, who has become so full of Theology and metaphysics that I'm afraid of her."[76]

Isabella had a busy schedule in Mount Carmel and New Haven, keeping house; caring for Isabel and Janet; making suffrage talks; attending faculty teas; volunteering for the Red Cross; working with a Town-Food Committee, part of the Connecticut governor's drive to promote agricultural interests to support the war effort; and serving as chairman of the education committee of the Mount Carmel Schools, personally leading schoolchildren in a village improvement project.[77] Thornton missed his mother and sisters, and his brother remained very much on his mind. Having finished his assignment with the Paris Service, Amos was driving in the American Friends Service ambulance operation during that autumn before the United States joined the war. He lived in a château in Neuilly with sixty other volunteer drivers, keeping a journal of his experiences and reflections in small black *carnets* (notebooks) like those that French schoolchildren used, and staying as connected with his family as slow, transoceanic wartime mail would permit.

Safe in Ohio, Thornton was beginning to worry about the war and his place in it. "Tell me about the brave French, give anecdotes of nobility in young men," he wrote again to Amos. "Stir me up over the war. Tell me, could I harden myself to hospital work?"[78]

THORNTON RECEIVED a visit from his father that December as Dr. Wilder made his way back east from Battle Creek. He wrote to his wife from Oberlin that the Battle Creek regimen had been good for his health. He noted that Amos was "presently remembered here [at Oberlin] as a gentleman-athlete." As for Thornton, he looked "well and brisk as ever," Dr. Wilder reported to his wife. "His room in the men's building is light and well ventilated; his clothes were properly hung up. He seems to be getting on well."[79]

9

DISTANT SONS

So writes a distant son, doting for your least considered moments,
the crumbs of your time.

—THORNTON WILDER TO HIS "DEAR OLD PAPA"
[May 1917?]

Oberlin (1917)

"Often I'm dissatisfied and unhappy; I want to leave college and live on a Desert Island. Would it cost much?" Thornton wrote to his mother in the fall of his sophomore year at Oberlin. "Everything I read or hear reminds me that I ought to be finished with all this and be at it."[1] During the second semester Thornton felt even more strongly: "I was not made for College; I was made for Plato's Republic where artists, on presentation of promising credentials, were supported by the state; or where Maecenases [the patron of Horace and Virgil] may be found to offer leisure and encouragement to those whose mental current no outer circumstances can interrupt without causing this quiet desperation."[2]

He argued his case forcefully in a long letter to his father in January 1917:

> *Why should we go to College at this time of our life it is hard to see. Our minds are in a ferment; we cannot realize an idea; or imagine a conviction. Art, sex and religion are driving us mad, and time or mood for reflection we have none. There are long periods, sometimes a whole week when I am so miserable because I cannot think of a beautiful thing to write that I seem to [be] beating my head in despair again[st] a stone wall. Sometimes when the din and voices of these years of my life become too insistent, I say:*
>
> *"Come, I'll stop all this. I'll try not to answer anything, or write*

*anything or aspire [to] anything. I will be an ordinary boy; I will eat
and study and wash and be full of polite attentions to other people. Then
after a few months I will come back to this inner room, and perhaps I
being older can put it in order."*

He couldn't tell whether his restlessness was more acute than that
experienced by other boys. "We all conceal it, and from our parents
first of all," he wrote. "But College is not an answer to it—not Oberlin
with its fat Christian optimism." If he had to go to college another
year, he wanted to go to Harvard. Better yet, he wanted to go live on
Monhegan Island, perhaps for a year, "until all this fever is over, and
I have grown up, or grown stiff or whatever it is that allows one to
accept the world, and be content with a life of Houses and dinners lived
on a life of Dreams and Cries."[3]

By February he was beseeching his father to let him go to Italy—
not to "relieve suffering" or "to see pictures and Classical landscapes"
or to "get away from the uninspired complacency of Oberlin"—but
simply to have some time to himself, perhaps six months.[4] He proposed
a "business arrangement" to his father: "Give me three or four months
on Monhegan, or a year alone somewhere, and I will give you something final and convincing."[5] He was determined to prove himself as
a writer—and as soon as possible. His father was equally determined
that, while his son might be outgrowing Oberlin, Thornton would
finish the academic year and then move on to the final two years of college elsewhere, most likely at Yale.

As he traveled on Yale-in-China business in March 1917, Dr.
Wilder visited Thornton at Oberlin and found him still campaigning
to be sent to Italy. Thornton had even tried to enlist the support of
Sherman Thacher for his idea of working in a hospital for wounded
soldiers in northern Italy.[6] He confided in his old schoolmaster
his recurring self-doubts: Was he "especially immature?" Was his
father "with his fostering solicitude unduly unjust?" Was his father
right that Thornton must be "forever self-distrustful?"[7] Dr. Wilder
was, in fact, surprisingly sympathetic to Thornton's situation that
March: "As I look over your beautiful letters read since my return,

some written before my visit, I realize what an inadequate Papa I am," he wrote,

> *how you long to exchange communications with me on many lines with much sincerity and openness and how I barrier you with misgivings and rebukes. It seems to be life that thus we should dark-glass even those we best love and to whom we would be useful, especially in this critical business of youth finding itself. Let it console to tell that as I looked you over from the train I thanked heaven for such a son; and that it pleasantly surprises me to find richer veins in my boy than even I dared to hope.*[8]

He reassured Thornton even further: "You *think* I will be content with small things for you, dear; but no one is keener to know your parts and there is nothing too high for you to attain. . . . Would I plan Italy and languages and voice cultivation and the best unless we were preparing for large things!"[9] But Dr. Wilder meant for the preparation for "large things" to take place at Oberlin for the time being, expecting that Thornton could finish his college course in one more year. Consequently Thornton trudged through his schedule, dreading two "dull classes" but still savoring Dr. Wager's Classics in Translation; reading Sophocles' *Oedipus Rex*; and exploring the work of the Irish poet, playwright, and novelist George Moore, with whom, Thornton said, he was "twin-knit." He thought he and Moore were "Affinities," and especially enjoyed Moore's aphorisms, his tone and mood, his "interest in the forms and spirit of the Catholic Church and his Cadence—his great contribution to the English sentence borrowed by him from the Anglo-Irish."[10]

His sophomore malaise did not stop Thornton from writing plays and reviewing those of others. He had written two of a planned series of three "spiritual stories"—"Caone and Acuthuna" and a florid, melodramatic short story, "The Marriage of Zabett," which he was trying unsuccessfully to sell to a literary journal.[11] It ultimately appeared in the *Oberlin Literary Magazine* in June 1917. Despite its melodrama, this was a well-written tale about a young woman whose wealthy father betrothed her to his business partner. The reluctant bride-to-be recoiled at any physical contact with her fiancé, longing instead to devote her life to God and the church. "Oh, to tell the torment of a life unaltered about an altered spirit," Thornton wrote of his heroine, who, by story's end, was hailed as "St. Zabett of Kaage." He was trying a new method in these stories—"plain narrative, with economy of ornament and absolutely with[out] comment; as innocent of labored footnotes as the book of Acts."[12] On his own Thornton was reading Ibsen's *Ghosts*, and the work of the English poet Rupert Brooke, who had been killed in battle on the Western Front in 1915, at the age of twenty-eight.

During that third year of the Great War, Thornton brooded over his future, his frustration at the paucity of time to write, his eagerness to get college behind him—and his anxiety about his family. "There are two insidious ghosts in our family," he wrote to his father in March. First, they were "not abundantly generous to one another," he felt; they were "a grudging family." And the second "ghost" was their "fear of poverty."[13] The seven Wilders were "so splendid individually," Thornton reflected. "If we were a sober, New England, around-the-lamp, co-praying family I insist, we should be less," he declared. "Amos would be more docile; I less modern, Charlotte less promising, Isabel less vivid, Janet more sophisticated, Mother less concentrated. You more demand-ative. We should be cut into pieces."[14]

His father no doubt thought that Thornton was just being Thornton. His mother worried that he was sinking into a "decadent period," but she also recognized that Thornton had "used up Oberlin, and hence his desire to cease." She believed that at a new institution—Harvard, Yale, or Columbia—"he would revive interest in his education and go through with it." Meanwhile, Thornton was "producing playlets and stories like an adding machine with scarcely a click," their mother wrote to Amos.[15]

Thornton missed his brother and his quiet understanding, for Amos was still a world away. After completing three months with the American Ambulance Hospital in Paris he had transferred on January 31, 1917, to the American Field Service and in February was assigned to the front in the Argonne. Sensitive accounts of transporting the wartime wounded filled the pages of his letters, often written at night in the dim light of improvised lamps in army dugouts. Back home his proud father offered "extended excerpts" for publication in the *New Haven Journal-Courier* and other newspapers.[16]

By early April 1917, with President Wilson leading the nation into the war, world events overshadowed Thornton's despondency, as well as his halfhearted academic pursuits and his dreams of writing. When Congress approved the declaration of war on April 6, 1917, Thornton wrote to his parents for guidance. He was almost twenty, and it was time to decide what part he would play in the war. Oberlin's president, Dr. Henry C. King, and Professor Wager spoke to students about the "bigger aspects" of the war, and some Oberlin men "hurried up to Cleveland to enlist hot-foot." Others decided to stay in college until the end of the semester. Thornton was inclined to wait and see, to "drill and cross" on campus, where military training was being organized as it was in colleges and universities throughout the United States.[17]

He agonized over the decision. For a short time he considered joining some Oberlin boys who were going to Paris to work as hospital orderlies, and his father encouraged the plan, as Thornton duly noted on a postcard: "You are very comforting in your description of an orderly's job as 'loitering along the corridors and being pleasant with the maimed.' I understand that it was to carry swill and help the undertaker. Please find out which one of us is right."[18]

Thornton imagined himself a soldier, and wrote to his family, "How absurd even to you I would look with a bayonet; I have no faint reflection in my mild make-up of the heroic! I should smile up to the last minute. And equally absurd with my illogical mind would I seem declaring myself after due process, a conscientious objector." And then there was the ultimate confrontation: "But all consideration leads to that moment when one shoots."[19]

"Thornton has had a 'quake of the soul' at last," his mother reflected, when she heard from her "mystical-minded boy" as the United States geared up for wartime. She predicted he was moving toward a "deep sincere visualization of a world of struggle and problem[s]."[20] Oberlin drills, marches, and field excursions began in earnest April

11, with 350 men participating. College men with on-campus training were promised eligibility to become noncommissioned officers. While Thornton's participation in the training exercises did not mean he had committed to enlist, he told his family, it did seem to him that he must do so—not because he was a hero, or because he felt "that the issues for an American are not great enough to risk everything for," but because of what the experience could do to him "in sudden maturing, completing," and for what it could do to inject "greatness" into his "Little Gift" as a writer.[21] He wrote his brother about the new routine: marching three times a week, undergoing endurance drills and sham battles. "It commits us to nothing however but strenuous exercise and a state of being nervously wrought."[22] He told Amos that he had almost decided that he should enlist.

By the end of April, Thornton was confiding his worries about the war and his role in it to Grandmother Niven: "What is being planned for me? I do not know." He wore eyeglasses, and had been told that his eyesight might keep him from being conscripted. But if he passed, he would be reconciled to the soldier's life. "In my funny, sensitive way of being distressed and despairing over my life and my fitness, I am always at odds with life," he told her. "I am a personality peculiarly isolated." He loved his country, but he had his doubts about the power of war to improve the human condition. He wondered if his father might send him to work on a farm; seventy Oberlin boys had already departed to "serve the agricultural need of their country and their country's allies," Thornton reported.[23]

In the midst of the "scorching" reality of wartime preparations, classes went on at Oberlin, as did the annual French play, in which Thornton played a small role. He wondered all the while if his "little practice in French" would prove to be significant in wartime.[24] He had just turned twenty, and he told his mother he was now thinking seriously about enlisting. When Isabella heard that Thornton's poor vision and dependence on eyeglasses might make him ineligible, she wrote to young Amos: "So I am *very* thankful. . . . One of you in the track of shellfire is all I can stand."[25]

"REALIZATION OF the war and Personal Determinations come to me with regular frequency, but between them I drift back to my pre-occupations with literature and with the little social life around me," Thornton wrote apologetically to his family that spring. He welcomed the company of Nina Trego, an Oberlin senior with "an elfin pointed oval" face, "dusky" skin, the eyes of "a mad Ariel," and a "salty" tongue.[26] Even though they quarreled often and heatedly, they enjoyed each other immensely. She held her own with Thornton, and never hesitated to criticize his writing, even his letters home. Once, when he asked her to read a letter, she told him "with a reproving smile that it was magnificent writing but that there were some things in it that she wouldn't send 'if she were I,'" adding, "although, of course, your parents must be used to that kind of letter." She was "sharply independent and warning-ful but elfin and super-intelligent," he wrote admiringly.[27] She was "a young seer."[28] All in all, he confided to his mother, he was "becoming absorbed in the entrancing Miss Nina Trego."[29]

Nina thought Thornton should do farmwork for the war cause, but he leaned toward going to Europe. They were living in "Great Adventurous Days."[30] His neglect of his college work was intensified by the reality that the war was disrupting life in general, and academic life in particular, with college students now leaving in droves to enlist. "All the boys are gradually going," he told his father, adding that the Oberlin dean predicted that two-thirds of them would leave by the end of the month.[31] Torn as he was about whether to enlist, Thornton rebelled when his father tried to discourage him. "I feel ashamed of myself for being so easily reduced to acquiesce by you," he wrote Dr. Wilder in May. "If I were worth my salt, I would fly into a fiery passion, demand your support for my enlisting and cow you into admiration—but instead I am a poet, a lover of the meek-eyed Peace and farthest Maine-coast solitude."[32]

But he grew increasingly anxious, believing he should serve in the military but fearful that, like so many young men, he might perish in battle before he had realized his aspirations. These exigencies led to Thornton's resolve to devote himself totally to his literary development.

"Other[s] fight for their country or for their sheer love of great action," he wrote to his family, "but the artist is the great egoist, and counts the world well lost for one created perfect thing."[33] But if he was going to die young in battle, he was determined to leave some good work behind. To that end he started keeping a journal. He began with an epigraph from *Twelfth Night*: "Not yet old enough for a man, nor young enough for a boy . . .'tis with him in standing water, between boy and man." This was followed by an aphorism: "When enthusiastic—make a note of. For what is not expressed dies."[34]

The pages of his journal were suffused with ideas for plays and short stories. First he would write out a draft of his prose in a leftover exam "blue book" or whatever was at hand, and then he would copy it with "meticulous neatness into a notebook."[35] Sometimes he escaped into daydreams—plays he would write, and stage and film stars he would cast in those plays, especially the handsome young Welsh actor Gareth Hughes. He copied portions of reviews of Hughes's performances, pasted a newspaper photograph of Hughes in the journal, and wrote a passage about how Professor Wager had actually seen Hughes play an "unimportant role" on Broadway, but remembered "more vividly his chance glimpse of the young actor striding splendidly down Fifth Avenue the next morning."[36] When Gareth Hughes disappeared from the news, Thornton worried that he had left for the trenches.

Into his 1917 journal also went accounts of Professor Wager's inspiring lectures on Dante and Euripides, Cardinal Newman and Saint Ignatius Loyola, and of his own stolen hours copying musical scores in the library. Thornton entrusted his ongoing literary work to the journal, which he hoped would "portray the various steps in the evolution" of his writings. He wrote out ideas for a play he soon condensed into a new three-minute playlet—*The Acolyte*—inspired in part by Professor Wager's lecture on the *Ion* of Euripides. A foundling left on the steps of the Temple of Apollo at Delphi, Ion was taken in by the priests to be raised as a slave. Thornton originally conceived his play expressly to star Gareth Hughes as a "lay-brother and caretaker of an old Mission in Southern California" who hesitates to become a monk because he was a foundling, left on the doorstep of the mission and raised by the brothers there. He does not want to commit his life to the church until he finds his birth family and learns why he was abandoned.[37]

Thornton worked hard over several days in May to honor Professor Wager with a sonnet, and began writing two other sonnets as well, trying to emulate the classical literary form and idiom he knew his professor admired. He would continue refining the Wager sonnet as late as December 1917. The May 17 draft in his journal does not inspire confidence that Thornton was destined to be a poet. It read in part, "Oh, let me listen on that saving word / That brings to leaf the branches of my mind.—/ As Saul leaned to Gamaliel, strangely stirred, / Urgent for God, and that dim work assigned."[38] Even so, when Thornton had polished the sonnet to his satisfaction, he sent it to Charles Wager.

Thornton also confided to the journal his fears about the war, filling pages with his apprehensions and his conflict about what to do. His imagination and empathy brought the horrors of battlefield into vivid reality, but he decided—for the third time—to enlist. Congress was about to pass the conscription bill, and soon the young men of the country would know the particulars—who would be called, and how, and when. "If I were one dummy among a thousand khaki dummies I believe that my thousand separate distresses would merge into one distress—the monotony of the military life, perhaps later, the terrible variety of military action," he reflected. "I am a tragical boy tonight, as despairing as a cat at sea."[39]

He wrote with foreboding:

I can see that I have always in the back of my mind the assurance that the war will end soon, that I was cultivated for a sudden term of violence at my twentieth year. And it is with this that I combine the—I deplore—little religious sense that I have. I can imagine myself believing up to the moment of my first "Company, fire!" that Providence would never bring me to active fighting. . . . Perhaps I am not all fool since I can see and ridicule (although I cannot correct) my illusions.[40]

He had nightmares: "Last night I dreamed of my first day in the trenches," he wrote in the journal.[41] He thought it was Belgium where he was fighting in his dream. He and the other new soldiers were asked to write on paper with torn edges. Then they were given gas masks and warned that poisonous clouds were about to enfold them. He donned his mask quickly and smelled the deadly bromine fumes. He could not remember the rest.

BACK IN New Haven, Amos Parker Wilder was gratified to hear in April that Thornton had been promoted to corporal, in charge of eight Oberlin men, and was taking an advanced military course to learn how to drill his charges. Pleased and proud, Dr. Wilder wrote, "You do not explain how you chance to be a corporal; you know a father is always surprised when his boy does better than the average boy! I confess this is power in an unexpected direction."[42] But soon, Thornton wrote in his journal, he had been "deposed from my corporal-ship in drill through sheer incompetence." He could not imagine how he was going to break the news to his father. "Our good Captain John Allen was grieved to do it," Thornton wrote, "for he placed me there from a kindly impulse, and the only thing I regret is the damage done to his opinion of me. But I have spoken to him this morning, saying that I am glad of the retirement, the complications of squads-on-to-left and squads-to-the-left-march harassed me, and his face showed relief."[43]

Now that he was a disgraced "deposed" corporal, Thornton decided that in his letters home, for the time being, he would maintain a "Furtive Silence" about his demotion.[44] Fortunately he was reinstated as a corporal on May 2, although "perhaps not permanently," but at least he did not have to inform his father of his temporary fall from grace.[45]

IN THE spring of 1917, that time of limbo when Thornton and countless other young men waited to learn if they would be conscripted, he and his father revisited an earlier battle—the question of whether and where Thornton would go to college for his junior year. The father lobbied for Yale. The son balked. He did not think he could pass all the Yale entrance exams, for one thing. He did not *want* to go to Yale, for another. Most of all he wanted to continue studying with Professor Wager, even though he believed that Wager was "not particularly fond" of him. "He likes the great, boyish, naive, accepting boys," Thornton wrote to his father, "and I am odd, over-learnèd, distressed and adrift, but ruddered by my own conceit."[46] Still, he was "no less fond" of his professor, and while he knew there were "brilliant and literary" professors at Yale and Harvard, they lacked "that spiritual almost ascetic magnetism of Mr. Wager." He thought it was better for him to "live in an ordinary routine college" with Wager than in a "World-famous University without him." Then Thornton offered an alternative that he knew would rivet his father's attention: "Albeit if you hear of some Catholic college I will discuss that seriously. I think that after all I am an acutely religious temperament and that beside it nothing else matters."[47]

The big question about Thornton's future was settled in May by the national conscription law, which proclaimed that only men between the ages of twenty-one and thirty would be drafted. "That leaves Thornton out," his mother wrote with relief.[48] She reported to Amos in Europe that Thornton had "suddenly become sane and calm again."[49] He wrote his own private letter to his brother about the outcome: "All the fever about my going into the army has passed—There were moments perhaps hours when it seemed to me the perfect thing for me to do—but with the news that the Registration age is from 21–30, the fever has passed with the necessity. For the present Father's plans carry."[50]

Dr. Wilder's plans for Thornton, as usual, included a summer of farmwork, this time at Berea College in Kentucky. At least agricultural work now had the larger purpose of helping the war effort. In the fall Thornton would resume his college program—most likely at Yale or Harvard. "I want to come back to Oberlin next year," he insisted in another letter to his father. "Other people are content to have Providence lay the school burdens on their children," he argued, trying another tactic, "but [you] have taken the work into your own hands;—it creates a different psychological reaction in the pupil's mind; mostly puzzlement."[51]

Thornton offered evidence that Oberlin had served him well, and would continue to do so: "During the last year under the tart instruction of Nina Trego I have civilized down a little from the Shelley manner and these people have understood me better and met me on a more generous footing." He was afraid that on another campus his "bedraggled despairing moods would increase. If the world is still going to College next year allow me to come to this nourishing back-stream."[52]

When, after a "long unproductive period," Thornton "suddenly wrote a story," he realized again, he told his father, "that whether I go or stay, whether I work or study or travel is all superficial. My real life is abstract and moves along on its own will and caprice, and all these outer things are a shrugging-of-the shoulders, a cork-on-the-stream. So do what you like; a hoe or a hospital pail or a bayonet in my hand are phantom, for my hand holds always a fountain-pen."[53]

Whether fate took him to war or to Yale or to another summer farm, he hoped that he could at least spend some time at home in Mount Carmel. He expressed that wish in a letter to his father, fusing his own dramatic bent with the style of writers he admired at the time, especially George Moore. Thornton was, he wrote extravagantly,

> *a distant son, doting for your least considered moments, the crumbs of your time. . . . As a mystic counts the troubles and irks of this life* nothing *compared to the felicities that shall be hereafter, so I dream beyond the plowed field and the dusty hay, to the moment when there is a rushing from the house to the Father returning and to the smell of Mother's risotto and the following of her about, talking to her as she works.*[54]

THORNTON HAD arrived at Oberlin an awkward adolescent, full of self-doubt and countless enthusiasms. He would leave Oberlin a more mature, self-confident young man with a much more clearly defined vision of who he was and what he wanted from life. He had been academically challenged in ways he had not expected, and Professor Wager played the catalytic role in his intellectual and artistic development, as well as in his growing acceptance by his fellow students. Thornton reveled in his friendships and in the acclaim he enjoyed when he shared his writing in campus productions and the college literary magazine. Like most of his peers, he agonized over the war—its transformation of the world as they had imagined it to be; his quandary about what role, if any, he should assume in wartime; the shock of the first recognition of his own mortality. The war galvanized him as a writer, provoking some subject matter, of course, but, more than that, solidifying once and for all his absolute determination to *be* a writer.

Thornton "talked" to himself about these matters in his first serious effort to keep a journal, using images in an entry on May 26 that would reappear in his later work: His journal helped him to see the incidents of daily life in a "new light," he wrote, leading him to the "surprising discovery" that "life is more a matter of strands and threads than the young platitudinous philosopher who uses the phrase erewhile realized. In the Rondo of life there are more recurrent themes than there appears at first hearing . . ."[55]

———

BY THE time he was twenty, two lifelong habits were firmly forged: Thornton would spend countless hours writing in his journal and writing letters. Of all the letters he exchanged with numerous people during his youth, Thornton was most consistently and completely himself with his brother. They were friends as well as brothers; they trusted each other absolutely, knew each other's history and foibles, and loved each other anyway. As Thornton approached the end of what would be his last year at Oberlin, he wrote a revealing self-portrait in a long, heartfelt letter to Amos. His brother was just winding up a much-needed leave from active duty with the American Field Service ambulance detail in France, reviving his health and spirit in London, and taking long walks and reading Wordsworth in the Lake District. "Your religious self-examination I cannot duplicate. I am a less conscientious nature and do not examine my faith," wrote Thornton, the perennial questioner.

> *I fling myself upon my knees as though at a divine compulsion, mostly when I am happy tho also in extremis. I am happiest in loving and being loved by human people and next to that in writing words and being commended for them, and next to that in mysteries of the spirit, into which I penetrate I believe more every year, until perhaps God will be my whole life.*[56]

He was deeply interested in the Catholic Church, and in his private moments had thought about becoming a priest. He had confided that idea to his mother, who in a letter dated May 30, 1917, promised the family's support if he made the decision to enter the clergy in the Episcopal Church instead.

In his letter to Amos, Thornton conjectured that "everyone feels that his nature cries out hourly for it knows not what," but he reflected that his situation was unique in one crucial way: he was a twin—a twinless twin, whose brother died at birth. Because of his twin's death, Thornton wrote, "an outlet for my affection was closed. It is not affection alone but energy and in it I live and because of it I believe I seem to see life as more vivid, electric and marvelous than others so placidly do."[57]

The Wilder brothers respected as well as loved each other, and, close as they were in age, there was surprisingly little if any rivalry between them. Even though he was not Thornton's twin, Amos wrote in later years, "there was some sort of occult affinity in my makeup for his fabulation, like the telepathic understanding between [the twin brothers] Manuel and Esteban in *The Bridge of San Luis Rey*." Amos understood that because his brother had lost his twin at birth, Thornton "was predisposed to fascination with this relationship. Indeed one could hazard that he was haunted all his life by this missing alter ego."[58]

The loss haunted Thornton when he was twenty, on the cusp of adulthood, holding on, despite everything, to his "vivid, electric and marvelous" vision of life as it might have been, life as it was, life as it could be.[59]

10

"FLOWERING INTO LITERATURE"

My whole family is flowering into literature it seems all at once.
—ISABELLA NIVEN WILDER TO AMOS NIVEN WILDER,
May 31, 1917

Berea and Yale (1917–1918)

The Wilders were as scattered as ever in 1917, but wherever they were, somebody was writing poetry or prose—Thornton in Ohio and then in Berea, in the mountains of Kentucky; Amos in France and then in Macedonia; Charlotte at Mount Holyoke; Isabel in Connecticut and then in Michigan. Amos Parker Wilder was continually writing speeches and fund-raising appeals for Yale-in-China in New Haven, and Isabella, in Mount Carmel, was penning poems and sending them out to national journals, as well as firing off letters to the editors of various newspapers and magazines. She was trying her hand at writing a one-act play for children, and was working on a book review as part of a contest sponsored by Doubleday, Page & Company, hoping to win the cash prize and use it to buy a Corona typewriter.[1] Only Janet, age seven, had yet to become a writer.

Isabella wrote to young Amos to praise his letters, and to tell him he was becoming a stylist. "My whole family is flowering into literature it seems all at once," she told him:

> The Wilders are saturated nearly to the typhoon point (to change figures). For Thornton has sent us a really number one Sonnet addressed to his adored teacher, Dr. Wager; and Isabel has started to write short stories by all that is extraordinary—not merely one or two with effort and compulsion, but spouting like a geyser—three at once and they

come to her complete without need of change or corrections as fast as she can write them down. And she says they clamour to be written. If only [William] James were alive, it would be worth his while to study your several mentalities to see how it happens that seven angels have entered into us all at once, as it were.[2]

The Wilder family, like the similarly creative, peripatetic James family, was composed of two parents and five children, some of whom were writers. Isabella Niven Wilder had been reading William James's *The Varieties of Religious Experience*, published in 1902, a book of significant importance in her own independent spiritual quest. She may have had in mind James's designation of two religious mentalities—the healthy minded, who tend to celebrate life, and the "sick soul" attuned to the tragic potential of existence. Thornton and his mother apparently discussed James's ideas in relation to their own family, for Thornton wrote to his brother, "Wm. James has a chapter somewhere on us two, the child of open nature and the self-clinging one"—although Thornton did not specify which he thought was which.[3]

The writings of the four older Wilder siblings quite naturally evolved in proportion to their individual "mentalities" and motivations. Half a century later, in his novel *The Eighth Day*, Thornton Wilder reflected: "Nothing is more interesting than the inquiry as to how creativity operates in anyone, in everyone."[4] For evidence of how creativity operates, for better or for worse, he did not have to look beyond his own family, composed of two driven, high-powered parents and their gifted children—striving to excel and yearning for parental approval and for authentic self-expression, two often-conflicting objectives. Through forces beyond their control, some innate, some prompted by circumstance, Amos, Thornton, Charlotte, and Isabel were already launched on the lifelong journey toward creative self-expression, some to fulfillment and some to failure.

———

WHEN THORNTON left Oberlin in June 1917 to begin seven weeks of summer work in Berea, Kentucky, it had been decided that he would return to Oberlin for his junior year, a decision that would be revisited over the summer.[5] Meanwhile his parents were happy, Dr. Wilder wrote to Thornton as he made plans for the Berea summer, "that you will be content with a soil fling there—, that for the present you will walk the humble round."[6] He wanted his son to serve an apprenticeship in grassroots America. Thornton would be interested in the people at Berea, Dr. Wilder predicted, and would find there "an enviable opportunity to see that segment of American life."[7]

During that summer the Wilders, except for young Amos, fanned out over the United States, some vacationing, some working, all doing Dr. Wilder's bidding—and it was not easy orchestrating all those plans for the family, he complained to Thornton: "It would be easier to plan many things if Ma would discuss; but it is not her way. Everybody has his burden; this is mine and after all, it is a minor one; think of all the dreadful things I might have in my quiver." The father mused to his son that "John Wesley had a wife who was absolutely impossible; he went about his business. I have one of the bright women of her time; why is it more than a minor matter that she declines to speak to her husband?"[8]

Undeterred by his wife's opposition, however, Wilder took Isabel as far as Albany, New York, to catch a train that went straight through to Battle Creek, Michigan, where she would spend the summer taking a physical-culture course at the Battle Creek Sanitarium. "It's her father's latest and least happy scheme (to my thinking) and besides, what shall I do without her," Isabella complained to young Amos.[9] She was going to miss her seventeen-year-old daughter, who helped her with the housekeeping, the errands, and seven-year-old Janet's care. "Isabel went off looking pale, pretty but tired herself," Isabella worried. "She had studied very hard," and made the honor roll again at New Haven High School.[10] After she got past her homesickness, Isabel had a wonderful time in Battle Creek taking classes in swimming, first aid, calisthenics, Swedish gymnastics, and dancing, at which she excelled.

Meanwhile, Charlotte, now nineteen, was enthusiastically working on the Mount Holyoke College summer farm project, designed to help increase the wartime food supply. Interested in becoming a doctor or a scientist, she was also doing her own original research project "on the subject of Protozoa" for the college zoology department, which had provided books and a microscope and other instruments for her. She was studying "heredity and medicine" as well, and writing poetry. Her poem "Hollows" would receive the Sigma Theta Chi Prize for 1918–19, with an award of twenty-five dollars and a personal message from Robert Frost commending her for having the "faith that seeks poetic form through poetic substance."[11]

Dr. Wilder had high hopes for Charlotte, and he wanted her, along with Thornton, to have some experience traveling and living in Europe, as had already been true for Amos, Isabel, and Janet. Over the years, however, Dr. Wilder had grown increasingly concerned about Charlotte's temperament. She was "very able & resourceful," he had written to Amos, "but she needs to be in a serene and cheerful environment during this formative period; for she has a disagreeable side which *must* be kept dwarfed or she will grow up unlovely in moods."[12] He believed that associating with "bright, happy, Christian girls" at Mount Holyoke would "surely mold her."[13] The college environment had in fact been good for Charlotte, stimulating and sheltering her during what would be some of the happiest years of her life. She was "full of rectitude," Dr. Wilder told Thornton, but added that "she lacks sympathy; frowns on sentiment; I can never make a college president of her while she carries a basket of chips on her shoulder and is too keen in judgments. Yet Mt. Holyoke is doing her good."[14]

EXCEPT FOR his father's campus visits, Thornton had not seen any of his family in nearly a year, and he devoured all the news from home.[15] He told his mother that he imagined his homecoming at the end of the summer: "dismounting at the car almost on to the laughing Janet, then Isabel bubbling half down the street and you drying your hands with [a] towel on the doorstep and grinning like a Cheshire cat."[16] "I am an unusually isolated personality," he wrote, and he felt he could reach out only to his family.[17]

He was in Kentucky in mid-June, quickly caught up in the farm routine—digging ditches, laying pipes for a cannery, excavating for cesspools, driving a team of mules to scrape and level ground, hoeing sweet potatoes and carrots, helping to unload thousands of empty cans for the cannery, tossing them from hand to hand until he was "bleeding in twenty places."[18] He registered to take a shorthand class at the college, and devoted some of his limited free time to working on the sonnets he had begun at Oberlin. He was also working on a "novelette" for his mother, he wrote her in July, instructing her to keep it a secret. The subject was foreign life in China. He predicted it would amuse her. "It's about people with damaged reputations who retire to the Coast for seclusion," he told her. "Aha, but you will yet laugh, albeit humour is only its incidental."[19] He called it *Genivar Wyatt*, and rapidly filled two notebooks with the first draft of fourteen chapters. It threatened to grow "to novel-size," he told his mother in late July, and he was eager to send it to her. There were certain literary influences, he wrote: "It is dripping with irony, often tragic, under the aegis of [George] Meredith.[20] Although he did not finish the novelette, he kept it in his portfolio and would later rework the idea as a play, *The Breaking of Exile*. He was beginning to learn that for the serious writer, no writing exercise is wasted, and everything is potential fodder for future work.

Thornton kept a grueling schedule at Berea, rising at 6 a.m. for breakfast, studying shorthand from 7 until 8:30, attending his shorthand class from 8:30 until 10, and then working on the Berea farm from 10 a.m. until 7 p.m. After quitting time he read or wrote, if he could stay awake, and then fell "eagerly" into bed.[21] Thornton polished his sonnet to Dr. Wager one last time, and mailed it to the professor, who proudly shared it with his wife and their friends.[22] The sonnet eventually made it into print in an anthology edition of the *Oberlin Literary Magazine*, called *Oberlin Verse 1908–1918*.

Thornton's roommate was driving him to "tears of vexation"—a feeling that was no doubt mutual. The boys worked their way into a respectful friendship, however, and soon the two were reading books aloud after work. They read *Treasure Island*, Thornton said, with his roommate fascinated because he had never heard of pirates.[23] In the letters he scrawled at night or on Sundays, Thornton griped to his father and talked literature to his mother. His mail brought the usual avalanche of advice from his father: "Become an authority [on] Kentucky . . . become an intelligent man after years of varying experiences. . . . Keep your New Testament at hand on the table. Learn the place of prayer as a bulwark against the storms of life—none of us escape." Dr. Wilder hoped Thornton would be "brave and cheerful and of good faith"—a daunting challenge, Thornton soon found, as he endured the daily drudgery at Berea.[24]

BEREA COLLEGE was established in 1855, and in keeping with its Christian affiliation and its motto—"God has made of one blood all peoples of the Earth"—it was the first interracial and coeducational college in the South. It was founded by abolitionist John G. Fee, who envisioned a college that would be, like Oberlin, "antislavery, anti-cast[e], anti-rum, anti-sin."[25] The college primarily served Appalachian students of limited means, who studied tuition-free at the college in return for working at least ten hours weekly on the college farm or in other campus jobs. Like Mount Hermon, Berea had as its mission learning, labor, and service—principles Amos Parker Wilder had long embraced for his sons and daughters, along with the college's anti-caste, anti-alcohol, and anti-sin credo.

Thornton was introduced to folk arts and crafts at Berea, and to mountain dialects, and, in the fields, to fellow workers who thought he was crazy. He lived in overalls as they did, slept in the same dorm, ate the same food, but he was always reading books and writing and using big words—and taking long solitary walks up and down the nearby hills, even in the rain. On Sundays, he attended the Berea church, where he had to listen to "vile, Mount Hermon-made hymns with rhythms worse than ragtimes: And judgment day sermons."[26] (Many of the hymns had been composed or gathered by the late Ira D. Sankey, the charismatic American gospel singer who traveled the world for years with Moody on his religious crusades; hence Thornton laid the "blame" on Mount Hermon.)

By this time his brother had enlisted for another three-months' duty with the American Field Service and transferred to Macedonia to serve with the French Army of the Orient. In the winter of 1917 the Thacher School had raised enough money to buy a new ambulance for the American Field Service in honor of Amos.[27] Thornton was very proud of his brother's work, and the ambulance service was receiving much-deserved international publicity. It reached Berea in the form of the *Saturday Evening Post*, as well as the Pathé weekly newsreel footage, which the college showed its students and farmworkers. Thornton was covetous as well. "Oh, that my hair was blown by an Aegean wind or that beneath my feet the prow folded the 'holy waters of Pauline memory,' " he wrote to Amos. "Instead I drag a hoe over a sod that only the tradition of Daniel Boone enriches, and that, but doubtfully."[28]

BY LATE August, Isabella, Thornton, Isabel, and Janet were vacationing at Highland House, a rambling summer hotel at North Truro on Cape Cod, where Thornton was invigorated by twice-daily swims far out into the ocean and long walks on the beach. He wrote to his father that he had found the "elixir of youth" in the "lashed and surging" windswept sea. He was enjoying the company of a new acquaintance, a "young instinctive Prince," he wrote to Dr. Wager. People told the two young men they looked alike, but they were "antipodal," Thornton said, and they were planning weekend visits when college resumed in the fall.[29] He had been in an "agony of indecision" about his college plans—"whether to return to Oberlin, come to Yale or go to Harvard."[30] Relaxed and rested, however, he wrote to his father that he would "go wherever you say, abounding in obedience."[31]

Isabella wrote to Amos from Cape Cod that at last the plans were firm: Thornton would transfer to Yale, she said, "so you two may graduate together after all, and Charlotte the same year!"[32] (Actually, Charlotte would receive her degree at Mount Holyoke in 1919, and the brothers would finish their degrees at Yale in 1920.) The logistics of Thornton's transfer to Yale were complicated, however. He had to

obtain his Thacher and Berkeley transcripts because the Oberlin reg-
istrar reported that Thornton's Oberlin records had been "mislaid."
"Now this is hardly possible—to mislay the entrance records of one
of their own students," Isabella wrote; "so I suspect they simply will
not take the responsibility of recommending him. They must think,
simply, that it would not be to the credit of Oberlin to pass him over
with or without a claim and then have him fall down and discredit
them. . . . I almost think Thornton might better have been left at Oberlin to finish."[33]

While Thornton had agreed to Dr. Wilder's plan to transfer, he wished
his father would just give him half the money about to be invested in the
year at Yale and let him "take a year of strenuous quill-driving about
Washington Square, talking til fifty-o'clock in the morning with the
young blood of American literature, instead of the corrected and sand-
paper etc. etc. from the prep. schools."[34] Besides, he had an offer to join
the Cincinnati Little Theater Repertory Company, which was, he said,
the practical experience he needed "to almost finish me off as dramatist,
but the family won't hear of it."[35]

While he waited for the Yale semester to begin, Thornton lived at
home in Mount Carmel and took typing and shorthand classes three
times weekly at a local business college—skills that would, in his father's opinion, prepare him for certain military jobs ("the 7th clerk
of a sub-quarter master," Thornton joked).[36] They would prove to be
invaluable skills for a writer as well. Thornton still wrestled with his
conscience about whether he should leave college for military service.
Once again his brother was the recipient of Thornton's innermost
thoughts:

> *My only feeling about not being in the war myself is: the audacity of
> it! There is no earthly reason why I should not be there except I cannot
> bring myself to be vengeful and slaughter-breathing and helmet-proud
> about it for more than 24 hours at a time. Then I slip back into my
> native, bee-like preoccupation with the rarities and tender uniques of art
> and letters and let the trumpeting die away down the end of the street.*[37]

ON SEPTEMBER 25, 1917, Thornton spent his first night in 414 Berkeley Hall, his dormitory room at Yale, waiting for Yale to assign him a roommate. He turned out to be a freshman who filled their room so full of tobacco smoke that it made Thornton sick. That first night he went to see the great Sarah Bernhardt perform, and then wrote a letter to Professor Wager at Oberlin. Thornton was "happy and expectant," he told Dr. Wager, but his family "was troubled" because the Yale entrance board had reviewed his academic record and decided to admit him as a sophomore rather than a junior. He hoped—to no avail—that the dean, a Yale classmate of his father's, could successfully intercede and allow him to enter the junior class. Once again Thornton was a sophomore, and he would spend three years completing degree requirements at Yale.[38] His Yale expenses were almost certainly paid in part by the "Sons of '84" fund established in 1891 by his father's Yale class of 1884 to "aid in the payment of tuition bills in Yale College of sons of members of the class."[39]

Isabel had been sent off, over her protest, to Northfield Seminary in Massachusetts. She was so unhappy about it that Isabella, Janet in tow, rented quarters near Northfield for several months to help Isabel adjust to boarding school.[40] Dr. Wilder's chess pieces did not always move willingly, and sometimes his wife did her best to check them—but ultimately, everyone moved as he ordained. He wrote to Amos about his satisfaction that Thornton was enrolled at Yale, and about his hopes for the boy. He had watched as Thornton wrote a play in ten minutes. "(I quietly observed him)—writing just as rapidly as he could; no changes; that seems to me tremendous." He believed that Thornton "certainly has genius." He hoped that the competition at Yale "with many bright youths" would "comb him out a little," however, and give him "a little more modesty as to his gifts." Dr. Wilder was concerned that Thornton

> lacks the power to tie down to anything he don't relish; and so is
> barred from high achievements, I fear; and yet genius has laws of its
> own. I could do much for him by way of suggestion of things to do as

foundations,—the great books etc.; but it is not his way and I must
accept it. His mother encourages his conceit I fear.

But Dr. Wilder was confident that Yale would "reduce him some."
Meantime, he said, Thornton was "in good humor; washes dishes; does
things about the house; after much pushing and withal I am thankful
for such a son."[41]

"I LIKE Yale more everyday," Thornton wrote to Amos that fall. He
especially enjoyed the campus in the evening, "A silvery autumn dusk
in the campus quadrangle is a stirring thing," he wrote.[42] Amos's reputation was "no less reverenced here than at Oberlin," Thornton told
his brother, because of the "combination of high Athleticism and a
sober, even grave personality." However, Thornton was a little disappointed in his professors, he confided.[43] He carried a hefty academic
load during his first semester as he tried to catch up with his Yale
classmates: courses in philosophy, history, anthropology, geology, and
literature, especially the works of Shakespeare and Milton. He also
studied Latin with emphasis on the works of Horace, Tacitus, and
Catullus.

He kept up his typing and shorthand classes three days a week—
"a sample of what I am preparing to do for my country in her extremi-
ties, as my father wishes me to look upon it," he wrote to Dr. Wager.

> *You won't believe me when I say that I had a terribly strong fit of*
> *militarism the last few days to go into the R. O. T. C., and my mother*
> *seemed to be inclining toward it for the ignoble reason I suspect of going*
> *down the street with a medium tall son in brown—it is a ravishing ex-*
> *perience I can perfectly see—but Father repeated that my aptitudes were*
> *not along the lines of Alexander the Great and that for the present this*
> *preparation for a quartermastership was my quota.*[44]

The war in Europe dominated campus life at Yale, as it had at Oberlin, with many college men enlisting in one form of service or another,

and those staying behind joining ROTC, drilling and learning to march on a campus that had been transformed into a military training ground. Prospective cavalrymen who could not ride learned to mount and dismount on wooden horses shipped out to military training stations by the War Department. In the *Yale Literary Magazine*, Thornton could read war poetry and essays written by Yale men such as Stephen Vincent Benét, another avid writer, a talented poet, and an outstanding member of the class of 1919.

For the time being, Thornton concentrated on his classes and made a strong first impression on at least one of his Yale professors, sharing the news in a letter to Dr. Wager: He was "being spoiled," he said, by the praise his Milton professor, Lawrence Mason, was writing in the margins of his papers: "Thank Heaven there is someone in the class that can illustrate their points as a cultivated Gentleman should," read one comment. "This is a triumph of critical wit and dexterity," ran another. "You have phrased this perfectly; the thing could be painted." There was the occasional caution about abusing metaphors, but his professor gave one of Thornton's papers the first "four plus" he had ever given.[45]

Lest he grow too cocky, Thornton was kept in line by letters from Nina Trego, who had received her Oberlin degree and was now working in Chicago at Marshall Field's department store. He reported to Dr. Wager that he had sent a recent manuscript to Nina, who pronounced it the worst thing he had ever written.

––––––

THORNTON FLUNKED three courses in his first two years at Yale— Latin, geology, and biology—but he quickly made a name for himself in other arenas. His friend Wilmarth Sheldon "Lefty" Lewis, who knew him first at Thacher and then at Yale, recalled years later that Thornton "became a character, and I think perhaps for the first time realized how much people liked him."[46] Lewis had served as an editor of the *Lit*, Yale's literary magazine, and by 1919, Thornton was also one of the "Powerful Pens" at the helm of the journal, the oldest such student magazine and literary journal in the United States.[47]

Early in his first year at Yale, Thornton met Stephen Vincent Benét, whose older brother, the author William Rose Benét, was also a Yale man, class of 1907. With his brother's help, Steve Benét's first book of poems, *Five Men and Pompeii: A Series of Dramatic Portraits*, had been published in 1915, when he was eighteen. At Yale he poured his energy into working on the *Record*, one of the college publications, and serving on the editorial board of the *Lit*. He was elected chairman of the magazine in April 1918. All the while Benét was writing and publishing poetry and fiction.

Thornton met Steve Benét at a *Record* meeting early in the semester, and found him a "perfectly unromantic looking person, although not commonplace. His hair is short and light and curly. His face is round and quizzical and snubbed and his eyes are mole's eyes. He rocks his shoulders from side to side while talking."[48] Thornton wrote to Dr. Wager that Steve Benét was "the whole power" of the *Lit*.[49] Benét invited Thornton to bring some plays and fiction to his room on the evening of October 4, to be considered for publication in the *Lit*, and "devoted himself" to Thornton's "smudgy typewritten sheets" without any regard for the author, Thornton wrote. They read *The Angel on the Ship* and *Solus inter Deos Potens* and then Benét "said some very nice things" and escorted Thornton out of the room and all the way down the hall.[50] "So. I've got a story—(-play I mean-)—on the first table of contents of the Yale Lit.," Thornton reported to Dr. Wager on October 16. He was also "being lured into a studio conversazione on Sunday evenings by Benét and Co. But too much tobacco smoke chokes me and the beer has no illusions—. . . . The playlet is the Angel on the Ship."[51] It appeared in the October 1917 issue of the *Yale Literary Magazine*, a brief but intriguing critique of organized religion.

To Thornton's pleasure, the Yale University Dramatic Association, in its quest to promote plays written by undergraduate authors, sponsored the performance of two Wilder one-acts on December 20, 1917, along with two other student plays. Printed invitations went out to students and faculty alike, and Yale president Arthur Twining Hadley and his wife were in the audience to see, among other student offerings, Thornton's *That Other Fanny Otcutt* and *The Message and Jehanne*, two of his three-minute playlets. Benét and company would publish several Wilder playlets in the *Lit*, and Thornton contributed essays to the magazine as well.[52] The December 1918 issue carried *In Praise of Guynemer*, his dramatic tribute to the French flying ace, born in 1894, and the victor in fifty-three missions during World War I. Georges Guynemer died in flight on September 11, 1917, and in 1918 the Yale University Press published a translation of Henry Bordeaux's biography, *Georges Guynemer: Knight of the Air*, with an introduction by Theodore Roosevelt. "Measure for Measure," a sonnet by Thornton, made it into the November 1917 issue of the *Lit* but is nevertheless proof that while he was already turning out promising plays, short stories, and essays, he was clearly not destined to become a poet.[53]

NOW THAT he lived in New Haven, near his parents, Thornton was freed of the weekly duty of writing letters home. (He was living almost too close to his father, who, from his Yale-in-China office, could keep uncomfortably close watch over his son's daily life.) Thornton wrote long letters to Amos, who was based in Bistrika (now Bistrica) on the Serbian front in the summer and early fall of 1917, still attached to the American Field Service. Amos was so ill with malaria in October 1917 that he had to be treated in a French hospital. He would resign from the American Field Service in Paris in November and enlist as a U.S. Army private, assigned to the Field Artillery Training School in Valdahon, France, near the Swiss border.

Thornton also corresponded with Charlotte, who was happily occupied with her studies, scientific experiments, and writing at Mount Holyoke. Released from the expectation of letters written home on Sunday afternoons, Thornton turned instead to writing long letters to Dr. Wager, who still held his loyal allegiance as the best teacher he had ever known. From Oberlin, Dr. Wager wrote to his former pupil, "I haven't said how I miss you and sigh for you and talk of you to all comers; nor how wise I think you were to leave us."[54]

During his first year at Yale, Thornton was invited to join the

Elizabethan Club, founded in 1896. Located in a historic colonial home on College Street, the club had a library stocked with first editions of Shakespeare—quartos and folios—and the works of Milton and others. On the walls of the house hung paintings and engravings—images of Erasmus, Henry VIII, Elizabeth, Francis Bacon, Shakespeare, and Ben Jonson.[55] This was a congenial place where faculty and students could gather for tea, tomato sandwiches, conversation, and intellectual exchange. Membership was offered only after nomination and election by existing members of the club, and Thornton's membership was no doubt encouraged by William Lyon Phelps, a longtime Niven family friend, who had been the club's president as well as chairman of its Board of Governors.

In December, Thornton wrote a minuscule playlet on a postcard, titling it *Dialogue in the Elizabethan Club* and mailing it to Dr. Wager. In this vignette Thornton is asked if he came from a college out west. "Yes, Oberlin, Ohio," he answers. The distinguished Yale professor of English, Chauncey Brewster Tinker, observes that Oberlin is where "the great Mr. Wager is." Thornton responds: "Yes, do you know him?" "No," Professor Tinker replies. "But his pupils come around praising him." Thornton tries to find words and "strains the language for eulogy and at last ends impotently, but impulsively . . . I should never have left." Professor Tinker "throws back his head with a kind of snort." Thornton wrote to Professor Wager, "By the great rivers, classical and Christian, I swear that every word of this is true. I have made myself to appear rude for you!"[56]

But he was finding himself at Yale, and basking in the stimulating company of his new friends. In fact, his mother reported to Amos, Thornton had been neglecting his courses and had to spend time in the Yale infirmary because he was so exhausted "by late hours talking with fellow students." He was "relishing the companionships almost too excitedly and almost at the expense of both his health and his studies."[57] Yet he found time to write his playlets, as well as to work on fiction and essays. One three-minute playlet to undergo several revisions and a transformation of title was *The Walled City*, which Steve

Benét published during Thornton's second semester at Yale. "Every soul dwells in its walled city," one of the characters says.

Eventually, some years after it was published in the Yale *Lit*, Thornton deleted that line, and changed the title to *Nascuntur Poetae . . .* The ellipses evoke the entire Latin saying to which Thornton referred: "Poets are born, but orators are made." In all its versions, this short play examines the life of the artist—the "chosen"—and the blessing of the artistic gifts, as well as the risks. "I am not afraid of life. I will astonish it," the gifted boy—the poet—says. "God's gifts are not easily borne; he who carries much gold stumbles, and is burdened," he is told by the Woman in the Chlamys in the early, unpublished version of the play. "*I* bring the dark and necessary gifts." When she warns that he will know himself "isolated, solitary, unlovable," the boy wants to relinquish the gifts. It is too late, she tells him, and he has no choice in the matter in any case.

The third character in the playlet, the Woman in Deep Red, asserts that his life is a journey and "has its destination." Because artists are "chosen," they are "breathed upon," set apart and given the power to create in words or images or music. Artistic responsibility and power isolate the artist—but then, the Woman in the Chlamys says, every human being is isolated. "Every soul is a walled city and [no] other may enter save at dusk and in strange moods, nor may thy soul visit another's save in rare and unknown hours."[58]

When his play was published in the *Lit* at Yale in 1918, Thornton, then twenty-one, was a restless, frustrated, gifted college boy, virtually alone in his belief that he was born to write. Ahead of him lay struggle and success far beyond what even his ambitious imagination could conjure in those days at Yale. He was a writer eager to be about his life's work, but temporarily required to be a college student and chafing at the bonds. Yale would indeed "reduce him some" as his father hoped, but it would also expand him, challenge him, urge him closer to his authentic voice.[59]

By the time *The Walled City* appeared in print ten years later, revised and renamed *Nascuntur Poetae . . .* , it reflected Thornton Wilder's emerging view of the challenge and the mission of the writer: "The life of man awaits you, the light laughter and the same misery in the same day, in the selfsame hour the trivial and the divine," one of the women tells the young poet prophetically, in words nowhere to be found in the earlier version at Yale. "You are to give it a voice. Among the bewildered and the stammering thousands you are to give it a voice and mark its meaning."[60]

"HEROES"

The veneration will grow. His place is beside the heroes he mused upon.
—THORNTON WILDER,
In Praise of Guynemer

New Haven, Connecticut; Washington, D.C.; Newport, Rhode Island (1918)

As he neared his twenty-first birthday, Thornton was idealistically given to hero worship. Foremost on his current roster of heroes were his brother, Amos, now a corporal in A Battery, 17th Field Artillery, 2nd Division, fighting at the front in Rupt Sector, southeast of Verdun; Charles Wager, the Oberlin professor he idolized; Georges Guynemer, the French flying ace he would eulogize; the actor John Barrymore; the producer and director Arthur Hopkins, and the latest in a long line of show business luminaries about whom he fantasized—the young Welsh actor Gareth Hughes.

"I am perpetually enthusiastic over some composition or book, some person or some friend," Thornton wrote to his brother.[1] He was "'writing' much," he told a friend, "both for the waste-basket and for posterity which is only a temporary postponement of the waste-basket."[2] A good deal of his writing was directed toward his current living heroes—long letters of self-revelation to Amos and to Professor Wager, and plays conceived for Barrymore, Hopkins, and Hughes—although the latter three knew nothing of Thornton Wilder or his writing. Not only had Professor Wager led Thornton through classical literature, occasionally suggesting related ideas for plays Thornton might write, but he often tantalized his former student with accounts of his occasional trips to Detroit or Cleveland or New York to go to the theater. "I missed seeing Gareth Hughes in Cleveland," Wager wrote, knowing of Thornton's admiration for the young Welshman. "If I had,

would have invited him to dinner and talked to him of you." Wager
had a friend who actually knew Hughes, and reported that he was
"quite as engaging as he looks."[3]

"Your wonderful many-sided letter has been in my head all day like
a dazzle," Thornton wrote to Wager in January 1918.[4] He shared, in
turn, an account of his own recent adventure in New York. Thornton
had so avidly followed newspaper accounts of Gareth Hughes's rising
career that he felt he knew the actor as well as he knew anyone of his
age, "and better."[5] When Thornton made his own trip into Manhattan to go to the theater, he decided on an impulse to call Hughes and
make an appointment under the pretense that "some of the boys of the
Yale Dramatic Association would like to have me discuss his appearing
with them in 'Everyman' about Easter time." Hughes agreed to meet
Thornton at four thirty in his apartment on Waverly Place near Washington Square.[6] Eagerly Thornton walked through "a bitter cold early
evening" and climbed four flights of dark stairs to Hughes's rooms.

Gareth Hughes surpassed Thornton's expectations. Starstruck, he
described Hughes to Dr. Wager: "He is Ariel, but more pathetic than
Ariel. He is sheer genius and poetry. And, when his glasses are off,
the divinest thing to look upon that I have ever seen. He was calling the comparatively gloomy and stone-like visitor 'Thornton dear'
within three-quarters of an hour."[7] Soon Thornton found himself playing Welsh hymns on the piano, and staying for supper, and playing
with the dog, Juba. Hughes told Thornton that he was "a peasant, the
son of a Welsh singer," and that he ran away with a Shakespearean
theater company when he was about fifteen. Hughes hated life, he told
Thornton, except when he was in a good play, but he found theatrical people especially hateful and disgusting. Thornton learned that his
hero knew Shakespeare "up and down," and that he was "very poor."
Even so there was a manservant, whom Thornton met that night—a
"whimpering, Irish 'decayed' actor."

Thornton stayed until one "talking excitedly" with Hughes. "He
didn't want me to go even then," Thornton reported to Wager, "and assured me it was the nightingale and not the lark I heard."[8] The next evening Thornton took Gareth to meet Isabella, who was visiting friends

in the city. "He was perfectly wonderful in company," Thornton wrote to Dr. Wager. "Talking not only of his experiences with famous actors, but telling old Welsh legends and quoting. My mother was delighted with him as were they all; no one can take his or her eyes off of him."[9] After Thornton returned to New Haven, a letter came from Hughes: "It is so grey here today and it has been so cold and cheerless and I am steeped in poverty and starving but soon the sun will shine. Oh it is so grey! I wish you were here to talk to me for I am lonely indeed."[10]

Thornton was enthralled and infatuated with Gareth Hughes, whom he had admired from afar for so long. He was even more determined to write plays for Hughes. (As it turned out, Hughes's burgeoning career as a silent movie star superseded his theater career through the late twenties. Hughes did not succeed in the "talkies," however, and tried to reestablish a stage career in the thirties. In the early forties he became known as Father David, and became a lay missionary to the Paiute Indians in Nevada.)

———

IN 1918 Thornton was simultaneously relishing his brief acquaintance with Gareth Hughes and worrying about some of the women in his life. He thought he understood women thoroughly because he was so close to his mother and sisters; nonetheless, at times he was baffled by them. He was shocked to learn secondhand of the engagement of Agnes Gammon, the cousin of his China Inland Mission School and Oberlin College friend, Theodore "Ted" Wilder. Agnes was a young woman whose company he had occasionally enjoyed, and he considered it "a model of womanly delicacy and fine feeling" that she did not send him "the embittering news herself." "I never could quite make out whether I was on the point of being engaged to Agnes or Nina Trego," he wrote to Ted Wilder.

> An alliance with the former would have been exhilarating, and the quarrels would have been fine, vigorous and tonic as [a] sneeze. With Nina life would be close-centred, nervous, with only oases of serenity and the quarrels would have been silent, repressed, dark and intense. In

considering a possible wife—and this is a real ipse dixit, Ted—choose
her in the light of her quarrels. Ascertain her style of argument, her
method in animosity. But I hear you laughing at me.[11]

"AMOS HAS won the Croix de Guerre," Thornton wrote Dr. Wager in January 1918.[12] To the end of his long life, with his usual modesty and self-deprecation, Amos reflected that the honor he received on October 28, 1917, was "a roll of the dice in the lottery with which our French division chose to honor several drivers of our departing Section 3, many of whom were more worthy than myself."[13] All in all 101 Yale men received the Croix de Guerre in World War I.[14]

Thornton won his own honor in the spring of 1918, far more modest than Amos's Croix de Guerre but significant in the Yale sphere nonetheless. His short story "Spiritus Valet" won the John Hubbard Curtis Prize given annually by the Yale English Department for an outstanding literary work by an undergraduate.[15] Thornton's prizewinning story, published in May 1918 by the Yale *Courant*, is an early example of a catalytic encounter between the writer's rich imagination and his copious reading. Thornton not only thought deeply and analytically about what he read but often posed hypothetical questions about a particular character, theme, or plot that captured his attention. "What if?" he seemed to ask. Wilder had steeped himself for several years in the writings of Henry James, and the echoes of plot and theme suggest that when he composed "Spiritus Valet," he thought about James's story *The Aspern Papers*. James's romantic tale of loss, greed, and intrigue is based on actual accounts of romantic letters written by Lord Byron to two of his mistresses. The letters and the mistresses survived Byron, and James had put his imagination to work on these facts to create a tale of an old woman living out her days in a shambles of a Venetian palace, holding fast, despite the efforts of others, to the love letters written to her long ago by an esteemed American poet, and to the life, love, and memories embodied in them.

In "Spiritus Valet," Thornton wrote of a fictitious poet, Sebastian Torr, whose life was full of "strange silent periods during which the poet seems to have entirely disappeared"—particularly a few years when "the only evidence of the poet's continued existence issued in the shape of the seven short but matchless lyrics to the 'golden-haired lady.'"[16] Torr's biographer seeks to illuminate the "dark ages" of his life, and embarks on a quest to identify the "golden-haired lady" and, he hopes, to obtain from her "many facts, letters, and perhaps poems." He locates Mrs. Judith Manners, who had indeed briefly known the great poet. She soon falls victim to a fusion of forces: She feels her youth slipping away; she is bored with her life; the biographer is beseeching her to turn over letters that do not exist, for she is not the lady in question, and the poet never wrote poems or letters to her, much less loved her. "I have no letters; I have no secrets," she protests honestly to the determined biographer. But he persists, and, finally, "starved" of excitement, Mrs. Manners wonders, "What harm would it do if I encouraged the rumor a little. . . . Why, that would be Romance. I might even, if I dared, write the letters myself."

She begins to think, defiantly, Why not? She proceeds to invent the letters, not attempting to forge the poet's handwriting, but copying the imaginary epistles "into an old diary, using diluted ink," under the ruse that "she had carefully copied the letters as they came, into a very private diary, and then had destroyed them."[17] So this polished, smoothly written, thoroughly intriguing tale unfolds—Thornton's variation on Henry James's extrapolation of a true story. What if there were letters? James asked. What if there weren't? Thornton seems to have wondered. It was a fascinating challenge, creating a fictitious world out of fragments of reading or memory or fancy—or an amalgam of those—and then animating that world with vividly imagined form, plot, characters, setting, and theme.

———

"I AM a wandering independent," Thornton wrote to his brother sometime during the spring of 1918, confessing that he often cut his classes to write plays "without end and then tear them up. . . . When someone has flattered me about something I go around like a bull in a China shop, cutting classes and neglecting duties and calling it Artistic

Temperament."[18] He was now a member of the *Lit* board; was escorting Grace Parker, a young woman from New Haven, to social events; and was resisting his father's efforts to make him "fit the mould of the practical, diligent, thoughtful American boy and *I don't fit*." Thornton told Amos that if he should be drafted after his twenty-first birthday, he would "very likely 'pick up and be a man,'" as his father urged him to do. He would then "cease writing illuminating dialogue and excited prose, and offer up my whole personality and impulses on the altar of 'Just-like-the-Other-Fella.'"[19]

The war was omnipresent in the life of his family and the nation. He was living and writing on a university campus that had become a virtual military installation, in a campus community whose professors and students had stood in the forefront of Americans challenging the country's isolationist stance on World War I. In 1915 Yale had organized the first artillery battalion of any American university.[20] That same year Yale professor Hiram Bingham III, the explorer and archaeologist who discovered Machu Picchu, had offered a silver loving cup as a reward to the class enlisting the most members in military training programs.[21] By the time Thornton entered Yale, hundreds of Yale students had gone off to Europe to help in the ambulance service or fight in military service, and one by one, the remaining men, Thornton among them, considered what role they should assume in wartime.

The published history of the Yale class of 1920 devoted an entire section to the war. "After all, there were some four hundred and fifty of us, in France, on the ocean, in training camps, in all the services and under all sorts of conditions," wrote Walter Millis, a member of the Class Book Committee and managing editor of the *Lit*, who went on to become a journalist, military historian, and author. "When you say that Nineteen Twenty, being a good average Yale class, did just a little more than good average service in a time of stress, you have really summed up the whole matter," Millis reported.[22] Many Yale men, like Amos Wilder in the class of 1917, served in the ambulance corps. Amos was the only member of the class of 1917 to receive his Yale degree with the class of 1920, as he had served in the war longer than any of his classmates.[23] Official records documented the Yale men who had served in the war—6,257 in the army, 1,431 in the navy, 65 in the marines, and 1,119 in foreign armies.[24] The official army and navy death lists included 186 Yale men, of whom at least six were members of the class of 1920. The class could also claim flying aces, captains in the balloon service, officers and enlisted men in the field artillery, two men in the "Tanks," one man in "Chemical Warfare," and a number of men wounded.[25] Those left behind at Yale drilled, marched, and took part in summer military camps.

Thornton was not the only aspiring writer wrestling with the question of how to join in the war effort, especially now that he was twenty-one and eligible for the draft. Ernest Hemingway, another unknown young writer with poor vision, was memorizing the army eye chart out in Kansas City, Missouri, so he could pass the examination. Closer to home, Steve Benét, now editor of the *Lit*, considered it an embarrassment and indignity to have to do military service behind the lines in some sort of clerkship. He had been afflicted with scarlet fever during his childhood, and the illness left him with impaired vision. Nevertheless Benét, the son of a career army officer, was determined to enlist in the army in July 1918. He, too, contrived to memorize the army eye chart because his eyes refused "to read the nice little black letters on the card."[26] He passed and was inducted into the army, serving for three days before an alert sergeant saw him peeling potatoes by holding them so close to his eyes that he risked stabbing himself in the nose. Benét was ordered to repeat the eye test, this time with a different chart. He failed and was immediately discharged from the army.[27] He got a job at the State Department in Washington, writing to a friend that he was relegated to "a legion of the halt, blind and heart-diseased."[28]

Meanwhile, Thornton had his own worries about being rejected because of his eyesight, a concern shared by Dr. Wilder. Unbeknownst to Thornton, his father was writing to Amos, urging him to save money "with remorseless care" because, he feared, "in the years to come you will have not only yourself but some of these others, especially hopeless Thornton, to finance."[29] Dr. Wilder pulled strings in Washington to land Thornton a civilian job for the summer of 1918 doing clerical work at the War Industries Board, the government agency set up in 1917 to mobilize industry to support the war effort and to protect the peacetime economy. Thornton's typing classes were finally going to pay off—to the tune of a desk job at a salary of thirty-five dollars a month. He headed to Washington, where at first he roomed with Yale men Benét and John Carter, but quickly grew uncomfortable in the "atmosphere of Perpetual Carousal" and the noise "created by that perpetual competition of cleverness which constitutes the relation of Steve and John."[30] By then he and Benét had established a respectful if wary friendship, not so much an overt rivalry as a quiet competition that may have served from time to time as motivation for both writers.

Thornton soon gave up on the "Perpetual Carousal" and moved into quieter quarters in suburban Chevy Chase, Maryland.[31] He set aside solitary time in the evenings to work on a new play, *Vecy-Segal*, which he wanted to share with Steve Benét's older brother, the poet and editor William Rose Benét, whom he had gotten to "know very well."[32] Bill Benét, eleven years Thornton's senior, had received his Yale degree in 1907, and in 1924, with Yale professor Henry Seidel Canby, would establish the *Saturday Review of Literature*. When he and Thornton met, Benét was associate editor of *The Century Magazine*, and had published four books of poetry, with another in the offing. He would become an influential editor, critic, and poet, and would win the Pulitzer Prize for poetry in 1942. He was in Washington in the Aviation Reserve that summer of 1918, and took an encouraging interest in Thornton and his work, praising his playlets "extravagantly," and leaving Thornton with a "renewed enthusiasm" to get ten of them revised, typed, and off to the Yale University Press, in hopes of publication.[33]

To do that he had to stay at his office after hours to use a type-writer. The combination of daily office work, surrounded by people, and nighttime literary work in the solitude of an empty office agreed with him. Thornton felt himself "engaged on really big things in my writing-self," and he relished putting in hours of "refreshing blessing work. Something new has come into my idea of what it is all about and I now take joy and solace in my work as though it were something warm and caressable," he wrote. In his plays he was striving for a "touch of acid" amid the idealism, so that there would not be even a "remote taint of sentimentalism."[34]

One of the playlets he was crafting that summer was entitled *Centaurs*, later called *The Death of the Centaur: A Footnote to Ibsen*. Into the compact intensity of his familiar three-minute, three-character format, Thornton deftly brought together Shelley and Ibsen, and Hilda Wangel, the young woman who worships the hero in Ibsen's play *The Master Builder*. This playlet foreshadows some of the devices to come in Thornton's more mature work: He takes liberties with time (Shelley died in 1822, six years before Ibsen was born); characterization (two historical figures interact with a fictional creation); and setting ("Miss Fosli, will you kindly push forward the wicker settee from the last act?" Hilda says, addressing another of Ibsen's characters who is not visible in *Centaurs*, and *"A wicker settee suddenly appears."*) The play's premise is that just before his death by drowning, Shelley was about to write a poem to be called "The Death of a Centaur." Hearing this, Ibsen says, "And I claim that I wrote it. The poem hung for a while above the Mediterranean, and then drifted up toward the Tyrol, and I caught it and wrote it down. And it is *The Master Builder*."

Shelley responds, "Well, it is not a strange idea, or a new one, that the stuff of which masterpieces are made drifts about the world waiting to be clothed with words."

He goes on to speak of the universal creative impulse, and the eradicating impact of war:

It is a truth that Plato would have understood that the mere language, the words of a masterpiece, are the least of its offerings. Nay, in the world we have come into now, the languages of the planet have no value: but the impulse, the idea of "Comus" is a miracle, even in heaven. Let you remember this when you regret the work that has been lost through this war that has been laid upon your treasurable young men. The work they might have done is still with you, and will yet find its way into your lives and into your children's lives.[35]

That summer of 1918, Thornton was continually aware of "the work that has been lost through this war"—and the work that might yet be lost, especially his own. There was solace in finishing, at least, this small play.

HE SPENT most of his summer evenings plowing through a draft of *The Breaking of Exile*, set in China, the new three-act play he was crafting from the novelette he had begun at Berea in 1917. He would compose for half an hour or so, and then pause to type what he had just written. He gave his mother a rousing synopsis of the play, which involved roles he had written expressly for John Barrymore and Gareth Hughes. It was, he said,

> *about people in a white heat of intensity and I no sooner sit down to write it than I am cast into a fever myself and the terrible thing pours out onto the page. It is a terrible play about What Happened in a Cheap French Hotel in a port on the Yangtze-Kiang River. The war broke out and caught all these social and political exiles longing to go back to their countries . . . I bet you that at the close of the Second Act, every one in the audience screams loud and long or else dies of horror.*[36]

The play not only drew on Thornton's impressions of China for theme, characters, and plot but utilized a setting he returned to often in his later work—the symbolic lonely boardinghouse, in this case a "Cheap French Hotel." He sent the finished play off to well-known producer and director Arthur Hopkins—another hero who did not know Thornton Wilder existed. Hopkins kept the manuscript for a long time before sending it back with a polite rejection letter.

Thornton enjoyed Washington life with Bill Benét and other Yale friends.[37] One of them, Bill Taylor, took it upon himself "almost boisterously" to make Thornton come out of his shell, encouraging him to be "more genial and approachable," and Dr. Wilder thought the experience was good for him.[38] All in all, he believed that the Washington experience would make Thornton "a little more confident—perhaps worldly," he wrote Amos. "I have noted his underlying penetration and poise (he is a leader among such, by reason of his abilities). He smokes some cigarettes frankly—but assures me no drinking and I believe him."[39]

"ARE YOU already laying out itineraries . . . ?" Thornton wrote to his father in June. True to form, various Wilders spent the summer of 1918 in various places. The brothers were doing their part in the war, Thornton in Washington, and Amos with his regiment in reserve after a month of fighting in Château-Thierry/Belleau Wood, and soon to be thrown into the second battle of the Marne. Charlotte was again working at Mount Holyoke for the summer. Dr. Wilder attended the Yale commencement in late June, a ceremony "full of high patriotism," he wrote to Amos in France.[40] Isabel had finished her year at Northfield and joined her mother and sisters for a visit with Charlotte, who was "doing finely," her father reported proudly. One of his Yale friends who had recently met her at Mount Holyoke wrote to tell Dr. Wilder "without blarney" that Charlotte was "the handsomest, most wholesome young woman he had met for a long time." Dr. Wilder was delighted, and found it "gratifying to a fond parent to know he is equipping the world with a whole quiver of whales."[41]

IN EARLY July, Thornton received the news that he had been drafted. His father thought it would be good for him to enter the army, but doubted that he could pass the physical examination for combat because of his vision. Dr. Wilder also believed that creative writers— especially poets—seemed to be temperamentally unsuited for combat in any case. Thornton filled out the standard questionnaire supplied by the draft board, noted in the newspaper that his draft number fell within the first two hundred chosen for the next national apportionment, and waited. Despite his vision problems and the heart murmur discovered in his physical examination, he did not ask for an exemption and expected to be called into service.

On the eve of his regiment's march to Soissons/Villers-Cotterêts during the second battle of the Marne, young Amos wrote to Thornton sympathetically about "the quandary of the dreamer and the aspiring artist in the nets of public and military hierarchy."[42] Amos felt it himself: "There seems to be a fundamental incompatibility of my temperament and the idea of military organization. One can't orient himself in any hierarchy of authority without giving a sad farewell to many gentle ways and actions. If I do this can I resurrect them afterwards?"[43]

Thornton had made up his mind to serve, however, and his father thought camp life and the military physical training would be good for him, especially "the mingling with men and reality."[44] But his father left matters up to Thornton and the draft board—although he said he would be willing to pull his "last string" to get Thornton into the merchant marine, where Dr. Wilder thought his son would "grow most." He told Thornton, "I will try to get a 'waiver' as to eyes and I usually get things I want where the welfare of my children is concerned."[45]

Worried that he would not be accepted in the regular army, Thornton took the necessary examinations in Washington in early August. He was directed to take a special eye exam, and the doctor predicted he was likely to be inducted in a "lower class" but would no doubt be accepted because of the high demand for fighting men. "I took my Advisory Board Exam. and probably passed it. But this is not certain," Thornton wrote his father August 14. "So I went today to the office of the Coast Artillery and put in my application for induction into that service. IT ONLY TAKES MEN WHO ARE IN GENERAL MILITARY SERVICE OF THE DRAFT (and of course general enlistments.) And Men who have had at least one year of College." Thornton had investigated all the options, and concluded that his best avenue of service would be the army's Coast Artillery Corps, writing to his father, "They take you as you come from the draft board and ask no questions."[46]

As of September 14 he was accepted and assigned to work as an office orderly for the 1st Coast Artillery Corps at Fort Adams outside Newport, Rhode Island, on Narragansett Bay. There would be a training period in September, followed by one or two months of training camp, which could result in the rank of second lieutenant. Then off to France to deal with "the very heaviest artillery, the Big Berthas etc." If all went well, Thornton expected to be in France before Christmas. He was eager to let his brother know that he would be in the artillery, too, even though it was, Thornton said, "the unskilled emergency-rush section of it."[47]

Their father was very proud of Amos's service in France, and saw to it that passages from many of his letters were published anonymously in the newspaper.[48] By late August, however, after nearly two years in the war zone, Cpl. Amos Wilder was suffering what he described as "a kind of chronic anguish"—"some kind of radical depletion, made up of battle fatigue, sleeplessness, and nervous strain"—demonstration that post-traumatic stress disorder affected combatants long before it received an official name.[49] This was the first recorded indication that Amos had ever experienced even a short period of depression, and his war journals reveal his efforts to analyze the source of his disability and to cope with it.[50] To further complicate Amos's recovery, military orders dictated that he, like thousands of other young men on active duty during World War I, should undergo a "minor operation"— circumcision—to diminish the possibility of venereal disease. Circum- cision at birth was still relatively rare early in the twentieth century, except for Jews and members of some other religious groups. During the war, however, military doctors in the field began to make up for lost time, operating on a generation of young army and navy men. Amos's procedure was performed on August 30. Afterward he found himself being carried to a hospital in a "speeding, swaying ambulance," just as he had transported so many soldiers earlier.[51]

Throughout September and October, Amos would be hospitalized in various convalescent camps and field hospitals, depressed, wonder- ing if he would ever regain his strength, thinking himself "on the point of insanity once or twice."[52] One September day he was allowed to get out on a baseball field at a convalescent camp, and after the exercise he felt more nearly himself than he had for two years. In mid-October he was declared well enough to make the seven-hundred-mile journey back to join his battery—a trip made miserable by freezing rain, cold victuals, and cramped, crowded conditions (the men in Amos's compartment would awaken "every hour" with foreheads "frozen from the window pane, or neck warped, or a leg paralyzed").[53] By October 20, 1918, Amos was back on the Western Front.

* * *

THORNTON WAS haunted by the tragic story of another hero—French flying ace Georges Guynemer, who died on September 11, 1917, at the age of twenty-three. Just as Thornton vividly imagined his own death in the trenches, he could graphically envision Guynemer's fatal plunge to earth in the *Vieux Charles*, his feisty SPAD, one of the experimental airplanes he had used as deadly weapons in fifty-three heroic sorties against the enemy. Guynemer was immortalized in the Panthéon in Paris.[54] On lined sheets of notebook paper, Thornton wrote a three-character playlet as his own tribute to the young French hero. "The scene is laid upon a medal, struck in honor of the aviator," the playlet begins, offering one of Thornton's most original settings. The characters: the Victory, the Horseman, and the Man.[55]

Sometime in the summer or fall of 1918 Thornton wrote a second playlet on the same subject, entitled *In Praise of Guynemer*, this time with only two characters—Senex and Juvenis, the classical old man and young man. Juvenis describes his initial idea for a tribute to Guynemer—an idea that echoes Thornton's first draft of the playlet—but, Juvenis explains, "the idea suddenly lost all its color." Senex then gives the young man directions about how to write his tribute: Above all, he must feel deeply about his subject. Senex predicts that "in after time Guynemer shall rise, like Hector undoubtable, from a mythic war."[56] This playlet was published in the December 1918 issue of the *Lit*, and Thornton's classmates liked the piece well enough to include an excerpt as one of five reprints from the *Lit* in the *History of the Class of Nineteen Hundred Twenty*.[57]

* * *

DR. WILDER and his wife carried a burden of worries about their sons—brave Amos suffering in France, inept Thornton embarking on

military service, full of his strong "writing passion" and writing plays
that were "certainly on a high plane."[58] Thornton had also reviewed a
play he saw in Washington and sold the article to the *Boston Transcript*.
His father found it "unquestionably full of promise" with its "sure
touch in the use of words and formations." Thornton was "certainly
a writer," Dr. Wilder told Amos. "His judgments are penetrating and
close; when one recalls that he is but 21 and has been his own teacher,
I am impressed."[59]

Even so, like the father Polonius to his son, Laertes, in Shakespeare's
Hamlet, Father Wilder lavished advice on Thornton, often in the form
of platitudes. He had done so all Thornton's life; he saw no need to
desist just because his son was twenty-one, a Yale student, a budding
writer, and now a military man. "Live economically as becomes your
circumstances, otherwise your dignity will suffer, you will be unfit-
ted to live modestly later, as you must; and you will be worried," Dr.
Wilder admonished Thornton that summer. "Wars, Washington experiences come and go; but character and obligation to God abide."[60] And
in another letter: "I am praying that the decadence in high-minded
youth I know so well may not be yours. You can't keep your enthusiasms and fine, irresistible fun and confidence in the goodness of life if
you drag your mind and soul thro' the sloughs of comic opera and the
like."[61] And still another: "Let us have a true man, a patriot, a Christian, a gentleman, Thornton dear, and all else shall be added."[62]

Dr. Wilder, the son of a dentist, knew that dental problems could
be a detriment to good physical health. He warned Thornton to take
good care of his teeth—apparently in the wake of reports about trench
mouth, a common and painful affliction for military personnel in the
trenches during World War I, deprived of even basic sanitary conditions.[63] Brush your teeth, Dr. Wilder cautioned his son, even though he
was laboring far from the trenches. "Public work is barred those whose
dentality is a poor, stuffed, faulty thing. Such are put on other work,
perhaps ushering or moving chairs. Poor Amos is far from a dentist; his
teeth and those of millions of men must go as a sacrifice."[64]

In the midst of these admonitions, Dr. Wilder also praised Thornton's *Centaur*, and asked if he could submit his son's work to the

Atlantic. No, Thornton replied. He was "very happy" to have his father's words, but he doubted the magazine would be interested in such "an extravaganza-fantasia." But his father's appreciation had "stirred" him, Thornton said, and "I cannot write a line in the two bigger plays I am at work on without asking myself whether you would be disappointed by it."[65]

PVT. T. N. WILDER was hard at work as an office orderly at historic Fort Adams, Rhode Island, in September 1918. His uniform didn't fit, and he was afraid he had the flu, but he enjoyed his morning and evening walks by the bay to and from his office. "Last evening I was there when the sudden noisiness and swishiness came that denotes the turn of the tide," he wrote to his mother. "I hadn't heard that since Chefoo. Knives of joy went through me."[66]

His duties over for the day, Thornton had time to write, and he was engrossed in a "big flaming character study" based on the legend of the pagan heroine Hypatia. He was working on an increasingly larger "stage," broadly expanding his vision of the dramas he could create. In fact, he confided to his mother, he had written "a magnificent fierce love-scene," and was "almost frightened at the size" of his "canvas" and the explosive nature of his "*dramatis personae.*" If he could only transfer his vision to paper, it would be "the most brilliant play" on his list.[67] The play would "ferment" in his mind "like sodium in water—explosions," but if he ever finished it, no copy survived.[68]

EVERYWHERE THAT autumn there were rumors of peace. On November 11, 1918, at eleven o'clock in the morning, U.S. time, the armistice was signed to mark the beginning of the end of World War I. In France, Amos spent the days following the armistice trying to sort out fact and rumor, and translating the French communications that came into the radio room at Beaumont, on the Meuse above Verdun. Thornton, back at his desk at Fort Adams, was promoted to corporal on November 12. He struggled with stacks of paperwork and criticized the circus atmosphere in the United States following the armistice news, when France was left "mortally weakened" and England "dreadfully awakened."[69]

Amos longed for home, and Thornton longed for normalcy. The Wilder boys were not going home anytime soon, however, for there was army work remaining to be done, and then the long, unpredictable mustering-out process. Thornton would not get home for Christmas, and he hoped Santa Claus would send him something to wear on his head because, he said, "I'm getting abjectly Bald. Not a day goes by without some colleague suddenly noticing and exclaiming, 'You're losing hair man!' "[70]

Father Wilder was tempted to try to pull strings to get his boys home, but Thornton warned him: "Nothing on earth can get me out of the Army that doesn't originate in this very building so please don't try."[71] He believed he would be out in January for sure, so that he could return to Yale to begin the new term. He was not enthusiastic about resuming his college work, however. His father thought he must get his college degree, but Thornton did not believe there was anything more for him at Yale. "Last year he slurred the work and his credits are low," Dr. Wilder worried in a letter to Amos. There had been a possibility that Thornton would flunk out of Yale, but he had managed to pass his courses. His father pointed out that "the college is good to heroes" and if Thornton could return to Yale in January, he might be admitted to the junior class.[72] As for Amos, he would have his father's support, financially and otherwise, if he wanted to stay in Europe to study for a year.

Dr. Wilder wrote to ask for Amos's help with Thornton:

You surely will not encourage any talk of quitting study now, tho you may feel that you need not get into the dispute very deeply. Mother admires his genius so much that she thinks Yale has nothing further for him, etc. If he does stop now it means a cheap room in N. Y. and hanging about newspaper offices with an occasional interview with a celebrity etc. However, I am not pressing him—"merely suggesting"; and it will work out all right.[73]

FOR THORNTON, dreading the return to Yale and longing for the freedom to write, there was another interlude of hero worship. "Forgive this long silence," began a letter he received in December 1918. It came from another handsome young actor who had caught Thornton's interest and imagination. He was Glenn Hunter, age twenty-four, and, like Thornton in 1918, struggling to find his way in the theater. Born in New York City in 1894, three years before Thornton, Hunter was beginning to appear regularly in productions mounted by successful producers Marcus Klaw and Abraham Lincoln Erlanger, in casts headed by the leading actors Alfred Lunt, Lynn Fontanne, George Arliss, and Helen Hayes, among others. The two men apparently met in Rhode Island during the war. By 1922 Hunter was the star of a Broadway hit, *Merton of the Movies*, and the film that followed it in 1924.[74] But in 1918 Glenn Hunter and Thornton Wilder were kindred spirits, dreaming of big careers in the theater, Glenn as an actor and Thornton as a playwright. They also dreamed about working on projects together. Glenn was reading Thornton's playlets as well as synopses of plays he planned to write, and predicted that Thornton would have a great career as a playwright.[75] He hoped Thornton would write a big play just for him, and promised he would "work like hell" to be ready for such a role.[76]

Thornton's letters to Glenn Hunter have not been located, but the handful of Hunter's surviving letters to Thornton hint of infatuation, if not intimacy. Hunter wrote that December that he hoped their relationship could grow through letters.[77] There was an invitation to Thornton to come and live in New York, to rent rooms on the floor of his apartment building so that they could be together.[78] On December 26 Hunter wrote to Thornton that he wished for a long talk so that he could share his dreams and hopes. He told Thornton he had loved being with him "that night," more than he could know.[79]

For years there would be speculation about Thornton Wilder's sexuality and his sex life, but he left behind little evidence of that very private matter. There has surfaced no other record of the nature of his relationship with Glenn Hunter, or what it meant to Thornton, except for these saved December letters, printed in Glenn Hunter's distinctive holograph, full of dreams and ambiguity.

————

CPL. THORNTON WILDER was discharged from the Coast artillery on December 31, 1918. Cpl. Amos Wilder received his discharge orders on June 12, 1919. On June 14, 1919, in the town of Hamden, Connecticut, just outside New Haven, citizens gathered to welcome 150 returning soldiers, all hometown men. The homecoming parade—"the most spectacular parade ever held in Hamden"—was followed by speeches and songs, and a spirited address by Dr. Amos P. Wilder.[80] There was a banquet that evening, followed by a grand march and dancing. For the Wilder family, the Great War, finally, was over.

12

"HIS OWN TUNE"

Thornton is light-hearted; I am pleased. Of course he studies not at all; yet is bright enough to "get by" as do many less bright. . . . On him too is the Puritan mark less affirmative than in you and me but let each singer choose his own tune.

—AMOS PARKER WILDER TO AMOS NIVEN WILDER,
April 25, 1919

Connecticut and Italy (1919–1921)

Military service leads to a man's asking questions of himself," Thornton wrote in an unpublished article titled "Student-Life at Yale Since the War"—a personal assessment of the unprecedented postwar challenges facing his generation, as well as a statement of his own discontent. He had reluctantly returned to Yale for his junior year after his discharge from military service. Yale men came back from the war "not only with a sheaf of particular problems," Thornton wrote, "but with the determination of acquiring in general, something of the power of clear thinking and the wide reading that would of [*sic*] helped them in the days they needed it most." He noted that while Yale seemed to be returning to the normalcy of prewar days, "Post-War Curriculum must take into account" that students returning from wartime service in the spring semester of 1919 were "restless" and "curious" about "knowledge in a very real, and in almost a new sense."[1]

His own restless prewar desire to go to New York to write, or to travel in Europe, had intensified, but his father objected to the first plan and was unable to implement the second, even though he was sympathetic. Amos, Isabel, and Janet had spent long periods of time in Europe but Thornton and Charlotte had yet to cross the Atlantic. For the time being Thornton resumed his classes at Yale. Meanwhile

Charlotte was finishing her last semester at Mount Holyoke, where she would receive her B.A. in June 1919, a year ahead of her brothers at Yale.

She had been lobbying for more than a year to go to Europe. "Father does not talk much of your going to Italy," Thornton wrote her. "He lives in terror of Mother's dissuading you. Mother (who is averse to the trip as you know) has suddenly burst into a brilliant acquaintance with the distressing economic condition of lower Europe; she can tell you the national debt down to a *lira*, and is full of disturbing intimations of panics, revolutions and wars."[2] Finally, thanks to their aunt Charlotte Niven, now one of the national YWCA secretaries in Italy, plans were made for Charlotte to work for the YWCA.[3] By August 1920 she was in Paris, awaiting her assignment to a YWCA youth hostel in Milan.[4]

Amos was still in Europe in the spring of 1919, on duty with the Allied Army of Occupation at Bendorf and Coblenz, and then taking courses at the American Army School Detachment at the University of Toulouse.[5] After his discharge on June 28, he spent the summer decompressing and attending a Workmen's Educational Institute at Balliol College at Oxford University in England, followed by Oxford's regular summer session. Finally, after three years away, he came home to the family and to Yale, where he and Thornton roomed together in Connecticut Hall throughout the 1919–20 school year, both finishing their senior-year courses.

Thornton had lived in his brother's shadow at the Thacher School and at Oberlin. At Yale he stood out on his own. Reginald Marsh, one of Thornton's friends and classmates, aspired to be an artist, was already moving in that direction while he was at Yale, and would carve out a distinctive career as a painter associated with the Social Realism movement. In 1919 he sketched a solemn portrait of a bespectacled Thornton—pensive eyes, cleft chin, sensuous mouth, dark hair combed slightly forward because he was starting to go bald. Thornton was beginning to be taken quite seriously as a writer. The legendary Yale professor William Lyon Phelps, who had known Thornton since he was a child, noted that he "showed remarkable versatility" as a Yale student. "He composed and played music on the piano, he wrote plays and short stories, he wrote professional dramatic criticisms for the newspapers."[6] However, at least one Yale professor looked askance at some of Thornton's work, observing of one of his proposed *Lit* pieces that he needed to learn grammar and spelling.[7]

His short story with an Irish mystical theme was passed over for the 1919 John Hubbard Curtis Prize, which went to Stephen Vincent Benét, then a senior. But Thornton was concentrating on drama, and working hard on *The Trumpet Shall Sound*, a full-length play that was published in four successive issues of the *Lit*, beginning in October 1919. His allegorical religious play in four acts, with its interwoven allusions to Plato, Prometheus, and the classics, received the college's Bradford Brinton Award in playwriting. He revised the play in years ahead until he felt it was strong enough to show to prospective producers. *The Trumpet Shall Sound* would eventually see the light of day in an off-Broadway production at the American Laboratory Theatre in New York in 1926, directed by Richard Boleslavsky, the theater's cofounder, with the legendary Russian actress Maria Ouspenskya. Boleslavsky would later try and fail to sell Thornton's play to the movies.

In 1928, in the foreword to *The Angel That Troubled the Waters and Other Plays*, the first published collection of his plays, Thornton wrote that most of his early dramas were religious—"but religious in that dilute fashion that is a believer's concession to a contemporary standard of good manners." He hoped "through many mistakes, to discover the spirit that is not unequal to the elevation of the great religious themes, yet which does not fall into a repellent didacticism."[8] He had grown up surrounded by religious didacticism—at Chefoo, at Thacher, at Mount Hermon, at Berea, at Oberlin, and in his father's house, or in his father's shadow during Dr. Wilder's prolonged absences from home. Religious didacticism, however well intentioned, offended the young writer's intellect and his spirit. Thornton wrote in his 1928 foreword, "Didacticism is an attempt at the coercion of another's free mind, even though one knows that in these matters beyond logic, beauty is the only persuasion."[9] At Yale after the war he was wrestling on paper with questions of spirituality and belief, striving for persuasion, not coercion, and most of all, striving for beauty of expression.

"AT NEW HAVEN, I frequently visited classes in which I was not enrolled," Thornton wrote decades later in an unpublished semi-autobiographical fragment. "I was never officially a student at Professor Tinker's Age of Johnson, but I heard all the lectures—many of them twice." During the first term of his senior year, when Thornton learned that a few very advanced students were being offered a course called The Fragments of the Lost Plays of Aeschylus, he decided to audit it.[10] Thornton appreciated the fact that "Yale was a vast emporium of lectures many of which were more tempting than those one was under obligation to attend."[11] Officially he majored in English and Latin, but he took full advantage of the "emporium."

During Thornton's senior year, Steve Benét, class of 1919, returned to Yale as a graduate student after a brief, unhappy stint as a copywriter in an advertising agency. Thornton and Benét were part of Henry Seidel Canby's advanced English 40 class, Literary Composition—a small seminar with very limited enrollment, and admission based on the submission of examples of the student's literary work. Canby, Yale class of 1899, had earned his Ph.D. at Yale in 1905. He taught at Yale beginning in 1903, and was an assistant editor of the *Yale Review* from 1911 to 1920. By the time Canby taught Wilder and Benét, his book *The Short Story in English*, published in 1909, had become a standard college and university text. Canby came to the English 40 classroom as a well-known teacher and editor on the brink of a national literary career: Beginning in 1920 he would edit the *Literary Review*, the literary supplement of the *New York Post*; and in 1924 he became one of the founders of the *Saturday Review of Literature*.

Canby remembered that it was a highlight of his teaching career to work with the class that included Thornton, Steve Benét, Walter Millis, William C. DeVane, who later became dean of Yale College, Briton Hadden, and Henry Luce, among others. They gathered around a long table, with Canby at the head.[12] Each student—whether an advanced undergraduate or a gifted graduate student—wrote constantly in the genre of his choice. Canby also instructed his students in literary criticism and literary principles. Much of the teaching took place in individual conferences, but the members of the class met weekly to read their work aloud, with lively discussion following. Already, Hadden and Luce were working their way toward their joint conception of the magazine that would become *Time*, and wrote journalistic prose in Canby's class. Benét the poet started working on a novel that became *The Beginning of Wisdom*, published in 1921.[13] In 1961, when Wilder scholar Donald Haberman asked Wilder if any of the three-minute plays or parts of *The Trumpet Shall Sound* were written in Canby's class, Wilder replied, "No—I vaguely remember a short story,—best forgotten."[14]

Like fine athletes who rise to greater performance in company and competition with other fine athletes, talented writers often profit by a catalytic relationship with other talented writers, especially in the presence of a challenging and skillful mentor. Canby demanded his students' best work, and Wilder and Benét brought out the best in each other. (To the end of his life, Thornton held on to a signed manuscript that Steve Benét gave him—a parody of Thornton's three-minute playlets titled "Passing Out.") Because Canby wanted his students to be able to place and sell what they wrote, he fostered a literary professionalism in them, as well as a practical knowledge of the literary marketplace. As Charles Fenton, another Yale professor and Benét's biographer, later observed, "Canby's English 40 was thus in effect a vocational training in the practice of letters."[15]

In 1919 and 1920 an ambitious original magazine made its debut at Yale through the auspices of literary-minded Yale men, energetically led by Norman Fitts of Northampton, Massachusetts, who set out to publish "True art," which, he wrote, "is unafraid, all embracing, multivarious, self-sufficient."[16] The journal was almost accidentally named *S4N*—a corruption of the note to the printer to leave "Space for Title," which evolved into "Space for Name," then "(S for N)," and, ultimately, *S4N*. Steve Benét was a driving force in the early years of *S4N*, along with other Yale men. The magazine—four by six inches for most of its life span—would be published for five years, and its roster included Benét, e. e. cummings, Jean Toomer, poet Ramon Guthrie, Malcolm Cowley, and Thornton Wilder, among other young writers.

Three of Thornton's three-minute playlets appeared in the pages of *S4N*—*Proserpina and the Devil* (*A Play for Marionettes*) in January 1920; *The Death of the Centaur: A Footnote to Ibsen* in April 1920; and *And the Sea Shall Give Up Its Dead* in January–February 1923—and he and Fitts discussed the possibility of a book-length publication of Thornton's playlets and fiction.

Thornton was writing prolifically at Yale despite the heavy course load he carried. He also participated actively in campus life. Since his first year at Yale he had been an active member of the Elizabethan Club. He was also elected a member of Alpha Delta Phi, one of the oldest junior fraternities at Yale, founded in 1836; and Chi Delta Theta, founded in 1821 as a literary society whose members were seniors and often involved in the *Yale Literary Magazine*. He served on the *Lit* staff, and was elected to the Pundits, an acknowledged group of class wits, serving in 1920 as secretary.[17] Thornton and Amos would not approach their father's status as a big man on the Yale campus, however. Amos Parker Wilder had been elected to that pinnacle of undergraduate achievement, the secret, elitist Skull and Bones, an enigmatic presence at Yale since 1832. But Thornton followed the trail of his keen interests, and in his senior year, when his classmates voted for superlatives, although he did not win, he received votes as "Most Scholarly," "Most Brilliant" (an honor won by his former Chefoo schoolmate and Yale classmate, Henry Luce), "Most Original," and "Most Entertaining."

———

"WHEN I graduated from Yale College in 1920 my father was faced with the problem of what to do with me," Thornton wrote decades later in an unpublished semiautobiographical manuscript titled "SS *Independenza*." His father may have had doubts, Thornton recalled, but he himself knew exactly what he wanted to do: write. Dr. Wilder despaired that Thornton would ever be able to earn a living in any profession, much less as a writer. While Dr. Wilder and his wife did not doubt their son's literary gifts, they thought that the only steady, income-producing profession realistically open to Thornton was teaching, and even this was not very promising. Thornton believed that his father's deeper concern had to do with his character: "I had been constantly reminded that I lacked concentration and perseverance," he wrote. "I was a woolgatherer. I was a dilettante."[18] To make matters worse, his father had warned Thornton that he feared that Amos would turn out to be "commonplace" and Thornton, "wayward."[19]

Amos, as usual, was an easier "chess piece" for their father to handle. He had taken one course in the Yale Divinity School in his senior year, and had almost decided to become a minister. He had considered this vocation before the war, but the wartime experience had "crystallized" it somewhat.[20] Haunted by his encounter with this twentieth-century apocalypse, Amos was reading the wartime work of French writers, and composing poetry about his own experience, exploring the war's ramifications in poems that would be published in 1920 in the *Yale Literary Magazine*.

As he had before the war, Amos loved being on the tennis court; there he found a great outlet for energy and stress. Furthermore he was a highly skilled player. In June 1920 he and his partner, Lee Wiley, won the National Intercollegiate Doubles championship in lawn tennis.[21] That summer, for once, he had ample time to play tennis because his father did not dispatch Amos, now almost twenty-five, to work on a farm. Instead, said Amos, "He put me in a Wall St. bank in New York."[22] Then it was back to Europe, for Amos received a Hoover Fellowship to study at the University of Brussels.

"Various strange plans are unfolding for my support next year," Thornton had written Charlotte the previous spring.[23] Professor Canby was preparing to launch his "rather grand Literary Review for the New York Evening Post" and asked Thornton to write some book reviews. He hoped a job might materialize.[24] He almost accepted a position teaching Latin in "a boy's boarding school in New Jersey," his mother reported to a friend. "In fact," she said, "he had several to choose from and always Latin as one of the subjects."[25]

But other opportunities intervened. First Dr. Wilder sent Thornton, now twenty-three, to work for six weeks on a farm near Litchfield, Connecticut. Then, wonder of wonders, Thornton, who had never laid eyes on Europe except in his imagination and in books, was actually going to spend a year in Italy. He wrote gratefully, looking back, that his allies in finally achieving this exciting plan were "Luck; an old family friend; and my mother's perspicuity."[26] As Thornton recorded events years later, this time Isabella set in motion the events that carried him to Rome. She regularly read the *New Republic*, and noticed with interest "some travel letters from Rome by Stark Young."[27] Discovering there that the currency exchange rate was advantageous for Americans, she decided to talk to Latin scholar and professor George Lincoln Hendrickson of Yale, the Wilders' friend since the early days in Wisconsin. Dr. Hendrickson, formerly director of classical studies at the American Academy in Rome, told Isabella about foreign study opportunities for college graduates at the academy. Might this be just the opportunity for Thornton? He could travel to Europe, as his parents felt he deserved the chance to do, and simultaneously, he could study Latin and better equip himself to teach.

When Clarence W. Mendell, Thornton's Yale Latin professor, assured Dr. Wilder that Thornton "was the boy in his classes who [would] get the most out of a year" at the academy, "the great project was launched," Isabella wrote.[28] Thornton was accepted as a visiting student in the School of Classical Studies at the American Academy in Rome. "So now the plan is for him to sail September first by the Fabre line steamer 'Providence' to Naples and attend the American Classical School at Rome for a year," his mother wrote. "He is going to study Latin, Italian and the usual local archeology."[29] Thornton was elated.

Even his father was pleased. The Rome experience would surely strengthen Thornton's credentials to teach Latin and, consequently, his ability to support himself. The experience might even lead to a master's degree. Besides, the foreign-exchange rate was attractive, and Dr. Wilder thought that Thornton's Italian year could be financed with nine hundred dollars—which he would not put into his son's "careless" hands all at once.[30]

"During my years in New Haven," Thornton recalled nearly half a century later in his semiautobiographical sketch, "my father was a stone's throw [from] my successive rooms in the dormitories. I was very much under his eye. I was in constant contact with many of his oldest friends, Dean Stokes, Dean Jones, Professor Hendrickson, who were like extensions of himself."[31] For Thornton and Amos Parker Wilder, the father-son relationship was a tangle of love and resentment, admiration and dismay, submission and rebellion. "In a son's eyes—and this is more true of this relationship than any other," Thornton wrote many years after Yale,

> a father carries with him like a pack on his back their total life together, not remembered in every daily [detail] but remembered as an uninterrupted presence. To the infant he was that tall stranger of unpredictable moods—alarmingly affectionate at times, alarmingly authoritative always. To the boy he was the one who punished or who rewarded (two faces of the same coin). To the youth he was the one who could give or withhold the money that could purchase those *sine qua non* that a youth's heart so passionately desires (decent clothes, tennis rackets . . .) To the full-grown man the father is the one who is felt as seeing, also, the total life of that son, all the foolish things he's ever done.[32]

Thornton concluded that it was difficult to live with a man who remembers everything about your young life, even when he remembers it "charitably."[33]

He clearly did admire and love his father, and always would, but Thornton was twenty-three, a man grown—a man civilized. At last, college was done. Six weeks of farmwork, and then—Rome. Europe. Freedom.

ON SEPTEMBER 1, 1920, Thornton boarded the French ocean liner *Providence*, bound for Italy and the future.[34] The voyage from New York to Naples took nearly two weeks. The ship accommodated 140 first-class passengers, 250 second-class passengers, and 1,850 third-class passengers, many of them, on the voyages from Naples to New York, Italian immigrants. Thornton traveled in second class, sleeping in an upper berth in a cabin for four persons. In seas tranquil or rough, he was a good sailor—had been ever since his transpacific voyages to and from China. Meals aboard ship were lively events in the second-class dining saloon, with "boisterous company" at the long bachelors' table, he wrote in later years. He recalled that his travel companions were civil servants, students, businessmen, and two Mormon missionaries. Most were "intoxicated" by their freedom and the prospect of the adventures awaiting them in Europe, not to mention "the carafes of wine on the tables." He found himself "largely in the company of young men who had *left their fathers at home*. Very exciting it was."[35] One of his fellow passengers was a New York lawyer and Harvard graduate, a native of Sorrento and a "traveller and dilettante" who introduced Thornton to an array of colorful local characters once he reached Sorrento.[36]

As a boy Thornton had fallen in love with sea travel, the exhilaration of being encapsulated aboard a ship, surrounded by the ocean and the incomparable air. He relished the freedom to choose company or solitude, work or play, and he craved the continual promise of new landscapes and new people to be discovered. He could sequester himself to think, to write, and, on this voyage, to immerse himself in the study of Italian. He could emerge from his seclusion, eager for company, and then withdraw again when he needed time alone. The 1920 voyage to Europe was the forerunner of a lifetime of such journeys at sea, where Thornton could live comfortably, if temporarily, and write and fraternize his way across oceans.

Aboard the *Providence* in 1920, he took Italian lessons from one of his cabin mates, an Italian American who was traveling to visit his grandparents. He tried to read Dante's *Divine Comedy* in Italian, and he memorized long passages. On the ship's top deck, "amid the careening smoke stacks and the flying spray," he practiced the Italian phrases he was learning, shouting into the wind, "When does the next train leave for Rome?" and other useful expressions.[37] He was a lucky man, he knew. "I have always been favored by luck," he wrote in later years, looking back on this journey and others. "A large part of luck is opportunity and the eye to recognize it. A large part of luck is readiness."[38]

After his ship docked in Naples in mid-September, Thornton made his way first to Sorrento because he was not due at the American

Academy in Rome until early October. He could stay in Sorrento cheaply and explore the medieval streets, churches, and cloisters, as well as the cliffs and the countryside and the islands in the bay. An avid tourist, he climbed Vesuvius—"a wicked mountain, half of every step you take is lost in the sliding blue-black dust, yet so steep that every step for two hours and a half is palpably *lift*."[39]

Coincidentally, Dr. and Mrs. Charles Wager were traveling in Italy just at the same time, and Thornton enjoyed seeing them in Sorrento before they moved on to Rome. He took a room at the Hotel Cocumella in Sorrento, encountering there a colorful international cast of characters with whom he could practice his Italian, French, and German. Barely a week into his stay he wrote to his family, "I love Italy now indissolubly; and the Italians; and the language."[40] He was storing away in memory and imagination the names, faces, and stories of the people he met, the vistas he saw, the conversations he overheard—rich material to be transmuted later into fiction and drama.

His Italian was improving day by day, and he was so enamored of Sorrento that he wrote to the secretary of the academy "with a moiety of truth, that the change of continent has had a temporarily upsetting affect on my constitution & a slight prolongation of my stay here is advisable." Thornton proposed that he register by mail and arrive at the academy on October 10, a week later than scheduled. Then he plunged into a "systematic study of the beautiful antiquities at the *Museo [Archeologico] Nazionale*."[41] Dressed in his "eccentric-looking baggy grey suit," Thornton went by boat from Sorrento back to Naples to walk "enraptured for hours among the bronzes and marbles" in the vast museum, home to countless artifacts and antiquities from ancient Greece and Rome, including treasures stolen from Pompeii.[42]

———

"LEARNING ITALIAN quickly, and beside myself with delight," he scribbled on a postcard to Amos from Sorrento October 14. Italy immediately inspired and liberated him, setting him free to write. He told Amos that he had already written "a whole play."[43] In a letter to his family he had shared the details:

The thing you should really know about me now is that I am writ-
ing my beautiful pitiful play about the American widow at Capri and
Dario Stavelli, the adventurer. Never did a play come to me more easily.
Day and day I sit down and this beautiful touching dialogue flows
from my pen. It is called "Villa Rhabani" but has no relation with the
other play I projected with the same name. . . . But no one short of Elsie
Ferguson, Gareth Hughes, Haidée Wright and Arthur Byron need at-
tempt to play it.[44]

A notebook among his papers reveals that in September in Sorrento, Thornton was working on act 1 of this new full-length play, completing the draft by September 30, 1920; by October 10 three acts were drafted, and he continued the work in Rome off and on from the fall of 1920 until February 10, 1921. He would revise the unproduced, unpublished play as late as 1924.[45] Not only did Capri and the Bay of Naples provide the setting for this new drama, but the major male character, Dario Stavelli, is an echo of Wilder's new friend in Sorrento, Dario Ercolano, one of two brothers introduced to him by the lawyer he had met aboard ship. Thornton wrote that Dario and his brother were "the most delightful type of Neapolitan,—lovable sharks. They know they are charming; it's a sort of profession among them to be beautiful and courteous and *sincere* (!) But you must pay for it as you'd pay for any work of art."[46]

———

"I HAVE this minute arrived in Rome, and am waiting up in my room at half-past ten for some supper," Thornton wrote his family on October 14, 1920. "The train was two-and-a-half hours late, and I know no more of Rome than can be gained on rainy evenings crossing the street that separates the station from the Hotel Continentale (The last room left for 22 lire)."[47]

He shared his growing excitement in another letter home: "How perfect it is, my being here! How much happier a chance has fallen than a year in Paris or London or New York. Rome's antiquity, her variety, her significance, swallow these others' up, and I feel myself being

irresistibly impelled towards saying of her that she is the Eternal City."
He told his family that he

> *went with an archaeological party the other day to a newly discovered*
> *tomb of about the first century; it was under a street near the center*
> *of the city, and while by candle-light we peered at faded paintings of a*
> *family called Aurelius, symbolic representations of their dear children*
> *and parents borne graciously away by winged spirits playing in gardens*
> *and adjusting their Roman robes, the street-cars of today rushed by*
> *over us. We were clutching at the past to recover the loves and pieties*
> *and habits of the Aurelius family, while the same elements were passing*
> *above us.*[48]

This profoundly significant experience resonated far into his future.
He conjectured that October day in 1920 that "two thousand years
from now," other people would be striving to recover the artifacts,
experience, atmosphere, and humanity of his own time.[49] He went on
to do that himself, in fiction and in drama. Over the decades to come,
in various manifestations, with diverse names and settings, he would
resurrect and revisit the Aurelius family—just people "clutching at the
past" for the universal and the timeless in the human experience, and
groping toward the future. Over time he would excavate and explore
the "loves and pieties and habits" of unique yet universal characters—
in *Our Town*, *The Skin of Our Teeth*, and other plays, and in *The Bridge of
San Luis Rey*, *The Eighth Day*, *Theophilus North*, and other novels.

Thornton took with him to Rome a grounding in classical mythology, history, and literature, including Dante's work. He was captivated
by the treasures of Rome—the paintings, sculpture, architecture,
music, literature, and especially his new enthusiasm, archaeology.
"One day our class in Rome was taken out into the country to dig
up a bit of the Etruscan world, a street," he wrote years later. "Once
thousands of people had walked it. The rut was very deep. Those who
have uncovered such a spot are never the same again."[50] He thought he
would be an archaeologist as well as a writer.

He threw himself headlong into his new life. On the day he had his first look at the house on the Piazza di Spagna where the poet John Keats died in 1821, Thornton wept. Then he recited the words from Keat's "When I Have Fears" (1818)—words he knew by heart, words that most likely evoked his wartime anxiety about his own mortality: "When I have fears that I may cease to be / Before my pen has gleaned my teeming brain . . ."

"My new school is too serene and beautiful to be described," Thornton wrote his family. He was living in Villa Ballacci, a small house belonging to the American Academy—"a villa overlooking Rome, all mine!" he wrote. "I have a bed-room, dressing-room and the bath all in a row."[51] He attended American Academy lectures and field trips; enjoyed the academy costume ball and other social events; met archaeologists, composers, artists, fellow students; encountered, he wrote to his family, "a number of American women who have married Italians, and this morning I left my cards on them and hope for an invitation to tea at least, if not a dinner-party, [with] the Marchesa de Johannis and Signora Malagola."[52] He was invited to formal luncheons and dinners at the academy, including one given by the wife of the academy secretary, who had known Isabella Niven Wilder at the Misses Masters School in Dobbs Ferry.[53] He went to the theater and to the opera, and explored the city, map in hand. "Just back from another day's wild wandering," he wrote home. "Picture me backing up against a wall in a side street and unfolding my 3-ft. sq. map to find out where I am! Too happy for correspondence, that can become merely a characterless rattling bushel-basket of superlatives."[54]

News reached him from home in October that plays he had sent out to the Theatre Guild had been rejected, and he was "cast down" by the negative response. He wrote a brooding assessment of his seemingly futile efforts to become a playwright: "All my other plays when they were returned to me I immediately saw as riddled with errors and undermined with incompetence," he wrote to his family.

The Rocket. *Mercifully destroyed and forgotten.* The Dreamers *having shaken off its ludicrous pseudo-psychoanalytical modern prologue and epilogue, is in process of being rewritten in a vein that candidly*

deprecates and retains the purple-patch rhetoric. . . . The Breaking
of Exile, *a good theme, a few sharp characterizations, three or four
vivid moments, eked out with half-hours of earnest young naiveté, poor
little Thornton's lucubrations on War, on disgrace, on morality!* The
Trumpet Shall Sound *is extraordinarily vague to me, and I cannot
tell whether the three or four pictures I have in my memory . . . may or
may not be on paper, may never have left my forehead.*[55]

He supposed he would just keep on writing plays, and he still had
hopes for *Villa Rhabani*. He promised to send a copy of the script to
Connecticut so that his mother could get it out to other producers and
directors. Temporarily preoccupied as he was with being a student, an
archaeologist, a socialite, a tourist, and a dilettante in Rome, Thornton
was still, underneath it all, an aspiring dramatist. He wouldn't give up
on that yet.

In a letter to his family from Italy that fall, he painted a vivid self-
portrait:

*Looking in the cheval-glass I see a young man . . . who implicitly, or
by reason of his large shell glasses, presents an expectant eager face to
the view. His shoes and clothes are in travel-state, but he is carefully
shaved and brushed. On his pink cheeks and almost infantile mouth lies
a young innocence that is not native to Italy and has to be imported in
hollow ships, and about the eyes there is the same strong naiveté, mercifully mitigated by a sort of frightened humor. He is very likely more
intelligent than he looks, and less charming. Alone in Italy? To study
archaeology!*[56]

An ocean away Dr. Wilder worried about his son, who seemed to
be having entirely too much childish, even dangerous fun in Italy. He
fired off a stern letter, laden with cautions: "Dear boy, I pray for you—
that you may be benefitted by these experiences and not return to us
impaired in soul." While his letters home were "interesting reading,"
Dr. Wilder wrote, they were full of "so many curious people, so many,
so many derelicts." He urged Thornton to beware of the "follies, the

emptiness of it all," and to strive "earnestly to come manfully through it, and not merely to save your own soul, but others along with you." He hoped that Thornton would "keep safe" his "precious gifts from despoiling."[57]

It seemed that Dr. Wilder's shadow could stretch across continents and an ocean, as it did back in the China days, and hover about as conspicuously and critically as it did at Yale—but Thornton, at twenty-three and a half, was not so vulnerable now to parental control as the much younger Thornton had been, except in the matter of financial dependence. Dr. Wilder was not in good health that fall, still coping after more than a decade with the chronic problems caused by the Asian sprue. However, he was making speeches with "more pep" after he recovered somewhat from the most recent breakdown in his health.[58] He relinquished his Yale-in-China work in 1920 and joined the staff of the *New Haven Journal-Courier* as associate editor, a position he would hold for nine years.[59] He was "quite happy in the office," he wrote to Thornton; "I find things I can do, partly under the editor—some editorial and at times a good deal; and some high class reporting for the managing editor. I am learning the town and the people."[60] In a sense the activist journalist and editor was starting all over again. He wrote "almost daily" editorials, was still in demand as a public speaker, still a respected figure in Yale circles, but as he neared sixty, he was keenly aware that he had never fulfilled the high expectations he had set for himself. His health had restricted him, and his income, his temperament, and his family had suffered accordingly. As he was able to achieve less and less, he needed and expected more and more from his children, and sought to live through them.

Amos Parker Wilder was a lonely man, he often told the children, intimating that it was because his wife held herself emotionally remote from him, even suggesting that she tried to deny him his children's full company and affection. But now he was at home "two or three evenings in the week," and all was going well, he wrote to Thornton. Isabel was attending a local art school, "eager for companionship." Janet was enjoying public school. He reported that Amos was "very happy with his friends and work" and that Charlotte was "full of vivacity."[61] But he worried that Thornton, far away in "that setting where there is so much to make you unworthy," would fail to keep alive "the consecration to high things."[62]

But Thornton was in his glory. He found his classes at the academy exciting, although he often missed lectures when sightseeing or social engagements diverted his attention. He reveled in his walks about the city, map in hand, and came to know Rome and its treasures so intimately that he could give an authoritative tour. As Christmas approached, Thornton and Charlotte made plans for her to travel from Milan to visit him in Rome. Like her brother, Charlotte loved Italy, and despite the rigors of her YWCA work schedule—ten hours a day, seven days a week, and then four days off at the end of each month—she managed to travel, enjoying it "immensely," and writing vivid letters home about her experiences.[63]

Thornton was surprised just before Christmas by the arrival of two Yale men, Henry Luce and William Dwight Whitney, both Rhodes scholars now, and eager to spend the holidays in Rome. Thornton found a cheap *pensione* for them within a stone's throw of the house where Keats died, and took them along to some of his social engagements.[64] He had met some girls from Miss Risser's School in Rome, a fashionable finishing school for girls, among them a vivacious Chicagoan, Lila Ross Hotz, to whom Henry Luce was introduced at a party that Christmas in Rome. The two began to correspond and write poems to each other, and would marry in 1923.

Wherever Thornton went in Italy—restaurants, parties, on streetcars and trains—strangers as well as friends or acquaintances told him their life stories, often confiding their dreams or their woes. He was accustomed to that role in his family, and encouraged it: "Tell me ALL, as they cry in books," he wrote to his sister Isabel when he heard about some of her romantic problems. "I should be ashamed if you didn't tell me the whole complicated affair, when I seem to be living in Italy for the sole purpose of receiving the confidences of ladies in distress. . . . There's something in the air over here: everyone is unhappily in love every ten minutes of their lives, and only too glad to find a sympathetic eye and ear."[65] On another occasion he wrote her, "A woman's heart, as you know, has no secrets from me, and my only prescription for its restlessness and sense of frustration is M-A-N. Woman is silly and man is stupid, but in one another's company they seem temporarily to surpass themselves, and this false and superficial elation is the only thing we can write plays about."[66] He had his own "strange little sentimental experience that made concrete the warnings that Continental women however impersonal, comradely and full of good sense they seem, cannot understand friendship that is without romantic concomitants."[67]

His Roman days were full of lectures and sightseeing, the occasional raucous party of graduate students, and the more sedate entertainments in the homes of new acquaintances—expatriates, the academy circle, and native citizens. He teased, in a passage that foreshadowed the novel he would soon begin about Rome and Roman society, that he was presenting himself "as a sort of *objet-d'art* of a most singular and quaint charm, rentable for teas, dinner-parties and dances; will read MSS plays to adoring ladies; will sit in their palaces and talk to them about their own uniqueness,"[68]

Early in 1921, father and son exchanged some angry letters about money, which Thornton thought his father had failed to send, and Dr. Wilder had sent but thought his son had squandered. Actually Thornton was managing his finances better than his father thought, and Amos Parker Wilder was dispatching funds more generously than Thornton could believe.[69] He apologized to his father for his strident letters about money.[70] He was a "great father," Thornton wrote—witty, charming, eloquent, making sacrifices for his children that were sometimes thoughtlessly received.[71]

Their lively father-son discourse through letters soon moved on from finances to the future. What would Thornton do when he left Rome, and when, and why? His mother's concerns were focused less on the future than on the present. Back home, Isabel was writing a novel, Isabella wrote to her son. Was Thornton writing? How was his play progressing—if at all? Right away he wrote to her, "I attach my poor play that has been lying all these months in a state of perpetual rewriting."

It's about an American millionairess at Capri with her fatal disease,
who falls into the toils of a beautiful Italian adventurer. Au fond there
seems to be much in [it] of [Henry James's] "The Wings of the Dove"
and your anecdote of the Dobbs girl who became infatuated with the
Neapolitan boatman. The play is a long hymn of love, profane love, of
course, most pagan. It fairly limps along until it comes to a love-scene,
Helen and Dario, or the Baroness and Dario, and then it develops some
of the most exquisite and tender conversations . . . etc. Strange to say,
Flora Hypatia Storey [one of the characters in Thornton's earlier play
The Trumpet Shall Sound*] and Mrs. Helen Darrall have much*
in common. They are both more in love than beloved, they are both
deceived.[72]

He was an artist who deftly sketched portraits of women in his
fiction and drama, and in his letters. There was his affectionate relationship with the mother whose mind and spirit he revered; the
vulnerability of the heroines he created in his plays; the old women
with their "malicious stories and their wise disillusioned comments"
who fascinated him, along with the "pseudo-motherly" attention they
paid him.[73] It was these old women he wanted to write about—and
he would, importing some of the women he met in Rome, mostly expatriates, into his later fiction and his plays.[74] He had a history of close
relationships with much older women—sometimes women more his
grandmother's age than his mother's. He had felt at home with them
when he was a teenager, read aloud to them, corresponded with them,
and treated them with gallant attentive courtesy and sincere interest.
Thornton had a gift for friendship that transcended age and gender,
and as he grew into his adult life, many of his closest friends would be
older women.

There were good friendships with men as well during the year in
Rome. Various Yale men came and went: With an American friend,
Bill Bissell, he visited Assisi that March, and the journey led to an
"impassioned return to Franciscan study."[75] In Perugia he happened
on a "complicated funeral service" in a dark candlelit church, where
"earnest-faced young Franciscan monks" intoned psalms.[76] Thornton

thought that Catholicism was "the most beautiful religious system that ever eased the heart of man; centering about a liturgy built like Thebes, by poets, four-square, on the desert of man's needs." He wrote to his brother, "You and I will never be Roman Catholics," but he encouraged Amos, reading theology at the University of Brussels, to study "this magnificent and eternal institution, and humbly sit down to learn from her the secret by which she held great men, a thing the modern church cannot do."[77]

There were other young American men in his ever-expanding circle of acquaintances, as well as young Italians. Thornton especially enjoyed the company of Lauro De Bosis, whose mother was an American and whose father was the Italian poet and translator Adolfo De Bosis. Lauro, four years younger than Thornton, was an aspiring poet and translator, and an intense, charismatic young man who was then studying chemistry at the University of Rome. Thornton thought of him for years afterward as one of his best friends. The De Bosis family invited Thornton to lunch, an event that turned out to be "twice as delightful" as he expected. He described it for his mother—"The reddish-yellow villa, hung with flowering wistaria at the end of a long avenue of trees; choked garden plots with various statues of Ezekiel glimpsed through the foliage; the rooms of the house furnished in rather ugly Victorian manner—all modern Italian taste in music and art being deplorable, perhaps because they are so discriminating in literature."[78] There were several other guests at lunch that day, including the young poet Ezra Pound.[79] In Rome, Thornton discovered the work of Luigi Pirandello, "an Italian playwright whose plays I adore."[80] He was deeply moved by a performance of Pirandello's new play, *Sei personaggi in cerca d'autore* (*Six Characters in Search of an Author*), in which the audience is greeted by a dark, empty stage with curtain raised, and one character is the Manager—the manager of the theater. Thornton would experiment with some of these concepts later in his own plays.

Rome was a continual feast for his eager mind and spirit, and his sojourn there certainly nourished his writing as well.

13

"CHOICE SOULS"

*It is a great opportunity—a few months—to learn your Paris, the language
and the rest—but of what avail if you become corrupted—perhaps cynical,
reckless—even coarsened: you can hardly escape this; yet you are the one
dedicated to speak delicate truths to choice souls.*

—AMOS PARKER WILDER TO THORNTON WILDER,
July 12, 1921

France and the United States (1921–1922)

As much as Thornton loved Rome, he began to feel overwhelmed and even intimidated by it. He found that "the very complexity of things flays one's peace of mind to the point of torment." He wrote to his father on February 1, 1921:

*You are haunted by the great vistas of learning to which you are
unequal; continuous gazing at masterpieces leaves you torn by
ineffectual conflicting aspirations; the social pleasures and cheap successes bring (against this antique and Renaissance background) more
immediate revulsions and satiety. . . . Your queer "aesthetic" over-
cerebral son may yet turn out to be your most fundamental New
Englander. . . .*[1]

He thought he should leave the academy about Easter time, spend a "week or two in Florence and the hill towns," and then go on to Paris for a couple of months before returning to the United States in late June.[2]

His father, no doubt pleased by Thornton's new assessment of Rome, was not opposed to more travel. Ideally he wished that Thornton could have a journey akin to Henry Wadsworth Longfellow's three-year exploration of Europe after he graduated from Bowdoin College in 1825. Longfellow had traveled and studied in Italy, Spain, France, England, and Germany, taking formal courses in universities and walking through country towns and villages, talking to people, learning their ways and their language, all to prepare himself to teach modern languages. Dr. Wilder wrote to Thornton, "My wish for you—the analogy is Longfellow's, if you know his story—is that you might have three intensive weeks in Germany; on the language and meeting as many people as possible; a walking trip etc. among the people. I would supplement that by the same in France, a month if possible; then for a bird's eye of England etc."[3] But the simplest and cheapest thing to do, he wrote to Thornton, would be to book passage and come home, although, Dr. Wilder mused, "If there is anyone who would be benefitted by even a look and dash through a number of countries, it is you; it is clearly the kind of education you need."[4]

Thornton did not want the family to sacrifice any further for such travel, however. He was grateful to have had the experience in Italy, he wrote, "and if those qualities have not been added to me that you sent me to Europe for, by my happiness here, no amount of eager gazing-about and applying historic quotations further can add them to me."[5]

Parents and son were also trying to plan what Thornton would do once he returned to the United States. He proposed that he go to New York to see if he could find a job writing drama reviews or a weekly column, perhaps for Henry Seidel Canby's new journal. If not, he could find a teaching job, and he was determined, no matter what, to forge ahead with the writing. "I am going to be at a frightful disadvantage for some years, sheepish and put-upon," he acknowledged to his father, "but when I am discovered things will be vulgarly resplendent; I vend a cake Americans will hug."[6]

But Papa had more practical ideas: Thornton could teach or get a civil service job in Washington, with status, stability, and a salary—and write on the side. Or he could find a job in a publishing firm or a bookstore. He needed to serve an apprenticeship in a steady, income-producing occupation, needed to have an insurance policy and a bank account. Once again Polonius preached to Laertes: Thornton should "get a grip on the deep solemn relation between God and Man." He should not exploit his "youth and high spirits, drifting from one play to another newspaper etc—the years slipping by until the late thirties when many have died off" and others had to get false teeth. He needed a "dignified permanent" life and career. Despite his "feverish plans for writing," he must commit to a trade or calling or profession. Otherwise, Thornton was in jeopardy of poverty, envy, even "moral deterioration."[7] But for now Dr. Wilder just wanted to get his son out of "poor old decayed Italy."[8]

As he contemplated his "chess pieces," Dr. Wilder decided to send his wife, Isabel, and Janet abroad that spring. Isabella had been ill with a chronic sore throat and general weakness, and her husband hoped that a change of scenery would provide the complete rest she needed, and settle her nerves. She wanted to go to Italy, but her husband held out for England, which he thought would be better for the children. He believed he could afford it, if they used part of the money that Isabella had inherited from a relative.[9] Amos planned to study at Oxford for a year, and Dr. Wilder insisted that it would be good for Isabella, Amos, and his sisters to spend the year in close proximity. "The girls will blossom out, I think, in the environment," he wrote to Thornton. "Most important, Mother Wilder will freshen up. . . . I am happy to think it may be possible."[10]

Finally matters were settled: Isabella, Isabel, Janet, and Amos would live in England. Thornton would go to Paris and, if possible, to England and Germany, and then come home and find a job. Dr. Wilder would provide the money for his travels—but Thornton would pay for it in guilt. His father spelled out the details:

> Thornton: to get this large sum together represents sacrifice that you can't understand—letting go things needed for the future of your "aging parents." I am telling you this, not to tax your sympathies, but to suggest that you handle it earnestly. It is a reflection, dear boy, that we are almost afraid to send so much, fearful you will lose it; or throw it about recklessly—later to be abroad without money, unhappy, humiliated, borrowing right and left. . . . France will shock you with

the high prices and the other places too; the money will slip away: I beg
you to watch every penny. . . . Faithfully economize at every point, and
have money to pay your bills in full, including the ocean passage [to
the United States] which will be high. Thus you will earn the respect of
your father.[11]

As the end of his sojourn in Rome drew near, Thornton realized
gratefully that he knew Romans "in every walk of life." Like "*a young
man possessed,*" he had thrown himself into the history and culture of the
Eternal City, as well as its contemporary life, until he was "frightfully
up to date in their arts and literature."[12] The city would haunt him in
memory and imagination, and figure powerfully in his future writing
life. But it was time to go. He left Rome on May 18 and headed for
France by way of Florence, Siena, and Milan, where he spent three days
with Charlotte. He read a hundred of her poems during their visit, but
was disappointed that it did not seem to occur to her to ask if he had
written anything new.

By early June, Thornton was in Paris. "Don't worry or think about
me," he wrote to his father. "I wear clean linen, brush my teeth, 'hear
Mass,' and drink much certified water. Without sticking to Americans I
meet many people you would like to feel near me in ambiguous Paris."[13]

AT FIRST glance he was shabby and shy, his blue eyes darting alertly
behind his spectacles, seeing everything. He found Frenchmen "not
so immediately 'sympathetic' as the Italians."[14] He was lonely, missing his family and friends, missing Rome, but determined to make the
best of "ambiguous Paris." As romantic as the bohemian writing life
had seemed from afar, Thornton found that living in penury in Paris
severely hampered his social life. At least in Rome he had the security
of comfortable quarters and good food at the American Academy, and
an ever-widening circle of friends and acquaintances. In Paris in the
summer of 1921, however, without money to buy new clothes or laun-
der the old ones, or to eat or drink in a decent restaurant, or to afford
anything but the cheapest tickets to the opera or the theater, and these

only rarely, the best he could do was "take long walks in this priceless city" and "stay home in this nasty little room and write as I haven't written for years."[15]

In his bedbug-infested hotel room in Paris, Thornton began writing about his experiences in Rome, not quite sure where they were leading—a novella or a memoir? Sometime that spring or summer he began a prose manuscript called *Memoirs of Charles Mallison: The Year in Rome*.[16] There is a veneer of autobiography in this fictitious memoir, complete with imagined footnotes and a citation of another fictitious memoir, *The Boy Sebastian*, which supposedly preceded *The Year in Rome*. The Roman memoir was conceived, according to Wilder/Mallison, to explore the "profound impression that a year in Italy can make upon a youthful spirit prepared by wide reading and a habit of reflection."[17]

Thornton's transformative adventures in Rome reverberated in his imagination in pages he would write in Paris and beyond. Every day that June of 1921, he stepped out of his Roman memories into the vibrant reality of Paris. The decadent allure of the city was irresistible. He loved strolling the quais, roaming about Notre Dame, eating in cheap restaurants and sidewalk cafés, hearing classical and liturgical music in the cathedrals and churches, and going as often as he could to the Théâtre du Vieux-Colombier. But the overriding fact was that he was writing once again, on fire with ideas ignited by the Roman adventure and fueled by his incessant reading, observations, and reflections.

After nearly a month in the city, Thornton decided that he knew the Paris theater scene well enough to write about it in a "chatty theatrical column" he called "The Boulevards and the Latin Quarter." He submitted his work to the English-language newspaper the *Telegram*—columns that apparently went unpublished.[18] He hoped to find some kind of job so he could stay in Paris until Christmas. He tried unsuccessfully to get hired to sell books at Brentano's, and hoped in vain to find work at the *Herald*. He was being very frugal, he assured his father, staying in his cramped, dirty room in a rundown hotel, using public baths for showers, buying "little penny paper copies of the great French classics" to read "indefatigably," but having trouble finding opportunities to practice speaking French.[19] He was amazed that his vast reading in French literature had not helped him in "the slightest in speaking or in grammar," he wrote to his mother.[20]

By accident, in his rambles around the Left Bank, Thornton found an extraordinary bookshop on the rue de l'Odéon. It was called Shakespeare and Company, and, wonder of wonders, it not only sold books but also lent them to customers. The business had been established in November 1919 by an American woman, Sylvia Beach, who found Thornton "rather shy and a little like a young curate." He seemed different from other young American writers of his generation who were in Paris then. For one thing, she said, he did not "wear cowboy shirts and corduroy pants." He was modest and unobtrusive, and moved into and out of the shop quietly.[21]

Shakespeare and Company was abuzz with excitement that summer of 1921 because Beach had undertaken the mammoth challenge of publishing James Joyce's controversial *Ulysses*, which had recently been the target of an obscenity trial in the United States after Margaret Anderson and Jane Heap of the *Little Review* had published excerpts from the novel in their journal. Despite their lawyer's defense that Joyce's work was "disgusting rather than indecent," the judge convicted Anderson and Heap of the obscenity charge, and American publishers (including Boni & Liveright) declined to publish the book.[22] Thus Sylvia Beach came to the rescue, sending solicitations to people around the world in order to sell the novel by advance subscriptions ahead of its publication in the fall. On one of Thornton's visits, Beach introduced him to Joyce, nearly forty, living what Thornton later called his "self-imposed exile" from Dublin, yet bound to it "in love and hate, parallel, irreconcilable."[23] Joyce had been at work on *Ulysses* for at least seven years, exploring a theme that would haunt Thornton's own later work: "the extent to which every individual—you and I, the millions of the people who walk this earth—is both sole and unique and also archetypical."[24]

American writers were just beginning to discover postwar Paris, and some were on the verge of settling there as expatriates. Ezra Pound was already there, as was the poet Edna St. Vincent Millay, living comfortably on the Left Bank, often on borrowed money, some of it from Edmund Wilson, whose heart she had already broken. Wilson, now writing for the *New Republic*, arrived in Paris on June 20, 1921. Scott and Zelda Fitzgerald had been there but had recently departed because, Fitzgerald wrote to Wilson, they "had just had a misadventure in Paris due to Zelda's having tried to make sure of the hotel elevator by tying it fast to their floor."[25] Ernest Hemingway would arrive in December 1921, and the Fitzgeralds would move back to Paris for a longer sojourn in 1925.

In contrast, Thornton, who had yet to meet these contemporaries, was a transient observer in Paris, far more at home in Rome. While others came to Paris and stayed on to write, Thornton Wilder came to the city of Proust, wrote briefly, mostly about Rome, and then went quickly home. Rome had captured his imagination when it came to the setting of his early work in fiction, but it was the style and substance of French literature that he would emulate. He was especially captivated by what he read and tried to decipher in Proust, whose work he was reading in depth by the summer of 1922. He would import into his early fiction and into certain novels that came afterward some Proustian devices—a richness of language and imagery; vivid portraits of eccentric characters, the strands of their lives interwoven in a novel's seemingly disjointed plot; themes of suffering and unrequited love; detailed attention to social mores and structures.[26]

Thornton knew the work of the French novelist, poet, and playwright Jules Romains (1885–1972) and, discovering his Paris address, worked up the courage to call on him—a visit Thornton looked back on with chagrin. He realized only afterward that such a visit out of the blue by an unknown young American—who purported to be writing an article about Romains—must have seemed "ludicrous," and, Thornton blushed to remember, "I had no suspicion what bad French I was speaking."[27] But Romains (the pseudonym of Louis Farigoule) was kind to him, giving Thornton an advance copy of his farce *M. le Trouhadec saisi par la débauche* (*Mr. Trouhadec Seized by Debauchery*). To help him with his alleged article, Romains directed Thornton to a 1918 journal essay discussing Romains's literary philosophy of unaminism, which held, Thornton wrote, that "drama is vital in proportion as it uses group-force and marshalls little crowd-psychology units; this eliminates most of Ibsen & a lot of Shakespeare, but throws a bit of light on some great plays," such as "the supernaturalism of Japanese drama, the ancestral curse of the Greeks, the perpetual faction of the German romantics."[28] Romains's concept of group force took root in Thornton's imagination and grew to support one of the four "fundamental conditions of drama" that he would set forward in a 1941 essay, "Some Thoughts on Playwriting." He wrote, "The theater is an art addressed to a group-mind. . . . It is the presence of the group-mind that brings another requirement to the theater—forward movement."[29]

As he did in his encounters with other writers of fiction and drama, Thornton ingested Romains's ideas, tested them against what he knew of Romains's writing to see if the author's theory materialized in his literary work, and then considered whether any of the ideas could energize his own work in progress. While Thornton thought originally and independently about his own fiction and plays, he also steeped himself in literary tradition, learning from an eclectic array of "teachers" whose work spanned centuries and cultures. He was their apprentice, experimenting, testing, trying—not depending on anyone else for encouragement or practical help. He would do whatever he would do in his own time, in his own way.

———

THORNTON WAS eager to get to England to see his mother and sisters and Aunt Charlotte, now general secretary of the World Committee of the YWCA, based in London, and making occasional trips to France and Italy. Perhaps, he wrote to his father dramatically, he would spend some of his passage money so he could visit his mother, even if it meant returning to the United States in steerage, or as a deck boy, or a hand on a cattle boat.[30] Dr. Wilder immediately provided more money. "I do want you and your mother to have a time together, and for you to see something of England," Dr. Wilder wrote to his son, who often cringed when he opened his father's letters for fear they would be full, as they usually were, of commands, advice, and recriminations about morality or money. This time, his father wrote, "Always feel free to ask me for things but if I decline believe it is for a good reason."[31]

Across the ocean from each other that summer, father and son wrestled in slow-moving transatlantic letters with the question of what would become of Thornton in the fall. Perhaps he could find work as a journalist in France or the United States, Thornton speculated. "I have long told you, journalism is so degenerate that young fellows are wanted not for their best work but for 'snappy stuff,'" countered his father, the journalist. He urged his son to come home. He would provide for Thornton, he promised, while they found him a "program—as constructive as possible."[32] Dr. Wilder was determined to get his son out of Paris: "The decay in much of French-city-life is so dreadful, and you thrown into the theatrical and degenerate ends—I need not tell you I am praying for you." He wanted his son to learn the language and the culture, but not at the risk of becoming "corrupted—perhaps cynical, reckless—even coarsened." Sternly he cautioned, "Get on pay roll (not occasional income) save gradually to a nest egg—be captain of your own soul."[33]

In July, Dr. Wilder received notice of the perfect solution to save Thornton from such peril: "The Blair School offers you a position as Latin dept. head," he wrote to Thornton, instructing him to cable: "Accept." Dr. Wilder would then negotiate "as favorable a contract as possible."[34] Thornton was not an outstanding scholar at Yale, but, for the most part, he was strong in Latin, as his professors affirmed. In addition to his flair for the language, he had demonstrated a deep comprehension of the literature, as well as a talent for translation. Before he left Yale, there had been preliminary discussions with Dr. John C. Sharpe, headmaster of the Blair Academy in Blairstown, New Jersey, about the possibility of teaching Latin there. Prodded by Thornton's Yale Latin professor, Dr. Clarence Mendell, matters had moved along to the point of a possible meeting in New York between Thornton and Dr. Sharpe. Now Thornton cabled his acceptance of the unexpected job offer, and wrote to his father in more detail: "Don't try to hold him up to a certain wage. I may not suit, and to be well-paid but unsatisfactory [is] horrible . . ."[35] He could imagine "the staggering difficulties of teaching Latin in a boys school—the study-hour discipline—the keeping down of rough-house in dormitories—the fixing of attention in class—But

I rather rise to the hope of being able to do it, not without a certain exhilaration."[36]

Ever conscious of expense, Dr. Wilder had notified Thornton of the Blair opportunity by mail—an economy that proved to be very costly. By the time Thornton received his father's letter and Dr. Sharpe received Thornton's cable in response, he had offered the chairmanship of the Latin Department to someone else. Dr. Wilder reported this fact to Thornton in a letter August 5, softening the news with word that Dr. Sharpe would like to meet Thornton on his return from Paris, "intimating that he might have something else to offer."[37] Dr. Wilder also informed Dr. Mendell at Yale about the disappointing news from Blair Academy, and Mendell suggested that he send a letter of inquiry to Mather A. Abbott, the new head of the Lawrenceville School in Lawrenceville, New Jersey.

If there was an offer from Lawrenceville, Dr. Wilder wrote to Thornton, "I shall assume you would accept the post and practically accept it for you—tho' writing you about it." Lawrenceville was a "great school," he reminded his son, and he was glad to know that Thornton was willing to come home and get to work. In the meantime Papa urged him to keep up his "intensive work on *French*" and to come home with a "working knowledge" of German as well—although, he added, "I must not ask the impossible!"[38]

Although he did not acknowledge his own culpability for the loss of the Blair Academy opportunity, Dr. Wilder worked fiercely to find his boy another job. He received good news in mid-August from Mather Abbott: Lawrenceville needed a French teacher and assistant housemaster, at an annual salary of fifteen hundred dollars. Could Thornton Wilder teach French? Dr. Wilder assured Dr. Abbott that he could and he would. Cables would be sent this time, the cost ignored by all the frugal Wilders. Thornton would make a quick trip to see his mother in England, and sail home from there in time to begin teaching.

"Lawrenceville you know is the smart prep. school for Princeton and entertains only big husky team material," he wrote to his mother. "Oh, how well dressed I must be! I'd better grow a mustache for maturity,"[39] All his life he had had to wear "strange wild cheap ballooning clothes," he wrote to his father with regret. "There are certain green years in the early teens when every boy and girl wants to dress *beautifully* before other girls and boys; in Charlotte and me such stirrings at Berkeley High were overwhelmed and betrayed and I doubt . . . whether we will ever be able to carry ourselves well, or (should the wind change) even wear expensive clothes properly in our life."[40]

"PEOPLE SAID to me *Never Teach school. You will be so unhappy. It will deaden you.*" These were Thornton Wilder's words to his own favorite teacher, Charles Wager, in November 1921 during his first semester of teaching at the Lawrenceville School. He went on: "But what happy surprises you find here; how delightful the relations of the teacher and an interested class; casual encounters with retiring boys on the campus, and at lights-out the strange big protective feeling, locking the doors against dark principalities and powers and thrones."[41]

The Lawrenceville School was established in 1810, and when Thornton arrived, thin, anxious, and poorly dressed, he stepped with trepidation into a long tradition of excellence. He had to learn quickly how to teach. He thought he was at least an adequate assistant housemaster at Davis House, and he found "times of great pleasure in the class-room when I know I'm not merely adequate but really good." Much of the time, however, he was "still in Europe," he confessed to his father. "I especially cannot forget Italy." But there were moments when he felt that he had an instinct for teaching and "that art of holding twenty intelligences in hushed attention" would justify his going to Lawrenceville "in the capacity of unprepared teacher and unsuitable companion."[42]

Thornton settled into the disciplined school schedule as the autumn leaves drifted over the beautiful Lawrenceville campus. He seemed always either to be recovering from today—grading papers, longing for rest, snatching moments to write—or preparing for tomorrow: lesson plans in the rudiments of French, which he often felt unqualified to teach; or in French literature, where he was very much at home. He found that it required "an awful lot of crude health to be a teacher," he wrote to his father that fall. "Even in one's best-behaved classes one must follow each recitation with deadly concentration, and keep glancing around the room at intervals with a sort of fierce nervous awareness—and yet at the same time appear serene and fat." He had to be a "monster of vitality."[43]

He carried the constant responsibility of supervising the thirty-two boys in Davis House. Four evenings weekly, from seven until ten, he sat in his study and the boys came to him as needed for help with their homework, or homesickness. When he heard the "sound of scuffling" he would "descend the stairs with majestic and perfectly audible advance, dispensing awe and order like fragrance."[44] He supervised the frantic preparations for lights-out, and then patrolled the house, locked the doors, checked the windows—and finally, as quiet settled over the three floors of the house, savored the respite, the privacy, and, if he was not too weary, the precious moments for writing.

He was growing more effective in the classroom, and more comfortable with the boys out of class. He organized an English Club, seven boys who gathered to read "very earnest bad original poems to one another." They took walks "through the bare tree trunks of a hesitant Spring," he wrote home. He liked working with "imaginative boys from homes and schools that never fed an imagination," and found that even his "flattest remarks on books or style or even people are manna to them." He treasured the "awkwardness and charm and rush of their opening minds."[45]

Thornton looked at other teaching jobs early in 1922, including one at Amherst, for he worried that his Lawrenceville contract would not be renewed. He was surprised and relieved to be offered a contract to return for another year. To Edwin Clyde "Tubby" Foresman, the Lawrenceville football coach and the master of Davis House, Thornton wrote, "I count myself especially lucky to have been assigned to your house; I owe you everything for having lifted me over my First Year so patiently."[46] He genuinely enjoyed the Foresmans; the coach was "a little stout man, an old football celebrity with blunt ideas and a jovial reticent manner," and his attractive wife was "much superior intellectually, a Cornell graduate, but domesticating rapidly." She spoke

French and Latin and played four-hand piano with Thornton. The Foresmans had a daughter, Emily, a "squirming little girl with a piquant French face."[47]

By spring 1922 Thornton began to contribute some of his salary to help support his mother, Isabel, and Janet, still living in England. Charlotte, working in Boston, was helping the family as well. Thornton was also sending modest amounts of money to Amos, still studying theology at Mansfield College, Oxford, and preaching in small chapels nearby. For a brief time Amos worked with Albert Schweitzer, who was giving a series of lectures in French at Oxford, and giving organ concerts to raise money to support his work in Africa. Because Amos knew French, he was engaged to help Dr. Schweitzer with his correspondence. This experience, combined with the reading of Schweitzer's *The Quest of the Historical Jesus* led, Amos wrote, to his "life-long interest in New Testament eschatology."[48]

His job secure for a second year, Thornton set out in July for Truro, Massachusetts, on Cape Cod, to rest, write, and spend some time with Charlotte, who had returned from Europe and was working in Boston. En route he stopped in Newport, Rhode Island, to "look at the old battlefield" at Fort Adams.[49] He decided to stay in Newport for a while. For four dollars a week, he rented a room in the small dormitory atop the Newport YMCA, where he enjoyed "abundant showers, clean beds" and the use of a swimming pool and gym. "Every day in the Gym I can be found hurling crowbars and fleeing among the trapezes," he wrote to his mother.[50] He swam each day in the high "menacing" surf at Newport Beach, and then stretched out in the sun and sand to read—or to think about nothing at all. He summed up the atmosphere in a letter to Charlotte: "I have a cheap little clean room, an intimate typewriter, a thousand vistas of an almost-Italian sea, the neighborhood of the Rich, excellent surf-bathing, and the use of a well-equipped Gym all to myself, an opportunity I am really using, and at whose results you will be pleased."[51]

When he was not admiring the "beautiful and dangerous mists" arising from the ocean, he was enjoying long walks in the "wild and upthrusting" countryside, exercise that relaxed him and gave him time to think.[52] He was only "a tepid believer in the efficacy of long walks as far as mere physique goes." While he had taken long walks wherever he was—"At Thacher, Berkeley, Oberlin, New Haven, Europe (what glorious ones) and around Lawrenceville"—it was Thornton's opinion that ten minutes of lifting weights or chinning on a bar yielded "twenty times the reaction" of a twelve-mile walk.[53] But those long walks paid off for the writer's mind if not his body, and he was often composing as he strode down country roads, untangling a snarl in a passage or dreaming up a new plot. He also explored Newport, as he had Berkeley, Rome, and Paris, until he felt he knew almost every inch of the place. Since Rome, he had habitually "excavated" the cities and towns he visited, absorbing their culture; probing their history, sociology, and psychology; wooing the people he met along the way into conversation and camaraderie, however temporary.

Sitting at an Underwood typewriter in his room at the Y, Thornton worked for several hours each day typing the novel he had been writing in fragments of time over the past year. He detoured briefly to polish "A House in the Country," a short story inspired by Chekhov. Thornton wrote a poignant account of a lonely clerk in a warehouse who had dreamed since boyhood of having a "big old house in the country and of filling it with relatives and friends over whom he saw himself playing the part of the benignant despot." In the gentle progression of the story, Old Malcolm gradually slips from the sad drudgery of his real world into the companion-filled fantasy of his dream world.[54] The tightly focused, understated story is a quiet counterpoint to the ambitious extravagance of Thornton's unfolding novel. "I will try and place it somewhere," he wrote to his mother, "but whether it is placed or not, it should have given pleasure to the little republic of Wilders."[55]

To help pay his summer expenses, Thornton posted an advertisement in the local newspapers, seeking a summer job. "TUTORING," it read. "An instructor in one of the foremost preparatory schools and a recent Yale graduate is willing to serve as tutor in French, English or Latin."[56] Meanwhile, as he typed, he was revising draft number six of the novel he was calling *The Trasteverine*, and "already a thousand and one felicities have been added and three thousand *gaucheries* cast out," he said.[57] It was set in Rome, and he needed books to augment his imagination and memory—Dante in Italian; Sidney Colvin's *Life of Keats*—but to his dismay he found the local public library sparsely equipped for serious writers. He was reading English biographer and critic Lytton Strachey, and took to heart Strachey's intimations about fusing "a host of disparate details" under one common trait "in order to give an impression of rich complicated romantic life."[58] Thornton was casting about on the wide seas of his reading, "fishing" for his own style and voice—and Strachey's words set him to practicing, and then incorporating such richly complex sentences into his novel.

His father had in the past, half in jest, cautioned his brilliant children about carving cherrystones when they were writing. Dr. Wilder may have had in mind the intricate, minuscule carvings some Asian and Western artists wrought on actual cherrystones, or he may have been thinking of certain metaphorical references to literary figures. One of his favorite writers, Samuel Johnson, had observed that John Milton was "a genius that could cut a Colossus from a rock but could not carve heads upon cherry stones."[59] Depending on how one regarded a carved cherry-stone, such an art could be a boon or a handicap. Thornton was carving some cherrystones, he confessed to his father that July of 1922, and he owed it to Lytton Strachey, sending along an example from his novel in progress. The passage, slightly revised, would appear in print that September in a new literary journal, the *Double Dealer*, published in New Orleans from January 1921 until May 1926. The magazine published the early work of William Faulkner, Jean Toomer, and Ezra Pound, as well as Thornton Wilder. He sent off a short piece to the *Double Dealer* almost before the ink was dry in July, and the magazine—which he had never even seen—published it in September. Titled "Sentences," and inspired by Rome, Dante, and Lytton Strachey, this one-page appearance marked Thornton's first published work after Yale.[60]

Just as Thornton's three-minute playlets were finger exercises in drama, these "Sentences," stimulated by his reading of Strachey, were finger exercises in prose, part of Thornton's intensive practice in the craft of fiction. He liked the immediate gratification of publication, as well as this advance exposure for his emerging novel.

He sent part of the flourishing manuscript off to the *Dial* in August. In a brief letter he offered the editors the first book—"ten to twelve thousand words"—of *The Trasteverine*, the current title of his "series of imaginary memoirs of a year spent in Rome." He added a disclaimer: "These give the appearance of being faithful portraits of living persons, but the work is a purely fanciful effort in the manner of Marcel Proust, or at times, of Paul Morand."[61] Thornton read Morand in French, and was no doubt drawn to his eccentric, often hedonistic characters, as well as his vivid imagery.

The editors of the *Dial* declined Thornton's offering because, they told him, they needed to see the whole. "Well, I can hardly send them books seven and eight," he told his mother ruefully, "when I have not yet begun Book Two. And I am unwilling to kill myself with the composition of an interminable Book Two without still greater assurance of their using it."[62] Still, this was an encouraging response from a prestigious literary journal.

Near summer's end Thornton returned to New Haven to fill in for his father at the *Journal-Courier* for two weeks so that Dr. Wilder could enjoy a vacation in Maine. During his short tenure at the newspaper, Thornton stepped into his father's shoes and wrote editorials headed "The Preparatory School versus the High School," "Preparing for a Coal Shortage," "The Theatre in America," and the "The Shelley Centenary"—which led to an invitation to turn it into a longer piece on the poet's centenary for the *Yale Alumni Weekly*. Thornton expanded and polished the piece, in part because he hoped it might impress his Yale professors, and perhaps even help his chances of teaching at Yale someday. Called "The Shelley Centenary—A Notable Exhibition of Shelleyana at the Brick Row Book-Shop," it ran on October 13, 1922.[63]

BACK AT Lawrenceville for his second year, Thornton was set to teach a heavy schedule of twenty-four hours weekly, but he felt much more at home—"settling down and getting so school-masterish," he wrote to his mother.[64] He had thirty-three charges in Davis House that fall, and there were almost a dozen new masters. But even with the added workload, Thornton wrote to his mother, he was "being extremely well paid for being happy."[65]

As was his reflex after all the years of the family separation, Thornton kept up a lively correspondence with his parents and siblings. After years of letters from his father, full of affection and admonitions, advice and reproof, Thornton, nearly twenty-five, composed a parody his father found "very funny," according to a note scrawled in Dr. Wilder's hand on the face of the letter. Thornton turned the tables on his platitude-spouting father:

> *Keep fat and well. Drink lots of water. When you're feeling unwell do as the animals do and eat nothing. Whatsoever things are indisputable, whatsoever things are common knowledge since the reign of Albert the Good so think on these things. If you see a task ahead say to yourself, This one thing I do. . . . Be kindly and impersonal in your relations to people, remember that they have their trials, too; even if a Bishop offers you liquor quietly and firmly turn your glass down. Remember Luther nailing his principles to the door of Wurtenburg [sic] and holding to a diet of Worms. You know how anxious I am about the particular perils that beset your temperament. Love, Thornton*[66]

ALTHOUGH HE was "caught in the quick-sands of Teaching" in the fall of 1922, Thornton wrote a new three-minute playlet, *And the Sea Shall Give Up Its Dead*, set after Judgment Day, when "time comes to an end like a frayed ribbon." In addition to this dramatic affirmation of the need to protect the self in the face of government, religion, art, and culture, Thornton was caught up in his novel, writing in his few private moments, and reading to research certain details. He was currently engrossed in Pierre de Labriolle's *Histoire de la littérature latine chrétienne.*[67] He wrote a detailed synopsis of his Roman memoirs for his mother that fall. The second book, he told her, featured a "wealthy maiden lady of

ancient lineage," Mlle. Astrée-Luce de Morfontaine. She and her compatriots, a group of royalists (including a cardinal, a critic, some minor
royalty, and an assortment of expatriates), begin to plan an ecumenical
council for 1938, although most of them know it will never take place.
Thornton was embroidering intricate details of setting and plot into the
story, including "interior decorating & culinary." He sketched the other
books, or sections, to come in the novel—"the death of Keats faithfully
documented and seen through the veil of 'my' dislike and revulsion";
the story of an American utopian experiment, replete with his "views as
to the special way of educating boys with gifts"; his play *Villa Rhabani*;
and the story of a "wonder-working Italian woman in the tenement of
Trastevere; how at her death her body was sliced for magical relics."
He also envisioned the "deliberate retelling of the strange relations that
bound together Cicero, Clodius and his sister Clodia-Lesbia, Catullus,
Julius Caesar and his wife, with all the ramifications of sacrilege, incest
and every other crime; an incredible novelette lying there to anyone's
hand these two thousand years. Don't ask me how much reading is
behind that."[68] Some of the ideas he had conceived and sketched by 1922
would make it into his first novel, *The Cabala*, but the "deliberate retelling" of the story of Julius Caesar and company would materialize many
years later, in 1948, in the novel he titled *The Ides of March*.

But the book he was writing after lights were out in Davis House,
and on weekends, and in spare moments here and there, was a hodge-
podge—a dazzling, mystifying panorama of a book; a first novel glut-
ted with his intense imaginings, his ambitious artistic impulses, his
endless curiosity and prodigious memory, his fascination with history,
philosophy, religion, languages, people, and every book he'd ever read.
How in the world would he weave it all together into an organic story?
He was conceiving this first novel as if he had to pack into its pages
all he ever knew, ever thought, ever believed, ever questioned, ever
wanted to say. It was hopelessly disjointed, overlarge, obscure, impossible—and he knew it. He confessed as much to his mother:

From all these eccentrics and madmen and scoundrels—thousands of
portraits—is supposed to arise the hot breath of a life more romantic

than Jules Verne—an escape from routine and weariness and stenog-
rapher's-anemia, and a reproduction of the feeling that Rome gives you
when you're no longer in it. Of course it is only written to please myself:
There is nothing in it except what I am madly curious about; no com-
promise made for people who do not like the particular forms of strange-
ness and disorder that I like.[69]

Most of the time Thornton was the teacher and assistant housemaster, doing every duty; endearing himself to students, colleagues, and
parents; earning money, as his father had feared he'd never do; and
sharing a good portion of it with his family. The rest of the time he
was living in the past and in the future—living in Rome—living in
his book.

14

"ALL MY FAULTS AND VIRTUES"

I've been consistent from birth—all my faults and virtues were just as marked in Chefoo and Thacher days as they are now, and by your letters then you seem to have been aware of it.

—THORNTON WILDER TO AMOS PARKER WILDER,
February 7, 1923

New Jersey and Connecticut (1922–1923)

In his midtwenties—a hardworking, wage-earning schoolmaster and erstwhile writer—Thornton Wilder was still squabbling with his father over money. He was applying for a summer camp job to augment his teaching income, he assured his father. But he still felt like a chastened schoolboy, defensively aware of all his shortcomings.[1] He was especially sensitive about his father's skepticism that he would ever find "a foothold in literature," but he plowed on.[2] He began keeping a new journal on September 4, 1922, while he was still in New Haven filling in at the newspaper for his vacationing father. The journal entries were written sometimes in English, sometimes in French, sometimes in shorthand. For a month he filled pages with notes on his daily activities and reflections on his prodigious reading—more of Morand's fiction and Flaubert's letters (which inspired him to write "painstakingly, religiously," and to compose a paragraph for his novel "describing the fountain at the Villa Pamphily-Doria").[3] He was absorbed in Proust's recently published *Sodome et Gomorrhe*, which Thornton called "the strangest book in the world, powerful & terrible." Thornton praised Proust for daring to "open a whole new continent" in psychology, and marveled that although he was a "pioneer," he was also the "complete master."[4] Long interested in the study of psychology, Thornton also admired Proust's perceptive psychological portraits.

He made a list in his journal of the books he had read or reread during his summer vacation in Newport: Walter De la Mare's *Memoirs of a Midget*; Henry James's *The Wings of the Dove* and *The Awkward Age*; four volumes of the letters of Horace Walpole, the eighteenth-century English writer and sometime publisher, best known for his copious correspondence and his Gothic horror story, *The Castle of Otranto*. Thornton also read Racine, George Meredith, the Greek poet Pindar, Jane Austen, and Cicero during those languid summer days in Newport.[5] He frequently immersed himself in the letters of Mme de Sévigné, Marie de Rabutin-Chantal (1626–96). A thousand or more of her letters, most written to her daughter, survive to document her personal life as well as life, art, and politics in seventeenth-century France. Mme de Sévigné's letters and life captured Thornton's imagination and would often make their way into his writing.

He was schooling himself in fiction, but drama was also very much on his mind. Thornton went to the theater in Philadelphia; in Trenton and Princeton, New Jersey; and in New York as often as his schedule and budget allowed. Most often he saw classical drama or new contemporary plays, but with Tom Dickens, a Yale graduate who was the new Lawrenceville football coach, he went to see movies and vaudeville. He was reading Sherwood Anderson and Eugene O'Neill, deciding they both had faults but showed "the same wonderful promise."[6] Most of all he was reading the texts of plays, "seeing" the dramas in his head, carefully analyzing the success and failures of certain writers—and drawing some fundamental conclusions about dramatic technique in the process.

The playwright who most caught Thornton's imagination and admiration that fall was the Spanish dramatist and poet Pedro Calderón de la Barca (1600–81). Calderón had been a knight, a soldier, and a priest as well as one of Spain's greatest playwrights—considered by most as second only to Lope de Vega, who would later absorb Thornton's avid attention. "I suddenly became possessed of a desire to get hold of a less-known Calderón play and reshape it for the Yale Dramat," he wrote in his journal September 11.[7] Once Thornton was drawn to a writer, his habit was to saturate himself in that writer's work, reading analytically, rereading a play or novel two or three times, taking notes along the way from the vantage point of the critic as well as the writer. He could dissect a work and then retrieve from its remains the techniques or themes he wanted to try with his own hand. As he plowed through Calderón's plays that fall, he found "delightful business" in them, but thought they were too "busily contrived" with as many as "thirteen noisy uninteresting plots."[8]

While he could read the work of French and German playwrights in the original language, he had to rely on translations of the Spanish, and disliked having to read a play secondhand. But he grasped enough of the theory inherent in the dramatic work of Lope de Vega and Calderón to decide that "unlike a book, a play must be seen quickly and quick projection in writing counts. Ibsen mulled over [his plays] with his sketches too much. I must never write one again without having a scenario first, as melodramatic as possible."[9]

At Lawrenceville School that fall, the necessary pleasures of reading and writing were quickly subsumed by the duties of reading student themes, grading papers, monitoring examinations, preparing for classes, and participating in community life. The journal entries ended abruptly on October 2, 1922. From that time on, Thornton's fall schedule was so intense that he began to suffer physically. "I haven't been awfully well for a number of days—nothing localized. Too late up nights and the nervosity of teaching," he wrote in his journal.[10] Some days he met five classes, with his "slightly difficult" third-formers just before lunch, and his "really dangerous" fourth-formers at the end of the day.[11] During his rare private hours he tried to relax, in company and in solitude. He went to the theater in New York and read plays in his spare time, often daydreaming about translating and adapting work by others—such as Pirandello. Though he had deemed the playwright's work "wonderful" since he had first seen it in Rome, he concluded that some of Pirandello's plays were "unadaptable."[12]

For physical relaxation he took long walks with colleagues or students, but most often by himself. Deep in the nearby woods, a fallen tree lay across a stream. The broad trunk was sturdy enough to hold a grown man, and Thornton liked to lie down on it and listen to the woods and water, or to nothing at all. When he needed solace or escape, he turned to music. As a boy in Berkeley, he used to sit "by the hour" to listen as the mother of one of his school friends played the scores of Puccini operas on the piano.[13] Although since childhood Thornton had studied piano, violin, voice, and organ, his lessons had been sporadic, often haphazard, except for his training at Oberlin's Conservatory of Music. It was a mark of his talent that he played and sang as skill-fully as he did, all the while studying music history and musicology on his own. Occasionally he composed lyrics and melodies—"lilts," he called them.[14] He followed the work of contemporary composers, went to concerts, loved playing four-hand piano, savored spending a private hour playing—the piano score of Mozart's *Così fan tutte* on one day, and on another, trying to find "almost in vain, the beauties that are universally reported to lie in the Slow Movement of the [Bach] Italian Concerto."[15] After Charlotte had visited Thornton in Rome in 1920, she wrote to her mother about his erudition: "If he goes on being edu-cated much longer, there won't be anyone left in the world of sufficient prestige in his eyes, to give him his 'come-up-ance.' "[16]

He had his faults and virtues, Thornton knew—and he regarded his faults with an anguish even greater than that provoked by his father's letters. He knew he was a dilettante, knew he was self-absorbed, knew he could focus single-mindedly on his interests and enthusiasms at the expense of other people, knew he could impose those enthusiasms on other people, knew he could be so excessively, reflexively polite that he could seem hypocritical and insincere. He knew he had a history of poor understanding and management of money, but he was working earnestly on that fault, and was stretching his salary in order to help his family. And he was in a frequent ferment about religion—pulled to the mystics and classical Catholic literature and liturgy, open to phi-losophy, rebelling against the conventional Christianity of his youth, searching for a spiritual compass. He had come to believe that "Chris-tianity has already strangled itself with its own inherent poisons and will have to be born again in a new quarter."[17]

As for his virtues, he believed that he was loyal, faithful, trustwor-thy, generally honest, eager for love and approval—and dutiful to a fault. He was trying to become a better teacher, and did not need his

father's advice about that. Dr. Wilder hoped Thornton would leave his
spiritual mark on each boy. He did not want his son to be "the graceful
figure, cigarette in hand, to whom the little mutes, frightened, hopeful,
nevertheless come in the holiness of childhood—only to go down the
corridor empty!"[18] Thornton in his midtwenties understood that his father's "scandalized air" in reprimanding his children could be "pretty
much assumed for our improvement."[19]

Most of all Thornton was determined to become a better writer. He
searched earnestly for what he later described, in reference to James
Joyce, as "his own subject, his myth-theme, hidden from him, but prepared for him every hour of his life, his *Gulliver's Travels*, his *Robinson Crusoe*."[20] Faults and virtues aside, Thornton was at twenty-five an
educated man, cultured, informed, highly civilized. His parents had
certainly done their part in that process, as had Sherman Thacher;
Charles Wager; Canby, Tinker, Phelps, and a few others at Yale; his
experiences in Rome and Paris; and the countless books he consumed
over the years. Yet Thornton had always been his own best teacher.

Unfortunately he had little time to write, giving himself up to the
school routine and the demands of his students, finding teaching to be
easier in the second year than in the first, but still feeling intensely
"burdened with more administrative trifles"—keeping attendance
and tardy rolls, and rewards and punishment records for Davis House,
being called "hither and thither" until he had "the illusion of being a
Secretary for Foreign Affairs or a Wall Street magnate."[21] In addition
to all his other duties, Thornton joined his parents in trying to keep
the far-flung Wilders apprised of each other's activities. Amos was still
writing poetry and studying theology at Oxford, and taking rigorous
bicycle trips through Italy on his vacation. During the 1921–22 academic year he had lived with his mother, Isabel, and Janet in a rented
house on Chalfont Road in Oxford. Then Amos moved into an apartment and Isabella and the girls moved on to London. Isabella had been
living in England since 1921, and wanted to spend some time in Italy
and France, but in the spring of 1923, her husband urged her to return
to the United States to care for her mother, whose health was beginning
to fail. Besides, he teased in a letter to Charlotte, "Mt. Carmel must

begin to wonder if it is really true that I hit her over the head with a talking machine and have a wife in Puxatawney [*sic*]."[22]

Isabella dreaded giving up her comparative freedom and going back to the drafty old "tumbledown house" in Mount Carmel where they had been living, with its wallpaper coming off "in ribbons," its wooden beams and floors "powdering into decay," and its frequent invasion by a "migration of ants." Never mind that the house was surrounded by blooming hydrangeas in the spring and summer—it was a nightmare to keep up. The family called it alternately Hydrangea House and the Sleeping Giant, and Dr. Wilder and Thornton promised Isabella that if she would come home she would never have to live there again.[23]

Dr. Wilder, meanwhile, traveled, made speeches, and held down his editorial post in New Haven, sharing with the family letters "from unknown or prominent readers of his editorials who have been struck or touched by certain passages," Thornton reported to his mother. He was always eager for news from London and pictures of his sisters. Eleven-year-old Janet was growing tall, and showing a strong interest in science and in horses. With all her brothers and sisters writing and publishing, Thornton teased, he would not be surprised if Janet wrote a book of reflections of a horse lover, calling it *Yeas and Neighs*.[24]

Isabel, now in her early twenties, studied Old English embroidery and design at the Oxford City-County Council School, and audited a "celebrated course" in Restoration drama at Lincoln College as well as an English literature course at Christ Church. She also took an acting course at the Ben Greet Acting School in London, run by the famous British Shakespearean actor-director whose company toured popular productions of Shakespeare's plays in the United States. Isabel played a "walk-on part for two weeks when the Ben Greet Company played a 2-week tour" in Oxford.[25] She studied typing and shorthand in 1922–23 in London, worked on a novel, and wrote at least two plays—a one-act called *The Empty-Handed* and a play in two acts entitled *At Dusk*, for which Thornton filed copyright protection on her behalf. He praised his sister's efforts, and began to send her books on playwriting, as well as advice about plays to study.

In a long letter to Thornton, Isabel confided that for a year she had

been "unpardonably, insanely in love" with a man who was "attractive, clever, charming—an incredible combination of everything." He
pursued her, wanted to make love to her, wanted to marry her. But
they had come to "an understanding" because Isabel couldn't make
a commitment to marriage, and she couldn't give in to her passionate
desire for an affair with this man—"he wants you & you need him terribly, awfully, but there is the Puritan background, feminine cowardice
(oh the courage of a prostitute) and modesty & a bit of ignorance." She
knew, she told her brother, that she had given up "one of the biggest
things I'll ever have" because of "that ever lastingly drilled in 'Thou
shalt not.'" She asked Thornton not to "enlighten" their mother about
it because "of all this Mother knows little."[26]

Isabel was casting about for a purpose in her life. There was writing, but she found that "oh, so tiring," and besides, she was "too
young for that—it is passive—I want to live *myself*. Then I will know
my powers." Isabel told her brother that she knew she would "never
be satisfied . . . until I have married and thoroughly explored sex."[27]
Thornton observed that the Wilders were "nervous and contrary" and
would "probably marry often and late."[28] And he wrote to a friend,
"Both of my sisters send me long accounts of MEN they meet, asking
me whether I find them ALL RIGHT and as an old schoolmaster I have
a passion for spreading advice."[29]

Amos, now nearly twenty-eight, was still a graduate student in
Mansfield College, Oxford, and was also playing tennis regularly as a
member of the Oxford University team.[30] He was also publishing an occasional poem in literary journals. Thornton was "elated" by his brother's "great success" in getting a poem, "Ode in a German Cemetery,"
published in the *Hibbert Journal* and reprinted in the *Literary Digest*.
He wrote to his mother, "In a sense the Ode is your first grandchild,
Mrs. Wilder." He went on to praise his mother for this accomplishment
by "one of the little school" she "reared so significantly."[31] Thornton
thought his brother's poetry was fine literature and recognized in it the
influence of the cadences and verse of the hymns of their youth.

Like Thornton, Amos got no affirmation from their father. Amos
was vindicated, however, when *Battle-Retrospect and Other Poems*, his

book-length collection of war poetry, was chosen for publication in 1923, the sixteenth volume in the prestigious Yale Series of Younger Poets—making him the first of the five young Wilders to achieve such distinguished national publication of a book.

All things considered, this was a remarkably happy and productive period for the Wilder family, scattered as they were. Thornton shared with the family in England the news that, up in Boston, independent Charlotte, now a writer and assistant editor for *The Youth's Companion*, had "changed from alpha to omega; she rushes out to call on people, and is ill unless people are calling on her; she wants me to give her address to any boys I might know in Boston; she scolds me for repaying her the money I owed her from Paris; is taking the part of Mary Magdalene in a church pageant."[32] He was very proud when his sister published an essay in the *Atlantic Monthly* in 1923, and he bragged that she was writing sonnets "that will make you hold your breath."[33]

Thornton urged Charlotte to be good to their father because, he wrote, "I'm not, very, these days; I can't send him enough money for him to deposit to my account, and he's afraid I'm incorrigible."[34] In letters to his mother and to Charlotte, Thornton affirmed his faith in Charlotte's future as a writer. "You and I must lie low in darkling obscurity perhaps for many years yet, knowing thousands of people and studying thousands of classics, until the hour or our emergence strikes," he wrote to Charlotte.[35] As he had for Isabel and her plays, he predicted that if Charlotte kept on writing she might "discover herself as something of a very high order."[36] He often praised his mother for her role in the accomplishments of her sons and daughters: "What is the secret, madam," he wrote to her, "of having astonishing children?"[37]

In February 1923 Thornton could report to his mother:

Great long stretches of my Roman Memoirs are now done, and I've a good mind to group together the Society sections and try and send them out into the world first, under the title: Elizabeth Grier and Her Circle. To many readers they will seem . . . too gossipy and feminine. Many passages however are of a valuable mordant satire, and others

drenched with restrained pity; I am not ashamed of it. You would be a
great help, but I cannot send my forlorn unique text across the ocean.[38]

He promised himself that he would teach one more year, and then concentrate on writing. He would earn some additional money working in a summer camp, and then he would go to New York, live on his savings, and write.[39] He would give himself a year, and if that plan did not work, he would "creep back into teaching." Meanwhile, he told his mother, he hoped that "the Memoirs I keep touching may in fourteen months have been finished and have found a haven."[40]

He announced his plans to his father in angry response to a birthday note in which Dr. Wilder wrote that he was resigned to the prospect that he could not expect any significant achievement from Thornton. In return Thornton chastised his father for his "moral pessimism," and announced: "I am fully decided now that next year is my last in teaching (if I live through it). I am going to move into the foremost city in the world, and do a little writing, tutoring, and, perhaps, acting. I'm not going to shatter into bits my prodigious mind for any number of boys or dollars."[41]

———

THORNTON DEVOTED every possible free moment to writing during the spring of 1923. He flirted briefly with Dadaism: "I'm going slightly Dada—you may have noticed it, and am trying to extract beautiful effects from an adroit use of nonsense," he wrote to his friend Norman Fitts, editor of *S4N*. He also proposed a publishing project: "I would like to consider laying down perhaps more than fifty dollars (would that go any distance?) towards making a pamphlet of my more radical and subtle tapestry pieces."[42] But after Fitts replied that he was willing to print such a book, Thornton begged off and apologized: He had "only four items ready for it," he wrote. "When it comes to actually getting a booklet out," Thornton told Fitts, he would draw on his savings to do so. Meanwhile, he wrote, "I must have had a rush of dreams to the head."[43] Although it went nowhere, the proposal signified Thornton's ongoing experimentation and his new determination to make his work visible. He also reported to Fitts that he was "turning to long plays," and if he had freedom to write, he believed he could "write four stunners a year."[44]

Thornton was soon the beneficiary of some helpful networking. Through Stark Young he was in touch with Edith Isaacs, editor and publisher of the influential *Theatre Arts Magazine*. He sent her *The Trumpet Shall Sound*, urging her to take her time reading it, and then, "When reckoning comes do not spare me: I learn meekly." Besides, he told her, this play came from a "closed chapter; after them came Dada."[45] When they met, she was quite taken with the shy, friendly, erudite young man. He had brought along portions of his Roman memoirs, and, at her invitation, read them aloud to her, bringing the characters to life with his animated reading. She praised his fiction, thought it had theatrical qualities, and was impressed enough with two of his plays to send them to director Richard Boleslavsky at the American Laboratory Theatre.

On May 2, 1923, Thornton went to Philadelphia to see the Moscow Art Theatre Company production of *The Cherry Orchard*, and to meet one of his theater icons. For years he had followed the theater career of Austrian-born producer and director Max Reinhardt. Coincidentally Thornton had read in the *New York Times* that Reinhardt planned to attend the very same performance for which he had already bought a ticket. Also providentially, Rudolf Kommer, who had befriended Thornton at Monhegan Island, was working with Reinhardt as his agent and interpreter. When Thornton spotted Kommer and Reinhardt, who was accompanied by "a gloriously beautiful actress setting off her face with the waftings of a huge feather fan in Paris green," he pushed his way through the crowd at intermission to speak to them.[46] As he had hoped, Kommer remembered him and introduced him to Reinhardt—whom Thornton found "astonishingly young and homely, but with bright eyes, and with a pretty, deferential manner."[47] He had dreamed for years about writing a play that Reinhardt would direct, and he was now many steps closer to turning that into a reality, however distant in the future.

To his surprise, Thornton had somehow set in motion this chain reaction of acquaintances who were impressed with him and his work.

Through Kommer he met Reinhardt. Through Stark Young he met Edith Isaacs and then Boleslavsky. As he turned his eyes beyond Lawrenceville to New York, Thornton was becoming his own best advocate. His father might doubt his future, but Thornton was enormously encouraged by these connections with professionals in the theater.

In May 1923, he began keeping a letter book, copying by hand his outgoing correspondence and occasionally recording the text of letters he received. The contents of his letter book document the range of his friendships, as well as his plans to relinquish teaching and move to New York. But as the spring term drew to its close, Thornton had to concentrate on school duties, including overseeing final preparations for his students who were taking College Board examinations. He was offered a new contract, with a raise to two thousand dollars for the coming year. The last days of the semester were crammed with teaching and house duties, and he tutored to earn extra money, ran two miles on the cinder path of the track every morning, and practiced playing jazz on the piano to prepare for his job as entertainment director at the camp where he was employed for the summer.

All in all he confessed to his brother that he was "right happy" in Lawrenceville: "Teaching is wonderful; I cannot tell whether I like it for itself, or whether my mind is such that in any walk of life I would be thus daily excited, moved, amused, surprised, and frightened."[48]

IN LATE May, Elizabeth Lewis Niven, Isabella's mother, suffered a stroke, which left her with aphasia. Thornton rushed to New York to see her, and he was sure his grandmother recognized him. She spoke in a "musical but incoherent flow of words" and when Thornton and his father made a motion to go, Thornton wrote, she "raised her hand and wrinkled her forehead in a characteristic expression of humorous reproach; so we sat down, until from fatigue or content she had closed her eyes and forgotten us."[49] She died soon afterward. Dr. Wilder and Thornton Niven, Isabella's brother, planned Mrs. Niven's funeral. Thornton wrote a sad letter to his mother in England on June 5, 1923, trying to comfort her: "Just a page," he said, "to supplement the letters Father and Uncle Thornton wrote you about Grandmother's last days. . . . To you who only received news of it by the cruelty of cablegrams it will seem more tragic than it has been for us who saw an end as gently disposed as is possible among us."[50]

In New Haven that June he and his father began to look for a house to lease for Isabella's return to the United States. Like their father, Thornton, Amos, and Charlotte thought it was time for their mother and their younger sisters to come back to the United States. "I am more concerned about Isabel than even [Mother], although she comes first," Charlotte wrote from Boston in July 1923:

> *Isabel [now twenty-three] may or may not have told you her anxieties, but she tells me it is a queer life they live, and I can well believe it. I would love to set Isabel up here, with a job. Of course, she will find an office job confining, but let her find she can do her own work, and stand on her feet and make her own friends, and I think she will be happier. . . . I would take pleasure in giving her many of the things that are simple "fun" that she misses, from lack of money. I shan't have any myself, but I can always turn out children's stories etc. and raise a holiday fund, and I can show her how to. We would go to music and swimming parties, and have fudge suppers; all the things she has little of, and ought to have. I don't know if Mother can spare her, though.*[51]

Amos was returning to the United States that summer as a member of the Oxford-Cambridge Tennis Team to play tennis tournaments with collegiate counterparts in the United States and Canada. The arrival of the Oxford-Cambridge team received national news coverage, and with most of his passage to the United States paid by the team, Amos told his family he was coming home to stay and to enter the Yale Divinity School in the fall. With this news Isabella began to think seriously about taking Isabel and Janet home to Connecticut. Thornton, meanwhile, set out for Litchfield, Connecticut, to begin a summer job that would, in some ways, be more frustrating and challenging than the strenuous farm labor that had defined so many of his earlier summers.

"THIS IS a noisy vexatious camp and I was a fool to come," he wrote his father from Sagawatha Lodge on Bantam Lake near Litchfield. [52] He had signed a contract to spend the summer of 1923 there as a counselor, and was immediately dismayed to learn that as entertainment director, he was actually expected to "sing and tell pirate stories and teach swimming, and other crosses." [53] He very quickly decided he had made a mistake when he took the job, but there was nothing to be done but see it through, which he did with humor, entertaining his family and friends with the comedy of his adventures. He wrote to his mother, "The whole problem of these camps is to keep the urchins amused on five acres for fourteen hours a day; nothing more difficult. They are pursued by boredom and fretfulness and homesickness." He found that "only story-telling can enthrall them long, and I hold that monopoly here, sitting on a piano-stool and narrating with my wiry hands and the changing horrors of my face. Two months of this and I see where I'll get thinner yet." [54]

Actually, there is probably no more difficult audience for a writer than a gaggle of rambunctious ten- and eleven-year-old boys, and Thornton's imagination got a vigorous workout that summer as he labored not only to subdue but to mesmerize his charges. Somehow, although he was on duty twenty-four hours daily, with only one day off a week, and even though he was sleeping in a log cabin with six boys, alternately listening to and tuning out their incessant chatter and their "perpetual nagging of one another," he was managing to read—Proust and Mme de Sévigné in French; Henry James's *The Ambassadors*; Henri Bergson's *Creative Evolution*; James Bryce's *Holy Roman Empire*; and the poet Carl Sandburg's *Rootabaga Stories*, American fairy tales written for his daughters. "Carl Sandburg is a Chicago vers-librist who writes a beautiful poem fifteen times out of a hundred," Thornton wrote to his mother; "his bright nonsense stories though are all delightful and very important because they are purely American." [55]

Thornton was also devouring novels, good and bad, about various periods and strata of society in Roman life. The determined writer somehow found moments amid the camp chaos to add "some handsome brocaded lengths to my Roman memoirs, vital, rich, crowded. Conscious of that inexhaustible invention that is so lacking these days where they can give you a thousand details without giving you a thousand lights, my portraits rise from my own pages to surprise me, solid, three-dimensional, speaking. All of them a little eccentric and all frustrated, wretched, but forceful, combative."[56]

Even the most fiercely disciplined writer must exert immense concentration if he is to keep writing a sophisticated first novel, set in Rome, while living in the rowdy jungle of a Connecticut summer camp for boys. Thornton not only succeeded in doing so, but in the process planted seeds that he would harvest later on, in plays and in another novel, this one set in Peru. "Now I'm staging Dramatics up here," he wrote to a friend, "and projecting real effects with a few benches and a station lamp."[57] (An early experiment in minimalist staging, perhaps—despite his disclaimer that "storytelling and the production of Shows raise my life slightly above that of a tree.")[58] To entertain his campers at the Monday-night marshmallow roasts, Thornton "ransacked the stories of Poe for material." He read *Treasure Island* to the boys on Thursday nights. Every Saturday night, he said, "I stage a melodrama *all* written by me, about purple rays, or ancestral ghosts, or pirates out kidnapping orphan asylums."[59] He cast the plays with other counselors, an occasional lady, and "a number of smart boys." Together they produced "finished pretentious four-act plays"—*The Perth Emeralds, The Idol's Eye, Bagdad* [sic], *The Kidnappers*, and *The Mean Trick*, among others. With relish they improvised many of their lines, Thornton wrote, "often making our happiest strokes, not in rehearsal, but during the performances."[60] On Sunday nights he told Bible stories, and because many of the boys had "never heard of Goliath or Esau or Belshazzar," they gave Mr. Wilder "credit for a great deal of talent."[61]

As for the future novel, Thornton was getting an education in the history of Peru and in the process, unbeknownst to himself, gathering material for a book he had not yet even imagined. Every Wednesday night he had to tell an Indian story at the camp's council. Rather than turn to Native American legends, Thornton "compromised on the Aztecs and Incas and got a great deal of pleasure out of it."[62] He read

William H. Prescott's *History of the Discovery of Mexico* and *History of the Discovery of Peru*, and in the foreboding shadows of firelit nights, transfixed his boys with mysterious, frightening, often bloody and violent Inca and Aztec lore. It took "everything short of parlor-magic" to keep his forty "shrill" campers amused, and Thornton entertained them expertly.[63] At the same time he was honing his narrative skills on an audience of little boys with short attention spans and no patience for the dull and lifeless. In return his usually obstreperous campers gave him their rapt attention—and invaluable practice in creating dynamic, enthralling stories, whatever the source or the genre.

Thornton grew a little mustache that summer, and it turned out to be red. He was lean, fit, and tan from hiking, swimming, canoeing, and keeping watch over his boys. He was counting the days till freedom. He wanted to spend some time in New Haven with his father, and do some work on his Roman memoirs in the Yale library "to verify allusions and collect those bits of false learning that give my pages the quality of stiff rich tapestry."[64] He hoped to visit Charlotte in Boston and North Truro, and go back to Newport, he said, "for my favorite solitary walks, and to refresh the memory of the sea-gulls to whom I read Shelley." He also longed for some time in New York to be a "professional theater-goer"—to see everything from the *Ziegfeld Follies* to Mrs. Fiske (Minnie Maddern Fiske, a famous American actress)—and then, he said, he would head back to "my dear School, to which I return with Joy and relief."[65]

AT LAST Isabella, Isabel, and Janet were on their way home from England, planning to sail in mid-September. Thornton and his father had found a house in New Haven to rent for the family, since Isabella insisted that they give up the "old matchbox" in Mount Carmel.[66] Thornton told his father he wanted to contribute $250 to the tickets for passage home for his mother and sisters, and to send his mother $100 of "serenity money."[67] This was not "for the necessities of travel," Thornton lectured his father with surprisingly candid disapproval, "but for the amenities that are so necessary for a Lady—details which you have always misunderstood; your obtuseness in such refinements has cost you more than money—a self-respecting 'compliment' to the Stewardess, a few minutes of taxi after the chaos of the dock, a lemonade on deck occasionally, 50 cents for the ship's concern, and so on."[68]

Thornton looked forward eagerly to his mother's return and to the reunion with the sisters he longed to get to know again. He gave his mother constant praise: She was, he wrote her, the "most rare of ladies, none in all my roaming have been so bright, so individual, so stimulating as you. Aren't I a lot like you? Claim it."[69] He told a friend that the family was about to be reunited, and that each of the five Wilder children had "either beauty, brains or goodness; several have two of these attributes; one has all."[70] Who was the one? Most likely Amos, but Thornton didn't say.

Conscious as he was of his own faults and virtues, however, Thornton was clear on another point: His father, he said, was "very much in doubt as to whether to be proud of me for having held a job for three years—I am the ne'er-do-well and black-sheep of a dreamer family—or angry because I am not rich or famous."[71]

15

"MILLSTONES"

I am ground between two millstones of an unsatisfying life and an unsatisfying art.
—THORNTON WILDER TO ISABELLA NIVEN WILDER,
December 2, 1924

New Jersey and New York (1923–1925)

In his midtwenties, Thornton Wilder was working hard to be an independent man, a self-supporting schoolmaster, and a part-time writer—but his self-esteem still turned with the weather vane of his father's approval. After his mother's return from Europe, however, his father looked more positively on Thornton's achievements. "You will not let my observations on your development perturb you; there is much I do not know, especially as to your and mother's gifts and interests," Amos Parker Wilder wrote to his son in September of 1923. "You are doing well now," his father continued, with uncharacteristic praise. "You are a good boy; it is probably that the environment is the super-thing for your unfolding; well-nourished, among good people; responsibility being developed. It is amusing to see how teaching gives one confidence."[1] Thornton bridled at the insinuation that his "good" qualities could be attributed to Lawrenceville rather than to his own nature and efforts.

There was more: Dr. Wilder wanted Thornton to go to graduate school, preferably in English, and thought he should try to get his work published in magazines. Or, as Dr. Wilder put it, "My two ideas you will consider for what they are worth: (1) advanced study preferably in English as your forum & support (2) some prose & poetry offerings to the magazines from time to time to get acquaintance and confidence."[2] When, in the same letter, Dr. Wilder told Thornton that he had recently seen Harry Luce and Briton Hadden, who were flushed with the great success of their *Time* magazine venture, Thornton read reproof between the lines. His aspirations were great, but his achievements so far were modest, greatly exceeded by those of some of his Yale classmates. His own brother had already published a book. Thornton needed no reminder of his lack of success—and being published occasionally in magazines was not going to satisfy him, or, he imagined, his demanding father. He answered with a four-page letter of his own, copying it into his letter book and then ripping out all but remnants of the pages.

Thornton wrote sympathetically to his brother, who was also enduring their father's remonstrations, confessing that there were times when he felt their father's "perpetual and repetitive monologue is trying to swamp my personality, and I get an awful rage. He has wonderful and beautiful qualities, but he has one monstrous sin. Mother, Charlotte, you and I (and lately Isabel) have lived in a kind of torment trying to shake off his octupus-personality."[3] During those years, as Amos approached thirty and Thornton and Charlotte were not far behind, they still grappled with their father's force in their lives. When the trio shared their perspectives on their father, as they often did in letters, Thornton and Charlotte were the rebels and Amos was the conciliator. "I have sometimes felt the queer warps we may have taken from our upbringing," Amos wrote to Charlotte,

> but I am philosophical enough to be sure that life has its powers of transmuting and equalizing all such handicaps by peculiar compensations. Father's influence on us was determined by his parents and so on back. He could not help it. And the good he did us was no doubt far greater than the other. Besides, we haven't the whole story of the family yet. If our lives are not altogether normal, they are at least extraordinarily rich in content, spiritual tact, artistic apprehension, imagination, etc. We have greater conflicts to resolve than most people but we develop thence unusually formidable personalities.[4]

In the fall of 1923 Thornton wrote letters to encourage his mother and his brother as they tried to acclimate to life in New Haven after the years abroad. Amos, Thornton, and Charlotte wanted their mother to be happy in New Haven, and the family, including Aunt Charlotte, agreed that Isabella's comfort would depend on "long-sufferingness on Father's part and peace in the family."[5] Even with young Amos close by, however, Isabella felt lonely and out of place in New Haven. It was an ordeal, she said, just to go out to dinner parties with her family. She dreaded even appearing with the whole family. "Looked at en masse no family appears well," she wrote to Thornton. "Especially the ageing and unfashionable parents. By myself I could perhaps chatter along and hold my own but before your Father and Isabel I am quite dumb and lost. I do not know how to face this light-hearted and busy town. It makes me feel very far away. . . . Do not lose sleep over my trouble. But comfort me somehow."[6]

He did his best. "But don't I know just what you mean!" he responded right away:

> It's the malady of the Wilders; each is better when the others aren't around. Father is ponderous when Amos and I are near; but I enter houses that he has just left and I hear wonders of his wit and nonsense. Hasn't Charlotte insisted a hundred times, almost with tears, that when we are not around she is Madame Recamier?[7] I have even a suspicion that Isabel is more buoyant at those parties where there is no chance of meeting my depreciating eye over the shoulders of the dancers.[8]

He went on to compliment his mother for her wit and charm, comparing her brilliance to that of his other heroine, Mme de Sévigné. He was convinced, he told her, that she had "the purest natural and cultivated talent for living" that he had ever seen. "You have something to talk with that hundreds of restless women have not,—the excellence of your own mind, with its monologue of temperate wise humorous content," he assured her, urging her to laugh at her fears.[9]

Thornton more than anyone else in the family could help Isabella restore her equilibrium. She would not or could not turn to her husband for any kind of comfort, financial or other, and she kept him keenly aware of that deficiency. From boyhood Thornton had been sensitive to his mother's moods and emotional needs, and had done his best to offset them. Now that he was earning his keep, he wanted to give her as much financial comfort as possible, even though Isabella discouraged that, not wanting to deplete his limited resources. He went to great lengths to provide concert tickets for her anonymously, and to supplement her income. Over her protest he made her keep a check, part of which she used, gratefully, to buy "a grand winter coat."[10]

The house their father leased at 96 Bishop Street was in a section of New Haven "which has no other distinction," Thornton wrote to a friend, "than that one carries into it. But wherever my Mother goes she surrounds herself with the same Chinese embroideries and books and delicious tea and personal charm and a troop of original sons and daughters, and calls it a Home."[11] He wished he could give his mother books, every luxury, vacations, a house, security. Maybe someday.

For the time being he was back at Lawrenceville School, busier than ever. Mr. Foresman's father and infant son died in the same week of September, and Foresman underwent complicated oral surgery, so Thornton could not leave the school. Enrollment had risen to more than five hundred boys, so that classes were larger and the faculty workload increased accordingly.[12] When some teachers were fired, Thornton had to step in until new ones were hired, teaching six periods a day. He had a nightmare, "the distant reverberation of a nervous breakdown—in which all night I lecture, lecture, without ceasing, on the pronouns and subjunctive."[13] Nevertheless, he could write to his mother, "I love teaching and have learned a hundred more of its secrets."[14] He scarcely liked the French, he told her, "or their country," but he adored their language and literature, and thoroughly enjoyed teaching French.[15] He still clung to the hope, however, that this would be his last year of teaching.

Thornton's connection to his mother was deeply affectionate, whimsical, and playful. He was coming up to see her, he wrote, and she should get used to the idea of his mustache before he arrived. He "understood some of the most delightful corners in international literature in the light of her personality." On the day after he wrote to scold his father, he wrote to "propose" to his mother: "Madam, I solemnly propose to you: will you be my mother," he teased. "Consider well; this is the most solemn step in a matron's life: are you sure we are compatible? Is my face one that you could endure at a thousand breakfasts? Divorce in this matter is not so easy as it was. Many wretched mothers are tied for life to unseeing sons."[16]

He saw her and the rest of the family as often as he could, inviting them to Lawrenceville or making the trip to New Haven when he had twenty-four hours free. His sisters came for a visit and "left a host of real admirers behind," he told his parents.[17] His weekend duties could be confining, so he had to satisfy his hunger for theater by attending previews of plays in nearby Trenton, which was suddenly "snowed under with try-outs."[18] He kept up with theater in New York by reading newspapers and journals, and stayed in touch with Stark Young and Mrs. Isaacs. Young encouraged Thornton to call on him in New York, but Thornton hesitated. After all, Stark Young kept company with Eleonora Duse and Charlie Chaplin. "You I dare not see," Thornton wrote to Young. "You do not know me if you do not understand my strange reluctance to go and see people who are busily and brilliantly occupied. Me, shy?—but it's true. I tell my Mother she must have punished me at the age of three for intruding and ever since I walk down side alleys."[19] In lieu of a visit he sent Young a long letter full of astute and witty commentary on current theater performances and personnel.

Thornton headed to New Haven for Christmas, stopping en route for what turned out to be a glamorous theater binge in New York. The overworked schoolmaster caught between two millstones stepped briefly into a dazzling parade of theater events. The first night he had dinner with Edith Isaacs and her family overlooking the lake at Central Park, and capped the evening with a three-hour conversation with Stark Young, mainly listening to Young's "extraordinary" anecdotes and verbal portraits of theater luminaries.

Thornton spent the next morning at rehearsals of Zona Gale's new play, *Mr. Pitt*, adapted from her novel *Birth*, and learned that Pirandello was due to arrive in New York the next day to supervise production of his cycle of plays. He had lunch with Stark Young and dinner with the playwright and author of musical comedies Clare Kummer, who invited him to go with her to see her musical comedy, *One Kiss*, adapted from a smash hit in Paris. From the actress Lola Fisher she had received a copy of Thornton's *And the Sea Shall Give Up Its Dead*, and professed to be "bewitched" by it. (Lola Fisher had most likely passed Thornton's script along from her friend William Lyon Phelps, the Yale English professor who was a lifelong friend of the Wilders.) The next day Thornton watched an acting workshop at Boleslavsky's Laboratory Theatre—"one of the most illuminating things" he'd ever seen.[20] As a finale to his enthralling New York adventure, he enjoyed the Theatre Guild production of *The Failures* by Henri Lenormand, directed by Young. "So beautiful, so beautiful," Thornton wrote.[21]

He was in paradise—but it did not seem to occur to him that these luminaries in the theater world could truly enjoy the company of a thin, shy schoolmaster with a dapper mustache, an eager smile, a brilliant mind, and a remarkable knowledge of and gratifying enthusiasm for the theater. All they knew of Thornton Wilder the writer was a handful of very short plays, a few letters, and, in some instances, scattered passages from an unfinished novel. It was Wilder the man they invited to lunch, dinner, rehearsals, workshops, and performances. Unwilling as he was to intrude, Thornton did not even imagine that these impressive people enjoyed his refreshing, exuberant company, and simply liked him for himself. He wrote to a friend afterward that the only fault of his new friends in New York was "their inability to see how unworthy of their lights I am."[22]

SOON IT was back to being the schoolmaster, but Thornton returned to New York briefly, at Edith Isaacs's invitation, to accompany her to a dinner in honor of Mrs. Edward MacDowell of the MacDowell Colony in Peterborough, New Hampshire. Mrs. Isaacs wanted to recommend Thornton for a summer residency at MacDowell, and to introduce her young protégé to Mrs. MacDowell in advance. Bill Benét attended the dinner that night, and introduced Thornton to his wife, the poet Elinor Wylie. Thornton found her "young and pretty and irritable," and soon came to admire her poetry. The British author Rebecca West was there also, seated between the poet Edwin Arlington Robinson and the leading stage designer Norman Bel Geddes. She was dressed in a "sack of deep blue-green," Thornton noted, and her "bright defiant flushed little face touched with an orange rather than a red rouge." He learned that she was traveling with her little girl, supposedly fathered by H. G. Wells, and was known as the "most famous living unmarried mother."[23]

Thornton's glitzy New York life was exhilarating, but his Lawrenceville life wore him "to a frazzle." On top of a rigorous daily schedule he was tutoring and translating to earn extra funds so he could stop teaching. He planned to spend most of his spring break in New Haven, he wrote his mother: "You may nurse me back to serenity." He hadn't heard from his father "since Moses was a pup," and Thornton assumed that his own "badness has at last got the disapproval it deserves." He asked his mother to put his father in a "gracious temper to receive me."[24]

In fact Dr. Wilder was not in the best frame of mind that winter and spring of 1924. The death of his friend and wealthy Yale classmate Edwin McClellan on January 20, 1924, had reminded him of his own mortality—and intensified his worries about earning money in his later years. To augment his income from the newspaper, Wilder still traveled to make speeches—"a sad melee of wholesome sentiment" with "a little patriotic appeal," he wrote to Thornton. He didn't earn much for them, but, he said, "it helps keep my family going in the latter rain—as the days draw nigh when Father's earnings grow less if not quit—and then . . . what will poor tense Mother do then!"[25]

When Dr. Wilder wasn't worrying about money, he was worrying about his grown children. At least Charlotte was nicely settled in Boston, doing well as an editor at *Youth's Companion*, and finishing work on her master's degree at Radcliffe. Janet, now fourteen, still lived under her parents' watchful care in New Haven. She was "horse mad" and caught up in "a stamp collecting craze" and "such an amusing, extraordinary individual!" Isabel, who had always been a homebody, was now living and working in New York. She was happily employed as an assistant to the literary agent Elizabeth Oñativia—and "having quite a lively time." She liked earning her own money, and made enough that spring to repay loans from her mother and from Thornton, and to save thirty dollars, "so I am terribly pleased with myself," she wrote.[26]

Dr. Wilder was not pleased, however. "Isabel is in the great city [New York]," he wrote to Thornton, asking him to keep an eye on his sister.[27] As for Amos, he was "sound and wholesome as a nut—no harm can befall a good man—it is well to give the world such," Dr. Wilder told Thornton. However, he professed certain reservations about his older son, who seemed to hide away with his books and studies when he should be "out slaying lions."[28]

As Dr. Wilder's own physical health deteriorated, a continuation of the long downward spiral generated by the Asian sprue, he worried about Amos's physical health as well as his mental and emotional well-being. He recognized that the war had left its mark on Amos. In France in October and November 1917, Amos had suffered malaria before effective drugs were available to treat and cure the disease. People who contracted certain types of malaria could be susceptible to relapses. Could that be one cause of Amos's occasional malaise, his seeming lack of energy—his failure to be "out slaying lions"? (This would be a lingering worry for the family, as indicated in lines from a letter Isabel wrote in 1925: "I'm afraid he'll never be really strong. The malaria, at least, malarious symptoms, shadow him. In tennis his strength is not equal to a sustained effort. His game is still good, too good for his vitality.")[29]

Once again calling on the Yale network, Dr. Wilder arranged for Amos to be examined by Dr. George Blumer in April 1924. "Sent him to the *best*—ex dean of Yale Medical School," Dr. Wilder scrawled on the back of a letter he received from the distinguished Dr. Blumer.[30] "I just wanted to tell you that I found nothing physically wrong with your son," Dr. Blumer reported after he examined Amos. "He presents a picture which is not unusual in young men who went through the period of the war and whose nervous systems have not yet quite recovered from that experience. I feel sure that ultimately he will come out all right."[31]

Dr. Wilder had his hands full trying to tend to his adult children. Thornton had apparently received—and decided to reject—an offer to teach at Yale. "As for yourself, dear Thornton: I counsel you to hold yourself in check until you have laid permanent foundations and obtained a card of introduction for the rest of your life by teaching at Yale, now the door is opened for at least two years," his father wrote.[32] It is not clear what the offer was, or why Thornton wanted to turn it down, but his father was dismayed, chiding, "We older men know one can do much who has a *Forum* and who is on some pay roll. 'Thornton of Yale' is interesting: and gets you hearers." Dr. Wilder had no faith that his son would "find a foothold in literature or call it what you will. I know you lad, your improvidence; you have kept but little ahead of the wolf even with a king's ransom income as youth goes."[33] However, Dr. Wilder acknowledged that Thornton had loaned him some money that "cleared a situation nicely," and was "a great service."[34]

THORNTON WOULD not go to teach at Yale, but he did hope against hope that the MacDowell residency would come through so that he could spend the summer writing in New Hampshire. William Lyon Phelps wrote a letter of recommendation for Thornton, as did Edith Isaacs and Bill Benét, whom Thornton was now calling Mr. Elinor Wylie as his admiration for her and her poetry grew. The Benéts would be at the MacDowell Colony that summer. "If I could spend a summer near by that tremendous mind I'd die at peace," he told his mother.[35] By late May he had been accepted for residence at the colony for July and August. "I didn't know how badly I wanted it until it was mine," he said. He promised his mother two weeks at the beginning of the summer and three weeks at the end, and "in the interim," he wrote, "I shall write you two of the most beautiful plays you can imagine."[36]

For the first time in his life, free of farms and summer camps and tutoring, Thornton could use most of a summer to write—and, better still, to write in a setting devoted to nurturing writers and artists. The MacDowell Colony, the first artists' colony to be established in the United States, was founded in 1907 by composer Edward MacDowell and his wife, Marian, on their 450-acre farm near Peterborough, New Hampshire. MacDowell, a founder of the American Academy in

Rome, appreciated the stimulation and fellowship that artists from different disciplines could share. Because he found himself inspired and immensely creative at the farm, he believed that other artists could profit by the chance to retreat and work there, surrounded by beautiful forest and meadowland. Rustic private studios scattered throughout the quiet woods provided ideal working conditions, and the artists gathered at night for company. Thornton lived in the men's dormitory with four other bachelors. Artists in residence that summer included, among others, poet Padraic Colum and his wife; Bill Benét and Elinor Wylie; and Tennessee Mitchell Anderson, recently divorced from Sherwood Anderson. She was "a handsome earthy free-speaking woman," Thornton said, who was "the center of Chicago's renaissance of a few years ago."[37] Thornton enjoyed her lively company, and perceived the undertones of sadness and bitterness in her exuberance. He called her "a real flame of mine."[38]

His favorite colonist at MacDowell, however, was the poet Edwin Arlington Robinson. He found Robinson a man of "few graces" and "difficult, austere, an infinitely conscientious workman, as yet little known of the casual public," despite the fact that he had won the Pulitzer Prize. Even though his fame was modest, many people thought of Robinson as "the foremost American poet." Robinson disliked contemporary poets, Thornton discovered that summer, and "would be quite content to finish his life with Shakespeare, Racine and a spare anthology."[39] But the taciturn poet liked the fledgling playwright and novelist enough to invite him to dinner during the Christmas holidays that year.

Thornton grew ever more enchanted with Elinor Wylie, and entrusted sheaves of his playlets to her and her husband, respecting their opinions. He reported to a friend, "I spent part of the Summer with Mrs. Bill Benét II, and singed my thinning wing at the blaze of Elinor Wylie."[40] After the hard work at the farms and summer camp of past years, Thornton was in his element, savoring the company of fellow artists, reading intensely, and turning out creative work, giving more time to his plays than to his novel in progress. He kept a list of the authors he was reading—Jane Austen, H. H. Munro (Saki), Beaumont and Fletcher, Elinor Wylie, Pirandello, E. M. Forster, Molière, Sherwood Anderson, Cocteau, Proust, Maurois, and Thomas Mann, among others. He looked forward to reading Amy Lowell's biography of Keats and Vincent d'Indy's book on César Franck. He told a friend, "I never cry for fiction (save when I'm composing it) but I weep myself ill over biography."[41] He kept working on the Roman portraits, and by mid-August was halfway through his play alternately entitled *Geraldine de Vere* and *Geraldine de Gray*. He had also assembled the book of collected writings that he hoped Norman Fitts would publish, with Thornton's subsidy. Its table of contents included ten three-minute playlets, three "Fables and Tirades," and five "Roman Portraits."

When he was not writing and socializing, Thornton was behaving as the model guest. "I think, dear Madam, I must have been well brought up," he wrote to his mother August 14. "How do you explain that I am the servants' favorite? I never arrive late at meals; I keep my room so that it has no terrors for the lady cleaning up; I am prompt about laundry; I can be trusted to close doors and windows & to turn out lights." He occasionally lit the boiler, kept it in wood and coal, and "actually worked a couple of hours stacking a woodpile today."[42] He hoped he would be invited back to the colony again.

BY MID-SEPTEMBER he was back in Davis House at Lawrenceville, with classes that were too large and duties that were too heavy, a schedule that put an end to the immersion in writing that had been a boon in Peterborough. He was excited to hear that "one of the best friends I have in the world, *Lauro de Bosis* of Rome," would be coming to the United States to lecture on Italian literature for seven months— a lecture tour that was so successful that he would be invited to lecture at Harvard, as well as to repeat the tour for several years.

Otherwise Thornton was "ground between two millstones," dissatisfied with both his life and his art. He was constantly worn down by the "daily threat," and the "wonder as to next year." He was "hankering after being recognized," and discouraged by "the indifference of a certain person I like!" (He did not provide any details about the "certain person"—or the where, when, or why.) He was anxious about his writings—"shame that I don't take more pains, that they aren't better and more numerous and that I don't think out the long ones carefully enough." But he was thankful, he wrote to his mother, that God, with all the "endless powers of invention and variety," had found for him "the astoundingly right family."[43]

BY 1925 Amos Parker Wilder was pleased and proud that two members of the Wilder family had earned advanced degrees—Amos, who had received his B.D. at Yale Divinity School in 1924, and Charlotte at Radcliffe, where she received an M.A. in English in 1925. In addition Isabel was about to enter the newly established three-year certificate program in the Department of Drama at the Yale School of Fine Arts, founded in 1924 with a million-dollar gift from Edward S. Harkness. The program was directed by renowned teacher of playwriting George Pierce Baker, wooed away to Yale from Harvard. Baker had trained or mentored such playwrights as Edward Sheldon and Eugene O'Neill.[44] Dr. Wilder knew his own Ph.D. had been helpful during his long, variegated professional life, and he was convinced that a graduate degree was a necessary credential as well as a dependable fallback for his brilliant children. He was determined that Thornton should go on for a master's degree.

Despite his longing for a life in New York, Thornton understood that his father was in dead earnest about "fallbacks." Dr. Wilder had preached to his children about fallback plans for years. Inexorably the plans began to take shape for Thornton to earn a graduate degree—but he still confided to Isabel and others his private hopes. He told a friend in January 1925 that he and Isabel were going to "rent an apartment in a bad neighborhood somewhere" and do freelance writing.[45]

Nevertheless, on January 16, 1925, Thornton wrote a letter of resignation to Lawrenceville headmaster Mather Abbott, explaining that he planned to go to graduate school, and notified his father that his bridges were "burned at Lawrenceville."[46] To his surprise, after his resignation, Thornton felt some regrets about giving up teaching—and at not having done a better job of it—but he could see more clearly the shortcomings in the school administration that rankled him. He would miss many of the boys, as well as the Foresmans, who had been like family to him. But it was time to leave, and he was determined to make the most of his freedom. It dawned on him that when he went to Princeton to work on the M.A.—in French rather than English—he was going to have much more time to write fiction and drama.

He wrote to Mrs. Isaacs about his plans for graduate school and the "secret writing" he hoped to do, reflecting that he was not going to "plunge into intensive literary life" until he could feel sure that his efforts would not be "full of odd rushes, superlatives, meaningless excitements and ridiculous adverbs."[47] Thornton shared his news with Edwin Arlington Robinson: "I'm leaving teaching and going to the Princeton Grad. College for an M. A. in Old French and the leisure for surreptitious masterpieces."[48]

Unknown to Thornton, his Princeton acceptance was granted with minimal enthusiasm: "Teaching French in Lawrenceville—seems a fair but not brilliant case," someone typed on Thornton's official record.[49] When she heard of Thornton's acceptance, Isabel was disappointed, but he tried to reassure her: "Don't jump to the conclusion that our retreat next year is off." He told Isabel that "all that can be said for Princeton is that of all the plans it's the cheapest & safest. If I go there it will be because I shall have had to *fall back upon it*."[50]

Graduate school acceptance in hand, Thornton was soon alight with high hopes about writing. In the absence of her regular drama critic, John Mason Brown, Edith Isaacs offered Thornton the chance to write the annual roundup of winter openings of new plays for *Theatre Arts Monthly*, a major publication in the drama world from 1916 until it ceased publication in 1964. Alternately thrilled at the assignment and afraid that he would fail, Thornton saw nineteen plays in New York, and then worried and worked over his article—"The Turn of the Year," published in *Theatre Arts Monthly* in March 1925.[51] He feared that the piece was too long at 2,500 words, and urged Mrs. Isaacs to cut and edit it as she saw fit. "If it turns out to be longer than most," he wrote to her, "please compress any payment down to the average without regard to the number of words." He was "proud and happy to have done it at all," and hoped the review would not disappoint.[52] "The article is really very good indeed," she replied, and she was "immensely pleased."[53]

Thornton's long, self-directed apprenticeship in the theater amply prepared him to write the review. He had a near-photographic memory where theater was concerned. His wide-ranging knowledge of dramaturgy and his years of sitting attentively in theater audiences equipped him to roam a spacious landscape, from classics to contemporary plays, and to offer informed views of the success or failure of the writing, the acting, the scenery, the direction, even the adaptations or translations. He could be witty and acerbic: He noted after one play, given in translation, that he "came away thinking of how rare and eloquent it would have seemed, if one had only been deaf."[54] He gave special praise to the actress Ruth Gordon (who would later become one of his closest friends) for forcing the audience "to breathless attention" despite her minor role in Philip Barry's *The Youngest*, which Thornton gave a mixed review.[55] His crisply written, candid, and authoritative article garnered good reviews itself, and introduced his name and credentials to a large, informed theater audience.

He was now working industriously to get his own plays and fiction out into the world as well. He was forging ahead with *Geraldine de Gray*, planning to send it out to directors at two theater groups who had asked to see it. Most promisingly of all, however, there was some interest in his novel. The overture came from his Yale classmate Lewis Baer, who had been impressed with Thornton's stories in their college days. Since graduation, Baer had worked at the *New York World*, and then in the advertising and publicity departments at Alfred A. Knopf, Inc. In 1924 he joined Albert & Charles Boni, Inc., a new publishing company founded by brothers Albert and Charles Boni in 1923, becoming secretary and treasurer of the firm.[56]

Albert Boni, previously of Boni & Liveright, brought significant publishing experience as well as a literary sensibility to his work, and would directly or indirectly launch some innovative publishing ventures. He had owned the Washington Square Bookshop in New York, and founded the Little Leather Library, publishing short versions of classics in a small, inexpensive format, and marketing them through Woolworth's stores. In 1917 he had sold his shop and gone into the publishing business full-time with Horace Liveright. The Boni & Liveright Publishing Company initiated the popular Modern Library of the World's Best Classics series. (One of their best salesmen was Bennett Cerf, who eventually bought the series, and went on to found Random House.) From the outset of their new publishing venture Albert and Charles Boni sought to publish contemporary authors. Their edgy list included Colette, Proust, D. H. Lawrence, Upton Sinclair, Leon Trotsky—and soon, Thornton Wilder.

When Baer approached Thornton about whether he had a book in progress, Thornton sent him a draft of the Roman memoirs. He waited half in excitement, half in dread, to hear what Baer would have to say. Biding his time as long as he could stand to, Thornton wrote to Baer in February to inquire about the manuscript, convinced that the Boni firm would turn it down.[57] Two weeks later came a heartening letter from Baer. He and the Bonis had "cleared away some of the piles" of manuscripts on their desks for the spring season, and had managed at last to read Thornton's manuscript—the first book of the Roman memoirs. "I am more than delighted to report that we are all crazy about it," Baer wrote. "Albert Boni feels so strongly about your style that he is very anxious to see more." He asked Thornton to send along more of the manuscript, as well as anything else he wanted them to see. "I do hope we will be able to get together a book which can mean the start of your career as an author (in print! I mean). No one would be happier than I."[58]

Elated, Thornton was "all a-whirr with the news that the Boni Brothers are most enthusiastic about the fragment of the Roman Memoirs." He was "hurriedly patching up" additional material to send to New York.[59] Now he was on fire to submit all his work for publication, but because he had the bad habit of sometimes entrusting his only copies of drafts to other people, he had to round up manuscripts to send. Bill Benét and Elinor Wylie had one folder, he thought, and Mrs. Isaacs had a gray folder of manuscripts that he needed back, he told her.

By mid-March he was working feverishly on the Roman memoirs so that he could send another segment to the Bonis. He was now calling the book *Marcantonio*, after one of the principal characters.

Slowly but steadily his work was being recognized, even sought after. He kept a rough list of his appearances in print: He had published "many plays and one essay" in the Oberlin College literary magazine, "many plays and two book reviews" in the Yale *Lit*, "seven or eight dramatic criticisms and one play [*Centaurs: A Footnote to Ibsen*]" in the *Boston Transcript*, and "many plays, sketches, etc." in *S4N*. His sonnet "Measure for Measure" had been included in *The Book of Yale Under-graduate Verse*, and he had been published in the *Double Dealer* and *Theatre Arts Monthly*.[60] Now there might actually be a book in the offing.

Thornton wrote to his good friend Bill Bissell, "Life's begun."[61]

PLEASED AS he was at the prospect of having his novel published, Thornton was still eager to concentrate on his plays. Thanks to his success at *Theatre Arts Monthly*, Thornton was invited to give a talk at Goucher College in Baltimore on the next ten years of American the-ater. He did not charge a fee because "the experience is valuable enough for me in that it will teach me further how to find my tongue."[62] All he asked for was a place to stay overnight. This event could be seen, in retrospect, as the launch of his career as a lecturer.

Despite his hectic schedule Thornton managed by mid-April, on the eve of his twenty-eighth birthday, to finish part 2 of *Marcantonio*. Because he hated the mechanics of preparing a manuscript, he hired a typist, and as soon as he had the manuscript typed and bound, he mailed it to New York. "There will be a good deal to recast if they decide to publish," he wrote to his mother, "but on the whole I can say that this thing which I began in Paris and which has dragged on behind me ever since is done tonight."[63]

As much as Thornton wanted to concentrate on his plays, the novel dominated his literary work that spring. He thought he must clearly indicate that *Marcantonio* was the first volume of a larger series called *Notes of a Roman Student*. His vision of the structure of his book was, in a significant way, Proustian: Marcel Proust's *In Search of Lost Time* included seven volumes.[64] Thornton envisioned his book on a far more modest scale, and was writing with greater economy, but the concept of related volumes was similar. His book as a whole would be constructed of a series of "novelettes that flow, so to speak, from the personality of each one of the demigods" who were emerging as central characters—Alix d'Espoli, the Cardinal, Marcantonio, Elizabeth Grier, and Astrée-Luce.[65] His reading of Proust also liberated Thornton to break away from linear time, and to explore such dark subjects as incest and suicide. He felt free as well to experiment with irony, comedy, and farce. He told Baer that he believed that the second part of his novel needed "more craziness, more high preposterous impudence, perhaps even some freaks of pagination and some grotesque interruptions. The thing is not to be mistaken for an Edith Wharton."[66]

Thornton worked out a narrative structure to which he would return again in fiction—a series of loosely connected "portraits" with enough interaction between characters to be welded together in a novel, but enough independence to stand alone, if need be. As it turned out, his first novel, finally titled *The Cabala*, and his last novel, *Theophilus North*, would be remarkably similar in their reliance on this device.

Word came back from Boni that the novel needed revision—more development, more clarity in certain sections, better proportion. Disappointed as he was, Thornton agreed with these assessments, although he estimated it would take him two years to accomplish some of the revisions and the additional writing. "As to the close of *Marcantonio*," he wrote, "I now see that by dint of trying to be arch and elliptical I have merely been ununderstandable. The boy suddenly discovers that his hatred of his half-sister is another disguise of passion. He gratifies it and with the revulsion that comes toward morning kills himself in the garden."[67]

A letter from Baer clarified what the Bonis expected, and Thornton wrote back that he had "resolved to write the rest for you," and had already begun, although he still longed to get back to work on his plays.[68] He and Baer began to talk about a possible edition of Thornton's playlets, which "morally," Thornton said, he owed to Norman

Fitts of *S4N*. But Fitts was gravely ill. Thornton proposed to send the playlets to Baer and, if Fitts, recovered, to offer him his full-length plays instead. Thornton and Baer also began to talk about the contract with the Bonis for the novel.[69]

THORNTON THE writer paced the Davis House floor after lights-out, or sat at his desk or on the foot of his bed, wrestling with his Roman portraits, stealing time as he could to work on his plays.[70] "I am still on Alix d'Esp's story. I hope it will move some people as it does me," he wrote to his mother.[71] Meanwhile Thornton the schoolmaster worked in a frenzy to finish his term at Lawrenceville and prepare to move himself and his few earthly possessions to nearby Princeton in the fall. And there was the summer job awaiting him in New Hampshire.

Before he left Lawrenceville, Thornton found himself the inadvertent star of a real-life comedy. The daughter of the man who owned the local soda fountain shyly approached "Dr. Wilder," as she called him, asking him to come to the local firehouse where members of the Village Congregational Church were rehearsing a play, *The Adventures of Grandpa*. They hoped that the newly famous drama critic from *Theatre Arts Monthly* would give them "a little advice." Thornton obliged, listening to the rehearsal, and telling "the Irish policeman and the heavy-comic Swedish maid not to turn their backs on an audience, to learn their lines, and to speak up." He attended two more rehearsals before the performance. When local newspapers reported that "Professor and Doctor Thornton Wilder" was directing the play, people who knew him bought tickets to the production, expecting something far more erudite than *The Adventures of Grandpa* was meant to offer. "Any suspicion of mortification however was appeased," Thornton said, "when I discovered that the little group was presenting me with a fountain-pen heavy with gold."[72]

16

"THE 'WAY WITHIN'"

*I don't know when or how or where I shall go. . . . My urge to go comes from
way within and the "way within" knows just what it is doing.*
—THORNTON WILDER TO AMY WERTHEIMER,
February 7, 1926

New Jersey and New Hampshire (1925–1926)

During his last month at Lawrenceville in 1925, Thornton was
thinking deeply about James Joyce's *Ulysses*, a novel he had just
finished, and one that he idolized.[1] While he was reading this
revolutionary book, Thornton reflected, he was "a little staggered by
its audacities," but that all had "merged into vast admiration." As he
analyzed the craftsmanship in Joyce's novel, he was struck most of all
by the book's "architectural plan." "Did you know," Thornton wrote
to musician Bruce Simonds, one of his Yale friends, "that each of its
inner chapters had not only its counterpart in Homer, but its own
colour; its presiding virtue, in the scholastic sense, and its complemen-
tary vice; and its own element?" (After he read this Thornton made a
fleeting attempt to identify the colors of his own chapters in progress.)
He went on to say that because Joyce had taken such good care of the
novel's form, he could afford

> to pack it with a million odd details, a writer's love for mere Shop, crazy
> whims, parading of scores of authors, rare old Anglo-Saxon words.
> Leopold Bloom turns on a faucet and we get a page from the encylop. on
> water; a 20-page conversation in a library about Shakespeare's private
> life; a screaming climax of all the most horrible thoughts one could
> entertain about death.[2]

These were matters to ponder as Thornton tried to finish his own novel. In his early years of work on the book he had characterized his imaginary memoirs as "formal portraits" with occasional commentary "dropped into [the] current, told by some character, like Canterbury pilgrims."[3] Now if he could, like Joyce, discover a clear, organic form—the solid "architectural plan" for his book—perhaps he could give his imagination freer rein and indulge himself in the "million odd details" that filled his mind and memory—the "writer's love for mere Shop. . . ."[4]

He took a summer job tutoring boys at Ira Williams's tutoring camp at Lake Sunapee, New Hampshire, just outside the village of Newbury. Williams was a math teacher at Lawrenceville, and many of Thornton's charges were Lawrenceville students preparing for college entrance examinations or making up academic deficiencies. "I tutor painfully all morning," Thornton wrote from Lake Sunapee to a friend—"good meals, distance swims in the afternoon, my belated athleticism; in the evenings, solitaire, movies or dancing at the Granliden," the resort hotel that sprawled comfortably on the western shore of Gardner Bay near Newbury.[5] Built in 1905, the hotel was noted for its modern conveniences, its excellent food, and its almost nightly dances. Handsome bachelors such as Thornton Wilder were encouraged to come to the dances, and numerous romances allegedly began on the polished Granliden dance floor or in the shadows on the spacious lawns surrounding the hotel.

"Let me describe some diversions of wistful bachelors," Thornton wrote to his mother.[6] He did the foxtrot with a beautician from New York, and danced with a medical illustrator from Maryland and a New York clothing designer who looked "exactly like Katharine Cornell."[7] In addition to waltzing and foxtrotting with unattached young ladies, Thornton found himself a popular dinner guest at various summerhouses around the lake, especially among the wives whose husbands, preoccupied in their offices in Boston, New York, or elsewhere, were in attendance only on weekends. One of the "merry wives," as Thornton called them, would become his lifelong friend. He wrote to his mother about Amy Weil Wertheimer, age thirty-five, describing her as a "proud sad Jewess with literary yearnings."[8] She was immediately drawn to Thornton and profoundly interested in his writing projects. She began inviting him to dinner and to social events, and showering him with gifts and letters. He found her attractive, stimulating, and—perhaps to his comfort—already married and therefore unavailable. They discovered an affinity of mind and interests and began a correspondence that lasted until her death in 1971.

Amy was infatuated with Thornton from the first, and soon fell in love with him. Aware of this, he wrote tactfully and whimsically—but candidly—about what he needed from her: "I'm looking for a wise intelligent and fairly tranquil friend. I should like it to be a lady, somewhat older than myself who will understand me so well (so humorously and with a touch of superiority) that I can write her conceitedly and she will understand that that's only my way . . . tragically, and that that's my nerves." He assured her that he would write her "long and frank" letters, however infrequent, about his life and work.[9] But he tried to establish the parameters of their relationship: He wanted to be sure that she too had "suffered at some time or other, and has come through," he wrote, as that would "constitute a bond, for enthusiastic carefree Thornton had an awful experience in Europe that left him so marred with woe that it is unimaginable that he will ever love again."[10] (The details of that heartbreak in Europe have never come to light, but, as will be seen several times in his letters, journal entries, and early fiction, he alluded to it and to at least one other disillusioning romance .)

Thornton tried to catch up on his letter writing that summer. He was carrying on a "clandestine correspondence," he teased Amy, with the beautiful blond aspiring actress Rosemary Ames, nineteen, whom he had met when she attended a prom at Lawrenceville School, a houseguest of Mather Abbott and his wife.[11] Rosemary was the daughter of Knowlton Lyman "Snake" Ames, a wealthy Chicago businessman.[12] When Thornton met Rosemary, nine years his junior, she told him that her family was not enthusiastic about her desire to become an actress, and she sought his advice. After all, he was a published theater critic, and he told her he was "going into criticism for earnest next year" and

might be of use to her as she assailed "the citadels of—ah—stardom."
He cautioned her, however, not to break her family's heart "unless you
feel you have a real vocation for real high stormy art. It's not worth
leaving a happy even home life to be merely an adequate average Broadway actress. A great actress or a great lady in daily life; but nothing in
between is good enough for you."[13]

Caught up in his summer social life and his correspondence—and
juggling the affections of at least two women—Thornton was neglecting his writing. "My conscience hurts me hourly for not writing on my
Memoirs—especially as I have at last found the subject for the third
and last nouvelle," Thornton wrote to a friend from Lake Sunapee.[14]
Despite the fact that he could "see the whole thing quite clearly," he
was having trouble with part 3.[15] But he was also working on a play,
and could report that he "suddenly finished the Second Act of Geraldine de Gray the other day, the obstinate, the insoluble Second Act. It
finished with unexpected simplicity and I begin to see the mists rising
from the Third."[16]

The author was also considering options for his professional name.
How should he sign his work? T. N. Wilder? Thornton Wilder? Thornton N. Wilder? Thornton Niven Wilder? That would be it, he decided,
writing to Amy Wertheimer, "The Niven is going to stay."[17]

———

THORNTON AND Amos paid a late-summer visit to the Wilders in
residence at their new address, 75 Mansfield Street in New Haven. "We
moved for more rooms and it is luxury indeed," Isabel had written
about the family's new home:

> Sun and light too. We have the second and third floors of a double
> house and the use of the garden. It had been redecorated and I think
> we shall be comfortable. It's more decent than we've been in years and
> years and years. With a heavy sigh I resigned all my jobs and I am
> taking Prof. George Baker's new Drama Course that Yale grabbed
> from Harvard. I'm lucky to get in. . . . It seemed best for me to stay
> home. This house is more than Mother can manage alone so the course

will be some compensation. . . . However I'll have a chance to take the
play-writing course too, and it's a venture. My heart isn't quite in it
yet, but expects to be.[18]

Amos, meanwhile, hoped to settle down and become a minister. He
had recently enjoyed nearly a year abroad as a traveling tutor and com-
panion for two teenagers, a job that took him to Egypt, the Holy Land,
Russia, India, and elsewhere. Dr. Wilder proudly published many of
Amos's letters home in the *New Haven Courier-Journal*. Back in New
Haven, Amos applied for two pastorates, including one at the First
Church of Christ (Congregational) in North Conway, New Hampshire.
He waited anxiously for the outcome, even though he knew his credentials were strong: He had studied theology in Europe, had done
some occasional preaching there, had received his Bachelor of Divinity
degree cum laude at the Yale Divinity School in 1924, and had been
ordained in the Congregational ministry in 1926.[19]

As usual Dr. Wilder was hovering, intensifying Amos's worries
about what lay ahead, "taking the matter foolishly (so desperately
hard)" that he added to Amos's stress. Thornton offered Amos his encouragement and support: "You must not let the deliberations of these
committees worry you. I'm now sure that you're not meant to be a
preacher at all; I've been rereading your poems. Now I think that some
passages in them are so fine that writing more should be your only business." Thornton urged his brother to spend six months with the family
on Mansfield Street in New Haven, and write full-time. "Anyway," he
concluded, "don't you be afraid of anything on earth. You have the
goods."[20]

According to Isabel, Janet, now sixteen, was "an original girl"—
"lean and lanky" and "stubborn, Oh!" Just entering high school, older
than her fellow students because the family's constant travels had
thrown her behind academically, Janet still loved horses, and had a new
hobby—raising chickens, four "pedigreed hens." Her ambition, which
surely pleased her father, was to go to an agricultural college and then
to run a farm.[21] Charlotte, her M.A. safely on her résumé, was working as "private secretary/daughter-in-the-house" for Mrs. J. Malcolm

Forbes, the widow of a wealthy Boston businessman and sportsman noted for his avid interest in racing yachts and breeding horses. Isabel thought the change from "third floor backs and everlasting female colleges" had done Charlotte "a world of good." She had been "so desperately poor for two years," Isabel wrote. "To take this job she had to get a nice wardrobe so she borrowed and did so and good food and no cares have done worlds for her."[22] Charlotte hoped to move to New York to take over Isabel's job at the literary agency, and to sell the "junior stories" she had been writing, all in support of her serious work as a poet.

Thornton was headed to Princeton to work on his graduate degree, while Amos still awaited news of his fate. In the fall of 1925 he accepted his first pastorate, as minister of the First Church of Christ (Congregational) in North Conway.[23] With Amos and Charlotte gainfully employed, and Thornton on his way to Princeton, Dr. Wilder now concentrated his attention on Isabel. He was not pleased that she would be studying drama. "At present struggling with Father has left me flattened," she wrote. "He considers the theatre an agent of evil and degeneration, etc. . . . How can I let him crush every atom of enthusiasm and interest I have [?]"[24]

Like Amos, Thornton, and Charlotte, Isabel was eager to get away from New Haven and home. She was saving her money so she could go back to England, as far away as possible.

"THIS PLACE is too good to be true," Thornton wrote from Princeton in the fall of 1925. "It may be spoiled by my having to work a little; they've signed me up for a course called Historical Grammar that makes my head sweat to write it down."[25] Despite the often tedious work his classes required—the work was "very hard and dry-as-dust," Thornton complained—he could spend far more time writing than was possible at Lawrenceville.[26] By November, Thornton Wilder the writer had superseded Thornton Wilder the graduate student.

At twenty-eight he had been writing seriously for nearly half his life, and at last he could call himself a professional novelist and playwright, thanks to good fortune on two fronts: The Boni brothers definitely wanted to publish his first novel and drew up a contract, and Richard Boleslavsky chose his *Geraldine de Gray* as one of four plays for the 1926–27 repertory season at the American Laboratory Theatre. This was unexpected good news, as Thornton had sent the newly finished play to Boleslavsky at the end of October, not expecting him to select it for production but hoping it would at least interest him in reading other plays in the future.[27] "He sent me the reports of the playreading committee," Thornton wrote to Amy on November 23. "They all conceded that it was good construction and [an] interesting subject, but asserted that it had *no literary value*. The sauce of them! That's almost as bad as my French professor who announced to me at the close of my analysis of an old sonnet that *I had no imagination*."[28]

Still Thornton was elated—and then very quickly inundated with work preparing the novel manuscript for publication and revising the play for production. He was especially eager to get the novel off his hands. "I long to be free of it; it's become a fretting burden," he wrote.[29] In his view it was a cluster of intertwined "novelettes," or books.[30] That fall he was wrestling with book 4, which would be entitled "Astrée-Luce and the Cardinal," although, as the manuscript was taking shape, the woman Astrée-Luce was called Mlle de Homodarmes.[31] He had written enough of book 4 to send it along for his mother's review. "I am very unhappy about the middle of it," he wrote to her.

> The more I look at the whole thing the more I see it as a bundle of notes that I should work over for months yet. But I must hurry. "It will have to do." I never thought I should have to say that of anything of mine, but I am frantic to finish this five-year thing and get back to my plays.[32]

When Boleslavsky offered 10 percent of gross receipts, and asked for extensive revisions to *Geraldine de Gray*, Thornton promised to do all he could to make his play succeed.[33] His melodrama, set "at the edge of Woodsville, Indiana," in 1872, stars Geraldine de Gray, a governess, beautiful and pure, who falls in love—like Jane Eyre—with the brooding master of the house, father of the little girl whom Geraldine is hired to tutor. Wilder explained to Boleslavsky, "My hope in casting the play into the form of a burlesque on dime novels was, partly, to see if I couldn't somehow force an eloquence out of the funny old romantic diction." But he had such confidence in Boleslavsky's "judgment and experience" that he would "gladly accede to any alterations" needed.[34] Thornton worked hard on the revisions in December, including re-writing the opening of the play. He was also touching up *Exile* and re-working a comedy he called *The Pilgrims*, planning, with Edith Isaacs's encouragement, to submit both full-length plays for Boleslavsky's con-sideration, along with *The Trumpet Shall Sound*, the four-act play he had composed at Yale.

Boleslavsky was a crucial link in the chain of theater history—firmly connected to Konstantin Stanislavsky, who had collaborated with Tolstoy and Chekhov in the nineteenth century, and who intro-duced new theories and methods of acting early in the twentieth cen-tury that would still resonate in the twenty-first. Born in Poland in 1889 and educated in Russia, Boleslavsky had been schooled in Stan-islavsky's famous Moscow Art Theatre, beginning in 1906. Boleslavsky starred in Moscow Art Theatre productions around the world, and his effectiveness as an actor, teacher, and director led him to be named director of the First Studio of the Moscow Art Theatre. After the Rus-sian Revolution in 1917, Boleslavsky returned to Poland, taught and di-rected in Germany, and by 1922 was living in the United States, where he founded the American Laboratory Theatre in 1923. "The Lab," as it came to be known, rigorously trained a repertory company of actors to perform classical as well as new, experimental plays. Boleslavsky was a gifted teacher who transmitted Stanislavsky's philosophy in Europe and the United States, and enhanced it with his own theories, articu-lated in the book Edith Isaacs would publish for him—*Acting: The First Six Lessons* (1933).

Thornton was surprised and "very proud and happy" when he heard the good news from Boleslavsky about *Geraldine de Gray*, al-though Boleslavsky soon changed his mind and decided instead to pro-duce *The Trumpet Shall Sound*. This was the first big break for Wilder the dramatist. The play would have an audience in New York—off

Broadway, but even so, a significant launching ground for a new play-wright.

As he migrated from novels to plays to French grammar that fall, Thornton kept "groping about for the subject of a new play," he wrote to Amy. "There are beautiful walks these days along the Raritan canal," he told her,

> *and almost every day (and twice a day) I push my feet before me among*
> *the leaves, constructing a whole new play every day from old germs*
> *of plots, and then discarding it when the excitement has ebbed. . . .*
> *Anyway, I'm hunting for my next play a happy subject and to fit myself*
> *for it I am running every morning at seven, renouncing cigarettes,*
> *avoiding artistic people, speaking slowly, refraining from frowns and*
> *trying to be good. Surely those charms cannot fail to work.*[35]

When he wasn't writing, running, or studying, he was going to the theater. That fall he was "thoroly [sic] excited" by Pirandello's *Six Characters in Search of an Author*, which he had first seen in Rome; Chekhov's *The Cherry Orchard*; Ibsen's *The Wild Duck*; and Aristophanes' *Lysistrata*, among others.[36] He found occasional escape in a longtime hobby—one he had enjoyed for years—collecting the records of German repertory theater. "I can hardly wait until the Univ. Library receives its weekly batch of foreign newspapers. I tear open the great Zeitung and fill out a diagram," he wrote to Amy. In red ink he charted openings of plays; in pencil he jotted down dates of the season's performances.[37] His new indulgence was movies. "I am a movie-goer and very enthusiastic," he wrote to his mother, encouraging her to see "Griffith's *Sally of the Sawdust* (you mustn't miss that), Lubitsch's *Kiss Me Again* and *The Gold Rush*."[38]

ON NOVEMBER 19, 1925, Thornton put his signature on his first publishing contract, for the novel he called *The Caballa* (at first using the preferred spelling of the *Concise Oxford English Dictionary*), and then changed to *The Cabala*. The Boni brothers scheduled the book for publication in the spring of 1926 by their firm, Albert & Charles Boni, Inc. "Tonight I am signing a heavy legal contract for the publication of my novel," he wrote to Rosemary Ames.[39] Despite his sensitivity over their age difference he had accepted her invitation to a dance later in November, and in spare moments, he teased, he was brushing up on his "polka and schottische," telling her to "hope for the best."[40]

A month later he wrote to congratulate his brother, who was preparing to preach his first sermon to his own congregation in North Conway. Like most siblings the Wilders were grateful for those moments when a brother or sister deflected parental concern, giving even a brief respite from their father's hovering. "I am happy that in spite of Father's 5 months of hysterical, fainting in coils on the hearthrug every time you got a letter and other demonstrations, all is well," Thornton told Amos. "He has now devoted his anguished attentions to minute brooding over Isabel's dramatic callers and the clauses in my publisher's contract."[41]

The brothers, especially Amos, did some hovering of their own over their sister Charlotte that year. She had proved herself a brilliant student at Mount Holyoke and at Radcliffe. She was a good editor, and would prove to be an effective teacher. But most of all she wanted to write. However, Charlotte increasingly felt the stress of her own self-imposed mission: to earn enough money so she could live on her own and write. She was constantly writing poetry, and Thornton had recognized and encouraged her gifts early on. He told their mother, "If she keeps on right she may discover herself as something of a very high order, that will scatter our magazine poetesses as a hawk does the hens."[42] Charlotte confided in Amos the worrisome news that she had discovered that the stimulating lectures and concerts she had always enjoyed now "really churned me up and gave way to periods of depression. I was being over-stimulated all the time. I could hear a rattling in my head when my thoughts, like rats, scuttled about."[43]

She was twenty-seven years old, more of a loner than any of her siblings, and most likely facing a more difficult struggle for independence than her two brothers because she was a woman, and, furthermore, a woman who longed to be a writer. Her struggle was intensified because she was beginning to suffer bouts of what would eventually become chronic depression. Charlotte tried her best in 1925 to ward off her melancholy and the "rattling" in her head by avoiding two pleasures she prized—the intellectual engagement of lectures and the emotional comfort of music.

———

THORNTON ENDURED an "awful crisis" during the Christmas holidays in 1925, and unrequited love was the crux of it. Only cryptic details of the experience survive in a few enigmatic letters and, almost a year later, in a startling entry in his journal. He first shared some of the experience in early January 1926 in a letter to Amy:

> *Just when I'd made the resolution to never think about anything else for the rest of my probably brief life than goodness and art. Yes, madam, I had an awful crisis over Xmas. You remember when I met you I let escape that I was coming to discover that Life slapped me sharply when I ventured outside those two pathways?*
>
> *Well, that was no pose. At last I resolved to do of my own free will what circumstances would presently force me to do anyway. And I killed myself. I am no longer a person. I am a heart and a pen. I have no brain. I have no body. I have no pride (oh what an amputation was there!) I have no fear (wish that were true!) There is something of all this in the Epilogue to The Cabala. Je n'existe plus.*[44]

Amy wrote back immediately, full of concern. "My dear Amy," Thornton replied, "I just meant I was awfully upset. It has nothing to do with you. I am in the middle of a kind of nervous breakdown." He wanted to run away to Florida or somewhere, he told her. He hated his work, dreaded his exams at Princeton, couldn't sleep, couldn't find the time to write. "How naughty of you to get so excited over mere phrasing," he scolded her, seeming to rationalize. "*To Kill oneself* in that sense, is a sort of religious idiom for shaking off one's old laziness and trying again. I'd quote you *its loci classici* [he used double underscores] only it would look like lecturing."[45] But Thornton's distress seemed to anxious Amy to be more than mere phrasing. She offered him comfort and affection.

"There is no affection in the world that I would be stupid enough to refuse," he answered.

> *All life is made possible by it. You have so much of mine. But the only kind I am ready for now is a clear serene understanding affection. When I see among my friends the kind that is touched with suffering I understand, but I draw back. I loved with all the exaggeration one can imagine; but I was not only not loved so in return. I was laughed at. The cleverest humiliations were set for me. And for a long time I am going to be the most cautious the most distrustful (of myself) man in the world. Again you find further hints of this in the Memoirs, most indirectly stated.*[46]

No trail of clues or facts leads to the identity of the person who failed to love Thornton in return, who "cleverly" humiliated him in 1925, and who wounded him so deeply. The impact was profound and enduring, however, leaving him by his own admission extremely cautious and doubtful about relationships, stripped down to "a heart and a pen." Regardless of the identity or the circumstances, Thornton responded by deliberately "killing" within himself the propensity to love with "exaggeration"—to idealize, to trust, to connect intimately with another person.

The experience continued to haunt him, and to be transmuted into his literary work, as his 1926 journal and certain letters reveal. These passages open a window on his innermost life and the often-shrouded revelation of self in his work. Months after his letter so alarmed Amy Wertheimer, he wrote in his journal about his intention in his first two novels—a passage that appears to have been wrung onto the page, if words scratched out are any indication. In that journal entry he resurrected words he had written to Amy in January 1926:

The Cabala was written because I brooded about great natures and their obstacles and ailments and frustrations. *The Bridge* was written because I wanted to die and I wanted to prove that death was a happy solution. The motto of *The Bridge* is to be found in the last page of *The Cabala:* Hurry and die!

In *The Cabala* I began to think that love is enough to reconcile one to the difficulty of living (i.e. the difficulty of being good); in *The Bridge* I am still a little surer. Perhaps someday I can write a book announcing that love is sufficient.[47]

The interval of a few months had at least restored in him a little hope that love might be someday be "sufficient" to "reconcile one to the difficulty of living," and Thornton began to embed in his fiction allusions to his "most secret life." In a letter to Amy he revealed the autobiographical shadows in his work, and so offered the key to others who might be curious about his inner life. He cautioned Amy not to think that he had disguised himself as the cardinal in *The Cabala*:

> *Be ready to get the flash that I am a little of Mlle. De Marfontaine too; and presently you will discover that I am Alix d'Espoli and Marc-antonio and a lot of people. If I went through the text with a red pencil and underlined every passage that somehow alluded to my most secret life I should have to resharpen the pencil several times. That's why I write fiction and plays instead of essays and poems: The things I have to say are so intimate that I would be ashamed to publish them under I [he underscored twice] and so pour them into men, women and children.*[48]

Thornton could be moved to tears, he had written to Amy in the fall of 1925, "when a great author is praised for some special beauty, above all for some transformation he has made of the troubles of his life into the gold of his art.[49] Early in 1926 he resolved with new determination that he would somehow find the way to devote all his time and energy to writing. He would transmute his own troubles into the "gold" of his novels and plays, tapping his recent painful experience for material—both dramatic action and emotional resonance. He would spin gold in the character of Alix and in the epilogue, "The Dusk of the Gods," in *The Cabala*, as well as in characters emerging in *The Bridge of San Luis Rey* and even later in *The Woman of Andros* and other literary works. "More and more I am retiring into myself to write," he told Amy in January 1926. "Twenty-nine years of material collected—goodbye, I close the studio door; a few beautiful books, a romantic play or two, then goodnight."[50]

THORNTON LEFT a convoluted trail of letters and manuscript drafts that make it difficult to trace with precision the evolution of the ultimate draft of *The Cabala* (which he pronounced, as the *Concise Oxford Dictionary* recommended, with the emphasis on the first syllable rather than the second).[51] But at last he finished the novel and turned it in to the Bonis. If only his novel would sell, he would tell friends and family good-bye and go "where there's sunlight. And Indians and sunsets and rattlers."[52] He was trying to work on his plays, "preparing a faultless text of 14 (fourteen) 3-minute plays" for Boni, and, if that firm didn't want them, for submission to the Dial Press and other publishers. The Bonis had planned "to use them as a follow-up book," Thornton told Amy, but he feared they might have "chilled toward them" over time.[53]

"Devil take me if I don't run away to Taos one of these fine mornings," Thornton wrote to Amy that January. He just wanted to get away from civilization and "respectability and nice clothes and the Whole Social Grimace." Maybe he'd head for Florida and the ocean, and sunlight, and write a children's book.[54] He didn't know "when or how or where" he would go, just that he felt compelled to. "My urge to go comes from way within and the 'way within' knows just what it is doing," he wrote.[55]

He was weary of his life at Princeton to the point of illness—"the 'nice' people, the cultivated conversations, the academic tone—do not permit me to be simple or sincere."[56] He was inordinately restless, wishing he could "say a long farewell to all civilization" and "return to ocean, sun and sleep."[57] He let his family know how he was feeling—and was soon inundated with letters urging him to come home for a visit. He went, stepping into a family drama that rivaled most of the scripts he had actually written to date. Thanks to his mother and his father, Thornton had a double dose of drama genes—the innate propensity to enlarge and embroider an event in the telling and retelling. His father warned him that the family would "fall to pieces financially at any moment" should Amos Parker Wilder retire or die; therefore it was Thornton's duty to get that M.A. so he could draw a salary for the rest of his life. His mother, hearing Thornton threaten to go to live in a Cuban village described in the February 1926 issue of *Scribner's Magazine*, fell into "hallucinations of snakes, revolutions, typhoid and the Inquisition." Dr. Wilder opined that an act of God could, at any moment, "easily precipitate the family into such straits that it would require a steady salary" from Thornton to provide food and shelter.[58] Thornton reflected that his father's chronic financial anxiety and caution amounted to a "mania, a distortion of essential values that I can excuse only in him who has worked so long & faithfully at dreadful tasks and still must way beyond the age when most men can begin to sit back. He is a dear soul, but with his two blind eyes—propriety and prudence—awfully hard to talk with."[59]

Thornton spent several days with his family, listening to their pleas that he not abandon Princeton and civilization and life in general. Somehow he left New Haven in better spirits, and set about making some practical changes in his life: dropping the course he hated at Princeton and substituting a course "worthy of a human's time"—Old French; promising his parents he would finish the academic year; meeting with his publishers in New York to see the book jacket and blurbs for *The Cabala*. While he was in New York he had a brief visit with the actor Glenn Hunter, he told Amy, describing Hunter as someone he used to know in the army, "long before he was famous."[60]

That winter Thornton and Amy waged a tug-of-war over their relationship. She idealized him, he told her, and described him in "rosy-tinted phrases" as if she had "invented someone." Here was the reality, he wrote to her: "There is a graduate student, harassed, prematurely aging, lazy, talkative but ill-informed, too analytical for many friendships, always hankering for friendships he can't have etc etc." She had simply transformed him into a fantasy, "with all the 'colors'" of her "beautiful nature."[61] Undeterred, she wanted to see him, and they met occasionally for lunch or dinner—but Thornton was increasingly uncomfortable about the secrecy of their meetings. They should not make any clandestine plans, for the "very implication" of secrecy had in it "the power to pain other people." Perhaps they should "work towards a kind of resignation to not seeing one another for a while," he wrote to her.[62] "I would like nothing better than to see you often," he wrote in late February; "to come and go naturally in your home. But that is only possible if I am a friend of the group. I want to be liked and understood and welcomed by Mr. Wertheimer, and the children and the neighbors."[63] He wanted their friendship to last but he rebelled "at anything that faintly looked like subterfuge," especially because it could ruin their "lifetime friendship."[64]

He was "in a bad way" emotionally and intellectually that winter, desperate for "some repose somewhere," he told her:

> *My inner life is so exciting that it refuses to take rests: the book, the next book, my hatred of the classes, my discouragement with myself, the high-pitched table conversations. I sleep pretty well, but every now and then there are hours when I stare into the darkness and my crazy mind goes on jangling, not thinking but merely running over its cheapest gramophone records. My friends tell me I am getting nervous twitches around the eyes and mouth. I must calm down, somehow.*[65]

Thornton kept up his correspondence with Rosemary Ames throughout the spring of 1926, in large part because she was an antidote to the burdens of his schedule and the demands other people made on him. He signed his letters "affectionately" and "Ever devotedly," asked for her photograph, and teased her about the "host of knights" and "scores of elegant young men" who admired her and surrounded her wherever she was.[66] "Just when I, through drudgery, and disappointed literary hopes, and divers cares, was stumbling into a premature middle age," he wrote to her, "you came along and made me make one more attempt to be simple and healthy and carefree."[67]

He gave her advice about her future, which she largely ignored. Despite his criticism of the American Academy of Dramatic Arts as a school that turned out "good slick competent Broadway actors" rather than "actors that work from within from a long painstaking experimental technique," Rosemary enrolled in the academy and went on to a modest stage and film career.[68] Their relationship gradually became a comfortable friendship, with Thornton, more often than not, giving avuncular advice whenever she asked him for it.

He hoped to spend Easter of 1926 in New Haven, staying for about six days and seeing "almost no one" so that he could rest, take long walks, wait somewhat apprehensively for the "first reviews of an outgrown book," and work on a new one.[69] The "outgrown book" was *The Cabala*; the new one, still in its early stages, was *The Bridge of San Luis Rey*. He had made an inventory of all the plays he had "ever completed—eight full length plays in all, plus all the three-minute playlets.[70] Novels and plays aside, he had to carry on his graduate work at Princeton. He enjoyed his literature course with "dear" Louis Con, distinguished author, scholar, and professor of French literature, who appreciated Thornton's work in return.[71] It was in Professor Con's class that Thornton had the idea for one of the first scenes in *The Bridge of San Luis Rey*.

———

IN LATER years Thornton was frequently quoted as saying that of his generation of writers, he was the only one who didn't go to Paris. Actually he went to Paris before many of the others but stayed a shorter time, yet still managed to find that favorite literary haunt, Sylvia Beach's Shakespeare and Company, and to meet Joyce, and to begin his first novel in a shabby hotel room in the summer of 1921. In Paris he had set out to re-create the Rome of his recent experience, fused with the Rome of his classical studies and his rich imagination. He had worked on the emerging story in fits and starts over the next five years, carving out time when his teaching, his summer work, and his other writing permitted, "but always with the sinking feeling that nowhere a publisher or friend would read it," he confessed to Professor Wager.[72] The Bonis and Lewis Baer had proved him wrong.

Early in the composition process he had developed a manuscript titled *The Memoirs of Charles Mallison: The Year in Rome*, replete with footnotes elucidating references in the story and citing another imaginary memoir, *The Boy Sebastian*, also by the fictitious Charles Mallison, published by the imaginary "Soochow Press in Soochow, China in 1913 in six unbound folio volumes."[73] There were other tentative titles for the novel along the way, including *Notes of a Roman Student, Roman Memoirs*, and *The Trasteverine*.

"Great long stretches of my Roman Memoirs are now done," Thornton had written to his mother in 1923. "I am not ashamed of it."[74] He had struggled with form and style, and found it difficult, he wrote, to combine "the real and the fantastic." At one point he had experimented with a few pages of a new novel "based on the survival of Greek divinities into modern Roman society" but set that aside and incorporated the idea of surviving dieties into *The Cabala*: One of the novel's principal characters, Miss Elizabeth Grier, believes that the members of the Cabala are actually reincarnations of Olympian gods.

Readers of *The Cabala* have frequently found in the novel traces of Proust or James or Edith Wharton, and Thornton acknowledged Proust's influence, along with that of Saint-Simon, La Bruyère, Paul Claudel, Ernest Renan, Lytton Strachey, and Mme de Sévigné, who would surface dramatically in his next novel in the guise of one of the main characters. Yet it is significant that during the last year of his work on *The Cabala*, Thornton was analyzing James Joyce's *Ulysses*, struck most by two devices Joyce employed—in form, an intricately, deliberately constructed "architecture," and in substance, an abundance of free-ranging themes, and allusions to everything under the sun.

The novel Thornton crafted was held together more by a fragile scaffolding than by the sturdy timbers and beams of structural, architectural design. The intertwined characters and episodes that he imagined play out freely with Rome as the stage, all witnessed by a narrator, a young American known to us only by his nickname, Samuele. The lovelorn Alix, princess d'Espoli, named him after her dog, a "beautiful setter" who "spent all his life sitting around on the pavement watching us with a look of most intense excitement."[75] Why Samuele? Asked that question many years later, Thornton wrote that he thought the choice was connected to the biblical child Samuel: "Speak Lord, I hear."[76]

Ultimately the novel was organized into five books. "First Encounters" introduces Samuele and an American scholar, James Blair, who meet on a crowded train bound for Rome. Through Blair we hear about the members of the Cabala, four of whom warrant their own books within the novel. According to Blair, they are rich, influential, powerful, bored, lonely, and intellectually snobbish, with a hatred and contempt for what is new. "Here's a group of people losing sleep over a host of notions that the rest of the world has outgrown several centuries ago," says Blair.[77]

The narrator soon encounters the members of the Cabala and begins to form his own relationships with them. There are Elizabeth Grier, a wealthy American spinster, Vassar College trustee, and dominant force in the Cabala; Her Highness Leda Matilda Colonna, duchessa d'Aquilanera, and her young son, the doomed prince Marcantonio, who has "fallen on bad ways"; the cultured Frenchwoman Alix, princess d'Espoli, unhappily married to an Italian prince; the ancient, reputedly wise Cardinal Vaini, who has spent his life on the mission fields of China; and the fervently devout Mlle. Astrée-Luce de Morfontaine. There is even a cameo appearance in the novel by John Keats.

Samuele, who is in Rome to study ancient history, charms his way into the inner circle of the Cabala, some of whose members enlist his help in solving seemingly insoluble problems. The duchessa d'Aquilanera implores Samuele to help reform her sexually promiscuous, self-destructive teenage son, Marcantonio, who ultimately commits incest and then kills himself. The unhappily married princess Alix d'Espoli turns to Samuele in hopes he can help her win the affections of the indifferent, unavailable James Blair. Alix confronts "that cavern of horror in her nature: she seemed always to be loving those that did not love her," Samuele observes.[78] He takes an almost prurient interest in Alix's despair: "I was trembling with a strange happy excitement, made up partly of my love and pity for her, and partly from the mere experience of eavesdropping on a beautiful spirit in the last reaches of its pride and suffering."[79] She considers suicide in the thrall of her hopeless, unrequited passion for Blair, but Samuele tries to set her on the road to redemption.

Into the imaginative fiction of *The Cabala* are woven strands of Thornton's own experiences with unrequited love, helping to explain why he devoted such detailed attention to Alix's rejection by Blair. Whereas Samuele narrates the stories of the other Cabalists from a more distant, third-person point of view, he paints a close-up portrait of Alix's unhappiness and her doomed efforts to seduce Blair. In doing so Thornton delineates characteristics that illuminate his own experience. He reflects that "while we are in love with a person our knowledge of his weaknesses lies lurking in the back of our minds and our idealization of the loved one is not so much an exaggeration of his excellences as a careful 'rationalization' of his defects." Through Samuele he observes that "the mere fact of being loved so, whether one could return it or not, put one under an obligation." In the concluding incident of Alix's chapter, the author demonstrates how deep and lingering such a wound can be.[80]

Samuel's next adventure involves the earnest Mlle Astrée-Luce de Morfontaine, an elderly woman defined by her absolute belief in the teachings of the church, and her conviction that only a return to the doctrine of the divine right of kings can ensure the future of European civilization. She hopes that Samuele can help her present her case to the cardinal, who so blatantly disappoints and disillusions her that she tries to kill him. Fortunately he is saved, only to die en route to China, where he had lived for many years, and where he had hoped to rediscover his own spiritual balance.

The final chapter of *The Cabala*, "The Dusk of the Gods," is a mystical and at times mystifying culmination of the novel. Samuele goes to Marcantonio's grave. He writes notes of appreciation and farewell, closes out his apartment, gives his dog to a friend. He has a long visit with Elizabeth Grier, who has pronounced Samuele the reincarnation or at least the avatar of the god Mercury—the messenger. On his voyage back to the United States, Samuele invokes the presence of the poet Virgil, who appears to give him the message that Rome cannot be the Eternal City because "Nothing is eternal save Heaven." Virgil goes on to say, "Romes existed before Rome and when Rome will be a waste there will be Romes after her."[81] In lines that foreshadow later work—*The Woman of Andros* and *Our Town*—Virgil mourns the earthly life he loved:

> When shall I erase from my heart this love of [Rome]? I cannot enter Zion until I have forgotten Rome.—Dismiss me now, my friend, I pray thee. These vain emotions have shaken me. . . . (Suddenly the poet became aware of the Mediterranean:) Oh, beautiful are these waters. Behold! For many years I have almost forgotten the world. Beautiful! Beautiful!—But no! What horror, what pain! Are you still alive? Alive? How can you endure it?[82]

As the ghost of Virgil "faded before the stars," Samuele's voyage continued "toward the new world and the last and greatest of all cities."[83]

The Cabala is more than an entertainment, more than a young novelist's first and sometimes affected display of talent and promise. There are glib, overwrought passages, some strained characterizations, and a smattering of esoteric literary allusions that verge on ostentation. But overall there is glittering style, replete with lyrical descriptive passages; metaphors deftly woven from musical terms; occasional comedy and parody; witty, sometimes biting irony—and, as Thornton described it, "mordant" social satire.[84] There is also high drama, at times farce, at times melodrama, at times tragedy. On one level the book can be read as a tragicomic allegory. The reader can laugh with and at Samuele and the Cabalists and at the same time pity them. As Samuele, at their instigation, becomes embroiled in the lives of the Cabalists, he sometimes witnesses and sometimes precipitates events, including tragedies—the suicide, the unrequited love affair with a desperately unhappy ending, the shattering crisis of faith.

"Marcantonio," the second episode, can even be viewed as a paradoxical allegory about the dangers of intemperately advocating temperance (echoes of Amos Parker Wilder's tendencies). Book 3, "Alix," dramatizes the intense suffering of unrequited love, and the compensations the rejected lover seeks. Book 4, "Astrée-Luce and the Cardinal," depicts the crisis when religious faith is challenged, and explores the impact of the loss of spiritual belief, as well as the harm that can be done when clergymen disillusion their most faithful followers.

"Who can understand religion unless he has sinned? who can understand literature unless he has suffered? who can understand love unless he has loved without response?" the cardinal says to Samuele.[85] These are the three central questions posed in *The Cabala*.

17

"MY REAL VOCATION"

*Dear Master, I cried, how shall I know If this be my real vocation? . . . I
was told that destiny herself was the mother of decision, and that my vocation
would be settled by events not by consideration.*

—SAMUELE TO SAREPTOR BASILIS, THE SEER,
in Thornton Wilder's The Cabala

New Haven, New York, and Europe (1926–1927)

The *Cabala* was published on April 20, 1926, by Albert and
Charles Boni, and to Thornton's chagrin, many pages were
marred by careless errors. Most of them were not his fault, he
wrote his brother, but some critics would pounce on them, blaming the
author whose name, after all, was on the text. "The final proofs were
perfect, I feel sure. But at that stage the firm suddenly decided that the
book was too short and began expanding it by all the devices known
to the trade. In the respacing of lines therefore many must have been
broken and crazily repatched by the typesetter: but a few of the errors
remain my maxima culpa!" He reported to Amos that almost no one
liked the last section of the novel, book 5, "The Dusk of the Gods." "I
should have 'prepared' it more consistently thru the earlier. Well—all
in all, I have learned lots of lessons."[1] He was preparing himself for the
possibility that the book might receive "a brief and decent" burial.[2]

The Bonis waited for the reviews, not planning to advertise the
book until "some blurbs begin." Even if his book failed to reach an
audience, Thornton consoled himself that at least he could earn his
living "elsewhere" and find "elsewhere" his "real pleasures."[3] He was
all too aware of his shortcomings as a novelist, he told Amos: "I am
too young and too undedicated a person to achieve a restrained Grand
Style (which I pretend after)—notes of burlesque, smartalecisms and
purple-rhetoric creep in and are only discovered when it is too late. Let

me promise you tho that tons of bunk were deported in the successive readings of the proof. Hope for the best."[4]

As it turned out, Thornton and the Bonis were pleasantly surprised by the reviews, which were mixed but overwhelmingly positive. Theodore Purdy, Jr., at the *Saturday Review* found the novel disorganized and the writing at times "imitative," but still he called *The Cabala* a "sophisticated extravaganza," and numerous critics praised Wilder's style.[5] Thornton's Yale friend John Farrar, writing in the *Bookman*, enthusiastically endorsed the book in a review headlined "Brilliant, Bitter, Imaginative," noting that even while Wilder's imagination was "bizarre," it was "restrained."[6] Some critics praised the book as charming, witty, authentic, brilliant, mature, beautiful, ironic, irresistible; others dismissed it as esoteric, strange, disorganized, imitative, inaccurate in its depiction of the Catholic Church, and full of inexcusable mechanical errors. Agnes Repplier in the Catholic journal *Commonweal* charged that Thornton Wilder did not "know the Church of Rome."[7] She said some "very harsh things," Thornton wrote to a friend. "Some of them are true and some are extravagantly unjust." Nevertheless he wanted to share the review with friends so they could, "for completeness' sake," read "the enemy's point-of-view"—one of the few times in his career that he would ever comment on a review.[8]

From his old friend William Lyon Phelps, in *Scribner's Magazine*, came lavish praise, especially for the author's style, although, Phelps said, "I am not quite sure what it is all about."[9] Wilder's debut, it was noted more than once, marked the appearance on the American literary scene of a promising new writer. In May a letter came to Thornton in Princeton from one of the critics who mattered most—his former professor Charles Wager. "It is just like you, full of your delightful airs and graces, but with what seems to me a sense for a situation that you did not even promise to have in the days of your former incarnation," Dr. Wager wrote. "It is the real thing, if I am judge, and of course I think I am . . . if one can be daring and clever and vivid and at the same time write like a gentleman and a wit, I cannot see why one would regret it. Besides all this, there is something curiously like wisdom in your book, and this strikes me as best of all."[10]

"If I deserved to be happy no letter could have made me happier than yours," Thornton replied:

> *How many hours I sat under your rostrum, burning with awe and emotion, while you unfolded the masterpieces. . . . I am an old fashioned believer and when I assert that I believe that lives are planned out for us I am always thinking of the fact that my father . . . sent his two sons to Oberlin where the younger could get the nourishment without which he would have remained a bright blundering trivial hysteric.*[11]

The Cabala quickly went into its second printing "with all the twenty-eight errata corrected," Thornton noted.[12] The book would be published in England in October by Longmans, Green & Company, Ltd. Although not a bestseller, it sold in respectable numbers—5,357 copies in the United States in the first year. The Boni brothers approached Thornton with an unusual proposition: If he would turn over to them $1,250 in royalties due him, they would match that amount and "plaster the country with adv'ts, to try and ram it down the public neck as one of the six bestsellers of the Spring and perhaps recoup all that was invested." Thornton turned them down. "In the first place I must eat," he wrote to Amy Wertheimer. "In the second, it would be absurd to make a little goldfish go through the antics of a whale."[13]

———

THROUGHOUT THAT hectic spring Amy sought Thornton's attention—asking to read his work in progress, wanting to give him a twenty-ninth birthday party, reproaching him when he did not write her long letters. He reminded her of the boundaries he had prescribed in January with "affectionate gentleness and affectionate firmness."[14] Even their correspondence verged on "Not Fair Play," he wrote to her in April, after a visit with his family in New Haven. Amy was married. She had children. He would continue to think about the limitations on their relationship, and he hoped she would as well. "It doesn't matter much what a poor unattached abstracted bachelor does; but it [is] very important what a lady with the network of attachment like yours does . . . your attention must be overwhelmingly centered where you are." Worst of all was his conviction that "I am cheating. New Haven [his family] implies that."[15]

She answered him with "beautiful pages" and "just in that vein of restraint with wistfulness which (haven't we decided?) must be ours." But he was worried that she was reading allusions to herself into his depiction of Alix in *The Cabala*. He cautioned her not to "wrench reflexions out of their context," reminding her that "the earlier books [of *The Cabala*] were written before we met and have elsewhere their application."[16]

He defined himself for Amy in late April. He was trying to juggle all his "existences": He was a graduate student; a "Sociable" who went to teas, dances, dinners, and movies; a teacher and a tutor; a published author concerned about the response to his new book; a writer filled with ideas for new books. It was a challenge to coordinate "all these persons I am," he wrote, "and it's too exciting."[17] Unknown to her, he confessed later, he was "leading the foxiest possible life trying to appear a gentleman and a Princetonian on a hobo's budget."[18] His life was a whirlwind: In his few spare hours he was trying to finish his revisions to the last act of *The Trumpet Shall Sound* and write at least a few sporadic pages of the new novel; he was signing "a perfect tower of books"; the "Fox Film Company" telegraphed the Bonis that they were considering *The Cabala* for a film; the theatrical producer Charles L. Wagner "whom I don't know from Adam," Thornton wrote, liked the characterizations in *The Cabala* and wanted to "discuss a play."[19] Despite these demands on his time and energy, Thornton finished his M.A. requirements and the degree was "all won and over." He was working on his new novel, *The Bridge of San Luis Rey*. "The book is going astonishingly," he told his mother. "The weather is glorious and my health is perfect. But I'm all 'sunk.' I'm coming to you about the 22nd or 23rd and sleep up in the hall and get cured. You are the only thing I can count on in a tiresome world."[20]

He was not very happy, he wrote to Amy, probably because

"through distraction and laziness I haven't written a word for so long, i.e. denied my *raison d'être*."[21] He would be all right once he got home, he told her, for "there is one place in the world I am really at peace and that is on the little cot up in the hall in Mansfield Street, with my Father and Mother and Isabel tiptoeing about their affairs." There was another reason for his weariness: "This little M. A. has been drinking a little too much lately having fallen into a crowd after his own heart— tough-guys, chemists and physicists and other non-introspectives," he confessed to Amy.

> *Their major ordeals are just over and they are all for stealing the distilled alcohols reserved for experimental work in the biological laboratories and infusing it with whole groves of lemons and shaking violently at the level of the shoulders. Then I am almost happy, accepted as a mere fella among fellas. . . . I long to be ordinary as Elinor Wylie longs to be respectable.*[22]

It was important to Thornton to be "a mere fella among fellas," but try as he might to be ordinary, he was remarkable. At twenty-nine, he was a successful teacher, his M.A. in French in hand; a published novelist, with a second novel under way; a dramatist whose play would open in New York in December. He would spend July on his second MacDowell Colony fellowship, where he could concentrate on writing the new novel and put the finish touches on *The Trumpet Shall Sound*, which Boleslavsky was "clamoring" to receive.[23] His first novel was being reviewed all over the United States and in England, and earning modest royalties.

For most of his MacDowell residency, Thornton was buried in his work on the *The Trumpet Shall Sound* and *The Bridge of San Luis Rey*, struggling with the "still shapeless mass of the first two books" of the novel, he wrote to a friend.[24] He found that *The Bridge of San Luis Rey* flowed from his pen "almost without effort, phrasing itself in a thousand beautiful accidents, but it is desperately sad."[25] He was "retelling the story of Mme de Sévigné's daughter, though under another name and in another age," he wrote to Amy.[26] After a few weeks, however, he tired of the "hothouse introspective conversation at Peterborough," and considered going back to Princeton for better working conditions, or accepting Boleslavsky's invitation to spend a week at his Connecticut farm.

Thornton also wanted to "get one unencumbered honest-to-god visit with my own mother," and enjoy some "congenial talks and salt-water swimming, the two enthusiasms of my life."[27] But when the director of the Lake Sunapee Summer School and Camp in New Hampshire asked Thornton to substitute for one of their French masters, he jumped at the chance to earn the extra income. In late July the camp director sent a roadster to MacDowell to take Thornton to Lake Sunapee, where he would stay until mid-September. He spent the morning hours teaching small groups of students and the afternoons swimming and taking long solitary walks. There was time for his own work, but he found it refreshing that most people at Sunapee paid no attention whatsoever to the fact the he had ever "meddled with writing."[28] "Once in a long while I add a paragraph to *The Bridge*," he wrote to his mother, "but it's a tender-growing lily and is never smudged with mere industry." He wished that he and his mother, just the two of them, could spend some time in September at "some sea-coast somewhere" while he finished the new novel. "It will go—again all right if you are near," he told her.[29]

The Wilder family was, as usual, scattered for the summer—with Thornton in New Hampshire, his mother in New Haven, his father and Isabel in Maine with various members of the extended Wilder family, his brother at his church in North Conway, Janet on a farm in northern New Hampshire, and Charlotte traveling in France with friends and writing an article about the journey entitled "In a Corner of France."[30] In mid-September, for once, the entire Wilder family was together in New Haven, albeit briefly—"every known Wilder around one table," Thornton wrote, "and a very emotional Grace from Father, who, as you remember, loves the Clan."[31]

Thornton marveled more than ever at his mother's spirit and achievements, and wrote a portrait of her in 1926, when he was twenty-nine and his mother was fifty-three:

She who is so bright and witty and feminine . . . for the last ten years has had to do her own housework. She is the delight of her friends— the committees of the Y. W. C. A. and International Girls Institute on which she serves (arriving late, with a collie on a leash, wilful and enthusiastic and capable) keep giving her flowers and odd and tender tributes. She has lived through the fretfulnesses of five stormy obstinate children and the humors of a husband from an opposite mould. With her hands scarcely dry from the dishwater she turns to read French, German and Italian. She enchants all the young men and women we children bring into the house.[32]

Isabella worried about what would become of unemployed Thornton in the fall, and he set her mind—and his own—at ease in late August. He had spent much of June tutoring Andrew "Andy" Townson, whose parents Thornton had met through his friend Robert Hutchins. Thornton despaired because Andy did not apply himself to his studies and, therefore, couldn't seem to "learn a thing."[33] The boy had failed all his college admissions exams and so was at loose ends for the fall. His affluent parents, who had decided college was clearly not for their son, hired Thornton to take Andy abroad in late September, to stay until Christmastime, after which they would situate Andy in the family business. They would pay all Thornton's expenses, plus a stipend of two hundred dollars a month. He would have to miss the opening of his play at the American Laboratory Theatre, but he assured Andy's father he was willing to do that.

Thornton and many others had expected that he would publish a book and see a major production of one of his plays when he was in his early twenties. Now he was twenty-nine, and looking at his novel and plays "impersonally." "I hope they're well done and well liked," he said, "but I don't want to mingle with actors and literary people and I fight to keep my life separate. Besides I always hope to earn my living in other ways so that I need never strain to write a word for money. In that way I can always contradict managers and withdraw my stuff if they want to alter it."[34]

ALBERT AND CHARLES BONI were poised to publish Thornton's second novel—with the stipulation that it should be longer than the first one—and they were willing to pay Thornton an advance on royalties that made it possible for him to settle some debts and to outfit himself for the trip to Europe. (He didn't need much, he wrote: "Three suits, a tuck, an overcoat, a raincoat, never more than five books, a sweater . . . some linen and some MSS. Behold my baggage in this world.")[35] He planned to go to New York to meet with the Bonis, and then with Boleslavsky about *The Trumpet Shall Sound*, now in rehearsals and scheduled to open at the American Laboratory Theatre in New York in December.

As he finished his preparations for the journey, Thornton wrote to his father, who was vacationing on Squirrel Island, Maine: "I wish I were out on the granite ledges of Squirrel with you, dear Papa, best of men—I'm twenty-nine and every year makes me understand and love you more, and just one tiny wait more and I'll be a help and not a hindrance. Be patient with me 7 x 7 + 1 times and things will clear. Your dreadful child Thornt."[36]

BY MOST measures, a young novelist, playwright, and teacher on a subsidized trip abroad might have felt a reasonable degree of pleasure. This was not the case for Thornton Wilder in October 1926, however, as he recorded in the journal he began to keep in London. By then he had spent nearly three futile weeks trying to interest twenty-year-old Andy Townson in the cultural, artistic, and architectural wonders of England, France, and Germany. Thornton wrote to his family that he was afraid Andy was "bored to extinction."[37] This usually affable young man was not inclined to spend his time or his generous allowance on edification in Europe. Andy and his chaperone/tutor were hopelessly incompatible travel companions, and Thornton had enough experience teaching and supervising young men to recognize that Andy much preferred the company of "certain roistering companions" he had met along the way.[38]

But Thornton had far more patience with Andy than he had with himself. "The impulse to keep a notebook derives from my great restlessness and dissatisfaction with myself," he wrote. Their journey was barely begun, but already he was eager to be free of his reluctant student, to go to the south of France where he could concentrate on finishing *The Bridge of San Luis Rey* and "relieve legitimately all this chaotic literature in my head."[39] He regretted undertaking this exasperating pilgrimage. "Why did I ever go into this thing?" he wrote after a visit with his friend Bill Nichols, a recent Harvard graduate and a Rhodes scholar at Balliol College, Oxford. "And now I groan for freedom, and fret, and fester. God knows that just seeing Oxford, and all the business of our good long talk filled me with perfect rage to get back to my fountain pen and commit something beautiful."[40]

He shared his frustration with his family as well: "Oh, I should never have entered into this contract," he wrote them from Rome on October 25, 1926. "I should have had the faith to come over alone. I am punished. My beautiful book would have been written by now instead of festering in me."[41] It was a great relief when Andy's brother Chick appeared in London and the brothers set off on daily excursions of their own. In those free hours Thornton walked the London streets thinking "absurdly, in 'fine phrases,'" he wrote in his journal. "I am alone most of the day in picture galleries and churches and I eat most of my meals alone, and all this talking to myself has become bad for me."[42] He was "nervously self-conscious" about his appearance in London as well, he wrote, and "a little so everywhere."[43] He was nearly thirty and belatedly, in his mind, gaining some recognition as a playwright and novelist. But he had learned all too quickly that even with good reviews and modestly good sales for a first novel, *The Cabala* was not going to produce a significant financial return, and he had doubts that his second novel would either. Lonely, self-conscious, restless, dissatisfied, he wanted above all to write, and he knew that this trip to Europe only temporarily deferred the problem of earning a living.

For the time being, however, there was money in his pocket, and his first obligation was to Andy. Thornton was known to his friends as a superb tour guide in Europe, but his best efforts to plan tours and events to interest Andy fell flat. Thornton had envisioned a journey that was "all adventure and all friendship and all important discoveries in art and archeology," but in fact Andy hated "museums and churches and walks and things." Because Andy loved to fly, they did so whenever possible. They flew across the English Channel, and Thornton found air travel "a very impressive experience," he wrote home. "Thank you for carrying on all my insurance these days," he wrote to his father back in New Haven. "I have to ride in airplanes so often with Andy that you may get the dividends before you know it."[44]

Thornton's new journal became the repository for scenes and ideas for *The Bridge of San Luis Rey*. The novel was growing slowly, but he found that whole passages could be inspired by a walk, a fragment of a symphony, an artistic detail in a cathedral or museum. Still he was adrift, uncertain about how to plan the next few months of his life, much less the next few years. He had made no firm commitment to teach or to study or to take any sort of job that might steadily, dependably pay his bills. He reflected in his journal that he had three "contracted books" for the Bonis: *The Bridge of San Luis Rey*, he noted, followed by an edition of *The Trumpet Shall Sound* (which would not materialize, as it turned out); and an edition of "plays long and short" which would appear with another publisher in 1928 as *The Angel That Troubled the Waters and Other Plays*, a collection of the three-minute playlets. But on his occasional solitary walks, doubting that he could make money writing, Thornton looked squarely into the future and decided that he would have to combine writing "with some kind of college work." After he finished the books he had promised to the Boni brothers, he reflected in his journal, "I must write a book of literary criticism that will get me a special lectureship at Yale or Harvard. Then can I be the first American don in Oxford or Cambridge?"[45]

He could be fatalistic—or perhaps, as the grandson of a Presbyterian clergyman, predestinarian in his views: "In fact, all my reading in cynical authors has not robbed me of the sensation of being a disobedient and foolish actor in a play whose author (in spite of me) gives me beautiful scenes and permits [me] to confront some rare and noble *dramatis personae.*"[46]

―――――

THORNTON AND Andy made brief stops in Rome, Naples, and Paris, where Thornton called on Sylvia Beach at Shakespeare and Company. Beach introduced him to Ernest Hemingway, whom Thornton described to his mother as "one of the two other good novelists of my generation, the 3rd being Glenway Wescott." Wilder and Hemingway had a "grand long talk."[47] They decided that their "immediate predecessors"—Sherwood Anderson, James Branch Cabell, Sinclair Lewis, Edith Wharton, and Willa Cather—were "quite inadequate."[48] Thornton gave Hemingway a copy of *The Cabala.*[49]

In Rome he visited the American Academy, where he was warmly welcomed by the director. "The book has been read by all with a sort of scandalous delight," Thornton wrote to his family. "Even old Romans take it as the hot stuff from the secret circles!"[50] He also had a reunion with Lauro De Bosis, who talked to Thornton about Mussolini, whom he knew well. To Thornton's great pleasure De Bosis had read his novel and understood that it was "preposterous" to regard *The Cabala* as realism. Thornton was sensitive to criticism from friends and critics when he felt that they failed to grasp his intentions in *The Cabala.* "I am mortified that you thot [thought] I put STYLE first," Thornton wrote to Nichols after they had discussed *The Cabala*, which was being published in England that fall by Longmans, Green. "I suppose you are right; but the next book . . . [*sic*]."[51] He appreciated a letter from his friend Harry Luce, and wrote to thank him with some illuminating lines about *The Cabala* and *The Bridge*:

> *Your remark that my C-b-la is more than style puts oil on an old bewildered wound. I thought the book was all about great natures in pain; but most of the reviewers tell me it is about eccentrics in ludicrous situations, and lean heavily on the style. I have buried a barbed sentence in my next book for them: "The Conde enjoyed the Marquesa's famous letters, but he [thought] that when he had admired the*

style he had extracted all their richness and intention missing (as most people do) the whole purport of literature, which is the notation of the heart. Style is but the faintly contemptible vessel in which the bitter liquid is recommended to the world."[52]

With only slight changes, this passage about the "purport of literature"—the "notation of the heart"—may be found in *The Bridge of San Luis Rey* in part 2: "The Marquesa de Montemayor."[53]

BY EARLY November, with London, Paris, Rome, and Naples behind them, Thornton and Andy were making their way by train from Florence to Munich. Wherever they went Thornton was the adventurer, imbibing the scenery and sunshine, walking the hillsides (Andy especially disliked walking), visiting with "friendly peasants" in the villages, savoring the food, and attending plays and concerts.[54] He wrote to his father from Berlin:

> *By some curious chance we found the one boy in the United States who was equipped to get just NOTHING out of a European trip. He liked England immensely because he could ignore it and sit indoors drinking whiskey with some friends. There are no friends to drink whiskey with in France, Italy and Germany so for the most part he sits in his hotel room, reads the foreign editions of the American papers, and smokes.*[55]

Throughout the whole trip Thornton was waiting "with clenched fists" until he could get back to work on *The Bridge of San Luis Rey*. The desire to write was "tormenting the life" out of him, he complained. "Oh god for independence and silence!"[56] He sent fragments of the manuscript to Andy's mother, Marie, who was fast becoming one of Thornton's bevy of women friends taking a great interest in his work. Mrs. Townson expressed some doubts about the book. "I am still hoping that when I finally get it out smooth, you will like it more than the C-b-la," Thornton replied:

It is going to be much longer and so varied that there will be parts that
will appeal to all moods. You will be surprised to hear that even on the
trip I have been able to do some work on it—on trains, at meals, late
at night, or on my walks, all sorts of notes, and anecdotes, and notions
keep pushing up to my attention in spite of myself, and I am like to finish
several blank books of odds and ends of suggestion before I can finally
settle down to work hard.[57]

He wrote Amy that he hoped to be free "to attack my book in
almost as much earnest as it's been attacking me. The Peruvians keep
visiting me at the most unexpected moments and I am filling quite a
large notebook with their doings and sayings and fretting and pining
to settle down and hug them and put them down masterfully on paper.
Perhaps the ferment and delay is even good for them."[58]

He was learning to be an objective, attentive editor of his own manuscripts, whose pages teemed with words and lines and even whole
passages stricken or completely rewritten as his hand worked busily
over the pages. Because Thornton had the novelist's eye and the dramatist's ear, a vital part of his revision process had long been to read
his plays and his fiction aloud—to friends if possible, but otherwise to
himself. The ear often catches problems in syntax, cadence, or vocabulary that the eye overlooks. And whether he accepted or ignored the
critical opinions of family and friends he trusted, their reactions could
be provocative. They made him think and rethink the story growing
on the page. For instance, when he shared portions of the *Bridge* manuscript with some New Haven friends in Capri, they told him that the
account of Brother Juniper and the accident "had the air of scoffing"
instead of the "humorously tender" effect Thornton intended. He revised accordingly.[59]

He wrote to Bill Nichols from Rome, "You have no idea how beautiful one's book [seems] *at this stage*. The Peruvians whom it treats
keep visiting me on trains, in front of pictures, in bed. Anecdotes
about them, bits of characterization, sometimes just one adjective
comes mysteriously floating to me across a dining-room."[60] He copied

on the back of the letter a passage from book 1 of the current draft of his novel—a fragment that, he said, "first came to me when I was reading the inscriptions on the left wall of Christ Church Cathedral" the day he had visited Nichols in Oxford.[61] The passage, considerably rewritten, appears in the final section of the finished novel, part 5, "Perhaps an Intention." Moments of inspiration were outweighed by hours of hard work, however. Thornton wrote to Nichols, "The process of literature seems to be to produce in tears and then rewrite as though in mockery."[62]

TO THORNTON'S relief, another Townson brother, Douglas, was coming to Europe to join Andy and Chick. Because Thornton was "bursting with material" for his novel, he began to think about turning Andy over entirely to his brothers, refunding the appropriate portion of his salary, and settling down somewhere in France where living was "ludicrously cheap," so that he could write full-time.[63] The one drawback to that plan, he wrote to his family, was loneliness: "I love you all more than tonguecantell [*sic*]," he wrote, "and dread even staying alone in the S. of France without somebody."[64]

"Andy sails Wednesday and the farce is over," he wrote to his mother and sisters on November 28, 1926. During that last week Andy had been "prowling around all night with his brother in dress-suits" and Thornton had more time to write. Consequently, he said, "*The Bridge* is getting along fast and is just filling up with beautiful passages that take your breath away."[65]

Now at last he could make his own plans. He imagined one option after another: He could stay in Paris for a month, rent a typewriter, and finish his novel there. Or he might spend a month in the south of France. Or he might share a studio with Ernest Hemingway, who had been living in Paris since 1921, with his first wife, Hadley, and later, their son, John, nicknamed Bumby. Hemingway's first novel, *The Sun Also Rises*, was published by Scribner's in the fall of 1926.[66]

When Hemingway wasn't writing in Montparnasse cafés and bars, he worked in his studio at 39 rue Descartes. "I'd love to go into the studio with Ernest," Thornton wrote home, "but there are no meals with it. He eats around with the enormous and flamboyant Rotonde crowd. And his wife is about to divorce him and his new wife is about to arrive from America, so I think I'd better not try. But he's wonderful. It's the first time I've met someone of my own generation whom I respected as an artist."[67]

Thornton enjoyed the occasional company of Hadley Hemingway, who was separated from Hemingway at the time. He escorted "the almost-ex Mrs. Hemingway" to a concert in Paris in December. "She is a nice brave little soul," he wrote to his mother. She looked "very like [movie star] Mae Marsh," he said, and no one knew how she really felt about "Ernest's cut-ups." He thought Hadley was "a brick" and, with other friends, hoped that Hemingway would go back to her and their "beautiful little 3-year old baby."[68] In Thornton's opinion Ernest was "just a Middle Western kid whose genius and health and good looks and success have gone to his head a little," and Thornton thought (perceptively, as it turned out) that Hemingway's current mistress and future wife, Pauline Pfeiffer, "was a mess."[69] He managed to sustain friendships with both Hemingway and Hadley, however. He wrote his mother, "I think she has ceased to be particularly in love with Ernest but dreads being alone and divorced and back in America. Fortunately she has the most beautiful little boy in the world and all the royalties of *The Sun Also Rises*."[70]

According to Thornton, Hemingway was "the hot sketch of all time. He bursts with self confidence and a sort of little-boy impudence."[71] Hemingway was working on a play about Mussolini, bragging to Thornton that he had "dabbled in secret service and plots" and "had access to highly secret dossiers," and that he knew that Mussolini "intentionally planted" attempts on his own life to "create a martyr-legend."[72] While Thornton listened skeptically to these claims, he encouraged Hemingway to "begin to think of a play" for Richard Boleslavsky, and Hemingway finished a one-act play in 1926—*Today Is Friday*, a drama set on Good Friday after the crucifixion.[73]

WHILE THORNTON was witnessing the breakdown of the Hemingways' marriage, he was facing the possible end of his own relationship with Amy Wertheimer. She was pursuing him in transoceanic letters, so much so that he considered ending their correspondence and their friendship once and for all. "I have always told you that I could only be a friend, but in the most valuable senses of the word," he wrote to her November 30. If she were divorced and single, he told her, they would have to see each other even less frequently because he did not "care to appear" to their friends as a "careless pilferer in other people's happiness." He told her he hoped for long years of "rich work" ahead, and a "steady honorable single-minded life."[74] Two weeks later he wrote to tell her that he was "very discouraged" about their correspondence, and the "dramatic" and "stormy" letters that arrived had left him "dejected" and unable to work. "I don't even go to see people: I must wander around looking in shop windows and feeling mad at a life in which you should decide to make a matter of suffering out of what should be a matter of delight."[75]

Perhaps there was nothing to do but to "cease writing: a painful measure," he wrote, "and the only one fair to your children, your husband and your friends." Yet intentionally or not, he kept them both in limbo, for Thornton couldn't bring himself to do it: "I think I had better try and see what one year's silence can do. However I won't begin the silence yet."[76]

"THIS CRAZY journey is drawing to a close and I may show up in Paris one of these days and drag you out to help me find a room," Thornton wrote to Ernest Hemingway.[77] All things considered, however, Thornton had decided by late November that he'd best leave Paris. "Between you and me," he wrote to his mother and sisters, "I don't like Paris. I never did. If I had somewhere to go in America I'd come straight home, but I don't want New York and I couldn't park with you adorable people in New Haven and that's that."[78]

He stayed on into December, however, feeling more at home now that he was free of Andy and the expensive hotels and restaurants the Townsons had paid for. Now Thornton was staying in a cheap pension in Montparnasse, taking his meals in cafés where writers and artists gravitated for cheap food and wine and lively company. He was making friends with his "motley crowd" of neighbors in the "dreadful pension"—impoverished Polish musicians, one "rich and famous and charming" Polish pianist who was hiding from a princess, "impecunious Russian composers and painters . . . a thickness of local color that would stagger Balzac."[79] Thornton loved it.

Another reason for lingering was that he was making plans to spend Christmas at Juan-les-Pins on the Riviera with Coleman Walker "(football star, U. Of Va. and ex-Lawrenceville master, and Rhodes scholar)" and a "whole horde of Oxonians," including Bill Nichols and a "pack of Rhodes scholars."[80] They swam, talked, and lolled about in springlike weather, Thornton wrote, finding "the air very fragrant but with a faint trace of spirits, explained by the fact that Sinclair Lewis and the Scott Fitzgeralds had passed through in the Fall."[81] Thornton wanted to stay in France and write, for he had been "frozen over" with his work on *The Bridge of San Luis Rey*, afraid that he'd never finish it, and he had just broken through again. The inspiration was Beethoven's Ninth Symphony. He went to a performance and was so moved that he returned to the pension and wrote "the pages you will someday know as the death of Manuel," he reported to his mother, going on to say, "and the next morning I wrote Doña Maria's visit to Cluxambuqua and I've been writing evenly ever since."[82]

He applied for a 1927 Guggenheim Fellowship to support a sojourn in Munich and Vienna to "learn the theatre from the inside out," especially the theater of Max Reinhardt and Rudolf Kommer, but he doubted he would get it—and he didn't. He was brimming with confidence in his novel now, however. He told his mother it was "going to be a riot. Every twenty pages there's a tremendous emotional situation and between times its as lyrical and beautifully written as . . . . [*sic*] It will help you build the most adorable little Engl. house and put a maid in it too. And then I'll never travel to

Europe again but will sit reading aloud to you while you punch rugs. Sweetest lady in the world, au revoir."[83]

––––––––––

CAUGHT UP as he was in the new novel, Thornton spent little time thinking about *The Cabala* as it made its way into British and French bookstores, but occasionally he wondered when *The Trumpet Shall Sound* would actually open in New York, and how it would be received. He feared the worst, for he could now see many flaws in his play, and as he anticipated, his debut as a novelist proved to be far more auspicious than his debut as a dramatist.

Boleslavsky had asked for revisions, which Thornton provided, but the director had no quarrel with the substance of the play. To the contrary, he praised the young playwright in a long letter to a colleague in June 1926, noting that Wilder's "point of view on life and art" was interesting, and adding, "He doesn't divide them—they are fused together—they are divine in his understanding—he looks for mystery in realism and realism in mystery." Boleslavsky called Thornton's drama "one of those realistic and common life plays at the first reading, and on the tenth reading it becomes a deep, rich confession of blind human souls, seeking for light and unable to find it, the eternal fairy tale of the Prometheus flame." He thought Thornton depicted "the lowest and the highest elements of the human soul in strange and unresolved relationships." This international veteran of the theater believed that the early work of this unknown playwright was far ahead of its time.[84]

Long before *The Trumpet Shall Sound* opened on December 10, 1926, Thornton was geographically and emotionally far removed from the play. "I feel awfully remote from the news about *The Trumpet*, though of course it's exciting," he wrote to his family. Thornton was "horrified" to learn in a telegram from Boleslavsky that he was going to have an actor in the play read the Lord's Prayer, and wired back immediately: *"Please no prayer."* Boleslavsky had telescoped the third and fourth acts; Thornton considered this a mistake, but he didn't care, he wrote to his family. "It's all sort of remote to me. If it's well-done or ill done, or successful or unsuccessful, it's all one to me: it's there on paper and someday when I'm older I'll revise it and get the ideas sound." He went on to critique his play objectively: "Its scenario is too pretentious. If Dante had gone into the theatre he couldn't have carved himself a more ambitious subject. On the eve of performance I shall telegraph the company my thanks and go to bed."[85]

Thornton's play was one of four on the American Laboratory Theatre's 1926–27 repertory calendar. (One of them, Clemence Dane's *Granite*, was so successful it went on to Broadway.)[86] "New American Play Is Quite Fantastic," read the *New York Times* heading December 11. The reviewer wrote that "Mr. Wilder is a novelist, best known for 'The Cabala,' a book which, one gathers, caused not a little waltzing in certain of the town's thoroughfares. It seems hardly likely that such definite indications of approval will follow the production of the play." The event was deemed a "rather murky evening among the better known symbols," however, and the plot was said to be derivative, predictable—a "rehash" of other works "from Ibsen to Sutton Vane."[87]

Years later, in his last novel, the semiautobiographical *Theophilus North* (1973), Thornton referred to the source of his first full-length play:

> While I was an undergraduate at college I had written and printed in the *Yale Literary Magazine* a callow play called *The Trumpet Shall Sound*. It was based on a theme borrowed from Ben Jonson's *The Alchemist*: Master departs on a journey of indefinite length, leaving his house in charge of faithful servants; servants gradually assume the mentality of masters; liberty leads to license; master returns unannounced and puts an end to their riotous existence. Lively writer, Ben Jonson.[88]

In his play Thornton transposed the action to a mansion in New York's Washington Square in the 1870s, and drew on the King James Version of 1 Corinthians 15:51–53 for his title: "for the trumpet shall sound, and the dead shall be raised incorruptible, and we shall be changed." As the *New York Times* critic described the play, there was a "motley, ragtag, bobtail assemblage" of characters, "each with his or her petty faults and vices . . . a woman of the streets . . . a sea captain who has 'got religion,' a wealthy Swedish matron who goes through life pretending to be a pauper, and a lunatic pyromaniac." There is also Flora, the young servant girl who has rented the house to provide a temporary home and some money for the "swaggering young sailor whom she loves," and who kills herself when she discovers his love is false.[89] And there is Peter Magnus, the owner of the mansion, who comes home to discover the sins of his servants, and to dispense justice and mercy.

Thornton did not see his play until February 1927. Homesick, and feeling "awfully unattached and unwanted" after Christmas when his friends returned to Oxford, he began to make arrangements for his return voyage.[90] He discussed them in a letter December 30, 1926, addressed to the Wilder family dog, Kelly—"Madam Kelly Wilder," he wrote on the envelope. Thornton reported that he was "hankering for you and the grand people who watch over you and the only bed in the world I can really sleep in (you sleep on it too and know which one I mean)." He asked Kelly to pass along to the family his regrets that

> *the reviews on* The Trumpet *weren't more cordial, but that I can't work up much resentment (or even disappointment) for I might perfectly well have said the same things if the play had fallen to me to review. . . . I'm awfully sorry for Mr. Boleslavsky's sake, that's all. . . . For my own rep. I don't mind:* The Bridge *will bring them around.*[91]

When he saw the play in New York, Thornton gave the production and himself a mixed review, tilted toward the negative. "There are lots of beautiful things in the production," he wrote to Nichols, "and the great technical virtuosity of Boleslavsky discovers lots of good things but there are some pretty distressing moments. . . . I don't like the play. It's remote from me. If I came upon it as the work of someone else I doubt whether I would see a grain of talent in it."[92] To the Townsons he wrote, "Between you and me and the critics the play isn't very good, but its few passages of emotion are so beautifully played by Boleslavsky's little troupe that every now and then I find someone who has been quite stirred by it—that is enough."[93]

He had traveled many miles, globally, intellectually, and creatively, since 1919 when he finished *The Trumpet Shall Sound* and saw it in print at Yale. He was more aware than anyone else of the play's shortcomings, of the gap between his dramatic intention and the reality. The flaws, he knew, were his, not Boleslavsky's or the actors'. But for a tenacious artist, no matter the shortfall between dream and creation, no creative work is wasted. Every play that would come after grew out of every word written before—every scene, every strand of dialogue, every stage direction. *The Trumpet Shall Sound* was a vital part of his apprenticeship as a playwright, just as *The Cabala* was for the novelist.

The Cabala was still selling in the United States and abroad, and the University of Michigan Comedy Club was going to produce *The Trumpet Shall Sound* in March. Thornton hoped to persuade Samuel French to publish an acting edition for the potentially lucrative amateur theater market. But for the time being, until *The Bridge* was delivered to the Bonis, Wilder the novelist had to take precedence over Wilder the dramatist, and Wilder the wage earner had to come first of all.

18

DR. JEKYLL AND MR. HYDE

I don't write in leisure. I don't write from any aspect of my life that daily life can exhibit. I am Dr. Jeykl [sic] and Mr. Hyde.

—THORNTON WILDER TO ISABEL WILDER,
August 22, 1927

Connecticut, New Hampshire, New Jersey, and Florida (1927)

He was closing in on thirty in the winter of 1927, a young man of many facets, trying to coax them into harmony, or at least into some order of precedence. Which was the overriding self; which was the innermost, authentic self? Wilder the loner? Wilder the friend? Wilder the son and brother? Wilder the teacher? The wage earner? The reader and perennial student? The writer? The philosopher? The vagabond? He resolved to give precedence to the writer, and to go back to New Haven for two months, finish his novel in three weeks, and be very attentive to his mother and father, giving them "a sort of autumnal comfort." At the same time, he would prepare himself "for writing (ten years from now) such beautiful books that all kinds of things will be forgiven me."[1]

Determined to reorganize and simplify his life, he urged Amy Wertheimer to understand his need to concentrate on his work. "Only do allow me these years to be self-centered," he wrote to her. "My whole talent will slip away from me if I don't learn to concentrate and cut out every distraction, even the apparently beneficent ones." He told her he was at his "wits-end." He absolutely had "to plunge about trying to teach myself to *fix* my mind and really work hard and plan, instead of just muddling through."[2]

He was working on himself as well as his writing. Beneath a gregarious exterior he was often shy, and insecure about how other people perceived him. In February of 1927, he sent a worried response to a critical letter from Bill Nichols: "I have been feared for my sharp tongue; I have been admired with a sort of distaste; only lately have I simplified out enough to be worthy of being liked (by men that is). I don't dare say that my silly egotism is entirely buried yet, but it is with you."[3] Thornton urged Nichols to be patient with him:

> *When various sides of me come forward that you do not like—the introspective side, perhaps . . . or the sentimento-demonstrative side (I have not known you very long after all and cannot be sure what strains make you impatient); or the I-did-this-and-that side . . . when such things come up, be patient and realize that after a long ill-adjusted awkward age I am only just beginning to be simple.*[4]

————

WHILE THORNTON carried on the occasional dialogue in letters, there were reflective soliloquies in the privacy of his 1926–27 journal. The pages were also filled with accounts of his travels, experimental pages of his novel, notes for plays he wanted to write, and critiques of plays he had seen or books he had read. He praised Max Reinhardt's production of Édouard Bourdet's *La prisonnière*, for instance, but took the play apart as a vestige of the "whole tedious theatrical cul-de-sac" of contemporary French playwrights.[5] He revealed in the journal the core intentions of his work: "Some day someone will discover that one of the principal ideas behind my work is the fear of catastrophe (especially illness and pain), and a preoccupation with the claims of a religion to meet the situation."[6] His literary approach to religion reflected his ongoing personal exploration: "There is the mood in which one distrusts religion because it so exactly fulfills one's need," he wrote in one journal entry. "You feel as though you had created religion because you wanted it so badly; instead of that it created you. (Most people feel this way about a life after death. Many do not want a life after death, but do want a loneliness mitigated in this.)"[7] He was simultaneously talking to himself about life as he sought to live it, and as he hoped to transmute it into fiction and drama.

By February 1927 he was reunited with his family in New Haven. He was slipping into a paternal role in the family, seeking to ease his parents' financial stress, worrying about Amos, Isabel, and Charlotte. Thornton feared that Amos was unhappy in his pastorate in New Hampshire. His brother had "a lonely scholar's and poet's mind" and an uncongenial congregation, Thornton felt, and, although Amos didn't say so, Thornton thought his brother longed to return to Oxford. But he worried that Charlotte's problems were the most difficult to solve. She was teaching at Wheaton College in Norton, Massachusetts, and when she came to New Haven to see the family, he found her in bad health, overworked, and "high-strung."[8] For once, however, he was not a problem to the family. "I am growing older (and high time) and serener," he wrote to Nichols. "My new book is finished up to the close of the penultimate chapter and is much simpler and more immediate than the other."[9] He had delivered the first installment of *The Bridge of San Luis Rey* to the Boni brothers, who were thrilled with it—but much work lay ahead.

Alternately shy and gregarious, Thornton was meeting interesting people wherever he roamed, "butting into turgid complicated lives," he wrote, always being "tangential to someone else's whirlwind."[10] This description of his own proclivities was an apt summary of Samuele's role in the lives of the members of the Cabala, and that dynamic would show up again in some of Thornton's later fiction—*Heaven's My Destination*, for instance, and *Theophilus North*. In both those novels he demonstrated an affinity for characters who butted into "complicated lives" and attached themselves to "someone else's whirlwind."

In real life, however, there was a continual tug-of-war: With his peers Thornton was at times still socially awkward and self-conscious—but his intellectual sophistication and elegant manners endeared him to his elders. He was still the loner, the outsider of his prep school days—yet he was gregarious and longed to be one of the crowd. He was a writer who wanted solitude but loved company. He craved opportunities to share his work, but he did not want to impose it on others.

During this time there were women he loved who loved him in return. He continued his often turbulent correspondence with Amy

Wertheimer, despite his intention of taking a year off. Finally, however, Amy's persistent letters so intruded on his patience and his need for uninterrupted time to work that he broke off communication altogether. "I asked for a year's pause," he wrote in a brief, straightforward letter. "I stick to it." She had refused "a strong helpful friendship," he told her. "I cannot give you anything else. . . . No one expects you to be happy. But to grip the elements of the situation *as they are* and to try and build up some kind of rich life for yourself from them." Circling both numbers, he wrote emphatically that he had to accept "the conditions of life as they are: 1. I have never implied that I could love you. 2. That you have a rare home and set of friends to whom you can serve as a great wonderful woman."[11] For the next few months there was silence between them.

To Amos he wrote, "Beware of women. I'm having a terrible time shaking off one. She can't decide whether to shoot me, herself or her husband. . . . Ernest Hemingway's motto: We have enough trouble with the women we do love, not to stand any from those we don't. It's the one realm where kindness don't work."[12]

He still wrote affectionate letters to Rosemary Ames, who was young and adoring, who sought his advice—and who was not a constant challenge. Rosemary's father was still standing in the way of her dreams of acting, and Thornton was her sympathetic confidant. At times, Thornton wrote to Nichols, he thought he might propose to Rosemary, or maybe to Nina Trego. But he had only to count to ten to realize "I hated such responsibilities" and "since I loved both girls so much it must be a sign that I don't love either *enough*, and so I refused and continue a celibate and a writer."[13]

Having had enough of high-maintenance women, Thornton turned with relief and new appreciation to his male friends, especially that kindred spirit Bill Nichols. Their friendship, which had begun in New York in the early twenties and had crystallized in England in 1926, would last a lifetime, but it was most intense during the twenties. Theirs was a deep bonding of two men of similar temperament, similar interests, similar circumstances in life. They gave each other advice about books to read, career strategies, and women they were involved with. (Nichols would marry, and would give up an academic post at Harvard for a successful career in journalism, culminating as editor of *This Week* magazine.) They confided in each other and encouraged each other in times of stress or sadness. When Nichols, who was spending part of the spring of 1927 in Wales, shared his worries with Thornton by mail, Thornton wrote back sympathetically from New Haven:

> *Your depressed letter found me in a similar condition. How real they are while they last, and how false: Three parts, chemical (digestion, a metabolism or the ductless glands, probably the pituitary body!); three parts, celibacy; three parts, religion (or whatever it will be called in the next century. Whitehead calls religion—"What a man does with his solitariness"); three parts, mere apprehension about the future, the whole mystery of tomorrow, physical, financial, social etc; and three parts homesickness. The respective appeasements are exercise, marriage, good deeds, hard work, and a return to America.*

Thornton's diagnosis grew out of his own experience, and he had come to think that some depressions "are so valuable and so important to personality" that you shouldn't "appease all of them; only keep one eye on the last."[14] He told Nichols, "I kind of dread making new friends. I like them so and that means letters and visits and thinking. And all life slips away as one loves more and more people."[15]

––––––––––

IN 1927 Thornton was still earnestly casting about for ways to earn money. Encouraged by Nichols, he was working on "the self-advertising business."[16] When Longmans, Green, the British publisher of *The Cabala*, sent him a scandalous French novel, Pierre Jean Jouve's *Paulina 1880*, "to translate and deodorize for them," he accepted the offer immediately even though, he said, "I have a low opinion of trans-lating. It oughtn't to take a week."[17] Desperate to earn the money for the translation, Thornton gave some thought that spring to going to a writers' retreat, perhaps in New Mexico. He had heard about the flamboyant Mabel Dodge and her "primitivo-sumptuous colony" of

artists, writers, and hangers-on at Taos, and he daydreamed about getting letters of introduction to her and paying her a visit there, where he
would take long walks, absorb the local color, listen to music, and concentrate on his writing—particularly the novel, which was nowhere
near completion.[18] Knowing that he couldn't live and work amid all the
distractions at home, much as he loved his family, he "engaged a rented
room in New Haven so that I could work without hearing the eternal
telephone conversations of my women-folk."[19]

Just in time Professor William Lyon Phelps came to the rescue with
a temporary job. He introduced Thornton to Gen. Charles Hitchcock
Sherrill, the wealthy former U.S. ambassador to Argentina, who told
Thornton that young Gibbs Sherrill had flunked out of Groton and
needed a tutor. Thornton immediately agreed to take the job, at a fee
of four hundred dollars, and headed to the Sherrill home in Briarcliff
Manor, New York, for "five weeks of *Hamlet* and *Virgil*, skating and
good cookery."[20] The money he earned would pay his living expenses
for a while, with funds left over to hire a typist to prepare the final
manuscript of *The Bridge of San Luis Rey*, and to have a publicity photograph made. By mid-March he was as sick of tutoring in New York
as he had been of chaperoning Andy Townson in Europe the previous
autumn. He was rested and healthy, however, thanks to the long walks
he craved for exercise, and the solitude that usually stimulated bursts
of creativity. "Isn't it great to feel as tho' you could chew rocks?" he
wrote to Nichols.[21]

He was habitually restless, with an innate yearning for the road,
barely finishing one journey before he wanted to embark on the next.
He acknowledged that he was living a "crazy vagabond life."[22] Maybe
he would go to Taos, or to Monhegan or to New York or back to Europe.
For the time being, Thornton wrote to Nichols, he would live in his
room in New Haven, with

a well-oiled typewriter. A little money and an occasional opera. De-
lightful family. Tea at the Eliz. Club and a faint smell of incense from
the undergrds. . . . Many swims up and down the shore with an awful
nice crowd that never heard of Tchekov. A few dances as I reluctantly

slip into the younger-married-set—and then, you get back. Hell!
That's my life as it looks from here.[23]

He was deeply discouraged about his future, and confided his doubts in a letter to his brother: "If you saw me closer, you'd wonder how any life could go on so crazily, at the mercy of this and that chance." He didn't see what he could do but "trail a meaningless life about from Mansfield St. to some little trip and then back again. I don't marry. In fact all I'm supposed to do is to make books as a cow gives milk and to live as little as a *person* as possible."[24]

———

"DON'T FORGET what you said about finishing the BRIDGE in a spurt," Lewis Baer wrote hopefully to Thornton on March 21, 1927. "We are anxious to get it to the printers soon so that we can get a lot of advance proofs."[25] Nine days later Baer tried again to nudge Thornton to some kind of action. "I am very anxious to set up the little bit we have of the BRIDGE," he wrote, "but it is rather difficult to choose the type since I have not the faintest idea of how long you expect to make it."[26]

Thornton could offer a dozen sometimes contradictory reasons why his novel lay unfinished on his desk: He had to seek work to earn money, and then he had to do the work once he found it; he had to work on his plays, especially when he felt he was "about to be brought to bed of a tragedy in 4 acts"; he needed to spend time in the Yale library to "verify some allusions"; he was lonely, and he needed to see his family; he needed to be away from his family and everyone else so he could concentrate; he had to work on the translation of *Paulina 1880*, but in order to do that, he teased, he had to study Fowler's *Dictionary of Modern English Usage* from cover to cover.[27]

Once he finished his tutoring job he went back to New Haven and tried to finish *Paulina* and *The Bridge*. In late May he received a letter from Edward "Ted" Weeks, then a junior editor of the *Atlantic Monthly*, praising *The Cabala* and asking if Thornton had a new book in progress that they might consider for serialization.[28] He sent Weeks "two very untidy portions" of *The Bridge of San Luis Rey*, with a letter revealing some of the dilemmas he faced as he struggled to finish the novel.[29] There were "two separate novelettes" in the existing manuscript, set in a " 'theological' frame." He had not finished "Parts Four and Five" of the book, and was "all flustered." Thornton anticipated that Weeks might not buy the serial rights—and he didn't.[30]

Thornton had finished the first three parts of the novel, which the Bonis set in page proofs in mid-June—but he was still "all flustered' by parts 4 and 5. Whether it was apprehension, procrastination, writer's block, or unavoidable distraction, he was struggling to meet his commitment to the Bonis, at the same time wrangling over contracts, royalties, and their future association. He wrote to his mother from Briarcliff in March 1927 that Albert Boni had offered him "15% and 500 advance on each of three novels."[31] Thornton wanted to publish his short plays as well, and Lewis Baer had written a letter in April to confirm their oral agreement for Thornton to proceed as he saw fit to publish the plays elsewhere in a "more or less limited edition," with the provision that the rights would revert to him so that Boni could eventually publish a "complete edition" of his works.[32]

In June, Thornton reported to friends that his English publisher was "setting up" to publish both his translation of *Paulina 1880* and *The Bridge*.[33] He had promised to have both manuscripts ready so Isabel, who was traveling to England on June 15, could deliver them in person to his publishers in London, but this was another deadline he did not meet.[34] By July 25 Thornton was writing to Baer at the Boni firm that the translation of *Paulina* would be ready within "a few weeks," and offering to sell it for three hundred dollars.[35] Then the project apparently lapsed unfinished, for reasons that are not clear. Any vestiges of Thornton's manuscript have yet to be found.

NO MATTER how overwhelmed with work he was, Thornton was first of all a brother, a son, and a friend. Therefore it was not only the financial and professional imperative but also his sense of responsibility to his parents and sisters, as well as to his Lawrenceville friends, that led him to return to the Lawrenceville School for the 1927 fall term. Clyde Foresman, the Davis housemaster, was critically ill, and Dr. Abbott offered Thornton that position, which he declined, agreeing instead to return as the assistant housemaster. But after Clyde Foresman's death on July 14, 1927, Dr. Abbott telegraphed Thornton, pressing him to accept the leadership of Davis House. Amos Parker Wilder begged his son "not to refuse," adding that "it would do a great deal to ease some of the problems in the family also."[36] Thornton gave in. (Abbott's telegram passed through their father's hands, Thornton told Isabel, and Dr. Wilder in turn sent his son "a series of pathetic telegrams begging me not to turn down four or five thousand bucks and residence. So I've accepted. Responsibilities and discipline and red tape galore—but I wouldn't write much anyway.")[37]

He explained his decision to return to Lawrenceville in other terms to Nichols: There was the "rueful thought that altho *The Bridge* is a much better book than *The Cabala*, it is a much less gaudy one" and an "undeniably sad" one, and he had "better not count on too many dividends."[38] He could not risk his family's well-being on the faint hope that he could earn any money as a writer. In fact he was finding it difficult to collect the money his first book had already earned. He wrote to Baer at Boni in July about the delays in the publishing house: "I have always been very grateful and loyal to you for having discovered me. . . . But my loyalty is being thrown away, if you cannot be normally considerate of me these early difficult years. You have not yet caught up to the January statement; you promised me some of the Spring royalties; and surely some of the Advance on a book of which four-fifths are set up." He asked Baer to send him his "five-hundred" so they could keep their association "cordial."[39]

Thornton felt it was his responsibility to help provide for his parents and two younger sisters. He wrote to his friend Leslie "Les" Glenn that "with a dear vague impractical family group like mine I don't dare stake on the margin of risk. If something happened to Father. . . . . [*sic*] etc." But his return to Lawrenceville would be just for a year, he insisted, and "In one more year I should be able to find a real niche some-where."[40] He also wrote to explain his decision to Foresman's widow, Grace, encouraging her to continue to feel a part of Davis House.[41]

Now he would have a house with seven rooms and a study and a housekeeper, as well as a large garden and a garage. He wished that his mother could live with him. She wouldn't have to run the house, he told her—just be there, and be herself, although he doubted she would agree. She was already begging off, mainly because there was Janet to consider.[42]

Because he was going to be a housemaster, stepping into a demand-ing full-time job, Thornton absolutely had to finish writing *The Bridge of San Luis Rey*, no matter how little faith he had in its prospects for success. He went for "a spell" to the MacDowell Colony, where he found Mrs. MacDowell seriously ill. Edwin Arlington Robinson was there as usual; the "dean" of the colony, Thornton called him.[43] New acquaintances that summer included DuBose and Dorothy Heyward, who were on the way to the New York opening of their play, based on DuBose Heyward's novel *Porgy* (his collaboration with George Gersh-win on *Porgy and Bess* would begin in 1933); and the writer Elizabeth Shepley Sergeant, who had been sent to Paris to cover World War I for the *New Republic*. She had been gravely wounded on the battlefield, an experience she reported in *Shadow-Shapes: The Journal of a Wounded Woman, October 1918–May 1919*, published in 1920.[44] There was "much talk" at the MacDowell Colony that summer about Glenway Wescott's new novel, *The Grandmothers* (1927). "I'm jealous," Thornton wrote to Marie Townson. "My only satisfaction is that the 3 musketeers aged 30 = Ernest Hemingway, Glenway Wescott and I may puncture the inflated rep's of the previous fashions: the Sherwood Andersons, Cab-ells, Cathers, what not. You'll scold me for that, but by dint of being modest most of the time I allow myself a little party of conceit every now and then."[45]

By the end of July, Thornton had finished his novel at last, and he moved on to spend a couple of days in August with old friends at the Sunapee summer tutoring camp at Blodgett's Landing in New Hamp-shire before returning to New Haven. As had happened before, however, he was asked to stay on and tutor at the Lake Sunapee summer school. "The usual crazy thing happened: I love it," he wrote to Isabel. "I take twelve mile walks almost every day; I swim over a mile; I'm brown-black and roaring with health."[46] Amy Wertheimer was in residence across the lake for the summer, and Thornton saw her once a week. "She's resigned and wistful," he told Isabel. "She always has house guests so that there isn't much occasion etc."[47] But there was occasion to visit Rosemary Ames, and he took advantage of it. She was the "star pupil" at the nearby Manarden Theatre Camp in Peterborough, and he went to see her. They were still affectionate pen pals: "Such letters— quite turn my head," he told his sister.[48]

NOW THAT he had delivered *The Bridge of San Luis Rey*, what would he "write next, by slow stages at the Davis? Plays, I suppose," he said. "Another letter from [producer] Charles Wagner wanting to see some and all that. But I have no burning ideas."[49] August brought word from Thornton's publishers that his new novel had caused a crisis in his publishing house. "We are in a quandary," Lewis Baer wrote to Thornton on behalf of Albert and Charles Boni August 18. "The page proofs of The Bridge just arrived, and the book only comes to 195 pages. We've announced it as a $2.50 book , and really should follow up The Cabala with a book of the same price, but we've explained to you the booksellers' stupid feelings on this subject. They'll take a book, say, Humph, only 195 pages, and immediately raise H."[50] There were two alternatives, Baer wrote: "To cut the price, which may be bad; or to put in 6 or 8 illustrations, which gives it in the booksellers' eyes anyway an added distinction and cuts down on his objections. What do you think? Do you believe the book would lend itself to illustrations."[51]

Thornton wrote to Isabel what he truly thought: "Boni is revolted that [the novel] isn't long enough to keep up the fraud of a 2.50 book. He wants six to eight illustrations, and the Canadian and Esquimaux [Eskimo] rights. I begin to see a lit. agent to keep Bonis quiet."[52]

The book would ultimately sport illustrations—ten plates, including the frontispiece, by the popular illustrator Amy Drevenstedt.

Albert Boni wrote Thornton on August 30, 1927, to let him know that the exact publication date of the novel would be left open until they heard decisions from the Book-of-the-Month Club, founded in 1926, and the newly formed Literary Guild, started in 1927, as acceptance by either might postpone publication until December or January.[53] Harry Scherman, the founder of the Book-of-the-Month Club, had been Albert and Charles Boni's partner in the Little Leather Books enterprise (an endeavor that had yielded more than 40 million books in its time), and Henry Seidel Canby, Thornton's creative-writing professor at Yale, was on the Book-of-the-Month Club board, which selected the books to send out to more than 46,000 members.[54] These connections were not enough, however, for club acceptance of *The Bridge of San Luis Rey*.

"The hurrying up of the last pages of the *Bridge* and the new arrangements of Lawrenceville were a lot to assimilate," Thornton wrote to Marie Townson as he juggled the responsibilities of the novelist and the schoolmaster.[55] In a later letter to Mrs. Townson, Thornton hinted at the ordeal of reading proofs for his books: "My mother has long been in despair over my spelling and even my grammar," he wrote, "and insists on 3 literate persons reading all my proofs after me."[56] By that time the fall term was well under way at Lawrenceville School, and Wilder the novelist had set aside his work in favor of Wilder the schoolmaster.

Many years later, after Wilder's death, Clark Andrews, one of his former students, reminisced about Wilder the teacher—"incurable insomniac, inveterate walker, fanciful conversationalist, friend." He described Wilder as a

> tall, thin man, about six feet, with an owlish face, a pencil mustache and brown tortoise-shell glasses which partly hid his darting, inquisitive blue eyes. . . . He was a nervous man—a very nervous man, constantly looking at his watch. His head jerked back and forth, his eyes jumped around as if he expected to see the unexpected happen at any moment.[57]

When Wilder entered the French classroom on the first day of the fall term, Andrews remembered, he wrote on the blackboard "in a neat, precise hand, MY NAME IS THORNTON WILDER. I AM YOUR TEACHER. THIS IS A COURSE IN CONVERSATIONAL FRENCH. AFTER TODAY, NO ENGLISH SPOKEN HERE."[58]

According to Andrews, Wilder made Conversational French "the most popular class at Lawrenceville." He was popular out of class as well, inviting students on weekend afternoons for tea and conversation (perhaps in the mode of the Elizabethan Club), sessions his students referred to as meetings of the Thornton Wilder Literary Society. Wilder usually concluded these gatherings with the dramatic recitation of a poem on the order of Robert Service's "The Shooting of Dan McGrew," declaiming every word by heart. (He had been required to learn that particular poem as a boy, he said, as "a punishment.")[59]

THAT FALL, Thornton began to suffer intense pain that led him to fear—correctly, as it turned out—that he was showing symptoms of appendicitis. His father's physician, Dr. William Francis Verdi, performed an appendectomy in New Haven in October. "The appendix was lifted out three weeks ago tomorrow," Thornton wrote to Marie Townson from New Haven on November 9. His surgery and recuperation kept him away from his school duties for three and a half weeks.[60]

He was back at Lawrenceville, still healing from his operation, when he began to realize that his harried life of the schoolmaster was about to change. On October 27, 1927, he had signed a contract with Longmans, Green & Company, Ltd., for the British publication of his second novel. The North American edition of *The Bridge of San Luis Rey* was published on November 3. To offset the brevity of the book, Albert and Charles Boni had chosen 235 pages of thick stock set with a generous-sized font and wide margins, accompanied in the first edition by the ten pen-and-ink drawings by Amy Drevenstedt. They added a map of Peru and Ecuador on brown endpapers. (A 1929 edition of the novel would be illustrated by wood engravings by the artist Clare Leighton; a special limited edition published in 1929 contained three-color lithographs by Rockwell Kent.) To the amazement of the author and the publishers, those advance proofs must have worked, for there were immediate enthusiastic reviews in the United States and in England, and *The Bridge* was successfully promoted for the Christmas trade. By the end of December the novel was in its seventh printing in the United States, and by January 6, 1928, Baer wrote to Thornton, the publishers would be "wildly busy getting ready the eighth edition of the Bridge."[61]

WHEN THE Lawrenceville School closed for the Christmas holidays, Thornton traveled to Florida and to Cuba to rest and continue his recuperation—but most of all, to recover from the excitement and stress of the year. From the Columbus Hotel in Miami, he wrote to Marie Townson that his novel was "selling like catnip . . . I'm almost getting RICH. But mind you I refuse to buy a car. A swimming pool, all right, a gold tooth, all right, but no CAR."[62] He didn't like Cuba, he told his mother, but in Miami he spent quiet, restful days in the sun. "Already I'm turkey-red," he wrote, "and I sleep nights for a change. And I have a friend in Town, oh what a friend! as the hymn says. And that's Gene Tunney." Thornton explained to his mother how they met:

> I wrote him a note asking for an hour's talk and telling him I had
> messages from Ernest Hemingway. He phoned back at once that he was
> delighted, would I please come to dinner Friday night, that right there
> on his table was The Cabala which had been highly recommended to him
> and which he was going to read as soon as he finished Death Comes to
> the Archbishop. I warned Father last October that I would get to know
> the champion and he made a disgusted face. Explain to him that now-
> days there are prizefighters and prizefighters.[63]

Thornton spent a fascinating evening with the movie-star-handsome world heavyweight champion, and wrote to Marie Townson about their meeting:

> I don't know what to say. . . . Most of the times, he's wonderful, as
> likable and naïf as the best Lawrenceville boy—and (don't quote me)

*exactly mental-age of 17. Then in the distance you hear a faint sound
of brass. Perhaps I imagined it. Heaven forgive me. Anyway I'm sure
of this: his famous aspiration after culture is perfectly sincere, only he
doesn't get 3 consecutive minutes to do anything with it. I wish someone
would engage me as his tutor. Anyway, I shall see more of him.*[64]

Thornton would indeed see more of Tunney—but before then, he
would come to know firsthand what it was like not to have three consecutive minutes to do what he needed or wanted to do. The retreat to
Florida proved to be the calm in the eye of a hurricane of totally unexpected literary success and acclaim, unrelenting public visibility, and
incessant demands on his time and energy—as well as a barrage of mail.
More and more people, Thornton wrote to Yale professor Chauncey
Tinker, were wondering why he didn't "leave the little chicken-feed
duties of the housemaster and teacher and go to Bermuda, for example,
and write books as a cow gives milk." He didn't know how to answer,
except to say that he felt "(though with intervals of misgiving) that
this life is valuable to me and, I dare presume, my very pleasure in my
routine can make me useful to others. Anyway no one, except you and
I, seems to believe any longer in the dignity of teaching."[65]

Thornton shared with Tinker some revealing details about himself
and his work: "As for your questions, oh, isn't there a lot of New England in me; all that ignoble passion to be didactic that I have to fight
with. All that bewilderment as to where Moral Attitude begins and
where it shades off into mere Puritan Bossiness. My father is still pure
Maine—1880 and I carry all that load of notions to examine and dis-
card or assimilate."[66] Had Thornton been to Peru? Tinker wondered.
What were his sources for the novel?

"No, I have never been to Peru," Thornton replied. "Why I chose to
graft my thoughts about Luke 13–4 upon a delightful one-act play by
Merimée, *Le Carosse du Saint-Sacrement* [sic], I do not know. The Marquesa is my beloved Mme de Sévigné in a distorting mirror. The bridge
is invented, the name borrowed from one of Junipero Serra's missions
in California."[67]

Tinker told Thornton that certain pages of *The Bridge of San Luis*

Rey had made him weep. "It is right and fitting that you cried for a page of mine," Thornton replied, with gratitude. "How many a time I have cried with love or awe or pity while you have talked of the Doctor [Samuel Johnson], or Cowper, or Goldsmith. . . . Between the lines then you will find here all my thanks and joy at your letter."[68]

19

"THE FINEST BRIDGE
IN ALL PERU"

*On Friday noon, July the twentieth, 1714, the finest bridge in all Peru
broke and precipitated five travelers into the gulf below.*

—THORNTON WILDER,
The Bridge of San Luis Rey

New Jersey and Europe (1928)

Thornton Wilder's second novel made its bow to the world
without the mechanical errors that had marred pages of *The
Cabala*. His novel may have been short, but thousands of readers got their money's worth in story and substance. Like *The Cabala*
before it, *The Bridge of San Luis Rey* pulls the reader into an intriguing
narrative composed of interlacing stories and characters—and, in the
process, confronts the reader with universal questions. In his second
novel, however, Wilder was far more at home in his craft, more skilled
in characterization, more assured in style and voice.

His journal and his surviving manuscript drafts and letters reveal
the evolution of the novel and the emerging habits of the writer.
For part of his inspiration Wilder gave credit to *Le Carrosse du Saint-
Sacrement* (*The Coach of the Holy Sacrament*), a comedy by the French
dramatist Prosper Mérimée (1803–70), whose novella *Carmen* was the
source of the popular opera. *Le Carrosse du Saint-Sacrement* was based
on a supposed incident in the life of Micaela Villegas (1748–1819)—
the Perichole—a great Peruvian actress and courtesan. For a time she
was the mistress of the Viceroy of Lima, Andrés de Ribera, and she
bore him three children.[1] Wilder was fascinated with the legendary
Perichole, but except for a few details, the complex character who
emerges in the novel is Wilder's fictional creation—and a tragic figure

rather than Mérimée's comic, even farcical one. Wilder transforms the Countess Montemayor, a minor figure in Mérimée's play, into the Marquesa de Montemayor, one of the three most important women he creates in his novel.

For two years he had filled the pages of his journal and notebooks with drafts, revisions, questions, and ideas, discarding many of them along the way. En route to his final manuscript, Wilder played with structures, sequences, and characters. One early plan, for instance, was to have a mysterious stranger perish in the collapse of the bridge, and then to dramatize the efforts to establish his identity, but Wilder abandoned that idea. The novel, dedicated to his mother, is at once more profound and more subtle than *The Cabala*. The tone is often conversational as the narrator speaks familiarly and directly to the reader. The style is pared back, clean, and taut, with a restrained beauty of expression. Stung by what he perceived to be the critics' overemphasis on his literary style in *The Cabala*, Wilder, as noted, wove into *The Bridge* a rebuke and a defense: When the marquesa's son-in-law failed to see past the style to the substance of her letters to her daughter, Wilder wrote that he missed "the whole purport of literature, which is the notation of the heart."[2]

Wilder insisted that *The Bridge* was a novel of unanswered questions—some of them questions he would explore all his life. "The book is not supposed to solve," Wilder wrote to a former student. "The book is supposed to be as puzzling and distressing as the news that five of your friends died in an automobile accident. . . . Chekhov said: 'The business of literature is not to answer questions, but to state them fairly.'"[3]

The questions proliferate as the novel moves forward: Why did this happen to *those* five people? Can the cause and the meaning of their fate be found in their secret, innermost lives? Is the event part of a divine plan? Do we live by accident and die by accident—or do we live by plan and die by plan? How do we cope with catastrophe? What is the significance of the religion of faith and fact, or the religion of mysticism and magic? These are the most obvious questions in the novel, and the questions that have garnered most attention, but there are other inquiries that merit close scrutiny: Wilder asks, How does one love, and why? What is the nature and purpose of art, and the function of the artist? How does one truly live and bear the burdens of life? And what does it all mean?

The plot of the novel is deceptively simple: A bridge collapses. Five people who happen to be crossing the bridge at this fateful moment fall into the chasm and die. Brother Juniper happens to witness the tragedy, and he resolves to investigate the lives of the victims in hopes of proving his belief that the accident is a "sheer act of God." He does not doubt that it is God's will that these five people should die in this catastrophe on this day, but he sets out to "prove it, historically, mathematically, to his converts,—poor obstinate converts, so slow to believe that their pains were inserted into their lives for their own good."[4]

To prove his case he will examine the lives and characters of the five victims—the Marquesa de Montemayor, a wealthy, bitterly lonely widow who is estranged from her only child, a married daughter living four thousand miles away to escape her mother's domination; Pepita, the marquesa's stoic servant and companion, an orphan girl who was raised by the noble abbess Madre María del Pilar; Esteban, like Wilder a twinless twin, but one who tries to kill himself after his brother, Manuel, dies; Uncle Pio, an adventurer, singing master, acting teacher, mentor, and dilettante, who has devoted his life to the Perichole, the finest actress in Peru; and Jaime, the Perichole's young son, whom Uncle Pio is taking to Lima so that he can nurture and educate the boy.

To resurrect and examine the lives of these five victims, Brother Juniper employs the tactics of the biographer—and in the process Wilder satirizes biographers and biographies. For six years Brother Juniper busies himself "knocking at all the doors in Lima, asking thousands of questions, filling scores of notebooks, in his effort at establishing the fact that each of the five lost lives was a perfect whole." He writes an "enormous book" which "deals with one after another of the victims of the accident, cataloguing thousands of little facts and anecdotes and testimonies."[5] Brother Juniper is afraid to omit any detail, putting everything down in "the notion perhaps that if he (or a keener head) reread the book twenty times, the countless facts would suddenly start to move, to assemble, and to betray their secret."[6] Yet despite his arsenal of notes and facts, Brother Juniper does not discover the "central passion"—the "very spring within the spring" of the lives he has examined. As the omniscient narrator observes, "The art of biography is more difficult than is generally supposed."[7]

Wilder was absorbed for many years in contemplation of the nature of art and the creative process, and the nature of the artist. One of the dozens of books he was reading during this period was French author and critic Paul Valéry's *Eupalinos, or the Architect*, an imaginary dialogue between Sophocles and Phaedrus, which contains a powerful parable of the artist and explores the processes of creation in art along with the philosophical and religious implications of certain works of art. The uses and abuses of art weave through *The Bridge* as a subtext. Two of the characters in Wilder's novel are immersed in the literary art of the theater and the art of acting; three others are caught up in the art or business of writing letters. The Marquesa de Montemayor, based loosely on the great letter writer Mme Marie de Sévigné, lives for and through the copious letters she writes to her estranged daughter. Unlike Mme de Sévigné, however, the marquesa becomes an eccentric, alcoholic recluse whose existence lies "in the burning center of her mind." The doomed twins, Manuel and Esteban, support themselves as scribes and copyists. Manuel falls in love with the great Perichole while writing secret letters dictated by the semiliterate actress. Over their long relationship, her "Uncle" Pio teaches the Perichole to act and sing, but not to read and write. He has done the Perichole's reading and writing for her for many years. Uncle Pio has a passion for "Spanish literature and its masterpieces, especially in the theatre."[8] He longs to be a poet, and has written songs for vaudeville that make their way into the world as folk music, but like the marquesa, he is unaware of the success of his art. The ultimate writer in the novel is, of course, Brother Juniper, obsessively researching and writing his epic religious treatise, which brings his downfall, and making a secret copy of it, which survives the destruction of the original manuscript by the clergy.

Wilder also borrowed a character from Valéry, as he acknowledged in his journal on December 22, 1926, a sea captain who, in Wilder's incarnation, has a keen mind that is "not buoyant but concentrated & enriched by the enforced chastity of long sea-voyages."[9] In Wilder's Captain Alvarado, "blackened and cured by all weathers," there are clear echoes of Valéry's sea captain, "bleached and blackened, gilded in turn by successive climes."[10] Like Valéry's captain, Wilder's memorable Captain Alvarado is a traveler and adventurer. He is invited by Uncle Pio to attend the nightlong symposia hosted by Don Andrés de Ribera, the viceroy of Lima. The symposia discussions are presented in concise summary in *The Bridge*, centered less on art, religion, and philosophy, as in Valéry's work, than on an array of topics—ghosts and second sight, the second coming of Christ, wars and kings, poets and scholars, and regrets about the human race.[11]

But for all the written words flying back and forth, and all the allusions to the dynamics of art and the artist, the novel is grounded in questions about the claims of religion and the meaning of love. As has been noted, Wilder wrote in his journal in 1926, "Some day someone will discover that one of the principal ideas behind my work is the fear of catastrophe (especially illness and pain), and a preoccupation with the claims of a religion to meet the situation."[12] In the forefront of *The Bridge* is Brother Juniper's conviction that theology should "take its place among the exact sciences." His quest grows out of his unwavering religious faith, not out of doubt or skepticism. Brother Juniper, we are told, is already convinced that he knows the answer to the question he raises: The collapse of the bridge of San Luis Rey, he believes, "was a sheer Act of God."[13] He is seeking "scientific" proof of his existing belief, not answers to questions about his faith. Brother Juniper dies willing "to lay down his life for the purity of the church," but longing "for one voice somewhere to testify for him that his intention, at least, had been for faith."[14]

It is the marquesa who poses the most profound and perplexing questions about religion. She exhorts the powers of paganism as well as of Christianity—religion as magic as well as religion as faith—to protect her daughter during her pregnancy. She maintains a belief in the "great Perhaps."[15] The marquesa's pilgrimage finally leads her to a certain peace: "She was listening to the new tide of resignation that was rising with her. Perhaps she would learn in time to permit both her daughter and her gods to govern their own affairs." She gives herself up to a certain fatalism: "What will be, will be."[16] The marquesa faces her own failures, and is ready to start a new life. "Let me live now," she prays. "Let me begin again."[17] The irony is that the marquesa's spiritual quest both saves her and kills her.

For all its examination of faith and belief, the novel is fundamentally a story of people who simply desire to love and to be loved, and who, in most cases, have failed. There is an exploration of many facets of love—romantic love; unequal love; unrequited love; platonic love; parental love; familial love; the unique love of twins; neurotic love; mistaken love; controlling love; self-love; the "disinterested" love of altruism; the love of God. Uncle Pio, whom Wilder later described as "all onlooker, all uncommitted participant" (and one of the most autobiographical figures in all his work) divides the "inhabitants of the world into two groups, those who have loved and those who have not."[18] He believes that love is "a sort of cruel malady through which the elect are required to pass in their late youth and from which they emerge, pale and wrung, but ready for the business of living."[19]

After years of suffocating parental love, when the parent seeks to control the child for her own good (echoes of Wilder's own father), the marquesa realizes that her love for her daughter "was not without a shade of tyranny" and that she has loved her daughter not for the daughter's sake, but for her own.[20] Between the twins Esteban and Manuel, orphans who, like Pepita, were raised by the abbess, there is an intense and exclusive love, a love that has its own private language, a love that, according to the critic Malcolm Goldstein, "is so intense that it approaches homosexual yearning."[21] When Manuel begins to love the Perichole, Esteban discovers "that secret from which one never quite recovers [echoes of Wilder's own heartbreaks], that even in the most perfect love one person loves less profoundly than the other. There may be two equally good, equally gifted, equally beautiful, but there may never be two that love one another equally well."[22] Disenchanted with Uncle Pio; with her lover, the viceroy; and most of all, with herself, the Perichole, who has known love only as passion, believes that you are loved for yourself only in plays in the theater.[23] So goes Wilder's provocative evocation of the varieties of love.

This novel, like much of Wilder's work, is notable for the presence of strong, complex female characters who empower the story—three in this instance: the marquesa, the Perichole, and the great abbess Madre María del Pilar. All three are inspired by real-life figures—the Marquesa by Mme de Sévigné; the Perichole by the great Peruvian actress Micaela Villegas, known as "La Perricholi"; and the abbess by Wilder's maternal aunt, Charlotte Niven, noted for her humanitarian work for the international YWCA. In the depiction of their lives and the conclusions they reach, the novel makes its strongest statement about the nature of love. In all three cases the prospect of peace and redemption comes only through selfless love. The marquesa realizes her own selfishness, her "tyrannical" love.[24] The Perichole despairs that she has always equated love with passion, that she has no heart, that she feels nothing. After Pio and her son die, she endures a "terrible incommunicable pain"—"the pain that could not speak once to Uncle Pio and tell him of her love and just once offer her courage to Jaime in his sufferings." She has failed everyone, she realizes too late. "They love me and I fail them."[25] The abbess, too, has wrestled with her own doubts, especially her fears that her work will not go on after her death. By the end of the novel she has "accepted the fact that it was of no importance whether her work went on or not; it was enough to work." She concludes that it "seemed to be sufficient for Heaven that for a while in Peru a disinterested love had flowered and faded."[26] The abbess, who hates men but loves mankind, has "allowed her life to be gnawed away" because she has "fallen in love with an idea several centuries before its appointed appearance in the history of civilization. She hurled herself against the obstinacy of her time in her desire to attach a little dignity to women."[27] Ultimately she practices a selfless love of her work, and of the sick and the blind and the lost whom she serves and comforts.

The abbess has the last word on love. She acknowledges the reality that every person who has ever lived will die and will ultimately be forgotten. "But," she adds, in lines that are among the most quoted in literature, the love will have been enough; all those impulses of love return to the love that made them. Even memory is not necessary for love. There is a land of the living and a land of the dead and the bridge is love, the only survival, the only meaning.[28]

FROM THE outset *The Bridge of San Luis Rey* was a commercial and critical success on two continents.[29] For the critic and editor Clifton Fadiman, the novel was "a very beautiful book," and its author was one of the "few young Americans writing today whose development will be watched by the discerning critic with greater hope and confidence."[30] The British novelist and critic Arnold Bennett wrote from England that he was "dazzled" by the book, praising the writing as "simple, straight, *juste*, and powerful" and "unsurpassed in the present epoch."[31] For the English novelist and poet Vita Sackville-West, it was a work of "genuine beauty and originality."[32] The positive reviews poured in, along with the occasional negative: Edwin Muir, novelist and poet, wrote in the London *Nation and Athenaeum*, "The book is hardly a good one, therefore; it is in many ways and at many points a bad one; but it is interesting, and the work of an unusual talent when he is genuine, and of considerable accomplishment when he is meretricious."[33]

The reviews abounded throughout 1928. The writer and critic Edmund Wilson, just two years older than Wilder, was impressed that "so young a man should display such unmistakable originality of style, of form and of point of view," although he wished Wilder would now "study the United States, and give us their national portraits."[34] The American poet and editor Louis Untermeyer called Wilder's success in England "unprecedented," and noted that major as well as minor critics had "responded to Wilder's sensibility, to his finesse of phrase, and what is most unusual—to his spiritual power."[35] Skepticism came from a seemingly disgruntled Hugh Walpole, the popular and prolific English novelist, whose own novel *Wintersmoon* (1927) had been superseded on the 1928 bestseller list by *The Bridge of San Luis Rey*. He wrote that he fancied that Wilder's book was "in danger of overpraise."[36]

According to *Publishers Weekly*, *The Bridge* was the number one best-selling novel in the United States for 1928. It was serialized in Hearst newspapers that summer, accompanied by garish headlines and illustrations. The novel won the Pulitzer Prize in fiction for novels published in 1927, a stellar group that included William Faulkner's *Mosquitos*, Willa Cather's *Death Comes to the Archbishop*, Glenway Wescott's *The Grandmothers*, Ernest Hemingway's *Men Without Women*, Sinclair Lewis's *Elmer Gantry*, and Upton Sinclair's *Oil!* (The Pulitzer Prize for poetry that year went to Wilder's MacDowell Colony friend Edwin Arlington Robinson for *Tristram*.)

"LETTERS AND telegrams from everywhere. What to do?" Wilder wrote to his mother from the Lawrenceville School in January 1928. "I could write you all day, honey, but I'm angry and distracted at the fact I can no longer even *live* between the claims of these duties real and imitation. I get some of the damndest letters and telegrams you ever saw." All he could think to do was to try to get away again. He confided in his mother that he was "probably going to travel through Germany, Austria, Venice and Greek islands with Gene Tunney and write a lovely travel book about it and us. 100,000 copies—all the boy scouts and their mamas."[37] Meanwhile there were the daily duties at Lawrenceville, compounded by the demands from his publishers: On February 4 they were hosting a party in his honor at Lewis Baer's Manhattan apartment, inviting, Wilder said, "all the critics and the New Yorker type of glib gossiphound."[38] When one reporter asked Wilder what he hoped to write next, he said he'd like to do a picaresque novel, and that the boyhood of Uncle Pio in *The Bridge of San Luis Rey* was a "hasty sketch" for the protagonist—"a purely parasitic, conscienceless gifted boy who carves out through endless trials and errors his own odd, but convincing, rules of right and wrong"—a harbinger of George Brush and *Heaven's My Destination*, the novel he would write in the thirties.[39]

He could not keep up with the burgeoning correspondence generated by the astounding success of his novel. He wrote his mother on

February 23 that books sales were "going to go well above 100,000 copies." The Bonis told him that on one day alone he "had earned over 600 dollars (5,000 copies by telegraphic order)."[40] If he wound up making the kind of money the Bonis implied he would, Wilder wrote to Amos that "the first thing to do is give Mama a few more rooms and a Finnish maid." But he was not "splashing around in worldliness," he told his brother; he was just overwhelmed. He asked Amos to be patient with him when he didn't answer letters, and to love him "thru thick and thin."[41] For the present he could only do his best to manage the new responsibilities without neglecting the old ones—and he made one decision that would affect his entire family. He wrote right away to tell his mother about it, in a letter headed "Dearest of mamas":

> *You and I and Isabel and Janet or everybody are taking a house near London (Oxford or the Thames-side) all Summer. And we, all or some or more, are staying there until March. Then I am coming back to lecture for two months under Lee Keedick (the best: Margot Asquith and G. K. Chesterton and Hugh Walpole). You stay on if you like.*[42]

Wilder wanted his mother to go over to England early in the spring to "find a house with a garden, please. . . . And a big house."[43] It needed to be spacious, not only for the family but for houseguests. He told her that he would be traveling abroad in July with three Lawrenceville boys "vaguely" under his care, that the boys would "drop in and out during the Summer," and that Gene Tunney would visit in the fall.[44] Not to worry about the expense; they could afford it: He had just received six thousand dollars from the Boni firm, he told his mother. Etching the words in deeper, darker ink, he promised her that there was "**More monthly**" to come.[45]

Wilder's sudden success, prosperity, and fame inundated him with opportunities, challenges, and frequent headaches. He was unhappy with his publishers, who had been, in the case of *The Cabala*, careless and even inattentive in the production of the book. The Bonis were often slow to promote his books, late with royalty payments, and not as supportive as Wilder wished of his ideas for future projects. He decided early in 1928 to take matters into his own hands. For one thing, he was being wooed by Harper & Brothers publishing executive Cass Canfield, just Wilder's age, a Harvard graduate, World War I veteran, reporter, and advertising man, and three years away from becoming president of Harper.

On January 16, 1928, Wilder wrote to Cass Canfield to say that he wished to commit himself to Harper on the condition that "the House of Harpers will consent to subsidize me to the extent of five thousand a year for three years beginning June 1929" even though that period would include some of the time when he would be completing the books he was obligated to give Albert and Charles Boni. In return Wilder would consider all future books to belong to Harper, except for the book of his short plays which was set to be published by Coward-McCann, since the Bonis were not interested in bringing it out. The fifteen thousand dollars from Harper would constitute an advance on royalties for "at least two novels of 50,000 words [each] or more." If it turned out that Wilder would not need the advance sum, he wrote, he would be "willing to enter into a contract along the ordinary lines" on terms satisfactory to the author and the publisher.[46] In what was a highly unusual arrangement, Wilder signed a secret agreement promising to move to Harper once his contractual obligations to the Boni firm were fulfilled.

"I've been going thru Hades; breaking with the Bonis," he wrote to the Townsons in mid-February. "I went about it all wrong and now there are scenes, and gore, and screams. Heaven help me, but [it] had to be. But gee I could have done it more nicely and I'm sunk in self-reproach."[47] By late June he was a "wore out schoolteacher just comin' back to life," and he was afraid he was going to have to resort to litigation over some of his snarled contracts.[48] At his father's encouragement, he turned to the New Haven lawyer J. Dwight Dana for legal advice. "A week ago I took unto myself a lawyer so that he could keep my poor contracts and papers and he found out that I had been vague and amiable and that my affairs were in a bad way."[49] From that time on Wilder relied on Dana and then his firm, Wiggin & Dana, founded in 1934.

In February, Wilder had faced another professional decision. He found in his stack of mail a letter from renowned lecture agent Lee Keedick, who represented and sometimes managed public figures including polar explorers such as Sir Ernest Shackleton and Capt. Roald Amundsen, and the controversial Arctic explorer Vilhjalmur Stefansson. Keedick usually had a waiting list of eager prospective clients, and it was significant that he solicited Wilder. "If you ever plan to do any lecturing I shall be glad to meet you at your convenience and discuss the matter in its many phases," Keedick wrote on February 4, 1928. "I feel confident that the public would welcome an opportunity to hear you on the lecture platform."[50]

Wilder replied in a brief note February 9, putting Keedick off.[51] But the impresario was a fast worker. On February 15 he met with Wilder in Lawrenceville, and departed with a signed contract in hand.[52] On February 21 he sent Wilder a copy of an advertising circular for his approval. "Of course, you may not approve of some of the statements," Keedick wrote, "but please remember that the committees realize this is our appraisal of you, and not your own opinion of yourself."[53]

Wilder fired back his objections on February 23. "I have never been in South America. And in the next sentence I could hardly have 'evolved the . . . Perichole' because she was a historic woman. . . . The heading: 'Greatest novel of the age' is liable to antagonize really cultivated people rather than win them. Tolstoi and Hardy and Conrad haven't been dead so awfully long." Wilder also objected to the statement that he was unsurpassed "'by any foreign writer.' Sure, I'm [un]surpassed by a good many foreign authors, but, my god, by all?? I suppose you meant scarcely surpassed. And even that's a bit thick."[54] He then added what had to be an unusual request: "Don't put me down as terribly expensive, Mr. Keedick. Or make it plain that there is a sliding scale for serious educational institutions. I couldn't face an audience if I thought they were astonished that such a 'humanitarian' author was after big cold prices."[55]

Wilder's first formal public lecture resulted from an invitation to give the Daniel S. Lamont Memorial Lecture on the topic of "English Letters and Letter Writers" at the Sampson Lyceum at Yale on May 4, 1928.[56] Wilder apologized to Keedick in advance: The lecture was "rotten," he wrote, and it was meant to be read rather than delivered with any drama or style.[57] He wrote at least two lengthy drafts of the lecture, the one he apparently delivered in 1928 and one he adapted and expanded to use on his lecture tour. In both texts he discussed such great English letter writers as Horace Walpole, William Cowper, and Edward FitzGerald, and gave special attention to the Frenchwoman he considered the greatest of all letter writers—Mme de Sévigné. In the more formal draft of the lecture—apparently the text he delivered in 1928—Wilder advocated reading the great letter writers on three levels: "the surface level, that is the *literary exercise*; the second level . . . the *profile of a personality*; and the third level, which is *news of the soul*."[58] (He called this trait "news from within" in the other draft.) The 1928 text is also notable for Wilder's reflections on the art of writing in whatever genre: "Art is confession; art is the secret told," Wilder wrote, adding later in the lecture,

> but art is not only the desire to tell one's secret; it is the desire to tell it and to hide it at the same time. And the secret is nothing more than the whole drama of the inner life, the alternations between one's hope of self-improvement and one's self-reproach at one's failures. "Out of our quarrels with other people we make rhetoric," said William Butler Yeats; "out of our quarrels with ourselves we make literature."[59]

WILDER'S NEW celebrity opened the door to new friendships. On the train home from Miami after Christmas in 1928, Wilder had met that "young wizard in the Broadway theatre," Jed Harris, who, before he was thirty years old, had produced and directed such Broadway hits as *Broadway* (1926), *Coquette* (1927), *The Royal Family* (1927), and *The Front Page* (1928). Although Harris and Wilder had overlapped at Yale, they had not known each other during their college days, and on the train, Harris actually mistook Thornton for Amos, the "tennis player at Yale."[60]

Wilder stayed in touch with Gene Tunney, who invited him to visit his training camp in the Adirondacks once the school year ended. "I'm sure you would find it interesting in seeing the way a 'champion' prepares for a contest," Tunney wrote to Wilder, "and healthful in trying to keep up with a 'champion' in his daily exercises."[61] Tunney would be training for his upcoming world heavyweight championship bout, defending his title against a challenge from the New Zealand boxer Tom Heeney. Wilder wrote back to accept the invitation to Tunney's camp, and to propose that they travel in Europe together in the fall. "I am particularly interested in two things," Tunney replied on January 30:

> First that you will come to my camp during the summer and spend more than I hope five or six days, as you suggest, and the idea of doing Europe in the way you suggest this fall. I have made up my mind to go abroad this fall but have had only vague notions of what I would do when there. Your . . . outline of a proposed trip with you is just exquisite. I love the idea. That, to me, would be the most perfect way of doing Europe. We will give the thought great contemplation between now and the time I see you this spring.[62]

By March the two men were making firm plans to travel together in August in England, France, or the Aegean Islands. Tunney told Wilder in confidence that he planned to box only once in 1928, in the summer, and the rest of the year he would be free to do as he liked. What he did not tell Wilder or almost anyone else was that for nearly two years he had been carrying on a secret romance with Carnegie Steel heiress Polly Lauder, and that he had decided he would retire from boxing after the Heeney fight, his last contractual commitment.

Admiring and befriending writers as he did, Tunney was genuinely pleased to observe Wilder's success: "Well, I see, old fellow, they are pushing you up, up, ever up and skyward," he wrote in March. "It certainly is most gratifying to me. It's amazing how rapidly one's star climbs. You have hitched your wagon to a star that soars as rapidly as a meteor falls. I am watching your rise from the side-lines, and I hope all this lionizing will not affect your well-balanced head."[63]

Then there was Scott Fitzgerald. When Wilder found a letter from

Fitzgerald in the mountain of his mail, he wrote back promptly to say, "I have been an admirer, not to say a student, of the Great Gatsby too long not to have got a great kick out of your letter." He hoped they might meet and "have some long talks on what writing's all about," Wilder wrote, adding,

> *As you see I am a provincial schoolmaster and have always worked alone. And yet nothing interests me more than thinking of our generation as a league and as a protest to the whole cardboard generation that precedes us from Wharton through Cabell and Anderson and Sinclair Lewis. I know Hemingway. Glenway Wescott, I think, is coming down here for a few days soon. I'd like to think that you'd be around Princeton before long and ready for some long talks. I like teaching a lot and shall probably remain here for ages; a daily routine is necessary to me: I have no writing habits, am terribly lazy and write seldom. I'd be awfully proud if you arrived in my guestroom some time.*[64]

He sent Fitzgerald a copy of *The Bridge of San Luis Rey*, and soon received an invitation to visit Scott and Zelda Fitzgerald in February at Ellerslie, the supposedly haunted nineteenth-century mansion they had rented at Edgemoor, overlooking the Delaware River, on the outskirts of Wilmington, Delaware. The two men apparently met in February when Fitzgerald spoke at the Princeton Cottage Club, for Wilder wrote to him that his speech was a "wow," and the audience wanted more. They were now "Thornt." and "Scotty," and in anticipation of his visit to the Fitzgeralds, Wilder wrote, "It is wonderful to have been liked by you and to have been told so, for the self-confidence I have exhibited toward my work I have never been able to extend to my person."[65]

Among the other guests for that particular one of the Fitzgeralds' legendary wild literary weekends was Edmund Wilson, then managing editor of the *New Republic*. Wilson and Wilder met on the journey to Ellerslie, and Wilson described their meeting in February 1928 in some detail in "A Weekend at Ellerslie," collected in his book *The Shores of Light* (1952). Wilson would first review Wilder's novels in August 1928, but had not yet read Wilder's books when they met on the train en route to see the Fitzgeralds. Wilson wrote that he had "the impression that [Wilder's] novels were rather on the fragile and precious side," and was, therefore, "surprised to find him a person of such positive and even peppery opinions."[66] He was further impressed that in the animated and, in some cases, inebriated company that evening, Wilder held his own in the conversation and the drinking, but "remained sharply and firmly" sober. (Wilder had long since forsaken his boyhood temperance pledge.) By one account, later in the evening the drunken Fitzgerald took Wilder up to the attic to show him something and accidentally fired a gun, just barely missing him.[67] In Wilson's version of the evening, however, "Scarcely had we left the table when the Fitzgeralds announced they were going to bed and left the guests to fend for themselves." Scott Fitzgerald slept all night, according to Wilson, but Zelda, refreshed after a few hours' sleep, rejoined the guests later in the evening, and, as Wilson recalled, Wilder left Ellerslie early the next morning.[68]

Fitzgerald answered Wilder's note of thanks with appreciation, a request, and a compliment: "Thank you for your friendship, for it is that," Fitzgerald said, "and for being such a hell of a nice person as well as a fine workman." The request: Zelda wanted to read some modern French writers in French—but writers who were "not so hard as Proust." Could Wilder recommend some books that Fitzgerald could find at Brentano's? The compliment: The Fitzgeralds' six-year-old daughter, Scottie, "announced that she liked you much the best of any of 'the people,'" and Wilder was "a hit" with the rest of the family as well. They hoped he would come to Ellerslie again soon. Fitzgerald teased that he was thinking of publishing two of his own novels in one volume and "calling them 'the Cabala.' What do you think? . . . I am writing this under difficulties," Fitzgerald joked at the end of his three-page letter. "There is a highball at my elbow but I keep drinking out of the ink bottle by mistake."[69]

Soon afterward came a note from Zelda thanking Wilder for sending her several books in French, and telling him he was "gargantuanly nice" to send them. "The books are divine and very depressing and I appreciate enormously your sending them," she wrote. "They are exactly right for my capacities in French and I am amazed that foreign words should actually make sense but not too much of it, like English ones do." She told Wilder that she, Scott, and Scottie were sailing on the *Paris* for France on April 20, and that they hoped to see him there later in the year. The sudden change of plans—for they had a two-year lease on Ellerslie—was, Zelda wrote, "All on account of a trip to New York and a bouncer and a taxi-driver, a doctor and the visceral system—and our attempt to condition the night clubs to us."[70]

ON MARCH 10, 1928, the president and fellows of Yale University voted to award Wilder an honorary master of arts degree at the commencement exercises set for June 29, 1928.[71] While grateful and flattered, Wilder was still uncomfortable with his sudden celebrity and did not believe he had accomplished enough to justify the honor. He worked over a draft of a letter, explaining his reasons for declining, and expressing his belief that "a number of years must pass before I feel sufficiently mature enough to take my place for what I hope may be some public usefulness."[72] (In 1947 Wilder accepted an honorary doctorate from Yale in a company of honorees that included the poet T. S. Eliot, the scientist Linus Pauling, and the theologian Henry Pitney Van Dusen, among others.)

Wilder labored through the spring of 1928 to carry on his Lawrenceville work, prepare for the Lamont lecture, and juggle the demands of his literary life. Meantime his friend Gene Tunney was preparing for a lecture of his own. Knowing of Tunney's love of Shakespeare, William Lyon Phelps of Yale invited Tunney to lecture to his Shakespeare class on April 23, 1928. So many Yale students wanted to hear Tunney speak that there was a standing-room-only crowd in a large auditorium on campus. Speaking informally, without notes, for about forty-five minutes, Tunney told his audience that when he was a marine during World War I he decided to read Shakespeare. He began with *The Winter's Tale*, which he read ten times before he believed he understood the play.[73]

For a writer everything is material: A few years later, in Wilder's novel *Heaven's My Destination*, the hero, George Brush, reads *King Lear* ten times trying to find the talent in it.

"You are a 'kindred spirit' and our 'kinship' started aeons and aeons ago on some spiritual plane of eternity," Tunney wrote to Wilder in June. "There is no measuring it by weeks or months or years. It seems to have always been." He told Wilder that he never discussed his "real" friends with journalists because those real friends were "too sacred for that."[74] There was already wide press coverage of the European jaunt Tunney and Wilder were planning, for they were two highly visible celebrities that summer of 1928—the book-loving heavyweight champion of the world, preparing to face a challenger for the title in July in Yankee Stadium, and the novelist who had just won the Pulitzer Prize, and whose book was an international bestseller.

Wilder arranged for a leave of absence from Lawrenceville for the coming academic year, wrapped up the semester, and, not long after commencement, traveled to Speculator, New York, to join Tunney at his spartan Adirondack training camp. There Wilder could see how Tunney trained and prepared for a fight, and at the same time, he could get some much-needed rest and vigorous exercise himself. There was little privacy, however, with curious reporters on the scene. "Tunney and Wilder Plunge into River as Canoe Upsets," reported the *New York Times* on June 29, 1928, noting that the champion and the author had no difficulty swimming to shore after their canoe capsized in the "chilly waters" of the Kunjamuck River.[75] According to Wilder, Tunney had taken along a copy of William Hazlitt's essays when they embarked, and he surfaced after the canoe flipped over holding the Hazlitt book between his teeth.[76] Years later Wilder remembered fondly "the fun we had at the training camp in The Adirondacks" and his "delighted surprise" when he was "trotting beside" Tunney, who turned to him "after stepping on a caterpillar" and solemnly and aptly quoted Shakespeare: " 'The humblest beetle that we tread upon in corporal sufferance feels a pang as great as when a giant dies.' "[77]

On July 7, when Wilder boarded the *Adriatic* for the journey to England, a telegram from Tunney awaited him aboard ship, wishing him well.[78] Isabella, Isabel, and Janet had gone on ahead, and had rented Axeland House near Horley in Sussex. There was room enough for the whole family, although Dr. Wilder would stay behind in New Haven to carry on his work at the newspaper, and Charlotte would spend the summer teaching English and literature in the Barnard College Summer School for Women Workers in Industry.[79] She had been teaching at Wheaton College for two years and would begin a new job as assistant professor of English at Smith College in September 1928. Joining the family in England would be houseguests, including Tunney and the three Lawrenceville students Wilder accompanied to England, Clark Andrews, Henry Noy, and Duff McCullough. Wilder wrote to Ernest Hemingway about his plans:

> *Sailing for 2 months in Eng. (Adriatic July 7); then walking tour with Gene Tunney (vide press passim) [see the press here and there]. As fine a person as you'd want to meet; not much humour, but I've always had a taste for the doggedly earnest ones. Then another tutoring job from Oct 20th on with Xmas in Egypt, then some readings & lectures in America (March and April.). Hawaii to write two plays. But I dread and lose my enthusiasm before all this leisure. I need routines.*[80]

Some of those plans would change, but this was Wilder's tentative agenda as he looked ahead in that summer of the most dramatic, most successful year of his life thus far: Literary success beyond his dreams. Financial success beyond his imaginings. Friends who lived visible lives on the world stage—Fitzgerald, Hemingway, Tunney—and treated him as if he belonged there, too. Friendships that meant the world to the man who had been a shy, awkward boy—the man who had far more confidence in his work, as he had told Fitzgerald, than he had ever been able to extend to his person.[81]

20

PREPARATION AND CIRCUMSTANCE

I know now that the [lecture] tours are Preparation. I don't know quite
what they prepare for: I prepare and Circumstance fulfills.

—THORNTON WILDER TO SIBYL COLEFAX,
February 20, 1930

Europe and the United States (1930s)

In the fall of 1928 sixteen of Wilder's three-minute playlets were published in *The Angel That Troubled the Waters and Other Plays*. He knew the playlets were "frail," he had told Lewis Baer, but he would "love to get these little things out somewhere, quietly and even unprofitably" so he could get "those Juvenilia" once and for all off his chest.[1] When Boni did not choose to publish them, Wilder turned them over to Coward-McCann, a new publishing house in New York. In his foreword to the collection Wilder noted that almost all of his playlets were religious, "but religious in that dilute fashion that is a believer's concession to a contemporary standard of good manners," and pointed out that the final four plays in the book, written in the past year and a half, "plant their flag as boldly as they may."[2]

With *The Angel That Troubled the Waters*, Wilder the playwright rode unabashedly on the coattails of Wilder the novelist. In advance of publication two of the playlets were published in the October 1928 issue of *Harper's Magazine*.[3] The issue also included an advertisement for *The Bridge of San Luis Rey*—"The most popular book in our generation. Now in its THIRD HUNDRED THOUSAND." *The Angel That Troubled the Waters* received mixed but largely positive reviews in England and the United States, far more attention than the young Wilder could have imagined when he was writing most of the playlets back in his high school and college days. According to the *New York Times Book Review* on November 18, 1928, "Mr. Wilder's miniature plays will yield most to those readers who bring the most to their reading of them. They have the perfection of intaglios, the delicate beauty of finest lace, the spiritual significance of poetry, the elusive music of the distant bird."[4]

The Bridge still reigned over the bestseller lists, Wilder's short plays were in print, and he was all of a sudden a man of wealth. Looking forward to joining his family abroad, he left the new and sometimes disconcerting public visibility of his life in the United States only to find himself thrown into the limelight big-time in England. The international press and paparazzi were bent on covering the forthcoming Tunney-Wilder walking tour of Europe—not so much because of Wilder's Pulitzer Prize and his international bestseller as because of Tunney's recent boxing victory and the announcement of his engagement to Polly Lauder. Tunney had defeated Tom Heeney (who had Jack Dempsey in his corner during the fight) on a technical knockout in the eleventh round of the July 26 world heavyweight championship bout in Yankee Stadium. Tunney immediately announced his retirement from boxing—the first champion to retire while still holding the crown—and soon afterward, Polly Lauder's mother announced her daughter's engagement to Tunney.

The forthcoming marriage of the beautiful heiress and the world heavyweight champion was called the romance of the century. Mobs of fans, reporters, and photographers tracked Tunney wherever he went, and stalked the bride-to-be and her family as well. Wilder, still unaccustomed to his own public visibility, disliked the hubbub intensely. "All the newspaper racket and the literary introductions leave a bad taste in my mouth," Wilder wrote from London to Bill Nichols (now a dean at Harvard). "And I wish the noble Gene wasn't so famous. I'm gnawing a curious discontent. Wish I were in Hawaii (one of the lesser islands) with dirty flannels, sunlight, surf, the works and correspondence of Jonathan Swift, and you."[5]

Even so, the Tunney-Wilder trek was, for the most part, exhilarating. "Actually," Wilder wrote to Isabel, "We do everything in an auto!! I long for walking and resting and staying somewhere. But at least we saw some splendid mountain roads."[6] Wilder had hoped that he and Tunney could visit out-of-the-way places in Switzerland, Germany, Austria, and Italy, and enjoy "literary walks" and the wide-ranging talks that were typical of their time together. Afterward he wanted to write a travel book full of their conversations and ideas as well as impressions of their favorite places. In Paris, Wilder and Tunney met Fitzgerald for drinks at the Ritz bar, and Wilder introduced Tunney and Hemingway. Tunney reported later that Wilder could "out-walk him, out-climb him and out-eat him."[7] Wilder was among the small, select gathering of wedding guests when Tunney and Polly Lauder were married at the Grand Hotel de Russie in Rome on October 3, 1928. Afterward the couple was besieged by the paparazzi in a mob scene that left some journalists with clothes ripped and cameras destroyed. Wilder was thankful to slip away to join his sister Isabel in the relative quiet and privacy of Munich, and then Wengen, Switzerland.[8]

AFTER A lifetime of the family's relentless frugality, he was thrilled to be able to take his mother and sisters to Europe, and to try to ease his father's habitual financial anxiety. After their summer together in England, Isabella had taken Janet home to New Haven in the fall of 1928 to enroll her in her final year of high school. Thornton and Isabel stayed on to travel in Europe, for Isabel had received her certificate from the Yale Drama Department in June of 1928, and Thornton's graduation gift to her was a tour of European theaters. He and Isabel discovered that they were congenial traveling companions. When they arrived in a new city he bought the local newspaper and pored over the theater and concert advertisements, circling the plays or concerts he wanted them to see, and plotting their cultural schedule. They spent their daytime hours separately—Isabel sightseeing or shopping or writing, and Thornton deep into work on his new book, *The Woman of Andros*—a novel he may actually have begun writing as a play.[9] In the evenings they went to the plays or concerts he had marked as events they would enjoy.

Some evenings were given over to another kind of pleasure: Thornton and Isabel loved to dance. He was a "very good dancer," Isabel recalled, but he "wasn't a disciplined one." He especially enjoyed the waltz and the tango, and frequently started out on the dance floor with a tango and wound up improvising, with Isabel gamely following, happy to see that her brother's delight in his unorthodox dance steps seemed to help him "relax completely." The Wilders danced their way through Europe in 1928 and early 1929, and Isabel remembered fondly that back in the times when "things were going so bad" for the family financially, Thornton would say, "Oh, well, it's all right. Isabel and I are going to be a dance team."[10] Her brother was so "mad about music," Isabel related, that he bought a traveling "talking machine" in Munich, along with a number of records so he could listen to music whenever he wished in his hotel room, or in his compartment on an overnight train trip from one European city to another.[11]

By January 1929 Thornton and Isabel were in London, where Isabel stayed with their aunt Charlotte, still world general secretary of the YWCA. Thornton tended to literary business, meeting with his London publishers, Longmans, Green, and being feted at literary dinner parties. Even amid the dancing, socializing, theatergoing, and traveling from place to place, he kept working on *The Woman of Andros*. His first glimmerings of the novel had come to him in the spring of 1928, he wrote on a manuscript draft. He had dashed off a note to his mother with the gist of the idea: "The Woman of Andros—after play by Terence—Aegean island. Paganism with premonitions of Xianty."[12]

He worked on his novel all over the map. He had written the first two conversations in the novel at Axeland House in Horley, Surrey, during the happy commotion of that summer with his mother, his sisters, and assorted houseguests. He copied completed portions of the manuscript into a notebook on October 11, 1928, while he was staying in the Pension Saramartel in Juan-les-Pins, France, one of his favorite places to retreat and write.[13] During the spring of 1929 he wrote passages on his lecture tour—snatching hours to work in hotels and on trains from Kansas and Missouri to Louisiana and Texas to California and Calgary. He worked on Chrysis's monologue in the Yale Law School dormitory at 76 Wall Street in New Haven in April 1929. He concentrated on the novel at the MacDowell Colony during the summer. "Lots more

Andros done," he wrote to Amos from Peterborough, "but confused about the direction to take in the fourth quarter of it. No hurry, and no worry."[14] He told his brother that *The Woman of Andros* could actually be considered his first novel "in the sense that the others were collections of tales, novelettes, bound together by a slight tie that identified them as belonging to the same group."[15]

But before he could truly concentrate on finishing the third novel, he had to deal with the financial repercussions of the second one. Accustomed as he was from boyhood to accounting for almost every cent, Wilder now faced the staggering challenge of managing an unexpected fortune. All his life, guilt had stained every coin he spent—and now there were many dollars to spare. In 1927 he had earned less than six thousand dollars—about three thousand for teaching at Lawrenceville, a few hundred for tutoring, and the rest in royalties from *The Cabala*. In 1928 he reported taxable income of $89,915.77—with $79,128.31 coming from royalties on *The Bridge*.[16] (Wilder's almost $90,000 of income equates to $1.15 million when measured by the 2010 consumer price index, and $13.6 million when measured by the 2010 relative share of gross domestic product.)

Dr. Wilder was still highly skeptical of his son's ability to handle money, convinced that Thornton would spend it extravagantly. As it turned out, Thornton was conscientious about the stewardship of this fortune and sometimes overly generous in sharing it. As he assumed financial responsibility for his parents and two younger sisters, and accepted the role of chief family breadwinner, he was becoming the actual if not the titular head of the Wilder family. As he told a friend later, it had "fallen upon" him to "sustain several members" of his family.[17] He would support his parents for the rest of their lives, and Isabel and Charlotte for the rest of his life and then, through his estate, until their deaths many years later.

In 1928 and 1929, at his father's behest, Thornton entrusted his business as well as his legal matters to experienced hands. One of the last good decisions Amos Parker Wilder urged on his son was his insistence that Thornton seek advice from the New Haven attorney J. Dwight Dana—and just in the nick of time. Dr. Wilder's health was beginning to fail, and he would soon be tactfully led to retire from his New Haven newspaper job. But by then, in large part because of his father's recommendation, Thornton's business and financial affairs, including his publishing and lecturing contracts, were safely in Dana's care.

After the publication of *The Bridge*, Wilder assumed the entire financial support of his parents and Isabel and Janet, financing Janet's college education. He contributed funds to Charlotte when she would accept them. Now thirty-one, she was teaching at Smith College, and Amos, thirty-four, was on the faculty at Hamilton College in Clinton, New York. As the Depression years bashed the U.S. economy, Wilder's income from writing and lecturing vacillated and then diminished so that he had to take on other work continuously to support his family and himself.[18] First and foremost, he was determined to take good care of his mother. He treated his musical family to the luxury of their own piano, after years of renting a secondhand one, or doing without one entirely, and it was a baby grand at that, selected for him by his musician friend Bruce Simonds. Wilder paid for it with part of the advance he "made the Bonis cough up" for his new novel in progress.[19] But he wanted to give his mother more than a piano and trips to Europe. Isabella had never had a house of her own, and he wanted to give her that security for the rest of her life.

He would build his mother a house on a wooded site on a hill in Hamden, on the edge of New Haven. Wilder paid $7,500 for the lot, and on August 8, 1929, he signed an agreement with Alice F. Washburn, an architect and contractor, to construct the house on Deepwood Drive, Hamden, at a cost of $21,500. The family moved into the house in March 1930, and christened it "The House *The Bridge* Built." There was a spacious living room downstairs, with a dining room, kitchen, and bath, and a small office. Upstairs were four bedrooms and two baths, as well as a study for Thornton. A comfortable porch overlooked New Haven, and there was a garage beneath the house. In 1929 Thornton bought himself a car, which he cheerfully shared with his mother and sisters.

A writer's income, under the best of circumstances, is an uncharted, unpredictable terrain of peaks and valleys, and Wilder the breadwinner poured new intensity into his moneymaking efforts. He still would not, however, fuse the need to earn money with his desire to write. Now that the windfall of *The Bridge of San Luis Rey* had been invested in savings accounts, stocks. and real estate, and now that he was enthralled with his new novel in progress, he was determined to earn the family's bread-and-butter income from pursuits other than writing. He would lecture. He would teach. He might even go to Hollywood and try his hand at screenwriting, which differed, he thought, from his serious, creative work in fiction and drama, and there was good money to be made in the movies despite the Depression economy. But he would not allow the need for money to propel his literary efforts or determine the creative choices he made.

"I *think* I'm going to positively enjoy it," Wilder wrote to lecture agent Lee Keedick about his forthcoming lecture tour.[20] By January 1929 he was on his way to Montreal; Pittsburgh; Chicago; Columbus, Dayton, and Cincinnati, Ohio; Kansas City, Missouri; and various destinations in Iowa, Indiana, Michigan, Kentucky, Tennessee, Texas, Louisiana, New York, Massachusetts, and Rhode Island.[21] He proved to be an immensely popular lecturer—witty and energetic, erudite but entertaining. In his early thirties he was balding, bespectacled, and handsome—looking something like the actor Douglas Fairbanks, one journalist thought, "with his small dark moustache, sturdy, athletic figure and incessant activity."[22]

With good humor he endured his baptism as a professional lecturer—experiencing almost everything that could go wrong, and trying to put on a good show in spite of the inevitable obstacles. He had to confront one problem most lecturers never bother about: Some of his first lectures were too short, and he had to work hard at expanding them. He discovered the importance of tailoring each lecture to each audience. He grew frustrated with the press, complaining that "the stuff they wrote is so bum that I'm going to refuse interviews one of these days. One woman in an entirely complimentary interview thought it was cute to call me the Tunney couple's honeymoon companion! And it got into the headlines."[23]

Wilder was his own harshest lecture critic. He gave a lecture in Kansas City, Missouri, that he thought was "rotten." In Pittsburgh he had to compete with a basketball game "going on quite audibly a few feet away." In St. Louis, he said, his heart sank when he had "to climb onto a platform full of the jazz band's instruments and speak to a dining hall, with wild orange night club festoons all over it, the whole room decorated to look like a coral grotto!"[24] There were bad acoustics, and the inevitable mix-ups on hotel and transportation arrangements. Some audiences didn't laugh when the lecture was funny and did laugh when it wasn't, and the size of the crowds was sometimes disappointing. The pace was exhausting: By April 19 he was "pretty well wore-out and looking forward to some sleep and some writing."[25]

Wilder built up a repertoire of speeches on drama and on literature—such general topics as "The Relation of Literature and Life" and "The Future of American Literature." He grew adept at packing his suitcase with clothes for various climates and degrees of formality—a tuxedo for some occasions, a suit for others—although he complained in December about having to pack "Tropical clothes for Pasadena" and a "Polar Express outfit for Michigan."[26] Along the way he accepted the invitation from his old friend Robert Maynard Hutchins, now president of the University of Chicago, to teach there part-time beginning in 1930.

In the summer of 1929 Wilder drove to Peterborough, New Hampshire, in his new car to sequester himself in the peaceful woodlands at the MacDowell Colony so that he could concentrate on *The Woman of Andros.*[27] "I've found a way of introducing Chrysis and her day into the novel," he told Isabel later. "A whole new second chapter. Awfully hard book to write, my god, but some beautiful places."[28] That fall Wilder took his mother back to England—incognito, he wrote to Isabel. (He sometimes registered in hotels as Niven Wilder, "very incog.," he said.)[29] In London they went to the theater, and Isabella and her sister, Charlotte, enjoyed some private visits, with "long heart-to-heart talks,"

Wilder wrote.[30] In Paris they saw Gene and Polly Tunney. Although Isabella's favorite city was London, she enjoyed being in Munich with her son, who delighted in giving her the grand tour of Europe, replete with music, theater, and fine food, unencumbered by financial worries and family duties.

He managed to work wherever they were: "I slowly write Andros and read a lot about the Grk tragedians for my college course," he said in a letter to Isabel from Oxford.[31] "I have been working well mornings in all these cities, making so many changes and insertions that I have to start copying the novel into a new cahier," he wrote from Munich.[32] But the two travelers missed the home folks, Wilder reported: "We pine after you often . . . and say what's Pa doing? And what's Isabel doing? And what's Amos doing? And is Janet happy? We're not perfect travelers because we adore the folks at home."[33]

By late November he and his mother had returned to New Haven. "This restless soul got back in due time and entered the Harbor with all sorts of swelling Whitmanesque emotions," Wilder wrote to a new friend in London, Sibyl Colefax, well known as a hostess and later as an interior decorator. "I get drunk on New York and go striding about as though the city were named after me and the Hudson River rolled slowly to please me. But after a few hard knocks and a few hotel bills I retired to my favorite university town and subdued myself to work." At times he was uncertain that his exotic new novel would speak to readers. He was assessing the contemporary American literary scene, concluding that "the American flowering, the American maturity is drawing nearer and nearer, though the evidence is all in works imperfect in themselves, like Ernest Hemingway's *Farewell to Arms*, Cozzens's *The Son of Perdition* and La Farge's *Laughing Boy*. The surest evidence lies in the audiences; the reading public is developing beyond all anticipation."[34] Wilder believed, however, that the theater was "in an awful turmoil," with dozens of "bad plays" running each week and "then being folded in the warehouse." Most theaters had "lost the courage to be adventurous," Wilder contended. He hoped that he might write something to counteract that.[35]

ON DECEMBER 18, 1929, Wilder signed a contract with the Boni firm for the publication of *The Woman of Andros*, the manuscript to be delivered on March 1, 1930, although he actually transmitted the final pages during the first week of January. Under Dwight Dana's supervision, Wilder's contract allowed him to keep the motion picture, serial, and dramatic rights, as well as the rights to publish a collection of his novels. Dana acted as his agent and attorney-in-fact, and Isabel began to act as his representative for translation rights.

Wilder was determined to avoid what he viewed as the undignified publicity events that had surrounded *The Bridge*. He still regretted the public hoopla about his trip with Gene Tunney, as well as the flashy exposure of the Hearst newspaper serialization of *The Bridge of San Luis Rey*—flamboyant headlines accompanied by cartoon illustrations in newspapers around the country. These two events undoubtedly helped sell his books, but Wilder insisted that "because of the very subject matter" of *The Woman of Andros*, there should be "no faint color of Hearst-Cosmopolitan" elements in the publicity for the new book. "I say as I did for the other book that as little publicity as possible is welcome to me," he wrote to Albert Boni.[36]

Nor was Wilder happy about the 1929 movie version of *The Bridge*—part silent, part sound, starring Lili Damita and Don Alvarado, and promoted by MGM as a spectacular romance. Wilder had no hand in the film, which focused on the Perichole and her "tawdry indiscretions." The novel came through "the movie mill with the usual bruises and abrasions," according to the movie critic Frederick James Smith, who was not surprised that Hollywood "switched" Wilder's novel into a "hot story of a rampageous dancer," and twisted "the study of why God cast five people in eternity into a peppy portrait of a heartless gamin[e]." Nevertheless Smith gave the movie three stars out of four.[37]

As Wilder worked on his new novel he was immersing himself in Greek drama and philosophy, spending time in ancient Greece in his imagination, his reading, and his preparations for the lectures he would give at the University of Chicago. He was rereading Aeschylus and

Euripides, and he wanted to learn Greek. He was exploring the concept that Greek religion was divided into two parts: ethics, having to do with the violation of rights; and the mystic, the identification with the gods.[38] In his journal he drew comparisons between Greek religion and religion as articulated in the Old and New Testaments, writing that the Old Testament conveyed the logic of passions, and the New Testament the logic of grace. One journal entry examines the parallels between concepts in Aeschylus's Orestian trilogy and precepts expressed in the Old Testament, reflecting one of the basic questions in the novel: What did the noblest type of person in pre-Christian paganism have to cling to in life's extremest difficulty?[39]

The Woman of Andros was drawn in part from an incident said to have taken place before the opening scene of the *Andria*, a comedy by the Roman playwright Terence (ca. 190–158 BC).[40] Terence had based his drama on two plays by the Greek dramatist Menander (342–291 BC)—*Andria* and *Woman of Perinthos*, or *Perinthia*. Out of the raw materials Terence and Menander provided, Wilder fashioned a tragedy rather than a comedy. Terence's play focused on the relationship between a father and a son, but in Wilder's novel the story is more complex. His heroine, Chrysis, is a beautiful courtesan, cultured and intelligent, an outsider, a stranger on the island, surrounded by the "stray human beings" she shelters and protects. She and her younger sister, Glycerium, are both in love with Pamphilus, the handsomest young man on the island, whose bride has already been chosen by their families. Pamphilus and Glycerium carry on an idyllic secret love affair that leaves her pregnant. The rest of the cast of characters includes two worried fathers, a contemplative priest of Apollo, some suspicious islanders, a battle-worn sea captain, and an avaricious pimp, all caught in a compelling concoction of myth, fable, and fantasy.[41]

The young man Pamphilus expresses some of the fundamental questions in the novel, questions that are the subtext if not the core of much of Wilder's work: "How does one live? What does one do first?" As Wilder himself further explained it in a letter, "What is the worst thing that the world can do to you, and what are the last resources one has to oppose it? In other words: When a human being is made to bear more than a human being can bear, what then?"[42]

His Greek studies also led to observations in his journal about the fundamental nature of literature. In one entry he wrote that "mere literature" is simply a "distraction from life," while "Good literature is observation of life: pictures of its delightfully varied appearance. Great literature is the explanation of existence and suggestion of rules of how to live it. Great literature is the Didactics of life made perceptible to the heart."[43] This last principle expressed his intention for *The Woman of Andros*.

His journal provides details about the logistics of his work: the time and place, even the conveyance—ship, or train, or a walk in the woods—where he wrote. Wilder had long been fascinated with aphorisms, and they abound in the novel, and in lists he kept in his journal and among his notes. He gave some of these lines to Chrysis, the hetaira—the Woman of Andros—writing to a friend that she was "developing into a sort of Dr. Johnson."[44] Pages of his journal record his ongoing critique of his novel in progress, details large and small: "Wish I could make up my mind as to whether the *chastity* sentence in the characterizing of the Priest is valuable or nonsense; also whether the opening nocturne is false or not," he wrote in Munich on October 5, 1929. The lyrical "opening nocturne" in *The Woman of Andros*, first drafted in his journal, was true enough to stay—and later to be frequently quoted as one of the most beautiful passages in American fiction: "The earth sighed as it turned in its course: the shadow of night crept gradually along the Mediterranean, and Asia was left in darkness."[45]

He indicated that there were autobiographical traits within three characters in the novel—Chremes, one of the leaders and fathers of Brynos; the young priest of Aesculapius and Apollo; and the Woman of Andros herself. He did not expound on the traits, but to speculate, Chremes resembles Wilder (as well as the narrator in *The Cabala* and in a later novel, *Theophilus North*, and the stage managers in Wilder's plays) in providing exposition and interpretation. Chremes also expresses forthright opinions in hopes of guiding or even engineering the actions of others.

The mysterious priest of Aesculapius and Apollo is an often-detached observer of events, and the occasional confidant of inhabitants of the island, as well as a healer and a celibate (by choice—or by repression or constraint?). There are echoes here of Wilder's own disillusionment about emotional and sexual intimacy. Not only was Wilder the product of an upbringing that left its intimidating mark on his emotional and sexual life as well as the lives of his brother and two of his sisters, but the heartbreaks that wounded him in the 1920s had made him a cynic, wary of intimacy, full of doubts about himself and distrust of others. Against that background Wilder's words about the priest take on more resonance. The priest foreclosed options of true physical and emotional intimacy and channeled his life force into his work. Such a choice could empower the priest—or the artist—at the expense of the man, sheltering and at the same time isolating him from the "unstable, tentative" sons or daughters of men.[46]

Wilder explored the harsh consequences of unrequited love and forbidden love in his early fiction—Alix's unrequited love and Marcantonio's incestuous love in *The Cabala*; the doomed love of Pio for the Perichole and Manuel for the Perichole in *The Bridge of San Luis Rey*; and the tragic, illicit love of Chrysis and her sister Glycerium for Pamphilus in *The Woman of Andros*. The heart and spirit pay a great price for loving where love is not returned, or for loving where love is forbidden. Best to deny, restrain, reroute the love, he seems to say; best to pour the love instead into art or religion or selfless service to humanity.

Like Wilder, Chrysis, the Woman of Andros, expresses her view of human experience "in fables, in quotations from literature, in proverbs and in mottoes." Like Wilder during the years he was working on *The Bridge of San Luis Rey*, Chrysis "regarded herself as having 'died'" and she reflects that "the only thing that troubled her in her grave was the recurrence, even in her professional associations, of a wild tenderness for this or that passerby, brief and humiliating approaches to love." She becomes acutely aware that she is alone, and that this loneliness is an essential part of the human condition. "Why have I never seen that before? I am alone," she wonders, adding. "The loneliest associations are those that pretend to intimacy."[47] Wilder, like Chrysis, believed in the supreme importance of the life of the mind. She says,"I no longer believe that what happens to us is important. . . . It is the life in the mind that is important."[48] The omniscient narrator reflects that "the most exhausting of all our adventures is that journey down the long corridors of the mind to the last halls where belief is enthroned."[49] Perhaps from his own private experience, Wilder scripts a lesson that Chrysis passes along to Pamphilus in her "strange command" to "praise all life, even the dark." As a result, Pamphilus "too praised the whole texture of life, for he saw how strangely life's richest gift flowered from frustration and cruelty and separation."[50]

In at least two instances the novel foreshadows *Our Town*, the play Wilder would complete in 1937. Chrysis entertains and instructs her banquet guests with the story about the Greek hero who begged Zeus to permit him to return to earth after death for just one day. Like Emily in *Our Town*, the hero discovers that "the living too are dead and that we can only be said to be alive in those moments when our hearts are conscious of our treasure." He then kisses "the soil of the world that is too dear to be realized."[51] Second, near the end of the story, Pamphilus, the young protagonist, climbs to "the highest point on the island to gaze upon the moon and the sea." His reflections foreshadow Wilder's *Our Town*: "Pamphilus thought of the thousands of homes over all Greece where sleeping or waking souls were forever turning over the dim assignment of life. 'Lift every roof,' as Chrysis used to say, 'and you will find seven puzzled hearts.' "[52]

ABOARD THE SS *Lapland* October 24, 1929, traveling home to the United States, Wilder made a fair copy of his book. Afterward he expressed his lingering doubts in his journal:

> From time to time the whole book seems mistaken. Is it drenched I ask myself with the wrong kind of pity? Have I let myself go again to a luxury of grief? I remember this haunted me through

the writing of The Bridge and I am still not sure whether that is the way the world is. Already I have begun to reduce some of the expressions. This perpetual harping on the supposition that people suffer within. Am I sufficiently realist?[53]

For Wilder the act of writing was an organic fusion of artistic endeavor and personal quest, as revealed in the last lines of his introspection, when he reflected that without effective irony, the book "must run the greater danger in committing itself to anguish & to the profoundest inner-life—if it fails artistically it will be all the more instructive to me, not only as a writer, but as a person."[54]

———

WILDER HAD been working on The Woman of Andros for nearly two years, and as he had done with the first two novels, he delivered the final manuscript to his publisher in stages. By the time he signed the official contract most of the manuscript was in his publisher's hands. He finished the book in early January 1930 at the Biltmore Hotel in Los Angeles, while he was lecturing in California. Soon afterward he made a side trip to the Thacher School in Ojai to keep his promise to Sherman Thacher to speak to the students at his old school.

Wilder sought his mother's help when it was time to read galleys for the book because he had to stay on the lecture circuit until March 10. "I begin to think I know why I am doing it," he wrote to Sibyl Colefax in February 1930. He was lecturing, he said,

> *partly of course to assemble money to pay for the new house and its Steinway; partly to buy the thirty-five volumes of Saint-Simon in the edition grands écrivains de France. All that is true but only vaguely felt by me. I know now that the tours are Preparation. I don't know quite what they prepare for: I prepare and Circumstance fulfills. . . . At all events I am burning out a host of awkward adolescent fears and maladjustments. I am actually serener. And the more people I meet the more I like people. I know America down to every absurd Keep Smiling Club, every gas station, every hot-dog stand.*

He told Sybil he would begin teaching April 1 at the University of Chicago—"'Tradition and Innovation—Aeschylus to Cervantes,' 40 lectures (including Dante) with the students writing a 6-minute paper every morning to prove that they read the long assignment for homework. It's absurd, but is very American and is exactly what I want."[55]

LEE KEEDICK had no trouble persuading Wilder to take on another ambitious challenge when he proposed that Wilder debate the popular British novelist Hugh Walpole, also a Keedick client, on the question of whether fiction or nonfiction "throws more light on experience."[56]

"Yes, I'd like to debate Mr. Walpole," Wilder replied: "Resolved: that reading great fiction and drama throws a better light on experience than reading great history and biography. Would be willing to attack either side."[57]

A telegram from Keedick confirmed the plans: "Walpole accepts debate takes fiction side." Keedick tried, without success, to persuade Gene Tunney to preside at the debates, originally scheduled for February 16, 1930, in New York; February 23 in Chicago; March 2 in Boston; and March 4 in Detroit.[58] Wilder soon began to have second thoughts, however. After nine months of heavy-duty travel and lecturing, he was worn out and unwell. The schedule was "cruel," he complained to Keedick, and asked that the February 16 date be pushed forward at least a day so he could be in "smart condition" for the "ordeal" of the debate.[59] It was difficult to find time to prepare for the debates as well as hone his lectures.

Concerned about Wilder's health and stamina, Keedick rearranged his tour schedule to minimize travel, and gave up the idea of debates in Chicago and Detroit. The "easier" itinerary he arranged for Wilder was still daunting—from California to Calgary to Chicago to La Crosse, Wisconsin, to Grand Rapids, Michigan, to lecture, and then to New York, where Wilder and Walpole would debate on February 16, with the second debate set for Washington the next day. The debates turned out to be hugely successful. A "record audience" attended the first, at the Selwyn Theatre in New

York.[60] In Symphony Hall in Washington there was a crowd of four thousand. "It looked like a football game," Wilder said afterward. "It was not a very good debate," but the crowd "scarcely coughed, while our humble little abstract ideas advanced and retreated in a very sedate combat."[61]

21

"VARIETY, VARIETY"

My life has variety. The other night I had supper (4 am) as the guest of Jack McGurn (Capone's chief representative and lieutenant) and Sam [Hunt] the golf bag killer. Tonight I dine at Mrs. Rockefeller McCormick's off the gold plate that Napoleon gave Josephine. Variety, variety.

—THORNTON WILDER TO J. DWIGHT DANA,
January 18, 1932

The United States and Europe (1930s)

When he was in his midfifties and working on a chronology of his life, Thornton Wilder looked back on the decade of the 1930s—years overcrowded with work, travel, and the demands and occasional pleasures of his new fame.[1] A few key events stood out in his memory: In 1930, his third novel, *The Woman of Andros*, was published, and he accepted an appointment as a lecturer in comparative literature at the University of Chicago, where, he said, he taught "for half of each year until 1936." In 1931, *The Long Christmas Dinner and Other Plays in One Act* was published.[2] His new lecture career began in February 1929 and, except for one hiatus, continued through the end of March 1937. Wilder traveled throughout the United States, sometimes for several weeks at a stretch, lecturing nearly all the way. Then, from 1930 until 1936, he would alight at the University of Chicago long enough to teach for part of each year. Between lecture commitments and teaching obligations, he made trips to Hollywood, Hawaii, Europe, and the West Indies.

Somehow, as he taught, lectured, and traveled during the thirties, Wilder found time and energy to write six new one-act plays and two novels. He worked for a stint doing screenwriting in Hollywood, and translated or adapted three plays, one of which had a respectable run on Broadway. He wrote two major three-act plays—*Our Town*, which enjoyed a huge success on Broadway and on tour, and *The Merchant of Yonkers*, which did not.

His first major publication in the thirties, *The Woman of Andros*, appeared on February 21, 1930, with thirty thousand copies printed in advance, joined by twenty thousand additional copies on the official publication day. For twelve weeks, beginning in April, the novel was on the bestseller list. The yield for the year: seventy thousand copies sold in the United States; $16,000 in royalties for Wilder, not including the $2,500 advance, which he had quickly earned back; third place on the 1930 list of the year's ten bestselling novels. Reviews were mixed but mostly positive, and an advertisement in the *Saturday Review of Literature* on March 15, 1930, published highlights: "Writing of this temper is rare in American fiction . . . 'The Woman of Andros' is the best book we have had from Thornton Wilder," according to the *New York Times*. "Wilder's third and best," wrote the *New York Herald Tribune* reviewer. "In every page one feels that Wilder is writing for the ages. . . . A creation of beauty," from the *New York Telegram*.[3]

Of the negative reviews, the most controversial was written by the communist critic Michael Gold, a champion of proletarian literature. Gold regularly used his critical platform in the *New Masses* and other leftist publications to attack writers and visual artists who did not conform to his views that art should be proletarian and political in purpose and subject matter. He was, Edmund Wilson wrote, one of the "more or less organized and highly self-conscious group of the social revolutionary writers," including John Dos Passos, John Howard Lawson, and others—although, Wilson observed, Dos Passos was "a good deal more intelligent" than Gold.[4] A passionate advocate of a Marxist approach to literature, Gold was one of the most strident voices in the contentious discourse in the thirties about the relationship between art and contemporary life.[5]

Michael Gold focused on Wilder and his work in a highly critical review in the April issue of the *New Masses*. Gold's platform expanded in October 1930 when the *New Republic* published his longer article attacking Wilder and all his novels and plays: Wilder's characters in *The Cabala*, Gold wrote, were "some eccentric old aristocrats in Rome, seen through the eyes of a typical American art 'pansy' who is there as a student." Gold intensely disliked *The Woman of Andros* and scorned Wilder's three-minute plays as "pretty" and "tinkling" and presenting "the most erudite and esoteric themes one could ever imagine." Alas, according to Gold, Wilder was no poet of the proletariat, but the "poet of the genteel bourgeoisie" whose goal was "comfort and status quo."

After reprimanding Wilder for how and what he *did* write, Gold spent nearly two columns of his four-column piece attacking Wilder for how and what he did not: He did not write with the language of the "intoxicated Emerson" or the "clean rugged Thoreau" or the "vast Whitman." Wilder did not write about cotton mills or child slaves or murders or coal miners. Gold presumed that Wilder, who in reality had worked hard all his life and worried about money since he was a boy, was "the perfect flower of the new prosperity." Furthermore, Gold sneered, Wilder was the "Emily Post of culture," and—in perhaps the only accurate statement in the essay—"the personal friend of Gene Tunney." In conclusion Gold challenged Wilder to "write a book about modern America."[6]

Gold's review set off a vigorous dispute in the pages of the *New Republic*. The nation at large was far too preoccupied with the economic impact of the Depression on Americans' own lives to worry overmuch about whether their national literature should be driven by economics, as Gold and his colleagues contended, or by classical, romantic, and ethical themes as advocated by the New Humanists and others, or by modernism—or by writers like Wilder who wrote independently of any critical school or trend. The tempest at the *New Republic* had its repercussions in the rarefied atmosphere of the literary world, where the "social revolutionists" were attacking mainstream writers and, on occasion, one another. Gold regularly attacked writers including Hemingway, Sherwood Anderson, Robinson Jeffers, and even Carl Sandburg, whom he usually admired as a proletarian poet.[7]

On May 4, 1932, in the *New Republic*, Edmund Wilson addressed "The Literary Class War," writing that Gold's "attack" on Wilder in 1930 "was an attempt to arraign Mr. Wilder at the bar of the Communist ideology." Wilson pointed out that Gold himself had been the target of criticism from "his own Marxist camp," having enjoyed "considerable success" with his semiautobiographical novel about the New York East Side, *Jews Without Money*, published in 1930—the same year as Wilder's *The Woman of Andros*. Wilson reported that communist critics had condemned Gold and his bestselling book because he had failed to mention "the mass" and "labor organizations and strikes," and had written about "merely poor people" and not "proletarians." Gold vigorously defended himself on principles that Wilder might very well have exerted on behalf of his own work: Gold accused one Marxist critic of being "too dogmatic in his application of the proletarian canon," arguing, "Each writer has to find his own way . . . I did not want to falsify the emotional values and bring in material that I did not feel. I do not believe any good writing can come out of this mechanical application of the spirit of proletarian literature."[8]

Although Wilder made no public response to the brouhaha, he was dismayed by the attack. "You can imagine my astonishment and disgust at the wretched controversy running in the New Republic," he wrote to Lee Keedick.[9] What Wilson and Gold did not know was that well before the flap, Wilder had been thinking deeply about the American experience and "the American flowering," as he called it in his 1929 letter to Sibyl Colefax.[10] His *Woman of Andros* was conceived and almost completely written before the 1929 crash of the U.S. economy.

Wilder's first public reference to the Gold episode apparently came in November 1933 during his two-week lecture appearance at the University of Hawaii, widely covered by the local press. Wilder told one interviewer that he believed radical critics to be "wrong in their claim that man is solely the product of the economic order under which he lives," and that he believed that the "fundamental emotions, love, hate, fear, anger, surprise are common to all mankind, in any milieu, in any age." He observed that "the left-wingers" thought that "all literature, all life, commenced somewhere around 1900, when they began." Furthermore, they had not themselves "met the first big test": They had yet to produce the kind of writing that in "their viewpoint would count as good literature."[11]

"Myself have dwindled to the least fashionable of authors," he wrote ruefully to Sibyl Colefax in 1932, when he was deeply absorbed in work on his new novel, *Heaven's My Destination*. "Few book reviews come out without a passing disparagement of my work. But I don't mind. I have a rather low opinion of my books myself, but am fairly conceited about the next ones."[12]

"I AM to be a 'special lecturer' in Comparative Literature at the University of Chicago during the Spring Term," Wilder announced to Sibyl Colefax. "Yes, Iliad and The Birds and Dante and Don Quixote and everything. And I can't even spell."[13] During the thirties Wilder's schedule was a jigsaw puzzle; still, he not only worked it out but enjoyed it—at least at first. He explained one of his major reasons for agreeing to teach at the University of Chicago: "The teaching work is really necessary to me; I write very little and slowly and I need a congenial daily routine to occupy me while the dim notions for books shape themselves. Apparently some writers write a great deal and can create a daily life out of it, but others work seldom and have a great deal of energy left over for another activity."[14]

The invitation to teach came from his longtime friend Robert Maynard Hutchins, a boy wonder, then a young adult wonder, and, at age thirty, a wonder on the national stage as the newly appointed president of the University of Chicago. Like Wilder, Hutchins was a product of Oberlin and Yale. Both men were the sons of fathers who were Yale graduates, and who embraced the religious and ethical traditions espoused by Oberlin (where Hutchins's father was a professor of homiletics from 1907 until 1920) and the intellectual and social expectations fostered at Yale. Like Amos Niven Wilder, Robert Hutchins had served in the ambulance corps during World War I. After the war he was an outstanding student at Yale, despite the hours he had to spend working to pay for his education. Handsome and charismatic, he was particularly acclaimed for his debating and public speaking skills. In 1923 he was appointed secretary of the Yale Corporation; in 1925 he received his law degree, magna cum laude, at Yale Law School, and accepted an appointment to teach there. He became acting dean and associate professor at the Yale Law School in 1927, and in 1928, at the age of twenty-eight, was appointed professor and dean. This was his launching pad for the presidency of the University of Chicago, which he assumed in 1930. In that role he was a catalyst for change and controversy with his vision of cooperative interdisciplinary education and innovative undergraduate programs, and his determination to reorganize the university and to give it a national rather than simply a regional presence.[15]

"Love my classes," Wilder wrote to his mother in the spring of 1930 soon after he began teaching at the university, "and they're sprouting that affectionate contempt for me which is the attitude I ask of my classes." He lectured on a range of topics, including *Don Quixote* and quixotisms, and the novel as a genre, working for hours each week to "frantically assemble stuff for four 50-minutes lectures and more." But he was thriving, as well as getting to know "droves of undergraduates" and, he hoped, winning their confidence.[16] He worked hard to prepare for his classes. "I worry in my sleep," he wrote to his mother, "and wake up wondering if I have enough notes to pull me through those eternal fifty-minutes."[17] In mid-February, when he lectured on five consecutive Tuesday evenings in the university's "downtown college" at the Art Institute of Chicago, his topic—"Sophocles for English Readers"—was advertised on billboards all over the city. His classes there, like those he taught on the university campus, were jam-packed, standing room only, with people on waiting lists: "Professor" Wilder was a star.

Back in New Haven, as the national economy worsened, Dwight Dana cautioned him about spending too much money and urged him to conserve. Wilder was spending most of his money on other people, however, especially his family. Isabella wrote to Dwight Dana in May 1931 to express her gratitude for his help to Thornton. "How fortunate for him that you can take these cares off him, insurance, contracts & these dreadful tax-problems. He is not very practical and his Father's mental state now is such that we can get no help there. In fact I carefully keep all questions from him as they only worry & excite him."[18]

Among other philanthropies, Wilder was financing an Oberlin College education for Tom Harris, a New Haven boy, the son of a blue-collar family. Harris had attended the Lawrenceville School, and Wilder paid his expenses all the way through Oberlin. "Your bank account is getting rather low," Dana cautioned, "and the prospects of its being replenished in the near future are not so very bright, and I am, therefore, writing to suggest that you go as slow as you can on expenditures, certainly until the new book comes out and until we see how it goes."[19] Dana recognized, he said, that Wilder was "under such heavy personal expenses in connection with keeping your family going and in other directions," but he warned Wilder again in October, "Your income is so irregular that it is really impossible to say whether you are living beyond your income or not, but I should be afraid that this coming year that would certainly be the case unless you can hold your expenses down to a considerably lower point than last year and also unless your income from lectures and from the book of plays is very considerable."[20]

Wilder responded promptly: "I have turned over an entirely new leaf," he wrote. "I have gone in for Voluntary Poverty. Voluntary Poverty is practically indistinguishable from Involuntary Poverty, but the hair's breadth of distinction makes a world of difference. . . . I don't drink. I don't smoke. I don't take taxis. And so on."[21]

Despite his "Voluntary Poverty," however, he wanted to contribute to various charities in New Haven and Chicago. He was also giving to a "secret Trustee's Fund" at the university to help students facing Depression-era hardship—"students who are fainting in the corridors for lack of food and doing unheard of feats to get an education." He wrote that it "makes education wonderful to see the price these students pay, and it makes Yale look cold, conventional, constipated and unlighted."[22]

WILDER THE successful novelist was also, simultaneously and fervently, Wilder the aspiring dramatist. During the thirties his escalating renown as the novelist, the lecturer, the professor, and the linguist helped open the doors of Broadway and Hollywood to Wilder the playwright. Since his teenage years he had been learning his craft as a playwright, immersing himself in dramatic literature—seeing every possible play; analyzing the texts, the acting, the directing, the staging; writing his short plays; and then leaping into ambitious experiments with the full-length drama. Living with self-rebuke in the aftermath of the failed production of *The Trumpet Shall Sound*, he filled notebooks with names of three- and four-act plays, and ideas and scenes for some of them. Then he reverted to the discipline of the one-act play, first as the laboratory for his experiments in drama, and then simply because he appreciated the one-act form for itself. On November 5, 1931, Coward-McCann and the Yale University Press published his second volume of plays, *The Long Christmas Dinner and Other Plays in One Act*— six plays in all.

It was fitting that Wilder worked on the one-act plays in Germany in 1931 with the volatile, charismatic director Jed Harris as his traveling companion. Their friendship had grown since their paths had crossed briefly on that northbound train in Florida in 1927. There would be a profound intersection of their professional lives in 1937. But in May 1931, Wilder was back in Munich, one of his favorite European cities, when Harris joined him for a few days. They went to the theater and to the opera—*Don Giovanni*—where they encountered Polly and Gene Tunney. The next day Wilder gathered Harris and the Tunneys and "threw a brilliant lunch at the Bayerischer Hof (the waiters fainted in coils)," he wrote to his family. "I'm very fond of Jed," Wilder added,

> *but if he'd stayed another week I'd have been in a Sanatorium. We had long ten-hour conversations about everything under the sun. He shopped the antiquarians for old furniture. Like Andy [Townson] (in the same hotel) he slept every day until noon, so I continued producing a new one-act play every two days. . . . Anyway I was sorry to see him go.*[23]

Wilder—too trusting, sometimes naive and gullible—could become too enamored of a friend. Such was the case with the mercurial Harris, who habitually alienated almost everyone who knew him. In the summer of 1933 Sibyl Colefax warned Wilder from afar to be cautious about Jed Harris, whose career, like that of many directors, seesawed between success and failure, with Harris's volatile temperament vacillating accordingly.

Wilder's friendship with Jed Harris expanded to include Harris's mistress, the actress Ruth Gordon, with whom he had a son, Jones Harris, born in 1929. Wilder's friendship with Gordon would last for the rest of his life, and he would write certain dramatic roles especially for her. From the first Wilder respected her as a remarkably talented actress, thoroughly enjoyed her company, and soon began calling her the "finest girl in the world" as well as the "drollest and most original."[24]

TOWARD THE end of the 1920s, Wilder recalled in later years, he "began to lose pleasure in going to the theatre." He "ceased to believe in the stories" he saw presented there.[25] At the same time, he reflected, "the conviction was growing in me that the theatre was the greatest of all the arts. I felt that something had gone wrong with it in my time and that it was fulfilling only a small part of its potentialities."[26] After the great success of *The Bridge of San Luis Rey*, Wilder could now command attention for almost anything he wanted to publish, and, as already noted, in 1931 Coward-McCann brought out *The Long Christmas Dinner and Other Plays in One Act*. At the same time Yale University Press issued a special signed limited edition of the plays. These one-acts were widely noticed and, for the most part, positively received. Right away some of them were produced, chiefly by amateur theater groups, with Samuel French, Inc., handling the dramatic rights.[27]

Wilder explained his intentions years later: "I began writing one-act plays that tried to capture not verisimilitude but reality," he wrote. "In *The Happy Journey to Trenton and Camden* four kitchen chairs represent an automobile and a family travels seventy miles in twenty minutes. In *Pullman Car Hiawatha* some more plain chairs serve as berths and we hear the very vital statistic of the towns and fields that passengers are traversing; we even hear the planets over their heads."[28] Well ahead of *Our Town,* Wilder was experimenting with theatrical time and space—departing from linear time; minimizing settings and props; using a stage manager to narrate and interpret events.

Looking back on these plays in 1974, he told an interviewer, "My earlier one-act plays, before *Our Town,* were free of scenery too and things went back and forth in time. . . . In my plays I attempted to raise ordinary daily conversation between ordinary people to the level of the universal human experience."[29]

ONCE *The Woman of Andros* and his one-act plays were launched, Wilder forged ahead with his fourth novel. In 1930 he had made a list of writing projects that were already under way on paper or in his imagination, some of them dating from 1929 or even earlier. Near the top of the list were two ideas for picaresque novels, for he had been reading Casanova, teaching *Don Quixote,* and ruminating on the picaresque form. Item three on the list in his journal on June 27, 1930, was "Picaresque: Baptist 'Don Quixote.' Selling education textbooks through Texas, Oklahoma, etc."[30]

That would be his next creative project. Edmund Wilson and others speculated that Wilder's decision to set some of his new one-act plays and his fourth novel in the United States came in response to Michael Gold's attack. Isabel Wilder perpetuated that idea many years later when she wrote that *Heaven's My Destination* was her brother's "riposte to the accusation from some quarters that he was refusing to deal with native American subjects," and that "Crossing the United States on several lecture tours had given him the material that he needed in order to write it."[31] But such motivation alone did not govern Wilder's creative choices. First, he had always chosen his subjects out of his deep-rooted artistic interests—characters who fascinated him; questions and themes he wanted to probe; literary challenges, including forms he wanted to tackle; stories he could not resist telling. He did not write for the marketplace or for money or for a particular audience—especially not for critics. Furthermore, like many American writers in the postwar twenties, Wilder had been thinking for some time about what he called the "flowering of America," especially American literature and culture.

He was soon absorbed in the picaresque form, and in his picaresque hero—his Baptist Don Quixote. This novel would be wildly different from its three predecessors in form, setting, and characterization, but it would be all of a piece with the major questions and themes that always engaged him; How do we live? How do we love? How do we cope? How do we bear the unbearable? Where do we turn for solace and survival? In *The Cabala* he gave us a decaying society and a declining religion—and in our last glimpse of the protagonist, we see him bound "eagerly toward the new world and the last and greatest of all cities."[32] *The Bridge of San Luis Rey* takes readers back two centuries before *The Cabala*, but despite the stark differences in place and time between the two novels, *The Bridge* treats many of the same themes and questions— and the characters who question orthodox religion in *The Bridge* are not treated kindly by the church or the society they inhabit. *The Woman of Andros* moves still farther back in time, long before the birth of the religion that has become stagnant and repressive in Wilder's first two novels. In *Andros* he searches the pagan soul for answers to his enduring questions. In the novel he decided to call *Heaven's My Destination* readers are catapulted to the American heartland in the 1930s to accompany George Brush, a tragicomic everyman, on his dogged journey to practice what his religion preaches, no matter the consequences.

From Lake Sunapee in the summer of 1932, Wilder wrote to Bill Nichols that he was "20,000 words advanced in [a] stunning new novel— Don Quixote—travelling salesman idealist; picaresque; Arkansas and Texas. Funny; vulgar; hotbreaking [*sic*]. From Baptist fundamentalist to sad tolerant wisdom in three years."[33] Hemmed in as he was with teaching and lecturing, Wilder had to work sporadically on *Heaven's My Destination*—but the story grew like yeast-rising bread even when he wasn't putting words on paper. Of necessity during the decade of the Great Depression, Wilder traveled the American landscape as a professional lecturer, hawking his ideas and his books—but in the process he was exploring the American vernacular and the American mind and spirit. Through his teaching and his travels, especially in the American

heartland, he was seeing Depression hardships close-up, and witnessing countless variations of American despair, grit, and ingenuity. One
by-product of the experience was the promise of gleaning rich material
with every mile he traveled on the lecture tour, every person he met
along the way, every conversation he shared or overheard in diners and
bars and hotels and railroad cars.

Riding the tide of his celebrity as a Pulitzer Prize–winning, best-
selling novelist, Thornton Wilder the man began to outgrow the shy
awkward boy who, during his earlier years, had stood on the outside
of society, looking in. He still worried, he said, that he grew "more
like Uncle Pio every day, all onlooker, all uncommitted participant,"
yet more and more often he was less the observer and more the active
participant who actually belonged in the social group.[34] Now he was
more often viewed as the handsome, dapper bachelor with impeccable
manners, an engaging wit, and an infectious ebullience for all his erudition—and he had become one of the most famous American writers in
the world.

His name even seeped into Chicago gossip columns: "The colum-
nists in town are linking my name with a certain xxxxxx xxxx [sic];
think nothing of it," he wrote jauntily to Isabel in May 1933. He was
also openly enjoying the company of new friends such as the flamboyant actress and speakeasy hostess Texas Guinan, then in her late forties. Wilder told Isabel, "I had a fine evening with Texas Guinan; we
rejoice in one another."[35] Guinan's colorful career included rodeos, more
than two hundred silent movies, two talkies, several Broadway musi-
cals, and a series of gigs as a popular speakeasy hostess, beginning at
bootlegger and racketeer Larry Fay's El Fay Club in New York. In and
out of trouble with the law, the glamorous Guinan starred in her own
revue in the early 1930s. When she was forbidden to stage it in France
because it was too risqué, she named the show *Too Hot for Paris* and
took it on the road in the United States and Canada, where it enjoyed a
roaring if scandalous success.

"My life has variety," Wilder wrote in a letter that must have at
least momentarily alarmed its recipient, staid Dwight Dana back in
New Haven. "The other night I had supper (4 am) as the guest of Jack

McGurn (Capone's chief representative and lieutenant) and Sam [Hunt] the golf bag killer. Tonight I dine at Mrs. Rockefeller McCormick's off the gold plate that Napoleon gave Josephine. Variety, variety."[36]

As Wilder's professional life expanded during the thirties, his personal world widened to encompass a variety of new friendships. Of course he still valued his longtime friends—Bill Nichols; Les Glenn; and Gene Tunney, who asked him in 1930 to consider another joint trip through Europe, although they couldn't make their schedules jibe this time. He enjoyed the company of a younger crowd of Chicagoans, among them some of his own writing students—Gladys Campbell, a poet and teacher; the budding playwright Robert Ardrey; the fiction writer Charles Newton.[37] "Lately I have been going up to New York a little and seeing people," he wrote to Sibyl Colefax in November 1932. "My best friends *there* (Chicago holds my real ones) are Jed Harris and Ruth Gordon. Lately Edward Sheldon. . . . Alex. Woollcott is a real pleasure too."[38]

Sheldon, the well-known playwright, was bedridden and crippled by a rare form of arthritis, and particularly savored lively company and letters. Alexander Woollcott, ten years older than Wilder, was the nationally known author and critic famous (and often feared) for his biting wit and his controversial commentary. (Woollcott's friend Harpo Marx claimed that the portly Woollcott resembled something that got loose from the Macy's Thanksgiving parade.) Woollcott would become one of Wilder's closest friends. In New York, Wilder sometimes played poker with playwright Noël Coward. He became a frequent guest at Woollcott's island retreat in Vermont, and Alfred Lunt and Lynn Fontanne's country home at Genesee Depot, Wisconsin, where Wilder, the Lunts, Katharine "Kit" Cornell, Woollcott, and other weekend guests "lived practically Nudist, eating wonderful things, playing anagrams and falling on the floor in coils" as Woollcott held forth on a variety of topics.[39] A visit to Lake Geneva evoked poignant memories of Wilder's boyhood on the shores of Lake Mendota, Wisconsin. He took walks at daybreak, enjoying the "early mist and horizontal sunlight and dew on the cobwebs" and "the lake's smell, and the particular seaweed moss on the stones at the water's edge and the cray-fish holes beside the piers:

that was my boyhood, too." He had known lakes in England, China, and Austria, he said, and others in the United States, but none of them shared the nostalgic light and the air and the "particular bundle of smells" of the Wisconsin lakes.[40]

There were other fascinating new friends and acquaintances: "Mary Pickford wants me to write a play with her," Wilder wrote to Ruth Gordon in the summer of 1933.[41] He told his family that Pickford asked him to collaborate with her on a stage play for Lillian Gish and herself. "She outlined the plot. . . . The same night I pushed Edna Millay in a ricksha for a mile at the World's Fair. When do I get my school work done? You ask?"[42]

He had a gift for friendship, and his coterie in Chicago included the city's foremost hostesses, such as the eccentric Edith Rockefeller McCormick. Wilder enjoyed a much deeper friendship with Chicago hostess and arts patron Mrs. Charles Goodspeed. Widely known as Bobsy Goodspeed, she was a personage in her own right—glamorous, intelligent, and passionately interested in the arts. She invested much of her husband's wealth and her own energy as a patron of Chicago arts and culture, and served as president of the Arts Club of Chicago. She was especially interested in music, arranging for Vladimir Horowitz to give a private concert, entertaining Arthur Rubinstein in a "quiet home dinner," giving a tea for George Gershwin. The Goodspeeds' apartment was the center of many congenial gatherings, and it was there that Wilder's friendship with Gertrude Stein and Alice B. Toklas would begin.

Robert and Maude Hutchins also paved Wilder's way to some of his Chicago friendships. The handsome couple had made a splashy entrance on the Chicago scene, although Maude Hutchins quickly demonstrated that she would not be the typical college president's wife. Tall, stylish—and charming when she wanted to be—she was also an artist and wanted to spend much of her time working on her often-controversial sculptures in the skylit studio on the top floor of the president's house. To the detriment of her husband's career, she did not have the patience or grace for large social events, and many university people joined other Chicagoans in considering her aloof and snobbish.

But she liked intimate gatherings, and came to think of Wilder as one of the family. He proved to be one of the most loyal friends and supporters of the Hutchinses as their tenure in Chicago grew more difficult and controversial.

Wilder mingled with faculty intellectuals and countless students at the University of Chicago—traditional and nontraditional students of all ages and all walks of life. At first there was some faculty resentment of his appointment, not so much because of Wilder as because of Hutchins's determination to transform the university, and his propensity for bringing in his friends to help him do so. In time, however, Wilder won over the skeptics, and Chicago rapidly became his hometown.[43] When he was young, poor, anonymous, and aspiring, Wilder had fallen in love with Rome, New York City, and Newport, Rhode Island—but when he was famous and sought after, and living in the heart of the city, he fell in love with Chicago. He carried on a love-hate relationship with Paris and Los Angeles, charmed by some facets of those cities, repelled by others. He felt at home in certain German cities, especially Munich and Berlin, and the Swiss-German city of Zurich. There were towns and villages, he loved—New Haven and Hamden, Peterborough, Juan-les-Pins, Martha's Vineyard, Monhegan Island. But all in all, there was probably no city he loved more than he loved Chicago when he lived there during the thirties.

In part he was glad to be reunited with the Midwestern landscapes of his childhood, but he especially loved the unique look of Chicago—the lake, the architecture, the sky. He wrote to a friend, "Every morning I wake up and see something very beautiful indeed. There lies the Midway looking like the Great Prospect at Versailles and there is the procession of towers of the University of Chicago, silver-gray and misty and ready for business."[44] But people, including his students, were at the heart of it all. Wilder enjoyed the company of *Chicago Tribune* literary editor Fanny Butcher and, for a time, met quietly and regularly in a writers' group with Butcher and five other Chicago writers—Dorothy Aldis, Kate Brewster, Arthur Meeker, Jr., David Hamilton, and Marion Strobel. Butcher recalled that they gathered twice a month in the home of one of the group,

had a bang-up dinner, and then got down to the business of listening to and criticizing what we had written in the interim. We
called it our writing class. Thornton's role, he insisted, was as
another writer, not as teacher, but his comments were the ones
we all craved and heeded. At our last meeting he read us the part
of *Heaven's My Destination* on which he was working. Everybody
had the same reaction: "Thornton, it's very funny."[45]

Wilder entertained a stream of guests during the time of Chicago's
1933 Century of Progress Exposition, otherwise known as the World's
Fair of 1933—a pivotal event in his ongoing exploration of the United
States of America. He rambled through the exposition as often as possible, especially during the weekends when he was "worn out with
talking in public and reading endless compositions and worn out with
eating in the Burton Court Dining Hall and making faintly mechanical conversation." After slipping away to the sprawling world's fair he
returned to campus "joyous and renewed."[46]

"The Fair is not serious; but it's fun," Wilder wrote to Ruth
Gordon. "Artistically it's one big lapse of taste, but on such a big scale
that it becomes somehow important. I love it; I trudge all over those
bright awkward acres, staring at my fellow-citizens. I see the back
side of it: the immense personnel a little frantically earning a living,
because scores of my students are selling hotdogs and pushing jin-
rickshas and holding information booths."[47] He cheerfully entertained
a parade of visitors who wanted to go to the fair during the summer of
1933. "I enjoy the Fair, great silly American thing that it is," he wrote
to a friend. "Scarcely a day goes by without a letter or phone call to
the effect that some old friend of mine (or my father's, brother's, sisters') from China, California, Oberlin, Princeton, Lawrenceville, Yale,
etc . . . is in town. I can't take 'em all to the Fair, but I take some. And
I enjoy it all."[48]

Texas Guinan telephoned Wilder for a favor that August. She
wanted to take over the Dance Ship on the midway of the fair for performances of *Too Hot for Paris*. The Dance Ship, boasting two dance
floors and two orchestras, was anchored in one of the two man-made

lagoons gracing the exposition complex, would be the perfect venue for her revue, starring her well-endowed showgirls, but she needed a letter of reference. The fair's director of concessions was former University of Chicago professor Col. George Moulton, who wanted to know, Guinan told Wilder, "if I'm all right, if I keep an eye on my girls—and you know, Thornton, if they were my own daughters I couldn't take better care of them. And all he knows is the worst about me, the headlines and all that. . . . Now if you could write him a letter." Wilder was happy to oblige, "making an honest woman of Texas Guinan and she got the job."[49] When Alexander Woollcott came to Chicago to see Wilder and the fair, Woollcott delighted in riding "in a Ricksha, his genial stomach pointing to heaven," and weaving about the grounds. He didn't care for the exposition at first, but wound up "loving it squarely to the square inch."[50] Wilder, too, loved it to the square inch. He was soaking up the American spirit embodied in the exposition, and it was coloring the atmosphere of his new novel. "The Fair is a great big silly *kitsch kitschig* thing," he wrote to Sibyl. "Bad educationally, bad aesthetically, and yet somehow very wonderful, lovable and impressive. . . . I go all the time, bewitched and warmed and almost in a state of gaseous exaltation. You know me—Walt Whitman's grandson, so sure of the immanent greatness and coming-of-age of the American people."[51]

He was delighted when officials of the exposition asked him to compose the text for a "certificate or diploma" that visitors might buy to prove that they had been to the fair. Although they asked for something straightforward, Wilder understood what a special event this was in the lives of many people in that Depression era who had saved their hard-earned money and traveled from all over the country to see the fair. He wrote:

> Be it known to my grandchildren, and to their grandchildren that I . . . . . . (John or Jane Doe) . . . . . . was present at the Century of Progress, an exposition raised in a time of doubt and hesitation by the gallantry of the American spirit; lighted through the genius of man by the rays of Arcturus; and that there I obtained instruction, enjoyment and the sense of wonder.[52]

WILDER HAD high hopes for *Heaven's My Destination*, a story served up from the delectable smorgasbord of his American experience from 1930 onward—part lecture tour, part world's fair, part Chicago, part "Variety, variety"—a kind of slapstick defiance of the Great Depression and the classics and, maybe, the critics. For the first time Wilder was out on the American hustings, living on his own. At last, no interference from Papa. He himself had stepped into Papa's role, building that house for the family, furnishing it, providing the money to run it. Thornton got his womenfolk comfortably and securely settled, and got out of Hamden and New Haven. He made Chicago *his* city.

He created his own world there, free from the strictures, no matter how well meaning, imposed by his family or anyone else. Despite that early temperance pledge, he could drink as much as he wanted to during Prohibition; spend his own money and make some more; and consort with people who consorted with Al Capone, or British royalty, or American theater wags, or Hollywood movers and shakers, or a fun-loving Chicago crowd.

Wilder's first three novels were set in exotic eras and foreign places, and his fourth was set smack in the middle of the American heartland. Yet time and setting are almost irrelevant in Wilder's early fiction. Literal setting and time seem incidental—ornamentation rather than scaffolding. He was experimenting with setting in fiction just as he experimented with sets onstage. The "sets" of his novels are draped in richer detail than the minimalist sets for his plays, but in Wilder's fiction, as in his drama, character and theme dominate.[53] The human personality and behavior, human conflicts, the plight of the human condition form the crux of his work; these universals defy time and place. The personalities, questions, and issues in each of his first four novels could be readily transported to other times and places. People can be lost, dysfunctional, suffering, struggling with how to live in any city, town, village, or countryside—anywhere, anytime. People can die unexpectedly and catastrophically anywhere, anytime. People can test the boundaries of society; can be outcast, alienated, isolated; can love and not be loved in return anywhere, anytime.

It was evidence of Wilder's cosmic mind and vision that he could work on *Heaven's My Destination* and simultaneously read Nietzsche ("Nietzsche has been my great discovery of this last year, my meat and drink," he said) and translate from German into English a contemporary comedy first produced in Vienna, and from French a contemporary play based on a Roman legend dating to 509 BC.[54] Fascinated with world literature and languages, he was eager to try his hand at translating and adapting the work of others. Two opportunities came his way in 1932: The producer Gilbert Miller asked him to translate Otto Indig's *Die Braut von Torozko*—"Not literature," Wilder said, "but a delightful play."[55] Not satisfied with Wilder's first version of *The Bride of Torozko*, Miller asked him to "alter it." Miller was still not happy with Wilder's second draft, and then had to shelve the play because of the Depression economy. A year and a half later, when Miller resurrected the project, Wilder, busy with other projects, released him from all obligations. Miller turned to another writer, whose efforts resulted in the script produced on Broadway in 1934, starring Jean Arthur, Sam Jaffe, and the young Van Heflin. The play closed after twelve performances.

Wilder's other opportunity was extended by Katharine Cornell, fresh from her triumphant role in 1931 as Elizabeth Barrett Browning in *The Barretts of Wimpole Street*. Cornell and her husband, producer and director Guthrie McClintic, invited Wilder, an unproven young playwright, to translate André Obey's *Le viol de Lucrèce* for a Broadway production to star Cornell. Obey, whose play opened in Paris in 1931, was one of a procession of artists to tell the story of the Roman matron, Lucrece, who was raped by Tarquin, the Roman prince. "I should be proud to translate *Le Viol*," Wilder wrote to Cornell in April 1932. "It is an eloquent play in itself and the freedom with which it overrides the conventions of the stage should make it very fruitful and additionally important."[56] Wilder had by then signed with a dramatic agent, Harold Freedman of Brandt & Brandt, and could expect to earn $180 a week if the play succeeded. As "only a translator," he felt "very remote" from the production, however—but he said he was "a great admirer of Kath. Cornell, the woman," and "happy" that the project would bring them together often.[57]

Cornell and company took the play to Cleveland, Ohio, in November 1932, and it opened on Broadway on December 20, 1932, with McClintic directing. The production was not a success but Cornell was praised for her portrayal of Lucrece. Wilder received generally favorable reviews for his translation, although there were those who believed he had not done justice to Obey's text. The play led to a breakthrough for Cornell, however, for the experience encouraged her to try Shakespeare. The director Arthur Hopkins told Cornell that *Lucrece* was her "most successful failure."[58] Wilder's translation was published as *Lucrece* in 1933—and, for better or worse, his interest in theater was now a matter of wide public visibility.

———

WILDER WAS putting down deeper roots in the thirties—not planting himself in one place, much as he loved Chicago, but grounding himself in fulfilling friendships and challenging work: He wrote to Sibyl Colefax about his appreciation for the "brightness and courage" of his students. He admired the Hutchinses and the "brave journey of the University of Chicago." He was pleased, he said, with "the humor and beauty of my new novel that I've quietly begun again now that [the] term is over."[59] But his busy social life was taking its toll. He wrote to Ruth Gordon, "I teach worse and worse, instead of better. I talk awful rubbish. My days are dissipated amid so many types of activity that I cease to be anybody. Nothing I do has been sufficiently prepared. I go through life postponing thinking."

Yet he had to teach. "I need the money for the running of Deepwood Drive," he wrote in confidence to Gordon. "I get $4,000 for a half-year, which is pretty good, considering that I can live here pretty cheaply myself. To be sure, if I settled down to write consistently I could make a good deal more than that, but I hate to feel any necessity-money aspect to my writing."[60]

He wrote to Sibyl, "Teaching and lectures make just enough to support me and my (very real) dependent household. If I gave over salary, it might ever so possibly happen that my pen on paper might be influenced by the needs of Deepwood Drive; and then something disastrous might happen. I'm not a martyr in supporting the family, since I greatly enjoy the Teaching, but surely if *Heaven's My Destination* does bring in something considerable I shall break away from both these activities and devote myself to writing seriously."[61]

22

"HOME"

I cried buckets of good old-fashioned unexamined tears!—not because it was
sad (those tears are all shed years ago) but because it was about a long lost
now archaeological phenomenon, the home.

—THORNTON WILDER TO MABEL DODGE LUHAN,
after seeing Little Women, *December 11, 1933*

The United States and Europe (1930s)

Wilder loved movies, and he saw Katharine Hepburn in George Cukor's *Little Women* two and a half times. He wrote to Mabel Dodge Luhan that it made him weep, not because he was grieving for the past, but because the movie was about a "long lost now archaeological phenomenon, the home." His choice of words was both resonant and prophetic, foreshadowing lines he would write five years later about *Our Town*, and echoing lines he had written more than a decade earlier about Rome. As noted, during his 1920–21 sojourn at the American Academy in Rome, where he was part of an archaeological group, Wilder had written to his family about "a newly discovered tomb of about the first century," resting under a busy Roman street. There he had "peered at faded paintings of a family called Aurelius, symbolic representations of their dear children and parents borne graciously away by winged spirits." Indelible in his memory was this vivid image of the strata of human history—"the street-cars of today" rushing over "the loves and pieties and habits of the first-century Aurelius family." He recognized that "two thousand years from now" there would be similar "humanizing" efforts to "recover" and understand the family life of his own century.[1]

During the thirties Wilder was exploring the archaeology of home and family in his personal life as well as his creative work, and those excavations were yielding pathways to future writing, most remarkably

Our Town, which would find its home on Broadway in 1938, and for
years afterward in the hearts of a global audience. He drew tight connections between his encounters with archaeology in Rome in 1920–21
and the methods he used in writing *Our Town*. In a preface to the play he
wrote that "the archeologist's and the social historian's points of view
began to mingle with another unremitting preoccupation which is the
central theme of the play: What is the relation between the countless
'unimportant' details of our daily life, on the one hand, and the great
perspectives of time, social history, and current religious ideas, on the
other?"[2]

He had already woven this theme into some of his one-act plays
in *The Long Christmas Dinner and Other Plays in One Act*. In 1933, en-
tranced by the film version of *Little Women*, Wilder revisited some of
the seminal details of his own family life. He felt, he said, "as though I
were the last person left on earth who had ever blown on and wiped a
lamp chimney; who had ever sat on the floor with brothers and sisters
in heaps and listened to reading aloud; who had ever stood in a fever
of expectation waiting for a parent to exclaim about the beauty and
rightness of a Christmas present one had spent hours in devising."[3]
He and his siblings had lived through hard times. They still looked
out for one another, called one another affectionately by some of the
old childhood nicknames—Charlotte was Sharlie or Charlie or Carla;
Amos was sometimes Amy or 'Mus; Thornton was Thornt. or Thorny;
Isabel was Isabello or Isabellina; their lingering favorites were Isaberry,
Charlieberry, Thornyberry.

But Wilder's response to *Little Women* was laced with more than
nostalgia, and his thoughts went beyond possible fodder for his literary work. In those years following his first great literary and financial
success, he turned homeward. He had built his family the comfortable
house on Deepwood Drive, had set up bank accounts to provide whatever they might need. After many years of living in rented quarters
around the world, Isabella could have her own permanent hearth and
kitchen, a baby grand in her own living room, and her own garden
where perennials could thrive. At last there was a house to which Isabel
would not be embarrassed to invite her friends, where Thornton could

have his own study, and where there was room for the entire family to gather for holidays.

Their father had suffered a stroke in 1928, and during the early 1930s, as his health broke down and he needed nursing care, he often lived away from Deepwood Drive, in private nursing homes in Connecticut or in the Berkshires or in Florida. He was now totally dependent for his financial support on his second son—the impractical boy who had grown up with his head in the clouds. Circumstances had enabled and then required Thornton to step into the paternal role his father, in the end, had been unable to play. The quintessential nineteenth-century patriarch, Dr. Wilder had managed despite the odds to educate his five children, and to see to it that his wife and children traveled the world, but he could never assuage their financial anxiety—largely because his own was so intense. His lifelong efforts to exert control over their individual dreams and actions grew out of his love for them, as misguided and oppressive as it could often be.

When he was a young man Amos Parker Wilder, abetted by his demanding mother, had set a remarkably high bar of expectations for the life he would live, but he had disappointed his most rigorous critic—himself. It was no small accomplishment to run a newspaper; to serve as a consular officer; to engage audiences as a popular orator; to work as an effective advocate and fund-raiser for Yale-in-China; and, most of all, to father five uniquely talented children who were, without exception, honorable people. But he felt himself a failure because he could never earn the money or the accolades he had expected.

In the last eight years of his life Dr. Wilder gradually succumbed to the inexorable hardship of years of chronic illness. On April 4, 1933, he updated his will. In September he suffered another stroke—emerging from two hours of spasms paralyzed on his left side. A nurse was assigned to care for him at home and to give him regular morphine injections. Dr. Wilder wrote to a friend in June 1935 that he was in "very broken health."[4] Still innately proud and stubborn in his sixties, Dr. Wilder saw his physical vigor ebbing away, and with it, his capacity to earn money and provide for his wife and Isabel and Janet, who even as adults were still dependent on their father and Thornton for financial support. There must have been a bittersweet mix of regret, resentment, and gratitude as Thornton supplanted him at the helm of the family.

Yet once Thornton had arranged for the construction and occupation of the house, and paid for it, and helped his family settle into it, he simply had to leave. He was part vagabond and gypsy, but something more than restlessness and the thirst for adventure regularly took him away from his family. He couldn't work at home in the new study in the new house surrounded by his family, much as he loved them. He couldn't concentrate, couldn't carve out the solitude his writing required. His life at the University of Chicago provided a part-time refuge. He embraced that city and its richly diverse culture, and the university served him as a much bigger Lawrenceville by providing the familiar daily structure he needed. He could also have his solitude and privacy there, and as much company as he could stand. His lecture tours kept him on the road, and he firmly established the pattern he would follow for the rest of his life: He traveled for months each year in the United States or abroad, writing on the go, settling down for a few weeks here or there, hibernating, retreating into his work, then pulling himself out of it because he needed to earn more money, or to enjoy some human companionship, or to avoid writing during those periods when it seemed a struggle something akin to wrestling alligators.

As always, letters tethered him to his family, and as his schedule permitted or demanded, he would go home to Deepwood Drive, stay for a while, and then shove off again. From Munich, Germany, in May 1931, he asked Isabel to help their mother understand his absence:

> *Explain to Ma that I go to Munich to write some long things—not because of any éloignement [emotional distance] from Deepwood Drive or its occupants (on the contrary I work to get them over [here]) but because the tepid sociabilities of an American city like New Haven tinged with envy, detraction, etc. make work impossible. Chicago I could stand except that the school routine altho' exciting as ever is too complicated for writing at the same time. There is no halfway solution.*[5]

Wilder was still working hard on *Heaven's My Destination*. "Am 15,000 words already advanced in the novel," he wrote to Les Glenn on July 15, 1932.

> *If it does not allude to some of your most cherished and secret hopes and problems I shall go into a decline. It's our old friend The Arkansas-Texas picaresque. From Baptist Fundamentalism to Gross-stadt toler-ance in three years: or How Rollo learned to be a Babbitt.*
>
> *Only my ending is not to sophistication, but to troubled wisdom. You'll see. All about the Depression.*
>
> *Funny, vulgar, heartbreaking—and a big socio-historical docu-ment.*[6]

In November 1933 Wilder wrote to Amy Wertheimer, "I think my new novel—half-done—will give you much pleasure. Comic, tenderly comic. It's high time I raised a smile. Aren't you in the mood to read a good thoughtful humorous novel?—well, I'm trying to give one to the republic."[7]

———

THE SEVEN Wilders were a remarkably close family, their relationships tightly interlaced despite—or even because of—years of geographical separation and the separate pathways the siblings traversed as adults. They had learned early how to rally around one another through let-ters, faithfully dispatched across oceans and continents. One's joy or achievement elated them all; one's illness or sorrow brought them all grief. In the 1930s, as the country and the world transformed around them, the members of the Wilder family were experiencing profound changes themselves, some perceptible, some too subtle for comprehen-sion at the time. In one way or another, however, all five siblings were searching for home. Especially during the thirties, this was a quest for Thornton, Amos, Charlotte, Isabel, and Janet, all of them working hard to establish vocation, relationships, home bases. Each and every member of the clan was caught up from time to time in living through high drama—individual dramas that fed the poetry, the fiction, and the plays that four of them would write.

In the haven of her own house Isabella gathered her five adult children around her as often as she could, encouraging them; delighting them and their friends with her company, her charm, and her cooking; reading and helping to edit the manuscripts her literary offspring were creating—Amos's poems and scholarly articles; Thornton's new novel and his experimental plays; Isabel's novels, three of them published in the 1930s; and Charlotte's prose and poetry: two books of poems published, one in 1936 and one in 1939. Isabella read and corrected galleys for Thornton and Isabel, and still wrote poems of her own. She looked after her husband as best she could, and when she couldn't provide the care he needed, or when she was exhausted by him, she and her husband's doctors found someone who could take care of him elsewhere—usually in a nursing home or a private home maintained by a practical nurse.[8]

Realizing that his mental powers were ebbing as his body was giving out, Dr. Wilder wanted to make a book of his own. In 1930 he began pulling together newspaper columns, editorials, and speeches, soliciting the help and advice of Charlotte, the most experienced editor in the family. She set her father to work pasting his columns and the text of his speeches onto pages that could be inserted in notebooks, and arranged according to topics and themes. She wrote an encouraging letter commending his "gift for striking & witty expression" but suggesting that some "careful cutting" would be in order to reach the "modern reader." Then, during the summer, when she was free of teaching, they could confer about which to eliminate and how to arrange the pieces.[9] The book did not materialize, but Dr. Wilder appreciated his daughter's "sensible" approach to the matter, and devoted much of his time to arranging and rearranging those pieces of the past.[10]

Like her siblings, Charlotte was still examining her relationship with her father, trying to make sense of it, and to come to terms with it. While Dr. Wilder's sons had suffered in many ways from his intense intervention in their lives, they had at least managed to establish their independence, and to achieve a truce, if not a semblance of harmony, in their relationship with their father. But his relationships with Charlotte and Isabel had been especially damaging. (For one thing, they had uncomfortable memories of being asked by their father, bedridden during one illness, to come to his bedside and brush his hair to help him relax.) Both daughters attributed to their father's strict, moralistic upbringing their eventual sexual repression and their consequent problems in intimate relationships. While Charlotte tried in the early thirties to make peace with her father, Isabel's anger toward him would last for many years.

In talks and letters Thornton, Amos, Isabel, and Charlotte shared their perspectives on their father's enduring influence, and Charlotte sought at least once to broach the matter in a letter to Dr. Wilder that could have been written by any of her siblings as well. "I had the feeling when I was last home, that you felt me very aloof and unknown to you," Charlotte wrote to him:

> I think that you brood over us too much . . . it does not make for a free and natural relationship. The talks we have trouble me, and make me confused. You speak with such anxiety, and put such apprehensions into my head. I know, I think, something of the nature of the disasters life may bring: but I believe strongly—(and if I am to have individuality—I must have a set of beliefs determined by my experience) that it is not helpful to dwell on fears; that it would unfit me for being aggressive and positive in useful ways. . . . You are troubled if I differ from you in any belief. I cannot agree with that. As I see human nature, in my many acquaintances, the beautiful relationships have come when each leaves the other free to choose; anything else is forcing, and one cannot dominate another, or suppose that his truth is all truth.[11]

While the older Wilder children struggled with their history of paternal domination, Janet, the youngest, and the least susceptible to her father's influence, had made her own choices freely. Amos, the eldest, buried himself in his work. Thornton's role in the family was circumscribed by his new duties as the breadwinner, the provider, and frequently, for the six other family members, the counselor and comforter—since he had by default displaced his father and his older brother as the head of the household. In particular he nurtured his three sisters, paying for Janet's college education and encouraging Isabel and Charlotte in their writing. Isabel's fiction and Charlotte's poetry would be published by Coward-McCann, which had published Thornton's plays, and there may have been a coattail effect in the decision to publish the Wilder sisters. But more than anything else, unlike their father, Thornton urged his sisters simply to be themselves.

Without neglecting his family responsibilities, Thornton tore himself away from the Deepwood Drive home and the family to secure the energy and solitude essential to the writer—not a purely selfish act but a practical necessity now that he had to earn the wherewithal to keep the home fires burning for the rest of them. Most of all, however, he had to get away from home in order to be himself.

WHEREVER HE was, Wilder was deeply connected, emotionally and practically, to the family. In copious letters to them, as richly detailed as diaries or journals, he recorded events as well as his work in progress, his reading, his thoughts, his advice and counsel. He worried about his aging father, who still wanted all his brood around him, preferably doing his bidding—and who wanted in vain to be, once and for all, the focus of his wife's love and care.

Wilder gladly sent his youngest sibling to college, paying her bills, encouraging her passion for science, enjoying her company whenever possible. Of all of the Wilders, Janet had the clearest, most precise, and most practical vision of what she expected from life: She wanted to be a scientist, and credited the Montessori school she had attended in Berkeley for imprinting in her "a love of animals and respect for nature" that led to her vocation. Direct and matter-of-fact, Janet seemed at home wherever she was—perhaps because from the time she was six months old her family had moved her from one country to another, first from Berkeley in the United States, where she was born, to China, and then from Shanghai to Paris, and on to Italy and England.[12]

As she looked back on her childhood, Janet recalled her parents' contrasting disciplinary techniques—Papa's delivery of an occasional spanking preceded and followed by long, boring lectures; and Janet's preference, Mother's "sound and proper" and instinctive way, reacting exactly like a mare to a foal: "Offense—followed by immediate punishment."[13] She remembered her sex education—or lack of it. "No information whatsoever from my parents; in fact as you will hear, negative instruction." Most of what she learned about birth she gleaned from watching the family's cat, named Billy Sunday, deliver a litter of kittens on her bed. At movies with her mother and Isabel, Janet was ordered to shut her eyes when the "film got to the kissing part." Once her father took her to a temperance lecture at a church on the New Haven green, and when the lecturer turned to the effects of alcohol on human reproduction, "Father took me firmly by the hand and we left."[14] Looking back in later years, Janet reflected that she never knew her father at his best, but a "cloud seemed to descend on the house when he came in." She believed, on the other hand, that their mother was "the sun and moon to Thornie."[15]

Although Janet clearly recalled the "acute poverty" of her family's life in New Haven, she loved her friends and her school life there, so much so that she "cried and cried" at the news that her mother was taking her and Isabel to live in England in 1921, when she was eleven. She was saved "from total misery" because her mother enrolled her in a riding school. Janet had not been a robustly healthy child, and when Isabella heard that horseback riding could help children overcome certain health problems, she arranged for Janet to take riding lessons with "an ancient and honorable old retired cavalry officer with a few riding horses stabled nearby," and then at the Oxford Riding School.[16] In her first lesson Janet fell in love with horses, and this passion stayed with her all her life.

Homeschooled in London, Janet entered public school in New Haven when she and her mother returned from England in August of 1928. After her high school graduation she enrolled in Mount Holyoke, as Charlotte had done, was elected chairman of the college judicial board in her senior year, and received her degree in zoology in 1933, magna cum laude. Thornton wrote proudly of his sister, "Janet graduated Phi B K and magna cum laude. The only Wilder to make the big grades."[17] She remained at Mount Holyoke to earn a master of science in 1935, and then went to the University of Chicago to work on her Ph.D.

Her mother must have been horrified to read Janet's description of her money-saving "mode of existence," preparing meals in her Ph.D. adviser's laboratory at the University of Chicago. She made her lunch in the lab, she reported, where the hens used for research laid dozens of eggs. "So I use those," she wrote. "Twice a week one pound of the best beef liver arrives to feed the fish and worms; they consume part of it, the rest gets thrown out. I think I'll try frying some tomorrow in my cute little frying pan. The students have done so before and not died."[18]

She survived, returning to Mount Holyoke in 1939, doctoral degree in hand, to teach zoology. Janet was not without her own record as a writer: At least one of her poems was published in the Mount Holyoke literary magazine during her undergraduate years. From 1936 to 1940, while her brothers and sisters were publishing poetry, novels, plays, and essays, she published scholarly papers drawn from her graduate studies of insect life. The capstone of her work as a writer would come in 1990, however, with the publication of a book titled *Jeffy's Journal: Raising a Morgan Horse*, described as "The touching story of a woman and the Morgan Horse she raised from birth." Dedicated to her mother, the book contains a series of monthly articles Janet published in the *Morgan Horse*, beginning in December 1952 and continuing through April 1956. Janet recognized that as the last-born child, thirteen years younger than her brother Thornton, she probably had "no early influence" in his life—but she felt she came "out strong" in his references to horses in two of his later works, *The Matchmaker* and *The Eighth Day*.[19]

DURING THE 1930s Isabel was the only Wilder sibling living full-time in the new house on Deepwood Drive, but she yearned for a home all her own. She was at work on a new novel in the late 1920s, "A thoroughly American story this time. I have the first thousand words,—began yesterday and I am entirely thrilled and wrapt in anticipation. Mother too is pleased and thinks it will beat the other all to pieces." But her social life kept her busy—perhaps too busy, Charlotte warned her. Isabel published three novels during the 1930s: *Mother and Four* (1933), *Heart Be Still* (1934), and *Let Winter Go* (1937). Her first, *Mother and Four*, tells the story of a mother with four children struggling to survive after her husband dies. People who knew the Wilders perceived strong autobiographical threads in the novel, which according to Amos "had a modest success."[20]

While her novels could not be classified as literary fiction, they were a cut above the usual popular fiction. Isabel had her own lecturing contract with Lee Keedick, traveling about in 1933 and 1934 to lecture on the reading and writing of novels, and on "The Modern Stage in America and Europe." But as much as she wanted to write, she found it awfully hard, frustrating work, and more than anything else, she wanted that home of her own, complete with husband and children. Isabel's desires are painfully evident in the second and third novels—wherein love comes belatedly to heroines who struggle for independence from home, and from loving but distant fathers. Disheartened by her literary life and her love life, she was increasingly eager to get married. "I look at every man, wondering, thinking, hoping,—*is it he?* I must get over caring and accept my status. Thornton says one can close one's mind to the whole subject, and says one must forget one wants to marry and if it is to be, it will happen. I'm trying and that's no good!"[21]

Disappointed by the modest success and benign neglect of her published novels, Isabel began to focus more and more on her brother's career. She enjoyed helping her brother as part-time secretary and agent, and eventual buffer and protector of his privacy and his writing time. Thornton appreciated and respected his sister's work on his behalf, and supported her financially in return. Gradually Thornton and Isabel moved into a symbiotic relationship that would last Thornton's lifetime: He traveled, wrote, taught, lectured, and earned the family income. She helped their mother run the house and, after Isabella's death, ran it herself; assisted with many of Thornton's business affairs, including his correspondence and some of his contracts; tended to family matters so he could be free to do his work; and often served as his hostess and traveling companion.

But Charlotte grew concerned about the path Isabel was treading. "I love your writing," she wrote to Isabel, and then expressed some astute observations about the evolving career choices of two aspiring writers who were sisters of a world-famous writer:

> In a way you are so identified, in emotion and energies, with Thornton's career, that you drain off the intensity that would otherwise go into [your writing]; and that is completely valid provided there is nothing in you that is being frustrated by it. I have a different orientation. I love his work, too, but I could not consider it so much mine that I would throw over mine, to absorb myself in it. . . . Somehow each person makes his own pattern, by some inner necessity, and then gives himself to it.[22]

As Isabel began to put down deeper and deeper roots in the Hamden home, surrounded by her brother's work, Charlotte, the middle child, took fiercely independent steps to make a new home for herself. Reluctant to be financially dependent on anyone, even a devoted older brother who sincerely wanted to help her, Charlotte struck out on her own in 1933, resigning her stable job as a Smith College professor to move to New York and have a go at writing full-time. During the years of teaching she had written poems and essays that were published in such journals as the *New Republic*, the *Atlantic Monthly*, *Commonweal*, the *Nation*, and *Poetry*. She explained to her mother in a letter in March 1933 that for the good of her creative life, she had to stop teaching. She had saved enough money to support herself for at least a year, she wrote, and she would not be a burden to her family. "I do hope you see it my way," she wrote. "I dreaded very much giving you this anxiety. And am so happy, and find so many people think I am not at all a silly ass to do it."[23]

Charlotte broke the news to Dr. Wilder only after the deed was done. "Dear Father," she wrote in 1933 from Yaddo, the writers' and artists' colony in Saratoga Springs, New York, knowing her father would be shocked by her decision. "I have resigned from Smith, after five years there. I want to live in another world from that of a woman's college; and want to write so much more than to teach, that I decided the choice must be made now. . . . With good health, so far, and a job to fall back on, I have as reasonable a chance as I can hope for, to do what I most want to do.[24]

Dr. Wilder was disappointed, but still proud of Charlotte even though she would not become the college president he had hoped for. As for her writing, he was pleased that *Poetry* had published her poem "Of Persons, Not Alive" in the March 1932 issue, but he was perplexed. He told her the poem was "too cryptic for Dad," but he knew it had to be good because it was published in a "distinguished magazine."[25]

Thornton wrote Charlotte to congratulate her on her residency at Yaddo, where she worked on a book of poetry, and he offered his financial help. "If your New York life becomes expensive, do not hesitate to call on me," he told her. "Do not crowd your soul by living on sandwiches and sausages." He went on to give her a family update: "Amos has finished his thesis, and is far cheerfuller. Isabel has made much progress in her novel and is cheerfuller. Mama is beginning to be aware of home-economic-security and is cheerfuller. I am full of new wonderful thoughts and am cheerfuller, so your new well being should sustain ours—less Wilder nail-biting, fears, and scruples and distrusts."[26]

Although Charlotte thought she had saved enough money to support herself for at least a year in New York, that did not prove to be the case. Too proud to take money from her mother or her brothers unless she could earn it, she would often live in poverty in the years ahead, ultimately sacrificing her mental and physical health to the unremitting struggles of the writing life. Unlike Isabel, Charlotte did not dream about a conventional marriage and family. In her midtwenties she had at least one serious male suitor, and saved at least one of his romantic letters to the end of her life.[27] By her late twenties she had been romantically if not sexually involved with at least one woman, and perhaps others. "No room except to say every thought of you is held close in my memory—that the blessing of your love is around me all the time," Charlotte wrote to one woman. "Come & be kissed," she answered.

"My love always." Charlotte wrote again, "Bye, sweetheart. . . . Please know deeply that I love you & am close to you always."[28]

Like Thornton, Amos, and Isabel, Charlotte had innate problems with intimacy. She faced them head-on: "The thing I'm learning now is that it would be well if, as children, one were trained in the technique of the 'shock and delicacy' of intimacy," she wrote to Amos in 1932. It was not easy, she reflected, to know how to be close to another person—"at once, self-responsible, and subtly dependent"—if you had grown up with suppressed emotions.[29] In April 1932 Charlotte wrote a frank and prophetic account of her emotional life: "All my life I have stated my experience to myself . . . often in words. My experience has passed through my imagination and mind; my emotion I have checked at every turn. . . . A Narcissism forced on me. I did not take into my heart any gestures of tenderness given me. . . . Yes rarely, in any gestures of love, did I have a gush of feeling welling in my heart." She remembered her first kiss from a woman. She was nineteen at the time, and the kiss, she wrote, "burned on my lips for a day." Yet there was little emotion. "Let me state," she wrote, "I have never had a homosexual consummation, nor come near it. I was too frigid to even experience the sensation of the kiss often."[30] She went on to write, with ironic prescience,

> I have the belief that all my suffering is ahead of me: that my inhibiting experience does not make me seem frustrated, because I have been expressing constantly, in social relationships (never *feeling* the happiness in sheer glow), and in writing. . . . I have intimations of what I must get through . . . or might, that approximate a sudden insight into insanity. . . . I would say I know no one who has been more alone from birth. And who now, at thirty-three, am for the first time knowing I have someone, in two women friends. My own worst enemy heretofore. I know no one (except Amos) who had no mother, no father, no lover.[31]

Through no fault of her own Charlotte had borne the brunt of the serial family separations, often the one child detached from the family, on her own. By choice and circumstance she repeated the pattern as an adult—profoundly bereft and alone.

Amos, the eldest, was scholarly, solitary, and often lonely. He had thought, studied, and prayed his way to some clarity of vision about the life he wanted to lead. He was an effective teacher at Hamilton College, where he served on the faculty from 1930 to 1933, so much so that the college awarded him an honorary doctorate of divinity in June 1933, the same year he received his Ph.D. at Yale. He moved on from Hamilton to become the Norris Professor of New Testament at Andover Newton Theological Seminary from 1933 until 1943. In 1929 Yale University Press had published *Arachne: Poems*, a collection of his poetry to follow *Battle-Retrospect and Other Poems* in 1923. Amos turned to biblical scholarship as he wrote his dissertation—"The Relation of Eschatology to Ethics in the Teaching of Jesus as Represented in Matthew."

Endowed with the Wilder/Niven drive, but with his physical energy still compromised by his World War I experiences, Amos often pushed himself too hard, studying, teaching, writing, working prodigiously. As early as 1930 Dr. Wilder wrote to Charlotte to ask her to reach out to her brother, who was suffering, the father said, from "nervous exhaustion."[32] Teaching was arduous work, Amos found—as did Thornton and Charlotte, all of them college professors in the thirties. "I am very sorry for your overtired state," Charlotte wrote sympathetically to Amos. "I know well what meeting classes is. I have compared them, in my mind, to restive horses."[33]

By the fall of 1934, overworked and anxious, Amos was physically ill with a stubborn case of grippe, and again lapsed into a state of "nervous depletion."[34] To his chagrin his doctor ordered absolute rest and required him to take leave from his classes and go to New Haven to recuperate. He was bedridden there during the Thanksgiving holidays, surrounded by his parents, Isabel, and Charlotte for company. ("Father is getting to be very much of an invalid," Amos worried.)[35] At his doctor's orders Amos traveled to Florida in December 1934 with instructions to recuperate in the sun and not to return to teaching until January at the earliest. "It seems my reservoirs, so to speak, had gone down so very low that it meant a really long time to fill them up again," he reflected. He had little physical energy, and could not "read anything solid for any length of time." He recognized that his efforts to work despite his illness "very ill-advisedly, got to my nerves some."[36] His physical illness was compounded by the lingering stress of the war. But his long recovery was made more bearable because in Geneva, Switzerland, in the summer of 1934, he had met a young teacher, Catharine Kerlin, from Moorestown, New Jersey. Many years later Amos described the life-changing encounter:

> As a long-time bachelor into my late thirties, I waited so long surveying the field and looking for perfection that I very nearly became a life-long Benedict. Then the rescue came from an un-expected quarter. Like many reluctant swains I felt especially on guard against red-haired maidens, against Kates . . . and against teachers. But then *this* Catharine turned up in Geneva who not only had bronze in her hair but turned to teaching. But I couldn't help myself. When we became engaged and married in 1935 we both saved each other from a dubious fate. She was being sounded out to be a head mistress in a private school. I was so far gone that I was thinking about founding a Congregational monastery of celibates.[37]

Their relationship grew despite the geographical distances between them. The miles were bridged by letters, and she saved most of his. From Andover Newton, he mailed a letter to her aboard the SS *Champlain*, due to dock in New York on September 18, 1934. He told her he treasured "very much" the memory of their meetings in Geneva, and would be "very much disappointed" if they could not see each other early in the fall. They had several weekend visits before Amos got sick. By Christmas he was recuperating in a "big quiet room" with an ocean view in an "ultra clean boarding house run by a very motherly and helpful woman" in St. Petersburg, Florida.[38] He and Catharine contin-ued to exchange long letters, and soon Amos was in love. He wanted to send her flowers but held back for fear that at the girls' boarding school where she taught she would have "been in for a general razzing." Instead he sent her a box of pecans from the Kumquat Sweet Shop in Clearwater, Florida. "If I ever bother you, you just tell me to slow up," he wrote, "and I will be perfectly amenable. Our relation started off so perfectly that it shouldn't ever have any misunderstandings—as so many; and we can have it so by speaking right out."[39]

Amos was still in Florida in late January, improving, but not strong enough to travel home and resume his teaching schedule. He was living for her letters, he told Catharine, and eager for a reunion with her.[40] Thornton wrote to Les Glenn about Amos's illness: "Amos had a kind of nervous breakdown. CONFIDENTIAL. Phobias and tics. Started off by intestinal flu. He feels much better now."[41] By mid-March Amos was planning his journey home.[42] Soon after his return Amos and Catharine were engaged. He reflected many years later that he "suffered the happy fate of being married to an internationalist, a can-doer, a nest builder."[43]

WHILE THORNTON was perpetually on the road during the thirties, events on the home front were always on his mind, and the family followed his achievements with pride, although in his father's case, with some skepticism. "Thornton's book a success," Dr. Wilder wrote to Charlotte after *Heaven's My Destination* appeared in January 1935. "London papers favorable. I presume conservatives not all favorable!" He went on to tell her, "I suspect Hawthorne and Geo. Eliot would handle certain aspects differently and shall tell Thornton so though I have not read it in full." He urged Charlotte and Amos to "sit in judgment" on Thornton's books so they could advise him of "obvious shortcomings" because, the father said, "the good fellow must learn things. Suffering is a severe school."[44]

To Grace Foresman, his friend since Lawrenceville days, Thornton wrote from Chicago to sum up his life: "I still enjoy teaching tremendously, and especially on this campus and in this city," he said. "My family is all well, except Papa whose health is uneven. Mother still is so attached to her house and garden that we can't budge her away more than one night." He reported that his delays in delivering his new novel had driven his publishers "insane." He warned her, "Be prepared for the fact that it's utterly unlike the other novels; nearer to *The Happy Journey to Trenton & Camden*. I hope it amuses you and touches you, Grace! An author really writes for a few friends; the indistinct public foots the bill."[45]

He wrote to another friend, offering an apology:

A good deal of the book is tough, full of bad words and life's un-lovelier traps; but I hope you will see that none of the coarseness is there for cheap display. The subject of the book goes quietly on under the surface din: the earnest humorless undefeated hero trying to live an extravagantly idealistic life in the middle of a cynical defeatist world—a Gideon-Bible travelling salesman. On the title page I placed the motto from The Woman of Andros so that readers wouldn't think it was merely a rowdy comic book—"Of all forms of genius, goodness has the longest awkward age"—namely priggishness, preachiness, confusion, etc. I hope it will be somehow useful to a lot of troubled young people.[46]

Wilder mailed an advance copy of the book to Grace Foresman in December, describing its intended mood: "Today I sent you a book that I hope will make you laugh right out loud once in a while, even tho' some parts of it are as sad as sad can be."[47]

Soon after *Heaven's My Destination* hit the bookstores, Thornton told Amos that he had "made a slip and got the actual name of a girl-evangelist in [the book], and may be seriously sued for libel" for showing her taking cocaine. "Sure I'll pay," Thornton went on, "but won't the trial be fascinating! Me as George Brush insisting on her taking all my money and more and then me as Sir Walter Scott diligently writing novels for years to pay a mountainous debt?"[48] Fortunately nothing came of the matter.

Thornton had his own longing for home during those years in the thirties, and he expressed it in a letter to his brother after Amos married his Catharine: "I think of you as having everything I haven't got," Wilder wrote from Vienna in September 1935. "You have a home, a continuity, a job. . . . I'm longing to settle down, as you have, and start a routine of working and reading and quiet evenings at home. I think I can begin it about next week, but until then I remain a hotel-room boy surrounded by cracked and overflowing suitcases."[49]

———

WHILE THE Wilders lived out their family saga in the thirties, George Brush, Thornton's picaresque hero, was searching for home and family in the fictional universe of *Heaven's My Destination*. As he turns twenty-three, this traveling textbook salesman believes he should already have put down roots and "founded an American home." He says to an acquaintance, "You know what I think is the greatest thing in the world? It's when a man, I mean an American, sits down to Sunday dinner with his wife and six children around him."[50] He aspires to "settle down and found an American home."[51] When he tries to persuade a young woman to marry him and share "a fine American home," he enlists the help of his prospective sister-in-law to convince Roberta, his reluctant bride. "Will you go and ask her to come here?" George pleads. "And, Lottie, listen: we'll have a nice home somewhere and you can come in all the time for Sunday dinner, and the whole family can come in from the farm, too. We'll have some fine times, you'll see."[52]

Later on, when Roberta wants to leave the marriage, George is in despair:

"I don't want to go on!" he cried. "What good does it do to go to work if I haven't got a home to work for?" He put his hands over his face. "I don't want to live," he said. "Everything goes wrong."[53]

To no avail he offers to give up his job "because my home's more important to me than my business is."[54] Alone again, George feels a "stab of physical pain" when "on the evening walks, he glimpsed through half-drawn blinds the felicities of an American home."[55]

In *Heaven's My Destination*, as in much of the work that lay ahead, Wilder the novelist, the dramatist, and the literary archaeologist would excavate and explore the felicities and challenges of family—of home.

23

"STRANDS AND THREADS"

Since I have been keeping this Journal I have seen the incidents of the day's life in a new light. One aspect of this consideration of events is the surprising discovery that life is more a matter of strands and threads.

—THORNTON WILDER,
journal, May 26, 1917

The United States and Europe (1930s)

During the thirties Wilder wove into his work the "strands and threads" of his family life, his teaching life, his life on the road—and, always, his rich imaginative and intellectual life. In 1941, writing of Joyce and Cervantes, Wilder said, "The history of a writer is his search for his own subject, his myth-theme, hidden from him, but prepared for him in every hour of his life, his *Gulliver's Travels*, his *Robinson Crusoe*."[1] Taking Wilder at his word, it appears that "every hour of his life" had prepared him to write, in a handful of years, *Heaven's My Destination* and then *Our Town*—two landmark works infused with his predominant myth-themes: How do you live? How do you bear the unbearable? How do you handle the various dimensions of love, of faith, of the human condition? How do universal elements forge every unique, individual human life? And where does the family fit in the cosmic scheme of things?

Wilder was offered a variety of jobs in the midthirties, turning down invitations to host a radio show, lecture aboard a luxury yacht in the Greek islands, and cover a sensational murder trial. When he received a tentative offer to edit a "class woman's magazine," Wilder was actually momentarily tempted, but the firm offer and the position never materialized. "Why should I even consider it?" he wrote to his lawyer.

For the same reason that I go to Hollywood: adventure, color, the exhilaration of even pretending that I have a part to play in the immense bright

stream of Twentieth Century activities. These things have no relation
to my midnight secret life of literary composition. I'm Jekyll and Hyde.
With the side of me which is not Poet, and there's lots of it, I like to do
things, meet people, restlessly experiment in untouched tracts of my Self,
be involved in things, make decisions, pretend that I'm a man of action.[2]

During the 1930s he was a man in constant motion, if not a man of action, juggling the parts he wanted to play—migrating from fiction to drama, from teaching in the university to lecturing in auditoriums and civic halls across the country, from fraternizing with literary lights and the intelligentsia to mingling with producers, screenwriters, and stars in Hollywood. Wilder's first formal movie contract was negotiated in 1934 by Rosalie Stewart and Harry Edington of the H. E. Edington–F. W. Vincent Agency, whose clients included Marlene Dietrich, Greta Garbo, and other luminaries. This agreement took Wilder to the RKO studios in Hollywood for two weeks in 1934 to discuss ideas for a possible movie about Joan of Arc, starring Katharine Hepburn, with George Cukor directing. Wilder was paid fifteen hundred dollars and engaged to write a forty-page outline, which, if accepted, would lead to the assignment to write the movie script and be present for the filming.

ENTIRE OFFICE ENTHUSIASTIC ABOUT YOUR MAGNIFICENT TREATMENT OF JOAN OF ARC, his agents telegraphed in May 1934, and Wilder waited to hear if he would be called back to work on the film for an additional fee of $13,500.[3] While there was perhaps gratuitous praise for Wilder's treatment, RKO declined to exercise his option on the grounds that they wanted to approach the film from a different angle. As it turned out, RKO abandoned the project, apparently because of lack of money, a growing concern even in Hollywood during the Depression.

It was no doubt a disadvantage to the Joan of Arc treatment that Wilder the scholar seemed to overtake Wilder the dramatist as he emphasized the authenticity of his research, occasionally burdened his characters with cumbersome dialogue, and justified the didactic intentions for certain scenes—such as those in heaven, which were important, he explained,

1. To please the adherents of the Roman Catholic Church.
2. To raise the closing scenes of the picture from the realm of physical suffering and torture to the realm of a triumphant moral victory.
3. To cast over even the homely passages an arresting awe-inspiring sense of divine intervention and guidance,— applicable to every member of the audience.[4]

Wilder wanted to satisfy what he presumed would be the audience's curiosity about what it felt like to be a saint, and what ordinary daily life was like for a "great historical character" (an idea he would revisit in his novel *The Ides of March*). He hoped the audience would come to "the final acceptance and willing grasp of death as a meaningful, triumphant and necessary ACT."[5] This lofty scenario did not suit Hollywood—but there are glimmerings of the third act of *Our Town* in Wilder's depiction of "ordinary daily life," and in his words about death.

Wilder was intrigued with the potential of the motion picture as an art form, and beguiled by the opportunity to earn so much money so fast for so little work. In the summer of 1934, Samuel Goldwyn asked Wilder to come to Hollywood to "add words to a former silent picture of Ronald Coleman's called 'Dark Angel'" and then to "write a new climactic closing scene to Anna Sten's 'We Live Again' (Tolstoi's Resurrection)." Wilder reported that he wrote three scenes that had been "shot," and so, he concluded, "I have had my baptism in the films."[6] When *We Live Again* appeared in 1934, Wilder did not expect or receive a film credit.

It was a heady existence, balancing the adventure and color of movieland with his "midnight secret life" as a serious writer. His Hollywood social life quickly grew to be even more fun than his exuberant life in Chicago—although not as emotionally satisfying because it was shallow and fleeting. While he often made fun of it, Wilder relished the glitz and glamour of Hollywood in what has been called its golden age. There were moments when his own life in Hollywood could have been a movie, starring some of the biggest names in films, with himself in a cameo guest spot. He even made the Hollywood Sidelights syndicated gossip column on September 14, 1934, hailed as a "Lion at Parties" and a "tremendous success" in the many divergent circles of Hollywood society that he had "penetrated." The columnist Mollie Herrick admired his "genius for laughter and play" and his ability to switch in an instant from "nonsense to profundity."[7]

Wilder dined at Pickfair with Mary Pickford. The actress Marion Davies, supported by her lover, William Randolph Hearst, "sent out a collaborator to cook up a story for Miss Davies' use in the movies," Wilder wrote to Mabel Luhan. "It's all about how a girl dressed as a boy and became the creator of all Shakespeare's heroines at the Globe Theatre: Willie Hewes, the dark lady of the Sonnets. Yes, Essex and Elizabeth are in it. Did you ever hear anything more foolish?"[8] The writer, film director, and composer Rupert Hughes (the uncle of Howard Hughes) took Wilder to a Hollywood Writers Club dinner, during which, Wilder said, he made a "short bad speech," Will Rogers made a "long heavenly one," and there was an earthquake.[9]

Ruth Gordon was in town for screen tests at MGM, and "dazzled the powers over there," Wilder wrote to the actor Charles Laughton, predicting that "something big will come of them."[10]

Wilder was spending time with Gordon, Laughton, and Helen Hayes, as well as screenwriters such as the playwrights Paul Green and Charles Lederer, the latter best known for his often edgy comedies. Lederer was "sick in bed of trying to build a movie about Mr. Wm. R. Hearst's scenario," Wilder wrote to Woollcott. "I am very fond of Charlie and to my great surprise he is very fond of me. We collaborated on a skit about censorship for the gala number of the *Hollywood Reporter*. I refused to sign my own name and used James Craven instead."[11]

The family back home in Connecticut followed Hollywood gossip and happenings with keen interest, and because the frugal Wilders could now afford to indulge in the occasional telegram, Wilder sent one to his mother on September 8, 1934: WAS OFFERED AND TURNED DOWN SOLO JOB ON NEXT GARBO PICTURE STOP ROLLER SKATED WITH WALT DISNEY.[12]

But Hollywood life was not all glamour, he wrote his friend Grace Foresman. "It's a mixture of very hard work and the industrious contrivance of untruths."[13] It was a dazzling, illusory, addictive, and often exhausting life with intense, deadline-driven work, and the drinking he was now doing at night with his new cohorts. It was enough to drive a man back to teaching. "Now I'm dying to withdraw from the whole business, refuse any money, and return to my university work, my correspondence, my reading and my thoughts," he said. "I haven't the strength to break off. Really."[14]

For Wilder, as for other novelists and playwrights who hired out in Hollywood during the Depression, there could be big payoffs, and Wilder had the chance to work on some serious projects in addition to the proposed Joan of Arc film. He collaborated with Paul Green to rewrite the final scene of Sam Goldwyn's *We Live Again*, based on Tolstoy's *Resurrection*. Goldwyn pronounced their work beautiful, but Wilder, Green, and three other writers did not receive on-screen credit for the finished product; the credit went, of course, to the principal screenwriters, Maxwell Anderson, Preston Sturges, and Leonard Praskins.[15]

All in all during that first year of movie assignments, Wilder worked more than two weeks for RKO, six weeks for Samuel Goldwyn, and two weeks for William Randolph Hearst's Cosmopolitan Productions—and the work was lucrative: Wilder earned $11,500 for ten weeks of work in Hollywood in 1934, more than double his half-time teaching salary, and five times the fees he earned out on the lecture circuit.[16] He needed the money as the Depression economy gnawed away at lecture fees, lowering them dramatically. Keedick found extra dates for him whenever possible, usually at reduced fees. "So many states have declared a bank moratorium that lecture committees everywhere have become frightened," Keedick informed him, explaining why some lecture dates had fallen through. "This country is in a deplorable state due to our wretched banking laws which were passed years ago when, I imagine, bankers controlled the government even more completely than now."[17] As if to fit the emotional atmosphere of the time, Wilder notified Keedick that lectures would "be a shade more serious from now on: I offer the Titles: 'Novel, Allegory and Myth' or 'The Novel versus The Drama.'"[18]

Wilder wrote to an old friend on October 13, 1934, "I work in

Hollywood a few months every year. I am very interested in the movies as a form; I am working very hard at its peculiar technique and after a few years of apprenticeship I hope to be allowed a chance to write one that is all myself and all deeply felt. Besides it has fallen upon me to sustain several members of my family and the earnings out there are a great help."[19]

In a demonstration of his serious interest in movies as an art form, Wilder later sent Lee Keedick a synopsis of a lecture he planned to give. "Motion Pictures and Literature," he called it, and it concluded with the prediction that the motion picture could become an independent art form and take its place as a form of literature.[20]

Wilder's love affair with Hollywood lasted for several years. He wrote to Dwight Dana from Hollywood in August 1938: "You will be interested to know that Columbia offered me $5000 a week to finish off the script of 'Golden Boy' and De Mille today wanted me to do some work on 'Union Pacific.' "[21] He found a certain security in knowing that earning money in Hollywood was an option. He could pay the medical bills for his father's "protracted invalidism."[22] He could provide certain luxuries for his family—sending his mother and Janet to Scotland, for instance—and certain necessities such as a new suit for himself, since his clothes were "falling to pieces." However, he assured Dwight Dana, overseer of his budget, except for an occasional dinner in a "dazzling" Hollywood restaurant, not a dollar he spent was wasteful.[23]

PART OF Wilder's discipline as a writer grew out of his pervasive sense of the artist's responsibility to his art, to his subjects, to his world, to himself. Bound up with that was his often-frustrating inability to create works of fiction or drama that lived up to his visions for them. He wrote to Aleck Woollcott in 1938, "Success is accorded to a work of art when the central intention is felt in every part of it, and intention and execution are good." As he endeavored to articulate his artistic intentions to readers—friends and strangers alike—who challenged him with questions, he was continually refining his ideas about the purpose of literature and art generally and his own creative endeavors specifically.[24] In particular Wilder found himself devoting a significant amount of time and energy in the thirties and afterward to clarifying for himself and his readers his intentions for *Heaven's My Destination*, as well as explaining the literary techniques he employed in the book.

His new novel traveled an unorthodox road to its publication in the United Kingdom on December 3, 1934, and in the United States on January 2, 1935. Wilder's original publishing agreement with Albert and Charles Boni had called for the publication of his next three books after *The Cabala*. The Bonis published *The Bridge of San Luis Rey* and *The Woman of Andros*, but, lacking faith in the market for Wilder's early plays, they had declined to publish, as the third book, *The Angel That Troubled the Waters*. That left *Heaven's My Destination* committed to the Boni firm. Wilder's secret 1928 agreement with Harper was still in place, however, and he stayed in touch with Harper's Cass Canfield, reporting to Dwight Dana in 1934 that Canfield "moans about, hoping that something will happen that will bring the text to him. If Boni's can't pay a just advance etc."[25]

By July 1934 Canfield's hopes were realized when the Bonis decided they did not like *Heaven's My Destination* well enough to publish it, and sold the rights to Harper & Brothers. A letter from Canfield to the Bonis on August 29, 1934, laid out the conditions of the sale: Four thousand dollars changed hands between the publishers, along with an agreement that the Bonis would receive a percentage of royalties for the book, along with proceeds from any serial sale transacted by June 1, 1935, and certain proceeds from any book-club sale.[26] By September 29, 1934, Wilder and his novel in progress were officially in the fold at Harper & Brothers.[27] In November, Wilder had the first inkling that *Heaven* would do well in the literary marketplace when the Book-of-the-Month Club bought the rights to the novel for the princely sum of ten thousand dollars—roughly the equivalent of $163,598 in 2010 dollars.[28]

Wilder had finished writing the novel in the fall of 1934 under Mabel Dodge Luhan's "humorous and disciplinary eye" at her ranch compound on a shady plateau on the edge of Taos, New Mexico. He had

promised Mabel that he was working "furiously" to finish his assignments with Goldwyn so he could visit her in the "glorious air" of Taos
and write the last chapter of his novel, which his publishers were clamoring to receive.[29] They had met through letters when Mabel wrote to
praise his first two novels and to invite him to come to Taos.[30] Before
her life there, she had been married three times, had befriended Gertrude Stein and Alice B. Toklas in Paris, had presided over a bohemian literary and political salon in Greenwich Village, and had been
the mistress of the radical John Reed. In Taos in 1923 Mabel married
her fourth husband, the charismatic Tiwi Indian Tony Luhan, who had
become her spiritual counselor, and then, pitching a tepee in front of
her house, had courted Mabel, despite the fact that he had a wife in the
nearby Pueblo community.

Like other writers (including D. H. Lawrence, Robinson Jeffers,
Thomas Wolfe, and Edna Ferber) and visual artists (Paul Strand, John
Marin, Georgia O'Keeffe, and others), Wilder gravitated not only to
Mabel's generous hospitality at her comfortable ranch, and the stimulating company she attracted there, but to flamboyant Mabel herself—
her energy, her "bracing" analysis of his work, and the "wonderful
and rich resources" of her intellect and spirit.[31] During the day Wilder
retreated into his work on the novel, but broke away gladly in the
late afternoon to take long drives with Mabel at the wheel, expertly
navigating the narrow roads twining up and down the hills of Pueblo
County. The two friends could talk about everything and everybody in
the world—including Gertrude Stein, whom Wilder had yet to meet.
He knew Stein's work well enough to write a wicked parody of it for
Mabel. His subject was Taos:

> There is something that you find—Throwing away is finding
> but there is no beginning to it.
>   There is a house but here is a current of air. Looking does not
> do anything. You go away and then you come back and so you
> are there. Nothing is black that is black only a waiting. You have
> lost a thinking, but you did not know you had a thinking until
> the throwing away became a finding.[32]

Wilder's letters to Mabel over the years were remarkably candid in his assessments of his own work, especially his anxieties about it. He hated to write, he told her. He was too lazy. As he worked to finish *Heaven's My Destination*, he was still stung by Jed Harris's critique of *The Woman of Andros*. Harris had pronounced the novel "so soft that wherever you touched it, it caved in like uncooked dough. I was all ears and all eager docility," Wilder told Mabel, "but he couldn't tell me why or where, so I merely went sadly away."[33]

AS ALWAYS, vivid strands and threads from Wilder's reading fed his imagination and were woven, subliminally or intentionally, into the pages of his work. He wrote that Nietzsche had been his "great discovery" in 1932—"my meat and drink."[34] Nietzsche's cautionary philosophy echoes in *Heaven's My Destination* in George Brush's rigid morality and his determination to live by a prescribed ethic, in his endeavors to improve himself, and in his efforts to rectify his errors by seeking to do good after he has done harm. ("If you have done harm," Nietzsche wrote in *The Wanderer and His Shadow*, "see how you can do good.—If you are punished for your actions, bear the punishment with the feeling that you *are* doing good—by deterring others from falling prey to the same folly.")[35]

Also entwined in the novel are the strands of Wilder's personal discovery of America—his sojourn at the University of Chicago, his visits to the world's fair, and his travels on the lecture circuit. There are memories of his father, his brother, and himself; his longtime fascination with the picaresque as a literary form, which intensified as he taught *Don Quixote* in his university classes; his "years among the missionaries in China"; his two years at Oberlin College; his friendship with Gene Tunney, who was part of the inspiration for George Brush; and Wilder's periodic sojourns in Hollywood. (If there was to be a movie version of the novel, Wilder wanted Frank Capra to direct and Gary Cooper to play George Brush.) He even transferred to Brush his concept of "Voluntary Poverty."

For the book's epigraph Wilder chose lines of Midwestern school doggerel that apparently sprang from Joyce's *Portrait of the Artist as a Young Man*:

> *Stephen Dedalus is my name,*
> *Ireland is my nation.*
> *Clongowes is my dwellingplace*
> *And heaven my expectation.*

From Wilder's pen the lines read *"George Brush* is my name; America's my nation; / *Ludington's* my dwelling-place / And Heaven's my destination." To follow those lines, Wilder pulled an aphorism from *The Woman of Andros*: "Of all the forms of genius, goodness has the longest awkward age." Given some of the questions later surrounding the novel, he wondered if he should have chosen "other phrases from Andros" instead—"How do you live? What do you do first?"[36]

Heaven's My Destination is an anomaly among American novels written during the Depression. While Wilder takes an informed, realistic look at the social struggles of that era, he often does so through the lens of farce and high comedy, believing that in dark and perilous times, people need and want the ballast of laughter. George Brush and his sometimes farcical escapades would be, Wilder hoped, the catalyst for such laughter. There are few heroes in American literature more wholeheartedly devoted to a rigid system of ethics—and more comically prone to trouble because of a puritanical conscience. George's dogged ethical system, enforced by his overbearing conscience, entangles him with evangelists, prostitutes, priests, and reluctant brides; he finds himself seduced, persecuted, misunderstood, arrested, incarcerated, married, and converted. Among Wilder's targets are evangelists, bankers, predatory women, self-help movements, and certain kinds of Christians and government officials.

Wilder quickly discovered, however, that what he intended as comedy many took for satire. "There's no satire in it," Wilder wrote to Dr. Creighton Barker of New Haven. "It's about all of us when young.

You're not supposed to notice the humor—you're supposed to look through it at a fellow who not only has the impulse to think out an ethic and plan a life—but actually *does* it." He acknowledged that he had made "a lot of mistakes" in the novel, "at the close especially," and time would tell, Wilder said, whether he had "made a big lapse of artistic judgment in presenting the matter so objectively."[37]

To another reader Wilder defended himself against the charge that he was making fun of George Brush. "His instinctive goodness and his instinctive view of what is essential in living is far superior to the groups among which he moves," he wrote, adding that Brush had been "badly educated—badly educated even in religion." Wilder believed that the "censorious, literal and joyless" traditions of some Protestant religions were based on "a misreading of the New Testament and a failure to see that most of that tone in the Old Testament is expressly superceded [*sic*] in the New." He "meant George Brush to be seen as learning in episode and episode better how to render his instinctive goodness and unworldliness effective. It's an Education Novel."[38] Wilder told a reader that he must not have written the end of the novel "clearly enough," and then he reiterated his purpose:

> *I intended that everyone should find something of his or her self in George Brush,—and of the best of themselves, too. I know that much of my father and my brother and myself is there, and many people recognize themselves in him. I was very glad to get your word to the same effect, and hope a second reading will remove your feeling that I wrote it to make fun of great and good qualities.*[39]

Wilder worried in a letter to Les Glenn that "people are still writing to tell me of their contempt for my book, that I made fun of religion to earn money for myself." He went on to say, "I didn't give Geo Brush enough of the intermittent moments of joy and reassurance. They are his due. . . . That was very bad of me; I was so intense about his troubles that I didn't *think* of it. SO my next book won't be harrowing, *it will* give pleasure . . ."[40]

DURING THE first months of 1935 Wilder was intensely busy with his heavy teaching load and other responsibilities at the University of Chicago, and his plans to welcome two new friends for an extended visit to Chicago. At Bobsy Goodspeed's apartment on November 25, 1934, Wilder had been introduced to Gertrude Stein and Alice B. Toklas when Stein arrived to lecture at the University of Chicago. It was the international success of her book *The Autobiography of Alice B. Toklas* (1933) that brought her back to her native United States for the first time in thirty years. Since about 1905 Gertrude had written and published (most often at her own expense) fiction, nonfiction, poetry, plays, and an opera libretto—but this book was her first commercial literary success.

In her 1937 book, *Everybody's Autobiography*, she wrote that she did not want to return to the United States until and unless she was a celebrity.[41] Stein was feted like the 1930s equivalent of a movie star. Her face had appeared on the cover of *Time* on September 11, 1933, to mark the publication of her book. Wherever she went on her cross-country tour in 1934–35, she drew crowds, press, and controversy. She and Wilder had spent very little time alone together during her 1934 visit to Chicago—but enough for the mutual recognition that they would like to see more of each other. Learning that Stein and Toklas would return to the university for two weeks in March 1935, Wilder conveyed his pleasure at the prospect, and offered them the use of his apartment. Stein and Toklas took him up on the invitation.

Before they arrived Wilder devoted much of January and February to directing the university's student production of Handel's only venture into comic opera, *Xerxes*, in celebration of Handel's 250th birthday. The ambitious production ran on February 16 and 17, 1935, and involved the University of Chicago Chorus and Orchesis (an orchestra in this case smaller than the symphony orchestra) as well as the symphony orchestra and dance group. Wilder translated the libretto into a lively English version, directed the opera, and even outfitted himself in a soldier's uniform—boots, cape, and all—to sing in the chorus in the third act.[42] Eager to immerse his audience and his performers in the authentic high Baroque style of the original production in London in 1738, he staged the opera with a raised curtain, so that audience members could watch stagehands finish preparations for the performance— a strategy he had used four years earlier in *The Happy Journey to Trenton and Camden* and, to some extent, in *Pullman Car Hiawatha*, and would employ again two years later in *Our Town*.

Meanwhile *Heaven's My Destination* was doing very well. It was a main selection of the Book-of-the-Month Club in the United States and the English Book Society in the United Kingdom, and would rank seventh among the top ten bestselling novels of 1935. The novel yielded $27,000 in royalties that first year (worth about $425,000 in 2010 buying power), and was "selling like pancakes," Wilder exulted, even though "almost everybody" misunderstood it. Once more he clarified his intention: "It's no satire. The hero's not a boob or a sap. George Brush at his best is everybody."[43]

Amos Wilder was one of the most appreciative readers of his brother's book, and wrote a perceptive assessment of it in 1943:

> The discerning saw in the hero, George Brush, an attempt on the part of the author to Americanize Don Quixote, and to give him the run of Main Street in the nineteen thirties. . . . George Brush is a Puritan who is under a misapprehension; he is a reformer wandering about in worlds not realized. It is his fate, out of zeal, always to overshoot the mark. In the field of ethics he is always doing the wrong thing for the right reason, and the right thing for the wrong reason. He has an undigested assortment of ideas and revelations from Marx, Tolstoi, Henry George and Gandhi and an outsider's over-simplifications about the common life. . . . He is not satisfied to hitch his wagon to a star but he must select the most remote and cloudy of all stars, perhaps the nebula in Andromeda or some galaxy entirely invisible to the naked eye.[44]

WHETHER HE was working in Hollywood or Chicago or New Haven, or traveling, lecturing, and writing throughout the United States and Europe, Wilder sustained an astonishing number and variety of friendships—steady ones, carried on largely through letters, with Alexander Woollcott, Mabel Dodge Luhan, Sibyl Colefax, Les Glenn, Jed Harris and Ruth Gordon, and Gertrude Stein and Alice B. Toklas, and more sporadic ones with people he met along the way. In Chicago in 1933, for instance, he had enjoyed a "galvanizing" talk with a discouraged young actor who had left the stage to become a writer, and Wilder gave the young man letters of introduction to friends in New York. He was a "rather pudgy-faced youngster with a wing of brown hair falling into his eyes and a vague Oxford epigrammatic manner," Wilder had written to Woollcott from Chicago in 1933. "The pose is from his misery and soon drops under a responsible pair of eyes like mine. The name is Orson Welles and it's going far."[45]

Wilder was connected to a powerful network of theater friends by this time, and he used it to benefit the eighteen-year-old Welles, who often gave Wilder credit for discovering him. Wilder gave Welles a letter of introduction to the illustrious, influential Woollcott, who took Welles under his wing and immediately gave him a new wardrobe as well as introductions to Katharine Cornell and her husband, Guthrie McClintic, who quickly cast Welles in three of their productions—*Candida*, *The Barretts of Wimpole Street*, and *Romeo and Juliet*. Wilder and Welles were later connected by other strands and threads: In 1940, as Welles worked on the script for his landmark film, *Citizen Kane*, he openly borrowed a pivotal idea from Wilder's *The Long Christmas Dinner*, telescoping time when he wrote the breakfast scene between Kane and Emily in which they traverse the history of their entire marriage as they sit at the breakfast table.[46]

In March 1935 Wilder, nearly thirty-eight, formed one of the pivotal literary friendships of his life when Gertrude Stein, just turned sixty-one, and Alice B. Toklas, fifty-eight, her companion-lover-amanuensis, arrived to stay in his apartment in Chicago. After Bobsy Goodspeed had introduced him to Stein and Toklas in November 1934, Wilder had

written to Mabel: "Gertrude Stein has been in town giving some beautiful lectures. I have met her over and over again, but usually with a
throng about her. I told her and Miss Toklas what I felt about Taos, my
affection for you and the beauty of the place."[47]

This message would not have entirely pleased either Stein or
Luhan, for the two were rivals as well as friends. They had known
each other since the spring of 1911 in Paris, and, by some accounts,
had been so attracted to each other that there was infatuation and
flirtation during a time when Gertrude, then thirty-seven, was already in her relationship with Alice, and Mabel, then thirty-three and
widowed by the first of her four husbands, was in the midst of one of
her many love affairs, this time with her son's twenty-two-year-old
tutor.[48]

On February 24, 1935, Gertrude and Alice settled into Wilder's
comfortable apartment at 6020 Drexel Avenue for two frenetic weeks
at the University of Chicago. While his guests took over his apartment, Wilder occupied the Visiting Preacher's Suite in Hitchcock Hall
at the University of Chicago, where he had stayed before and felt "perfectly at home."[49] Gertrude was to deliver four public lectures to audiences limited to five hundred, and, in a special course, Narration,
lead a series of two-hour "conferences," as Wilder described them, in
which she "amplified the ideas contained in these lectures by means of
general discussion with some thirty selected students."[50] The university students were handpicked by Wilder, and according to him, there
were ten conferences in all. In *Everybody's Autobiography* Gertrude
acknowledged that Thornton made all the arrangements, including
choosing the participating students.[51] Wilder wrote to Les Glenn, "At
present I am the secretary, errand boy-companion of Gertrude Stein
who is teaching here for two weeks—a great, sensible, gallant gal and
a great treat."[52]

Delighted by the American custom of "drive-yourself" cars, Stein
rented a Ford and drove all over the city. ("Gertrude with the wheel
of a car in her grasp was like Jehu with the steering reins of a racing
chariot," said her friend Fanny Butcher. One evening in Chicago Gertrude was arrested for driving erratically—and without a license—but

managed to prove that she had a license at home in France and to intimidate the police into believing that she was in Chicago as a guest of the government and therefore had diplomatic immunity.)[53] Looking back on her sojourn in Chicago, Gertrude wrote that piloting the "drive-yourself" car around the city was the most exciting aspect of the experience.[54]

In addition to keeping up with Gertrude and Alice and his teaching schedule, Wilder welcomed two other special guests to Chicago, and the flurry of social events intensified. March 4 marked the arrival of Alexander Woollcott, whom Gertrude had met in New York, and on March 9, Isabel Wilder came to town to promote *Heart Be Still*, her second novel. The Wilders, Fanny Butcher, and her husband, Dick Bokum, joined Stein and Toklas for a festive lunch in Wilder's apartment, no doubt prepared by Alice, a notable chef. (Alice would leave Wilder's refrigerator full of gourmet treats when she and Gertrude vacated the apartment.)

It was not surprising, all things considered, that Wilder found himself "a little shaken in health" during that hectic time or that he had AN ODD LITTLE UNIMPORTANT NERVOUS BREAKDOWN, as he described it in a telegram to Stein on April 2.[55] Actually, he was totally exhausted and very worried about his health. Encouraged by the book royalties coming in, Wilder requested a year's leave of absence from the University of Chicago in 1935. He was still "very proud of the university and the *wunderkind* president."[56] He wrote to Les Glenn:

> *The University has now given me one year off—April to April. Maybe with plays on Broadway or something other I shall not return. But I don't know any reason now why I shouldn't, except that I teach worse and worse in the classroom itself—tho' if I do say it, I get better and better as a "campus character" in general circulation, accessible to all comers. Some mornings I rise up and swear that I shall never teach again, that I must go away and become a writer etc. Other days I rise up and love it . . . the classes, the tumult on the stairs of Cobb Hall.*
>
> *What a silly pathless creature I am.*[57]

He was also mentally and physically exhausted, as he confided to Amy Wertheimer. "I was in a strange state ever since Christmas," he wrote to her from Hamden.

> *I was working like mad: eight classroom lectures a week; lectures outside; the long rehearsals of Xerxes; the gregarious social life; endless conferences over MSS with novelists, dramatists, etc., many of whom were not even connected with the University; and finally Gertrude Stein's [two-week] visit for which I was guide, manager and secretary. Naturally nature could not stand this any longer and I was suddenly brushed by light warnings of a nervous breakdown. I began fainting for apparently no reason in public and found that after any conversation an hour long my hands began to tremble and I was filled by an irresistible desire to run away. I saw the warning and immediately changed my life; day before yesterday I came home here and my family is putting the last touches to my convalescence.[58]*

Free of his university commitment, and with money in the bank (and, like his hero George Brush, with a history of attributing other people's illnesses and "nervous breakdowns" to psychogenic roots), Wilder decided that the only path to his own renewed good health and vigor and the essential time to write led to one destination: Europe. He had not been there for three years, and he was determined to embark on that journey in early July 1935. However, he was caught in the web of family concerns about his father's rapidly declining health. Dr. Wilder had been a virtual invalid for several years, and although Thornton believed that his father's illness was almost entirely psychogenic, he suffered from seizures and strokes and intermittent paralysis.[59] Thornton dutifully paid the mounting medical bills, along with the other family expenses. He had been the family's dependable financial father since 1930, and, with Dwight Dana's guidance, planned to continue that support indefinitely. While Wilder was in Europe, Dana would oversee financial matters and serve as liaison between Wilder's literary interests and his publishers, past and present. His Hollywood agent, Rosalie Stewart, was working on "the possible sale of the movie rights" to *Heaven's My Destination*. Playwright Marc Connelly had entered negotiations for the rights, and then withdrawn, but Stewart had hopes—eventually dashed—of making a sale.[60]

"I feel like a cad to be going abroad," Wilder wrote to Stein and Toklas, who hoped to entertain him at their country home at Bilignin in the south of France. His "women-folk" were "standing by," he said, "attending the protracted exasperating unlovable death of my father. I pass through the house having come—in their eyes—from a brightly lighted gay life in Chicago en route to a life of pleasure and glamor in Europe."[61] One roadblock to his journey was averted when Amos and his bride-to-be, Catharine Kerlin, offered to move their planned September 1 wedding to late June so that Thornton could be there "and usher in striped trousers and a camellia."[62] He reluctantly agreed—how could he not? But he was "really not well," he mused. "I have funny moods. I have to withdraw when there are large groups of people, etc. . . . What fetishes there are about us. This notion that one must be present at weddings and funerals."[63]

———

"THERE ARE some new notes to report to you on the Wilder saga," Wilder wrote to Mabel in the summer of 1935 after the landmark family event. "Wednesday we got Amos married on a sunny lawn."[64] Catharine and Amos were wed on June 26, 1935, in the garden of the Kerlin home in Moorestown, New Jersey, with Thornton as the best man and Isabel as a bridesmaid. It was on his brother's wedding day that Thornton discovered the custom that the groom was not allowed to see his bride until the ceremony—a detail that would later show up in *Our Town*. Amos was "marrying a fine girl," Thornton reported to Mabel, "and we're delighted for him."[65]

Wilder had very little uninterrupted time for writing in 1935, but by July 2, soon after his brother's wedding, he started a draft of a play he titled *M Marries N*, clearly a forerunner of the first two acts of *Our Town*. A stage manager takes on the role of a minister and tells the audience that "M. . . . marries N. . . . millions of them." [66] The stage manager oversees "an American village," in which two young people are in love.

The intertwining threads of courtship, love, and marriage lingered in Wilder's mind that year: When his friend Fanny Butcher married Dick Bokum in February 1935, Wilder had discussed the "awe-full character of the Marriage Service" with Gertrude Stein. It was "one of the best written scenes in all drama," Wilder said. "I wish I'd thought of it first."[67]

—————

"EAGER TO get abroad; the correspondence over that blame book swamps me," Wilder wrote to Amy Wertheimer.[68] By June 28 he was bound for Europe aboard the RMS *Ascania*, with George Brush tagging along. Wilder took with him letters from his readers—pages full of questions and complaints about *Heaven's My Destination*, and occasional praise. Wilder's actual traveling companion on the crossing was Robert Frederick Davis, one of his University of Chicago "children" as he called the group of talented scholars and writers he had taken under his wing, including the playwright Robert Ardrey and the artist John Pratt.[69]

Wilder had taken a special interest in Robert Davis, a "grave yet turbulent" philosophy major who had just received his undergraduate degree at the University of Chicago. "Don't be mad," Wilder had written to Dwight Dana in the spring of 1935, explaining that he wanted to invest in the future of this "very brilliant student" by funding a year's study abroad, since the university's graduate school was at that time "very poor in Philosophy." Davis was from a large family in Chicago, where his father worked for the Swift meatpacking company. Wilder had discussed with Davis's parents his offer of six hundred dollars to subsidize a year abroad for Davis to study philosophy, psychology, and German, and the funds were accepted.[70]

After Davis left the ship at Plymouth for a tour of Scotland, Wilder went on to Paris, and then he and Davis went to Bilignin to see Gertrude and Alice. He described their eight-day visit in a letter to Mabel:

> *Automobile trips in the environs; an intense preoccupation with two dogs; Alice B. Toklas's sublime housekeeping; and Gertrude Stein's*

difficult magnificent and occasionally too abstract and faintly disillu-
sioned alpine wisdom about the **Human Mind,** *identity, the sense of time*
and How we Know. I am devoted to both of them, but in the presence of
Gertrude's gifts one must occasionally scramble pretty hard to realize
one's self, collect it, encourage it, and trust it.[71]

After some "splendid Tyrolian hiking and some great music at Salzburg," Wilder moved on to Vienna, where he craved solitude and long
walks in the woods. He would be a "surly hermit" for a while, he explained to the poet H.D.[72] When he was ready he would settle down to
work again. "My head is hot with three fine fiction subjects and three
for non-fiction," he wrote to Mabel. "I keep jotting down notes toward
all six and finally one of them becomes more insistent than the other
and that will be my task."[73]

24

OUR LIVING AND OUR DYING

Well, people a thousand years from now, this is the way we were—in our growing-up, in our marrying, in our doctoring, in our living, and in our dying.

—THORNTON WILDER,
early draft of Our Town

The United States, the Caribbean, and Europe (1930s)

In the midthirties an eclectic array of subjects filled the pages of Wilder's working notebooks—a drama about a caliph in the *Arabian Nights*; an homage to the British humorist, novelist, playwright, and screenwriter P. G. Wodehouse; a farce about an exuberant matchmaker; and a quiet play about life in a mythical New Hampshire village. Ultimately this last drama emerged from the cluster of Wilder's plays in progress to claim his energy and attention. *Our Town* was years in the making, and he wrote much of it in transit, in American and European towns. He was a perpetual traveler, habitually living "in two suitcases and a brief-case," a mark of his transient lifestyle as well as the relative ease with which he could transplant himself from one place to another.[1] This time he had gone abroad to rest and recover from the strenuous months of overwork in Chicago and on the lecture trail—and then to make serious progress on the unfinished manuscript drafts packed in his briefcase.

He liked railroad stations, especially in Austria, he wrote to Gertrude Stein from Salzburg in late August 1935. Wilder rose early every morning and walked to the Salzburg railway station for "a prebreakfast," which he especially enjoyed on Sunday mornings when the station was packed with people attending mass in the second-class waiting room, or singing folk songs in four-part harmony in the third-class restaurant, or embarking on a day trip to the mountains.[2]

When he was not dining with the crowds in the railroad station, he was socializing with such luminaries as the director Max Reinhardt, whom he had revered since his boyhood in Berkeley, and the German novelist and Nobel Laureate Thomas Mann, introduced to Wilder by Reinhardt at a midnight supper he and his wife hosted at their castle after a performance of *Faust* at the Salzburg Music Festival.[3] That night Max Reinhardt offered Wilder the directorship of the theater school he hoped to establish in Los Angeles, but Wilder turned it down.[4]

Wilder seesawed between convivial hours spent with friends new or old, and solitary hours sequestered in his work—indulging his gregarious self until he tired of company, and then retreating into his writing self until weariness or frustration or fulfillment drove him away from his desk and manuscripts to socialize once more. He saw his aunt Charlotte Niven in Innsbruck, and in Salzburg spent time with Bobsy Goodspeed, Sibyl Colefax, Katharine Cornell, and the violinist Fritz Kreisler, as well as Reinhardt, one of the cofounders of the Salzburg Festival. Wilder and Robert Davis immersed themselves in the festival— Toscanini and the Vienna Philharmonic, Reinhardt's lavish version of Goethe's *Faust*, and Bruno Walter's *Don Giovanni*. During the festival, for fun, Wilder and Bobsy Goodspeed took a class in symphony conducting from the Austrian composer and conductor Felix Weingartner.[5]

Throughout, Wilder was serving as patron or mentor to a variety of friends and acquaintances. As his friendship with Sibyl Colefax flourished, they exchanged long letters, and he began to confide in her about his writing projects. In person or in correspondence, he was a confidant and literary adviser for Mabel Luhan in New Mexico and Gertrude Stein in France, sometimes even acting as Stein's publishing agent. He was both patron and mentor to Robert Davis, paying his way to Europe, funding his year of study there, seeing to it that he had German-language lessons, and introducing him to people who might be helpful to him. An inveterate walker and hiker, Wilder insisted that Davis accompany him on hikes through the wild splendor of the Dolomites. They bought "leder-hosen and complete rig," and posed for a photograph that Wilder sent to Stein and Toklas.[6]

Before long, however, Wilder was "cranky from travelling, from not being in one place more than two days at a time" and "from having to speak and think in French, German, and Italian and English (every now and then I have amnesia and can't remember one word in any)."[7] He was eager to focus on writing, and he needed "silence and solitude" and long walks. He found them in nearby Kobenzl, at the Schlosshotel, where he began a "new life":

> *On a hilltop—nobody near. Long walks through woods stretching on every side of the hotel, with great prospects of the city in the distance with St. Stephen's tower, the Danube winding about the plains that stretch toward Hungary.*
>
> *And the hours falling like leaves.*
>
> *At last I shall hear myself and when the inner monologue gets too loud I can go into town.*[8]

At the same time Wilder was reading, traveling with a book in hand. He gave up on eighteenth-century dramatist Carlo Goldoni's realistic comedies because the Venetian dialect was too difficult, but he devoured *Der Zerrissene* and other farcical comedies by Johann Nestroy, Austria's popular nineteenth-century playwright. He read Voltaire's *Zadig* and Goethe's *Faust* twice, the plays of the great nineteenth-century Austrian dramatist Franz Grillparzer, and the fiction of the nineteenth-century Austrian novelist Adalbert Stifter.[9] Wilder's German was improving so steadily that he could "tear up and down Goethe and Thomas Mann and Freud like they was English," he wrote to his brother and sister-in-law.[10] He reported that his farce-comedy was "shaping up" in his mind; this was an early stab at *The Merchant of Yonkers*, influenced by Nestroy's work, which Wilder had been reading for several years.[11] He would base his *Merchant* on Nestroy's *Einen Jux will er sich machen* ("He Intends to Have a Fling" or "He Just Wants to Have Fun") with a little help from a scene from Molière's *The Miser*.

The more time he spent in Europe in 1935, the more he began to worry about the world scene: "I guess there's going to be a War soon,"

Wilder wrote to Amos and Catharine from Vienna in September. "Italy had 500,000 men in manoevres [*sic*] in their northernmost mountains when I was there and now your Geneva is on pins and needles. . . . Amputated, strangled Austria hasn't money enough to buy a cannon even, so the Austrians sit in cafés all day over one *mokka* and wax witty about dictators and empires."[12]

But he had to force his eyes away from world issues to read the page proofs of Gertrude Stein's latest book, *Narration*, the University of Chicago Press edition of the lectures she had given at the university—and a book whose publication in 1935 in large part hinged on Wilder's agreement to write an introduction. He could be diplomatically forthright with Stein about her lectures and writings, and sometimes he simply told her candidly that he had no idea what she was talking about. Stein also asked Wilder to read the manuscript of her unpublished *Four in America*, which she had begun writing in 1932 and finished in 1933. In this treatise on creativity, Stein wrote hypothetical biographical portraits speculating on what Ulysses S. Grant, the Wright brothers, Henry James, and George Washington might have accomplished if they had devoted their lives and creative energies to different professions. Wilder wrote to Stein from Berchtesgaden, Germany, "I am all happy and grateful about Grant; scarcely understand a word of Wilbur Wright; and still have the other two to read—read slowly and aloud."[13] Having read further, he wrote from Vienna, "I cast myself out into the open sea of friendship and hope to be supported and understood. SO: there are long long stretches of the *Four in America* where I don't understand a word."[14] Stein thanked him for his observations and hoped that they could talk them over. That manuscript would not be published until 1947, the year after Stein's death, and Wilder contributed a long introduction that was part literary criticism, part affirmation, and part eulogy for his friend.

When Wilder wrote introductions to Stein's *Narration* (1935) and *The Geographical History of America* (1936) he not only lent his highly visible name and literary reputation to Stein's ongoing effort to establish herself firmly with the American audience, but also served as her emissary and intermediary with American publishers, especially Bennett Cerf at Random House. In Wilder's elucidations of Stein's work he functioned as her virtual translator, distilling the essence of her often dense and convoluted prose. In the introduction Wilder highlighted some of the ideas he and Stein had explored in their conversations, especially those that had stimulated or coincided with his own thought: The question of how creativity operates. The concept that repetition is a dynamic in all of nature as well as in human life, and, as Wilder put it, foreshadowing *Our Town*, "Repeating is emphasis. Every time a thing is repeated it is slightly different." And Stein's belief, first stressed to him by his parents, that, as Wilder summarized it, "the richest rewards for the reader have come from those works in which the authors admitted no consideration of an audience into their creating mind."[15]

He had to lobby aggressively with Cerf for the publication of Stein's *Geographical History of America*. "G. Stein has written a very good book," Wilder wrote to Aleck Woollcott, who by 1935 was one of the most formidable literary and theater critics in the United States. For years he had written reviews and commentary for the *New York Times* and the *New York World* and then, from 1929 to 1934, for the *New Yorker* in his column, "Shouts And Murmurs." From 1929 to 1933 he reviewed books on CBS radio, and beginning in 1933 he had his own popular CBS radio show, *The Town Crier*. It was said that if Woollcott merely mentioned a book it could sell a thousand copies, and he could make or break plays and actors.[16] He had promoted the careers of Katharine Cornell, Ruth Gordon, Orson Welles, Paul Robeson, and Helen Hayes, among others. But it was mutual friendship rather than promotion that prompted Wilder's letter about Stein's book:

> *I don't know yet whether it's a very great book. She does. Bennett Cerf says the rewards of her previous ones were so slender that he doesn't dare publish this one ("The Geographical History of America, or the Relations between Human Nature and the Human Mind") . . . Gertrude . . . and P. Picasso (and Bennett Cerf) want it to be published with the text on one side and my explanatory marginalia on the other, reproduced in my own handwriting. I don't want to do that. It's true*

that I can clarify many an apparently willful inanity and (with the help
of those wonderful conversations show it to be brilliant phrasing and
thinking), but there are long stretches I cannot; and it's those stretches
where the pretentious explicator ought to be strong.[17]

Many readers have observed that Wilder was influenced by Stein, and he himself acknowledged her influence—but few have noted Wilder's influence on Stein, as documented in her published work. In *The Geographical History of America*, which she wrote in the early years of her friendship with Wilder, and which is often called her culminating work, Wilder is a presence, called by name, and a strong voice who sometimes affirmed, sometimes challenged, and occasionally crystallized her own ideas. In one of their conversations Stein talked about inspiration, and Wilder later recalled that she told him, "What we know is formed in our head by thousands of small occasions in the daily life," emphasizing the importance of all the "thousands of occasions in the daily life that go into our head to form our ideas." She did not like the word "inspiration," he remembered, "because it suggests that someone else is blowing that knowledge into you. It is not being blown into you; it is very much your own and was acquired by you in thousands of tiny occasions in your life"—an idea akin to Wilder's later reflection in his essay on Joyce that a writer's subject or "myth-theme" is "prepared for him in every hour of his life."[18]

Wilder devoted hours to reading Stein's manuscripts and commenting on them, and then performing some of the tasks a literary agent would normally do in getting the work to potential publishers. Stein was not alone in seeking Wilder's advice and support. He read and praised Mabel Dodge Luhan's *Winter in Taos*, published to critical acclaim in 1935, one of her seven books published in her lifetime. Later, at Mabel's request, he responded in detail to the manuscript draft of a novel she was working on in 1936. In that exchange he was the willing teacher in the equivalent of a private tutorial in advanced creative writing. He reminded her, "The greatest idea-men in the world when they really wanted to convey always found themselves moving into a story: think of Plato and his Cave and his Charioteers; think of Christ and his 'there was once a man who . . .' "[19] Mabel apparently gave up on the novel and returned to writing nonfiction.

In Vienna, Wilder was beleaguered to the point of vexation by "authors, playwrights, stage directors, phone calls and strangers at social gatherings"—everyone wanting some favor from him, seeking to "make an engagement for a good long talk, freighted with self-interest."[20] Some of the hubbub may have been connected to a forthcoming production of Wilder's one-act play *The Long Christmas Dinner*. He wrote to Woollcott that the play was "about to be performed in Vienna in a wildly expressionistic fashion. It's been given 500 times, but for the first time as far as I know they're going to use those wigs to indicate the passing of time."[21] He was also grateful to Woollcott for including *The Happy Journey to Trenton and Camden*, another of his one-act plays, in the bestselling anthology *Woollcott's Reader* (1935). "I loved your afterward [*sic*] to the Happy Journey," Wilder wrote to Woollcott. "The Reader is going to be under every Xmas tree and I'm proud to figure in it with the best pages I was ever permitted to write."[22]

A WELCOME compensation for all the public attention in Vienna came in the form of an invitation from Sigmund Freud for a private visit in his villa in Grinzing, just north of the city. On the afternoon of October 13 the two men spent an hour and a half together, and Wilder recounted their conversation in a letter to Stein and Toklas. Freud, then seventy, was "Really a beautiful old man," Wilder wrote.[23] They talked of Shakespeare (Freud believed he was really the Earl of Oxford) and religion. "I am no seeker after God," Freud said, but he "liked" gods and collected cases full of Greek, Chinese, African, and Egyptian icons. He told Wilder, "Religion is the recapitulation and the solution of the problems of one's first four years that have been covered over by amnesia."[24] They discussed their work, including Wilder's novels. Freud liked *The Bridge of San Luis Rey*, but not *The Cabala* (in which the cardinal reads Freud) and especially not *Heaven's My Destination*. He couldn't read it, he said, and he threw it away. "Why should you treat of an American fanatic; that cannot be treated poetically," Freud complained.[25]

They also spoke of Freud's daughter Anna, the youngest of his six children. Anna, then forty, was not at home that October day. "Can you come again?" Freud asked, seeming to have decided that Wilder might be a worthy candidate to marry Anna and become his son-in-law. "She is older than you—you do not have to be afraid," he told Wilder. "She is a sensible reasonable girl. You are not afraid of women? She is sensible—no nonsense about her. Are you married, may I ask?"[26]

By 1935 Anna Freud had established her own international reputation as a psychoanalyst, specializing in the analysis of children. She had been general secretary of the International Psychoanalytical Association for seven years, beginning in 1927, and in 1935 was appointed director of the Vienna Psychoanalytical Training Institute.[27] There was much speculation that she sustained a long homosexual relationship with her close friend and colleague Dorothy Burlingham, granddaughter of Charles Tiffany, one of the founders of Tiffany & Company. Anna Freud was devoted to her father, was psychoanalyzed by him, and would care for him during the last years of his life when he was suffering from cancer.

The two men met again on October 23—and it may have been at this meeting that Wilder talked with Freud about Charlotte.[28] He and their family had begun to worry about Charlotte's mental and emotional health. Years later Wilder explained that during one of their visits he had told Freud about his "several brilliant brothers [*sic*] and sisters—and of this invalid sister." Freud had reflected that in "every lively family there is one who must pay."[29]

The trip to Europe that fall of 1935 was a tonic for Wilder—a much-needed rest, and an abundance of stimulating company—from Stein and Toklas to Max Reinhardt, Freud, and Pablo Picasso. On October 31 Stein took Wilder to Picasso's house to hear the painter read the poetry he had begun to write that spring. Picasso read his poems, some in French and some in Spanish, and after a time looked up at Wilder and asked if he could follow them. Wilder told him he could, and he found the poems interesting.[30] Later, in private, Stein and Wilder agreed that Picasso's poems were definitely not poetry, but they also agreed not to tell Picasso.

"SOMETHING'S HAPPENED to me. I'm crazy about America, and I want to go home," Wilder wrote to Stein in October. "Yes, I'm crazy about America. And you did that to me, too. . . . My country tis of thee. I always knew I loved it, but I never knew I loved it like this."[31] Stein did not deserve all the credit for Wilder's patriotism, however. Earlier in the decade he had called himself Walt Whitman's grandson, and had emphatically articulated his love for the United States. Stein, the longtime expatriate, had embarked on her rediscovery of America in 1935, sharing with Wilder her new vision of the country of her birth. Together they explored the American language and the American spirit, both of them energized by the exchange of new ideas and perspectives. Stein returned to the United States in the thirties and then went back to her life in France. Wilder went to Europe in the twenties and thirties and afterward, but always returned to the United States. "I'm a citizen by God's inscrutable grace of the greatest country in the world," he wrote to Woollcott, "and I don't like to be out of it for long at a time, esp. not out of it to wander in those great aching echoing museums that are the countries of Europe."[32] He wrote to Stein and Toklas, "The trouble with me is that I can't be soul-happy outside of my beloved U.S.A. and that's a fact."[33]

Something more than Wilder's love of country and his innate restlessness pulled him back to Connecticut that autumn, however: By December, Amos Parker Wilder was "*in extremis*, surrounded by nurses."[34] He had suffered a series of strokes and major surgery for an intestinal blockage. The family needed Thornton—not just the ever-growing sums of money he paid for his father's care, but his ebullient, reassuring presence. His mother and Isabel were exhausted from caring for Dr. Wilder, even with the help of nurses. "I came back to discover my father very ill indeed," Wilder wrote to Gertrude and Alice from Connecticut in late November. "While I was on the ocean he had a major operation and now we call on tiptoe through the ranks of nurses. There's nothing anybody can do, so I invent activities for the girls who have been under tension for three years over this matter. . . . I could a tale unfold re papa's illness."[35]

Wilder returned to a family whose lives at that time ran the gamut of issues and emotions: a dying father; a weary mother; happy newlyweds beginning a life together; one sister—Janet—thriving in her life and work; and two sisters—Charlotte and Isabel—struggling in theirs. Exhausted and despondent, Isabel was at work on her third novel, but now she was her mother's primary aide and supporter during Dr. Wilder's long illness. Charlotte was still living in New York and now working as a journalist for the WPA Writers' Project. Her first book of poetry, published in 1936, was corecipient of the prestigious Shelley Memorial Award, given by the Poetry Society of America. Charlotte occasionally shared a few poems in progress with her mother, but sheltered most of her work from the eyes of her literary family, working largely in secrecy, striving for creative as well as financial independence from those who loved her most and wanted to be of help to her. When her book came out, Thornton telegraphed his praise: DEAR SHARLIE I THINK ITS SPLENDID POWERFUL AND GLORIOUSLY ORIGINAL HAVE NO QUALMS HOMAGE AND CONGRATULATIONS.[36]

Charlotte dedicated the book to the two women closest to her— the novelist Evelyn Scott and Ernestine Friedmann, who had been an industrial secretary of the YWCA and had worked for years on behalf of women's rights—especially education and equality for working women. Because of the erotic textures of some of the poems, especially five "Monologues of Repression," Charlotte felt compelled to offer "Words of Annotation"—four pages of prose at the end of the volume. This disclaimer defended the "subjective implications" of the book, which, she wrote, "may not be taken as constituting the record of an actual life."[37] The apparent record of her "actual life" was the subject of a novel she was writing and shielding from would-be readers, especially her family members.

In spite of everything, the Wilders gathered for a "Very happy"

Thanksgiving, with Amos and Catharine joining them at the house on Deepwood Drive.[38] From Hamden just before Christmas, Wilder wrote to Stein and Toklas, "My father with the tenacious physique of an exemplary life amazes the doctors and nurses by surviving strokes and convulsions and paralyses."[39]

As the chief breadwinner of the family, Wilder had to get back to work soon after Christmas. He had lecture and teaching commitments to fulfill in 1936—two months booked out on the lecture circuit—and then classes to teach at the University of Chicago through the spring and summer. "The tour is an ignoble affair: I no longer believe what I say, no longer 'hear' what I say," wrote Wilder, now seven years into the contract he had signed with Keedick in 1929. There were compensations, as he told Sibyl Colefax: He was getting to know American cities firsthand—on one trip, Tulsa, Oklahoma, and Salt Lake City, Utah.[40] "I've seen an oil well, and an old Creek Indian—from that tribe the Americans transported from Louisiana with such graft and blood," he wrote to Alice and Gertrude. "In Salt Lake City a granddaughter of Brigham Young told me a set of appalling stories of grandfather. In Hollywood Walt Disney showed me five of his masterpieces that I happened to have missed and I danced at the Trocadero. At Tucson I dined at a tuberculosis sanatarium and wearied a few patients back to life."[41]

With a contract to honor and a family to support, he plowed on. As his father's health waned, his medical expenses soared. "My father continues to linger in the expensive luxury of a *bravura* hospital," Wilder wrote to Stein and Toklas, who understood what it was to worry about money. As the lecture tour wound to its close, Wilder felt more than ever that his lectures were "nullenvoyd," and wished he could get out of his contract.[42] He could not escape the lecture commitments for another year, but by April he had decided it was time to resign from the University of Chicago. He told Mabel, "I was five years at Lawrenceville and I've been five years at the University and that seems to be my unit-measure of giving and getting any vitality." He didn't know what he would do next, or where he would live. "Perhaps first thing in the Fall I'll have to go to Hollywood and make some money," he mused.[43]

Unfortunately he was not engaged for any Hollywood projects in

1936, so he had to rely on the teaching, the lecture fees, and his royalties. And all the time, despite classes to teach at the university, there were pressing family matters to tend to. "Father's still outliving the predictions of science with a State-of-Maine tenacity," Wilder wrote to a friend after a trip to Hamden. "I go to cheer the onlooking womenfolk up. They're wonderful."[44] Back in Chicago, Wilder tried to bolster the flagging spirits of his mother and sisters by mail. He had returned from Connecticut armed with advice from his mother about how to prepare his own meals in Chicago, apparently to save money. He obliged and sent her the menu (complete with footnotes) for three meals he prepared for himself on Monday, May 25: muffins purchased at a nearby Irish bakery; creamed spinach; broiled ham ("Brown, not pink; candied edge, with cloves"); and fresh tomatoes with Heinz mayonnaise, with a Scotch Highball to accompany his lunch ("What fun men do have," his footnote for this item read).[45]

On the back of his letter is a draft in Isabella's hand of an unfinished sonnet—words and lines crossed out and some of them illegible—but the gist of the poem is a reflection on motherhood.[46] Even in adulthood her children still valued her advice and wisdom, and depended on her steady presence at the heart of family life.

———

TWO OF the very few people in Wilder's life who seldom made any demands and who gave him as much as they received from him were Aleck Woollcott and socially ambitious, largely self-educated Sibyl Colefax, the wife of the London barrister Arthur Colefax, who was knighted in 1920. Sibyl Colefax turned Argyll House, their home in Chelsea, into a notable salon where she gathered writers, artists, actors, composers, politicians, war heroes—people who were "interesting, interested and sincere," according to the British diplomat and author Harold Nicolson in Lady Colefax's obituary. She entertained Virginia Woolf (who did not much care for Sibyl), Vita Sackville-West (Harold Nicolson's wife and Virginia Woolf's lover), Max Beerbohm, H. G. Wells, George Gershwin, Charlie Chaplin, Cole Porter, Laurence Olivier, Somerset Maugham, the Duke and Duchess of Windsor, Bernard Berenson, and

Woollcott and Wilder, among countless others. While three of his other chief female correspondents—Gertrude Stein, Mabel Dodge Luhan, and Amy Wertheimer—were more often than not asking Thornton to give advice or do a favor or read a manuscript or arrange an event or an introduction, Sibyl Colefax never asked him for anything. She only gave—ever the kind and generous hostess, the thoughtful conduit to people Thornton might enjoy, and, most important of all, his attentive listener.

Wilder seldom discussed his own literary challenges and work in progress in his letters to Stein. His role was to listen to *her*, to read and comment on *her* manuscripts, and to do literary errands for *her* in the United States. Their correspondence was largely about Gertrude. Her letters to him usually centered on herself and her own activities; his to her usually centered in turn on her and her activities, with occasional passages of lively gossip or entertaining accounts of his travels and adventures.

In contrast Wilder frequently entrusted some of his own concerns and worries to Mabel, and he could write at length and in depth to Sibyl about his teaching, his lecturing, his writing, his family. She was a willing, perceptive listener and encourager, and he could be frank with her, as he could be with Mabel. He poured out his pervasive doubts about his creative work in long letters to Sibyl; she responded with encouragement and sound advice. After the death in 1936 of her husband of thirty-five years, Wilder had an opportunity to reciprocate, serving as a "lifeline" as she coped with her loss, and had to sell her house and go to work full-time as an interior decorator.[47] Some of Sibyl's friends and acquaintances dropped her as her fortunes declined, but Wilder remained her correspondent and devoted friend—his words—until she died in 1950.

———

"BETWEEN CORRECTING papers & preparing poor undigested lectures at the University of Chicago," Wilder could report that his resignation from his university post was official, effective in September 1936. He wrote to tell Mabel about it on July 1: "Then I shall be that dreadful thing: a writer. Without visible duties; without fixed appointments; without residence."[48]

He was abruptly called back to the family residence in Hamden the next day, however, for his father died July 2. Dr. Wilder's obituary ran on the front page of the *Wisconsin State Journal*, which he had edited for so many years. He was hailed as "the dean of Connecticut newspaper editors" for, it was noted, his journalistic life had begun and ended in New Haven. "Mr. Wilder, before attaining his outstanding record as a diplomat, was a forceful editorialist, a republican [*sic*] whose writings attracted attention of the party not only in Wisconsin but in Washington. He was also an effective and entertaining public speaker."[49]

"Did I tell you that my revered papa died? Yes. . . . . . . Yes. . . . . All of us five children were back," Wilder wrote to Stein and Toklas.[50] Over the years Amos, the eldest of the five, retreated into his studies and his writing, keeping the peace with his father largely through acquiescence to his father's wishes, or with occasional passive resistance to them, or the reinterpretation or rationalizing of events. Thornton and Charlotte, the most forthright with their father and, as young people, the most openly rebellious, had as adults come to at least an affectionate truce with him. Isabel still harbored a deep anger that often surfaced years later in her letters and interviews. Janet, the youngest Wilder, a Phi Beta Kappa graduate of Mount Holyoke and now a "single-minded biologist" with her M.A. degree in biology from Mount Holyoke, was still enrolled in the Ph.D. program in zoology at the University of Chicago. Janet knew her father the least, and therefore suffered the least from his strong-willed, often overwhelming love and ambition for his five children.[51]

Thirty-one years after his father's death, on hearing of the death of Harry Luce, Wilder reflected on one of his enduring themes, especially in *Our Town*—the significance of the family. He wrote that he, his brother, Luce, and Bob Hutchins were

a very special breed of cats. Our fathers were very religious, very dogmatic Patriarchs. They preached and talked cant from morning til night—not because they were hypocritical but because they knew

no other language. They were forceful men. They thought they were
"spiritual"—damn it, they should have been in industry. They had
no insight into the lives of others—least of all their families. They had
an Old Testament view (sentimentalized around the edges) of what a
WIFE, DAUGHTER, SON, CITIZEN should be. We're the product
of those (finally bewildered and unhappy) Worthies. In Harry it took
the shape of a shy joyless power-drive. And like so many he intermit-
tently longed to be loved, enjoyed, laughed with. But he didn't under-
stand give-and-take. Bob and Amos and I—bottom of p. 148![52]

Wilder was referring to words spoken by the character John Ashley
in a passage in his novel *The Eighth Day*, published in 1967. Ashley
realizes that he has "formed himself to be the opposite of his father"
and that his life has been "as mistaken as his father's." Then he wonders, "Is that what family life is? The growing children are misshapen
by those parents who were in various ways warped by the blindness,
ignorance, and passions of their own parents; and one's own errors
impoverish and cripple one's children? Such is the endless chain of the
generations?"[53]

———

IN THE fall of 1936, after completing the summer quarter at the University of Chicago and satisfying himself that his mother and Isabel
were reasonably rested and settled at home, Wilder set off for St.
Thomas in the U.S. Virgin Islands and Castries, St. Lucia, in the British
West Indies, among other ports of call. He told Mabel that as soon as
his classes were over he "left with the speed of light to become a shaggy
rum-soaked West Indian."[54] He would spend six weeks there in sun and
solitude. "It's beautiful here," he wrote Janet from Castries, but it was
so hot he couldn't take his long walks and the water was tepid.[55] He
was homesick: "I miss Chicago and the campus, honey, and you in the
middle of it," he wrote. "Whatjadooin? Are you well? Are you heart-
whole? I feel a thousand miles away."[56]

But he loved the solitude, he wrote to Woollcott. "Of course the wonderful part of it for me is the aloneness. . . . I enjoy it so. No ill-digested

speeches to make, none of the wild grasping at approximations which is conversation. And I'm improving at it every day. What is Art? What is Religion? I'm writing, too, but that's still a secret."[57]

The solitude spawned introspection: He could be "pretty contented" when he visited foreign places. He was not a born traveler, he said, "But Travel I shall and travel I must."[58] He left the West Indies "a new fellow," he wrote to Stein and Toklas, "remade by solitude, by the long straight lines of the sea, and with my notebooks full of projects."[59] Wilder concluded that "there are only two things in the world that are fresh, unpredictable, and inspiriting, and the beauties and marvels of nature, nor the customs and conditions of foreign peoples are not among them. The only two things in the world that are rewarding are: The masterpieces of the fine arts, and one's friends."[60]

BACK IN the United States, Wilder visited Aleck Woollcott, resplendent in his dressing gown as he received friends in his grand new Gracie Square apartment in New York, full of "a corps of secretaries, stewards and ministers."[61] Wilder was a guest at Woollcott's dinner party on December 20, joining John Gielgud, then playing *Hamlet* to rave reviews on Broadway; Ruth Gordon, currently a Broadway hit as the star of *The Country Wife*, William Wycherley's Restoration comedy; and Gerald Murphy, friend, playmate, and sometime patron of Scott and Zelda Fitzgerald. Then Wilder spent a quiet Christmas in Connecticut with his mother, Aunt Charlotte, Isabel, and Charlotte. Sometimes in the evenings he stretched out on the floor before the fire to read aloud from his work in progress to his "little, pretty, apparently fragile but in reality strungle [*sic*] on gold-wire, my gentle, garden-making, sock-mending, French translating" mother. He was glad for the reunion with Isabel, and "independent self-tormenting home-fleeing Charlotte." Janet chose to spend the holidays in Chicago "engrossed in discovering which of the four methods for determining the oxygen-content of water is the best."[62]

"There are some members missing from our family circle," Wilder wrote to Bobsy Goodspeed on Christmas Day. "Father. And Janet whom I saw last week, however, well, and violently occupied over her microscopes, and not pining. And Amos who could not leave his bride about to present us with another Wilder." The Christmas tree was surrounded by the "bright-colored wrapping paper" that had adorned the gifts, and the aroma of roasting turkey filled the house.[63] The New Year brought a new family member: Amos and Catharine's daughter, Catharine Dix "Dixie" Wilder, was born January 31, 1937. Thornton told a friend that she became "her grandmother's joy as well as everybody's."[64]

WILDER'S *Our Town* was shaped by his imagination and memory, his experiences with family and friends, his love of country, his concern about world events, and his passion for theater. He had fallen in love with the theater the first moment his mother took him to see a stage play all those years ago in Wisconsin, and had avidly followed the theater world ever since. By the thirties, however, something significant was changing: "I no longer get much pleasure out of theatre-going, but I never get tired of the atmosphere about theatres," he wrote to Sibyl in 1936.[65] He shared that view with Stein and Toklas as well: "I no longer get much real pleasure from going to a play, but I get more and more from hanging around theatres."[66]

He had been hanging around theaters since boyhood, when he had been so infatuated with the Greek Theatre in Berkeley that he would sneak in or climb a tree to watch rehearsals or performances. When he started writing his own plays as a teenager, he dreamed about casting them with his favorite movie stars, stage actors, and directors. Now thirty-nine and a playwright with a few modest credentials, he was not only hanging around theaters but partying after the performances with luminaries—Katharine Cornell and Guthrie McClintic; the "brilliant and waspish" Aleck Woollcott; Raymond Massey; Pauline Lord; Helen Hayes and her husband, the playwright Charles MacArthur; the "insolent and brilliant" Jed Harris and his mistress and mother of his child, the "sublime" Ruth Gordon. Harris and Gordon's son was now seven, and a "wonderful vivid" little boy, Wilder wrote to Stein and Toklas.[67]

He became a surrogate uncle to little Jones Harris, who remembered him warmly as one adult he could count on. Wilder called Jed Harris "the bat out of Hell."[68]

Wilder especially loved Ruth Gordon and was probably in love with her.[69] Wilder shared with Sibyl some of Gordon's history: She had employed her "intelligence, will and character" to triumph over "a host of disadvantages. The disadvantages," Wilder went on,

> *were voice, appearance, lack of a sense of "dress," undependable taste arising from her environment when a girl, and the heart-wrenching and career-blocking association to Jed. All New York giggled fifteen years ago when she forced a doctor to break her knees in order to straighten her legs; well, it's a sample, anyway, of the incredible determination. Fortunately, on top of it she has genius and intelligence. Within five years she'll be the first actress here.*[70]

His predictions about her career were right, and he would have a hand in making that happen. For the time being, however, he was seeing plays with less and less satisfaction. It was gratifying that his one-act play *Love and How to Cure It* was being staged in London in 1937, directed by Tyrone Guthrie at the Globe Theatre and starring the movie and stage actress Ann Harding, who also played the lead in George Bernard Shaw's *Candida* at the Globe. This double bill of Shaw and Wilder marked the first professional production of a Wilder play abroad.[71]

While he grew ever more convinced that the theater was "the greatest of all the arts," Wilder believed that "something had gone wrong with it" in his time, and "that it was fulfilling only a small part of its potentialities."[72] He complained to a friend that there were "only about 3 good plays in every five years."[73] As the Depression wore on and as ominous clouds gathered over the political landscape in Europe, Wilder was searching for positives in the theater and in the world around him. To Stein and Toklas in Paris, Wilder wrote from Oklahoma, "The newspapers over here read very threatening about your peace of mind over there."[74] He expressed his concern about the impending war in

Europe in a letter to Mabel early in 1937: "The rush to the abyss is visible all over the world."[75]

———————

AS OF April 1, 1937, lectures and classes done, Wilder was a free man. He spent April and May working in his study in New Haven, looking after his family, and stepping into his fatherly role one more time. With their mother's knowledge, he conspired with Amos to fund "legacies" for his sisters that, Thornton said, "Father might have but did not leave them."[76] Apparently Dr. Wilder had left money from his modest estate to his wife and sons, but not to his daughters. Thornton insisted that he should contribute twice as much as Amos to this "legacy" for their sisters, since his brother had a wife and child to support, and he let Amos know that their mother wanted to participate. "Ma is going through protests that she wants to contribute also from her thousand," Thornton wrote, "but, Lordy, she must keep what was coming to her from so long and money-worried a married life."[77] Before he knew it, however, "Ma got hysterical—generous and disobeying me and behind our back sent off a cheque for $300.00 to Charlotte. . . . So now there's $300 to be placed for the other two."[78] By this loving subterfuge Isabella and her sons rectified Amos Parker Wilder's final oversight.

———————

"THE NEW life's begun. Taught my last class. Delivered my last lecture," Wilder wrote to Amy Wertheimer. His new life was "wonderful and alarming," he said as he "plunged jubilantly into work."[79] He poured his energy into his plays, working simultaneously on three of the manuscripts in progress in his briefcase. "My first play on my new life-plan is almost done," he wrote Amos about the farce he first called *Stranger Things Have Happened* and then *The Merchant of Yonkers*. "Have spliced a brilliant scene from Molière right into the middle of the 1st Act. . . . The whole play is based on the 1st two acts of an Austrian classic—Nestroy's *Einen Jux will er sich machen*."[80] Then there was *The Hell of the Vizier Kabäar*, also titled at various times *Haroun al-Raschid*, *The Prince of Baghdad*, *The Diamond of Baghdad*, and *Arabian Nights*—a play he considered at one point to be better than *Our Town*.[81] He told Amos, "The second play will be about Haroun Al Raschid—in love and in government only the concession of free will to the beloved and the governed can bring any satisfactory rewards."[82]

He made steady progress on *Homage to P. G. Wodehouse*, and on *M Marries N*, which he renamed *Our Village* and then *Our Town*. He was writing that play, he told Amy, "in the style of Happy Journey & Long Xmas Dinner," and it was "all planned out," along with "several more" plays.[83] At times during the late thirties he also made notes for *The Fifty Dollar Play*, which would trace the progress and history of a certain sum of money as it changed hands.[84]

Soon he was ready to share the draft of the first three acts of his farce with discerning listeners, first of all his old friend the playwright Ned Sheldon, blind and paralyzed from ankylosing spondylitis, a severe, chronic, crippling form of arthritis that can also affect the eyesight. Sheldon was known not only for his successful career as a dramatist but for the astute advice he generously offered to playwrights and actors. Imprisoned in his body, confined to bed in his penthouse quarters, totally dependent on the care of servants, nurses, and physical therapists, Sheldon received a daily parade of visitors, mainly personages in the theater who came to cheer and bolster him—and went away cheered and bolstered themselves. As Wilder put it in 1948 in the dedication of his novel *The Ides of March*, Sheldon "though immobile and blind for over twenty years was the dispenser of wisdom, courage, and gaiety to a large number of people."[85] Wilder trusted Sheldon's theatrical sensibility and his vibrant sense of humor, and Sheldon praised the draft of the play. "Oh, it's a darlin' play," Wilder joked to Woollcott. "And it has all the shades of wit: savage, graceful, grotesque, fanciful, and tender."[86] By the end of May, however, Wilder's farce had "suddenly gone stale." He invited some Yale friends to a reading of the play but at the last moment found he just couldn't do it. Instead he read "the First Acts of Play No#3 and Play No#5, namely 'Our Town' and 'Homage to P. G. Wodehouse.'" They were enthusiastically received. Wilder wrote to Woollcott afterward, "I know that Hell is paved with good first acts, but I think I'll be able to finish 'em."[87]

25

THE VILLAGE AND THE STARS

*These are but the belated gropings to reconstruct what may have taken place
when the play first presented itself—the life of a village against
the life of the stars.*

—THORNTON WILDER,
"A Preface for Our Town," New York Times, *February 13, 1938*

The United States and Europe (1930s)

With his one-act plays in *The Long Christmas Dinner and Other Plays in One Act*, and his novel *Heaven's My Destination*, Wilder had moved deep into an American odyssey—an exploration of American landscapes, characters, and spirit. However, no matter the literal settings of his plays and novels, he habitually worked with a universal palette. In the one-act plays he launched in 1931, Wilder had in effect practiced for the unique staging and substance of *Our Town*. Some of these plays can be viewed as prototypes, even dress rehearsals for *Our Town*—employing stage managers, taking liberties with time and space, stripping scenery and plots to a minimum. On the bare stage welcoming curious theatergoers to *Our Town* in 1937 and 1938 and afterward, Wilder experimented with deceptively simple subjects and themes. The family had become a powerful symbol in his plays and novels—not only the individual family unit but the vast human family interconnected in their local yet universal "villages." He peopled the stage with American families whose seemingly ordinary lives at once reflected and transcended the place and the era in which they lived. Simultaneously he contemplated the perennial dramas of ordinary life as they played out again and again on a cosmic stage, one person at a time, one place at a time, throughout the ages.

He would recapitulate this theme in 1957 in a preface to his major plays:

Every action which has ever taken place—every thought, every emotion—has taken place only once, at one moment in time and place. "I love you," "I rejoice," "I suffer," have been said and felt many billions of times, and never twice the same. Every person who has ever lived has lived an unbroken succession of unique occasions. Yet the more one is aware of this individuality in experience (innumerable! innumerable!) the more one becomes attentive to what these disparate moments have in common, to repetitive patterns.[1]

His fascination with the patterns in "many billions" of individual lives had, as noted, been born that autumn day in 1920 when, as a student in Rome, he saw a freshly excavated first-century tomb. By candlelight he and his fellow students had examined the "faded paintings" of the Aurelius family and other remnants of their lives that, after nearly two thousand years, were frozen in time under a busy street in the center of modern Rome, with streetcars clattering overhead. Wilder realized in that moment that two thousand centuries later, his own era could be the subject of such curiosity and speculation—the quest to recapture and understand the very "loves and pieties and habits" that he himself had lived and witnessed in his lifetime.

"For a while in Rome I lived among archeologists, and ever since I find myself occasionally looking at the things about me as an archeologist will look at them a thousand years hence," he wrote in a preface to *Our Town* in 1938. "An archeologist's eyes combine the view of the telescope with the view of the microscope. He reconstructs the very distant with the help of the very small."[2] In his play Wilder was groping, he said, to reconstruct "the life of a village against the life of the stars."[3] This was his creative compass: the juxtaposition of the village and the stars—one town and the cosmos, one person and the galaxy.

In his fiction and his plays Wilder continually excavated and resurrected universal, time-defying human dramas, and probed the enduring questions: How do we live—survive, surmount, even transcend the struggles implicit in the human condition? And why?[4] As he worked on *Our Town* he reiterated that the fundamental concepts in the play had been forged in large part during those student days in Rome as he hovered on the edges of archaeological excavations in the ancient city, studying the water systems, the pathways, the architecture, and even the stage designs of the ancient Romans—and the repeating patterns of human existence despite differences in cultures, civilizations, and eras. In the twenties, after his discoveries in Rome, Wilder wrote in a manuscript fragment:

> We bend with pitying condescension over past civilizations, over Thebes, Ur and Babylon, and there floats up to us a murmur made up of cries of war, cruelty, pleasure and religious terror. Even as our civilization will some day exhale to its observers the same cries of soldiers, slaves, revellers and suppliants.[5]

These exhalations, at once ephemeral and eternal, empowered his work. This fragment also foreshadows the words the Stage Manager speaks in the first act of *Our Town*:

> Y'know—Babylon once had two million people in it, and all we know about 'em is the names of the kings and some copies of wheat contracts . . . and contracts for the sale of slaves. Yet every night all those families sat down to supper, and the father came home from his work, and the smoke went up the chimney—same as here. And even in Greece and Rome, all we know about the *real* lives of the people is what we can piece together out of the joking poems and the comedies they wrote for the theatre back then.[6]

With these reflections the Stage Manager confirms the crux of Wilder's play—and at the same time affirms the historic importance of the theater as a mirror of life in any given time.

In the 1930s Wilder created twentieth-century incarnations of the Aurelius family in the American family—the Bayards in *The Long Christmas Dinner*; and then the Harrisons in *Pullman Car Hiawatha*; and then the Kirbys in *The Happy Journey to Trenton and Camden*. Late in the decade Wilder pulled his audience into the theater again to witness, with the help of the Stage Manager, the growing up, marrying, living, and dying of members of the Webb and the Gibbs families in Grover's Corners, New Hampshire, their mythical American yet thoroughly universal hometown. In a handwritten note, most likely dating from the sixties, Wilder further explained himself as a dramatist as he defined Emily's discovery in the last act of *Our Town*:

> She learns that each life—though it appears to be a repetition among millions—can be felt to be inestimably precious. Though the realization of it is present to us seldom, briefly, and incommunicably. At the moment there are no walls, no chairs, no tables: all is inward. Our true life is in the imagination and in the memory.[7]

IN JUNE 1937 Wilder traveled again to the MacDowell Colony for his first sojourn there in five years. Time in "that deep pine-wood is what I need most of all," he wrote to Gertrude Stein and Alice B. Toklas. "I have an Arabian Night play-subject that's a house-afire, and I could only grasp it and devour it in the Green Isolation up there."[8] Gratefully, he settled into the "long hours in the cabin in deep woods," where he soon had several new plays in "well-advanced stages," including the one he was still calling "Our Village."[9] When he was not writing he was reading—finishing "all 925 pages of the unshortened edition of Gertrude Stein's *The Making of Americans*," which Wilder pronounced "the greatest American book since *Leaves of Grass*."[10]

By this time Wilder had publicly announced more than once that from now on he was going to be a playwright first and foremost. No more novels. Only plays. He gave Woollcott a progress report:

> *My darts thrown at perfection are being whittled, feathered and pointed in many tranquil hours in these woods. . . . I always think of Our Village as yours. It is intended to give you pleasure. The Happy Journey is no longer a part of it. The last act in the cemetery will be prodigious, and it will no longer remind you of Spoon River. Nobody tells their life*

story. In fact, I have received "guidance" to the effect that the dead are
no longer interested in the doings on this painful planet.[11]

Years of living and writing led Wilder to create *Our Town*, and he
sometimes had little patience when readers quizzed him about the how
and why of his work. He believed there were no definitive answers
to such questions imposed on the work of an artist.[12] He tried to discourage a proposed thesis by Dorothy Ulrich (Troubetzkoy), one of
his former students at the University of Chicago, and now a graduate
student exploring influences in his novels:

> *Lordy! My influences—Saint-Simon, La Bruyère, Proust, Morand—*
> *all kinds of things in all kinds of languages and literatures—and in the*
> *final count so unimportant. So far-fetched and elusive are they that it*
> *would seem as though they were unobtainable and unguessable unless*
> *I sat down and made a list of them: page by page and paragraph by*
> *paragraph; and I do hate to do that. . . . You are up against an author*
> *who hates to look backward at former work, ever to think of it—*
> *indifference, boredom and even repudiation have a part in that.*[13]

Wilder drew from an amalgam of sources as he worked on *Our
Town*—Ibsen and Nestroy, Dante and Molière, Gertrude Stein and
Alfred North Whitehead, Alexander Woollcott and Mabel Dodge
Luhan, Fred Astaire and Ginger Rogers on the movie screen, his
mother and his father, Rome and New Hampshire, Paris and Zurich.
Themes in the play, already evident in his earlier work, emerged first
from his own thought and spirit, shaped in part by writers whose work
he found resonant—Dante, Goethe, Balzac, and Nietzsche among an
ever-expanding company of others. He credited *The Oxford Book of Re-
gency Verse* for helping him give the last act its "ultimate affirmative
Ring."[14] But most of all the play emerged from his own vivid imagination and memory.

Gradually the play evolving as *Our Town* overshadowed his homage
to P. G. Wodehouse and the Arabian Nights and even his farce about
a matchmaker and money. He began to focus on the ordinary lives of

ordinary people in the mythical village he had created as their habitat. Some events in the plot of *Our Town* came from his own family life—his brother's wedding, his father's illness and death, his and his sisters' yearnings and joys and disappointments, his mother's anchoring presence in the family and her own unfulfilled dreams. Fragments of dialogue were sparked by conversations, in person and in letters, with his parents, his brother and sisters, his friends—Stein, Luhan, Colefax, Woollcott, Sheldon, and Freud, among others. ("That's the way black-birds make their nests," Wilder told Sibyl Colefax.)[15] Always listening and observing, Wilder found the idioms and cadences of the American vernacular in snatches of conversation on ships and trains; in bars, boardinghouses, shops, university classrooms, and the civic and cultural meeting halls across the country where he gave his lectures; and in the voices of the citizens of Peterborough, New Hampshire, where he had often retreated to work in the summer.

He was writing *Our Town* in 1937 against the daunting backdrop of the Depression (one-third of the nation, said FDR in his second inaugural speech, was "ill-housed, ill-clothed, ill-nourished," and unemployment stood at 14.3 percent nationwide) and the expanding conflict in Europe, led by Hitler and Mussolini. As Wilder worked on the play, he went for a second time to see Fred Astaire and Ginger Rogers in *Swing Time*. He found inspiration in the movies to feed his creative work—not only his choice of an American subject but his concerns over what he saw as the impending decline of Europe. He wrote to Mabel an "amorphous defense of the still-amorphous possibilities of greatness in the American people."[16] He realized that as the Depression and the looming war threatened to fracture the world as they knew it, Americans needed diversion and some kind of hope. He believed that the American art form of the motion picture could help to provide both. "In Austria or France go to see a Ginger-Rogers-Fred-Astaire movie," Wilder wrote:

> *Watch the audience.*
> *Spell-bound at something terribly uneuropean—all that technical effortless precision; all that radiant youth bursting with sex but not*

sex-hunting, sex-collecting; and all that allusion to money, but money
as fun, the American love of conspicuous waste, not money-to-sit-on,
not money-to-frighten-with. And finally when the pair really leap into
one of those radiant waltzes the Europeans know in their bones that
their day is over.[17]

Even in its seeming frivolity, Wilder suggested, this American film
was a cultural harbinger of a shift in world influence from Europe to
the United States.

He was reading Alfred North Whitehead during those months, and
found Whitehead's "Christian-Platonic" philosophy provocative. "I
think you'd be pained and shocked to hear my views on international
affairs," he wrote Mabel:

They'd seem to you an optimism too easily arrived at in the light of
the daily news; but more and more (under the shadow of Whitehead's
philosophy—Christian—Platonic) I see a long-time, a planetary curve
and that I cling to. . . . I have decided that the human race as a whole
can be given the benefit of the doubt; and the set-backs of one year and
one decade and one century no longer completely obscure the sky. But I
hate Hitler and the Spanish rebels.[18]

As Wilder the citizen gave his fellow human beings the benefit of
the doubt, *Our Town* was taking deeper root and seeds were being sown
for a later play—the one he would call *The Skin of Our Teeth.*

———

"THE FAMILY'S fine," Wilder wrote to Stein and Toklas from Hamden
in the spring of 1937. "Ma loves having two chillun in the house; she
darns my socks; listens avidly to all radio news-reports, detective
stories and serial dramas. I lie on my stomach on the floor playing solitaire and listen to the concerts."[19] Isabel was at home on Deepwood
Drive, in love with a New Haven doctor and hoping for a marriage proposal. She had just finished *Let Winter Go*, her third novel. According

to Thornton, it was "a light novel that may run serially in one of the woman's glazed-paper magazines and make her an heiress."[20] As the reviews of her novel came in, Wilder proudly shared the good ones with his friends.[21] Amos, Catharine, and their baby daughter lived in Newton Center, Massachusetts, where Amos was still teaching at the Andover Newton Theological Seminary. Charlotte, meanwhile, was still writing her poems and her novel, supporting herself by working on the WPA Federal Writers' Project in New York. Her poems appeared, along with work by Kenneth Rexroth, Richard Wright, Claude McKay, and other struggling writers, in *American Stuff: An Anthology of Prose & Verse by Members of the Federal Writers' Project with Sixteen Prints by the Federal Art Project*, published in 1937.

Wilder left Hamden hoping to spend most of the summer of 1937 sequestered at the MacDowell Colony, hard at work on his plays ("June and July would bring real work from me, reluctant writer that I am," he wrote to Woollcott), but he changed his plans to accept an unexpected and irresistible invitation.[22] He was asked to attend the Paris conference of the Institut International de Coopération Intellectuelle of the League of Nations as the American delegate, substituting for Frederick Paul Keppel, president of the Carnegie Corporation. The Second General Conference of National Committees for Intellectual Cooperation would take place in Paris July 20–26, with sessions to be led by the philosopher and Symbolist poet Paul Valéry on "The Immediate Future of Letters." Wilder wrote to Mabel, "This is the first time there has ever been an American delegate and he'll have to defend the charge that the U.S. is corrupting the world."[23]

Because his round-trip fare would be paid, he planned to stay on in Europe after the conference. "It's about decided I shall spend eight or nine months in Zurich next year," he had written to Stein and Toklas that spring. "I'm in no doubt about my country and countrymen being the best there are, but I got to get away from them for a while."[24]

Once the conference was over, Wilder planned to go to Salzburg for the festival, and then settle in Zurich for a few months away from "the whole overinsistent hammering American scene," and temporary "immersion in old wise tired Europe."[25] As much as anything, he needed to get away from Deepwood Drive and the family he dearly loved in order to find peace and solitude for writing.

Wilder's speeches at the 1937 Paris conference marked his first appearance as an American emissary and a spokesperson for American literature and culture.[26] When he arrived he was intimidated. "It's all a little alarming for a provincial little intellectual," he wrote to Stein. "The stenographic report of our conversations is being published by the League of Nations."[27] He had prepared "about six little speeches" on various topics—and in his typical generous way, gave Stein credit for some of the pivotal ideas he contributed to the conference discussion. "Yes, defense of the American's right to remake himself a language from the fabric of the English language, with a diagram of the difference between the American and English minds. All Gertrude."[28] At the same time he was reading the 1936 edition of H. L. Mencken's classic, *The American Language: An Inquiry into the Development of English in the United States*. In their catalytic hours of conversation over the years, Stein and Wilder shared numerous ideas and theories, and Wilder was careful in his attribution—sometimes verging on overstatement—if he elaborated on her thoughts.

After the Paris conference Wilder spent two weeks with Stein and Toklas in Bilignin at the house they rented in the country. "It's lovely here," he wrote to his mother and Isabel. "Drives, calls on neighboring gentry, walks, Conversation and wonderful meals."[29] That summer Stein begged Thornton to collaborate with her on a novel, and they discussed the idea at length.[30] He told Stein and others that he didn't fully understand her concept of the novel and ultimately said no, and Stein wrote several drafts of *Ida A Novel* before it was published in 1941.

Gertrude was "a heady drink of water," Wilder wrote to Woollcott, but he appreciated her "heroic" laughter and her "sense of enjoyment," and her ability to talk "like an inspired being."[31] Wilder loved the view from Stein's terrace—the lush valley in the lap of the hills of Ain, with Mont Blanc etched on the horizon. He prized their lively conversations. That summer he read the manuscript of Stein's *Everybody's Autobiography*, in which he himself appeared. "You will be enchanted by the description of me in the New Book!" he wrote to his mother and Isabel.[32] He devoured the exquisite meals prepared by Alice and worked in her garden every morning, bare shoulders and chest soaking up the sun. "Mama, every morning I garden for Alice," he wrote. "I take off shirt and undershirt and hoe obstinate weedy paths and I like it and so I'll do it for you someday."[33]

He went on to Salzburg, where he met Sibyl Colefax for the music and a whirlwind of social events they often attended together—the famous writer, fit and dapper at forty, and the patrician widow, still glamorous at sixty-three. They were "such a success" at one party, Wilder reported to Woollcott, "that we were promptly invited for the next night, too . . . musicale and supper, probably the Crown Princess of Italy."[34] But most of all he enjoyed taking walks with Sibyl, and reading parts of his plays in progress to her, welcoming her thoughtful opinions. Their "big social whirl" in Salzburg and their "tranquil country walks" cemented their friendship, and "I love her very much," Wilder wrote to Woollcott. He especially appreciated her "long generous letters packed with information":

> *Golly, her knowledge of places and pictures and people and her memory. And under it all, the constant pain of her widowhood. And the grueling distasteful hard work of her shop. . . . She's a trump and I intend to know her and love her all my life.*[35]

Before her husband died, Sibyl had worked occasionally as an interior decorator to augment their income, but this became a serious business of necessity when she was widowed. In 1938, with young decorator and designer John Fowler, Sibyl founded Colefax & Fowler, an interior decorating company that came to be lauded as the foremost decorating firm in England in the twentieth century.

IN LATE August, Wilder the writer and social gadfly was superseded by Wilder the older brother when a letter from Isabel reached him in Salzburg. She was heartbroken over her breakup with the man she had hoped to marry. Wilder immediately cabled his sister and mother to come to Europe. Then he wrote a long letter full of brotherly advice: Isabel and their mother should come to Europe, he reiterated. "Would even help my work," he contended, as if that might persuade Isabel to make the journey.[36]

Isabel had felt "pretty sure" she wanted to marry this workaholic surgeon, she said, although she recognized that it would "not be the marriage one plans and dreams of as a girl. It would not be the kind of companionship one would want." He was "a restrained, even eccentric man," a "seasoned bachelor" who didn't send notes or flowers, although now and then he surprised her with a gift. Yet she had believed he loved her "deeply" and needed her, and would marry her as soon as he was less "harassed and worried."[37] Isabel was thirty-seven, eager to be a wife and a mother—and she had been so confident that this would soon happen that she was cleaning the Deepwood Drive house from top to bottom "so that if I step out, everything will be in order here." She was also excited that her mother had bought herself a car as "part of her plan for getting used to being without me."[38] But by August the relationship was over, and Isabel was bereft.

Thornton answered her despairing letter by tackling her worries one by one. She was not "old plain and poor," as she had described herself in her letter. "Don't overdo that notion that a woman has nothing to say or be or give unless she's wife-mother-and-home-decorator," he wrote. "We're all People, before we're anything else," he told her. "People, even before we're artists. The rôle of being a Person is sufficient to have lived and died for." There was "lots of" pathology in the whole business, Wilder wrote. The man who broke Isabel's heart had a "psychic fear of going thru a thing. He's ill." But Isabel had her own problems, her brother told her: "From some deep infantile Father-love-and-hate you brought up a lack-of-confidence in that realm that colored the air without your knowing it. . . . Out of these infantile conditionings we make our strengths as well as our weaknesses." His prescription for her convalescence? "Better take a trip to Europe. There's plenty of money."[39]

Isabel and Isabella decided to stay in Hamden, however, and Thornton was soon caught up in the Salzburg Festival, living "entirely for pleasure" before settling down to work in Zurich. From Salzburg he wrote to Stein and Toklas about a night of drinking, first at the Mirabell Bar and then, after the bar closed, in the third-class waiting room at the railway station with the novelist Erich Maria Remarque; the German playwright Carl Zuckmayer; a "wonderful German Archbishop" incognito in civilian clothes; Lucy Tal, the wife of Wilder's German publisher; and "a Swedish street-walker."[40] But soon he was sober and hard at work in Zurich. He planned to spend some time in the mountains at Sils-Maria, he told Gertrude and Alice. "I must face the fact that I shall be very lonely," he wrote to them, "but there at the least, in terrifying loneliness, Nietzsche sent out his Zarathustra into the world, the time-bomb that took fifty years to explode and then what havoc."[41] Yet he was "very happy" in Zurich, despite the fact that he had "scarcely spoken a word to a human being in over a week."[42]

Gertrude wrote in early September to tell Wilder he had left a vest in Bilignin, and sent him a postcard shortly thereafter to say she was sending it to him via a young writer and college professor who would be passing through Zurich. He was Samuel Steward, twenty-eight, a native of Ohio and the author of a controversial novel entitled *Angels on the Bough* (1936). Gertrude liked him and hoped Wilder would have time to see him. Because Wilder knew "scarcely anyone in town," he was eager for company. He left a note at the American Express office in Zurich inviting Steward to visit him at the Carleton-Elite Hotel.[43] According to Steward, this "began the casual acquaintance with Thornton Wilder that lasted through the war years and beyond, ending sometime in 1948."[44] Also according to Steward, he and Wilder had sex in Zurich.

Opinions diverge as to whether a writer's sex life is a legitimate field for public examination unless it serves as subject matter and/or thematic matter for the artistic work, or unless it has, with the writer's complicity, emerged into public view as a defining force in the life and work. A very private man who often saw his fame as an intrusion into his personal life, Thornton Wilder seems to have studiously kept to himself the details of his sexual experiences, whether homosexual or heterosexual or both.

Five years after Wilder's death, and forty-three years after they met, Sam Steward published his first account of a sexual experience with Wilder, and then included the account in a memoir in 1981.[45] Several years later Steward talked about Wilder in interviews that linger in the public record. The surviving documentary evidence seems to give only a partial record of exactly what transpired between the two men, and when, and where, especially since some of Steward's later recollections do not always coincide with his letters written at the time.

Letters of the period document the fact that Sam Steward called on Wilder on September 10, 1937—an unexpected stop on the unorthodox literary pilgrimage Steward undertook in what he called the "Magic Summer" of 1937 in his memoir, *Chapters from an Autobiography*, published in 1981. Steward had begun a correspondence with Gertrude Stein in 1933 when he wrote to notify her of the death of a mutual friend. As their correspondence grew he got the idea of writing to other authors he admired—Thomas Mann, Carl Van Vechten, A. E. Housman, Eugene O'Neill, Sigmund Freud, André Gide, W. B. Yeats, Somerset Maugham, and others. Steward hit on a letter-writing strategy that worked: He commented on the author's work, and he never asked for a thing—no questions, no autographs, no request for a reply.

Steward had set out on his unique literary pilgrimage after he heard Hamlin Garland mention in a lecture that he had known Walt Whitman and had actually touched him. Steward said that this "electrified" him."[46] He wanted to touch the man who had touched Whitman, to be physically "linked in" with Whitman. That moment of contact inspired him to write to Lord Alfred Douglas, who had been Oscar Wilde's lover. Steward was now "linked in to" Whitman by the touch of a hand. Perhaps he could be "linked in to" Oscar Wilde by going to bed with Lord Alfred Douglas, who was then sixty-seven and not especially attractive, Steward mused in his autobiography. Nevertheless, Steward wrote, if he wanted to "link" himself with Oscar Wilde more directly than he was "linked" to Walt Whitman, it had to be done.[47] With the help of generous quantities of gin and bitters, Steward accomplished his mission.

After Steward's first meeting with Stein and Toklas in France, he headed for the next stop on his "pilgrimage"—his scheduled visit in Switzerland with Thomas Mann. But first, at Stein's behest, he would deliver Wilder's errant vest. Steward had met Wilder in 1929 and asked him to autograph a copy of *The Angel That Troubled the Waters*, but he was sure Wilder would not remember him. He agreed to call on Wilder in Zurich because Stein asked him to deliver the vest, but Wilder was not on the itinerary for Steward's amorous literary pilgrimage. In fact, Steward's opinion of Wilder's work had declined after Michael Gold's 1930 criticism of *The Woman of Andros*.

Steward and Wilder immediately began a "whirlwind of talk" covering a wide range of topics. As Steward reconstructed their visit in Zurich forty-three years later, some of his facts were slightly askew. They spent "six or seven" afternoons and evenings together, Steward wrote in 1980.[48] Their letters to Stein and Toklas give a different account, however: "Steward was here two days and a half and he's a fine fella and it was a pleasure," Wilder wrote to Stein on September 13, 1937, just after Steward's departure.[49] Steward wrote to Stein and Toklas on September 15, "I did see Thornton in Zurich, and Thornton was charming, and we talked like madmen for two days (because, he said, he hadn't talked to anyone in English for ten) and anyway, I always like to talk or listen."[50]

According to Steward, that rainy night in Zurich marked the beginning of another "lengthy literary pilgrimage" for him.[51] He wrote in his autobiography that Wilder lectured him about religion and about how to handle his homosexuality—among other things, urging him to "study the lives and careers of the great homosexuals from the beginning down to the present day—Leonardo and Michelangelo to Whitman and beyond." And then, Steward wrote, he and Wilder "climbed into bed together," Steward "half-drunk" as he said he had to be "in those days to have an encounter."[52]

In what appears to be the only published account of an instance of Wilder's sexual intimacy, Steward described an inhibited man with a "puritan reluctance" who "could never forthrightly discuss anything sexual," and for whom "the act itself was quite literally unspeakable." Nothing happened between them that "could be prosecuted anywhere," Steward wrote, and "there was never even any kissing."[53] He and Wilder met for sex in Chicago, Stewart wrote in his autobiography. He told others that they also met in Paris. In 1973 Steward sold letters, Christmas greetings, and postcards he had received from Wilder between 1937 and 1948 (an average of slightly more than two items per year), and they were sold in turn to the Beinecke Library at Yale University, repository of the Wilder papers. Wilder's last extant letter to Steward was written September 14, 1948. Steward published the article about his relationship with Wilder in *The Advocate* in May 1980, and edited it for inclusion in his *Chapters from an Autobiography* in 1981.

In a 1993 interview with the columnist and author Owen Keehnen, Steward, then eighty-five, mused that Wilder "was afraid of sex and unfortunately I was put in the position of outing him but I never did it until after he had died." Steward did not explain why he was "put in the position" of outing Wilder, but went on to say, "We were lovers in Zurich. He was very secretive about his homosexual inclinations but they were definitely there. We had quite an experience. Thornton always went about having sex as though it were something going on behind his back and he didn't know anything about it. He was more than a little afraid of it I think."[54]

In his 1980 and 1981 account of events, Steward moved from the subject of sex, which was for Wilder a very private matter, to the subject of literature, which was a very public matter. Steward said that Wilder told him that he "wouldn't dare criticize anything" Stein wrote, but the Wilder-Stein correspondence and Wilder's letters and commentary reveal his forthright public and private questions and concerns about her work. According to what Steward wrote forty years later about what Stein and Toklas told him, his need for an umbrella on a rainy night in Zurich inspired Wilder not only to write the third act of *Our Town*—but to write the entire third act in one morning after their meeting.[55] Wilder's letters, however, contradict this second- or third-hand observation. They document that act 3 was well under way at least as early as June 1937, before Wilder and Steward met, and that the text of the play, including act 3, would not be completed until December, with more revisions done in January 1938.[56] Wilder's correspondence documents the progress of his play, and it includes a letter he wrote to his mother and Isabel shortly after Steward's departure from Zurich revealing that he had just finished the second act of *Our Town* and written the opening of the third.[57]

More serious by far, Steward circulated the erroneous story that Wilder stole from novelist Wendell Wilcox the plot for *The Ides of March* (1948). Wilcox had published short fiction, and his only published novel was *Everything Is Quite All Right*, which appeared in 1945. Wilder was by then the author of four novels; was the recipient of three Pulitzer Prizes, one in fiction; and was one of the best-known American writers in the world. He would generously mentor Wilcox, Steward, and other writers in Chicago and elsewhere. Documents clearly confirm that Wilder did not appropriate a plot from Wendell Wilcox. Wilder told a journalist in later years that he first thought of the plot of *The Ides of March* while he was in Rome in 1920–21.[58] More significantly, Wilder's correspondence confirms beyond question that he began conceiving and planning the novel as early as 1922, soon after his first trip to Rome. On November 5, 1922—twenty-six years before the novel's publication and long before Wilder met Steward or Wilcox—Wilder had written to his mother about his idea for a "retelling of the strange relations that bound together Cicero, Clodius and his sister Clodia-Lesbia, Catullus, Julius Caesar and his wife."[59]

As has been noted, Wilder was steeped in Latin language, history, and literature from an early age. He had long been fascinated with Catullus, Caesar, Cleopatra, and company. His strengths and background in Latin and classical literature had led him to study at the American Academy in Rome in 1920–21. In 1931 Wilder had written to the classicist and translator Sir Edward Howard Marsh about his idea for the "conversation-novel" he wanted to write someday, "turning upon the famous profanation of the mysteries of the Bona Dea— with Clodius, Clodia, Catullus, Caesar and Cicero."[60] In 1935 he listed among his projects "The Top of the World—(Caesar, Cicero, Catullus,

Clodius, Clodia)," and by 1939 he was writing about the novel in his journal, still calling it "The Top of the World."[61]

Steward did not know the facts of the matter in the late 1940s or in 1980 and 1981, when he spread the untruth about Wilder and his novel. Steward also wrote that many of Wilder's friends in Chicago "disappeared or grew cool or distant" as the story "gained wider circulation," and that he ended his friendship with Wilder at this time. If Wilder himself or his host of close friends in Chicago or elsewhere made any reference to such an event, that evidence has not been found.[62]

Wilder's longtime friend Glenway Wescott, openly homosexual and the author of novels with homosexual subjects and themes, recalled in 1957 that Steward gave him "an amusing, resentful little account of his having sex with Wilder passingly in Paris some years ago; no one else ever told me any such thing."[63] Other gay men who knew Wilder over the years agreed that whether they believed Wilder was homosexual or heterosexual or bisexual or asexual, his personal life was intensely private, seemingly impervious even to rumor.[64] A case can be made that Wilder was bisexual in his emotional affinities, celibate by choice or circumstance more often than not, and private about his sexual relationships. Other than Sam Steward's posthumous outing of Wilder, no evidence has surfaced to reveal whether he consummated physical relationships with women, especially the women who loved him, or with other men he knew in Rome or New York or Chicago or Paris or Zurich or elsewhere.

Wilder's private writings suggest sexual constraint, repression, sublimation, and at times, self-imposed celibacy, but he did not leave definitive answers. It is clear, however, that through his ongoing intellectual, philosophical, and intuitive inquiry, Wilder was keenly attuned to the subliminal forces in life and in art, that he thought deeply over a number of years about sexual implications for art and the artist, and that he affirmed and even celebrated sexual energy as a vital life force that can fire and empower the creative life. He discussed issues of human sexuality with Freud, studied them in the work of Jung and Henri Bergson and others, and reflected on them over the years in passages in his journals. Wilder's study of Walt Whitman and Herman

Melville in the 1950s sheds light on his own evolving views on love and sex and "harmonious sexual adjustments." (He wrote in his journal on July 20, 1953, for instance, that "the term *sublimation* is misleading: it implies only a *higher* transference of the sexual drive.")[65]

In 1940, as he worked on *The Skin of Our Teeth*, Wilder considered plans to insert "jokes about sex" at regular intervals in the play. He was thinking about women in general and actresses in particular as he considered the "vast phenomenon" of sex, writing this revealing passage in his journal while he was "mildly drunk on a quart of Bordeaux":

> Laughter is not itself sexual, but how closely it is allied to that same censor that holds guard over all the confusions, the humiliations, and (to state the more positive side) the unspoken, unspeakable gratifications of life. . . . Sex is a vast phenomenon, a maw seldom pacified, never circumvented, and perpetually identified by the subconscious mind with the refractory exasperating, not to say unappeasable, character of external circumstance itself. . . .
>
> A laugh at sex is a laugh at destiny.
>
> And the stage is peculiarly fitted to be its home. There *a* woman is so quickly All Woman [*sic*].[66]

Wilder was not a novelist who chose to write graphically about sex, but his fictional characters are by no means sexless. This journal entry about the stage as the fitting home for sex encourages attention to the sexuality of the characters in his plays, especially from *The Merchant of Yonkers/The Matchmaker* onward—Dolly Levi; Mr. Antrobus, Mrs. Antrobus, and Sabina in *The Skin of Our Teeth*; Alcestis in *The Alcestiad*. Wilder offers his deepest speculations about sexuality in his nonfiction treatment of Melville, Whitman, Emily Dickinson.

When he met Sam Steward in Zurich in 1937, did Wilder, at forty, understand and embrace his own sexual identity? Did he explore or repress it, experiment or deny it, affirm or channel it, deplore it or celebrate it? Over the years his literary, spiritual, and philosophical belief and practice unfolded, evolved, and transformed. This kind of evolution seems to have been true as well of his sexual belief and practice. But Wilder was essentially a deeply private man, the product of a repressive upbringing in an intolerant, unforgiving, legally repressive era. Heterosexual, homosexual, bisexual, or asexual—whatever his inclinations and involvements may have been—he was a product of his era and his family, supremely conscientious and thoughtful by nature and by upbringing. He would have instinctively protected his own privacy as well as that of his sex partners, not out of hypocrisy but out of affection, out of courtesy, out of propriety, out of respect for others, and himself.

"I CAN no longer conceal from you that I'm writing the most beautiful little play you can imagine," Wilder wrote to Stein and Toklas September 13, 1937. He had finished two acts, he told them. "It's a little play with all the big subjects in it; and it's a big play with all the little things of life lovingly impressed into it." He described the play as "an immersion, immersion into a New Hampshire town. It's called 'Our Town' and its third act is based on your ideas, as on great pillars, and whether you know it or not, until further notice, you're in a deep-knit collaboration already."[67]

Some of the ideas that served as "great pillars" for act 3 of *Our Town* may have been triggered or ratified in Wilder's conversations with Stein, augmented by his reading, in 1937, of *The Making of Americans* (1925), a sweeping family saga that, as Stein proclaimed, offered a description of "everyone who is, or has been, or will be."[68] Wilder also knew intimately Stein's *The Geographical History of America or The Relation of Human Nature to the Human Mind* (1936), for which he wrote the introduction. This short essay sheds light on what Wilder had in mind when he wrote of Stein's influences on the third act of his play. In this book she was considering the treatment of time and identity in literature and, by extension, in life, Wilder wrote. ("And what's left when memory's gone, and your identity, Mrs. Smith?" the Stage Manager asks in the third act of *Our Town*.)

Wilder also observed that Stein was exploring the metaphysics of repetition, an idea that had long preoccupied him in his own work. Since his Roman awakening Wilder had been fascinated by the repetition of universal events and themes in individual lives. He had written about it in *The Woman of Andros*, as noted: "Pamphilus thought of the thousands of homes over all Greece where sleeping or waking souls were forever turning over the dim assignment of life. 'Lift every roof,' as Chrysis used to say, 'and you will find seven puzzled hearts.' "[69] Wilder was intrigued by the view of the self repeating the universal patterns, whereas Stein was more attuned to the idea of the self repeating the self. As he worked on his play in Switzerland in 1937, Wilder was haunted by "The great ghost of Nietzche [*sic*]."[70] Whether Stein read Nietszche—as Wilder avidly did—these ideas about repetition evoke Nietszche's concept of eternal recurrence or eternal return, "linked, not to a repetition of the same, but on the contrary, to a transmutation."[71]

The major ideas in act 3 of *Our Town* are uttered by the Stage Manager in his soliloquy on the "something way down deep that's eternal about every human being," and by Emily, who returns to earth for one day and asks, "Do any human beings ever realize life while they live it?—every, every minute?" A search for possible evidence of Stein's influence in that third act yields a passage from *The Making of Americans*, which Wilder did not read until 1937. Stein described her novel's protagonist as a man who understood the need to live every minute of life, and to fully realize every moment.[72]

Stein went on in this vein page after page in her novel, but Wilder had already addressed this very premise with considerably more economy, power, and beauty in *The Woman of Andros* in 1930, before he met Stein. In a scene that foreshadows the third act of *Our Town*, Chrysis tells the story of the hero who asked Zeus, as a reward for services rendered, to allow him to return to earth for one day. Lacking that power, Zeus turned to Hades, the king of the dead, who reluctantly granted the hero permission to return to earth to live over the day in "all the twenty-two thousand days of his lifetime that had been least eventful." The hero chose a sunlit day in his fifteenth year:

Suddenly the hero saw that the living too are dead and that we can only be said to be alive in those moments when our hearts are conscious of our treasure; for our hearts are not strong enough to love every moment. And not an hour had gone by before the hero who was both watching life and living it called on Zeus to release him from so terrible a dream. The gods heard him, but before he left he fell upon the ground and kissed the soil of the world that is too dear to be realized.[73]

"Oh, earth, you're too wonderful for anybody to realize you," Emily says near the end of act 3. "They don't understand, do they?" she asks her mother-in-law, who replies, "No, dear. They don't understand."

———

IN MID-SEPTEMBER, Wilder wrote to his family that he had finished the second act of *Our Town*, which he pronounced "just lovely, as is the opening of Act III. I'm just a dandy dramatist, looks like."[74] For all of Wilder's deference to Stein and Woollcott about their inspiration, it was to Sibyl Colefax that he entrusted his play in progress, reading sections aloud to her, and copying into his letters to her entire sections of the play as they evolved. "You never saw such a play!" he exclaimed in a letter to Sibyl September 25. He wrote at length about the first act, including a two-page transcription of lines and stage directions. He had finished a draft of act 3, he told her, although it had to "be cleared and enriched." Still it had "some awful strokes in it," transcribing passages to demonstrate, and adding that he had woven "hymn-singing" into every act of his play, just as spirituals "bathed and supported" Marc Connelly's 1936 play *Green Pastures*.[75]

Wilder worked on the third act of *Our Town* in a hotel five miles outside Zurich, where for a time he was the only guest. His room's small balcony overlooked the slope of a mountain and the lake below. In October he described his daily schedule to Woollcott: "Late every afternoon I walk into town, call for my mail, get a cocktail, dine on a kilogram of Hungarian or Italian grapes and return home on a little suburban train. I'm very happy, but the happiness does not prevent little accesses of home-sickness for the greatest country of the world."[76]

26

"CHALK . . . OR FIRE"

*There are the stars—doing their old, old crisscross journeys in the sky.
Scholars haven't settled the matter yet, but they seem to think there are no
living beings up there. Just chalk . . . or fire. Only this one is straining
away, straining away all the time to make something of itself.*

—STAGE MANAGER,
Our Town, *Act 3*

Princeton, Boston, New York, Tucson, Hollywood, Taos, and Other Destinations (Late 1930s)

Jed telephoned from London for 20 minutes the other night," Wilder wrote to his mother and Isabel on October 28 from Zurich. "He wants to know if 'Our Town' would be a good play for the Xmas season in New York. Would it?!! And guess who might act the lanky tooth picking Stage-manager? Sinclair Lewis! He's been plaguing Jed to let him act for a long time."[1] Harris, who badly needed another Broadway hit, had in turn been "plaguing" Wilder for a play. He had promised Harris years earlier to let him have the first look at his first full-length play, and Wilder was a man of his word.

Wilder had already had a hand in one Broadway hit that year, for he had adapted Ibsen's *A Doll's House* from existing English and German scripts for production by Harris, starring Ruth Gordon. The play had opened in the Central City, Colorado, Opera House on July 17, touring to enthusiastic audiences for thirteen weeks before heading to New York for its opening on December 27. The play's successful run on Broadway would continue until May 1938—144 performances in all. When Harris and Ruth Gordon did the play for Ned Sheldon in his penthouse, Sheldon called it "the best performance" of Ibsen ever, lauding Wilder's adaptation as "positively magnificent."[2]

By this time Gordon and Harris were working together even though

their turbulent love affair had ended. Gordon could no longer toler-
ate Harris's serial affairs with other women—although she herself had
been one of the other women during Harris's first marriage. Harris was
now romantically involved with movie and stage actress and socialite
Rosamond Pinchot, who had been separated for several years from her
husband, William "Big Bill" Gaston. Quite a beauty—called by some
the loveliest woman in America—Rosamond had been discovered by
Max Reinhardt, who cast her in movies as well as plays.[3] She was befriended by Aleck Woollcott, and pursued by Sinclair Lewis, George
Cukor, and David O. Selznick, among others.

Wilder arranged to meet Jed Harris in Paris on October 31, 1937,
and read him *Our Town* as well as *The Merchant of Yonkers*. Wilder made
it clear to Harris that he had promised Max Reinhardt first refusal on
Merchant, but even so consulted with Harris about some problems in
the third act. Harris pronounced the second act of *Merchant* a "perfect
piece of farce-comedy writing," and gladly set in motion the production plans for *Our Town*, aiming to rush it into rehearsal in New York
by mid-December.[4] First, however, Wilder had to finish writing the
play. In a letter from Paris November 24, he described it to Amy Wertheimer as "a New Hampshire village explored by the techniques of
Chinese Drama and of *Pullman Car Hiawatha*."[5]

By December 9 Wilder was back in the United States, where Harris
had "installed, or rather imprisoned" him in a cottage in the "swanki-
est section" of Long Island, with a butler and a cook—and orders to
finish *Our Town*.[6] Wilder soon discovered that his "prison" was chosen
for its proximity to Ballybrook, the estate near Old Brookville, Long
Island, that Pinchot was renting. Some of Wilder's closest friends cautioned him to watch his back with Jed Harris, whose reputation for
a volatile temper and questionable integrity and trustworthiness expanded as the years passed. Sibyl Colefax in particular warned Wilder
never to trust Harris in business dealings, and Ruth Gordon sent the
most serious warning: "There is a stage in the creative act where one
rises up to destroy the work in creation," she wrote to Wilder. "The
same mind that is intelligent enough to create something is also at
every moment intelligent enough to see every fault in the work and to

turn and destroy it. That impulse must remain in the subconscious as corrective power." She told Wilder that already, with *A Doll's House*, Jed had "opened the trapdoor to the destructive impulse and was tearing his work to pieces."[7] Fortunately that production survived and went on to its Broadway success.

By the time Wilder arrived in New York, Harris was thinking of casting the actor Frank Craven to play *Our Town*'s Stage Manager, and was putting other production details in place, although he and Wilder had no written contract. Wilder was still finishing act 3, and rehearsals were about to begin in New York. He found himself in "such a mess of friendship-collaboration sentiment with Jed, and with the sense of guilt about the unfinished condition of the play" that he couldn't bring himself to insist on a contract immediately.[8]

Soon the play was cast, and the script was finished, with some revisions by Harris—"admirable alterations in the order of the scenes, and some deletions that I would have arrived at anyway," Wilder wrote to Sibyl, plus "a number of tasteless little jokes" that "don't do much harm," although they gave Harris "that sensation of having written the play which is so important to him."[9] At the first rehearsal, Wilder said, when the actors sat around a table reading the third act, they all wept, "so that pauses had to be made so they could collect themselves."[10] He wrote to Dwight Dana, "There's a possibility that the play will be a smashing success—an old theatre-hand like Frank Craven seems to be thinking so." Then he added cautiously, "Maybe not."[11]

"ON THE WHOLE everything has been pleasant, exciting and friendly," Wilder wrote to Sibyl Colefax on January 2, 1938, soon after the play went into rehearsal. Harris planned to try out the play in Princeton, New Jersey, with "perhaps an advance performance in New Haven, too," Wilder wrote. Then they hoped to head for Broadway. For the duration of rehearsals, Wilder was staying in New York, revising the play and sitting in on readings, meetings, and practices as needed. Behind the scenes, however, despite and even because of their long friendship, the "pleasant" and "friendly" atmosphere of the high-stakes

Wilder-Harris association was quickly deteriorating. Harris, desperate for another hit on Broadway after a drought of a few years, and Wilder, staunchly possessive of his text and vision for *Our Town*, began to clash over the script, the lighting, the acting, and even Harris's choice of a theater in New York. It would probably be the Henry Miller's, Wilder wrote to Sibyl, but that would be "all wrong; that's a drawing-room theatre; my play should be in a high old-fashioned echoing barn of a place with an enormous yawning stage on which is built the diaphanous 'Town.' "[12]

Wilder had been repeatedly warned by Ruth Gordon, Gertrude Stein, the Lunts, Sibyl Colefax, Woollcott, and others about Harris's temperament and tactics, and he finally confessed his growing concerns to Colefax and Woollcott. One night, "under an angry insomnia," he had even considered withdrawing his play, he wrote, "but the thoughts of 3:00 a. m. are very unreasonable things and in the morning I knew it had been nonsense."[13] He worried that Harris was trying to "make the play 'smoother' and more civilized, and the edge of boldness is being worn down," but rationalized that the play remained "bold enough still."[14] He was afraid that the second act was the "least solid of the three," and copied a page of the Stage Manager's opening lines into his letter to Sibyl—lines that deviated slightly in word choice and cadences from the published script.[15] Harris was constantly changing and interpolating lines in the play, often without Wilder's knowledge. Wilder wrote to Gertrude Stein on January 12:

> *As you predicted Jed got the notion that he had written the play and was still writing it.*
>
> *As long as his suggestions for alterations are on the structure they are often very good; but once they apply to the words they are always bad and sometimes atrocious.*
>
> *There have been some white-hot flaring fights. At present we are in a lull of reconcilement.*[16]

To his own detriment, despite warnings from people close to him. Wilder put his friendship with Harris ahead of his obligations to himself, his work, his lawyer, and his dramatic agent, Harold Freedman. Inevitably, as in many of Harris's productions, there was a morass of trouble. Over the years Harris had alienated a string of theater luminaries—the director George Abbott, the actor Henry Fonda, the playwright George S. Kaufman. Wilder was still working without a contract with Harris—a foolhardy approach under the best circumstances, but especially treacherous with someone who often did business the way Harris could do business—selfishly, single-mindedly, sometimes unscrupulously, and often heedless of the rights of other people. Wilder greatly admired Harris's proven skills as a director, but now he also trusted himself as a playwright. His self-confidence had been fortified by Ned Sheldon and Aleck Woollcott—the dramatist and the critic. "How proud I was to be told by Ned that I had the resources of a playwright well in hand," Wilder wrote to Woollcott in January 1938. "And I learn. I am an *apprenti sorcier.* That's all [that] matters."[17] Of all the people with whom Wilder shared his work in progress, Ned Sheldon was the one, Wilder said, who had never lost one of his manuscripts, never tried to compete for his audience, just generously "*shared* a thing in a state of growth."[18]

Early in 1937, with one of the first rough drafts of *Our Town* in hand, Wilder had called on Sheldon at his penthouse on the fourteenth floor of an apartment building at Eighty-fourth and Madison. Countless friends (including Woollcott, Ruth Gordon, Edith Wharton, the actress Ruth Draper, the composer Deems Taylor, the violinist Jascha Heifetz, and Helen Hayes and Charles MacArthur, the brother of Alfred MacArthur, who was married to Sheldon's sister, Mary) found in Sheldon's company a "haven of repose in the hectic life of Broadway."[19] Wilder sat beside Sheldon's bed to read his play aloud, knowing his friend would not interrupt until he had finished. Wilder read all the parts, beginning with the Stage Manager, who would guide the audience through *Our Town*, just as a Stage Manager had functioned early in the decade in his one-act plays *Pullman Car Hiawatha* and *The Happy Journey to Trenton and Camden.* Wilder played with time in *Our Town*, as he had in the one-acts and even in some of his early playlets, liberating his characters from the strictures of conventional linear time into a malleable, dynamic stream of time and being. And in the apparent simplicity of their lives in the mythical village he created as their habitat, Wilder surrounded his characters with the primal questions he had been exploring for years: How do we live? How do we survive? What is love—and is love sufficient "to reconcile one to the difficulty of living (i.e. the difficulty of being good. . . .)?"[20]

"You broke every rule," Sheldon wrote to Wilder after the reading:

> *There is no suspense, no relationship between the acts, no progress; but every seven minutes—no, every five minutes—you've supplied a new thing—some novelty—in the proceedings, which is at once a pleasure in the experience, and, at the same time, a contribution to the content of the play. Most plays progress in time, but here is a progression in depth. Let us know this town more and more![21]*

Wilder had followed Sheldon's advice, reporting to him from Zurich that summer of 1937 that before Emily Gibbs appeared in act 3 "in the Elysian Fields on the hill above Grover's Corners, New Hampshire," the whole second act of the play was devoted to her wedding and the events leading up to it.[22] Furthermore, Wilder said, he thought the audience would love Emily.[23]

Wilder quickly learned that in Jed Harris he had to confront a nearly invincible adversary. Constitutionally averse to conflict, Wilder fought for the integrity of his script but internalized much of his anger and frustration. By mid-January he told Harris he had a "whole set of Nature's Warnings = twitches, and stutterings and head aches." He was going to have to "retire" from the production for a while, to sleep and rest and regain his "fresh eye" for the play. His perspective, he said, had "become so jaundiced that I can no longer catch what's good or bad."[24]

At noon on January 22, 1938—before the opening of the Princeton tryout that evening—a deeply worried Wilder recorded his concerns about Harris's production and sealed them in an envelope that was not opened until 1944, when Isabel Wilder took out her brother's notes and read them at the time of *Our Town*'s first revival in New York. That snowy day in Princeton in 1938 Wilder wrote that he was very much afraid certain of Harris's production elements would "harm and perhaps shipwreck" the play's effectiveness. He feared that the play was "in danger of falling into trivial episodes," that Harris had not "vigorously directed" some of his actors, that he had an "astonishingly weak sense of visual reconstruction," that his interpolations in the text robbed it of "its nervous compression."[25]

The play opened January 22 in Princeton's McCarter Theatre—the theater where Wilder had seen so many tryouts during his years in New Jersey. He wrote the details to Dana, calling the performance "an undoubted success," and noting that there was standing room only in the theater, with a box office "take" of nineteen hundred dollars. He observed much laughter, some "astonishment," and "lots of tears" and applause from his audience.[26] One critic, writing in *Variety*, was not so kind, however, finding the performance "not only disappointing but hopelessly slow. . . . It will probably go down as the season's most extravagant waste of fine talent." The play "should never have left the campus," the reviewer charged, "for once the novelty has been worn thin, the play lacks the sturdy qualities necessary to carry it on its own."[27]

But Wilder's worries about the Princeton performance and his director's decisions were abruptly overshadowed by a tragedy that would haunt the play, the cast, and its director. Jed Harris, the classic brooding bad boy, magnetically attracted women. By 1937, at the age of thirty-seven, he was long divorced from his first wife, Anita Greenbaum (the person who, years earlier, had suggested that he change his given name, Jacob Horowitz, to something else), and he had begun a relationship with the actress Louise Platt, who would later become his second wife and the mother of his daughter. His long relationship with Ruth Gordon, the mother of his son, had been transmuted from a turbulent romance to a civil friendship and professional relationship. His current romantic interest, in addition to Louise Platt, was Rosamond Pinchot, whom he had met at a Hollywood party in 1935. The glamorous society matron, mother, and movie star, separated from her husband, was very much in evidence at rehearsals for *Our Town*. Harris set her to work backstage with the few props and sound effects the production required, and she may have designed Emily's wedding dress. Jed and Rosamond apparently boosted their energy during the final grueling days of rehearsal by taking Benzedrine.[28] According to Harris's principal biographer and to interviews Isabel Wilder gave decades later, Harris often treated Pinchot rudely in the presence of his cast and crew. Also according to Isabel, she and Thornton overheard Jed's side of a telephone quarrel with Rosamond on January 22, after the Princeton performance.[29]

By Monday, January 24, Wilder, Isabel, Jed, and the cast of *Our Town* were in Boston for the play's tryout there—and Rosamond Pinchot was dead. Sometime before dawn on January 24 she parked her car in the garage of her rented Long Island estate and died of carbon monoxide poisoning. Her suicide "fell like a bomb into the middle of everything," Wilder wrote to Woollcott. "She had loved the play and was at rehearsals."[30] Her death was sensationalized front-page news in Boston and elsewhere. The January 25 edition of the *Boston Post* bore the headline "LINK SUICIDE TO NEW SHOW HERE. Rosamond Pinchot Said to Have Been Brooding Over Failure to Win Part in 'Our Town.'"

A distraught Jed Harris was the first to publicly deny the alleged cause of Rosamond's suicide. The *New York Daily News* quoted him as saying, "Any report that Miss Pinchot wanted to get into *Our Town* is fantastic. She attended a rehearsal in New York, along with about fifty other persons. But she hadn't asked for a part, and there wasn't a part—not even a small one—for which she could be considered." But not only did he understate her involvement behind the scenes of the play; his general manager, Sidney Hirsch, reportedly denied that there was any romance between Harris and Rosamond Pinchot, calling her instead "one of Mr. Harris's many friends."[31]

Although there is no evidence that Pinchot wanted or sought a role in Wilder's play—and ample evidence of the complicated challenges she faced in her personal life—the link to *Our Town* stuck, giving the play a sad notoriety just as it opened in Boston, a link poignantly heightened by reports that one of Pinchot's suicide notes quoted Emily's farewell speech in *Our Town*.[32]

Despite the pall, however, the show went on. Some members of the cast and crew thought Harris drove the cast too hard in those days after Rosamond's death, and that he even exploited her death to heighten the emotional response of his actors. To the contrary, Wilder wrote, "Jed has been kind and controlled to all the actors, except in overtiring them with interminable rehearsals, delays and all night work." Wilder escaped when he could and lost himself in work on *The Merchant of Yonkers*, breaking to take long walks to clear his head. But he kept fighting with Jed over the script for *Our Town*, telling Woollcott that he'd rather "have it die on the road than come into New York as an aimless series of little jokes, with a painful last act."[33]

Woollcott sent Wilder a letter of support January 26: "I have an abiding faith in this play of yours and others that you are going to write."[34] In a letter to Woollcott, Wilder poured out his anguish over what was happening to his play in Jed's hands. "Success is accorded to a work of art when the central intention is felt in every part of it, and intention and execution are good," he wrote. "Jed lost courage about my central intention and moved the production over to a different set of emphases. The result is that the vestiges of my central attention that remain stick out as timid and awkward excrescences."[35]

Woollcott answered immediately, urging Wilder to stick to his guns, and to "trust that hard core you have—rock-ribbed and ancient as the sun—upon which the Jed Harrises and the Frank Cravens and the *haute noblesse* of Boston will break like spray."[36] Woollcott had used the popular podium of his weekly radio broadcast to give *A Doll's House* "the effect of adrenalin [*sic*], " and he would do the same for *Our Town*.[37]

In the audience at the Boston opening of the play sat forty-one citizens from the small New Hampshire towns surrounding Mount Monadnock and Peterborough, the home of the MacDowell Colony—the village equivalents of Wilder's mythical Grover's Corners. After the performance their spokesman, A. Erland Goyette, presented a cherry-wood gavel to Wilder, along with "an eternal membership" in the Mount Monadnock Region Association of New Hampshire. The *Boston Evening Transcript* reported that the inscribed gavel was "made of native wood grown at the MacDowell Colony," noting that Wilder had spent six summers at MacDowell and that "that association with life in a small New Hampshire town" was "responsible for" *Our Town*.[38] Wilder was moved by the pleasure these people had taken in seeing a play that was "about something they knew."[39]

To his lawyer Wilder wrote, "Boston reviews cautious but not unfavorable. . . . Business in Boston very bad; but even so better than [Orson Welles's production of] Julius Caesar which had rave reviews."[40] But there were encouraging signs amid the turbulence in Boston: Edmund Wilson, who just happened to be in Boston, saw the play and called the last act "the most terrific thing" he had ever seen in the theater, and playwright Marc Connelly, summoned to Boston on Thursday by a worried Harris, found the play "magnificent."[41]

"So with all those plus and minus marks," Wilder reported to Dwight Dana, "Jed cancelled the second week in Boston (losing, he says, $2500 on the two weeks) and opens at the Henry Miller's Theater in New York on Thursday."[42] Although *Our Town*, with its dearth of scenery, might look cheap, it was actually very expensive to produce, Wilder noted: "45 actors; and not two but five electric switchboards."[43]

Marc Connelly, Jed Harris's longtime friend and sometime champion, and an occasional investor in his productions, hurried to Boston to see the Thursday-night performance at Harris's urging. Eavesdropping on the audience in the lobby between acts, Connelly heard people say they liked the veteran actor Frank Craven, who had come out of retirement to play the Stage Manager. They found Martha Scott, making her debut, "lovely and talented." But the consensus seemed to be displeasure that the play jumped about in time, and had very little plot and scenery, so there was "nothing to see except the theater's steam pipes on the back wall of the stage." Nevertheless Connelly "found the play utterly delightful."[44] When Wilder's play moved to the Henry Miller's Theatre in New York on February 4, Connelly wrote, "The day after *Our Town* opened, without a word changed, the accolades from all the critics made it suddenly desirable to every theater owner in New York with a faltering tenant."[45]

WILDER TOOK time out just before the Broadway opening to see the first television production of one of his plays. On October 19, 1937, the

British producer, director, and librettist Eric Crozier's television film of *The Happy Journey to Trenton and Camden* was broadcast in England. Wilder first saw the telecast in New York on February 1, 1938, and found problems with the acting and the production. He wrote to his mother, "I don't think television will ever make good theatre."[46]

He was in New Haven when he got the good news about *Our Town*'s Broadway debut. "Funny thing's happened," he wrote to Dwight Dana:

> *Ruth phoned down it's already broken a house record.*
>
> *In spite of the mixed reviews when the box office opened Saturday morning there were 26 people in line; the line continued all day, and the police had to close it for ten minutes so the audience could get into the matinée; and that $6,500 was taken in on that day—the two performances and the advance sale.*
>
> *Imagine that!*
>
> *Friday night both Sam Goldwyn and Bea Lillie were seen to be weeping. Honest!*
>
> *It was very expensive being a dramatist.*
>
> *Three opening-nights—telegrams to some of the actors, bouquets to leading ladies; a humidor to Frank Craven; gift of seats to a few friends; hotel expenses at Princeton & Boston (the contract says Jed should have paid.) . . . Isn't it astonishing, and fun, and exhausting!*[47]

The morning after opening night Wilder and Isabel had taken the train back to Connecticut. They had promised each other that if the reviews were great they would splurge and take a taxi from the New Haven station to their house in Hamden. If not, they would take the trolley. The reviews were mixed, however, and accustomed as they were from childhood to being very frugal, they rode the trolley home.[48]

FROM THE outset *Our Town* enchanted some theatergoers and bored or baffled others. Eleanor Roosevelt, then the outspoken, influential first lady of the United States, found the play "interesting" and "original," but she was "moved and depressed beyond words," she wrote in her popular, nationally syndicated newspaper column, My Day. While she was glad she saw it, she "did not have a pleasant evening."[49] The *New York Times* critic Brooks Atkinson, a champion of Wilder's play, gently took Mrs. Roosevelt to task for her "Standards in Drama Criticism," writing, "I fear that Mrs. Roosevelt has done less than justice to a distinguished work of art."[50]

By mid-February, despite the excitement of two hits on Broadway, Wilder was "broken by a Cold, and by a long tug-of-war with Jed Harris, and crammed with subjects for new plays," he wrote his old friend Harry Luce, who had sent congratulations for the success of *Our Town*. Luce had especially liked the hymns sung in the choir rehearsal in Wilder's play—hymns that reminded both men of their boyhood days at Chefoo School. "I'm about to go to Arizona for two months," Wilder continued. "Long walks among the tumbleweeds & rattlesnake nests, liquor, and more work."[51] But before he departed for the desert, he deposited the first batch of Gertrude Stein's papers in the library at Yale University—notebooks and manuscripts he had hand-carried from France, in part to honor her literary legacy and in part because he was concerned about the safety of the papers if Stein remained in Europe during the war. He wrote to Stein and Toklas in late February to tell them the deed was done, adding, "Oh, oh,—I wish I could a long Tale unfold: Jed Harris. You diagnosed him to a T."[52]

Together, through their contentious collaboration, Thornton Wilder and Jed Harris, the idealistic Broadway neophyte and the hardened Broadway veteran, brought *Our Town* to vivid life on Broadway, first at the Henry Miller's Theatre, and then at the Morosco, where it would run more than ten months, closing November 19, 1938, after 336 performances. The Wilder-Harris friendship did not survive the play, however, and while their estrangement was par for the course for Harris, this was the most turbulent, conflicted professional relationship of Wilder's life. The weeks after the play opened in New York found Wilder bitter and disillusioned—and bound for Arizona, where he planned to hide away; recover the balance of work, rest, and exercise that had served him so well in Zurich; and make headway on his new plays. He was writing Stein and Toklas "the flurried letters of a crazy man," he apologized, "but when I get to Arizona, I'll be myself again. The whole blame of my state rests at Jed Harris's door."[53]

Wilder expressed his strongest, most critical assessment of Harris to Ernest Hemingway, who was in discussions with Harris about producing Hemingway's play, *The Fifth Column*. Harris did not like the play but had been persuaded by Hemingway's agent to fly to Key West and discuss the project anyway. Wilder wrote an adamant warning to Hemingway on March 1:

> *You've seen him now, and know that extraordinary bundle of lightning flash intuitions into the organization of a play; vivid psychological realism; and intelligence, devious intelligence.*
>
> *But maybe you don't know the rest: tormented, jealous egotism; latent hatred of all engaged in creative work; and so on.*
>
> *Use him for his great gifts—one play at a time only. But don't presuppose a long happy collaboration.*
>
> *My distrust of him is bad enough, but others go far farther than I do and insist on a malignant daemonic force to destruction in him. Anyway, his professional career is one long series of repeated patterns: trampling on the friendship, gifts and love of anybody who's been associated with him.*
>
> *I feel something like a piker to write such a letter as this. Because he has done, in many places, a fine job on my work. But the friendship's over all right. He's the best in N. Y., Ernest, but after this I'm ready to work with duller managers, if only I can get reliability, truthfulness, old-fashioned character, and coöperation at the same time.*[54]

As Wilder was trying to come to closure on his unhappy relationship with Harris, he was just beginning the association with the great director Max Reinhardt that had been his dream since boyhood. He had sent Reinhardt the script of *The Merchant of Yonkers*, and had just about given up on hearing from him when a "thunderbolt" of good news came in a telegram from Hollywood. Reinhardt was "truly delighted" with what he had read, awaited the rest of the script with "the greatest suspense," and "eagerly" wished to "put it on the stage."

Reinhardt, of course, knew the Nestroy play that had given rise to
Wilder's farce, and so he recognized that Dolly Levi was Wilder's creation. Reinhardt found her to be a "precious addition to the play."[55]

———————

Our Town settled in at the Morosco, receiving mixed but mostly favorable notices, and drawing largely enthusiastic crowds. All the Wilders
celebrated, and Thornton probably never saw one of the most affirming
"reviews" of his play—the letter about *Our Town* written to Amos by
their sister Charlotte. "The Play is the Thing," she commented.

> *It is doubtless selling like wildfire—sometimes I walk by just to see, and
> there are always people getting tickets; it stays in my imagination as
> magically graphic, touching, original, and powerful, in its few mor-
> dant spots—the umbrellas of the funeral; the young husband flung on
> the ground; and the fascination of that exquisite expressive keenness, in
> humor, and nostalgic reference. Thornton's genius, as I see it, besides the
> wealth of his imaginative evocation, his verbal virtuosity, is for perfect
> taste in relation to form.*[56]

Thornton's income from *Our Town* would set him free to write more
plays, even though royalty payments lagged behind the reviews and
the box-office receipts. Amos and Janet were not dependent on Thornton for financial support, and Charlotte, struggling to stay afloat on her
paltry earnings in New York, was too proud and stubborn to accept her
brother's offers of help. But Thornton's income from *Our Town* would
provide additional security for his mother and Isabel—and Charlotte,
if she would allow it. Frugal Isabella celebrated by indulging in a new
hat and a "black cotton lace dress with bolero" that fitted perfectly,
and she could have bought more: Wilder's income jumped from a net of
$4,854.23 in 1937 to a net of $29,768.16 in 1938, and $37,154.80 in 1939
(the estimated equivalent of more than $720,000 in 2010 purchasing
power). Slightly more than two-thirds of the 1939 income came from
the publication of *The Bridge of San Luis Rey* as one of the first ten books
in the new Pocket Books series.[57]

Worried about Isabel, who was still grieving over her broken romance, Wilder used some of his income to try to hasten her "convalescence" by providing "a complete change of place and tempo." He invited her to travel with him to help him with various matters surrounding the production of the play.[58] He also funded a trip for her to spend April in London, believing that she needed "a rest and change very much; that 'heart' trouble slow a-healing."[59]

———

BY MARCH 8, 1938, free of teaching, lecturing, and Broadway duties, Wilder was at the Arizona Inn in Tucson, and by March 16 he was comfortably settled in a "tiny apartment" at 732 North Sixth Avenue, surrounded by desert air, Arizona sunlight, and at night, the "wild magic" of the moon. He found himself to be the lone walker in the town. "Everybody else drives dusty cars, or stands leaning against store-fronts with half-closed eyes," he said. "But I still walk right smartly."[60] "The desert's wonderful," he exulted in a letter to Stein and Toklas. "I just returned from spending the day at a ranch sixty miles away,— between 20 and 30 thousand acres, the cows browsing among the cacti and rattlesnakes. I climbed the nearest hill and looked out over a tremendous prospect of mountains, plain, clouds and mesquite."[61] After the prolonged stress in New York, the desert retreat was just what he needed for rest, rejuvenation and work. He was thriving in his new daily regimen of "baking sunlight, long walks and hard work."[62] He fixed simple, "primitive, but good" meals for himself, and took time to enjoy "Wonderful piercing hot days" and the flowering of the cactus.[63] He was living a monastic life, he wrote his family. "Haven't spoken to a soul; walked and saw sunset from Sentinel Mountain! And spent the mornings on the play." *The Merchant of Yonkers* had its ups and downs, he said. "Some mornings fancies run down my forearm like ants, and other days I just copy the *status quo*. Writing's a damnable profession. But rain or shine, I write."[64]

The new play was growing, so much so that one evening he read portions of it aloud to friends at a nearby ranch. "Some of it's very funny—sly deep deep records of 'human nature' getting itself into frightful predicaments. Max Reinhardt wrote that he was very pleased with the first two acts I sent him and as soon as I can I'll be in Hollywood showing him the rest."[65] By March 21 he had finished the fourth act, but the third was giving him trouble. "The Fourth Act's developed fine," he reported to his mother and Isabel.

> *I who never could finish a novel correctly seem to have the knack of Last Acts.*
>
> *But the Third Act has been terrifying me.*
>
> *Ever since I got here I've been in a cold sweat about it. It wouldn't come right.*
>
> *I had thoughts of laying the play aside and telling Reinhardt that maybe I'd be a year or two at it.*
>
> *And then last night I got the Key. The direction.*
>
> *All my plots—count 'em—and idea-themes all come to a head at the right moment, with Mrs. Levi ruling the Roost.*
>
> *Rejoice with me. Now it'll go very fast.*[66]

Physically and mentally restored in the "wonderful desert air and penetrating sun light," Wilder could turn his attention to the mountain of mail generated by *Our Town*.[67]

After his Oberlin professor Charles Wager read the Coward-McCann 1938 readers' edition of the play, the first publication of *Our Town*, he pronounced it the finest work Wilder had ever done. Wilder was still perplexed, however, to discover the contradictory conclusions the play provoked: Some people found it sentimental, while others saw in the play an "embittered pessimism" about human nature and its "being in the dark."[68] He recognized that "for every person that thinks the last act is easy, sentimental and soft, there's always another person who thinks it hard, embittered and cruel."[69]

Another letter caught Wilder's attention, and elicited a detailed response about the sources for the play. It came from Christina Hopkinson Baker, the widow of George Pierce Baker, one of the founders of the drama program at Yale, and the mentor and teacher of numerous playwrights. In answer to her question about the influences in the third act, Wilder responded at length. "Lordy. I'd built my house with those ideas so long they seemed to have the character of simple self evidence," he wrote:

> *I suppose that I got it from Dante. I had to teach the Inferno And the first half of the Purgatorio at Chicago. I had in mind especially the Valley of the repentant Kings in about the 8th Canto of the Purgatorio. Same patience, waiting; same muted pain; same oblique side-glances back to earth. Dante has an angel descend nightly and after slaying a serpent who tries to enter the Valley every evening, stands guard the rest of the night. Most commentators agree that the allegory means: from now on the Dead must be guarded from memories of their earthly existence and from irruptions of the old human nature associations . . .*
>
> *At all events I do not mind from critics the charge of immaturity, confusion and even pretentiousness. It's a first play; it's a first sally into deep waters. I hope to do many more—and better—and even more pretentious. I write as I choose; and I learn as I go; and I'm very happy when the public pays the bills.*[70]

"THE PULITZER announcement is to be Monday," Wilder's proud mother wrote on April 29, 1938. "How can I wait?"[71] She had just entertained twenty-five friends at tea, and found it difficult to keep the secret that Thornton was about to receive the Pulitzer Prize for *Our Town*, becoming the first writer to win the award for both fiction and drama.

Isabella Niven Wilder had lived many years of her own life through her children—her literary ambitions materializing in their achievements, her disappointing marriage more than offset by the devotion and affection lavished on her by her sons and daughters. Those were especially gratifying years—the last years of the thirties—when her children were flourishing and, except for Isabel's disappointment in love, happy, as far as a mother's eye and instinct could tell. Isabella was proud of all her children, hovering over them in person or through long, chatty letters; avidly following their projects; bolstering their spirits during hard times; and, as she had done all their lives, cheering their aspirations and achievements.

Although Isabel was on the brink of giving up her career as a novelist, Charlotte was working relentlessly hard as a poet. Coward-McCann had just accepted Charlotte's new book of poetry, *Mortal Sequence*, to be published in 1939. "I never had a moment's doubt that Mr. Coward would accept the book," Isabella wrote to her daughter:

> *Your "Moon" [Phases of the Moon, published in 1936] was a "distinguished book of verse," as Thornton phrased it and you know he is a very good and a very exacting critic—none better—and this book has the further joy & distinction of lyric qualities external as well as internal.*

Isabella predicted that Charlotte would "wake up some day to being judged in your own field as a dominant figure—unique and distinguished and justified in all the decisions you have made."[72]

Like Thornton, Isabella kept up with New York theater and Hollywood movies. "Hollywood is in a big depression," she wrote in 1938 as Thornton and Max Reinhardt began serious talks about the production of *The Merchant of Yonkers*. She predicted that the Pulitzer Prize would help attract backers to her son's new play.[73] The Pulitzer award no doubt boosted ticket sales for *Our Town*, and the play would run until November 19, 1938, when Harris closed the show and inaugurated the national tour. Almost immediately there was extraordinary national demand from amateur and stock companies for rights to perform the play. Coward-McCann had published a hardcover reading edition of the play in March 1938, and collaborated with Samuel French on the production of the first acting edition, published in 1939. The first amateur production rights for *Our Town* were granted on April 5, 1939, to a theater group in Salt Lake City, and next came Tucson on April 8, 1939. Over the next twenty months *Our Town* was produced in at least 658 communities across the United States and in Hawaii and Canada.

With the success of the plays, Wilder's whole view of life had changed, he said. "Now I make no plans—I'm a theatre-gypsy," he wrote to Sam Steward. "Come and go, without home, address, or citizenship."[74] His life in Tucson was a daily calibration of "desert, sun, walks, and work. Some days work goes fine; other days nil; writing's an awful business, punctuated by ecstasies."[75] For now, he focused all his attention on *The Merchant of Yonkers*, which he described to another friend as a "broad low comedy, based upon a Viennese classic of 1845, into which is inserted that wonderful scene in Molière's *L'Avare* where Louise, the marriage-broker, tries to interest Harpagon in a young girl. This time I'm out for trenchant, not to say, cutting laughter."[76]

In addition to the ever-growing public interest in *Our Town*, Wilder now found himself and his earlier works much in demand. Many of his one-act plays were being widely done, and there was interest in England for a production of *Lucrece* starring Laurence Olivier, whom Wilder called "the best new actor of all."[77] Amateur and stock theaters all over the map were eager to produce *Our Town*—from Burlington, Vermont, to Ann Arbor, Michigan, to the Honolulu Community Theatre in Hawaii. But for the time being, writing *The Merchant of Yonkers* absorbed all Wilder's creative energy, especially when the words spun across the page "like silk off a spool."[78]

Since the star-struck days of his boyhood, when Thornton began poring over reviews and reports of German and Austrian theatrical productions, it had been "the height" of his ambition to write a play Max Reinhardt would be interested in directing. After the encouragement Reinhardt had given him, Wilder believed *The Merchant of Yonkers* would be that play. Reinhardt was now a distinguished member of the fast-growing community of European artists, directors, writers, and other intellectuals who sought refuge—and work—in Hollywood and New York. When Hitler ascended to power, the Nazis had begun to take over Reinhardt's theaters in Germany. He fled to the United States in 1934, forced by circumstances to start his life over at age sixty-one. By 1938 the Nazis had also taken over Reinhardt's beloved home near Salzburg—Schloss Leopoldskron, the Baroque palace he had spent years and a fortune restoring. He and his wife were now permanently exiled from Hitler's Germany and Austria.

Before Wilder left the East Coast to work with Reinhardt, he went to Philadelphia to see Ruth Gordon in the closing performance of *A Doll's House*, and escorted "dead-tired but adorable Ruthie home."[79] Since Rosamond Pinchot's death, Jed Harris had turned to Ruth again for friendship. Wilder admired her performance in his adaptation of Ibsen's play, and his enduring affection for Ruth inevitably intensified his growing animosity toward Harris. Wilder lent her his practical support whenever he could, checking on young Jones Harris when Ruth asked him to. "Jones has no fever," he wrote to her while she was visiting Woollcott in Vermont. "A little coughing in the a. m. but wears off later in the day. Sends his love and divers kissing noises to you and Mr. Wo'cot. . . . Boy's lungs in good condition, seems like."[80]

On June 11 Wilder accompanied Gordon to Hoboken, New Jersey, to see her off on a voyage to Europe. Harris was not on hand to say good-bye because Gordon's ten o'clock departure was too early in the morning for him. "As for me I loathe him," Wilder wrote to Woollcott from aboard the Santa Fe Chief, en route to Hollywood. "And if the train weren't rocking so I'd tell you some more stories about him, each more tiresome than the other."[81]

Wilder headed to Hollywood in June fully expecting to get right to work with Reinhardt on his proposed lavish productions of *Faust* and *The Blue Bird*, as well as the more modest production of *The Merchant of Yonkers*, all three planned for the California Festival. Reinhardt was famous worldwide for his colossal theatrical productions, magnificently staged and splendidly costumed. As a young director in 1905 he had orchestrated *A Midsummer Night's Dream* on a revolving stage decorated with a magical forest. In 1934, by then a theatrical legend, he made a two-million-dollar movie of the play. His stage productions of *The Miracle*, a religious epic, were international sensations—two thousand cast members in London, accompanied by a two-hundred-piece orchestra. The show ran for 298 performances on Broadway in 1924, and then, with a smaller cast, toured the United States for five years. On Broadway and during part of the tour, the Nun, one of the lead roles, had been played by the beautiful young Rosamond Pinchot, the socialite with no acting experience, whom Reinhardt had "discovered" aboard ship during a voyage to the United States in 1923.

In 1938 Reinhardt was fresh from his 1937 Broadway success with *The Eternal Road*, depicting the history of the Jews, with a cast of 350 actors, a wardrobe of seventeen hundred costumes, and the Manhattan Opera House on West Thirty-fourth Street renovated to accommodate a set that was an acre in expanse and four stories tall. The mammoth theater, which seated about 3,100 people, had been built by Oscar Hammerstein I in 1906, and by 1927 was being leased by Warner Bros. as a sound stage.

Reinhardt had staged Goethe's *Faust* many times at the Salzburg Festival he cofounded, and he was determined to do it again at the California Festival in 1938, but even for an international impresario, funding was almost impossible to find in that difficult Depression year.[82] Reinhardt was so overwhelmed with efforts to raise money and mount his festival that he had very little time that summer for Wilder and his play. But for the maestro, Wilder would wait.

Isabel joined Wilder in Hollywood, where they shared an apartment in the Villa Carlotta, a charming residential hotel on Franklin Avenue, built in 1927 and, at one time or another during the 1930s, housing such Hollywood folk as George Cukor, David O. Selznick, Edward G. Robinson, Louella Parsons, and Marion Davies. While Wilder waited for Reinhardt to summon him, he revised the first two acts of *The Merchant of Yonkers*, making some minor cuts, some changes in characterization, and a name change for one of the leads: Mr. Geyermacher became Mr. Vanderguildern and then Mr. Vandergelder—to evoke the "background of the Hudson River Dutch."[83] Wilder read the finished script of his play to Reinhardt and his second wife, the actress, Helene Thimig, whose "wonderful face and exquisite voice" Wilder admired.[84]

They loved the play, and he was growing very fond of them. "They've lost everything, live frugally," he wrote of the Reinhardts. "Obstacles arrive every day. The Chamber of Commerce has just vetoed the Blue Bird in Hollywood Bowl, and may cancel the Faust. Only my play will be left. . . . Think of what their daily mail must bring them as news of Vienna every day. Think of what they once knew, the palace on the Tiergarten in Berlin. But they never wince or sigh or allude to all that. I simply love them."[85]

Reinhardt made some helpful suggestions, which Wilder incorporated into the script of *The Merchant of Yonkers*, and he praised Dolly Levi's new monologue in act 4. Was it too earnest? Wilder asked nervously. Reinhardt assured Wilder that he was a poet, and that "in a comedy—near the end—there should always be one moment of complete seriousness and by that the audience can see that also the comedy parts are not just pastime."[86]

———

AS WILDER waited for Reinhardt in Hollywood, he contemplated the ruins of the summer. He could have been in New Hampshire, Maine, or Europe. But he understood Reinhardt's delays and his frustrations about money. In the end able to raise only a hundred thousand dollars, Reinhardt realized he could mount just one production for the California Festival, and chose to invest all his resources in *Faust*, which would open on August 23 in the outdoor Pilgrimage Theatre in Hollywood.[87] Because carpenters worked in the theater all day building the elaborate set—an entire village—Reinhardt held rehearsals at night. Wilder attended every rehearsal, marveling at the great director's stamina, drive, and attention to detail. During the days Wilder polished *The Merchant of Yonkers* and worked on a new play that had been fermenting in his imagination for some time—an ambitious drama based on the story of Alcestis. His imagination was crowded that August with seemingly disparate images. His own exuberant, often irreverent Dolly Levi and now the regal, tragic Alcestis mingled with Reinhardt's visions of Goethe's *Faust, Part One*—all these figures weaving into and out of Wilder's restless mind in the illusory light and shadows of Hollywood.

His *Merchant* had "improved immensely" under Reinhardt's "discrete suggestions," to the point, Wilder believed, that "a stone would love it."[88] But the theater world was one of "postponements, uncertainties and deferred hopes," he was learning, and more and more, it appeared that *The Merchant of Yonkers* would open not, as he had hoped, in Los Angeles in the summer, but in New York as late as December.[89]

BY SUMMER's end Wilder was caught up in a new adventure. "You shall be the first to know," he wrote to Woollcott. "I'm going on the stage." With very short notice Jed Harris asked him to replace Frank Craven as the Stage Manager in *Our Town* for two weeks so Craven could rest. "That is to say: I'm memorizing the lines. I'm insisting on two days' rehearsal with the Stage-manager before Jed sees me. (You can imagine how even the most shy and considerate suggestion from Jed would dry up my hypothetical art)." Wilder also confided in Woollcott that he had a "far better and more experienced and congenial coach" lined up to "encourage and guide" him. He was Dr. Otto Ludwig Preminger, who grew up in the Austro-Hungarian Empire, joined Max Reinhardt's acting company when he was seventeen, became a successful director, and arrived in Hollywood in 1935 to direct films for Twentieth Century-Fox. In 1937 Preminger had a disagreement with producer Darryl Zanuck over the script of *Kidnapped*, which Zanuck had written and assigned Preminger to direct. The conflict cost Preminger his job, and he was turning back to theater when he and Wilder met. Wilder hoped that with Preminger's help, he could "transfer the best of the lecturing experience" to acting—if he could only memorize the words he himself had written. "The memory hazards are *immense*," he wrote to Woollcott. He was afraid that he would make his play "spineless and boring," but he depended on Preminger—"honest as the day"—to tell him if he did.[90]

"All that memorization!" Wilder wrote to his mother. "On the train, in hotel rooms, etc. Jed only rehearsed me the last afternoon. The other days I worked with the Stage Manager. The day before the opening I was in despair. I thought I'd disgrace everybody, but 'opening night' was all right. And it's getting better every time."[91] Still he found that memorizing lines—even lines he had written himself—was "like walking a tight-rope of danger."[92]

What a year it had been. After his long apprenticeship in the theater, he had in the space of a single year achieved two successes on Broadway, and another Pulitzer Prize. *Our Town* had been runner-up to John Steinbeck's *Of Mice and Men* for the New York Drama Critics Circle Award as the best American play of the 1937–38 season.[93] *The Merchant of Yonkers* awaited its Broadway opening. He had stepped onstage into the role he had written for others to play, and survived without too much embarrassment. He wrote to Woollcott, "Anyway: what's life if it isn't risk, venture, taxes on the will-power, diversity, and fun?"[94]

27

"PERSEVERANCE"

Working perseverance: These two years of taking up subjects and dropping them, of desultory reading as an evasion from writing, of mixed activities have undermined what little collection-to-work I used to have.

—THORNTON WILDER,
journal entry 36, November 1, 1940

The United States and Europe (1938–1940)

Brought up to be a citizen of the world, Wilder was increasingly disturbed in 1938 by what he called the "new Ugliness abroad among the Children of Men who hate one another."[1] Sadly Wilder read in the newspapers about "Freud, 82, standing by calming his family while the [Nazi] Troopers ransacked his house."[2] What would become of the Freuds? What would happen to Gertrude Stein and Alice B. Toklas if they stayed in France in wartime, and how would Sibyl Colefax fare in England? There were countless other friends and acquaintances who lived in Europe—and others, such as Max and Helene Thimig Reinhardt, who had already taken refuge in the United States. President Roosevelt was struggling with Congress for authority to strengthen U.S. Army and Navy forces. Germany had taken over Wilder's beloved Austria. Maps were being fractured and reconfigured: Part of Czechoslovakia was ceded to Germany; Mussolini annexed Libya as part of Italy; Hungary wrested Slovakia from Czechoslovakia; and so it went.

Amid all the commotion in 1938, Wilder's personal and professional worlds seemed, at least temporarily, to be stable, harmonious, and full of promise. He had successfully translated and slightly adapted *A Doll's House* into a fresh English version of the play, which was promoted as a new acting edition.[3] Heartened by the Broadway success of *Our Town*, he was still waiting confidently for Max Reinhardt to turn his attention to a production of *The Merchant of Yonkers*, the new play Wilder described as "a broad farce with social implications," in a letter to Albert Einstein, who had written expressing his admiration for *Our Town*.[4]

The Merchant of Yonkers is an amalgam of stories and scenes from Johann Nestroy (who borrowed from English playwright John Oxenford's 1835 comedy, *A Day Well Spent*) and a passage from act 2, scene 5 of Molière's satirical *L'Avare* (*The Miser*, 1688), mingled with Wilder's long fascination with farce and a sampling of ideas about the psychology of money that Wilder and Gertrude Stein had discussed. These disparate elements coalesced in Wilder's imagination, and led to his invention of Dolly Levi, one of the strongest, savviest, most exuberant of the long line of remarkable women he created in drama or fiction.

When Wilder sat down for an interview with John Hobart of the *San Francisco Chronicle* in September 1938, he said, "Everything I have written has been a preparation for writing for the stage—my novels, my two volumes of one-act plays, my adaptations of Obey's *Lucrèce* and Ibsen's *A Doll's House*. I like to think of all that as an apprenticeship. For the drama, it seems to me, is the most satisfying of all art-forms."[5] His apprenticeship in writing drama actually gave way in 1938 and 1939 to a tough apprenticeship in getting his plays produced. At age forty-one he had achieved the remarkable feat of having two successful plays running simultaneously on Broadway—one translation/adaptation and one highly original drama, both directed by Jed Harris. In the contentious process of mounting *Our Town*, the Wilder-Harris friendship dissolved, with recriminations on both sides, but out of their bitter conflict the two achieved a stellar success and launched an American classic. Wilder had gladly entrusted his four-act farce to Max Reinhardt, the iconic director he had idolized since he was a teenager. He was convinced that Reinhardt would do his play masterfully. But if Wilder now regarded Harris with too much skepticism, he regarded Reinhardt with too much awe.

———

IN MID-SEPTEMBER in Hamden, still waiting for Reinhardt, Wilder the playwright and actor was supplanted by Wilder the son and brother. His mother and Janet were in Scotland when Isabel had to be hospitalized in New Haven for "a considerable operation," and the house and grounds on Deepwood Drive were badly damaged by the great New England hurricane of 1938 that struck Long Island and New England on September 21—the deadliest natural catastrophe to hit Connecticut since the great hurricane of 1815.[6] Wilder was playing the Stage Manager in *Our Town* the night the storm hit. Throughout New England an estimated six hundred to eight hundred people died and more than sixty thousand structures were demolished by the massive storm, which leveled forests and wiped out bridges, telephone service, and electricity. By the end of September, Wilder had dealt as best he could with the storm damage at home. Isabel was recuperating well from her surgery, and he was preparing to meet his mother and Janet at the boat and "break the news" of Isabel's operation and "the hurricane-torn house and grounds."[7]

Soon he was in New York, working full-time with Reinhardt at last on the production of *Merchant of Yonkers*, set to open in December.[8] "Rightly or wrongly I am being leaned upon," Wilder wrote to Woollcott as his days were crammed full—listening to readings as the play was cast, inspecting stage designs, and polishing the script.[9] At first he was thrilled. There were 'glorious uproarious times going on at the Windsor Theatre," he reported to Woollcott. "Reinhardt a great great man; his comic invention is dazzling; the actors adore him."[10]

Reinhardt and his producer, Herman Shumlin, conferred with Wilder on all major production matters, especially cast and set design. There were "casting agonies," Wilder confided to Bobsy Goodspeed.[11] He lobbied aggressively for Ruth Gordon to play Dolly Levi. Shumlin believed that she was too short, that she "might not satisfy us at the close of the play"—but Wilder knew that "she would be very funny, very brilliant, and carry all before her in the first three acts" because he had seen her "prodigious success" in London in the "low broad farce," William Wycherley's Restoration comedy *The Country Wife*. Wilder persuaded Shumlin, but when Gordon was approached about the role she did not commit to it. "She said that she liked the play and she knew that she would be good in the part," Wilder reported. "Perhaps she has some other production in mind; perhaps Jed Harris has prejudiced her against me."[12] He hoped they could persuade her, but in the end she wouldn't agree because, Wilder said, she distrusted Reinhardt as a director.[13]

The role ultimately went to Jane Cowl, although Wilder feared—correctly, as it turned out—that she was too much of a "tragedy-queen."[14] At first Cowl declined to take direction from Reinhardt, but soon she progressed, Wilder said, "from offended Bernhardt to adoring slave. Now it's all 'Professor, will you please read that line for me,' and 'I never worked under a great director before.' "[15]

Wilder was also asked his opinion of noted Russian painter and set designer Nicolai Remisoff's drawings for the sets—and he objected to them emphatically. "They are very attractive and skillful and full of wonderfully caught accuracy in details of architecture and furniture," Wilder wrote. "But they are very different from what I imagined for the play" because they were "thick, solid, heavy, actual and over-rich in detail and idea." He wanted the actors to have "the full attention of the audience—of painted canvas, none too fresh, just enough for sug-gestion of time and place." As *Our Town* had demonstrated, Wilder the playwright was convinced that the audience should put its imagina-tion to work on the stage settings, and the set should not "weaken" the "vitality of gesture and word." Wilder asked for and got another designer, Boris Aronson, who designed for the Group Theatre during the thirties.[16]

Reinhardt had his heart set on music for the play—singing as well as dancing and some instrumental background. Wilder resisted, however, afraid that music would "introduce an operetta unreality into the action," would "upset the characterization of the persons on stage," and, most of all, would "upset the American audience's attitude. Dance and . . . song does not, for them, mix well with real story-telling and real activity," Wilder explained.[17] Reinhardt won out in the end, and Wilder admitted that he liked the Vandergelder Recreational and Burial Society band, the Harmonia Gardens Restaurant waltzes. "But best of all," he said, "is the veiled pathos and sweetness of 15 lovable people out for a holiday."[18] (Reinhardt's determination to mix Dolly Levi and company with music and dance was vindicated with the metamorphosis of *Merchant* into *The Matchmaker* in 1955 and then into *Hello, Dolly!* in 1964.)

Wilder quickly found himself involved in every aspect of the production, as well as with ongoing revisions of the script in the mornings, and then sitting in on eight-hour-long rehearsals. "This afternoon the Professor, for the first time, ran through the Fourth Act," Wilder wrote Reinhardt's wife at midnight on November 20. "Even in a first reading like that what one saw was dazzling virtuosity in direction. Wonderful! As each character and situation developed all of us involved—including the Professor—would be shaken with laughter."[19] Wilder just hoped that everyone involved in the production, from producer Shumlin to the actor with the smallest role, would realize "the aspects of comic abandon and joy of life in the play."[20] His enthusiasm during rehearsals waned as time approached for the Boston tryout at the Colonial Theatre, beginning December 12. With a little more than two weeks to go until the December 28 opening, Wilder was increasingly distressed by what he saw onstage. Reinhardt's propensity for pageantry and high drama led to a heavy-handed, sometimes stiff and awkward production. The play was not coming to life as Wilder had envisioned it.

Woollcott spent one evening in Boston "helping the sorely beset Wilder get tight at the Copley-Plaza," he wrote to their friend Bob Hutchins.[21] After Woollcott saw the Boston tryout, he predicted that the production would fail, and he was right. He immediately discerned the major problem: Because Reinhardt inevitably infused the play with his European expectations of farce, there was a disconnect with the American audience and its affinity for broader, less stylized, more slapstick comedy. Jane Cowl as Dolly was ill at ease with farce, and openly nervous, with "near explosions daily."[22] Wilder believed that Percy Waram was miscast as the male lead.

The play opened in New York at the Guild Theatre December 28, 1938, starring Jane Cowl as Dolly Levi, Percy Waram as Horace Vandergelder, and the young Tom Ewell as Cornelius Hackl. Reviews were mixed but largely negative, box-office business was bad, and the play closed in January 1939, after only thirty-nine performances, and probably would have closed sooner but for the subscription tickets already sold to Theatre Guild members.

A FAILED play, like a successful one, is an equation of many parts—script, director, producer, actors, audience, the events that transpire onstage, and those that swirl around offstage and on the larger world stage. Wilder wrote a terse recapitulation to Stein and Toklas: "Suffice to say that that play which had taken from July to December to get produced, was damned by the critics and withdrawn."[23] He wrote to Sibyl Colefax that he hoped Woollcott was right to predict that *Merchant* would have a revival after a few years "in the American idiom, and declare and justify itself."[24]

He had learned "a great deal from the association with Reinhardt," Wilder wrote to a friend in January 1939, looking to the future. "I shall continue to write more and all I ask is that the public attend them sufficiently to subsidy the expense of my long apprenticeship. I recommend my plays ten years from now."[25] He told the Reinhardts that "no words could express the richness of such a privilege as watching the Professor work on a text of one's own, and all the stimulation of the personal association as well."[26] Harper & Brothers published the reading edition of the play on April 13, 1939, with Wilder's dedication to Reinhardt. Later Wilder called *Merchant* his "Ugly Duckling," and reiterated his hope that someday it would come into its own.[27]

He was discouraged and disillusioned in 1939, not only because of the failure of his play and his disappointment in himself—and in his hero, Max Reinhardt—but also because of "an unbroken succession of skullduggeries" perpetrated by Jed Harris. *Our Town* was still doing "good business," but was "withdrawn by Jed Harris in a paroxysm of spite against the leading actor and against me," Wilder said.[28] Harris was reportedly unhappy when he discovered that Frank Craven was earning more money each week than he was. Wilder wrote to the Reinhardts about Harris's action: "Jed Harris, in a fever of self-destruction, has closed the run of 'Our Town' in Chicago, although it was doing good business. Yes, something's the matter with a theatre where both my plays were closed, though they were doing better than $9,000 a week." He began to think that the American theater needed cheaper seats, and scripts and stages that fostered a "closer relation between the actor and the audience."[29]

Enthralled as he had been with Reinhardt's power and presence, Wilder ultimately had to accept the demise of *The Merchant of Yonkers*—but he was philosophical. He wrote to the Reinhardts from Mexico City in February 1939, "Lots of things turned out badly about our *Merchant of Yonkers*, but they fade into nothingness compared to the wonderful value for me of watching the Professor work, and the great privilege of learning to know you two better."[30]

Before the final curtain had come down on *The Merchant of Yonkers*, Wilder decided he would travel to a new place, and throw himself into work on a new project. He decided to pour his creative energy into the play he was calling *The Alcestiad: A Tetralogy, including The Alcestis of Euripides*, and he would go to Mexico to concentrate on his Greek drama.[31] He planned to spend two and a half months there, giving himself up to "Solitude; long walks; and work." He didn't want to "emerge into civilization" until he had finished two plays.[32]

He had sailed from New York January 20, but quickly discovered that while Mexico was beautiful and fascinating, he couldn't work there. The sunsets were enchanting—"red-gold over the foreground, with its bougainvilleas and oleanders and the mountains in the distance are in blue and purple veils and the tops of the volcanoes are rose snow," he wrote to Sybil.[33] But for a month he struggled with his work and then gave up on Mexico: "The altitude, the alkali dust, the national food, the misery and unrest below the surface, and the reminders of centuries of cruelty and bloodshed,—all combine to upset one's concentration," he told the Reinhardts. Nothing helped—not even his customary long walks.[34] ("I'm always harping on my walks," he wrote to Sybil, "but my walks are my work.")[35]

It is impossible to tell whether Wilder couldn't work in Mexico because of Mexico—or whether he just couldn't work, period. He was "wrestling" with his new play, *The Alcestiad*. The structure was clear to him, the "idea-life" was exciting, but he couldn't find the voice, the diction. "I keep trying to find an utterly simple English prose," he wrote to Sibyl, "but it keeps coming out like a translation of a Greek classic, at one moment, and like a self-conscious assumption of homely colloquial speech at the next. I foresaw that it would be hard, but not as hard as this."[36] He began to think he would have to write the play in blank verse, difficult as that would be. He was searching for "a plainness, a purity" of rhetoric, and he hoped that Texas would show him the way to it.[37]

Wilder was grappling with another major distraction by long distance. Not only had Jed Harris "gone into paroxysms of self-destruction" by closing the tour of *Our Town*, but he was threatening litigation over the amateur rights to the play. Wilder's agent and lawyers and Isabel were inundated with telegrams about Harris's demands for a "huge advance" and his "hairsplitting" arguments over percentages.[38] Desperate to escape into his work, Wilder moved on to Houston and Corpus Christi, Texas, which he found "cold and rainy and uncongenial"—except for a local gambling place where people called him Doc and, Wilder reported to Woollcott, he threw away some of his money, but discovered that "like all descendants of Scotch Presbyterian clergymen," he was "very lucky at dice."[39] Soon he abandoned Texas because he couldn't work there either. Where to go? For the time being he was needed in Hamden, as his mother was alone while Isabel was spending a month in New York "under the impression that 'life is passing her by.' "[40] He doubted he would get any work done in Hamden either, but duty called.

Wilder's goal of finishing *The Alcestiad* in 1938 had been deferred by his work on *Our Town* and *The Merchant of Yonkers*, but even when he was free of those projects, the new play was a struggle. It was a "golden subject," and if it defeated him, he thought the defeat would be only temporary, for there were many other subjects "crowding in the notebooks," he wrote to Sibyl, "and most of them come with innovations (i.e. revivals of lost excellences) of form." But he was absolutely sure of one thing: "There will be from me no repetitions of 'Our Town' but there will be the freest possible treatment of time and place."[41]

Back in Connecticut, Wilder found his restlessness intensifying, along with his frustration with Jed Harris, who was blocking all attempts at negotiations with "his exorbitant demands."[42] He dealt with the Harris business as best he could; conferred with Dwight Dana on other business matters; turned down an invitation to teach at Princeton; caught up with mail; at Dr. Freud's request, tried to help his nephew-in-law, now a refugee in the United States, find a job; spent time with his mother—and planned another trip to Europe. He decided to sail in early May for a week in London, a visit with Stein and Toklas in France, and a month working, and walking in the Fontainebleau forest.[43]

"Everyone is trying to dissuade me," he wrote to Reinhardt, "saying that even if I do not find war I will find such uneasiness that the trip will be valueless."[44] But he was determined to go to Europe anyway. Before his departure he accepted several acting engagements for summer theater performances of *Our Town*, and dealt with another headache: "The ugly possibility of having to go to law hangs over me," he told Reinhardt. "Mr. Jed Harris is threatening to sue me for not selling 'Our Town' to a certain motion-picture company. I hate lawsuits, but I am eager to establish that a writer cannot be forced to sell his work to a film company without some guarantee and safe-guard of sympathy and fidelity to the spirit of a text." Wilder hoped that the matter would be settled out of court, "but," he wrote, "it further delays my making plans and upsets my concentration of mind."[45]

Reinhardt was then directing his acting students in Los Angeles in what Wilder called his "hitherto almost neglected *Pullman Car Hiawatha*" and he asked if Wilder had a new play near completion. Wilder replied that since his aborted Mexican journey he could "feel many subjects hesitating, preparing, building,—and each one trying to clothe itself in its own appropriate form." He believed that a dramatist not only had to create a new play but also had to "each time create a new form." That ambitious but perhaps impossible challenge may have been at the crux of Wilder's inability to go forward with *The Alcestiad* or any other of the subjects "hesitating, preparing, building" in his imagination. He had created a new form with *Our Town* but was determined not to repeat himself. Besides, rooted as it was in Greek drama and mythology, the dramatization of the Alcestiad was not the most likely subject for innovations in form. Honoring the classical Greek dramatic convention of following a tragedy with a comic, often farcical satyr play, he had already conceived *The Drunken Sisters*, to conclude productions of *The Alcestiad*—but the play itself continued to defy him.

Wilder alluded to this search for form in an essay he was writing on Sophocles' *Oedipus Rex* in the fall of 1939: Noting that the play received the second prize at the Greek festival where it was first produced, Wilder suggested that the second prize "reminded us primarily that masterpieces are difficult. Their survival and the diversity in their appeal are evidence that they come to us from a removed thought-world not easy to penetrate. Sometimes their difficulty proceeds from an inner necessity on their authors' part continually to innovate in form and subject matter."[46]

He was possessed of that "inner necessity," and this helps to explain Wilder's migration from one genre to another and his "perseverance" in pursuit of his craft, as well as his "evasions"—the recurring periods of what appeared to be writer's block, and the long, sporadic intervals between the completion of one work and another. Vulnerable as he was to distractions, many of them self-imposed, Wilder was not so much a writer of fits and starts as one bent on a prolonged, continuous evolution and growth as an artist. He had learned early that no unfinished novel or play was a total waste of his time and creative energy, and that the creative struggle could be a concomitant and even a catalyst of growth. Wilder wrote to Reinhardt that his next play would "have been greatly helped exactly by the *fights* and resistances I had with the *Alcestis*-subject."[47] Meantime he put that play away, confessing to Max Reinhardt months later that he was "bitterly disappointed" that *Alcestis* "failed to come to birth."[48]

In Hollywood, Wilder's agent, Rosalie Stewart, was presenting him offers to write movie scripts, and "hammering" Jed Harris on "his likelihood of losing" his threatened lawsuit over the *Our Town* movie rights in arbitration.[49] Stewart, with Wilder's approval, proposed that Harris accept an outright cash offer of $7,000 from Wilder instead of the $12,500 he wanted. By early May, Harris had dropped his threat of a lawsuit, and Wilder could sail for Europe on May 6 with a clear conscience and a release from stress—at least until July 10, when he had to be back in the United States to begin rehearsals for his summer stock performances.

DESPITE ESCALATING tensions in Europe, Wilder spent six weeks of the summer of 1939 in France and in England. He especially savored his leisurely visits and talks with Stein and Toklas, and sometimes walked ten miles a day through the "endless" Fontainebleau forest. Wilder saw Harry and Clare Boothe Luce in Paris and, at their request, arranged for the Luces to visit Stein and Toklas. (Luce had left his wife and sons, obtained a divorce, and married Clare Boothe Brokaw in 1935.) Wilder enjoyed "some fine talks with Louis Jouvet and Jean Cocteau."[50] He had a poignant visit in London with Sigmund Freud, who was dying of cancer, and his daughter Anna. "Oh, I love him," Wilder wrote to Stein and Toklas afterward. "As always the occasion flowered into characterizing anecdote but it takes all my face and hands to tell it correctly so I'll save it until our next visit."[51]

Back in the United States in July, Wilder the writer tried to ignore his guilty conscience as Wilder the actor plunged into rehearsals for upcoming performances as the Stage Manager in *Our Town* in four different theaters (three in Massachusetts and one in Pennsylvania) with four different casts. Isabel helped her brother immeasurably that busy summer, driving him to Massachusetts and Pennsylvania, and taking care of business matters as well as the Deepwood Drive house. His performances that summer were "better and better," Isabel told Dwight Dana.[52] Wilder gave a lively account of his onstage role to Stein and Toklas. "It's been very successful. In places we've broken house records; chairs in the aisle; ovations; weepings. Being present at these repetitions I get to know the play pretty well and I find a lot to wince at in addition to some fine wincing at the actors' renderings, but I hope I've learned a lot that can go into future plays."[53] The acting stint that summer confirmed Wilder's belief that a playwright needed some first-hand experience as an actor in order to do justice to a script. Even so his conscience hurt, for he had not written a thing other than letters, most of them perfunctory, since he gave up on Mexico and Texas and abandoned *The Alcestiad*.

He was due a rest, however, after a remarkably productive decade of work—two novels, several one-act plays, adaptations of plays, collaboration on movie scripts, his work on several new full-length plays, and three Broadway productions. He began to relax by spending hours on a new literary obsession—James Joyce's new novel, *Finnegans Wake*, published in May 1939. Already it was one of his "absorptions and consolations" and his "midnight recuperation," he wrote. He spent most of his limited free time that summer "digging out its buried keys and resolving that unbroken chain of erudite puzzles and finally coming on lots of wit, and lots of beautiful things."[54] Wilder's keen interest in *Finnegans Wake* would last for the rest of his life, often providing diversion, stimulation, and companionship, but sometimes causing him a good deal of trouble.

———

GERMANY INVADED Poland on September 1, 1939, and England and France, as they were treaty-bound to do, declared war on Germany on September 3. Nearly 50 percent of Americans surveyed in a Gallup poll now believed that the United States would become involved in the war. Wilder was deeply worried about his friends in Europe, especially Stein and Toklas. "All the time I keep wondering what you are and will be doing?" Wilder wrote in September, as Stein and Toklas hunkered down to wait out one more war in Europe.[55] (They had survived World War I in England, France, Spain, and Majorca.) "Here we read newspapers and listen to radios all day. We built dream-myths of hope and alarm," Wilder wrote to Gertrude in September.[56] On their side of the Atlantic, she wrote him, she and Alice were linked to the world only by radio.[57]

The news from Europe in September 1939 reported catastrophe after catastrophe—on the Western Front, in Poland, in the Atlantic. Looking about for even some small way to help, Wilder made arrangements to give his Swiss *Our Town* royalties to an Austrian-German exile fund.

He would donate his English royalties to Paternoster Row in London after the December 29, 1940, Luftwaffe bombing of that traditional home of many publishers, including Wilder's British publisher, Longmans, Green.[58]

In late September 1939 Wilder retreated to Woollcott's island in Vermont, knowing that the private sanctuary would be full of congenial companions, including the actress Ethel Barrymore. There were "endless games of savage croquet, and crippling badminton and head-breaking pencil games," but Wilder managed to work, "cleaning up a lot of chores," reading some of the countless manuscripts people sent for his critique, and working on two new projects of his own. He was adapting the text of George Farquhar's 1707 Restoration comedy, *The Beaux' Stratagem*, at the request of the producer-director Cheryl Crawford.[59] Even though Wilder was making progress with the adaptation, he began to doubt that it would be a "practical entertainment" and he eventually set it aside unfinished; it would be completed by another playwright and performed after Wilder's death.[60]

In Hamden that September, Wilder was caught up in final negotiations for the sale of the *Our Town* movie rights. The independent producer Sol Lesser wanted to buy them and produce the film, and he wanted Wilder to write the screenplay. Wilder accepted the financial deal but declined to write the script, giving approval for Frank Craven, who had written a few minor screenplays, to work on a script with Lesser. A longtime friend and colleague of Walt Disney and Charlie Chaplin, Lesser was a shrewd, trustworthy businessman whose Principle Pictures and Principle Distributing Company were well-respected in the movie industry. He had made a lot of money producing B Westerns and a string of successful Tarzan movies, and *Our Town* would be a step in a new direction for him. Lesser paid $35,000 for the movie rights to the play, with 60 percent going to Wilder and 40 percent to Harris.

From the outset of the deal Wilder made it clear that he did not want a major role in planning or writing the movie because that would "inevitably lead to the general impression" that he had "completely authorized and was responsible for the final picture."[61] He was willing to meet briefly with Lesser in New York, and he would "always extend" to Lesser and the film his "cordial best wishes."[62] Wilder conferred with Lesser as promised and refused any payment for the consultation. Astounded that a writer would actually decline an offer of money, Lesser sent Wilder a snazzy radio in appreciation.[63]

In early October, Lesser sent Wilder the first rough draft of the script, prepared by Craven, and Wilder could not resist responding with detailed notes.[64] He believed that a stage play and a screenplay were essentially two different entities, two different art forms. He wrote to the ever-solicitous Sol Lesser in October:

> *I feel that now the point has come in the work, as I foresaw, when my feelings must often give way before those of people who understand motion-picture narrative better than I do. It's not a matter of fidelity to my text—since I doubt whether there has ever been a movie as faithful to its original text as this seems to be—it's just a matter of opinion, and my opinion should often give way before that of those who know moving pictures thoroughly.*[65]

Nevertheless Wilder sent Lesser pages of notes over the next few months, and Lesser more often than not embraced Wilder's suggestions. He urged Lesser to be bold, and to avoid the "danger of dwindling to the conventional. . . . I know you'll realize," Wilder wrote, "that I don't mean boldness or oddity for their own sakes, but merely as the almost indispensable reinforcement and refreshment of a play that was never intended to be interesting for its story alone, or even for its background."[66]

WILDER WAS restless to the point of rootlessness that fall, as writers often are when they are not deeply grounded in their work, but even for a self-anointed theater gypsy, the new plays wouldn't come. They eluded him, frustrated him, stymied him. *The Merchant of Yonkers* had left scars yet to heal, and Wilder seemed almost relieved to be distracted by Lesser and the movie. He hadn't been able to work in

Mexico or Texas or Connecticut. He had not written a page during his six summer weeks in England and France—and now, thanks to Hitler and company, working in Europe was at least temporarily out of the question. His head was "full of European places all the time," he wrote to Stein and Toklas. "I'm fretful not to be there,—there as place; I have no wish to be near it as war." He reiterated his concern about their safety: "If the war is to be long and terrible, should you be there with it all around you—especially should you be in Paris?"[67]

He could not work in his writing room in the house on Deepwood Drive, much as he loved his family. He needed a few weeks of work "in solitary confinement," and went to Atlantic City, New Jersey, where he followed events in Europe from the daily papers, with "hope and dread in every muscle."[68] For escape from current events and from writing, he lost himself in *Finnegans Wake*. He soon abandoned his solitary life in Atlantic City for New York, where he found an apartment, and tried to help arrange a U.S. lecture tour for Stein in hopes of getting her and Toklas safely out of France for the duration of the war. They refused to leave France, however, unless they were positive they could quickly and safely return.

By mid-November, Wilder was reasonably content in his new apartment at 81 Irving Place near Gramercy Park in Manhattan, enjoying the quiet and the privacy, exploring the city, and probing *Finnegans Wake*, which, he said, made "great inroads" into his time. He had "untangled some more of its knots, but there remain a million."[69] He loved having daily access to the theater—even Clare Boothe Luce's "dreadfully easy, emphatic and vulgar" anti-Nazi play, *Margin of Error*, and *Thunder Rock*, written by his friend and former student Robert Ardrey, directed by the young Elia Kazan for the Group Theatre, and "so immediate a failure that it is being withdrawn after a week."[70] Aleck Woollcott was starring as Sheridan Whiteside, the colorful character modeled on Woollcott himself, in *The Man Who Came to Dinner*, Moss Hart and George S. Kaufman's new smash hit on Broadway. (The actor Monty Woolley first played the role of Sheridan Whiteside in the original 1939 stage production of *The Man Who Came to Dinner*.

Wilder spent time with Charlotte, taking her to restaurants and theater performances. She was working on her mysterious new book, all the while patching together a meager living from her ongoing work for the WPA, and doing freelance editing and typing manuscripts— still refusing offers of financial help from her mother and her brothers. Thornton and Charlotte had seen "considerably more of each other, while he was in town in this more leisurely way," Charlotte wrote to Amos. "He seemed to enjoy walking across town to take in my neighborhood," she said, and her landlady, "although she manages to conceal it behind a worn discouraged harridan's aspect, is a-flutter. I get the benefit of the prestige."[71]

Mabel Dodge Luhan, also in New York, arranged for Wilder to read and interpret eight pages from *Finnegans Wake* at one of her salons. For that gathering Wilder passed out mimeographed sheets "reprinting the first three paragraphs" of Joyce's novel, along with "the Nocturnes on p. 244 and the close from 626," he wrote to Edmund Wilson afterward. It turned out to be a boisterous evening at Luhan's apartment, overcrowded with people coming out of curiosity about Joyce's novel, or about Wilder or Mabel herself, and latecomers being turned away and "pounding on the door."[72]

Wilder was addicted to the novel, he told Stein and Toklas, obsessed with decoding that unbroken chain of complicated, erudite puzzles: "I've only skimmed the surface, but I know more about it than any article on it yet published. Finally I stopped, and put it away from me as one would liquor or gambling."[73] He soon relapsed, however, reopening *Finnegans Wake* and spending "hundreds of hours" on it, and planning a visit with Edmund Wilson so that they could discuss the novel at length.[74]

Looking back on the past few months, however, Wilder was exasperated with himself for his inertia and his "shocking busyness over trifles."[75] Despite his adamant disclaimer that he could not help with the *Our Town* film script, he had spent hours during those months in New York poring over letters and screenplay drafts from Sol Lesser, attentive down to the smallest detail of script and camera angles. Lesser not only solicited and encouraged him, but at least as far as their letters reveal, genuinely welcomed and incorporated most of Wilder's ideas, respecting his wishes to restore certain cuts to the original script, and to abandon certain changes. Lesser proposed, for instance, that the film set up some conflicts in Emily and George's marriage—conflicts that were Emily's fault and that she would understand and regret only after her death. Wilder replied that for several explicit reasons, he felt "pretty concrete about trying to dissuade you against showing Emily returning to her fifth wedding anniversary and regretting that she had been an unwise wife."[76]

The most significant change Lesser made had to do with Emily's death. "The first serious thing to decide is whether we should let Emily live or die," Lesser wrote to Wilder, offering the reasons for and against such a major departure from the stage play.[77] The ultimate decision was to let Emily live. "In the first place, I think Emily should live," Wilder responded:

> *I've always thought so. In a movie you see the people so close to that a different relation is established. In the theatre they are halfway abstractions in an allegory; in the movie they are very concrete. So insofar as the play is a Generalized Allegory, she dies—we die—they die; insofar as it's a Concrete Happening it's not important that she die; it's even disproportionately cruel that she die. Let her live—the idea will have been imparted anyway.*[78]

In late November, Lesser considered and then decided against calling in Lillian Hellman to help Frank Craven with the screenplay. The on-screen credit went to Wilder, Craven, and screenwriter Harry Chandlee. Lesser hired Sam Wood, the director of *Goodbye, Mr. Chips*, to direct the film. By early December 1939 the script was in such good shape, and Wilder had done so much—without pay—to make that possible that Sol Lesser looked about for a tangible way to express his appreciation. On December 4 he telegraphed Isabel Wilder: WHAT MAKE OF CAR WOULD THORNTON LIKE FOR CHRISTMAS.

Isabel telegraphed Lesser in Hollywood the next day: THORNTON DOESN'T DRIVE ANY MORE BUT HAS ALWAYS SAID IF HE HAD CAR

WANTED A CHRYSLER CONVERTIBLE WITH RUMBLE SEAT.[79] A surprised and delighted Wilder wrote to Lesser the day after Christmas
to tell him he now owned "the most beautiful car in town." Everyone
home for Christmas was "squealing" with pleasure. "Everybody had to
be taught all the gadgets," Wilder wrote:

> *When they found there were little red lights that went on when your*
> *oil and gas were low—that slew 'em; and the two speeds on the wind-*
> *shield—oh, and the defroster; and a top that goes up and down without*
> *anybody losing their temper. Well, well—first I was so astonished I*
> *didn't know what to do, but ever since I've been getting more proud and*
> *pleased every hour. A thousand thanks, Sol! I wish you were here to see*
> *what a big success it is.*[80]

Wilder decided that when he left New York he would take his new
car "and drive far away."[81] He wrote to Gertrude and Alice, "That
movie producer gave me a beautiful car for Xmas and soon I shall be out
on the road—sleeping in tourist-camps and drawing near to the first
tumble-weeds and the desert." After his city life he was ready for "air
and light and sky."[82]

———

AS THEY moved forward in the new decade, all the Wilders were fine,
according to the roundup of family news Thornton sent to Stein and
Toklas. Isabella was in good health and enjoying her life in Hamden,
content to stay at home for a while after her recent journey to Scotland,
especially with the growing tumult in Europe. Isabel "at last" had a
job—as assistant to the supervisor of the Connecticut branch of the
Federal Writers' Project. Janet was teaching at Mount Holyoke after
finishing her Ph.D. at the University of Chicago. Amos's new book,
The Spiritual Aspects of the New Poetry, would be published by Harper &
Brothers in 1940, and he and Catharine were expecting a baby. Their
son, Amos Tappan Wilder, was born in Boston on February 6, 1940.
    Charlotte's second book of poetry, *Mortal Sequence*, dedicated to her
mother, came out in 1939, to small sales and mixed reviews, unlike her

first book, *Phases of the Moon*, winner of the Shelley Memorial Award, given annually by the Poetry Society of America to honor a living American poet on the basis of merit and need. Charlotte had shared the 1936 prize with the poet Ben Belitt, and the honor had opened doors to ongoing friendships with other writers, including the Irish poet and novelist Padraic Colum.[83] This award, over time, was remarkably prophetic of distinguished careers in poetry: Previous winners included Conrad Aiken, Archibald MacLeish, and Lola Ridge, and among those in the 1940s would be Marianne Moore, e. e. cummings, Edgar Lee Masters, Robert Penn Warren, and John Berryman. Charlotte's career, unfortunately, would be short-lived.[84]

Like her versatile siblings, Charlotte was writing in more than one genre. "Charlotte will have after many years a volume of prose ready this spring—Proust-like evocations of her childhood in Berkeley and China," Wilder told Stein and Toklas, unaware, like the rest of the family, of how hard his gifted sister was struggling to finish her book.[85]

Meanwhile Wilder had embarked on a writing project of his own in February 1939, beginning a new journal "in order to discipline my thinking, in order to have thoughts, and in order to improve my thinking."[86] This 1939–41 journal turned out to be the most profound instrument of self-revelation and analysis that Wilder had yet created. In 1940, when he was filling pages and pages with single-spaced text, the journal also absorbed much of his creative energy and, as intense journal writing can do, satisfied the urge to write to the point of subverting his literary work. He had kept journals before, filling them with ideas for novels or plays, passages from works in progress, copies of letters written or received, notes on his reading, random accounts of his nocturnal dreams, and sporadic reflections on his daydreams and doubts. For the most part those journals were repositories for the strivings and experiments of a working writer.

The journal he wrote in 1939–41 was a different endeavor, however. It would focus on the inward life of Wilder the man more than that of Wilder the writer. In it he wrestled with what he called his chronic "easy fatigue, flagging concentration, and bad habits." While he analyzed in depth his failings as a writer, he was far more profoundly

concerned with his failures as a thinker. "I had long noticed," he confessed, "that my thoughts on some given subject . . . ran into confusion
or ran off the track or fell into a meretricious elaboration which was
able to bedazzle (yet untrouble) the unthinking but which left me with
despair and self-contempt."[87]

He could edit and berate himself ruthlessly after a speech or even
a conversation. The Wilder who could "bedazzle" an audience with
his eloquence and wit was privately beset with doubts and "stage-
fright"—"so much," he wrote, "that I turned with hope and yet with
alarmed self-distrust and *watched myself* try to jump the gate." His intense search for modes of thought and speech carried over to his search
for literary form. He sought to make all his expression, whether written
or spoken, substantial, profound, original, unique. His expression had
to be organic to the subject. It had to be masterly. "I soon came to see
that the practice of reflection alone—even on the long walks which
have provided me for twenty years with all that is my best in that very
different activity, imaginative composition—would for me, be fruitless," he wrote.

Instead of doing some of his best thinking on those habitual
walks, he decided, he would now "require a more exacting method"
of thought. He believed he could best achieve that by writing in his
journal with disciplined precision "to prevent mere word mosaic and
self-deception." He aimed "to create a habit and a relation between
thinking and writing," and to record in the journal "a reservoir of
more codified ideas on which to base the judgments I am so often
called upon for in conversation." He hoped that from these practices
he could "proceed to the ability to reflect without writing and build
up the power of 'unflurried' thinking in the thousand occasions in
daily life."[88] As the journal unfolded, this "unflurried" thought would
encompass his explorations of *Finnegans Wake*; his theory of the novel
as a literary form; his search for the subject of his next play; his work
on the novel about Julius Caesar that he was now calling *The Top of the
World*, a novel that would not be published until 1948, when it was
titled *The Ides of March*; and his thoughts on moralizing, on happiness
and unhappiness in fiction, on motion pictures, on tone in tragedy and

comedy, on actors, on sentimentality and obscenity, on religion and psychoanalysis—and on the war.

He longed to see Stein and Toklas and to hear their close-up perspectives on the war. "I don't like my own and I don't like anybody else's," he wrote to them.

On many nights during his sojourn in New York he had walked down to the Battery to listen to "the waves slapping the sea-wall" and to think of his friends "across the million waves."[89]

IN THE spring, back in Hamden, Wilder took driving lessons so he could prove to his family that he wasn't incompetent, and so he could take his "beautiful car" out on the road.[90] He wanted to travel "in and out of hundreds of American villages."[91] He passed his driver's license examination in late March, he reported to Woollcott. This was a significant feat, for in earlier years, to the dismay of his family, Wilder had declined to get a license. When he was learning to drive in Peterborough, New Hampshire, years earlier, he had obtained his first license only after being "tactfully" warned by the local sheriff that one was required. Later, after Wilder skidded and broke the back axle and a wheel of his first car, he stopped driving for a long time. He preferred for someone to drive him "hither and yon," Isabel confided to Dwight Dana in 1931. But sometimes, she said, "in the enthusiasm of the moment," he would set out alone in his car, "zig-zagging down the road," leaving his anxious family behind. Wilder did many things well, but driving was never one of them.[92] "At present," he wrote, "it seems to me that I hate driving and automobiles. Like I hate typewriters."[93] He preferred walking to riding in cars, traveling by ship to flying, and writing with pencil or ink on paper to typing. Sometimes, however, certain modern conveniences were unavoidable, even if they were basically just a "lot of metal."[94]

Wilder set out in the Chrysler convertible on April 1 for a long, leisurely trip south, paying a brief visit to his aunt Charlotte in Winter Park, Florida, and going on for a solitary stay in Saint Augustine. As he traversed the East Coast in his new convertible, he paid far too little attention to his driving, as he noted in his journal May 2, 1940: "Having resumed automobile-driving after eleven years I notice more clearly that my real danger as a driver is that my 'thinking' employs such concrete imaginative forms that it steals my attention from the process of driving." He found that even his "banal" thoughts about passing scenery, or people he saw along the roadside (especially the convicts working along Florida's highways), or memories of past events or anticipation of future ones, were "dramatized to such an extent that I am, as it were, wrapt up into them."[95]

Fortunately he managed to drive himself safely to Florida and home again, staying in tourist camps along the way "On this trip I've lived in Tourist Camps," he wrote to Stein and Toklas, "elbow-close to my fellow-census numbers among the 130 millions."[96] Forerunners of the American motels, tourist camps evolved as alternatives to hotels, which were not the most convenient accommodations for dusty, road-weary travelers or for their automobiles, which had to be housed some-where, often in livery stables. When automobile travelers took matters into their own hands and camped out overnight along the roadside, in parks, or even on private property, many towns and cities began build-ing free municipal tourist camps equipped with cabins, picnic tables, fireplaces, showers, and toilets. When the camps began to be overrun by riffraff—criminals, prostitutes, and noisy college students—owners imposed rental fees, and the modern motel was born.

Wilder was back in Connecticut in mid-May. On June 18 he was scheduled to be the guest of honor at a reception and dinner at the Hotel Taft in New Haven when *Our Town* opened in the movie theater in that city, just in time for the twentieth reunion of his Yale class. But first he would escort Isabel to the gala premiere of Sol Lesser's film in Boston on May 22. The governors of Massachusetts and New Hamp-shire joined Boston's mayor at the premiere—an event so dazzling that Wilder feared it was enormously inappropriate during a time of war. The news from Europe was grim: The Nazis had taken Antwerp, Bel-gium, on May 18. There were reports that the French 9th Army had been destroyed. The Allies were gearing up for Operation Dynamo, a mammoth effort to save Allied troops at Dunkirk. The Germans were within days of subduing Calais, and Luftwaffe bombers were pummeling targets in France. Against that global backdrop, Wilder had little heart for the Hollywood-style celebrations of *Our Town*.

The movie was welcomed with "glittering fanfare" in Boston instead of the "indifference" that greeted the opening of the play in that city in 1938.[97] According to the *New York Times* critic Bosley Crowther, "There is reason to hope this morning, to find renewed faith and confidence in mankind—and, incidentally, in the artistry of the screen." He found in the film a "tonic and reassuring avowal of the nobility that resides in just plain folks."[98] The film garnered good reviews and good box office, and received an Academy Award nomination for Best Picture (although the prize would go to *Rebecca*, the first American-made film directed by Alfred Hitchcock). More important, just as *Our Town* spoke to theater audiences during the Depression, the movie resonated with the American audience in what Wilder described to friends as that time of "vast and terrible events," when each day seemed "more in crisis than the last."[99]

28

"SEEING, KNOWING AND TELLING"

In fact, it's not so much a matter of emotion at all, as it is of seeing, knowing and telling.
—THORNTON WILDER,
journal entry 34, November 1, 1940

The United States and Canada (1940s)

In the summer of 1940 Wilder planned to settle down to hard work at the MacDowell Colony, occasionally indulging in the distraction of *Finnegans Wake*. He had picked it up again "after a long recess," he wrote to Edmund Wilson, one of the few people he knew who shared his avid interest in the novel. He told Wilson, "I think I'm stuck," for he was alternately obsessed and exasperated with Joyce's "damned tricks."[1] On June 3 he told Wilson:

> I discovered the key to Finnegans Wake, "the figure in the carpet," and the meaning of 1132.
> The subject matter of this letter is plain nasty, but it'll be over soon.
> F———gans W———treats anal eroticism plus coprophilia plus stercophagia and that's all it's about and it isn't about anything else. It's buried in every five words of it. Even that beautiful last eight pages is deep in it.
> Millions of those words are to be read backwards, sometimes slightly anagramatized, sometimes as a whole word, and sometimes syllable by syllable.[2]

At first, Wilder wrote, "I thought I was imagining it and that I'd fallen into a prurient miasma." But he went on to give Wilson vivid details to support his thesis. All in all, Wilder contended, the novel read this way revealed a "triumph of Neurosis," along with some "secondary thoughts," including: "How overwhelmingly the book illustrates Freud's definition of the type anal-erotic: order, neatness, single-minded economy of means. The neurotic's frenzy to tell and not tell. . . . Joyce's beady-eyed delight as the critics grope for the cosmological message. . . . The unsettling thought of the figure in the carpet of many works in literature."[3]

"I was very much interested in your letters," Wilson quickly replied, "but I think you're exaggerating the importance of the anal element—which has always been present in Joyce. . . . Don't you think, after all, that he means to present it as merely mixed up with all the other elements of the human situation?" Wilson agreed, however, with Wilder's earlier idea that the family was the "fundamental symbol" in the novel.[4]

There was "a lot more evidence there that I didn't feel like committing to the Postal Service," Wilder retorted, but he joked that he "tore up" his notes "in wild indignation," and hoped later in the summer to visit Wilson and discuss the issue further.[5] In his letter rejecting Wilder's latest theory about *Finnegans Wake*, Wilson sent along another compliment for *Our Town*, which he had greatly admired on the stage, and had just read in a paperback edition he bought at a newsstand. He still found it "certainly one of the few really first-rate American plays."[6]

In June, Wilder was once again sequestered in the "deep green shade and solitude" at the MacDowell Colony, and—"at last"—he found the subject for his new play. He recorded it in his journal on July 6, 1940: He had begun the play on Monday, June 24, in the Veltin Studio at MacDowell, and quickly finished the first act. During those years of global upheaval Wilder had despaired over the "difficulty of finding a subject." He wrote in his journal that summer, "During the last year subject after subject has presented itself and crumbled away in my hand. Can this one hold out?"[7] He fervently hoped so. He was calling the new play *The Ends of the Worlds*. As the first draft of the first act began to take shape on the page, Wilder wrote, "I've at last found a subject that 'permits' perseverance."[8]

THE WAR was very much on his mind, as his journal reveals. "What are some of the primary reflections that keep returning to the mind in the face of so vast an irruption of evil?" he had written in his journal in late May. He was increasingly cut off from communication with friends in England and France, and, with daily dread, he depended on radio and newspaper accounts to track the proliferating war. He speculated about what it all meant and where it would lead. "Democracy is the government-form toward which the world moves, but one which requires as long an education of the people to maintain it as it requires a painful struggle to acquire," he reflected.[9] He wrote in his journal about the role of the artist in the modern world: "This irruption of evil should show all the more clearly that [the artist's] work is to write Pure poetry, pure novel, and pure drama."[10]

As his thoughts on the war crystallized his theory of the artist's role in society, Wilder resolved to write "pure drama." Soon afterward he began writing *The Ends of the Worlds*, which he eventually renamed *The Skin of Our Teeth*—a title evoking Job 19:20: "My bone cleaveth to my skin and to my flesh, and I am escaped with the skin of my teeth." Wilder decided that his new play about the "ordeals that man has had to pass through, including the Ice Age" would be a comedy—at first glance a strange choice for a drama about war, catastrophe, and the universal human family. He wrote to Austrian dramatist and poet Richard Beer-Hofmann, "In this one it seems I call upon still free-er uses of the stage, as to scenery, time, abstraction and audience collaboration." He recognized that it would be "Difficult, difficult," he said, "but I hope I can 'get it right.'" The method would be "buffoonery and *lazzi* [jokes]." The play, Wilder wrote, "has all colors in it—violence, anguish, detailed realism of the contemporary American scene, and low comedy."[11]

Wilder had spent two years in a fruitless search for subject and form, and now his play emerged full force from the firestorm of war. The world war compelled him to confront the universal sweep of human experience. He was writing a play "in which the protagonist is [a] twenty-thousand-year-old man and whose heroine is [a] twenty-thousand-year old woman and eight thousand years a wife."[12] He tried to describe it to Max Reinhardt: "All I can say of the play is that it is about the sufferings of the human race—including the Ice Age, and the Flood—told in riotous low comedy, with a pathos that never comes to the surface."[13]

Why comedy, for such a tragic subject? Like Joyce, Wilder would have to invent a style that would do justice to the subject. "Happier ages than our own could do it—or some aspects of it—in the purity of the lyric, the morality play, or in the relative simplicity of the *Prometheus Bound* and the *Oedipus*," he wrote in his journal, "but in this century and above all, in these times, there has been added to the difficulty that of avoiding the pathetic, the declamatory, and the grand style. The only remaining possibility is the comic, the grotesque, and the myth as mock-heroic."[14]

This play was in many ways the most difficult creative work he had ever undertaken—but in the process he was discovering essential lessons about his craft. Heretofore he had often begun writing a novel or play only to abandon it when it didn't go well. Then he had come to recognize that the half-born or stillborn projects in his notebooks had, for the most part, not wasted his creative energy but redirected it. Now he was so committed to this new idea for a play that he felt he could not give up on it even if he was "writing it all wrong." He wrote in his journal, "It presents problems so vast and a need of inspiration so constant that all I can do is to continue daily to write it *anyhow* in order to keep unobstructed the channels from the subconscious and to maintain that subconscious in a state of ferment, of brewing it."[15]

Throughout his writing life he had "been convinced of the fact that the subconscious writes our work for us, digests during the night or in its night the demands we make upon it, ceaselessly groping about for the subject's outlets, tapping at all the possibilities, finding relationship between all the parts to the whole and to one another."[16] He was even more sure of this one night when he was "turning over the play in feverish insomnia," and suddenly saw the resolution of his dilemma about a particular scene. "A few more such revelations," he wrote, "and I shall be building a mysticism of the writing process, like Flaubert's: that the work is not a thing that we make, but an already-made thing which we discover."[17]

He wanted to infuse his play with pure, genuine emotion—no "false pumped-up emotion—or an anemic emotion which ekes out itself in whimsical fancies. In fact, it's not so much a matter of emotion at all," he concluded, "as it is of seeing, knowing and telling." He applied that formula to his play in progress: "In so far as I see, know, and tell that the human race has gone through a long struggle (Act One) it is legitimate that I cast the consideration in the form of modern man and his home; and precisely to avoid false heroics—in this time, of all others—that I cast it in comic vein." He hoped, he said, that "at least, I bring to it my sense of making the whole stage move and talk, and my characteristic style, which weaves back and forth between the general and the particular."[18]

By mid-July, when Wilder packed up his journal and manuscript and left the MacDowell Colony to return to New Haven, he had finished the first act of *The Skin of Our Teeth*.[19]

"EARLY FALL, I was busy talking and broadcasting and signing manifestos for the British, etc., and for Roosevelt," Wilder wrote to a friend. "Then I retired from the whole whirlpool and went to Quebec for two months—work, long walks and reading the papers."[20]

"I love it here, but it's not reciprocated," Wilder wrote to Woollcott from Quebec in October 1940.[21] He had driven his Chrysler to Canada in pursuit of solitude and a "working hermitage" where he could immerse himself in the new play.[22] He could see the steep streets of Old Quebec and the glistening St. Lawrence River from the window of his comfortable room in the Château Frontenac—a far cry from the tourist camps where he stopped overnight en route to Canada. He had barely gotten settled, however, when he was summoned to the local post office. "My family carelessly forwarded to me a magazine edited in Zurich," Wilder explained to Woollcott:

I was called into the Post Office and the words "printed in Germany" were pointed out to me on the third page. It is being carried up to higher and higher authorities who are looking for cryptograms in the pages of Corona whose only fault is that it's overprecious. I suspect my rooms of being sifted while I'm out. . . . While I take these endless walks—I presume some poor Intelligence Officer is darting behind trees and burning up shoe leather at my heels.[23]

Unknown to Wilder as he joked about being under surveillance in Quebec, the FBI was actually investigating him in earnest in the United States. During the summer of 1940, Wilder had crisscrossed New England, driving his Chrysler from New Haven and Hamden to Woollcott's Neshobe Island on Lake Bomoseen, Vermont, to the Mac-Dowell Colony in Peterborough, New Hampshire, back to Hamden, and then back to Neshobe. He also drove to Gloucester, Massachusetts, for a stint as the Stage Manager in *Our Town*, a role he had played more than sixty times by early December 1940.[24] "I'm acting in my play again," he wrote to Stein and Toklas. "The world's weather has done something to the reception of the play—the last act always was sad—now it's convulsive—Lordy, I never meant that!"[25]

On or about July 19, 1940, as Wilder drove from Hamden to Neshobe Island in Vermont, he apparently stopped to visit friends in Keene, New Hampshire, for his car was spotted at an alleged Austrian "Refugee Camp" located on an estate near Keene—"under suspicion as a possible center of operations for a group of German spies." An FBI agent investigating the rumor of espionage based his information largely on an interview with "a girl who is employed at the Eskimo stand," an ice-cream shop and dance pavilion near the estate. The proprietor of this enterprise told the FBI agent a hair-raising tale about the supposed goings-on at the alleged spy camp: The Austrian refugees appeared to the Eskimo-stand staff to be engaged in secret activities led by a man they called the "Captain," who had supposedly commanded a "U-Boat or a destroyer in the World War" and was now "dominating" the "elderly lady" who owned the estate. Some people who sounded as if they were Germans came and went in cars, but the FBI investigator had obtained only one license number for an automobile observed at the camp—Connecticut 1940 License WW-69. The FBI set out to "ascertain all available registration data" on the car, and to "conduct a preliminary investigation to determine the apparent activities and occupation of the person to whom this car is registered."[26]

The culprit who owned the car was Thornton Niven Wilder of Hamden, Connecticut, who, when he was not possibly consorting with alleged spies, was a man of "excellent reputation" and a World War I veteran, according to a subsequent FBI report filed on January 9, 1941. "His occupation is that of a writer and teacher and he has spent a great deal of his time at a writers' camp in Vermont. No information received would link subject Wilder with any espionage or subversive activities."

Another report issued on December 8, 1940, divulged that Wilder had "lived in Hamden a good many years and has a good reputation, no police record and no credit record."[27] It reported details of his World War I service (including the fact that at that time he was five feet nine inches tall, with blue eyes, dark hair, and a medium complexion). The FBI report further noted that Wilder owned his house at 50 Deepwood Drive, that it had an assessed tax value of $25,000, and that he lived there with his mother and sister. While Wilder's name was on the Republican voting list of Hamden, he had "boosted for President Roosevelt this last election." Two cars were registered in his name—the green Chrysler that had gotten him into trouble, and a 1937 Plymouth coupe he had bought for his mother and Isabel.

The Hamden sources also "disclosed that Wilder has an excellent reputation in Hamden and that it was not felt that he is engaged in any activities inimical to the welfare of this government."[28] Even though Wilder was cleared, the refugee camp was the subject of ongoing surveillance—and the FBI file on the matter continued to bear his name. Furthermore, in December 1941 "a source of known reliability" alerted the FBI that Wilder's name appeared on a list of supporters of the National Federation for Constitutional Liberties in New Haven. The FBI could not substantiate this information, but that organization and others showing Wilder's name on mastheads, pamphlets, or petitions were later cited by the U.S. attorney general "as subversive organizations within the purview of Executive Order 9835."[29]

With or without Wilder's knowledge, his name appeared on the roster of numerous organizations—including the National Committee of the American Committee for Struggle Against War (1933), the American Committee of the American League Against War and Fascism (1935), the Second National Congress of the League of American Writers (1937), the American Committee for the Protection of Foreign Born (1940), and the National Committee for People's Rights (1941). In addition, the FBI reported, in 1939 Wilder was one of "36 prominent writers" who wrote to Congress urging support of federal arts projects.[30] FBI attention to Wilder, as to many Americans, accelerated.

For the time being, however, as an active, concerned, highly informed, true-blue American citizen, Wilder was working hard to help friends and friends of friends who were exiles from Austria and Germany. He was "deep in Austrian exiles," he wrote, trying to find "teaching posts and pension grants etc., etc., for teachers and writers," including Freud's nephew-in-law, Dr. Ernst Waldinger, a poet, essayist, and translator. He was also trying to help Max Reinhardt establish a drama school in New York or in a New England college.[31]

During those months in 1940 when the FBI was checking out the information provided by the Eskimo-stand employees and various anonymous sources, Wilder was engaged in a number of patriotic activities, including picnicking with Eleanor and Franklin Roosevelt at a gathering of writers and artists at Val-Kill Cottage in Hyde Park, New York. The Roosevelts invited them for a cookout and a discussion of world events, and Wilder and others sat around an open fire cooking hamburgers and hot dogs, and talking about vital issues of the day with the first lady and the president. Mrs. Roosevelt was so impressed by the conversation that she invited some of her guests to speak on September 17, 1940, on an NBC radio program sponsored by the Women's Division of the Democratic National Committee. Participants along with Wilder were Marc Connelly, Edna Ferber, Katharine Hepburn, the playwrights Elmer Rice and Robert Sherwood, and the mystery writer Rex Stout, among others.

Even though she had found Wilder's *Our Town* sad and depressing, Eleanor Roosevelt greatly admired Wilder and his work. He inspired the country, she said as she introduced him to the radio audience, with his "true picture of all the 'Our Towns' which make up our country," and with his "deep faith in America." Wilder spoke on the broadcast about the importance of every single vote—the blood that had been shed to make voting possible, and the significance of each vote in the "slow rising tide of curbs against absolute power." He had briefly doubted the power of democracy early in the Depression, he said, when the country was "in confusion and distress" and the government seemed "sluggish, timid and self-centered." He had worried that "it takes the administration in a democracy scores of years to move from any one point to any other point." Then, he said, President Roosevelt stepped in and showed him that "democracy can move and create and represent us all." Wilder reminded the radio audience that in a "still larger world of confusion and danger," Americans must vote "not only with the country, but with the whole world in mind."[32] His afternoon with the Roosevelts at Hyde Park, followed by the radio broadcast, and then a long talk with Woollcott, also set Wilder to thinking about "the nature of the Public Mind and how it can be coerced or persuaded," and about the dangers of propaganda, whether its purposes were good or evil.[33]

"Our country is being rent by the coming election," Wilder wrote to Sybil Colefax September 26, a few days after his picnic with the Roosevelts. "There is something exhilarating about the very violence of the partisanship. I am fanatically for Roosevelt and of course a large part of my feeling is that more than any man in the country he sees all that we can and must do for the Allies and can put the measures into effect, skillfully driving through the oppositions." He predicted that Roosevelt would win. "The opponents' charges that he is usurping autocratic powers, that he is 'conceited', that he is buying the people's votes with public works, that he is inciting to class-warfare, that he is corrupting the American character by creating a dole population—each of these can be answered so easily," Wilder wrote. He thought this opposition to the president came from "deep visceral resentment envy-grudge against the Superior Man. Roosevelt is not a great man, but he's disinterested, tireless, and so instinctively active and creative that *his bravery* about it *does not look like bravery*; free from fanaticism; without spite or retaliation. . . . The great thing is that he's always doing things and most of them are good."[34]

IN QUEBEC that autumn Wilder worked steadily on his new play, but there were days when he knew he was "writing it all wrong."[35] He believed he had "one advantage," however: "the dramatic vehicle as surprise. Again by shattering the ossified conventions of the well-made play the characters emerge *ipso facto* as generalized beings."[36] As he sculpted his female characters in the play—where "*a* Woman is so quickly All Woman"—Wilder recorded in the journal his "favorite principle that the characters on the stage tend to figure as generalizations, that the stage burns and longs to express a timeless individualized Symbol. The accumulation of fictions—fictions as time, as place, as character—is forever tending to reveal its true truth: man, woman, time, place." He reflected that "the operation of such an activity must be recognized: when man and woman are regarded in their absolute character that character is pejorative: man is absurd; woman is sex."[37]

It was no accident, he noted, "that since the beginning of the theatre the actress has been regarded as the courtesan." His Perichole in *The Bridge of San Luis Rey* is a classic demonstration of that historical fact. Behind his journal reflections on women in the theater, there is a glimpse of the psychic history of a forty-three-year-old bachelor who had been badly hurt by a mysterious lover some two decades earlier, and who had retreated into himself, despite his loving friendships with numerous women—many of them unavailable because they were married, or in other relationships, or a generation older, or a continent away. He wrote in his journal:

> Woman lives in our minds under two aspects: as the untouchable, the revered, surrounded by taboos (and a taboo is a provocation-plus-veto); and as the accessible, even—in spite of

the mask of decorum and dignity-indignity—*inviting*. To maintain the first of these two roles all the buttresses of society and
custom are necessary: the marriage institution, the prestige of
virtue, the law, and custom. A woman on the stage is bereft of
these safeguards. The exhibition of her bare face in mixed society, for money, under repetition, speaking words not her own,
is sufficient. But far more powerfully is she delivered into the
hands, into the thought-impulse life, of the audience by the fact
that she is on the stage—that realm of accumulated fictions—
as *Woman*, as prey, victim, partner and connivance—that is,
as bird-of-prey, hence attacker,—and as willing victim, that is
piège [trap]. Under those bright lights, on that timeless platform,
all the modesty of demeanor in the world cannot convince us
that this is not our hereditary ghost, the haunter of our nervous
system, the fiend-enemy [or friend-enemy? Wilder's writing is
murky here] of our dreams and appetites.[38]

Private man that he was, Wilder kept to himself his own hereditary ghosts, his dreams and appetites, making his disclosures—if he
disclosed anything at all—in his novels, plays, and essays. He would
revisit the theme of women with and without "safeguards" from another angle in fiction many years later in *Theophilus North* (1973). In
that instance Theophilus has a conversation with Sigmund Freud about
a man who "in the presence of 'ladies' and of genteel well-brought up
girls . . . is shy and tongue-tied, he is scarcely able to raise his eyes
from the ground; but in the presence of servant girls and barmaids and
what they are calling 'emancipated women' he is all boldness and impudence." Freud pointed out the "relation of the problem to the Oedipus
complex and to the incest-tabu under which 'respectable' women are
associated with a man's mother and sisters—'out of bounds.'"[39]

Wilder created conventional women—traditional wives, mothers,
and daughters—in *Our Town*, and the infectiously unconventional
Dolly Levi in *The Merchant of Yonkers*, although Dolly was as eager as the
next woman of her era for a man to support her financially. The women
in *The Skin of Our Teeth*, foreshadowed in Wilder's journal, are far more

complex, however. Just as the play breaks the mold of traditional theater, Mrs. Antrobus and Sabina step out of the gender stereotypes and turn them upside down. First, however, they and their creator tease the audience. On first meeting, Mrs. Antrobus is the traditional wife, "the charming and gracious president of the Excelsior Mothers' Club." She is "an excellent needlewoman" and, like her husband, an inventor, although on a different scale. While he invents the alphabet and the wheel, she invents the apron, the hem, the gore, the gusset, and "the novelty of the year,—frying in oil." Most important, over thousands of years she keeps the home going.

Sabina, the maid in the Antrobus household, is, also on first meeting, the standard unconventional woman. In fact, she is the traditional fallen woman—a would-be actress, working as a maid as she waits for better times in the theater, not averse to seducing another woman's husband. She takes on roles an audience would expect of an actress, the ones Wilder described in his journal—woman as "prey, victim, partner and connivance—that is, as bird-of-prey, hence attacker,—and as willing victim, that is *piège*." Sabina plays several parts in the play: a reluctant servant; a beauty queen (Miss Fairweather, Miss Atlantic City of 1942); a siren and seductress as she seduces George Antrobus; a Napoleonic War camp follower—"la fille du régiment."[40]

Mrs. Antrobus has Sabina's number early in act 1: When Sabina chastizes Mrs. Antrobus for not understanding her husband, she whips out a response:

> Oh, Sabina, I know you. When Mr. Antrobus raped you home
> from your Sabine hills, he did it to insult me. He did it for your
> pretty face, and to insult me. You were the new wife, weren't
> you? For a year or two you lay on your bed all day and polished
> the nails on your hands and feet. . . . But I knew you wouldn't
> last. You didn't last.[41]

In the second act, not long after Mr. and Mrs. Antrobus celebrate their five-thousandth wedding anniversary, it appears that Sabina, alias Miss Fairweather, will have another chance at wifehood. She has

successfully alienated George Antrobus's affections, with considerable collaboration from George. He tells his forbearing wife that he is
"moving out of everything. For good." He is going to marry Miss Fairweather. He will provide generously for the first Mrs. Antrobus and
their children. She will come to see that "it's all for the best."

Maggie Antrobus responds with eloquent dignity to this news. "I
didn't marry you because you were perfect," she says, according to
Wilder's stage direction, *"Calmly, almost dreamily."*

> I didn't even marry you because I loved you. I married you
> because you gave me a promise. That promise made up for your
> faults. And the promise I gave you made up for mine. Two
> imperfect people got married and it was the promise that made
> the marriage.

Soon she throws into the Atlantic Ocean a bottle containing a letter
she has written about "all the things a woman knows"—secrets never
before told, she claims. "We're not what books and plays say we are,"
she declares.

> We're not what advertisements say we are. We're not in the
> movies and we're not on the radio. We're not what you're all told
> and what you think we are: We're ourselves. And if any man can
> find one of us he'll learn why the whole universe was set in
> motion. And if any man harm any one of us, his soul—the only
> soul he's got—had better be at the bottom of that ocean,—and
> that's the only way to put it.[42]

George Antrobus's decision to abandon his family for Miss Fairweather coincides with his five-thousandth wedding anniversary—
and the occasion in Atlantic City when, as president of the Ancient
and Honorable Order of Mammals, Subdivision Humans, he presides
over their six-hundred-thousandth anniversary convocation. Antrobus has proclaimed as the year's watchword for the organization,
"Enjoy Yourselves." Mrs. Antrobus warns that this is "very open to

misunderstanding." Her watchword for the year is "Save the Family." "It's held together for over five thousand years," she says. "Save it!"[43]

And what new vision of woman and her role emerges from the catastrophes and cataclysms the human race has survived? Sabina sums it up for Mrs. Antrobus, now reunited with her husband:

> And he's got such plans for you, Mrs. Antrobus. You're going to study history and algebra—and so are Gladys [the daughter in the Antrobus family] and I—and philosophy. . . . To hear him talk, seems like he expects you to be a combination, Mrs. Antrobus, of a saint and a college professor, and a dancehall hostess, if you know what I mean.[44]

THE PLOT of *The Skin of Our Teeth* can be condensed to man and woman at war—individually and collectively—with each other, with nature, with time, with social and political forces. It was the most difficult challenge Wilder had ever undertaken as a playwright—"the most ambitious subject I have ever approached," he wrote in his journal on November 1, 1940. He worked with the heavy knowledge that "the theatric invention must tirelessly transform every fragment of dialogue into a stylization surprising, comic, violent or picturesque. Here lies the increased difficulty over the writing of Our Town where the essence of the play lay in the contrast between the passages of generalization and those of relaxed and homely tone."[45]

Interwoven in *The Skin of Our Teeth* are strands and threads of sources and allusions, biblical, classical, and contemporary: Moses, Adam and Eve; Cain and Abel; Noah's ark; Homer, Spinoza, and Plato; Wilder's talks with Freud and his studies of Joyce's *Finnegans Wake*. There are autobiographical threads as well: conventions and conventioneers from Wilder's recent sojourn in Atlantic City; exiles from the war; FDR's reelection campaign; the Wilder children's complicated relationship with their father and his paternal expectations of perfection; and snippets of rare but vivid dreams recorded in Wilder's journals. The play is infused with inchoate, dreamlike, often nightmarish events. As he was working on *The Skin of Our Teeth,* Wilder speculated that "the dream is the true vital norm of our intellectual experience, to which waking is but an incoherent and comparatively 'uninteresting' life. Perhaps what art does for us is to remind us of the true absorption of our life, the nightly life in dream."[46]

In this most imaginative of all Wilder's works, drama or fiction, he manipulates subject and form, time and space, confronting the audience watching the play and the actors performing it with surprises that test and tantalize the imagination. This is a cosmic play, defying time by demolishing its normal constraints and sequence, and then reinventing it. The characters are vibrant figures in an engaging farce—on the surface the pejoratives Wilder described in his journal—but underneath multidimensional, deeply moving figures in a universal drama.

Undergirding everything in the drama is the war itself. Wilder opened the first two acts of the play with a montage of lantern-slide images and an announcer narrating "News Events of the World"— a world riven by ice, flood, war, and other catastrophes. Wilder was living in such a world, and he devoted the pages of his 1940 journal to his ongoing struggles with his play and his profound anxiety about the war. When he heard from Woollcott that Robert Sherwood, Averell Harriman, and others were forming a Defense of Democracy League, Wilder laid out in his journal detailed suggestions for such a body, based on the assumption that the war would last for five to ten years. "The frightened, the misguided, and the ignorant cannot be directed without a certain element of fear also," he wrote. "How [can we] employ this without ourselves falling into the Fascist model?"[47]

His concern about the incoherence of wartime political thought and discourse was an extension of his preoccupation with the insufficiency of his own thought. On November 1 he wrote that his play seemed "—as is being said of the Italian army in North Africa these days—to have bogged down again, halted in irresolution and a sense of lacking any vitality." He was revising, reshaping, doing away with "whimsical digressions," inspecting the manuscript for contrivances or insincerity. He concluded that if he was "bogged down, the reason is not far to seek: my mind's daily thinking for twenty years has not been of sufficient largeness to prepare me to: rise to the height of this Argument."[48]

As he worked, Wilder was obsessed with the daily papers, reading several editions for the latest news of the war and the U.S. presidential election, ashamed that he sometimes viewed the war and the election "as a game in which one is emotionally immersed, wishing, deploring, pushing, despairing."[49] Yet to his surprise, despite the "omnipresence of the War" and the doubts about his work, Wilder was "singularly happy" in his self-imposed solitary life in Quebec in the autumn of 1940. He endured "periods of great doubt and even despair about accomplishing" his intentions for his play. He put up with the "perpetual vexation of solitude, the choosing of places to eat," and the inevitable self-consciousness of "forever reappearing alone." He missed good music, good bookstores, good theater. Countless people who knew or thought they knew Wilder, who valued his company, who admired his brilliant lectures and conversation, would most likely have been stunned to learn that he regarded himself "unfailingly inept at the social relation." He confessed in his journal:

It is not only the *gaffes* that I make—and which worry me far less than they used to; even when things are going well, when a congeniality or friendship is well established as that with Aleck or Bob H. [Hutchins] I am never free of a sense of inadequacy; I feel that I am forever dry when warmth is called for, and warm when judicious impersonality is called for, and this inadequacy is primarily represented in the spoken word.[50]

He confessed to a "mortified condemnation of the quality of my mind particularly in its expression in social life and public life. Hence my loathing for my lectures; hence my eagerness to be gone from any place I have been staying, my carefully concealed delight at goodbyes." Perceptive as he was about others, Wilder seemed to have little idea about the impression he actually made on friends, colleagues, and strangers who beheld and appreciated the articulate, eloquent, learned man who knew how to listen as well as to speak, elucidate, and entertain.

Instead, Wilder wrote, it was "as though I were haunted by the idea that the spoken word should be as precise as the written, and that the encounters of friends should have the character of a work of art."[51]

Unable to live up to the burden of this unrealistic if not neurotic expectation of himself and others, Wilder chose the "luxury" of silence—"that is = absence." That "luxury" was an escape that could also result in loneliness—the absence of sustained close companionship, the absence of intimacy, perhaps the absence of a lover. It was a "luxury" that carried the risk of repression, denial, isolation. The innate loneliness that was a reality in his personal life was both a necessity and a consequence in his literary life. He was fond of quoting Gertrude Stein's observation that "the business of living was to make a solitude that wasn't a loneliness," and he could keep himself company, as he did in Quebec, through daily pleasures, such as the beauty of a place.[52] "I seem to be seeing landscape for the first time; perhaps the silence is a therapeutic element bringing me to the present state of unprecedented well-being in which the eye particularly profits." He found congenial and stimulating company in books and music, as he always had done, and in his writing. He believed, he wrote in the journal, that "one of the elements" in his happiness that fall was

> the play and that even during these last three days when it
> seemed to me that what I had written was all wrong, that there
> would be no "right," even then my subconscious knew that the
> play would come out all right. All I can say about that is that
> through it all my "happiness" has been unshaken, my gratitude
> for the effects of morning and evening light on the river and
> its shores no less spontaneous, my mental health no less béat
> [blessed], and that the work done on the play today has been
> more encouraging.[53]

He gave himself a weeklong change of scenery in November, driving out to Lac Beauport and taking a tiny room at the Manoir Saint-Castin. He was getting so distracted in Quebec by "the glorious sweep" of the St. Lawrence River and its boat life that he could "scarcely continue" with his work. The evergreen forests near Lac Beauport reminded him of Switzerland, and he enjoyed walking along the "wide brimming streams" with their cascading waterfalls. For the first time in his life he actually wanted a camera—an instrument he had always believed before to be "incapable of telling a truth." He wrote to his mother and Isabel that his play was "wonderful"—that it had "come out of its 'bogging down' of last week." He had rewritten the opening over and over, and believed he had written some "stuff" that would "lift audiences out of their chairs."[54] He had briefly considered having the women's parts played by men, but had discarded that notion. He had no idea when he would finish *The Skin of Our Teeth*, for he wanted to get as near to perfection as possible.[55]

WILDER CONFESSED to his family that fall that at last he loved his car. "Yes, I just love the perfect motion of it and the quietness and obedience of it." It even had a name, given to it by a group of admiring little boys, who said, "Oo-oo-ou! The Green Hornet!"[56] There were many miles ahead to travel in the Green Hornet, many pages to write and revise before *The Skin of Our Teeth* would be finished, but Wilder had regained his momentum. He wrote to Woollcott,"The play exceeds a dreamer's dream."[57] He felt confident enough to read the manuscript to Ned Sheldon in New York. "He thinks well of it," Wilder told Woollcott, "and has refired my furnace—soon after the new year, I retire into the cell that Archie MacLeish has offered me in the Library of Congress. Until that moment everything is impediment and obstruction."[58]

He was going to Washington in January 1941 for two reasons: The Roosevelts had invited him to attend FDR's inauguration; and, prompted by the librarian of Congress, Archibald MacLeish, Secretary of State Cordell Hull had asked Wilder to embark on a three-month-long goodwill visit to South America—Colombia, Ecuador, and Peru. "The emphasis is not on lectures," Wilder said, "but 'just live there; get to know them and let them get to know you.'"[59] He would receive no salary, just a modest expense account, but he relished the opportunity to travel to these new countries—especially to pay his first visit to Peru, the setting for *The Bridge of San Luis Rey*. MacLeish had offered Wilder a "cell" at the library so that he could bone up on South American history, read the work of South American writers, and improve his Spanish. Woollcott shared the news with Lynn Fontanne: "Thornton is being dispatched by the State Department to South America where his name, thanks to 'The Bridge,' is the most potent of all American writers," he wrote, adding that Wilder could already think in Spanish.[60]

Wilder joined other inaugural guests at a buffet luncheon at the White House, where he had "protracted conversations with such pillars of our commonwealth" as Dorothy Thompson; Charlie Chaplin, who "lectured us on the Brotherhood of Man," Wilder said; Douglas Fairbanks, Jr.; Nelson Eddy; Felix Frankfurter; Raymond Massey; and Wilder's old friend Les Glenn and his wife. In 1940 Glenn became the rector of Washington's Saint John's Episcopal Church, known as the Church of the Presidents.[61] Throughout all the inaugural events, the first lady was a fine hostess, "dizzyingly capable and yet always human in that ocean of people," Wilder wrote to Sibyl Colefax.[62]

He was spending eight hours daily at the Library of Congress, working on the third act of his play and reading the novels and essays of the writers he would meet "in Bogota, Quito, Lima and other cities." He showed a young Brazilian novelist around Washington, met with Colombian officials, and on his private walks delivered, "not silently either, long lectures in Spanish."[63]

———

THE WILDER family celebrated some happy news in January 1941 with the announcement of Janet's engagement to Amherst native Winthrop Saltonstall Dakin, who practiced law in nearby Northampton. "She has already received a large diamond and a string of pearls and bland dreams of parasitism drift through the other Wilders' minds, like cats dreaming about firesides," Wilder joked to Woollcott.[64] Janet was teaching at Mount Holyoke, and she and "Toby" Dakin began planning a June wedding. Thornton would be home from South America by then, and could give her away, with all the Wilders on hand for the celebration.

Before his departure Wilder spent time with the family in Hamden, enjoying the long-standing family Sunday tradition—eating ham and eggs for breakfast, reading the newspapers, and writing letters. Then he was off to Washington and New York, planning to sail February 28 for his three-month assignment in South America. Hoping to have lunch with Charlotte a couple of days before he sailed, Wilder went to her Greenwich Village apartment twice but did not find her at home. He left a note on his calling card: "Dear Sharlie—Called at 1:10 1:45 Will stroll around neighborhood and call again at 2:10."[65] When he couldn't reach his sister, he wrote a note inviting her to go with him February 27 to a private, late-night screening of Orson Welles's new film, *Citizen Kane*. Although the movie would not have its New York premiere until May 1, Welles was eager to show it to Wilder before he left the country. "Whether I see you or not, lots of love for the present," he told his sister, "& see you at Janet's wedding circa June 15."[66]

Once again Wilder looked forward to a sea voyage and to adventures in new landscapes, filling his briefcase with the manuscript drafts of *The Skin of Our Teeth*, his journal, and novels and essays by some of the South American writers he would be meeting. He hoped he could speak Spanish "with complete ease." His budget would be tight, and he predicted that Dwight Dana would "shake his head sadly" as Wilder spent his own money to pay for "dinners for the writers and professors and students and flowers for their wives."[67]

29

"THE ETERNAL FAMILY"

The germ of my play, once started, began to collect about it many aspects which had nothing to do with Joyce. It fixed its thoughts on the War and the situation of the eternal family under successive catastrophes.

—THORNTON WILDER TO ISABEL WILDER,
December 17, 1942

The United States and South America (1940s)

Isabella, Isabel, and Charlotte Wilder planned to meet Thornton at the West Sixteenth Street Pier in New York at noon on February 28, 1941, to see him off on the SS *Santa Lucia* for his official goodwill tour of South America.[1] At the last minute Isabel was ill with a bad cold and stayed at home, and without explanation, Charlotte failed to appear. The Wilders were concerned when she did not join them as planned. Isabella stayed at the pier until Thornton boarded ship, and then went directly to her daughter's apartment in Greenwich Village. When Charlotte finally answered the door, her worried mother found her in her nightclothes, "bewildered, but quite gentle, and entirely normal most of the time."[2]

Isabella begged Charlotte to dress and go out to lunch with her, and then to travel home to Hamden with her for the weekend, as they had planned. Charlotte agreed, but just before they reached the restaurant she "simply ran away, calling out that she had changed her mind—that her 'inner voices' told her not to go—to remain at her own room." Alarmed, Isabella hurried back to Charlotte's apartment, but Charlotte refused to let her in. Finally Isabella took the train home to Connecticut "frightened and exhausted," in hopes of getting advice and help for her daughter in New Haven.[3]

That night the news came by telephone that Charlotte had suffered "a complete nervous breakdown" and had been taken to Doctors

Hospital in Manhattan, a fairly new private hospital. Because Thornton was at sea, and Janet and Amos were in Massachusetts, Isabella and Isabel coped with the immediate emergency, hurrying to Manhattan to begin what would prove to be a long vigil. The preliminary diagnosis was schizophrenia, and the doctors directed that Charlotte should be moved to the psychopathic department of the Payne Whitney Clinic at the Cornell Medical Center for thirty days.[4] There Isabella and Isabel were referred to Dr. Lincoln Rahman, a young psychiatrist who not only was "pleasant and understanding," according to Isabella, but was already doing groundbreaking research into schizophrenia.[5] Dr. Rahman and his colleagues hoped that thirty days would be enough time for Charlotte's recovery, and Isabella told them she would then take Charlotte home to stay "indefinitely."[6]

Isabel took her sister's breakdown "very hard," Isabella reported to Dwight Dana. As for herself, she was a mother in full armor, taking charge of the oversight of her daughter's treatment, conferring with doctors, living "one day at a time," worrying about finances—and adamantly insisting that for the time being Thornton must not know what had happened. "I shall not spoil Thornton's trip with its responsibilities by any anxiety over home matters," she declared to Dana and her family. "Have not decided yet how much to tell him or when. The fact that he got happily away without any of us knowing that a blow was to fall seems indicative to me that he should *not* know while he has to give himself so entirely to a new untried & perhaps difficult rôle in South America."[7]

"I think you were wise not to tell Thornton the whole story," Dana wrote to Isabella, adding that "for the time being at least it might be as well not to refer to Charlotte at all, pending more information as to how things are going to work out." Meantime, he reassured her, "Don't worry about the financial part for I know Thornton will wish to take care of all of this, and his bank account is amply sufficient to do so."[8]

———

THORNTON WAS in Bogotá, still protected from the news about Charlotte's illness, when he received a cable from the family that Janet and

Toby Dakin were married. "Janet's wedding was sudden," Isabel explained to Dwight Dana,

> *for the young man was drafted. By marrying now they had her Easter*
> *holiday for a trip South, and the hope of at least the spring together. . . .*
> *But it did make lots of excitement and complications. It was held in the*
> *pretty chapel of Winthrop's church—Episcopalian. Amos gave her away.*
> *Just we four and my brother's wife; the retired rector of the church,*
> *his wife, and a young couple, friends of Janet's were present. They left*
> *at once after we had tea at the Dakins' home and met Mrs. Dakin, an*
> *invalid of many years' standing so she could not be at the ceremony.*[9]

When Thornton got the news of the wedding, he wrote to his new brother-in-law: "May you be very happy. May you found one of those American homes which is really one of the triumphs of civilization. . . . A thousand blessings on you both from Your brother Thorny."[10]

FROM HER first day at the Payne Whitney Psychiatric Clinic, Charlotte was "up and dressed and busy," thanks to the "elaborate routine" arranged for the patients.[11] At first the family continued to receive good reports about her progress, and on March 8 Isabella and Isabel were heartened to receive a note from Charlotte herself. It was, Isabel wrote to Dana, "most reassuring, so affectionate and gentle, proving she connects nothing of that dreadful Friday with having seen Mother earlier in the day. She is fully conscious that she is ill and glad the past, which she felt she had not made a good job of, is over; and that she will not have to go on thus, and spoil the future."[12]

The Wilder family gathered around, unified in their support of Charlotte, endeavoring to provide the best medical care for her, but still determined to keep the news from Thornton. What could he do from South America that he was not already doing (through the attentive auspices of Dwight Dana, who promptly wrote checks on Thornton's bank account to pay every bill for Charlotte's medical care, as well as the bills for Janet's trousseau)?

The family insisted that Janet and Toby Dakin go on with plans for their southern honeymoon during Janet's spring vacation from Mount Holyoke. Isabella and Isabel would keep watch over Charlotte. They commuted between Hamden and New York, and Amos traveled down from Massachusetts to see Charlotte in the hospital as often as her doctors would permit her to have company.

Charlotte's "nervous breakdown" was actually a psychotic episode that marked the onset of schizophrenia, and from the first, she was fortunate to be under the care of some of the best doctors at one of the best psychiatric clinics of the time. Standard treatment in 1941 included psychotherapy, various physical therapies, electric shock treatments, insulin shock therapy, and, as a last resort, lobotomy. The first antipsychotic drug would not be identified until 1952, or approved for use until 1954. Isabella and Isabel had frequent conferences with the doctors, providing family history, answering the questions the doctors raised based on what they understood at that time about schizophrenia and other mental disorders, trying to help shed "any light on Charlotte's past that might add to the picture of the case."[13] There was no family history of mental illness or clinical depression—although Amos had certainly suffered depression from time to time, especially in 1934, and their parents may have done so from time to time as well. There were, however, physical issues: Charlotte skimped on food, smoked a great deal, had serious dental problems, and had undertaken a fast that further undermined her health.

Isabella and Isabel thought that Charlotte's childhood history of being separated from the family might be a factor. Some of the Wilders wondered if part of Charlotte's illness was rooted in her relationship with their father and his ambitious drive for perfection in his children. There would be glimmers of Amos Parker Wilder's relationship with his children in George Antrobus and his daughter, Gladys, in *The Skin of Our Teeth*: "Papa, do you want to hear what I recited in class?" Gladys asks him. " 'THE STAR' by Henry Wadsworth LONGFELLOW."[14]

She strives to please her father:

Look, Papa, here's my report card. Lookit. Conduct A! Look, Papa. Papa, do you want to hear the Star, by Henry Wadsworth Longfellow? Papa, you're not mad at me, are you? . . . Papa, just look at me once.[15]

With her mother's encouragement, she tries to be perfect: "And, Gladys," Mrs. Antrobus says, "I want you to be especially nice to your father tonight. You know what he calls you when you're good—his little angel, his little star."[16]

AS AN adult Charlotte alternately defied her family's advice and desired their approval. Her daily life in New York was defined by her struggle to earn even a subsistence living, all the while trying to hide her dire situation from her family. Poets seldom survived on the proceeds from poetry alone, Charlotte knew, and she pinned her hopes on the new prose book, under contract to Coward-McCann. But at the time of her breakdown it was giving her trouble—"vignette tales, about 20 or 25," she wrote her mother, "all standing far off from subjective stuff, nothing intimate or involving personal stuff; each the kernel of some person, place, or tiny happening, which, if it happened, happened far away and long ago."[17] She continually assured Thornton, Isabella, and Amos that she was not "in a jam" about funds, even though she was. Amos had offered her a place to live and work near him and Catharine—"something to fall back on." She appreciated it deeply, she had written to him in the fall of 1939, promising "not to get into a nervous jam—but to stay well and unworried; and ahead of myself as I am now."[18]

She had applied for a Guggenheim Fellowship in the fall of 1939 in hopes of receiving a year's financial support, writing an application narrative so densely esoteric as to be incomprehensible. "I have known, and am knowing now, real privation—although I have, what many have not—the security of a home background, which saves me from experiencing these ultimate crises of nervous anxiety that come with insecurity," she wrote to the novelist Rollo Brown in 1939, after she had pinned all her hopes on the Guggenheim Fellowship application.[19] She was bitterly disappointed to be turned down.

Charlotte had written a prose disclaimer about her sexuality in her first book of poetry, *Phases of the Moon,* for there were lesbian undertones in the poems. Charlotte sustained long, intimate friendships with the novelist Evelyn Scott and the educator and activist Ernestine Friedmann, the women to whom she had dedicated *Phases* in 1936. After the book was published, she had written to Amos about the "distasteful aspect of the confessional" in poetry. "I shall never again, doubtless, 'let go' in emotionalism in just that way, for I think an objectivity in me now functions in that material, absent then." She wrote further in this letter to Amos:

> *I was so explicit about the sex-frustration, because I wanted it to be understood, beyond a shadow of a doubt, that I was not a sexual pervert, experiencing sex in a woman's world. It seemed necessary to me because so much emotion was shown as directed toward women that a natural inference might have been drawn. The reading public—used to the disguise of such things, achieved by a mere change of pronoun . . . would not, I argue, realize that had I been, I would have felt it necessary to be explicit about that—and might have jumped to a conclusion, unjust to me, from so much show of feeling for women.*[20]

Amos Wilder wrote with surprising candor about these themes in his sister's poetry in his book *The Spiritual Aspects of the New Poetry* (1940). He had hired Charlotte to type his manuscript, encouraging her to comment on its substance and structure, but Charlotte apparently did not request changes in his treatment of her own work. In his chapter entitled "A World Without Roots," Amos discussed the modern poet's alienation from nature, including "the desolation wrought in the lives of sensitive and mature moderns by the frustration of the sex relationships, and we are speaking solely of the area of personal and psychological hurts." To illustrate, he quoted poems by T. S. Eliot, Francis Thompson, Dante, Geoffrey Scott—and Charlotte Wilder. He cited the "ravages done to the will, to the life force itself, by traumatic experiences in the area of sex, especially by the record of sex conflict and irreparable injustices and remorses." The "records and ravages" in the "secret lives of men and women" may be found in their art, Amos wrote. He contended that "there is abundant evidence of the costs of frustration in this area largely consequent upon the character of our civilization: man 'burned by the ropes of his own flesh' [a line from one of Charlotte's poems] as a result of false sex attitudes, delayed marriage, or the febrile overemphasis on and exasperation of sex by commercialism and amusements."[21]

Amos surely had himself, his brother, and two of his sisters in mind when he wrote, "More particularly such frustration is due to paralyzing inhibitions, resultant from Puritan attitudes and training." Referring to Charlotte by name only in a footnote, he wrote, "The author last quoted has expressed both the oppressions and the struggle consequent on frustrations in this area in a series of 'Monologues of Repression,'" and then offered lines from one of Charlotte's poems to illustrate. In this literary exposition of his sister's "secret life" and, by extension, of a shaping force in his and his siblings' upbringing, Amos, the devoted elder brother, may have diagnosed even more astutely than Charlotte's doctors one significant root of her breakdown.

Charlotte's first book of poetry, *Phases of the Moon*, was stunningly unorthodox in style and subject matter; heart-wrenching in its emotional content, whether grounded in imagination or experience; and, in either case, portending what might lie ahead. Near the end of her book, in "(For the Two)," a poem about parting with someone beloved, Charlotte wrote,

> ... but in the heart, in the place of being: *what will become of me?*
> The years wheeled; spun in the iron hub, I was torn on the spoke-ends
> and standing aloof—the intricate ghost-ridden—knew nothing, felt
> nothing. Destroyed ... or fore-doomed to destruction. ...[22]

Her second book, *Mortal Sequence*, was by comparison sedate, muted, constrained—and, for the most part, conventional in style and subject. There are many instances of rhymed verse, of structure, order, boundaries, conformity. There seemed to be two poets—two Charlottes—foreshadowing the greater chasm in personality that was to come. She had written in 1936, in the defensive coda to *Phases of the Moon*, "At the close of the narrative suggested, we are left on the threshold of a future in which expanding experience, re-orientating the individual with respect to human relationships, effects a cathartic resolution of the particular conflict that troubles the pages here."[23] Unfortunately that would not be true for Charlotte.

In part the family blamed Charlotte's breakdown on Evelyn Scott, one of her closest friends, as well as her confidante and mentor. Isabel wrote to Dwight Dana, noting that Scott had always believed—unjustly—that the Wilders had neglected Charlotte and failed to support her financially. "Two years ago I feared and was prepared for this break," Isabel wrote to Dana. "It had to come and we had to wait until it came; so did Charlotte, apparently. Now from bedrock, there is hope she can have a fresh start toward a more normal kind of life and especially, more natural and open personal and family relationships."[24]

By mid-March, however, it was clear that Charlotte was gravely ill, and that her treatment would last far longer than thirty days. She alternated between euphoria and rebellion, going on a hunger strike. Her doctors told the family what they had always known—that Charlotte was an "unusually strong-willed type."[25] Isabella was relieved to hear from the doctors that Charlotte demonstrated no suicidal tendencies. She was well enough on April 22 to write to Amos herself, and by early May Isabella and Isabel believed that Charlotte seemed completely normal.

––––––––––

THORNTON HAD for years been the financial head of his family, and that role would irrevocably expand and solidify as Charlotte's illness progressed. With Charlotte incapacitated, Janet newly married and on her honeymoon, Thornton in South America, and their mother now growing more and more anxious about Charlotte's health and the accelerating cost of her treatment, Isabel, by default, began to pick up the

emotional reins of the family. As Isabel described the family dynamics, Amos and Charlotte were especially close, and Amos was deeply
concerned and conscientious—but despite his own "difficult year of
mental depression in 1934" he was "too overworked and full of responsibility to be able to give the time" to fully realize the extent of Charlotte's illness. Furthermore Amos had a demanding job and a wife and
two children. Besides, Isabel wrote to Dana, Amos was "so sensitive
and quick to respond emotionally, that he takes things very hard without always working it out mentally." As for their mother, Isabel wrote,
"she understands more than Amos for she knows Charlotte so much
better and has seen so much more of her. She knows this is very serious
and yet to protect herself she has to shy away from it. And Mother, too,
suffers so acutely from worrying over the financial end, that she's got
to have C. quickly well to stop that leak."[26]

Dwight Dana tried repeatedly to reassure Isabella and Isabel that
they need not worry about "the expense of Charlotte's illness." The
money was available in Thornton's accounts, he said, "and I know that
Thornton would want to have no expense spared which might expe-
dite his sister's recovery."[27] Dr. Rahman and his colleagues assured the
Wilders that Charlotte's case was not hopeless, but that she would need
at least six more months of hospitalization, and after that, "a sanatarium or quiet country retreat for a very long time." The doctors were
particularly interested in Charlotte "because of her individual case
history, and family background of New England clergymen, etc., and
no history of mental illness or hereditary insanity."[28] They hoped as
soon as possible to move Charlotte to their "branch in the country, the
Westchester division of the New York Hospital at White Plains," Isabel
wrote, because there she would have more privacy and enjoy some freedom to roam outdoors. It would also be good for her to be cared for by
new staff and live among new patients who had not seen her in the first
throes of her breakdown.[29]

———

BY APRIL 1 Thornton had received the news of Charlotte's collapse.
"From home, good and bad news," he wrote to Stein and Toklas from

Colombia. "Janet got married and Charlotte had—long deferred—her nervous breakdown."[30] He urged them to understand "the three volumes between the lines."[31] From various cities in Colombia, Peru, and Ecuador he communicated with the family and Dwight Dana by cable and letter, trying to allay his mother's financial worries.

Isabel, in concert with Dana, was also handling literary business on Thornton's behalf while he was in South America. There were overtures about a radio script for the sale of radio rights to *Our Town* (Isabel worked long and hard on a script, but the project did not find a buyer); and inquiries about anthology rights to *The Woman of Andros* and *Heaven's My Destination* (Thornton eventually said yes to *Woman* and no to *Heaven*).[32] Meanwhile he had to concentrate on the work that was before him.

He made "friends-til-death" everywhere he went. When a copy of the movie of *Our Town* was discovered in "far-off Cartagena" it was "air-posted" to Bogotá, where Wilder and thirty friends watched the film at 11:30 one night in early April. "I spoke. They spoke. We separated at 1:30 with embraces and tears and promises of return," Wilder wrote to Woollcott.[33] In a letter to Ruth Gordon he described the landscapes and terrain: "Everywhere mighty peaks . . . eternal snow . . . Cotopaxi . . . Chinborazo . . . El Misti." In Colombia, a country split by great mountain ranges, "you visit the other cities either in an hour by plane, or in a month by donkey back." In Peru, which he had visited in his imagination in *The Bridge of San Luis Rey*, he saw, instead of foot travelers on a bridge, "a handful of Spaniards or almost Spaniards driving Rolls Royces through a myriad Indians."[34] He wrote to Stein and Toklas that he wished the Inca had won.[35] He pronounced Ecuador the "most beautiful country in the world."[36]

As the journey came to an end, Wilder believed he had "done pretty well" what the State Department had sent him to do. He had lectured in English and in Spanish, given radio interviews, and met people from all walks of life. Two of the writers he met along the way dedicated books to Wilder—the Colombian novelist Fernando González Ochoa and the Brazilian author Erico Verissimo. "I have been made an honorary member of the chief 'cultural' society in Quito [the Sociedad

Jurídico-Literaria], and am first names with all the poets and novelists in sight," he wrote Stein and Toklas.[37] He hoped that his success in South America would lead to a similar assignment in Europe.[38]

At the outset Wilder had made it clear to the sponsors of his trip that he would not write about it. "Writing's only fun when you can tell your truth," he told Ruth Gordon, "and my truth about these countries is winning, appealing, complex, aching, frustrated, hopeful and dejected." Nevertheless Wilder wound up writing twenty-one pages advocating measures for better cultural understanding and attacking "the majority of the devices which they [the State Department] are employing as propaganda."[39] He wrote to Stein, "It was from you I learned that no souls are won by flattery, argumentation or coërcion; that description paints no pictures and that purity is the only propaganda."[40] He might also have given his own ideas credit, for his 1940 journal documents his ongoing ruminations about the dynamics of "Propaganda and Anti-Propaganda."[41]

Wilder's densely packed schedule in the fall of 1940 and the spring of 1941 apparently accounts for the fact that he stopped writing in his journal in Canada in November 1940 and did not resume until May 23, 1941, in Peru. That day he wrote a "Sketch for a Portrait of Tia Bates"— "for forty years the famous, kind, roaring, strongwilled, childhearted mistress of the best inn on the west coast of South America." Wilder called her "*tía*," Spanish for "aunt," but her first name was Anna. Her husband was a mining engineer, "and she could tell wild stories of gaiety and dangers of the 'Wild-West' days of early Bolivia and Peru." She was reported to have "adopted and settled in life" scores, even hundreds of "children abandoned or orphaned by unfortunate gringos; to have 'set right' financially and morally a host of shipwrecked persons; to have refused payment from a large number of her guests. The Truth is better."[42] Wilder stored Anna Bates away securely in his journal—the only person he encountered in all his travels in South America to merit such attention—and he filed her in his memory. Twenty years later he would pull her out into the light of day, name her Mrs. Wickersham, make her the proprietor of the best hotel in South America, and set her down in his novel *The Eighth Day*.

The last journal passage Wilder had written in November 1940 was titled "On Happy Endings, and the Pessimist." There, thinking about his play, and the year, he had contemplated the catastrophes of nature, the preponderant "dark" character of human experience, the "pessimism" in Christianity, and the omnipresent knowledge of the brevity of life and the inevitability of death. In that context Wilder found it interesting, he declared, that there are "no great works of literature that assert this pessimism."[43] If there could be optimism and a happy ending in his play about "the War and the situation of the eternal family under successive catastrophes," he was determined to find it and express it.[44]

BY EARLY June he was at home in Hamden, immediately caught up in the efforts to understand and treat Charlotte's condition. To Thornton fell the sobering legal responsibility of signing commitment papers in case his sister would not voluntarily make the recommended move to the Payne Whitney hospital in White Plains—although she agreed to make the change and was moved to Westchester. By this time, Isabella told Amos, Charlotte "is not writing to anybody anymore and no doubt is blaming the family for her detention."[45] She seemed to adjust well enough to her new surroundings, however.[46] The hospital director reported that if Charlotte continued to cooperate, she would soon be moved to a convalescent wing and "be able to have her typewriter and papers as she so longs to do."[47]

Charlotte periodically underwent standard electric shock therapy, which worked briefly but "did not hold," and insulin shock therapy, which was not effective.[48] She wrote to her mother after one electric shock treatment that she was greatly improved. "If it is sustained I am on the road to recovery and we all certainly hope it is," Charlotte wrote, adding that she was "shocked" at the expense of her long stay in the hospital. "I can't bear to think how big it must be," Charlotte told her mother,

and however slow I shall have to be to return it, shall always consider it my debt, and pay back in installments. Also I must insure vacations and

more conventional living when I next go to New York. I shall put that
first—building a career as editorial assistant is something I am experi-
enced in by now—and should charge well for it. I won't ever again go
as bohemian as I did; and I wouldn't have if I dreamed it would run me
into this charge on the family.[49]

By this time, however, her doctors believed that "Charlotte would eventually recover but would never be able to live on her own again or do a regular responsible job."[50]

———

ONCE THORNTON had done all he could to help arrange Charlotte's treatment for the coming months, and to relieve his mother and Isabel from some of their anxiety and stress, he had to pack his bags and his briefcase in the Green Hornet and head west to keep his commitment to teach ten weeks of summer classes at the University of Chicago— and to try to get back to work on *The Skin of Our Teeth*. He would live in the apartment he had rented before, and earn four thousand dollars for the summer's teaching. Every dollar was welcome now that Charlotte's medical expenses were mounting, with no end in sight. Now there was also a pressing financial imperative to finish his play and get it into production.

In Chicago the academic work was intense, the hours were long, and Wilder felt he was teaching "worse and worse." He got into his car on hot summer weekends and drove to Michigan or Wisconsin in search of a cool, quiet place to work on the third act of *The Skin of Our Teeth*. "It is hard to sit in remote hotel rooms, the perspiration rolling down one's naked sides, and write pages of world-embracing gaiety," he complained in a letter to Stein and Toklas. During the school week Wilder was up at six, preparing to teach his classes from ten until one—Homer, Sophocles, Dante, and *Don Quixote, Part One*. Then he took an afternoon nap. In the evenings he dined with the Hutchinses or drove uptown to "get a good dinner and get the least bit drunk." Then it was another hour of work and early to bed. Two afternoons weekly he held office hours, "crowded with all Chicago's hall-bedroom poets, waiting their turn as in a dentist's waiting room."[51] In late July he hosted a spaghetti supper in his apartment for the "Chicago Chapter of the Society of the Friends of Gertrude Stein," as he described it in a letter to Stein. Present were Wendell Wilcox and his wife; the painter Gertrude Abercrombie and her husband, Robert Livingston; the writer and teacher Gladys Campbell; and Sam Steward.[52] By then Wilder was exhausted from teaching, and from weekends devoted to the third act of *The Skin of Our Teeth*.

Wilder had somehow managed to set aside his animosity toward Jed Harris by this time, and had shown him the first two acts of his new play, in hopes that Harris would direct it. Despite the history of hard feelings associated with the production of *Our Town*, Wilder had no doubt that Harris was the director most likely to do justice to his innovative drama. "Jed Harris has begun casting the new play *The Skin of Our Teeth* even before the last act is finished," Wilder wrote to Stein and Toklas from Chicago on July 28.[53]

Wilder still counted University of Chicago president Robert Hutchins among his closest friends and one of the greatest influences in his life. Nevertheless Wilder was distressed by Hutchins's very public anti-interventionist position on the war, believing it was "badly argued" and "deeply sentimental." After Hutchins made an NBC radio address titled "America and the War" in January 1941, Wilder had conveyed his disagreement directly in a letter to Hutchins: "As I see the matter of our relation to the War I hold exactly opposite views . . . but I hold my tongue, listen with unprejudiced mind to all views, eagerly accord others the reasoned statement of their positions, and continue to cultivate my own garden."[54] He concluded, "Let the world ail. . . . Til the last bomb I shall unpenitently hold that the masterpieces of literature are the highest concretions of life and that nothing in the world has priority over the conditions of friendship."[55]

As the year wore on Hutchins got "a good deal of unpleasant notoriety" for his views, which he would change only after the bombing of Pearl Harbor.[56] Wilder had a great deal of sympathy for the private "war" Hutchins had been going through, and tried to befriend both Hutchins and his wife as their marriage was clearly unraveling. "I summarize it by saying that Maude's going crazy and in such a way that one is torn between pitying her for a desperately sick mind and hating her for a vulgar pretentious tiresome goose," Wilder had written to Stein and Toklas. "Such dances as she leads Bob, with tantrums, caprices, changes of mind and talk, talk, talk. . . . And the effect of it on the two daughters!"[57]

DURING THAT summer in Chicago, Wilder decided he should live in New Haven during the coming fall. The State Department was already pressing him to go on a goodwill tour of Argentina, but he resisted. With any luck his play would be finished and in rehearsals by fall, and he could spend intervals in New York as necessary. But the rest of the time he wanted to be close to the family as they kept an anxious vigil over Charlotte. They still hoped she would be well enough in a few months to come home to Deepwood Drive.

"I have a good mind to move into my study and release my bedroom to our enlargening family. What do you think?" Thornton wrote to his mother. "Yes, ma'am. There'll be poaching of eggs in your kitchen at 6:15 a.m. but I'll clean up so you'll not know anyone's been there. If Sharlie's home by that time, we'll find diversions for her."[58]

For decades the resilient, resourceful Wilders had survived any number of catastrophes. With imagination, fortitude, and devotion to each other, they had managed over many years to withstand extended separations, Dr. Wilder's illness and death, and the perennial anxiety about money. But Charlotte's illness was a crisis beyond their capacity to resolve. No one had the power to make Charlotte well again, and she would live most of the remaining years of her long life in psychiatric institutions.

Thornton was now solely responsible for supporting his mother, Isabel, and Charlotte. For the rest of his life he worked to sustain his family and to put aside money in trusts for Charlotte and for Isabel that would provide for them even after his own death. Reams of medical, financial, and legal records document the long, hard journey of Charlotte's lifetime of illness, and the family's unflagging efforts to provide the care and support she needed. For nearly forty years, until her death in 1980, family members paid Charlotte visits when her doctors allowed them to; tried to facilitate her independence; wrote her affectionate letters; bought her clothes, typewriters, and television sets; took her home for birthdays, holidays, and vacations; and secured the best treatment and the best doctors in the best institutions. Together the family formed a compassionate circle around their Sharlie, even when she was unaware or, as she often was, bitterly resentful and difficult. For the Wilders this was simply what family did—the eternal family, bound by blood and history, by love and pain.

———

WILDER THE cultural emissary could not resist an invitation to join John Dos Passos, best known then for his *USA* trilogy, in serving as the two American delegates to the 17th International Congress of PEN in London in September 1941. (This international association of writers was originally called Poets, Essayists, and Novelists, but had expanded over its twenty years of existence to include dramatists and writers in other genres.) When Librarian of Congress Archibald MacLeish realized that he himself could not attend the conference, he had recommended Wilder, writing, "No one can speak for American writers with more authority and understanding than Thornton Wilder."[59]

He was eager to make the journey, not only because of the congress, which would consider the theme "Literature and the World after the War," but because he could witness the impact of the war firsthand. He would be in London for three weeks, spending time with Sibyl Colefax and other friends, and would gain a graphic understanding of the wartime perils of daily life and nightly blackouts in London. He had spent "four days in Washington and NY wading through bolts of red-tape," he wrote Stein and Toklas. He had "begged and hammered" the State Department for a visa for France without success, and was terribly disappointed not to be able to see them.[60]

He was a highly visible American abroad that fall. As a speaker at and delegate to the PEN congress, he wound up as one of four international authors appointed to the organization's presidential committee, along with H. G. Wells, Denis Saurat of France, and Hu Shih of China. Wilder served on the committee until 1947. At the 1941 congress, along with Rebecca West and E. M. Forster, he opposed the British author Storm Jameson's proposal that during the war, PEN members devote themselves to writing Allied propaganda. Wilder had expressed in his journal his strong aversion to writing propaganda rather than art, believing that pure art was a far more powerful force than propaganda. He articulated his convictions persuasively in London. His voice was also heard on BBC broadcasts, at meetings in Glasgow and Edinburgh, and at a luncheon in his honor given by the English-Speaking Union in London.

"I saw plenty," Wilder wrote to Bob and Maude Hutchins. "Brick-dust heaps and Achilles-airmen reserved for death; old working women bombed out of three successive homes and duchesses in becoming uniforms."[61] From Bristol he wrote graphic accounts to Woollcott:

> *The nights of fury brought wide destruction. There is no stretch of ruin as large as you will see in Moorgate, north of St. Paul's, London. But there are whole blocks of ploughed brick and riven iron. Halves of great warehouses from which all the interiors have been burned out and which resemble, with their regular rows of windows, a Roman viaduct, or the baths of Caracalla.*

Wilder marveled at the "resilience of the city" and the "orderliness that the British nature can impose even on a ruin, and the distinctness with which a store or hotel or church spared can go about its normal business next to a yawning edentate hole."[62]

He welcomed his time with Sibyl and his visit with his aunt Charlotte, who was in London training YWCA workers for wartime work with refugees, especially women and children. Charlotte, who had served as World General Secretary of the YWCA from 1920 until 1935, was still active in the organization as a teacher and speaker, and toured the United States speaking on the role of the YWCA during the war. "Can silk stockings be assembled for Aunt Charlotte and Sibyl?" Thornton had asked his mother once he knew he would be making the trip to England, and it may be assumed that if they could be, they were.[63] He would also have shared with his aunt Charlotte the full details of her namesake's illness.

After Wilder's return from England and Scotland, Rex Stout interviewed him about his impressions of wartime England and Scotland on "Speaking of Liberty," an NBC radio program broadcast on October 30. Wilder reported that the war was "being waged directly against every man, woman, and child." He observed: "As a result, everyone is filled with their resistance and their resolve. It gives new meaning and new weight to everything they do." He could see that much of the blitz and the bombing was directed at the civilian population rather than at military targets. He was profoundly moved by the "powerful sense of community responsibility, the responsibility of each individual to his neighbor," which he called "the finest thing a democracy can show." He concluded that "the Nazi spirit with its contempt for the human being as anything else but a tool has clarified for all of us just what a democracy is. A democracy has greater things to do than to organize itself towards a total war. But when it sees itself threatened with extinction, it can do that too."[64]

In December 1941 the *Yale Review* published "After a Visit to England," Wilder's account of his journey. He paid particular tribute to the "total magnificent achievement of civilian defense in Britain under the unheard-of conditions of the air raid," and the "unity and resolution exemplified in the self-imposed restraint and the co-operation of all citizens in the emergency." He observed that the British made it clear that what the Germans "effected, first with rhetorical oratory, and finally with threats and coercion, a democracy can achieve with composure and free will."[65]

———

THE JAPANESE attack on the U.S. Pacific Fleet at Pearl Harbor at 7:55 a.m. local time on December 7, 1941, transformed allegiances, politics, and policies around the world, in a fiery instant sweeping away the opposition of anti-interventionists and galvanizing the American war effort. In the aftermath of Pearl Harbor, Wilder joined the multitudes who decided to volunteer to go to war. Before the attack on Pearl Harbor, American men twenty-one to thirty-one years of age were being drafted. Beginning on February 16, 1942, however, men from twenty up to forty-four were required to register for the draft and were eligible for active service as needed. On April 27, 1942, men forty-five to sixty-four had to register, although they were not liable for military service. Wilder was eager to serve, and he would turn forty-five on April 17, 1942, ten days before his eligibility for active duty expired. He was determined to enlist before then, and he swore he would not be content to write propaganda or to sit in an office in some safe place. He wanted active overseas duty, and he believed his "first command" would be to "learn the Japanese language."[66]

Wilder was in Hamden for the Christmas holidays, although there was little to celebrate: More bad news came in a letter from one of Charlotte's doctors: "I have to report that your sister fails to hold the improvement which followed her last electric shock therapy course. She has again become withdrawn, restless and delusional." He advised that the family postpone further visits to Charlotte until she was "again improved."[67]

Amid travel and turmoil, surrounded by global and family upheaval, Wilder spent New Year's Day 1942 in the house on Deepwood Drive. He lost himself in his work, writing the last lines of a draft of the final act *The Skin of Our Teeth*, believing his war play to be more relevant now than ever before.

Thornton Niven Wilder, Berkeley, California, in 1906 or 1907, at the age of nine or ten. (*Courtesy of the Wilder Family LLC and Yale Collection of American Literature, Beinecke Rare Book and Manuscript Library, hereafter TCAL.*)

Thornton, about three, standing beside the baby carriage that holds his sisters Charlotte and Isabel, who are ready for a ride, Madison, Wisconsin, circa 1900 to 1901. (*Courtesy of the Wilder Family LLC and YCAL.*)

The Wilder family in China, 1906: (front row, left to right) Isabella Thornton Niven Wilder, Amos Niven Wilder, Isabel Wilder, Charlotte Elizabeth Wilder, Thornton Niven Wilder, Amos Parker Wilder, and an unidentified man in the background. (*Courtesy of the Wilder Family LLC and YCAL.*)

Isabella Thornton Niven Wilder (front row, third from left) in China with members of the Ladies' International Tea Cup Club. (*Courtesy of the Wilder Family LLC and YCAL.*)

Consul General Amos Parker Wilder and Wu Ting Fang, Chinese minister to Washington, April 4, 1908, Washington, D.C.; autographed by Wu Ting Fang: "May the two nations we represent remain friends forever." (*Courtesy of the Wilder Family LLC and YCAL.*)

Thornton, Amos, Charlotte, Isabel, and Isabella, holding baby Janet, Berkeley, California, 1910. (*Courtesy of the Wilder Family LLC and YCAL.*)

Isabel, Thornton, Isabella, and Charlotte with little sister Janet in the center, Berkeley, California, 1914 or 1915. (*Courtesy of the Wilder Family LLC and YCAL.*)

Amos Parker Wilder with his sons, Amos and Thornton, New Haven, Connecticut, 1915 or 1916. (*Courtesy of the Wilder Family LLC and YCAL.*)

Thornton Niven Wilder at Oberlin College. (*Courtesy of the Wilder Family LLC and YCAL.*)

Thornton Niven Wilder, Yale student and U.S. Army Coast Artillery Corps corporal, Narragansett Bay, Rhode Island, World War I, 1918. (*Courtesy of the Wilder Family LLC and YCAL.*)

Thornton Wilder aboard a ship en route to Europe, 1928. (*Courtesy of the Wilder Family LLC and YCAL.*)

Gene Tunney and Thornton Wilder on their European journey, hiking in the French Alps at the Mer de Glace, October 28, 1928. (*Courtesy of the Wilder Family LLC and YCAL.*)

Isabel, Thornton, Isabella, and Janet in Surrey, England, celebrating the international success of *The Bridge of San Luis Rey*, 1928. (*Courtesy of the Wilder Family LLC and YCAL.*)

Isabel Wilder, 1933.
(*Courtesy of the Wilder Family LLC and YCAL.*)

Charlotte Elizabeth Wilder, 1930s.
(*Courtesy of the Wilder Family LLC and YCAL.*)

Janet Frances Wilder,
Mount Holyoke graduation, 1933.
(*Courtesy of the Wilder Family
LLC and YCAL.*)

Amos Niven Wilder, 1930s.
(*Courtesy of the Wilder Family
LLC and YCAL.*)

Thornton and Isabel, 1933.
(*Courtesy of the Wilder Family
LLC and YCAL.*)

The house at 50 Deepwood Drive, Hamden, Connecticut, built by
Thornton for his family. The Wilders called this "the house *The Bridge*
built," because Thornton's royalties from the novel paid for the design
and construction. (*Courtesy of the Wilder Family LLC and YCAL.*)

"OUR TOWN"

FIRST FULL (Act II missing) *a play in Three Acts.*
SCRIPT

(No curtain.
(No scenery.
(When the house-lights go down, the stage-manager
in overalls, has been leaning for some time against the left proscenium pillar,
smoking a cigarette, and staring drily at the late arrivals in the
audience. At last, in a very Yankee accent, he begins to speak:)

The Stage-Manager

This play is called "Our Town." It was written by Thornton
Wilder. It is produced and directed by Jed Harris, and it is
acted by Miss X, Miss Y, Miss Z; Mr. A, Mr. B, Mr. C, and
many others.

The First Act shows a day in our Town; the second act
shows a ~~family in~~ ~~for~~ century in our first family's
home, and the last act shows — well, you'll see.

Between the First Act and the Second, there will
be played an interlude called The Pleasures and Penalties
of Automobiling; and between the Second and Third
Acts, there will be another interlude — a propaganda
piece, called "Is the Devil Entitled to a Vote?"

Are you ready?

(He looks at the lady who arrived
late. She shakes her head amused,
saying Ts-Ts-Ts, implying what'll
~~they do~~ he do next.)

This is our Town, Grover's Corners, New Hampshire.
It's near the Massachusetts line — Latitude 71° 37',
Longitude, 42° 40". The date is Friday, May 7, 1907.

(He looks hard at the lady again
and repeats "1907.")

It's dawn.

The sky is beginning to show some streaks of
light behind our mountain, over in the East there.
The morning star is doing that last excitement it
always goes into just before dawn.

I'll draw the plan of the Town for you.

(Chalk in hand he goes to the back
of the stage and draws two parallel
lines down the center of the
stage toward the footlights.

Way back here is the railway station and the

A page from the first manuscript draft
of *Our Town*, 1937. (*Courtesy of the Wilder
Family LLC and YCAL.*)

Thornton standing beside his Chrysler convertible with a rumble seat, his 1939 Christmas gift from producer Sol Lesser for his help with the film adaptation of *Our Town*. (*Courtesy of the Wilder Family LLC and YCAL.*)

Thornton Wilder with Ellen Weston and Robert Hock in *Our Town*, Williamstown Theatre, Williamstown, Massachusetts, 1959. This was Wilder's final theatrical performance as the Stage Manager. (*Photograph by William Tague. Courtesy of the Williamstown Theatre Festival.*)

Lieutenant Colonel Wilder serving as an intelligence officer in the U.S. Army Air Forces, World War II, 1945. (*Courtesy of the Wilder Family LLC and YCAL.*)

The novelist, playwright, lecturer, and global citizen in midcareer, undated photograph. (*Photograph by LeTrelle. Courtesy of the Wilder Family LLC and YCAL.*)

Thornton Wilder and American actress and singer Ethel Waters after their arrival at West Berlin's Tempelhof Airport, September 11, 1957, for performances in Wilder's one-act plays at Congress Hall. *(Photograph by Kreusch/AP Photo. Courtesy of AP Images.)*

Wilder with Ruth Gordon and Garson Kanin in Williamstown, 1959.
(Photograph by William Tague. Courtesy of the Williamstown Theatre Festival.)

Thornton Wilder, the perennial traveler, on his way to board the train in New Haven for one more departure, May 1960. (*Courtesy of the Wilder Family LLC and YCAL.*)

Wilder receiving the first-ever National Medal for Literature from the National Book Committee, in a ceremony at the White House with Lady Bird Johnson and Donald McGannon, television broadcasting executive and president of the National Book Committee, May 4, 1965. (*Courtesy of the Wilder Family LLC and YCAL.*)

Wilder sails for Italy aboard the American Export Lines SS *Independence*, November 18, 1955. (© *Bettmann/CORBIS. Courtesy of CORBIS Images.*)

He was a refined gypsy, wandering the world, writing, he said, for and about "Everybody."

30

"THE CLOSING OF THE DOOR"

*The closing of the Door—that to Civilian Life—is almost pure joy and the
anticipation of what's ahead: being pure instrument, however moderately, in
a movement-wave that's so important to me . . .*

—THORNTON WILDER TO ROBERT M. HUTCHINS,
June 15, 1942

The United States (1940s)

Wilder finished *The Skin of Our Teeth* at "three o'clock on New
Year's Day," he reported to Alexander Woollcott. "It shows
how that fine American family, Mr. and Mrs. George Antrobus, their children, Henry and Gladys, and their girl, Sabina, of Excelsior, New Jersey, go through the Ice Age, the Flood and a War, with
a lot of screaming, absurdity and a few shreds of dignity."[1] The play
represented, he told Sibyl Colefax, his "thoughts about endurance and
fortitude in War."[2]

He spent the first months of 1942 revising the text of *The Skin of
Our Teeth* and working on production plans—hoping to secure the best
director, the best producer, the best actors—and hurrying to finish
The Alcestiad. Charlotte's illness and his upcoming military service
prompted a new urgency to make money—an imperative that would
override his earlier resolve never to write for money, and that would
drive many of his personal and professional decisions from that time
on. "I have two dependents—a 69 year-old mother (mighty alive still)
and a sister—Charlotte—who has been a whole year in a hospital for
mental diseases," he wrote to Stein and Toklas in March. "These two
play-subjects are all that I have in my knapsack and when they are
written I temporarily close the door on the whole matter of writing and
turn to other things"—chiefly military service.[3] He fervently hoped

that both plays would make it to Broadway and "sustain" his family in his absence.[4]

At Archie MacLeish's request, Wilder wrote scripts for two military-training films—*Manuelito Becomes an Air Cadet* and *Your Community and the War Effort*, both for the Office of War Information. There were other overtures: "Now the Government's asked me to do—and really plan—a large movie 'like Our Town'—how a small community collects itself to live under War condition," he told Woollcott, but the project did not come to pass.[5] Wilder marveled at the swift mobilization of personnel and factories in the United States now that the country was at war. The "basic American" was "swinging into view," he said, appreciating "the miraculous conducted as though it were the matter-of-course. Old America."[6]

He raced against the clock during the first three months of 1942, trying to finish *The Skin of Our Teeth*, get it into production, and get himself into uniform. He wrote to Woollcott in February, "I sign up for conscription soon. I'm within two months of the Limit. I feel somehow as though I were in better condition to face a board now than I was 25 years ago."[7] He found himself mired in decisions to be made about the play, and certain key decisions were thwarted by tentative acceptances, long silences, rejection. After weeks of delay, Jed Harris—"the Ideal Director and the Atrocious Manager," as Wilder called him—turned down Wilder's invitation to direct the play, ostensibly because he saw problems with acts 2 and 3, which Wilder himself recognized.[8]

He began to see that the play needed serious revisions. "Lately, my eyes have been opened with a shock to one aspect of it," he wrote to Alfred Lunt and Lynn Fontanne on February 5, 1942:

> It's struck some people as "defeatist." I have only read it to a few friends, mostly our academic group in New Haven. One distinguished doctor said that it haunted him for days but that "the government ought to prevent its being shown"; others variously said it was "anti-war" or "pacifistic." And I suddenly remember that Sibyl, who heard the first two acts in London, said that the second Act was "so cruel."[9]

Now Wilder said, "I could see with amazement that I had given so wrong an impression of what I meant." He blamed himself for his "New England shame-facedness and shyness of the didactic, the dread of moralizing, the assumption that the aspirational side of life can be taken for granted." He recognized that he needed to weave in a scene of "conjugal love and trust between Mr. and Mrs. Antrobus," and to give "open voice" to their "confidence, through discouragement, in the unshakable sense that work and home and society move on towards great good things." He was mortified to see that "the Second Act—vindication of the unit of the family—exhibits only the exasperating side of children and the 'nagging' side of Mrs. Antrobus," and he recognized now that "the positive affirmative elements of Act Three are muted and evaded to the point of spiritual thinness." Wilder decided to revise the play with the chief purpose of infusing it with "the tone of warmth and courage and confidence about the human adventure" he had "too much 'taken for granted.'"[10]

As Wilder revised *The Skin of Our Teeth*, he also had to change his expectations about a director and actors. He turned to two new colleagues to bring the play to life in the theater: the producer Michael Myerberg, manager of Leopold Stokowski's recent tour of South America with the American Youth Orchestra, and the director Elia Kazan, whose work Wilder knew through the Group Theatre. Wilder had met Myerberg with Stokowski at Mabel Dodge Luhan's house a few years earlier. Myerberg was young—about thirty-eight—but Cordell Hull had recommended him highly, on the basis of his work in South America. Wilder thought Myerberg would be good at "dickering, middleman, promotion"—managing all the behind-the-scenes logistics that were essential to a play's success on Broadway.[11] Furthermore he was "honest" and "very effective and capable," Wilder told Dwight Dana—and "very enthusiastic about the play." While Wilder would have preferred Jed Harris at the helm, and after him, Orson Welles, Jed had said no, and Welles was "deeply engaged in a new movie."[12]

"I think Kazan is the director I've been hunting for," Wilder decided in February. "Fine comedy; superb stage movement; and dry economy in emotion." In addition Kazan was also "very enthusiastic about the play."[13] Fredric March, who had a distinguished career in Hollywood (he had won an Academy Award in 1932 for his role in *Dr. Jekyll and Mr. Hyde*) and on Broadway, was eager to play Mr. Antrobus, and Wilder said he would "settle" for Mrs. March—Florence Eldridge—as Mrs. Antrobus "with the proviso that she and ourselves might find her unsuited as rehearsals advance."[14] But Kazan and March were tied up with other projects until late spring, and if the production had to be postponed until fall, Wilder thought they might have to "begin from scratch and try for Orson [Welles] who is an old friend of mine and never forgets that I 'discovered' him."[15]

It was difficult to cast the crucial role of Sabina. Myerberg considered the comedienne Fanny Brice, and Wilder thought she would be a good choice, but nothing came of that. Although many people assumed Wilder had Ruth Gordon in mind when he created Sabina, the record is not clear, and in any case Gordon was tied up with another show. "So about Sabina," Wilder wrote to Gordon on June 11, 1942, implying that she was on his mind when he created the role:

> *You were Sabina in Quebec; just as you were Mrs. Levi in Tucson. I roared at you. I knelt before you. I carried home your flowers after the first performance. Never have I been so happy in the theatre.*
>
> *I feel quite calm in the fact that you will one day be Mrs. Levi and Sabina in the future. . . . Besides, it looks as though you were going to insinuate yourself into my future plays, too.*[16]

Myerberg was determined to persuade a big star to play Sabina—and, although he did not think she was "a big theatre personality," he sent the script to the flamboyant, controversial Tallulah Bankhead, who was reportedly suggested for the role by Ned Sheldon.[17] Bankhead was almost as notorious for her spicy vocabulary and her myriad love affairs as she was lauded for her film and stage career. Although she had a Paramount Pictures contract beginning in 1931, during the thirties she did most of her best work onstage in New York (*Dark Victory, Rain, Something Gay, Reflected Glory, The Little Foxes*) and most of her notable film work in the 1940s (Alfred Hitchcock's *Lifeboat* in 1944; Otto Preminger's *A Royal Scandal* in 1948). The glamorous woman with the deep voice had a reputation as a diva—and, as it turned out, the name recognition and celebrity to pull people into the theater. However, she could and would be capricious and uncontrollable as "the obstreperous daughter of nature, Sabina," Wilder wrote to Woollcott. "She not only loves the part, but knows every corner of the play. Already she's asking that such-and-such a line be transferred to her rôle. That's right. Sabina's greedy—to thrust herself forward, and she can scream and protest and interfere and raise hell as much as she wants."[18] Wilder remembered years later that Bankhead as Sabina was "a wonderful being, but she never gave the same performance twice."[19]

Florence Reed, a skilled character actress who had first appeared onstage in 1902, would be hired to play the Fortune Teller. The handsome young Montgomery Clift joined the cast as Henry Antrobus. In the spring of 1942, with rehearsals for *The Skin of Our Teeth* set to begin in the fall, Wilder had done all he could do about the production except revise his play. He turned his focus to other work, especially *The Alcestiad*, sending Woollcott a list of his "Various plans" for the upcoming months: First on the list was "Removing Charlotte to a less expensive but equally conscientious hospital." Next he was thinking about renting out the house on Deepwood Drive and persuading his mother and Isabel to move into a "bungalow in some college town farther South—Chapel Hill or Winter Park." The last item on the list was the preparation of the text of the reading edition of *The Skin of Our Teeth*, to be published by Harper & Brothers on December 18, 1942, just a month after the show opened.[20]

For all the delays and detours with the play, Wilder was not "downcast" except about one thing, he told Harold Freedman, his theater agent: "I'm always forgetting that I'm the head of a household and am presumed to be earning my living by my pen. Jed used to foster that notion that I'm a gentleman of vast private means; I'm damned if I'll fall in with that rôle forever."[21]

"I JUST got a thousand-word telegram," Wilder wrote to Woollcott on May 12, 1942. "Mr. Hitchcock of the Thriller movies wants me to come out to California for six weeks and write the screen treatment of a movie. He recounts the plot. It's about American small-town life and [a] big-city murderer. I'm a consultant on small-town life to the tune of fifteen thousand dollars and murder has no secrets for him."[22] Because of his admiration for *Our Town*, Hitchcock wanted Wilder to write the script for *Shadow of a Doubt*. This would only be Hitchcock's sixth movie to be made in the United States, although he had been working on motion pictures in his native England as a crew member, actor, or director since 1921, when he was twenty-two.

Wilder inherited a scenario called "Uncle Charlie," which Hitchcock had purchased from the writer Gordon McDonell, who based his story idea on a newspaper article reporting on a serial killer who had strangled several women, and had been discovered and arrested while he was visiting his family in Hanford, a small California town.[23] True crime aside, Wilder thought the plot as Hitchcock outlined it was "corny," and doubted whether he could "supply one convincing small-town speech." Besides that, he didn't have six weeks free, for he was tentatively scheduled to begin his army training July 1. But he was determined to find a compromise "with time, art and money." Perhaps he could go for five weeks for ten thousand dollars.[24] His agent, Rosalie Stewart, worked out a favorable contract that accommodated his schedule and still secured the fifteen-thousand-dollar fee.

"My dependents are much on my mind," Wilder wrote. "Charlotte is not getting better and must be moved to a less expensive institution. If my play should fail—or be unproduceable because of a bombing in New York—I should be supporting my kith-and-kin from capital. If the War should be very long my family would be living in a Florida cracker's house on a captain's pay. . . . So I'll go to California."[25] He said good-bye to family and friends on the East Coast, and after an exuberant weekend in New York on May 16 and 17, Wilder found himself with a "diffused hang-over," he wrote Woollcott, "and God knows what I will be saying next. I am on the verge of the beautiful inane, spent my youth there, but never again."[26]

He was in Hollywood by May 20, at the Villa Carlotta again. Wilder rented a "Drive-U-Self Chevrolet" to get himself back and forth between his apartment and the Universal Pictures studio where he would be working, although he was reluctant to drive in Los Angeles traffic. Just starting the car was an ordeal, punctuated by "lurches, leaps and a screaming of gears."[27] When he reached the studio, however, Wilder immediately found himself "very interested" in the movie, and from the first he enjoyed working with Hitchcock and his producer, Jack Skirball.[28] "The other trips I came out with naif illusions about making good movies and fumbled," Wilder wrote his family. "This time I came out to make money and am really caught up in the thing. Mr. Hitchcock and I get on fine and he and Mr. Skirball are very excited by the way the script is going—for *already there is a lot of script!!!*"[29]

The intense schedule left him "tired all the time," however, as he socialized with the Sol Lessers; George Cukor, whose party included "Barbara Hutton Reventlow and Cole Porter. Glamor-food. Footmen"; and his former student Robert Ardrey, now a playwright and screenwriter, and his wife, among others.[30] Wilder and Hitchcock met at ten each morning for their story conference, and Wilder spent the rest of the day writing. Hitchcock showed Wilder his 1941 suspense thriller, *Suspicion*, starring Cary Grant and Joan Fontaine, pointing out technical details and procedures all the way through the film.

"Work, work, work," Wilder wrote to Isabel. "But it's really good. For hours Hitchcock and I with glowing eyes and excited laughter plot out how the information—the dreadful information—is gradually revealed to the Audience and the characters. And I will say I've written some scenes. And that old Wilder poignance about family life [is] going on behind it."[31] Hitchcock, like Wilder, was fascinated with the family as a focus for drama. The Newton family in Santa Rosa in *Shadow of a Doubt* is a stark counterpoint to Wilder's Gibbs and Webb families in Grover's Corners, New Hampshire, in *Our Town*, and his Antrobus family in Excelsior, New Jersey, in *The Skin of Our Teeth*. There are resonant "shadows" in the film—the interplay of dark and light, innocence and depravity, truth and illusion, characters who are not what they seem, and characters who are blind to reality. "We think up new twists to the plot," Wilder wrote, "and gaze at one another in appalled silence: as much as to say 'Do you think an audience can *bear* it?' "[32]

With chilling irony and foreshadowing, Wilder played with the concept of twinship between two family members who could not be more different:

YOUNG CHARLIE:

Uncle Charlie, you and I aren't just any uncle and niece. Mother's always said that you and I are alike. And I know we are . . . We're kind of . . . twins. . . .

UNCLE CHARLIE (*taken aback*):

Twins? That's a mighty fine thing to be.

YOUNG CHARLIE:

It's a very serious thing to be, too. Because we can read one another's thoughts.[33]

"I'm fascinated," Wilder wrote to Bob Hutchins. "Our work is very good. It's not literature. But the wrestling with sheer craft, the calculations in a mosaic of exposition is bracing."[34] Wilder's respect for the motion picture as an art form was growing. He had observed in 1940 that "the movies have risen to surpass the play."[35] Under Hitchcock's tutelage Wilder embraced each step of work on the film script, especially the "complicated plotting and of course that gets denser and more complex as it goes on." He and Hitchcock were pleased with the emerging screenplay. "There's no satisfaction like giving satisfaction to your employer," Wilder wrote. "I hope I give it to the Army too. Satisfaction to *yourself* is fleeting, [in] spite of what the moralists say. And satisfaction to the public does not interest me."[36] There was definite satisfaction, however, in receiving his first paycheck. "Never did I love money more purely," Wilder wrote to Isabel as he banked the funds for his family.[37]

THE SCREENPLAY was nearly finished as time drew near for Wilder to report for military duty. "I'm a tiny speck in this War," he wrote to Woollcott. "But my relation to it is so real that I have the sensation of entering it for the happiest and most selfish reasons."[38] Because the requirements for civilians becoming officers had become more demanding, Wilder received new orders to report to Miami for a six-week training course in "basic soldiery" to begin June 27. As there were now certain wartime restrictions on cross-country civilian air travel, Wilder would have to make part of the trip by train. Hitchcock decided to join him for the journey, and the two men left Los Angeles by train June 22, bound for Chicago, finishing and polishing the script for *Shadow of a Doubt* on the way. The change in orders had forced Wilder to cancel plans to visit Woollcott at Neshobe. "Anyway," he joked, explaining the change, "I should think the picture of me at bayonet practice (muttering 'Jed Harris' and leading the class in ferocity) would be so tonic that no one could wish me anywhere else."[39]

"Honest, Ruth, the picture is good," Wilder wrote to Ruth Gordon after he had finished his work with Hitchcock. "At the end we descend to a little fee-fo-fi-fum, but for the most part it's honest suspense and poignancy and terror."[40] After Wilder's departure from Hollywood, Hitchcock's wife and collaborator, the actress and writer Alma Reville, and screenwriter and short-story author Sally Benson (*Meet Me in Saint Louis* and *Junior Miss*) added dialogue to the script, under Hitchcock's supervision. Wilder was not happy to discover this later on when he first saw the film in a movie theater.

Shadow of a Doubt was released in 1943 to rave reviews, and was frequently reported to be Hitchcock's favorite production. One of Hitchcock's biographers later observed that the Wilder-Hitchcock collaboration was "one of the most harmonious" of Hitchcock's career.[41] Wilder received screenwriting credit and a special acknowledgment for his contributions to the film. Credits also went to Reville and Benson, and Gordon McDonell received an Academy Award nomination for Writing—Original Motion Picture Story. Teresa Wright and Joseph Cotten starred as Charlie and Uncle Charlie, with a strong supporting cast including MacDonald Carey, Hume Cronyn, and Patricia Collinge. In 1943 Wilder wrote to Sol Lesser about the film, noting that the text was about 80 percent his, and suggesting that he and Lesser do a film after the war—provided Lesser thought, on the basis of *Shadow of a Doubt*, that Wilder could "write movie-telling."[42]

"IT SEEMS both diplomatic and army-air intelligence needs Thornton's type," Isabella Niven Wilder wrote to her son Amos on May 13, 1942. She was already worried that Thornton would be sent to "dreadfully far, dangerous posts."[43]

Capt. T. N. Wilder, 0908587, age forty-five, was sworn in on June 16, 1942, and received orders to begin six weeks of training in "basic soldiery" June 27 in Miami, Florida, and then to report to Army Air Intelligence Officers Training School in Harrisburg, Pennsylvania.[44] In Miami six thousand officer candidates were being trained, and a smaller number of "re-treads," or veterans of World War I, were undergoing "refresher training."[45] In the tropical heat and humidity Captain Wilder kept up with the best of the younger men, with "unflagging vitality." Men in uniform often collapsed in the summer heat, to be carried off the parade ground. But Wilder, his khakis and his overseas cap soaked with sweat, actually appeared to enjoy the exercise. At forty-five he was in better shape than he had been at twenty, when he had difficulty passing the physical examination for service in World War I.[46]

After one sweltering daily parade in Miami, Wilder met the writer Paul Horgan, who was traveling as an official "Expert Consultant to the Secretary of War" to inspect officers' candidate training programs across the United States, and then to write a script for an army training film with Maj. Frank Capra. Horgan and Wilder had corresponded occasionally but had never met until that particular July afternoon. Horgan asked Wilder about his next assignment. "In a few weeks I go to the Air Corps Intelligence School at Harrisburg [Pennsylvania]," Wilder said. And what would he be doing after that? Horgan wanted to know. Writing training manuals or historical records of the air services? "Never!" Wilder answered "in a subdued sort of shout," Horgan wrote. "He kept his smile but it became severe and his heavy brows seemed to bristle. 'Never: *I shall not write for my country!* '"[47]

Wilder had taken this same position with Archie MacLeish, insisting that he did not want to serve in the relative safety of Washington or Hollywood, using his skills as a writer to turn out propaganda and training films. MacLeish promised to help him find an interesting assignment, perhaps in Army Air Force Intelligence, where there was a need for people with analytical prowess and fluency in foreign languages. Wilder was determined to serve overseas: "The dream of most of our lives is to become that Intelligence Officer in the Combat Zones," he wrote to his family.[48]

For the most part Wilder would have his wish. He was "still healthy, hot, hardworked and happy" in Miami in July. He complied with requests from the Bureau of Public Relations to do broadcasts and lectures, and to meet the press with the popular actors Capt. Clark Gable and Capt. Don Ameche, but he found the most satisfaction in the achievements of Squadron M, to which he belonged. They won the pennant for best marching and got the highest marks ever recorded by the training program for a test on judgment. Captain Wilder made a score of 400 out of a possible 400 points in "Company Administration."[49] He was excelling mentally and physically in his work, sleeping well, even enjoying reveille, and feeling "the War coming nearer and nearer—a huge concrete thing that diminishes everything one has ever known except friendship, love of places, and the few occasions one has known of good hard work."[50]

From Miami he was dispatched to Harrisburg, and from this point on letters with explicit details of his whereabouts and his duties gradually diminished, in accord with army policy. "It's supposed to be a secret: where we are and what we do and who we are," he explained to Woollcott in August 1942. He could say only that he was in "the most exclusive school in the world," and that he and his compatriots were "being trained and polished to very specialized and very responsible duties."[51] He was being schooled to be an Army Air Force Intelligence officer—"a new kind of officer at the interrogators' table" where Allied pilots were debriefed. Young pilots were "emotionally immature,"

Wilder wrote. "Returning from raids where they have killed, or where their friends behind them, gunners, etc., have been killed, they approach the Interrogators Table in inner turmoil. They do not wish to speak to a human being for 24 hours. They fantasize or worst of all develop mutism."[52] As for the officers doing the interrogating, "it's not enough to know maps, read photographs and compute ballistics. There must be a psychologist, etc. He must know with which pilots he must be hard as nails, with which he must be patient and indirect. Yes, all War is ugly, not less so when it tries to be humane."[53]

Still he was thriving. "Say, we come of good stock," he wrote Amos that summer, looking back on his training in Miami. "Those Hebridean parsons; those Maine farmers . . . your kid brother never missed an appointment, a roll-call, a class, a drill. . . . My colleagues were fainting on the drill field, or getting excused from this or that . . . but Brotherboy was up at 5:15 and enjoying it."[54] At Harrisburg he underwent training in "map reading; aerial photography; codes; celestial navigation (!); structure of planes, etc.—so that we can at least talk adequately to the young flyers whom we interrogate and whose lives, meals, payrolls, service records we must direct."[55]

Civilian life intruded now and then: Myerberg and Kazan traveled to Harrisburg to meet with Wilder about the script for *The Skin of Our Teeth*. He was able to get leave in late August to go to New York to confer with them about the play, and he looked forward to meeting Montgomery Clift and having dinner with Isabel, Tallulah Bankhead, and Clift at Sardi's. He was able to spend nearly twenty-four hours with his family at Deepwood Drive.[56] By mid-September, Wilder had done all he could do for the time being with the script and was ready to put it aside. "I reckon that I believe that a text counts 95% of a show," he told Isabel, "and I let all the rest go hang. . . . Anyway, now the text's established and I don't have to think one more iota about that part of it."[57]

In early fall Wilder reported to the 328th Fighter Group headquarters at Hamilton Field, Novato, California, near San Francisco. In addition to his training classes he performed various administrative duties, including drafting a history of the 328th, noting that the general order activating this fighter group was originally secret, and that many of the "most interesting facts about the beginning of the Group" could not be disclosed until after the war. Hamilton Field was "a post widely envied for its beauty, its handsome and comfortable original buildings and its proximity to San Francisco," he wrote.[58] Pilots of the 328th trained in P-39 Airacobras, small fighter planes that possessed sufficient speed and power at altitudes under fifteen thousand feet but were vulnerable and virtually useless above that range, and consequently were not suited for the high-altitude combat in the skies over Western Europe.

Wilder was also assigned as investigating officer in a court-martial case involving "A little 18-year old Mississippi scrub farmer's son who hitchhiked home for a month to help his father with the harvest." Wilder helped get the desertion charge reduced to AWOL.[59]

His daily routine provided free time most evenings—time he had habitually used for reading and writing. He picked up his "several-times attempted and discarded" play, *The Alcestiad*, which had already accompanied him on so many journeys.[60] "I write only about 10 speeches an evening," he wrote to his mother. "If I find that it moves into the center of my interest, or keeps me awake at night, I'll have to give it up. But so far it contributes its fragments tranquilly every night. And on Sundays I can do a larger portion.—As I see it now it's very Helen Hayes."[61] But, he warned, that was a secret.

Civilian life encroached more frequently as the time grew near for the opening of *The Skin of Our Teeth* in New Haven. Then the show would go on the road for six weeks, "being licked into shape" for New York. Isabel was serving as her brother's proxy and his eyes and ears at rehearsals. Wilder shared Isabel's report with Sibyl Colefax:

> *Rehearsals have gone swimmingly as far as the text is concerned, though there have been many clashes of personalities. Tallulah has tried to show all the other actresses how to do their job and when they have not taken her advice she has flounced off to her hotel and resigned. So far she has returned almost penitently each time. She loves her rôle (Sabina) as well she might, and is very acute about the whole play when the demon is not*

possessing her. The text is almost established. My last week at Harris-
burg I wrote them a new close to Act II and some crowning motto lines
for Mr. Antrobus in Act III. Last Sunday from San Francisco I sent
them a new treatment of a middle portion of Act I . . . heightening the
atmosphere of impending cold and danger.[62]

His third act, Wilder said, had at its core "the conflict of Father and Son and the statement of War as the anguish of the 'emptinesses.'"[63] Whether the battle between George Antrobus and his son, Henry, is seen as mirroring the universal father-son relationship, or the particular Amos Parker Wilder–Thornton Niven Wilder relationship, or both, it is intense, bitter, and complex. Henry returns from war sullen and angry. He has risen through the military ranks from corporal to general. He has spent seven years, he tells Sabina, "trying to find him; the others I killed were just substitutes." He wants to burn his father's old books because "it's the ideas he gets out of those old books that . . . that makes the whole world so you can't live in it."

Sabina intervenes to save the books, and scolds Henry for suggesting that his family doesn't care about him. "There's that old whine again," she chides. "All you people think you're not loved enough, nobody loves you. Well, you start being lovable and we'll love you." Outraged, Henry replies, "I don't want anybody to love me. . . . I want everybody to hate me."

Face-to-face, father and son battle over the past and the future. "I'm not going to be a part of any peacetime of yours," Henry swears. "I'm going a long way from here and make my own world that's fit for a man to live in. Where a man can be free, and have a chance, and do what he wants to do in his own way."

"How can you make a world for people to live in, unless you've first put order in yourself?" George Antrobus counters. Before there is violence, Sabina intervenes: "Stop! Stop! Don't play this scene. You know what happened last night. Stop the play."[64] Father and son come to a kind of truce, perhaps too swiftly for credibility—but this is, after all, a play meant to seduce an audience into a willing suspension of disbelief.

Wilder would also rework the ending of the drama. As he explained to Amy Wertheimer in 1943:

> I've always assumed a very slow curve of civilization. But I always affirm too that my "toleration" of humanity's failings is more affirmative than most "opportunists." When I first wrote Skin of Our Teeth it lacked [the] motto-humanity-climbing-upward speeches of Mr. Antrobus at the end. I assumed that they were omnipresent in the play and didn't have to be stated. I assumed that they were self-evident,—that's how highly I believe in mankind. But more and more of the early readers found the play "defeatist." So I wrote in the moral and crossed the t's and dotted the i's.[65]

The Skin of Our Teeth was now on tour in Baltimore, Philadelphia, and Washington after its world premiere at the Shubert Theater in New Haven on October 15. Myerberg had hired the legendary press agent Richard Maney to manage publicity for the play and, according to Maney, on opening night, after fifteen people left the theater before the play was over, Myerberg directed him to write a synopsis of the plot for a program note. Perhaps if the audience knew something about the plot ahead of time, Myerberg reasoned, they'd stay put for the entire show. Maney complied, overnight producing words Wilder later approved, and they were added to the playbill and have been part of the play's acting edition ever since.[66] Even so, word got around that taxis hovered outside the Shubert Theater like getaway cars to collect unhappy patrons who gave up on the play after the first act, or the second. Variety reported that although ten or fifteen patrons stalked out during every performance, the play was "thriving on controversy, holding to much bigger grosses than expected."[67]

"Wreathed in controversy, The Skin of Our Teeth was an immediate hit," Maney confirmed later. He did his part in "raising a din" over the play, pleased when its "champions hailed it as a comic masterpiece," as well as when "motion-picture actors and other dolts denounced it as gibberish." He recalled that this "medley of cheers and jeers was music to my ears. Furtively I prodded both camps to further excesses."[68]

AT HAMILTON FIELD, Wilder found that it was simpler to coordinate pilots and fighter squadrons than it was to persuade feuding producers and actors to work together congenially. As the pre-Broadway tour progressed, there was near-mutiny from the cast. Hearing from Tallulah Bankhead and Florence Reed that Michael Myerberg had dismissed three actors and was undermining the play, Wilder tried to untangle events from his vantage point on a California military base. Isabel confirmed that Myerberg, prone to an arrogant disregard for others, and Bankhead, prone to an excessive confidence in her own talent and power, often clashed. Bankhead did not get along with other members of the cast, especially Florence Eldridge. Wilder was bombarded with letters of complaint about Myerberg. He urged Myerberg by mail to "do everything to establish so fine a company into the harmonious working unit they have a right to be."[69] He pointed out that the stars of the play had "almost a right to such agitations—being artists going through the throes of bringing to birth."[70]

Wilder was eager, as always, for Woollcott's opinion of the production of his play. Before he had seen the play himself, Woollcott reported to Sibyl Colefax that Edward Sheldon had called *The Skin of Our Teeth* "a work of indisputable genius and Helen Hayes thinks of it as the finest script she ever read."[71] After he saw the play in previews in early November, Woollcott wrote Wilder his frank opinion:

> Having seen "By the Skin of Our Teeth" [sic] and thought about it and read it, I know what I think about it. I think no American play has ever come anywhere near it. I think it might have been written by Plato and Lewis Carroll in collaboration, or better still by any noble pedagogue with a little poltergeist blood in him. I had not foreseen that you could write a play that would be both topical and timeless, though I might have remembered from "The Trojan Women" [by Euripides] that it could be done.[72]

However, Woollcott wrote, "Tallulah does not know how to play Sabina and cannot be taught to. She has some assets as an actress, but she is without comic gift. . . . . Tallulah is not a comedienne and thinks she's a wonderful one." Woollcott told Wilder that Sabina's every scene and every line "aches for Ruth Gordon."[73]

Backstage feuds continued long after the play opened on Broadway at the Plymouth Theatre on November 18, but reviews were strongly positive, and Talullah Bankhead and Fredric March had the marquee appeal to draw crowds. The play was a critical as well as a box-office hit, playing to nearly full houses night after night, with a box-office take approaching twenty thousand dollars a week.[74]

Wilder saw his play onstage for the first time in November, just before its New York opening. With the play's successful debut, he hoped he could be free of civilian distractions and concentrate on his military duties, which had grown more and more demanding. That fall Wilder was assigned sixty days of "Detached Service" to travel the country visiting airfields as part of a committee preparing an Air Force document. From Spokane, Washington, on November 24, he mailed notes on *The Skin of Our Teeth* to Harold Freedman, his dramatic agent, asking him to pass them along to his producer and director, as well as to Isabel. He was "overwhelmingly grateful" for the "fine things about the performance," Wilder wrote. The only flaw he perceived in the performance was the "hurry-hurry-hurry"—the "lack of variation in pace" in act 1.[75]

By December 1942 Captain Wilder, part-time playwright, had been assigned to the Pentagon in Washington and, to his astonishment, found himself under siege from the *Saturday Review of Literature*. The December 19 issue of the magazine carried "The Skin of Whose Teeth?—The Strange Case of Mr. Wilder's New Play and *Finnegans Wake*," the first half of a two-part article by Joseph Campbell and Henry Morton Robinson challenging the originality of *The Skin of Our Teeth*, and charging that Wilder's play was "an Americanized re-creation, thinly disguised, of James Joyce's 'Finnegans Wake'"[76] The second installment, "The Skin of Whose Teeth? Part II: The Intention Behind the Deed," appeared in the February 13, 1943, issue. Campbell, a thirty-eight-year-old teacher of literature at Sarah Lawrence College, was at that time working with Swami Nikhilananda on a new translation of *The Gospel of Sri Ramakrishna*, published in 1942, and *A Skeleton Key to Finnegans Wake* with Henry Morton Robinson, which would be published in 1944. Robinson, forty-four, had taught English at Columbia University, was a senior editor at *Reader's Digest*, and would make his fortune as the author of a popular novel, *The Cardinal*, a bestseller in 1950 and 1951, made into a movie by Otto Preminger in 1963. Campbell would become an award-winning teacher, editor, and popularizer of mythology and folklore.

At the time of their attack on Wilder and his play, however, Campbell and Robinson did not have a publisher for their proposed key to *Finnegans Wake*, having been turned down by Benjamin W. Huebsch, who had published the first American edition of Joyce's *A Portrait of the Artist as a Young Man* in 1916. Huebsch was a pioneer in publishing the work of modernists in the United States, working as an independent publisher before joining Viking Press in 1925. In June 1940 Wilder had written to Huebsch that he and Edmund Wilson were conferring on the "knottier problems of *Finnegans Wake*," and that some of them were "mighty dirty."[77] In his reply to Wilder, Huebsch mentioned that Campbell and Robinson had submitted some "good" preliminary material for a proposed key to Joyce's novel, but that it had been turned down. If Wilder—or Wilder and Wilson—should decide to write about some of their discoveries in *Finnegans Wake*, ("including the 'mighty dirty' ones"), Huebesch said he would be interested.[78]

In 1942, working on their proposed key to Joyce's *Finnegans Wake*, Campbell and Robinson attacked Wilder's play. Without using the term "plagiarism," they insinuated that Wilder was guilty of it, and that he had appropriated his play from Joyce's novel. It was no secret that Wilder was studying *Finnegans Wake*. His tribute on the occasion of Joyce's death in 1941 had been published in *Poetry* that March, and his commentary on Joyce and myth-theme in literature would surely have caught Campbell's attention.

The ensuing brouhaha drew welcome publicity for Campbell and Robinson and their proposed book on Joyce, and to the *Saturday Review*, which was trying to build circulation (then about twenty thousand) under the aegis of its founder, Henry Seidel Canby, one of Wilder's Yale professors, and its new chief editor, Norman Cousins. A long, heated exchange of letters to the editor ensued, most of them defending Wilder. This brought more publicity for *The Skin of Our Teeth* but some unwelcome notoriety for Wilder, who, on his lawyer's advice, declined public comment, other than to suggest that people read Joyce's novel and make up their own minds.[79] Perhaps the most spirited defense of Wilder came from Bennett Cerf in "Trade Winds" in the *Saturday Review* in January 1943: Quoting the opening sentences of Joyce's novel, Cerf declared that it was "utterly incomprehensible to ninety-nine percent of the literate public," and that "anybody who can turn that sort of thing into a smash hit on Broadway is entitled to everything he can get."[80]

In his few free hours after his military duties, in response to a telephone request from the editor of the *Saturday Review of Literature*, Wilder drafted a letter documenting his response to the Campbell-Robinson attack. He never mailed the letter, but fortunately it survived among his legal papers, for it provides invaluable insight about how *Finnegans Wake* did and did not figure in Wilder's creation of *The Skin of Our Teeth*. "At the time that I was absorbed in deciphering Joyce's novel the idea came to me that one aspect of it might be expressed in drama," Wilder wrote:

> *the method of representing mankind's long history through superimposing different epochs of time simultaneously. I even made sketches employing Joyce's characters and locale, but soon abandoned the project. The slight element of plot in the novel is so dimly glimpsed amid the distortions of nightmare and the polyglot of distortions of language that any possibility of dramatization is out of the question. The notion of a play about mankind and the family viewed through several simultaneous layers of time, however, persisted and began to surround itself with many inventions of my own. If one's subject is man and the family considered historically, the element of myth inevitably presents itself. It is not necessary to go to Joyce's novel to find the motive of Adam, Eve, Cain, Abel, Lilith, and Noah.*[81]

Wilder went on to say that he had received from Joyce's novel "the idea of presenting ancient man as an ever-present double to modern man," but that the "four fundamental aspects" of *Finnegans Wake* were not to his purpose, nor were they present in his play. Furthermore, he wrote, "The germ of my play, once started, began to collect about it many aspects which had nothing to do with Joyce. It fixed its thoughts on the War and the situation of the eternal family under successive catastrophes." Then, echoing his conviction that a literary work often determines its own form, he said, "But principally the play moved into its own independent existence through its insistence on being theatre. . . . I can think of no novel in all literature that is farther removed from theatre than 'Finnegans Wake.'"[82]

Wilder's unsent letter offered a compelling rebuttal of Campbell and Robinson's contentions about his alleged pilfering from Joyce's novel. For instance:

> In the most wonderful chapter in the novel, *Anna Livia Plurabelle*, river and woman, looks for a match to search for some peat to warm her husband's supper. The authors of the article quote this passage and tell your readers it resembles Mrs. Antrobus and Sabina asking for fuel to warm the household against the approaching glacier. By such devices your authors could derive "*Junior Miss*" from "*Lady Chatterly's* [sic] *Lover.*" The ant-like industry of pedants, collecting isolated fragments, has mistaken the nature of literary influence since the first critics arose to regard books as a branch of merchandise instead of as an expression of energy.[83]

Wilder never did mail his letter, and the controversy eventually died down, but the charges lingered in some academic and critical circles for several years, besmirching Wilder's literary reputation in some of those venues. In 1943 the influential drama critic George Jean Nathan (who, with H. L. Mencken, founded and edited the *American Mercury*) persuaded his fellow critics that because of the charges brought against Wilder's play, and because Wilder had offered no public defense, the New York Drama Critics Circle Award for best American play for 1942–43 should go to Sidney Kingsley for *The Patriots*. Tallulah "Sabina" Bankhead expressed her opinion on the matter a decade later, noting that "Padraic Colum, the Irish critic and friend of Joyce, said Joyce had mined *Finnegans Wake* from the works of the Spaniard, Lope de Vega, one of the most prolific dramatists of all time. Nathan's charge was as ridiculous as it would be to denounce Shakespeare because he found some of his material in Hollingshead's *Chronicles* and Plutarch. It's my guess Wilder is more familiar with De Vega than is Nathan with Joyce."[84] Unlike the New York Drama Critics Circle, the Pulitzer Prize committee was undeterred by the *Saturday Review* flap and awarded Wilder and *The Skin of Our Teeth* the Pulitzer in drama in 1943.

In a preface to an edition of *Our Town, The Skin of Our Teeth*, and *The Matchmaker* in 1957, Wilder wrote that *Skin* was "deeply indebted to James Joyce's *Finnegans Wake*," and went on to say, "I should be very happy if, in the future, some author should feel similarly indebted to any work of mine. Literature has always more resembled a torch race than a furious dispute among heirs."[85]

Wilder had alluded to that torch race in 1940 in a playful letter to playwright and screenwriter Zoë Akins, telling her about his "thefts" from Molière and Francis Bacon in *The Merchant of Yonkers*. "I'm like a woman I heard about who was arrested in Los Angeles for shoplifting," Wilder wrote. "Her defense was 'I only steal from the best department stores, and they don't miss it.'"[86]

31

"WARTIME"

Entering the Army in wartime is like getting married: only the insecure feel called upon to give the reasons for their decision.

—THORNTON WILDER TO ROBERT MAYNARD HUTCHINS,
June 16, 1942

The United States, North Africa, and Italy (1940s)

At Hamilton Field as the intelligence or planning officer at various times for the 324th, 327th, 328th, and 329th Fighter Squadrons, Captain Wilder had bonded with his men, especially the fighter pilots who were assigned not only to defend San Francisco Bay but also to train for overseas battle. Wilder soon discovered that wartime casualties could hit hard close to home. He happened to be Officer of the Day when "everything happened that can tax the resources of an Officer of the Day," he wrote to his mother: a major general arrived at the post unexpectedly; an officer accidentally shot another officer ("fortunately not badly") while cleaning his gun; and, worst of all, one of the pilots in Wilder's squadron crashed to his death on a training mission six miles north of Hamilton Field. It was Wilder's job to go to the scene of the accident to help investigate the tragedy.[1]

He had written to Amy Wertheimer that fall, "My writing life has been set aside for the duration, and very willingly," a message he had shared with other friends and associates, as well as with family.[2] But he was "aching to get back to my Fighter Group, and to hell with military bureaucracy," Wilder wrote to Woollcott December 8, 1942. At that time he was ordered to serve on a team inspecting Air Force bases and operations all over the United States, and in twenty days, Wilder traveled on military business to "Spokane, Tampa, Los Angeles, Fort Worth and many other places," he wrote. "Often grounded by bad weather but never by priorities."[3] While he bristled with impatience at the assignment, he acknowledged that he "should be grateful for having seen the U.S. once more, though once over lightly."[4] Wilder took pride in doing his job well—so much so that he had been crestfallen the day he received his first U, for "unsatisfactory," on a written test. "I went out with some other U's and got doleful-drunk," he reported to Woollcott.[5]

By December he was stationed in Washington and assigned "extra chores"—writing a chapter of a training manual—and other jobs he was not at liberty to describe in detail, but "so far outside the type of any writing I have ever done that I think (in spite of every effort of my own) I won't be assigned any more," he wrote to his mother on January 1, 1943. By then Wilder was careworn, not only from work, but from concern over the family. With Isabel often in New York preoccupied with *The Skin of Our Teeth*, Thornton worried that his mother was alone so much of the time. "This d——d war and that damned play have blown some solitary hours through Deepwood Drive," he wrote to her. "Let's hope that the former is short and the latter's long."[6]

During the fall his mother had been very ill but had refused to see a doctor. He had to "get administrative" about family affairs, he scolded her roundly in a letter: "I still shake my head helplessly when I think of your illness. . . . I suspect that you should not only have called a doctor, but ordered yourself firmly to a hospital as well. I share with you the delusion that if you don't recognize illness it won't increase, but we're both wrong and we can both punish ourselves needlessly and punish those about us by holding to any such nonsense."[7]

His mother was not the only person in his life who could be heedless of personal health. Aleck Woollcott, his longtime friend, confidant, and champion, had suffered multiple heart attacks in the past two years and had been in and out of hospitals. He underwent major heart surgery in 1942, but despite cautions from his doctor, Woollcott insisted on resuming a schedule that by his own acknowledgment would overtax five or ten men. He had barely convalesced before he was traveling; lecturing; doing radio broadcasts; writing magazine articles about, among other topics, *The Skin of Our Teeth*; and editing *As You Were*, a "portable library of American prose and poetry intended for the nourishment and entertainment of men in the armed forces and the merchant marine."[8] He wanted to include Wilder's *Happy Journey*, along with the Declaration of Independence, Lincoln's second inaugural address, and excerpts from the work of Mark Twain, Carl Sandburg, Robert Frost, Oliver Wendell Holmes, O. Henry, Dorothy Parker, and others.[9]

During what proved to be the last month of his life, Woollcott went to the Saturday matinee of *The Skin of Our Teeth*, and was disappointed to find an understudy standing in for Florence Reed, who was very ill. He was afraid to go backstage to inquire about Reed, Woollcott wrote to Wilder, "because of Tallulah who played the first act like a female impersonator."[10] On Saturday, January 23, just four days after his fifty-sixth birthday, Woollcott suffered a heart attack while he was on the air on a broadcast of "The People's Platform" at CBS radio, discussing with Rex Stout and others the question "Is Germany Curable?" Woollcott was rushed to the hospital, where he died that night. For more than a decade Woollcott had been one of Wilder's closest friends. Wilder had dedicated *Our Town* to Woollcott, and in their prolific, multilayered correspondence there are intimations of the conversations they enjoyed over the years, at Neshobe, in New York and Chicago, and wherever they met. The letters brim with mutual affection.

As a letter writer Wilder usually tailored his voice to fit the recipient of the letter. In his copious correspondence with his family, he often shielded them from bad news, editing himself and his own needs and concerns out of his consideration for their needs or worries or expectations. Wilder exchanged many letters with Gertrude Stein and Alice B. Toklas but was, for the most part, Gertrude's witness, listener, and encourager. During his long, rich correspondence with Sibyl Colefax, she was, most often, Wilder's witness, listener, and encourager. In his letters to Woollcott, Wilder could be completely himself, confiding the details of what he was doing, seeing, thinking, feeling, writing. He counted on Woollcott for forthright advice; lively and sometimes wicked gossip; private counsel and public support. Woollcott was at times Wilder's mentor, at times his critic, and very often his advocate.

They had great fun together, in person and on paper, and had many friends in common—Ned Sheldon, Ruth Gordon, Sibyl Colefax, and Orson Welles among them.

Years later, in 1951, Wilder would agree to write about Woollcott, the friend and correspondent, in "Five Thousand Letters to Alexander Woollcott" an essay unpublished in his lifetime, but intended for the *Harvard University Bulletin* to commemorate the deposit of Woollcott's letters and papers in Harvard's Houghton Library. Woollcott enjoyed a gregariousness "not primarily of talent or brains, but of the heart," Wilder wrote. Woollcott believed in maintaining, cultivating, and defending his friendships. He was a "born letter-writer" who knew how to communicate one-to-one. Woollcott had been engaged all his life, Wilder said, in

> *constructing for himself a persona, a façade-characterization, by virtue of which he was able to live with such buoyancy and such intensity among his fellow beings. . . . Woollcott's persona was delightful, clamorous for attention, exasperating, sentimental, moralizing, and could have strains of rigorous moral elevation. . . . It combined the elements of being a kindly and indulgent uncle with those of being a willful, crotchety domestic tyrant.*[11]

A decade before Woollcott died, Wilder wrote to thank him for "sitting at your desk, loyally refusing to believe your ears while I try to disentangle my foolish thoughts, loyally listening to my character and not my words, loyally editing me."[12]

CAPTAIN WILDER was promoted to major April 15, 1943, and assigned to the 12th Air Force intelligence section in Constantine, Algeria, attached to the Army Air Forces Mediterranean Theater of Operations headquarters. "I felt no yearnings for advancement," Wilder wrote to his brother, "except for one thing: a Captain at my age level is not allowed to go overseas. Now I can and shall soon. (But would it be fun to see Father's and S. D. Thacher's face on receipt of the news.)"[13] He echoed that sentiment in a letter to Dwight Dana: "Picture my father's face if he'd been told that Thornton had been advanced to a Major and in a HQ Department called Management, Control, Organizational Planning."[14]

Before he departed for overseas duty Wilder wrote to his brother, "First sign of old age is the often warned and often pooh-poohed one that bachelorhood is less a single blessedness the older you grow. All my colleagues at the office here have fine wives and children, and I confess to the first signs of envy. Yours are the best, and give 'em my love."[15]

ONE OF the pleasures Wilder drew from military life was that he could concentrate on one job, rather than juggle dozens of matters, as he had to do in his complicated civilian life. *The Skin of Our Teeth* had been running on Broadway for six months, and problems behind the scenes mounted rather than subsided. In a very short time Wilder, Isabel, and Montgomery Clift had formed a friendship that would last over the years, so that Wilder was far more worried about Clift than the play when illness had forced him to drop out of the cast in March 1943. Wilder's relationship with Michael Myerberg was anything but cordial, however, and Wilder's last deed before going overseas was to write a stern letter of advice to Myerberg about his mishandling of *The Skin of Our Teeth*. With their standard six-month contracts running out, Fredric March, Florence Eldridge, and Tallulah Bankhead were leaving the play. Wilder blamed their departure on Myerberg, who had "locked up" his mind "in a steel brace,—and transferred the operations of the reason over to sheer blocked unlistening will." He urged Myerberg to do his best to safeguard the production.[16]

It was too late, however. Had the original cast stayed on, the play would no doubt have survived for a much longer run on Broadway. Without its original stars, the last curtain would fall on September 25, 1943, after 359 performances, and the projected national tour fell through after only one week. Nonetheless, as happened with *Our Town*, amateur and stock rights would be immediately in demand.

THAT MAY, as he prepared to go overseas for the duration of the war, Major Wilder also took care of necessary legal matters—updating his will, and solidifying Dwight Dana and Isabel's authority to administer his business and literary affairs in his absence. At the request of his attorneys he also drafted a detailed six-page discussion of "MATERIALS To use in my absence if stupidity, malice, envy or avarice should institute a plagiarism suit against The Skin of Our Teeth."[17] Wilder's New Haven lawyers had in mind recent plagiarism suits filed against George S. Kaufman and Moss Hart for *The Man Who Came to Dinner* and Noël Coward for *Blithe Spirit*. Wilder's scathing dissection of the Campbell-Robinson charges was kept on file by his lawyers but never had to be used, as no litigation materialized.[18] Still, Wilder's forceful defense of his work revealed his passion about the episode, and his astute analytical powers—powers that had served him well as a teacher and scholar, and would make him a highly effective military intelligence officer. "Divide the defense into two parts," he wrote in his contingency "brief":

> Against the charge that the whole play is a theft of the whole novel or any extended portion of it; Against the charge that there are many parallel passages. Concede that the play bears the influence of many works and that among others it reflects the influence of Joyce's novel.
>
> Show that both novel and play have in common that they represent *all mankind represented in one man*, and *the institution of the family represented in one family* . . . Generalized *man* and generalized *family* is a characteristic of modern literature.[19]

He noted that he had employed the universal generalization in his previous work: *Our Town*, for instance, "is about all Towns, and all existences; *The Happy Journey to Trenton and Camden* is about a million American families; etc."[20] Wilder pointed out numerous traditional literary, biblical, and mythological sources which had influenced Joyce and countless other writers, including himself.

His unsent letter to the editor of the *Saturday Review of Literature* had been carefully controlled in tone. Early in the uproar over the attack, Dwight Dana had counseled Wilder that it was important that he not make statements to anyone—advice Wilder had scrupulously honored, perhaps to his detriment.[21] Now Wilder's anger animated this memorandum to his lawyers: Campbell and Robinson were "faking" and "throwing sand," Wilder wrote. They deserved "plenty of ridicule" for their "cooked-up analogies," their "tissue of vague nothings." They were "unable to furnish one real piece of evidence between the two works." Most of all, they clearly did not understand the literary tradition within which he and Joyce and other writers worked.[22]

Satisfied that his family and his lawyers were armed for any domestic battles in his absence, Major Wilder flew out of Presque Isle, Maine, on May 21, 1943, bound for his new assignment in the North African theater of war. Fighting was particularly widespread and intense in Tunisia when Wilder arrived in Algeria, where Gen. Dwight D. Eisenhower was in charge of the U.S. command structure in the prolonged battle for North Africa. Wilder was first stationed at Northwest African Air Force (NAAF) Headquarters as an intelligence officer. After a month he was transferred to NAAF Headquarters, Rear, as a planning officer. He wrote Dana that the next time he visited his law offices he was "going to cast an eye around and see how it's administered." He went on to write that while he loved his work, he hoped that when the war was over, he would "never have to administrate again" and could "return to that excruciatingly 'lone wolf' profession: authorship."[23]

Wilder actually proved to be a highly effective administrator with a knack for strategic planning. He found the preparations for the Italian campaign "fascinating" with the focus on "maps, reconnaissance photographs and computations."[24] It was on an epic, global, life-or-death scale the kind of tantalizing puzzle he had welcomed all his life, whether he was documenting German and Austrian theatrical productions, memorizing musical scores, playing with anagrams or crossword puzzles, or deciphering *Finnegans Wake*. His assignment required a good deal of travel, and he was stationed at times in Bouzaréah, La Marsa, and Algiers as well as Constantine. He traveled on military business to many North African towns and cities—Tunis, Sousse, Oran,

Casablanca, Marrakech. As he moved about North Africa, his quarters, shared with other officers, ranged from a "wealthy Mohammedan's villa," with seven rooms and a large central court, to a five-room city apartment, with a housekeeper who cooked, cleaned, and did laundry, to basic military tents and billets.[25]

Wilder found his civilian life catching up with him even in North Africa, however, when a traveling entertainment group appeared in Constantine, led by the London producer Hugh "Binkie" Beaumont, and starring Vivien Leigh and Beatrice Lillie, who proudly announced that she was singing songs to the troops she had sung "at the end of the last war."[26] "I've been reading Italian and talking Italian to the (happy) Italian prisoners who work at the Post," Wilder wrote to his mother in September 1943.[27] His Italian- and German-language skills were important tools in his work. When he wrote to his family he endeavored to paint a positive picture of his daily life and his work. Yes, he was safe. Yes, he was warm enough, or cool enough, depending on the season. Yes, he had plenty to eat. Yes, he was healthy and strong. Yes, the scenery was beautiful; he would bring his family to see it one day. Mail call one day brought him a "lovely note from Charlotte," he wrote to Amos. "What hopes that raises."[28]

"Nothing so lifts a soldier's morale as getting a letter from home and nothing so depresses him as reading it," Wilder had once written to Woollcott.[29] He was writing not from his own experience so much as from his observation of the young pilots he worked with, especially those whose girlfriends broke their hearts. But in July 1944 Wilder's mail brought him a depressing letter from Charlotte's friend Evelyn Scott, who was convinced that Wilder and his family were deliberately "incarcerating" Charlotte in psychiatric hospitals, and that she was not only completely sane but quite capable of living a normal life on her own. Charlotte was then a patient in the New York State psychiatric hospital at Wingdale, New York, where she was treated with electric shock therapy, insulin therapy, and drugs. Nothing worked for long; the treatments left Charlotte sometimes responsive and stable, sometimes irrational or depressed, sometimes withdrawn, and sometimes aggressive. The family never knew which Charlotte would greet them on their visits.[30]

Wilder wrote a firm but tactful letter to Evelyn Scott in return, noting that he and his family understood that Charlotte could give "every indication of being restored to herself," only to have that "lucid interval" evaporate without warning. Charlotte maintained an "implacable silence" toward her doctors, pretending "not to see nor hear them," and this behavior made it difficult for the doctors to help her. Wilder was reassured, he wrote to Scott, that Charlotte was where she needed to be for her treatment and recovery because Dr. Tom Rennie, "one of the most distinguished doctors for mental illness in the country" and the chief of the Psychiatric Section of New York Hospital, was his friend, and was taking a personal interest in Charlotte's case. "He assures me that there is still a measure of hope that she may rejoin the outside world," Wilder wrote, "and that he will continue to follow her case and let us know when he thinks that she has sufficiently recovered to justify a change of background."[31]

IN APRIL 1944, almost a year into his North African duty, Wilder was nearing exhaustion, feeling every now and then as though he "couldn't flog one more step out of the old horse."[32] He now understood how his father must have felt "those last years on the top of his ill health trying to churn out editorials for the Journal Courier."[33] Wilder wrote to his friend the actor William "Bill" Layton, "God almighty, I shall be 47 this month, and my life has not been such as to prepare me for inflexible routines. I arrive here at 8:15 and seldom leave before 7:15 in the evening and no Sundays off." Nevertheless, he was still "crazy about the work" and his colleagues and his boss.[34] But he constantly hoped, he wrote to his aunt Charlotte, that "this horrendous smashing crashing war will soon be over."[35]

There was some good news from home when some of his literary properties seemed to take on a wartime life of their own. Back in the United States, Isabel and his publishers were fielding requests for translation rights for some of his novels and plays. The Red Cross was showing Howard Estabrook and Herman Weissman's 1944 film version of *The Bridge of San Luis Rey* in Algiers, and all Wilder's clerks were going to see it—without Wilder, who declined. Marc Connelly was performing as the Stage Manager in a 1944 New York revival of *Our Town* directed by Jed Harris at the City Center.[36] Harris had also mounted a successful "London military" production of *Our Town* in 1944, performed by GIs and WAACs for military audiences.[37]

That summer of 1944 Major Wilder hoped to have a few days' leave "at a new rest camp" where he could enjoy the sun and the sea and some time for playwriting. "Another subject has been sneaking up on me that's as promising as the Alcestiad," he wrote to his mother:

> *It's still in the very germinal stage which is about the most fun of all but requires the largest stretches of uninterrupted meditating. All the developments of the plot that one rejects. One rejects so many that the final shape seems not so much a thing created as a thing discovered from the ready-made. You will be horrified to learn that the title of the new one will contain the word Hell! Yes, "The Hell of ——(then an Arab name)".... Isn't that awful?*[38]

The name he would choose was Vizier Kabäar.

———

AFTER HIS promotion to lieutenant colonel on August 27, 1944, Wilder was assigned to Caserta, Italy, headquarters of the newly established Mediterranean Allied Armed Forces (MAAF). As a staff officer in the Air Plans division, Wilder interrogated prisoners of war, gathered and prepared intelligence, briefed and debriefed Allied pilots, and worked on plans for air attacks in Romania, Germany, Austria, and Yugoslavia, as well as strategic plans involving designated sites in Italy and France. Lieutenant Colonel Wilder was no cloistered celebrity soldier, safe at a desk in the United States. He was stationed in the heart of the MAAF control center, dispatched to travel all over Europe when he was not working long hours seven days a week in Caserta.

In addition to his valuable service as a planning and intelligence officer, Wilder made his own unique cultural contributions to the Allies, directing a military production of *Our Town* in Caserta in November

1944, and a Serbo-Croatian production of *Our Town* in February 1945 in Belgrade, this one produced by Tito's partisans, the guerrilla force commanded by Marshal Tito after Germany's invasion of Yugoslavia in 1941. These enterprises gave Wilder a change of pace—sometimes amusing and refreshing, sometimes frustrating and exhausting. He found his days "more and more cluttered" with duties beyond his military assignment, especially as he directed "a group of soldiers with very little theatre and professional experience and some WAC's" who wanted to produce *Our Town* in November 1944. He was "pushed" into serving as acting chairman of a committee supervising an epidemic of theater productions at military headquarters in Caserta—everything from *Our Town* to Sutton Vane's *Outward Bound* to Noël Coward's *Blithe Spirit*, Joseph Kesselring's *Arsenic and Old Lace*, and Gilbert and Sullivan's *Pirates of Penzance*.[39] Nevertheless, overworked as he was, Wilder liked getting to know so many of the airmen, WACs, and WAACs, and "being able to ask them to tell me the stories of their lives."[40]

To relieve himself of some of the burdensome details of these productions, Wilder somehow finagled a transfer for M. Sgt. Lester Martin Kuehl from another air combat unit to his. Before the war, Kuehl had been the assistant stage manager for Jed Harris's Los Angeles production of *Our Town*. Kuehl quickly relieved Lieutenant Colonel Wilder of some of his theatrical chores, especially with *Our Town*. The Stage Manager was played by Sgt. John Hobart, former drama critic for the *San Francisco Chronicle*, who documented the production in "Grover's Corners, Italy," an article in *Theatre Arts* in April 1945. "For exiled Americans overseas," Hobart wrote, "*Our Town* inevitably stirred thoughts of home, and it also summoned a feeling of deep and honest pride. Grover's Corners has never before seemed so wonderful a town or held so tangible a meaning."[41]

Although these amateur productions had their own share of "underground politics and some very bitter feuds," Wilder complained, they still served as a welcome relief from the demanding work and duty schedule: "Day follows days with a featureless uniformity, a sort of winter quarters monotony."[42] Officers and enlisted men came and went, and Wilder especially enjoyed his colleague from British intelligence,

Roland Le Grand, who asked him to serve as best man when he was married in October 1944 in Rome. Their friendship would last far beyond the war, and Wilder was godfather to Le Grand's son, Julian, who was born in 1945.

During his first several months in Caserta, Wilder lived in a tent, a weary forty-seven-year-old sleeping on winter nights huddled under several blankets and his heavy raincoat, with rolls of New York Sunday newspapers for insulation. But as a lieutenant colonel Wilder got his own private tent with a cot, a small table, and a chair, one of many military tents on the grounds of the palace at Caserta, which served as MAAF headquarters. There was no heat or electricity, however. His mother inundated her son, he teased, with "earmuffs, cummerbunds, toe-warmers, velvet kidney protectors, tonsil-guards and candle comforters."[43] He reassured her that he had been issued a B-10 field jacket made of alpaca and mohair with a fur collar. It kept him warm and looked "like a million dollars and twelve distinguished service medals," he wrote.[44] Later he was assigned more comfortable quarters in a trailer on the grounds.

When his Christmas box arrived from Connecticut, jammed with good things to eat, Wilder kept some of the goodies and donated the rest in a collection box for "402 Italian orphans whom some nuns are maintaining at the ragged edge a few miles from here," he wrote to the home folks. "I even re-wrapped them in their bright colorings, so that Isabel's spent time will have a double reception and a double success."[45] During those war days Wilder came to fully appreciate the scale of his aunt Charlotte Niven's ongoing work with the YWCA in Europe. During a trip to Rome he went to the local YWCA, introduced himself as Charlotte Niven's nephew, and was impressed by the affection workers expressed for his aunt. "I see enough of the life of the WAAF and WAC's to know what a tremendous need the YW's fill in their lives," he wrote to her.[46] He commended her for drawing on "heroic resources" to continue her work "so unremittingly all this time."[47]

By year's end Wilder was still "working like a fool," but he occasionally found solace in walking through the Italian countryside. "I feel an even stronger continuity of strong life," he wrote to his mother and sisters, recalling a Carducci sonnet about the patience of oxen in the fields, one that his mother had most likely translated:

> *The oxen pull the plough. Do you remember, Mama, teaching me*
> *Carducci's sonnet, "O Pio Bove,"—here it is. The Lombard pine*
> *and the umbrella pine are all around us; a wonderful eleventh century*
> *church is on the hill; forceful Roman ruins to the west. Oh, there are*
> *lots of times when we all get deeply war-weary with the tragic nonsense*
> *the Germans have raised in the world, but I'm always snatching gratifi-*
> *cations as they come to hand. The Wilders and the Nivens transmitted*
> *to me sufficient vitality to make everything I could out of what I had.*
> *I'm no moper.*[48]

IN FEBRUARY 1945 Wilder learned that Hugh "Binkie" Beaumont and Laurence Olivier had obtained the rights to produce *The Skin of Our Teeth* in London. Olivier's military schedule would permit him to direct the play but not to act in it. Beaumont, head of the theatrical production company H. M. Tennent Ltd., would oversee this success-ful production of Wilder's play in March 1945, starring Vivien Leigh as Sabina. Wilder wrote to Olivier to express his pleasure at the news. "My idea is that the play could give practically the sense of improvisa-tion," he wrote, "a free cartoon, 'The History of the Human race in Comic Strip.'"[49] "The play was magnificent," Beaumont wrote after-ward to Wilder's agent, Harold Freedman, and Olivier did a "first class production job."[50]

Wilder was "galvanized by the tempo of progress in the Pacific Theatre and by the dismay that must be sweeping over Germany." He was quietly arranging for royalties from his plays in Europe to be given to writers and actors in those countries who seemed to be "in distress," or to hospitals.[51] He received the news that Assistant Secretary of State Archibald MacLeish, already planning for postwar days, had recommended him for a civilian post in the American For-eign Service as cultural relations attaché at the American embassy in

Paris, to take effect once he was released from the army. Encouraged by his success in Latin America, Wilder was eager to accept the post. He was ideally suited for this multifaceted assignment, and he hoped it would begin soon, but nothing happened on schedule in the last months of the war.

"I'm tired and I'm in a decline," Wilder had written to his brother and sister-in-law in February. "I'm not tired in body—you never saw such constant health,—nor in mind, exactly. I'm just tired in nature."[52] He had been working nonstop, seven days a week, eleven or twelve hours a day, for nearly two years, deprived, most of the time, of his habitual long contemplative walks and his customary restorative hours devoted to reading or to listening to music. He realized that the "regimen" of "long hours" and "unrelieved singlemindedness finally drains many of one's centers." He wrote to Aunt Charlotte, "My participation in the terrible overwhelming war was microscopic but it was sufficiently related to it to have its reality, and by reason of that I can say I don't regret a moment of it, even though it may have impoverished some of these other centers."[53]

By the end of March he was confined to bed in a military hospital in Italy. On March 29, 1945, Wilder wrote to Amy Wertheimer, "I'm mortified to say that I'm in a military hospital bed!!! For the first time in my life in two wars. A deep-lodged cold not improved by two trips to Jugoslav moved into one ear. However I will be discharged in a day or two. My, I'm ashamed; my record of perfect health is broken."[54] Since boyhood he had been prone to painful ear infections, and as he grew older, they recurred and often left him temporarily deaf in the affected ear. Apparently it was a painful abscess of the inner ear that forced him to be hospitalized. While he was in the hospital, Wilder amused himself reading Plato's *Republic*, *Moby-Dick*, and various detective stories. He also mulled over the themes of three plays that, he said, were "ready and waiting to be written." However, he reflected, "Now that I'm old they don't come so spontaneously; they're built and calculated more carefully, and weighed from all sides." Yet he felt that "their dramatic form seems to get bolder and more adventurous all the time."[55]

When he was well enough to leave the hospital, Wilder spent the rest of April awaiting his discharge from the army and his final instructions from the State Department about the Paris assignment. He took a few days' leave at an air force rest camp on Capri, wrapped up his duties at Caserta, and began to say good-bye to friends and colleagues. He was still in Caserta when the news came of President Roosevelt's death on April 12, 1945. The president had looked gaunt and haggard when he posed for photographs during the Yalta Conference in the Crimea February 4–11, 1945, and was too ill by late March to carry the burden of wartime responsibilities. He died of a cerebral hemorrhage on April 12, 1945. "We're having a memorial service for the President this morning," Wilder wrote to his family from Caserta April 14. "His death had a tremendous effect in this headquarters."[56]

Wilder was still there when the Germans signed a surrender agreement on April 29 at Caserta. By V-E Day, May 8, 1945, he was back in the United States, awaiting discharge orders in Miami. The paperwork was delayed by one bureaucratic snafu after another. "I'm in such a mess of red tape as has never been seen," he wrote to Harry J. Traugott, his clerk in North Africa and Italy, describing the convoluted reassignment process.[57]

Wilder had served in the war with distinction, confirmed by the award of the Bronze Star, the Legion of Merit, and the Chevalier de la Légion d'Honneur. He received an honorary membership in "The Military Division of the Most Excellent Order of the British Empire" for his "ability, enthusiasm and indefatigable energy together with painstaking accuracy," and the official citation noted that his work had "contributed materially to the efficiency and success of air operations."[58] ("Hah! Everybody laughed when little Thornton entered the Army," he wrote.)[59]

He received the news of the MBE in 1945, although the final paperwork was issued in stages by the British War Office and the U.S. War Department in 1946 and 1947, and his receipt of the actual Bronze Oak Leaf emblem that accompanied the MBE was delayed for more than two years because of the postwar "scarcity of supplies and material necessary to manufacture the British insignia."[60] But that summer of

1945, awaiting his discharge orders, Wilder wanted Sibyl Colefax to be "among the first to know" about the Military Order of the British Empire. "That with my Legion of Merit brings my three years of the war to a happy close," he wrote to her. "There are few satisfactions greater than knowing you have the approval of your superiors in a job which involved their responsibility as well as your own. When I heard of this, I thought of my favorite Britisher in the world: 'Sibyl will be pleased,' I said."[61]

He did not regret a moment of his service, but he was eager for the war to be over. "Some of my colleagues are cynical when I talk of how wonderful the day of peace will be," Wilder reflected. "I'm not; it's wonderful enough to know that conscious death dealing has come to an end; the difficulties beyond may be formidable, but I am grateful enough for *that* cessation."[62]

WILDER SPENT more than four months in limbo, in Miami, New Haven, Hamden, and Washington, waiting in vain for his military discharge to come through. As for the assignment in Paris, he was simply physically unable to fulfill it, and had to notify Archie MacLeish that his doctors would not allow him to take it on. "It's all off," Wilder wrote Stein and Toklas in July. "The doctors say I must take 6 months' to a year's rest. . . . What's my sickness? I don't know. Everything and nothing. . . . There's nothing organic the matter. There's nothing that a revolver won't cure. So as soon as I get out of the Army I'm going to Colorado to write plays."[63]

He was, in fact, badly run down, and his "long torpor" and "paralysis of the will" dragged on.[64] In those post–World War II days, long before post-traumatic stress disorder was given its clinical name in 1980, "gross stress reaction" was the formal diagnostic term applied to problems such as those Wilder and other World War II veterans experienced. The profound aftereffects of war had been called combat fatigue or shell shock after World War I, and "soldier's heart" after the Civil War. For Wilder there seemed then to be no cure but rest and time. His family alternately rejoiced in his return and worried about his health, and Isabel alerted friends to the seriousness of Wilder's problems: He had come home "an exhausted, grey-green, limp image of his own former self," she wrote to Sol Lesser.[65] After eight weeks in the United States, he was "just beginning to show signs of being himself," she wrote. Physically he was plagued by lingering ear trouble, occasional deafness, and "a fatigue so great that he will be many more months overcoming that and being in good enough shape to overcome the deafness and head congestion. He is weary to some inner core of being; ill to a point that it is a physical, nervous and with him, spiritual, illness too."[66]

After years of helping to make life-or-death decisions in the war, Wilder couldn't seem to make the simplest decisions at home. He was restless and distracted, as if civilian life were too much for him. After a few days of driving the Green Hornet, he stripped the gears, but fortunately, spare parts for the expensive repairs were available in a nearby town. He had come home from the war "hungry and thirsty for music," Isabel said, and he spent a great deal of time at the piano with an "unconscious sweetness of touch" although he didn't always hit all the right notes. He seemed to take "infinite pleasure and comfort" from the portable Victrola they bought to replace the ones Isabel and her mother had given away to the prisoner-of-war drive.[67]

As the summer wore on, Wilder would occasionally travel in to New York to see his theater agent, Harold Freedman, and his wife, or the director and producer Arthur Hopkins. When Thornton was up to company, Isabella and Isabel invited a few friends at a time to quiet luncheons or dinners at Deepwood Drive—Elia and Mollie Kazan, and Montgomery Clift, who was sometimes invited to spend a couple of days with the Wilders. Thornton had "discovered a most rewarding and happy friendship in Monty Clift, surely our rising great actor, only 24 now," Isabel wrote.[68] The bond between the two men grew stronger when Wilder learned that Clift was also a twin, and they talked at length about the significance of twinship.[69] "I have a new friend—one T. N. Wilder—novelist—playwright," Clift wrote in July 1945.[70] He claimed Wilder as his uncle and his mentor.

Wilder and his mother and sister hoped that writing might help to restore his health, and he began working again on *The Alcestiad*.[71] Later in the summer Jed Harris traveled to Hamden for lunch and an afternoon of intense conversation that stimulated and even agitated Wilder. After Harris departed, Isabel wrote, Wilder "paced up and down the terrace" and not only delivered long scenes of *The Alcestiad* "in full dialogue, but acted out the parts, described the setting, even the props, the costumes." He had shared parts of the play before, but as he walked and talked that sultry summer night, the whole play seemed to come clear to him. Isabel marked his return to writing as a turning point in her brother's homecoming.[72] Now Wilder went into his study each morning and came out energized and excited.

More than thirty years later Isabel remembered that while her brother was "in a camp near Boston" waiting to be separated from the Army Air Forces, "his papers were lost" and that the commanding officer granted him a three-day pass to go to the Boston Public Library, "where he drowned himself once more in the Golden Age of Greece."[73] Wilder was at Camp Devens in Massachusetts in September 1945. On July 23, however, Isabel wrote to Sibyl Colefax that Thornton had lost the manuscript of the "almost completed first act," but "doggedly and courageously he began again, from memory and also from beginning again." The exact circumstances are unclear, but the fact remains that at some point Wilder lost his only copy of the working draft of his play, and reconstructed parts of it from memory, at the same time creating new versions of certain scenes. His own note about the loss does not record exactly when it happened, but the title page of the 1945 draft among his papers reads "THE ALCESTIAD/A PLAY OF QUESTIONS." On the back of the page are Wilder's brief annotations:

Sketches up to and including the Tiresias scene of Act One had been made before the War and lost. Draft One of the first act, May and July 1945. Draft Two, begun July 8, 1945. This Draft Three begun (after the Completion of the First Drafts of Act II and half of Act III) on Dec [*sic*].[74]

At last Thornton was again finding joy in writing.[75] It seemed to his family that word by word, page by page, day by day, the act of writing was "restoring him."[76] There were flashes of his sense of humor in the few letters he wrote that summer of 1945. "In a word I have psycho-physico-somatic-hypsobybalic symptoms, and am enjoying them very much," he said.[77] Two activities were helping him: He was reading Kafka, and he was reading Kierkegaard. He wrote facetiously in a letter, "Just read twice Kierkegaard's Fear and Trembling and know that I haven't got religious faith, that nobody ever has had it, and that it need not concern us."[78]

WHEN HE heard the news on August 14, 1945, that the war was over, Thornton was having dinner with his sister Janet in Washington, where his brother-in-law, Toby Dakin, was still stationed in the International Law Branch of the Judge Advocate General's Office. They "wandered around among the crowds until two a.m., and gazed at the front of the White House," Wilder wrote.[79] He was "full of thoughts about the Atomic Bomb," Wilder told Bill Layton. Those thoughts were going to "explode in the play I do when I've finished The Alcestiad, namely The Hell of the Vizier Kabäar; about the necessity of finding a non-religious expression for the religious (The Alcestiad); and always, always, about the War: and the millions of aspects there are to it."[80]

By August 20 Wilder was back in Miami again, still waiting for his official discharge. As he had often done in the past, Wilder wrote to Sibyl in detail about his work in progress. He hoped the acclaimed actress Elisabeth Bergner, an Austrian refugee, would star in his Alcestiad because she had the range to play the young Alcestis in the first act, the "golden young matron" in the second act, and the "agéd slave, water-bearer in her own palace, with scenes of tragic power and mystical elevation" in the third. "And all to be played," Wilder wrote, "against that crazy atmosphere of the numinous that is possibly hoax and the charlatanism that may be divine. And the preposterous-comic continually married to the shudder of Terror."[81] The play was very difficult, if not impossible, to write, for it "must be subtended by one idea," he said, "which is not an idea but a question (and the same questions as the Bridge of San Luis Rey!). . . ."[82] He was keenly aware as he wrote that every scene must be "balanced just so," and not resort to "dazzling theatrics."[83]

His other play in progress(*The Hell of Vizier Kabäar*, as he now referred to it) would be even more difficult, "but in a different way," Wilder reflected.

> *That will require the good old-fashioned plot-carpentry that I've never done; the joiner's art that must be then rendered invisible, as though it were perfectly easy. . . . The danger of the Alcestiad is that the effectiveness may be greater than the content (to which Jed replied, quoting an old Jewish exclamation:* "May you have greater troubles!" *But what greater trouble could an artist have?) The Hell of . . . can't run into that danger. Its content is not a hesitant though despairing question.*[84]

WILDER LEFT Florida with more manuscript pages in hand, but still no discharge orders. "From other people's stories, I judge that postponements are the order of things in the Army," his mother had written to him. After all, she observed, millions of men had had to be gotten into the army in "record time" and it was predictable that it would take time and some occasional "muddling" to get them out.[85]

Lieutenant Colonel Wilder, soldier and playwright, finally received his separation papers at Camp Devens in Massachusetts on September 19, 1945.[86]

32

"POST-WAR ADJUSTMENT EXERCISE"

[The Ides of March] was, in fact, my post-war adjustment exercise, my therapy. Part almost febrile high spirits and part uncompleted Speculations on the First Things.

—THORNTON WILDER TO GLENWAY WESCOTT,
April 7, 1948

The United States, Mexico, England, and France (1940s)

It is not only work which has kept me silent and interrupted my correspondence with even my best friends," Wilder apologized to Eileen and Roland Le Grand in March of 1946. "It is a sort of post-war malaise which I won't go into further lest I give the impression of self-pity or misanthropy or melancholia. It's none of those things. Call it out-of-jointness, and forgive me. I think I've recovered now."[1] He was too optimistic, however, for his postwar adjustment and recovery would take far more time and effort than he anticipated, and he was only slowly "reacquiring habits of concentration and perseverance."[2] Another factor, no doubt, was that a military intelligence officer's life is governed by the persistent protocols of secrecy—and prolonged enforced secrecy can exacerbate the isolation of an already intensely private man. In 1947 Wilder wrote to British friends June and Leonard Trolley, whose wartime wedding he had helped to arrange in Rome in 1945, "I had a sheltered life during the War and have no right to talk of post-war maladjustment, but that uprooting in my middle age did have bad after effects on me. One of them was a relapse into melancholia, lethargy and unsociableness. . . . What I needed was to work and in order to work, solitude."[3]

His work was his therapy, he said, and he threw himself into it, drafting scenes in his plays, working on the novel that would become *The Ides of March*, and taking up a "compelling" new enthusiasm— trying to establish the chronology of the estimated five hundred plays of Lope Félix de Vega Carpio (1562–1635), the great playwright of the Spanish golden age. At times Wilder devoted ten-hour days to research- ing Lope de Vega in the Yale University Library, and traveled to other libraries as well to examine additional sources and collect new data. "I think this passion was a useful therapy," he wrote; "pure research has nothing to do with human beings." When he realized that this quest to date Lope's plays could be a "Life-work" and that it was an escape from rather than a solution to his problems, he "willed" himself to "quit it," but couldn't stop.[4] Instead, when he was supposed to be writing, he was often preoccupied

> *all day and far into the night on the chronology of the plays of Lope de Vega (but out of the 500, only those between 1595 and 1610). Passion, fury and great delight. Yes, a compulsion complex. Sherlock Holmes as scholar. . . . It is perhaps my harbor from the atomic bomb. In the meantime, letters mount up, duties neglected.*[5]

The time was not entirely wasted, however, for Wilder actually found a kindred playwright in Lope who, as his essay "The New Art of Writing Plays" (1609) reveals, believed in departing from the tradi- tional stage treatment of time and place, and suffusing his plays with both comedy and seriousness of purpose, contending that whether he was writing comedy or tragedy, a playwright could entertain an audi- ence and at the same time communicate a moral purpose.[6]

Lope soon had to make way for another of Wilder's enthusiasms— existentialism, an interest that had fallen on already seeded ground. He had been reading Kierkegaard and Kafka since before the war, and now turned in earnest to the work of Jean-Paul Sartre, who lectured at Yale, Harvard, Columbia, and Princeton, as well as at Carnegie Hall in New York on his 1946 visit to the United States, his second such tour. Wilder was absorbed, he said, "by Existential philosophy and its literary diffusion, especially in France."[7] Sartre and Wilder met on

February 24, 1946, when Sartre gave two lectures at Yale, and they saw each other often that year. Later Sartre invited Wilder to translate *Morts sans sépulture*, his controversial new play, which would open in Paris that November. Sartre did not give Wilder a copy of the play until two years later, but he described it. "Jean-Paul Sartre has given me the American disposition of a play he's written that would freeze your gullets," Wilder wrote to Ruth Gordon and her new husband, the writer Garson Kanin. "Will any American manager produce it? Five French Maquis are variously tortured and raped by some Pétain militiamen. But it's not about the Resistance movement; it's about the dignity of man and the freedom of the will."[8]

By March 1946 Wilder believed he had almost finished *The Alcestiad*.[9] He told his brother that the play was "about how Alcestis had real Kierkegaardian despair"—the despair born out of the struggle over whether and how to realize and connect to the Self, and to become the Self "grounded transparently in the Power which constituted it."[10] Wilder doubted whether Alcestis could resolve this dilemma by the time a three-act play was over.[11]

Meanwhile he was working on *The Ides of March*, his "novel-in-letters about Julius Caesar and the scandal of the profanation of the mysteries of the Bona Dea."[12] The Roman "good goddess," or goddess of fertility, the Bona Dea was worshipped in secret rites by aristocratic Roman matrons and the Vestal Virgins, and at least one ceremony had allegedly been violated by the presence of a man in disguise, said to be the Roman politician Clodius Pulcher. Wilder incorporated the character and the event into the novel he had been thinking about since his first Roman sojourn in 1920–21. He was also filling his manuscript with Caesar's ideas about leadership, politics, power, and liberty, as well as Cicero's thoughts on the poetry of Catullus.[13]

The work was going slowly but he kept at it, dispatching Isabel to New York and then to London in his stead to represent his interests in Jed Harris's revival of *Our Town*—an assignment that proved to be a full-time job for Isabel, who welcomed the travel and the excitement, even though Harris was as difficult and demanding as ever. Already Isabel was becoming the historian and archivist of her brother's work, as well as his proxy and his agent on the scene. When Amos wrote to inquire about how Thornton's plays were faring, Isabel gave him an accounting: The Italian dramatic company run by Wilder's friend, the great Italian actress Elsa Merlini, had produced *Our Town* in Italy in 1939, despite Fascist efforts to disrupt the performances. She was now touring Italy with the play in her repertory. Merlini had told Wilder that while many Italians did not "completely understand Act I and II," they "adored and understood Act III" and waited patiently to see it.[14]

Isabel also reported to Amos that *Our Town* had been performed in Switzerland, Sweden, Argentina, and Hungary, and, in a pirated production, in Spain. *Our Town* was the first foreign play to be performed in Berlin soon after the occupation, with audiences transfixed as they sat or stood in the rubble of buildings. Plays could be performed only by approval of the occupying powers in each country, and Isabel noted that "the Russian authorities stopped it" in their zone in Berlin after three days, purportedly because the play was "unsuitable for the Germans so soon,—too democratic." *Our Town* was successfully performed in Munich, however, and Wilder's Swiss-based agent, who handled the German-language productions of the play in Switzerland, Austria, and Germany, let them know that it was being done all over Germany. *Our Town* had played during the war in military prison camps, and in a USO performance in Holland. The leaders of a festival to celebrate the liberation of Holland sought the rights to perform *The Skin of Our Teeth* because, they said, "it speaks for them" and "the whole world at this time rising out of ruins." Authorities in Japan requested permission to translate and perform *Our Town* in native Japanese theaters because of its reflection of the "American and democratic way of life and the art and literature it represents."[15] American occupation authorities were already beginning to turn to Wilder as an artistic voice during what would become the Cold War.[16]

Wilder said to an interviewer in 1948:

One of the greatest gratifications of my writing life has been the reception of *Our Town* and *The Skin of Our Teeth* in Germany. During the run of *Skin* in New York I was already in the service, but I was astonished at the fact it was never listed among plays dealing with the war, the preoccupation then in everyone's mind. The Germans not only had no doubt that it dealt with the war, but found that the role of Cain throughout the play, and the third act, had for them all but unbearable actuality.

He noted that the Russians said they banned *Our Town* because it glorified the family, and *Skin* because it represented war "as inevitable." But, Wilder said, "To a half-attentive listener *Skin* says the very contrary."[17] In those postwar days, when people were hungry for normalcy and hope, Wilder's plays were establishing him as a familiar voice, American as well as international. In half-destroyed, makeshift theaters around the globe, diverse audiences were finding personal as well as universal resonance in his characters and themes.

———

ISABEL WILDER stood at a crossroads in the 1940s as she took on more and more of the responsibility for overseeing her brother's literary affairs, as well as Charlotte's medical treatment. In 1939 Isabel had entered into a publishing agreement with Coward-McCann, which held the option to publish the novels she hoped to write after *Let Winter Go*. For an advance of three hundrd dollars, she agreed to deliver a new novel in the fall of 1939, a deadline later postponed to September 1, 1940. During that time Isabel also worked on a play, and while she did deliver the novel in 1940, she withdrew it just before it went to the printer, recalling that she did so because of "the outbreak of the War."[18] Tim Coward had earlier admonished Isabel to make prudent decisions about her own literary career. "You have got to get going with your own development or you never will," he chided. "I know this business of the theatre is fascinating and can eat up the years. If you want to be a sort of general advance agent, stage manager, and go-between for Thornton, that is all right, if you do it with your eyes open. But you are not going to do much creative stuff yourself as long as you do the other."[19]

Isabel kept trying to write after the war, but gradually set aside her own creative work and concentrated on Thornton's. During the war, with her brother far away, Charlotte hospitalized, and her mother growing older, Isabel had become the family's official "stage manager"—orchestrating Charlotte's care, Thornton's literary business, her mother's daily life. Whether these duties served as the reason or the excuse, they increasingly consumed her attention and energy, and Isabel set aside her own writing—with some relief, it may be speculated, for she had always found writing hard work. She could never be certain that she hadn't ridden her brother's coattails to her first publishing contract with one of her brother's publishers. Marriage and a home of her own had eluded her, but now she had a brother, a sister, and a mother who needed and depended on her, and she devoted her energy to them.

Charlotte, meanwhile, faced her own battles throughout the forties, still declining, for the most part, to acknowledge that she was or ever had been physically or mentally ill, still refusing to cooperate with her doctors and nurses, alternating between lethargy and depression, and periods of aggression and hostility—toward her family, her caregivers, and her fellow patients. Sometimes she spent hours writing poetry or prose, or letters, some cogent, some irrational, to friends, relatives, or strangers. Often antisocial and belligerent, she did not want to engage with other patients, or, at times, with her family members when they came to visit. She also began to suffer gastrointestinal and other serious physical health problems.

While Thornton had moved during the war years from the United States to North Africa to Italy and home again, Charlotte had moved to the Westchester branch of New York Hospital in White Plains, then to Harlem Valley State Hospital in Wingdale, New York, and finally to the Long Island Home, a private psychiatric hospital in Amityville, New York. She was transferred there in January 1945, on the recommendation and referral of Wilder's friend Dr. Thomas Rennie. By 1944 Charlotte was convinced that there were at least three people masquerading as Thornton Wilder, disguising themselves with makeup, using her brother's name, and even writing his books and plays. "The Thornton Wilder who wrote *The Skin of Our Teeth* is not the same man who wrote *The Bridge of San Luis Rey*," she told Isabel.[20]

Charlotte clung to her own dreams of writing. She had not lost her "devotion" to her "expressive needs," she wrote to Evelyn Scott, but she had no privacy at Amityville, and she felt that her words were "read and returned to her mockingly."[21] In November 1945 Charlotte wrote Evelyn that she had to throw away "about eight months' work, some of it . . . the most 'precious'" she had ever done. She couldn't see visitors at Amityville, she said to Scott, "not even you." When people came to see her they seemed like strangers, she wrote, "some of them nicer than in life; but—the psychiatrist's ace trump, I suppose, a club. Thornton twelve feet high, without the hat!"[22]

Charlotte wrote angry, often incoherent letters to her family, including one to her mother on April 15, 1945, about how no one in the family appreciated her poetry, or Isabella's. Charlotte spoke of her mother's demands of "impossible perfection."[23] She wrote to Amos in 1946 asking him to return to her the manuscript she called "I Remember," which she had entrusted to Evelyn Scott, who in turn had given it to Amos for safekeeping. "Could you at, at your convenience, send it to me?" Charlotte asked her brother. "It is so personal in character that I doubt I shall ever offer it for publication: that too, is why I do not suggest that you read it, before sending it, should you feel the inclination to do so."[24] Charlotte chastised Amos: "I am well, not ill, never having been ill, and should be allowed to leave here," she wrote, blaming Amos, Thornton, and their mother for withholding permission.[25]

Difficult as it was, the family believed that Charlotte was where she had to be, and they worked closely with her doctors, visited her when the doctors approved, and provided generously for all her personal needs—right down to, later, the pipes and tobacco she enjoyed smoking.

IN HAMDEN, Isabella and Isabel collaborated long after Thornton came home from the war to buffer him from stress and shield him from people he did not want to see. They entertained friends whose company would be good for him, however. "Our house is honored this weekend by two Golden Guests, Laurence Olivier and Vivien Leigh," Thornton wrote to Amos in May 1946. "Larry, the greatest English actor in 200 years, says he is using the drive down here to study Lear which he brings to London in the Fall!"[26] He called Olivier and Leigh "the Dioscuri" because he said, "I like to think of happy married couples as twins."[27]

Thinking that rest by the sea would be good for Thornton and his work, Isabella and Isabel decided they should spend part of the summer of 1946 on Nantucket. It was there, near the end of June, that Isabella finally acknowledged to her children that she was very ill and needed help. She had cancer and had been trying to conceal the gravity of her illness from the family, including her sister, Charlotte. "She was suddenly taken ill last Thursday and we lost her Saturday morning," Wilder wrote to Amy Wertheimer. "During the illness all her dear traits were before us in a new light—her self-effacement, her unwillingness to be a subject of concern, her Scots independence—her wanting to go through it all in her own way—all unforgettable and finding its way into the book I'm working on."[28] He wrote to his longtime friend William Rose Benét, "Henceforth the big things and the small things of life lose half their force because we cannot share them with her."[29] A poet to the end of her life, Isabella wrote about death in what was to be her last poem, found on the table next to her bed after she died. It began, "This earth is my favorite heaven! / Oh do not bid me go hence."[30]

When Isabella died Wilder lost an encourager and a trusted critic as well his mother and the center of his family life. Facets of Isabella's personality and character are etched into the mothers Wilder portrayed onstage and in the pages of his fiction, especially in the dreams that they nurtured in their children. After his mother's death Wilder immediately set out to reconfigure his family life. He relinquished plans to go abroad, in order to stay at Deepwood Drive with Isabel, at least until Christmas, "finishing the novel and sort-of re-establishing a home. Important for Isabel is the feeling that she is needed and useful somewhere; otherwise—you can see—she seems to hang in mid-air."[31]

FOR WILDER 1946 was a year of continual losses, his mother's death first of all. Charlotte was growing worse. His friend and confidant Ned Sheldon died April 1. Gertrude Stein died July 27, after undergoing cancer surgery. In the fall Wilder wrote to Alice B. Toklas of "the several Gertrudes"—of "the Gertrude who with zest and vitality could make so much out of every moment of the daily life," of her capacity for friendship and "intellectual combat," and the "giant-Gertrude" who "broke the milestones behind her."[32] He would understand if she had chosen someone else to be her literary executor, he said. In fact, in a clause in her will written just before her surgery, Stein had put her longtime friend Carl Van Vechten in charge of decisions about her unpublished work. Wilder offered Toklas his assistance with Stein's papers at Yale in any case, especially since he had persuaded her to deposit them there originally, and had recently "interested the editors of the Yale University Press in a possible publication of *Four in America*."[33]

When Yale University Press published *Four in America* in 1947, Wilder provided in the introduction a clear summation that probably endowed Stein's work with more clarity than it actually possessed. Her work was unorthodox, Wilder emphasized, encouraging readers to "relax your predilection for the accustomed, the received, and be ready to accept an extreme example of idiosyncratic writing."[34] He paid special note to a question that had fascinated him long before he met Stein: He thought that it could be said "that the fundamental occupation of Miss Stein's life was not the work of art but the shaping of a theory of knowledge, a theory of time, and a theory of the passions. These theories finally converged on the master question: What are the various ways in which creativity works in everyone? That is the subject of this book."[35] Twenty years later Wilder would pose the question in his own way as a motif in *The Eighth Day:* "Nothing is more interesting than the inquiry as to how creativity operates in anyone, in everyone: mind, propelled by passion, imposing itself, building and unbuilding."[36]

WILDER SET aside the manuscript of *The Ides of March* so that he could take care of matters at home after his mother died. Once he felt he could leave Isabel, he drove without mishap to the Gulf Coast. In Biloxi and Pass Christian, Mississippi, and in New Orleans, Wilder forged ahead with his novel, doing "some fascinating Cleopatra-Caesar business," and then moving back to the Catullus story and the Clodius conspiracy. "My narrative interest is threatened by too much colorful digression," he said.[37] Wilder spent most of the winter at Mérida on the Yucatán Peninsula. "The novel's going fine. It talks to me all the time," he wrote to Isabel. "Last night it woke me up just as The Skin used to do in Quebec."[38]

All his writing life Wilder craved solitude, the long, unstructured blocks of time that were essential for unfettered imagination, and then the patient work of creating the story and the characters and rendering them on the page. But the solitude often came with a price of loneliness and renunciation. While he often hated the solitude, he found it was "the only way to work."[39] In Mérida he quickly settled into a daily routine of work, breaking about five in the afternoon to "go over to the ruins until dark, taking the best guide with me or some learned treatise from the hotel's library."[40] He was fascinated with the Mayan ruins at Mérida and Chichén Itzá. "The ruins are overwhelming," he wrote to the poet and translator Leonard Bacon:

> *Were life 200 years long I'd love to set aside 5 to "fix" the infinitely complex symbolism of Gods and forces on the sculptures. . . . I feel in my bones the archaeologists are wrong,—as they were wrong in Greece for a hundred years. Those dandruff-covered library mice, the savants, are not the men to interpret the violence and fear-haunted imagination and the ceremonial magnificence of a race like Maya-Toltec.[41]*

His explorations of the Mayan ruins provided an evocative parallel to his literary explorations of the ruins of Caesar's Rome, as he interpreted in his novel the "violence and fear-haunted imagination and ceremonial magnificence" of Caesar's empire and era. By late March

1947 in Mérida, where it was "hot as hell," Wilder was thinking about returning to New Orleans—although he hated to move just then, he wrote Isabel, "because the daily novel-writing thing is going fine." He had written some "new stuff" and "some more that's very wicked and very funny. The book's yelling with life."[42]

He was back in New Orleans in April 1947, and then in Washington through May, reading Roman history and literature at the Library of Congress, and settling once and for all on the title of the novel. In late July he was at Saratoga Springs "working like a beaver" because he had promised to deliver the text of *The Ides of March* to Harper by August 1, 1947, "a wild and irresponsible engagement that I cannot live up to."[43]

As his absorption in finishing the novel grew, his attention to *The Alcestiad* had declined. Once more he gave up his work on the play, in part because of his postwar "malaise," but mainly, he wrote to the Trolleys, because "my ideas about life had changed and I felt it to be sentimental. Instead I'm working on my novel about Julius Caesar, told in letters exchanged between the characters—and such characters!! Caesar, Cicero, Catullus and Cleopatra!!"[44] He came to this subject naturally, having grown up reading the classics at home and at school. From his early teens he was especially intrigued with Caesar and Cleopatra. The idea for *The Ides of March*, as has been noted, took root when he was a student at the American Academy in Rome in 1920–21, and he had sketched the plot in a letter to his mother in 1922.[45] Over the years he explored the concept in his journal, as in this entry in February 1939:

> Suppose I wrote *The Top of the World* and prefaced it with this
> note: "in this novel I have put into Julius Caesar's mouth words
> gathered from many authors in many different ages. The discourse
> to Catullus on nature is a paraphrase of Goethe's 'Fragment' of
> 1806. The arguments on the immortality of the soul in the con-
> versation with Cicero are from Walter Savage Landor and he in
> turn was indebted for several of them to Plato and Cicero."[46]

He had been gathering sources for *The Ides of March* for more than twenty-five years, sometimes unconsciously, sometimes intentionally. He was "deep in the politics of 44 B.C.," he had written to Stein and Toklas from Austria in 1937 when he was reading a "very good and frightening book called *Der Kampf um Caesar's Erbe* by Ferdinand Mainzer."[47] In 1942, on his cultural mission to South America, he had discovered a "new enthusiasm" in the figure of the legendary Venezuelan general Simón Bolívar (1783–1830). "I read the thousands of letters by him and laugh all the time at the contemplation of such gifts," Wilder wrote.[48] He was so drawn to Bolívar's combination of despair and hope that he modeled his Caesar in part on the general: "For a Caesar I was richly fed by a great admiration for the thousands of pages of Simón Bolivar's correspondence: a lofty smiling half-sad unshakenness in the face of the betrayal of friends and beneficiaries."[49] Wilder also immersed himself in the letters of Cicero. He acknowledged the influence of other writers, such as his longtime affinity for Goethe; his deepening knowledge of the work of Kierkegaard, thanks in part to his brother Amos, and to their friend Walter Lowrie, a noted Kierkegaard scholar and translator; and his reading of Sartre and his translation of Sartre's play. *The Ides of March* was also shaped by Wilder's talks on leadership with Gertrude Stein, and his own wartime encounters with military leaders and the politics and propaganda of military and civic power.

Like the novels that preceded it, *The Ides of March* is character- rather than plot-driven, and two characters occupy center stage: Caesar and Cleopatra. "The novel's full of glitter now that Cleopatra has arrived in Rome," Wilder wrote Ruth Gordon and Garson Kanin, "but it's also getting deeper, wider and more preposterous,—yes, that's the word for the burden of vast implications I've assigned myself."[50] But from time to time the "work on the novel stumbled," and when that happened, Wilder wrote to Sibyl Colefax, "I rolled up my sleeves to do a page or two to keep it in hand, and it came fine." He wrote a "funny" scene in which Cicero had dinner with Cornelius Nepos, and as they talked about Caesar, Cicero's "fear, envy, and incomprehension" came out as "wit. Very funny." The novel needed color, Wilder said, and he tried to juxtapose "very funny places" with "much that is painful" and much, he hoped, that was "beautiful."[51] He fused antiquity of subject with timelessness of theme in the novel, and encapsulated them in an innovative form that broke the fictional boundaries of structure, time, point of view, and voice. Wilder chose the epistolary form for his novel because, as was his habit and desire, he was experimenting with structure. He also wanted to avoid the omniscient narrator typical of most fiction.

"All art is pretense but the pretense of the historical novel is particularly difficult to swallow," he wrote about *The Ides of March* when an excerpt from the novel was published in 1950 in *105 Greatest Living Authors Present the World's Best Stories, Humor, Drama, Biography, History, Essays, Poetry*. Wilder went on to explain his methodology: "I therefore moved the pretense over to a different terrain: I pretended to have discovered a large collection of letters and documents written by these notable persons. I attempted to coerce belief by submitting a sort of apparatus of historical method and scholarship." In addition, he said, he "had approached the effect of the theatre." He believed that in a "novel-in-letters each document tends to give the impression of a speech, a cry, at which we are present." Furthermore he surrounded his work "with a veil of irony, offering it as a sort of parody of historical scholarship. I begged the question in that I not so much asked the reader to 'believe' me as to 'play this game' with me."[52]

Looking back on his novel in 1956, Wilder wrote to Maxwell Anderson:

> Of all the works I've done that book comes nearest to what one would call fun. Fun to shift from voice to voice; to build up the complicated time-scheme (there are several howling boners in it); fun to parody the apparatus of a work of scholarship; fun to force the reader to assume that people have been much the same in all times and ages.[53]

———

THERE WAS growing concern in the Wilder family in 1947 because, six years after her breakdown, Charlotte was getting no better and her future seemed hopeless. Dr. Mildred Squires and her staff at Amityville considered recommending a prefrontal lobotomy as the only remaining option for Charlotte's treatment. She was referred to Dr. John E. Scarff, a neurosurgeon and a principal member of the staff of the Neurological Institute at New York–Presbyterian Hospital. Dr. Scarff thought Charlotte would be a good candidate for the procedure—which was controversial but frequently used in the 1940s and 1950s, when more than forty thousand lobotomies were performed in the United States.

The surgery severed the nerve fiber system between the prefrontal region of the brain and the thalamus, "the seat of emotional feelings."[54] The family was warned of the seriousness of the operation and the great risks involved: If positive results did not materialize within two years, there was little hope of recovery, and danger of a permanent vegetative state. The Wilders decided there was no choice but to take the risk, however, and Charlotte was lobotomized by Dr. Scarff at the Neurological Institute of Presbyterian Hospital in the spring of 1947.[55] Charlotte came through the surgery well and seemed herself immediately afterward, although she had no memory of what had happened to her. Doctors told the family that although it was too early to know how she would respond, her personality appeared to be intact.[56]

Within a few weeks, however, Charlotte had regressed and reverted to her presurgery behavior—alternately withdrawn and passive, or depressed, or hostile and aggressive. At times she had to be confined in a special ward "under complete supervision." She wrote letters that were sometimes lucid and normal, and at other times irrational and paranoid. She often wrote poetry, which the family hoped they might get published to encourage her, but the poems were only shadows of her earlier work.[57]

About two and a half years after her lobotomy Charlotte suddenly, for no apparent reason, seemed to come back to life. She was pleasant and responsive, and eager to see her family. Soon she was well enough to go by herself into the village of Amityville to a coffee shop or to the movies. More than anything else, she wanted to go back to Manhattan—to live in her own apartment again, to have her own independent life, and to write.[58]

WILDER HAD to finish his novel in 1947. He and his family needed the infusion of income, but most of all his immersion in *The Ides of March* had helped him regain his creative energy and momentum. He delivered the final manuscript to Harper & Brothers in the fall of 1947, and the novel was published on January 16, 1948. At the request of *New York Times* critic Brooks Atkinson, who was preparing to review *The Ides of March* in February 1948, Wilder wrote a detailed accounting of the sources that had helped to shape certain characters and episodes in the novel: His severely disabled friend and mentor Ned Sheldon was the model for Caesar's friend and confidant Lucius Mamilius Turrinus, who had survived wartime torture that "was progressively cutting off his limbs and depriving him of his senses."[59] Caesar confided in Turrinus as Wilder had confided in Sheldon. Wilder dedicated his novel to Sheldon and to the Italian poet Lauro De Bosis. "To Edward Sheldon," Wilder wrote, "who though immobile and blind for over twenty years was the dispenser of wisdom, courage, and gaiety to a large number of people."[60]

Lauro De Bosis was, in part, the model for Gaius Valerius Catullus. Wilder had known De Bosis since his first journey to Italy, and their friendship continued when De Bosis came to the United States in 1928 as executive secretary of the Italy-America Society in New York. De Bosis had at first been sympathetic to Mussolini and Fascism, but by 1924 had begun to oppose the Fascist regime and its totalitarian policies. By 1930 he had resigned his job with the Italy-America Society and returned to Italy, where he organized a resistance group, the Alleanza Nazionale, hoping to facilitate a coalition of opposition forces to thwart the spread of Fascism in Italy.

Inspired in part by Percy Bysshe Shelley's political tracts, De Bosis wrote letters and pamphlets attacking Mussolini and the Fascists, and urged people to pass them on as chain letters to sympathizers. When he heard that activist Giovanni Bassanesi had dropped 150,000 anti-Fascist pamphlets in a flight over Milan in 1930, De Bosis began to plan his own similar flight over Rome—despite the fact that he had never flown a plane. He raised funds to purchase a small plane, took a few hours of flying lessons, armed himself with 200,000 anti-Fascist letters, and set out on his quest. When his plane was damaged en route as he stopped to refuel, De Bosis had to abandon the aircraft and its cargo of letters. The purpose of his foiled mission was discovered, and he went underground in Switzerland, raised funds for another small plane (this time with a contribution from his mistress, the actress Ruth Draper), and had 400,000 copies of his letter printed.

On October 2, 1931, De Bosis made the flight to Rome, scattering letters over the city in his wake, and flying so low over Mussolini's headquarters that spectators said it looked as if the plane were actually climbing the Spanish Steps. He managed to penetrate Roman air defenses as he flew into the city and as he climbed skyward on departure—but after he left the city his plane disappeared, never to be found.[61]

Wilder wove the device of "The Broadsides of Conspiracy" into his novel—creating a "chain letter" that "was circulated throughout the Peninsula by the thousands" by the Council of Twenty, conspirators who hoped to "Shake off the Tyranny under which our Republic groans."[62] He wrote in the dedication to *The Ides of March* that Lauro De Bosis was a "Roman poet who lost his life marshaling a resistance against the absolute power of Mussolini; his aircraft pursued by those of the Duce plunged into the Tyrrhenian Sea."[63] Actually Mussolini's planes were not able to take off in time to pursue De Bosis, and no trace of the poet or his plane was ever reported. De Bosis was thirty years old.

"I have just finished your book," Ruth Draper wrote to Wilder in March 1948. "I am fairly dazzled by its brilliance. . . . Of course I felt a deep emotion when I read the dedication. I felt too a great pride in my association with a work of such beauty, dedicated to the memory of my lover, & my beloved friend—both heroes,—both men of lofty vision." She had always hoped Wilder would write something about De Bosis and Sheldon. "I am so grateful to you," she wrote, "so proud & happy thinking of their pride could they know that their names & a record of their achievements stand together on your page."[64]

Wilder modeled at least one of his characters after someone who was still vitally alive—Tallulah Bankhead. His reflections on Roman women born into great houses in "the Old Roman Way" were illuminated by his knowledge of Bankhead's background. He told Maxwell Anderson, "I'll give you 2½ guesses as to what lady well known to the U.S. public—daughter, granddaughter, descendant of senators, governors, etc., etc. gave me some 'lights' on how a Clodia ticked (the revolt against being duped by society's genteel facade)."[65] Clodia Pulcher was a controversial woman, according to various Latin sources of the period, "an important and ruthless political force and an ostentatiously abandoned hussy."[66] Wilder's Caesar writes in his journal that Clodia lived "only to impress the chaos of her soul on all that surrounds her."[67]

The Ides of March is a complex novel about the dynamics of religion, ethics, leadership, power, politics, love, and art, especially literature. Wilder explores the nature of the written word—the introspection and self-revelation of the journal; the intimate communication and occasional subterfuge of the letter; the disclosing or withholding of the self in poetry; the truth or the distortions of history and biography. He was surely thinking of Charlotte—and perhaps Amos and Isabel and himself as well—when he had the poet, orator, and historian Asinius Pollio draw a portrait of poets in a long letter to Vergil (Wilder's chosen spelling of the name in *The Ides*) and Horace in book 1 of the novel. According to Wilder's Pollio, poets were thought to be "inept in all practical matters," as well as absentminded, impatient, and subject to "excessive passions of all sorts." Furthermore Pollio believed that "all poets in childhood have received some deep wound or mortification from life which renders them forever fearful of all the situations of our human existence. In their hatred and distrust they are driven to build in imagination another world."[68]

"THIS CAESAR is the most personal expression of mine in the book, and yet I am not aware of running counter to 'facts' at any point (save, of course, the chronology of his wives)," Wilder wrote to Brooks At-kinson.[69] Wilder knew before the novel was published that his "liber-ties with 'history'" would "annoy the learnéd and render the layman vaguely uneasy." He wrote the latter words to the poet Rosemary Benét, who was preparing a profile of him to include in the Febru-ary 1948 *Book-of-the-Month Club News*, featuring *The Ides of March* as a March selection.[70] He was surprised that his novel was even chosen for the Book-of-the-Month Club, and was happy to cooperate. "It wouldn't hurt to mention that I spent two years of my life in Central and South-ern Italy,—one studying archaeology; the other in the War," he told Benét (who was the wife of Stephen Vincent Benét). "That won't make the book any more 'factual' but it will tend to give the impression that most of the time I at least knew where I was inventing. In addition, my novel is my second one about Rome, (and I certainly would love to do one about that city in the Renaissance, too!)."[71]

Despite Wilder's concentration on *The Ides of March*, his journal, his imagination, and his writing hours were still haunted by another com-pelling figure—Alcestis, the heroine of the play he had put aside. By now the stories of Caesar and Alcestis were so interwoven in Wilder's imagination that as he suspended his work on *The Alcestiad*, he im-ported the story into book 1 of *The Ides*, retelling the legend of Alcestis in a letter that Asinius Pollio writes to Vergil and Horace.

Wilder had written a "fantasia on certain events and persons of the last days of the Roman republic," he explained in a brief preface to the novel, and he played with time, as he made perfectly clear to his read-ers: *"The reader is reminded,"* he wrote at the outset of book 2, *"that the documents in each Book begin at an earlier date than those in the preceding Book, traverse the time already covered, and continue on to a later date."*[72] This kaleidoscopic refraction of time and events is shaped by different characters, different voices, different angles of vision. Wilder's epigraphs in the novel forecast his major themes. First he renders a slightly flawed translation of lines from Goethe's *Faust, Part Two*: "The shudder of awe is humanity's highest faculty / Even though this world is forever alter-ing its values. . . ." Then he offers a "Gloss": "Out of man's recognition in fear and awe that there is an Unknowable comes all that is best in the explorations of his mind,—even though that recognition is often misled into superstition, enslavement, and overconfidence."[73] When asked about his intentions for *The Ides of March*, Wilder told an interviewer that his novel "attempts to show the mind of a man like Julius Caesar, with enormous experience of men and affairs, trying to separate the elements of superstition from those of religion, the elements of exploitation from those of government," and endeavoring to determine whether his own role as the Roman emperor was "of his own making or whether he was an instrument of a Destiny Force beyond his knowledge."[74]

Within his major themes in *The Ides of March*, Wilder examines topics he had explored in his preceding work: love, family, religion, fate, chance, and destiny. In this novel he also contemplates power, leadership, politics, propaganda, and mortality. Although Wilder's penchant for irony must be taken into account, he seems to answer his earlier questions about whether love is sufficient when he has Catullus write to Clodia, "Never, never, can I conceive of a love which is able to foresee its own termination. Love *is* its own eternity. Love is in every moment of its being: all time. It is the only glimpse we are permitted of what eternity is."[75]

———

The Ides of March, published when Wilder was almost fifty-one, is far richer, more mature, more complex, and more accomplished in form, theme, and characterization than his earlier works of fiction. The novel is beautifully written; its strong, clear passages are infused with wisdom. It is a testament to his continuous evolution as a novelist and stylist, as well as a thinker. Although Wilder still probed the meaning of love, of religion, of fate, of destiny, he seemed at least to have made a measure of peace with some of the old questions, as if he had come to recognize and accept the unknowable. He also tackled new questions: His experience in the prewar and war years led him to a prolonged contemplation of the nature of leadership, the risks and obligations of power, the dangers of propaganda, and the dynamics of freedom and individual responsibility.

He had wanted to write a novel that was like a play, and he

succeeded.[76] His tactics in the epistolary novel led to the creation of complex characters vividly revealed through dialogue in letters and journals. Rightly or wrongly, his characters speak definitively for themselves—and Wilder's Julius Caesar is the most complex, fully developed, multidimensional character he ever created. In some ways *Ides* is also a novel of manners, as *The Cabala* had been and, later, *Theophilus North* would be—not glib, superficial commentary but astute, ironic observations on the human condition as reflected in the trappings and interactions of any society in any era.

THE NOVEL appeared in January 1948 and was already a bestseller by mid-March 1948. Explaining why the Book-of-the-Month Club had chosen the book for its March selection, John P. Marquand pronounced it "more than a literary *tour de force*. It is actually literature."[77] While some critics found the book cold or limited in appeal, the reviews were largely favorable, with more than one reviewer joining Marquand in calling *The Ides of March* a tour de force, and praising its maturity and its lustrous prose.

Some women, however, thought the novel was unfair to women. They included Amy Wertheimer, to whom Wilder protested, "Those parts about women that make you bristle weren't me—they're Cicero! I've made a novel like a play—i.e.—*I* [Wilder underlined the word twice] am not there; just other people."[78] He acknowledged in a letter to Alice B. Toklas, however, that he could not resist an allusion to his mother and Isabel in *The Ides of March*. Isabel, like their mother "and like a great many women," felt that she had "an instinct for medical matters that is superior to eight years' exclusive study of them," he wrote. "I put that into the Ides of March, and I remember rocking with laughter in my chair while I wrote the lines."[79]

Wilder's own view of women is more accurately expressed not by Cicero but by Caesar: "I am beyond any man I have ever met the admirer of the essential feminine; beyond any man I have ever met I am least censorious of their failings and least exasperated by their vagaries. But then!—what advantages I have had! I ask myself in amazement:

What opinion must that man hold of womankind who has not had the advantage of living in the proximity of great women?"[80]

BY THE time his novel was published, Wilder was in England to consult with Laurence Olivier on his upcoming production of *The Skin of Our Teeth*. He spent a night in the country with the Oliviers, as well as one in their London house; had a reunion with his friends Sibyl Colefax and Michael Redgrave; and met and had tea with T. S. Eliot. In the aftermath of the war, Wilder was heartened to see England and then France emerging "from the season of despairing confusion," and in both countries there was "stout-hearted 'coping' and resourcefulness," as well as a remarkable "flowering in theatre. . . ."[81]

He spent time in Paris with Sartre, who gave him a copy of the final text of his play, *Morts sans sépulture*, asking Wilder to go forward with the translation. Entitled *The Victors*, the play was directed by Mary Hunter (Wolfe), one of the first successful female directors in the United States, and produced by New Stages at the Bleecker Street Playhouse off-Broadway. It ran for a limited engagement from December 26, 1948, to January 22, 1949, with mixed reviews.

AFTER HE returned from Europe in 1948, Wilder was restless:

> But here I am this very funny fellow, glad to drop in at cocktails anywhere in New Haven, speaking at any Veterans Wives sewing circle, if it's in New Haven; going to New York "on business," then getting a fit of shyness rather than call up friends, and eating alone at little boites in the West Forties and dropping in alone at whatever trembling pianist may be coping with a début at Town Hall.[82]

He found himself caught up in the "sideshows" of an author's work—writing "prefaces, translations, recommendations, political statements."[83] In April 1947, for instance, he had written a long letter to Lillian Gish, who sought the theater and motion picture rights to *The*

Woman of Andros, explaining to her in diplomatic detail why his novel would not make a good play or movie.[84] He had accepted an honorary doctorate at Yale in 1947, and written a series of dramatic sketches for the 1947 centennial of the Century Association, of which he was a member.[85] In October 1947 he had contributed an article titled "Gertrude Stein Makes Sense" to *'47: The Magazine of the Year*, an essay condensed and adapted from his introduction to Stein's *Four in America*. Also in 1947, for the National Conference of Christians and Jews, Wilder had written a short play, *The Unerring Instinct*, for their "Scripts for Brotherhood" series—scripts provided without charge to dramatic clubs and high schools.[86] He frequently read and commented on manuscripts, many of them sent to him by people he didn't know. Some of these "sideshows" were necessary, and even enjoyable—but most of them ate away his time and energy.

Wilder was onstage again himself in the summer of 1948, playing George Antrobus in summer stock theaters in Pennsylvania, Connecticut, and Massachusetts, and this work would at least generate some income. He performed as Mr. Antrobus in sold-out shows in Cohasset, Stockbridge, and Westport. Glenway Wescott, who had known and admired Wilder the writer for years, was also an "assiduous . . . lifelong and international" theatergoer. He was in the audience one night, and so could give a firsthand account of Wilder the actor. Wilder characterized his Antrobus "with humor," Wescott wrote:

> temperamentally: a familiar type of tired but sturdy, more or less indomitable man in a raincoat or trench coat. . . . As he came on stage he immediately established the reality of the scene by glancing all around it, taking possession of it, flashing his eyes; then turned and faced the audience and immediately began his portrayal of himself, gesturing strongly, as though wielding a brush, painting [a] great everyman's portrait on the canvas of air between him and the audience, up over our heads.[87]

Wilder told Wescott about sending a two-page letter to a sixteen-year-old boy from Long Island who had written to ask how he should enact Mr. Antrobus in his school play. The nexus of Wilder's advice to the lad: "Pick out a few places where you'll be real loud."[88]

IN AUGUST 1948 Isabel was afflicted with severe arthritis, and had to be hospitalized for two weeks and "strung up by the neck in traction" in order to have "all those top vertebrae pulled out of their lethargy."[89] She came home from the hospital much improved, but having to wear a leather neck brace. Wilder chauffeured her to and from her treatments, took her shopping, and drove himself back and forth to the Westport Country Playhouse for his acting job. He had accepted Robert Hutchins's invitation to lecture in Germany in November 1948 under the auspices of the University of Chicago in its program at the University of Frankfurt-am-Main. There and at other German universities, he would speak on "The American Character as Mirrored in Literature." He and Isabel traveled to Ireland in September, and then to Germany for his lectures.

Wilder was constantly ruminating about what to write next. A play? A novel? An original screenplay? His travels would help clarify the decision. He vowed, however, that although he would never write about World War II directly, he hoped that nothing he wrote would "ever fail to contain" what he had experienced there.[90]

33

SEARCHING FOR THE RIGHT WAY

The play [The Emporium] as it now projects itself will be all right,
but it will have for me the draw-back of being all about one thing:
the baffling search for the Right Way.

—THORNTON WILDER,
journal entry 412, September 25, 1948, Dublin, Ireland

The United States and Abroad (1948–1950s)

In 1948 Wilder applied for a military permit to enter Germany, the necessary official sanction to travel to Paris and then on to Frankfurt-am-Main for three weeks "to deliver lectures at the Universities of Frankfurt and Heidelberg, on the recommendation of the Military Government for Hesse, Education and Cultural Relations Divisions."[1] His longtime friend Robert Maynard Hutchins, former president and now chancellor of the University of Chicago, had invited Wilder to lecture in the university's programs in Frankfurt. Wilder would also lecture to university students in Heidelberg, Marburg, and Berlin. But first he and Isabel would spend a month in Dublin, and then go on to Paris.

In September, when he packed for the Atlantic crossing on the RMS *Mauretania*, bound for Cobh, Ireland, Wilder deliberately left his Lope de Vega research material at home, hoping to wean himself from his addiction to it. He had told Maxwell Anderson that he planned to write a "short book, 'The Early Plays of L. De V.' for scholars only, all footnotes, no 'literary' appraisal." He should have taken up this work in his twenties, Wilder said, "but I'm still living as though we were to live until a hundred and fifty."[2] Instead of his work on Lope's plays, Wilder took his journal on the voyage, and quickly began to fill it with ideas for a new play of his own.

Whether they were lost or destroyed, or never existed at all, there is a gap in Wilder's journals from 1942 until a one-paragraph entry on June 6, 1948. It was not until his ship approached the Irish coast on September 21, 1948, that he took up his journal again in earnest. Although his topic was his new play, his subject was himself at age fifty-one—his doubts and indecision about what to write, and how; about where to spend his energy; about, from this time onward, how to live his life. In the confines of this postwar journal in the 1950s, Wilder created as compelling and revealing a self-portrait as he had ever written.

In 1950 he would clarify the purpose of his journal: It was not to be a receptacle for descriptions of events, or conversations, or parties, or books he was reading, or plays he was seeing. Instead it was to be a vehicle for reflection, a "repository only for ideas which are *moving* and *gathering*, which promise to reward me with greater extent and definition if I note them here, which are *snowballing.*" In essence his journal would concentrate on two questions: "Why One Writes and What One Writes."[3] He might have added a third, for the journal also reveals his own struggles with the question of how one lives.

The journal would absorb and consume much of his creative energy in the 1950s—and, at first glance, even seems on the surface to deflect it. In reality Wilder's journals through the decade contain some of his most important creative work, as well as unprecedented revelations of his inner life. There are 539 pages of entries from 1948 through 1961, with two short entries in 1969. For the most part all these entries are handwritten, single-spaced, on lined paper. Each of these handwritten pages contained an average of 500 words. By this measure Wilder wrote an estimated 269,500 words in his journals alone from 1948 to 1961. In addition, more than a thousand manuscript pages of Wilder's notes on Lope de Vega survive, as well as more than 600 manuscript pages of notes on Joyce's *Finnegans Wake*, along with the "hundreds of annotations" in his copy of the novel.[4] That is 2,139 pages plus an estimated 400 pages of earlier journal entries—or more than 2,500 pages Wilder thought about, composed, and wrote out by hand, as was his habit when writing his novels and plays. The pages in his surviving journals, added to his surviving Joyce and Lope de Vega notes, yield an estimated total of at least 1,250,000 words—words he put on paper beyond all the words in his novels and his plays, unfinished as well as finished, and in the thousands of letters he wrote. This total far exceeded the word count in his first five novels, combined. *The Bridge of San Luis Rey* contains an estimated 34,000 words, for instance; with the words Wilder put to the page in his journals and scholarly investigations, he could have written thirty-six novels the length of *The Bridge* and still have had words left over.

He was often criticized as a writer of slight output—by 1950, five novels; four full-length plays, if *The Trumpet Shall Sound* is counted; a number of playlets; and a collection of six one-act plays. But if the text in his journals and his scholarly investigations is counted, Wilder was actually prolific, and he had compelling reasons for investing his creative energy as he did. He expanded his experiments in his own literary work and his inquisition into the works of Joyce and Lope to search for the "right way" to interpret the American experience and the American character as revealed in nineteenth-century American literature; to define what it meant to be an American in the twentieth century; and to examine the role of America and Americans in the global community.

IN A lecture Wilder gave at Harvard in 1950, he speculated that after Herman Melville finished writing *Moby-Dick*, "something broke" in him. Melville "lost his concentration," Wilder said.[5] He recognized in Melville what he knew to be true of himself after he had finished writing *The Ides of March*. Throughout the months after his novel was published, Wilder wrote in his journal, "I groped about for the theme of my next piece of work,—a play, a novel, or an original motion-picture. I turned over some of the old themes, the Alcestiad. The Christmas pageant [a proposed play he called 'The Sandusky, Ohio Mystery Play']. The pure detective story. The Horatio Alger form, rejecting them all without much exploration."[6] A chance remark from a friend led him to consider writing a play juxtaposing his unfinished "Empress of Newfoundland" story with a Horatio Alger theme, told in the atmosphere

Kafka created in *The Castle*. After two shipboard nights of "almost total insomnia" Wilder believed this new play was "in a fair way to determine itself as the next work I shall offer."[7] He called it *The Emporium*, and began filling page after page of his journal with notes on character and plots, and fragments of possible dialogue.

His work on the dating of Lope's plays encroached again, however, despite his good intentions. He had been working on that project for nearly three years, and reckoned that if he concentrated on it for ten years he could date most of the plays "within a three-year margin of error" and, in the process, make significant discoveries about Lope as a playwright and a "builder and destroyer" of drama companies.[8] But he had to face the reality: What difference would it make? Would the book he envisioned "be worth that time"? He postponed the answers, deciding that when he returned to the United States in February, he would "devote solid months to Lope," and assess where he stood. Then he would have to decide whether to continue, or whether the "whole pursuit in reality" was a "dangerous flight from the difficulty of thinking and writing."[9]

In Dublin, when he was not drinking shandy and exploring sites depicted in *Finnegans Wake*, Wilder was engrossed in his new play, pulling together events, characters, and ideas from his earlier, unfinished work. It would take place in an emporium, a symbolic department store, where metaphorical material goods and life itself were bargained, bought, and sold. Once again he made a firm decision to challenge the audience's imagination with "bone-bare staging" and the "incoherence and the absorbing intensity of dream-experience," with the whole play "touched with the unexpected and the disconcerting."[10] By September 23 he was "well along in Part Two," and had changed the name of the play to "Pluck and Luck," in deference to the Horatio Alger theme and Alger's series of novels by that name. The play was "straining to be born," he believed, because it was still giving him insomnia.[11] He could feel "the central idea of the play tearing around" in his head.[12] He was writing at white heat, but he had no idea how the play would end: "Of course, I should be frightened that I do not see my conclusion, but all writing is a Leap."[13]

His play as it unfolded presented him with "the drawback of being all about one thing: the baffling search for 'the right way.'" He did not want to write a play that turned "endlessly on one subject"—an objection he had always felt to Shakespeare's *Othello*.[14] He looked at his play from "every angle," seeking to "establish the angst"—in part I, the angst of an orphan boy who felt "the wild homelessness that longs to 'belong.'" He would write about the angst of longing for recognition from "those Higher Up"; about the angst of "self-seeking"; about "love under the conditions of angst"; and, finally, about "the liberty found in the *angst*, the self-reliance that is the only answer to the bafflement, and then the slightest intimations that the Emporium approves the exploitation of one's liberty however erratic." It was painful, he acknowledged in his journal, to tease his subject from every angle, and to "color" the "inner state" of his characters with "the dragging search for the right way."[15] Wilder turned back to Kierkegaard's ruminations on sin, guilt, and freedom of choice in *The Theory of Dread* as he thought through his plans for the play "at its most profound level."[16]

He had promised his next play to director and producer Arthur Hopkins, whom he had long admired. In fact, he allowed his concern for Hopkins's expectations to influence some of the creative choices he made in *The Emporium*.[17] By early October, Wilder was beset by doubts about the emerging drama, especially the device of using the audience as if they were characters in the play—a device he employed out of consideration for Hopkins's need for a small cast. Was this going to be "valid theatre"? Would the audience tire of the word "emporium"? What were the perils of using "the Store as a figure of the Absolute" and of employing a "sustained metaphor"? (A sustained metaphor was bad enough in a sonnet, Wilder wrote, and even worse in a full-length play.) "But my real basic fears—when I allow myself to admit of a fear—are that the whole thing may be a wild preposterous lapse of judgment on my part (and oh, how badly I can write); and that I may not digest and compass a true ending."[18]

During the month Wilder and Isabel spent in Dublin he split his time between writing—and fretting over—the new play, and preparing for the lectures he had promised Bob Hutchins he would give in

Germany in November and December. He would address two topics. The first was "Some Reflections on the Theatre," an updated version of a lecture that had been a staple on his speaking tours in the 1930s, and the subject of a major essay he entitled "Some Thoughts on Playwriting."[19] The other topic was "American Characteristics as Reflected in American Literature," a lecture he had been developing for years, especially during and after his South American tour in 1941. He expanded the lecture as time and world events dictated, and it would serve as the foundation for lectures he would deliver in the future.

In these upcoming lectures in Germany, Wilder would speak not "of man in his social and political relationships but of the Human Condition in general," he wrote in his journal.[20] He would speak about art as one principal resource mankind could summon in the face of "potential catastrophe," along with religion, technology, and "Frivolity—distraction." In "Some Reflections on the Theatre," he would focus on the art of the theater, which, he wrote, "hangs balanced in suspension between two resources: it both offers a flight and relief from dread by being as completely occupying as frivolity is, and it also, like religion, provides an escape from the insecurity of the human condition by offering a promise that there is order and relatedness in the world."[21] The lectures were well received, and he appreciated his encounters with German university students, especially in Berlin, which was then blockaded by the Soviets and dependent on British and American airlifts to fly in food and fuel—more than three hundred thousand tons by November, when Wilder visited the city.

By December 27 the Wilders were in St. Moritz, after a short stay in England. He could finally pick up the pages of *The Emporium* again, but now Wilder realized that his momentum, his energy, and even his original vision for the play had disappeared. "During the last few weeks I almost lost my play several times," he wrote in his journal. "Totally lost it. Even now it may be lost."[22] He thought he might have to destroy everything he had written. "I see that I don't yet know how I can write this play," he worried in his journal. "I haven't thought deep enough. If this is all I've got I'd better throw it away now." He diagnosed his problem astutely: He was not feeling his themes "validly in my self . . .

I have found them in books (in Kierkegaard), but if they are not in me (or . . . with passion potentially in me) they have no business messing up my play."[23]

ON FEBRUARY 19, 1949, the Wilders were homeward bound on the *Queen Mary*; they arrived in New York on February 25. Wilder did not pick up his journal again until May 7, when he took refuge at the Claridge Hotel in Atlantic City, his first opportunity for "true solitude" in months. He was going to try again, he wrote, to collect his thoughts "toward the Emporium and toward the two tasks that await me this summer: the short address of opening at the Goethe Festival and my own forty-minute discourse there."[24] He berated himself because the five-month lapse in his journal was proof of his "continued inability to organize" his life so he could work. It was also evidence of his "lifelong" habit of "barefaced substitution of occupying diversions."[25]

Overwhelmed with doubts, he wrestled with the play. "I hate allegory and here I am deep in allegory," he wrote. He revisited Goethe's work hoping to reinvigorate his own play in progress, as well as to glean ideas for the lecture he had been invited to deliver at the Bicentennial Goethe Convocation in Aspen, Colorado, in July 1949—another invitation extended by Bob Hutchins. Wilder was indebted to Hutchins for some of the most significant experiences in his career—the opportunity to teach at the University of Chicago, and to enjoy there some of the happiest years of his life; the chance to meet Gertrude Stein and launch a pivotal literary and personal friendship; the journey to lecture in postwar Germany; and now the invitation to go to Aspen to experience what would be a galvanizing summer.

Hutchins and two of his friends, wealthy businessman and University of Chicago trustee Walter Paepcke, and university vice president Wilbur C. Munnecke, had established the Goethe Bicentennial Foundation in order to orchestrate a celebration of Goethe's bicentennial in 1949. The event would take place in Aspen, where Paepcke's Aspen Company was rescuing the old silver-mining town in the high Rockies and transforming it into a mountain resort that would also be a sort of

Chautauqua of the West. The Goethe festival would lead to the creation of the Aspen Institute for Humanistic Studies. Although the Modern Language Association first conceived the notion of honoring Goethe's legacy, the idea was brought to fruition by Hutchins and the Italian classical scholar Giuseppe Antonio Borgese, who saw the bicentennial celebration as an opportunity to "honor Goethe the cosmopolitan humanist and universal man—poet, philosopher, scientist, administrator, and exponent of the cultural unity of mankind—and thereby to help heal the wounds of war and to promote world government."[26]

Hutchins was largely responsible for securing the speakers and raising funds for the event in an era when Germans and Germany were still viewed as suspect by many in the United States. He succeeded in recruiting two world figures as speakers—the Spanish philosopher and author José Ortega y Gasset and Dr. Albert Schweitzer, musician, biographer, teacher, theologian, and, for thirty-six years, physician ministering to the people of Gabon in French Equatorial Africa. This would be Schweitzer's first and only visit to the United States. Naturally Hutchins relied on his old friend Thornton Wilder as an adviser, and invited him as well to speak at Aspen, where more than two thousand people gathered during the three-week run of the celebration.

On July 7, 1949, in a letter from Aspen, Thornton described the event to Amos, who in 1922 had worked briefly with Schweitzer at Oxford, and assisted him with French-to-English translations. Wilder wrote, "Batteries of concerts and lectures assault you—often three a day," adding, "I've become the pack mule of the convocation." Dr. Schweitzer lectured in French at Aspen, but when a translation into English proved to be "terrible," Wilder was asked to "touch up the English text for its German presentation," and to read the English text antiphonally as Dr. Schweitzer delivered his lecture in German. "Ditto Don José Ortega y Gasset," Wilder wrote to his brother. "Only for him I am to be first and sole translator of his Second Lecture and I am to read it with him from the Podium."[27] Not only did Wilder translate German to English for Dr. Schweitzer and Spanish to English for Ortega, but at Hutchins's "command," he delivered his own lecture twice as new guests and subscribers arrived at different times.

Wilder spoke at the festival not as a novelist or playwright, but as a student of Goethe's work, and an advocate of certain of Goethe's principles, which he had long ago incorporated into his own work: Goethe's concept of the unity of mankind and the potential unity of human minds; his prediction, in 1827, that the era of world literature was at hand; his belief that "from the heart of the universe . . . there pours out a stream of energy ceaselessly operative," and that this energy's "action is to mold chaos into significant form."[28]

Wilder loved the convocation, he loved the mountains, and, he wrote to Amos, "I love the schoolteachers who stop me on the street, and the students who've hitchhiked across the country to sample this. But most of all I love Goethe. Nobody ever loved anybody like I love Goethe."[29] He thought he'd stay on in Aspen after the festival and finish his play. "I realize this letter sounds like *euphoria*," Wilder wrote to his brother, "and you are putting it down to the altitude or to drink,—no, no, mostly it is Goethe. Perhaps too it is the elation of plain brute fatigue. Pack-mule fatigue."[30]

Now in Aspen—and again, thanks to Hutchins—Wilder was launching his work as an advocate for the global community, the champion of the planetary mind—a worldview that transcended national borders. His Goethe lecture not only articulated one writer's debt to another but crystallized fundamental tenets in the literary work Wilder himself had already done—and, if he would only pay attention, it could guide him toward the work ahead. As Wilder's lecture on Goethe reveals, Goethe, like Kierkegaard, Nietzsche, Joyce, and Stein, was a catalyst for the expression of some of Wilder's quintessential themes: There is the theme Wilder first recognized in the archaeological ruins in Rome, "that billions—not merely millions—have lived and died and that no description of mankind is adequate which does not find its proportionate place within a realization of all the diversity of life on the entire planet over a vast extent of time."[31] There is a second theme—a corollary of the first—the principle of the particular in the universal, and the universal in the particular. There is the vision of a planetary consciousness, and an understanding of the unique identity of each soul among the multitude of souls.[32]

As he composed his lecture Wilder seemed to resolve the quandary about the role of chance, fate, and destiny in human life, a recurring question in his own work, hovering throughout *The Bridge of San Luis Rey*, *The Woman of Andros*, *Heaven's My Destination*, and *The Ides of March*. In his allusions to Goethe's ideas, Wilder was offering a possible answer to himself as well as to the two thousand people who gathered in Aspen that July. "What do we do while we await" being "carried on to our goal?" "We work," Wilder said. "What do we work at? There the life of Goethe helps us as much as the writings—through *Faust* rings wide the conviction that *Wirken*—effective action—alone reconciles us to life and leads us into the sense of the oneness of all existing."[33]

And after life on this planet, what? In Wilder's novels and plays, various characters ponder this question, among them Brother Juniper, Chrysis, George Brush, Emily, Caesar. Again, Wilder found an answer in Goethe's ideas—one answer, if not *the* answer—continuous practice of one's art, and continuous evolution as an artist and a person. According to Wilder, Goethe said when he was "very, very old":

> If I remain ceaselessly active to the end of my days nature is under an obligation to allot me another form of existence, when the present one is no longer capable of containing my spirit. . . . I do not doubt the continuance of our existence. May it then be that He who is eternally Living will not refuse us new forms of activity, analogous to those in which we have been tested.[34]

Wilder concluded that Goethe could envision a planetary literature and not be frightened by the prospect because "he had found his place among two hundred thousand billion and had accepted his moment in uncountable light-years."[35]

———

IN HIS private hours in Aspen, as Wilder thought over his conversations with the Goethe specialists at the convocation, some of them related to questions about Goethe's sexuality. "It seems to be agreed that Goethe was psychically impotent until the Italian Journey," Wilder wrote in his journal, adding, with reference to Goldsmith's play, that some scholars had concluded that Goethe had "the She-Stoops-to-Conquer" situation—he could connect only with a woman of inferior social class. "This would indeed give rise to fantasies."[36] Wilder concluded that "Goethe's genius is all sublimation," observing that sublimation involves both a "normal" animality and "the Twisted—the price which must be paid for that very offense against nature which is sublimation."[37] It was not so much sublimation resulting in "the Twisted" that Wilder had in mind, but, as he later defined it, sublimation as "a *higher* transference of the sexual drive," for instance, into art or science or religion or some other worthy endeavor.[38] As Wilder reflected on Goethe's sexuality in his journal, he may have revealed part of the rationale for the choice he was making for himself—the sublimation of his own sexual energy in his creative work.

———

WILDER STAYED on for a time in Aspen after the convocation concluded, socializing and working sporadically on *The Emporium*. He wrote a new prologue for the play, restructured certain elements, and felt that, at last, he had regained his momentum even though it was "still far from written or even foreseen."[39]

He answered a pile of mail in Aspen, and wrote a long letter in response to a telephone call from the actor Cary Grant, who, with the producer Howard Hawks, wanted Wilder to write a film script based on the first two books of *Gulliver's Travels*. Wilder replied that there was "no possibility" that he would undertake the Gulliver project. Still he thought it was a "fine idea" and if "certain difficulties" could be mastered, it would make a film that "would delight millions." Wilder suggested what should and should not be done with such an adaptation—including a whimsical reflection on the "real difficulty" in such a script: "*Do you need to add some plot?* Love-interest (given the difference of size!) is out of the question; but what is lacking is any person-to-person relation between *anybody* and *anybody*. . . . Can you hold the interest of audiences for two hours on the situation GIANT-PYGMY?"

Perhaps Grant could take some liberties, Wilder said, and let

Gulliver "really have an absurd but touching *tendresse* (and farewell) with the Queen of Brobdingnag." He would be in Aspen until September 3, Wilder wrote, in the event that Grant and Hawks would like to travel to Colorado to see the majestic scenery and "talk over this very exciting project."[40] Grant and Hawks didn't make the trip or the movie, and in early September Wilder was aboard the Zephyr, traveling back to Connecticut.

In late September he went on from Hamden to Newport, one of his favorite writing retreats, but despite his solitude and long walks on the familiar shore, he remained discouraged about his play. He wrote in his journal, "Never have I had a work at once so far advanced and so far from completion."[41]

WILDER'S LIFE in the decade of the 1950s was a dichotomy: There was his public face, famous on both sides of the Atlantic, increasingly visible in lectures and public appearances. There was his private face, revealed only in his journal and certain intimate letters. As his artistic and intellectual interests continued to evolve, it was a decade of doubt and indecision about what to write, and how, and why—and where to live, and how, and why. Wilder migrated from public appearances and accolades to private angst, from Europe to the United States, and back again, restless, searching. He was, he wrote in his journal, "a canoe in mid-ocean."[42]

He was bound this time for Holland, England, France, and Spain. He would see Alice B. Toklas, lonely in Paris. He was forced to cancel plans to drive through Tuscany with Sibyl Colefax, for she was too ill to make the trip. Other than seeing very close friends, he hoped against hope for a "solitary Trappist work-siege."[43] Wherever he traveled these days, there were distractions—people he wanted to see, people who wanted to see him, reporters who wanted interviews, some of them annoying. Gone were the days when he could travel anonymously, at his leisure, on his own terms. In a letter written in Paris, he recalled fondly, "the happiest occasions in my life were those days when as dreamy student-vagabond—boundlessly un-noticed—I visited foreign countries; to recover that is all my aim."[44]

He had escaped to Europe to work on *The Emporium*, and on that omnipresent compulsion, the Lope de Vega project, planning to do some research in the playwright's archives in Spain. He was also thinking about more lectures he had recently committed himself to give. He had accepted the invitation to be the Charles Eliot Norton Professor of Poetry at Harvard University in 1950–51. This distinguished professorship obligated him to deliver a series of at least six public lectures on American literature that would then be published by the Harvard University Press.[45]

Meanwhile *The Emporium* was still giving him trouble, and he had long since put away the drafts of *The Alcestiad*. Wilder was searching for ways to impose new order in his daily life as well as his literary life, but longtime habits were hard to break. In his usual fashion his search for innovative literary forms led him to revisit his own portfolio of work for characters and themes, as well as to reread Kafka, Goethe, and Kierkegaard. As he sought the cutting edge in form and style, he turned back to Euripides and the distant past for inspiration for characters and themes.

In his ongoing self-examination in the privacy of his journal, Wilder acknowledged his propensity for fixations, intellectual obsessions, such as his intense focus on dating Lope de Vega's plays—a preoccupation that he knew was "irrational," and grew out of "an appetite parading itself in the guise of an intellectual discipline." He recognized that the Lope studies obstructed not only his writing, but his "very 'thinking.'" He wrote, "They are like a banyan-tree in my garden which sap all shoots save their own. Already they have robbed the life of *The Emporium* of whatever energy it possessed."[46] He had promised Arthur Hopkins the first look at his new play, and had just received news of Hopkins's death—an event that led to the death of *The Emporium*. Wilder would never finish the play.

ON SUNDAY, March 26, 1950, less than a month before his fifty-third birthday, Wilder sat alone in a hotel room in Saint-Jean-de-Luz, France, and took a hard look at himself and his life, literary and personal. He did not like what he saw. In his journal he wrote an unsparing self-analysis headed "A Look-around my Situation." He was exhausted and sick with a cold that brought on, as always, partial deafness. He was eager for isolation "as promise of the new mode of life which I must enter resolutely or abandon all hope of significant experiences or work." He wrote at length in his journal about his frustrations: He had had his fill of "false" situations—superficial social engagements, whether in London or in New Haven; meaningless polite conversations; the prevailing assumption by strangers and some friends that he *was* the books and plays he had written, that his success as an author was his only identity, and the consequent failure to recognize him as a person who possessed any identity apart from his work.

Wilder was working hard in the fifties to break some old habits and to establish "a new mode of life" that would facilitate his creative work and make him a better person. He wrote in his journal,

A lover burns to share himself and to compass also the life of the beloved; but the artist-lover burns in addition to share his thought-world, his *Schauen* [view or perspective], self-evident to him, and communicable not in living-together but only in the finished works. For the artist, love then has always something of the false position; and particularly marriage which I profoundly believe in *for others*, but which I am glad not to have entered into.[47]

In his journal Wilder searched for reasons for the "disarray" in his "psychic life" and his writing life. Perhaps it was caused, he wrote, "by the uprooting which was the War and which has been so advanced by the even deeper immersion in the 'false positions' I have recounted." In his unflinching self-examination, Wilder acknowledged that "all these activities have been *flights from seriousness*." He confessed, "I am deep in *dilettantism*. Even my apparent preoccupation with deeply serious matter, e.g. the reading of Kierkegaard, is superficial and doubly superficial because it pretends to be searching." Despite his angst he knew the solution to his predicament—if only he could summon the will, discipline, and energy to achieve it. "Gradually, gradually I must resume my, my own meditation on the only things that can re-awaken any writing I have to do = I must gaze directly at the boundless misery of the human situation, collective and individual."[48]

IN HIS painfully candid "Look-around," Wilder confronted himself and his future, full of insight and resolve. But all too soon he was distracting himself again, flooding his mind that spring with "Lopeana," with Kierkegaard, with Shakespeare and Goethe, and with Melville, Poe, Thoreau, Whitman, Emily Dickinson, Henry James, and other American writers who might appear in his Norton lectures. That amalgam of Wilder's imagination and those other voices and ideas yielded, during one sleepless night, an idea for a novel he called *The Turning Point*. It could be composed in "short stories and fragments of narrations representing action from all places and ages—a sort of *Decameron*, except that the stories are of varying length." It would be written in a "really new form" which could "serve as a vehicle," he wrote in his journal, without elaborating in detail,

> for two of my compelling preoccupations: man seen in all his history; mind seen as a force struggling out of the biologic undergrowth—to say nothing of the secondary preoccupations: woman as instigatrix; narrations as the means of depicting the scientific process; and so on.[49]

But the idea for the novel faded as quickly as it had materialized, and soon Wilder was back in the United States, busily looking outward at events, instead of inward at the bothersome questions that had surfaced in his journal soliloquy, now pushed aside as he began to prepare in earnest for his year at Harvard. He spent part of August playing the Stage Manager in *Our Town* at the Wellesley Summer Theatre in Massachusetts—the twelfth company with whom he had performed the role. He advised every playwright, he wrote to the Laurence Oliviers, "to get somehow somewhere *that* side of the footlights," for there were certain lessons a playwright could learn only by putting his feet on the floor of a stage.[50]

As a citizen and a former soldier, Wilder was deeply concerned that summer about the prospect of war in Korea, writing lengthy passages in his journal about the nature of war, about wars of aggression versus wars of liberation. On July 8 he wrote that the Korean War was "about here in part due to this mixture of relief, alerted self-protection and outraged responsibility. Tragically, it is also due to the fact that in our time we are accustomed to war, and custom is almost habit and habit is almost appetite."[51]

In his journal that summer Harry Truman and Korea shared space with Goethe, Palestrina (the sixteenth-century composer whose liturgical music Wilder had studied for years), and Kierkegaard, and then with American literary figures as Wilder moved closer to the beginning of the Harvard year. By August he was almost as engrossed in analyzing Thoreau's *Walden* as he had been in analyzing the work of Lope and Joyce—and that earlier experience and those skills and tactics proved immensely useful as he built his Harvard lectures. As he embarked on detailed examinations of the work of Whitman, Poe, Thoreau, Dickinson, and Melville, what began as scholarly analysis soon transformed into a deep absorption in the sort of research that he called high adventure. Soon Wilder was making significant discoveries about the American experience, the American character, the American time sense, and the American language—the "syntax of freedom."[52]

He also wrote in his journal about the loss of people he loved. Shortly before he arrived in Cambridge to begin the Norton year, he received the news of the death of Sibyl Colefax. He had spent time with Sibyl in London in March 1950, finding her thin and fragile, bent with arthritis, and often confined to bed—but still full of spirit, curiosity, hospitality. He visited her on three consecutive afternoons, and her house, as always, was full of company, including that week T. S. Eliot and Noël Coward. She died at home September 22, 1950. She was for Wilder an irreplaceable friend and an indefatigable listener, witness, encourager, and adviser. In his journal he mourned the loss:

It is as though with the death of Gertrude and Sibyl and the removal by distance and situation of others I have been left not only high and dry of objects [of friendship] but that the very faculty itself has cooled. I accept the condition within myself . . . with a theoretical concern, for have I not always believed emphatically that all and every derivation of Eros is the sole fount of energy?[53]

―――――

AS WILDER's residency at Harvard began on October 1, 1950, he settled into his quarters at Dunster House and tackled his lectures with excitement. He also agreed to teach, although he was not obligated to do so. He very soon found himself overextended, with a jammed schedule. As he explained later,

> *every time the phone rang I said "yes"—not to "social" events (I made the rule never to cross the River Charles) but to speak; and the forums and discussion groups and hospital benefit committees and Harvard Dames clubs and so on are legion.*[54]

From the outset of his Harvard year, however, he tried to concentrate on his Norton lectures, outlining them in detailed pages in his journal. In November he worked on "The American Writer as a Speaker and to a Multitude," a title he would change, and on Herman Melville's *Billy Budd, Foretopman*, as well as Thoreau's life and work. In December he concentrated on the nature of a work of art, especially literary forms, drawing examples from the work of Walt Whitman, Henry James, Emily Dickinson, and Benjamin Franklin.[55] The first of the three eventually published Norton lectures explored the evolution of the American language, with special attention to Melville; the American loneliness, focusing on Thoreau; and American loneliness and individuality in a rich biographical discussion of Dickinson and her work. Whitman, Poe, and Melville were Wilder's subjects for the other lectures.[56]

He delivered the first Norton, "Adapting an Island Language to a Continental Thought," to an audience of eight hundred in Harvard's New Lecture Hall on November 8. Next, on November 15, came "Thoreau, or the Bean-Row in the Wilderness," followed by "Emily Dickinson, or the Articulate Inarticulate" on November 29, and "Walt Whitman and the American Loneliness" on December 6. On February 20, 1951, Wilder devoted his fifth Norton lecture to Edgar Allan Poe. His sixth and final lecture, "Melville: The Real and the Forged Ambiguities," was given May 16. All the lectures were laced with observations about the evolution and significance of the fundamental American characteristics Wilder identified: First, the evolution of the American language—the transformation, especially by nineteenth-century American writers, of "an old island language into a new continental one."[57] Second, the fact that "Americans are still engaged in inventing what it is to be American."[58] Third, the idea that Americans "are disconnected. They are exposed to all place and all time. . . . They have a relation, but it is to everywhere, to everybody, and to always."[59] Next, the view that for the free, independent, and individualistic American, there is a "loneliness that accompanies independence and the uneasiness that accompanies freedom."[60] Finally, the observation that it is not easy to be an American, and that American writers offer various solutions to this difficulty. These key characteristics are also descriptive of Wilder's own work—his transformation of the American vernacular into a continental language; his attention to what it means to be an American; his sense of the connections of everyone to every place and every time; his awareness and his experience of the American loneliness; and his appreciation for the varieties of expression in American life and literature.

Wilder discovered a particular affinity for Emily Dickinson, writing that while she was "in all appearance the loneliest of beings," she "solved the problem in a way which is of importance to every American: by loving the particular while living in the universal."[61] As Wilder explored these American characteristics and their manisfestations in nineteenth-century American literature, he drew on the lives of the authors to provide context for their work, constructing insightful biographical portraits, especially of Dickinson. There are autobiographical echoes in his analyses as well, especially in his discussion of father-daughter relations in Emily Dickinson's life—dynamics that reflect the experiences of his own sisters, and of his brother and himself. Dickinson, Wilder wrote, was the daughter of "a very grim patriarch" who had, as she herself said, a "lonely life and lonelier death."[62] What daughter and father both desired was to win from each other "love, attentive love, and the sense of one's identity rebounding from some intelligent and admired being." Knowing all too well the dynamics of his parents' marriage, Wilder observed that a patriarchal father may also have "long since quenched any spontaneous femininity in his wife. (Unquestionable authority is an offense against love, as it is against anything else, and it is ever seeking new territories to overwhelm.)"[63]

WILDER WAS an enormous hit at Harvard, but he wore himself out in the process. On Monday, March 1, he awoke to sharp pains in his back, thigh, and left leg. He managed to hobble to his ten o'clock class, but the pain grew so intense that he was taken to the Stillman Infirmary, and from there, to Massachusetts General Hospital, where he was treated for a strained or displaced sacroiliac. Wilder would be hospitalized for a month—a time of "immobile days and largely wakeful nights." He was unable to sit up even to write in his journal. His mind, sharpened by pain and by the drugs he was given, was "very active," so much so that in two and a half weeks he had reread *Moby-Dick*, *Great Expectations*, and *War and Peace*, among other books. He longed to write in his journal about his reading, as well as about pain, and the "professional formation and deformation of nurses," but he had to postpone writing anything at all so as not to arouse "the slumbering sciatic nerve."[64]

He believed that his "whole illness has been obviously a retort of offended Nature against my excessive exertions."[65] He enumerated them in his journal when he could safely write again: the Norton lectures; his two classes; his correspondence, more than twenty items a day; his ongoing literary work; the engagements he agreed to undertake, sixteen classes and lectures in less than a month in February alone.[66] Gertrude Stein used to warn Wilder that every individual possessed a "quotient of solitude and gregariousness" and if those conditions were not in balance, illness could result. That was exactly his plight, Wilder wrote in his journal. "My requirement for solitude is high and I was leading a flagrantly gregarious life."[67] He was paying a steep price for it.

During that period of recuperation and enforced rest, Wilder's desire to write in his journal soon overcame his incapacity. He refused to mark time. Unable to sit or stand to write, he stretched out facedown in his hospital bed and filled page after page for what he now thought of as his Norton book. He was released from the hospital at the end of March and moved to the Hotel Continental in Cambridge to continue his recuperation. His left leg still ached "faintly" and writing was still "very awkward" because he still could not sit comfortably. Nevertheless, he managed to write long accounts of past experiences, an extended analysis of George Bernard Shaw, a passage on Dr. Schweitzer, and new assertions about the American experience: Americans "are inventing a new kind of human being—a new relationship between one human being and another—a new relationship between the individual and the all."[68]

He grew to love the idea of the Norton book, but, he insisted, he was not an essayist, not a critic, "not a 'non-fiction' man." He was an experienced lecturer and public speaker, however, and thus understood that there is a great difference in speaking to the ear and writing "for the eye." Because he believed firmly that his lectures could not be published as they had been spoken, he set to work rewriting them with that in mind.[69]

FOR WILDER the decade of the fifties was a period of unfinished business—chiefly the Norton book and *The Emporium* and other plays he wanted to write. For several years he would carry around the Norton manuscript, saddled with guilt because he had not finished it, somehow *could* not finish it. As he often did, he envisioned a project much vaster than he could accomplish, or was obligated to deliver. Rather than write down his lectures, already brilliantly presented from the podium, he conceived a book of elegantly crafted essays on American literature, coupled with profound essays on world literature. He was ultimately thwarted by his own grandiose expectations.

Even so, Wilder's most important work in the decade of the fifties was accomplished not as the playwright or as the novelist, but as the lecturer/scholar, the teacher, the public citizen. For the next five years he often turned to his journal in the ongoing effort to articulate, craft, and test his ideas about American characteristics as revealed in nineteenth-century literature and applied in twentieth-century life. He was driven in part by the obligation to ready the Norton lectures for publication, but even more, as a writer and a citizen, he wanted to understand the national experience, to interpret it, to speculate about its implications for the future.

He gave his final Norton lecture on May 16, 1951. As his Harvard year wound to its close, Wilder expressed a hope and a promise in his personal quest for the right way: "I shall yet produce a work—a work and a self—which in its relative and limited proportions will be its justification."[70] He thought of himself as "an observer and an onlooker," he wrote to Howard Lowry, president of the College of Wooster in Ohio. During the Harvard year Wilder made an earnest effort, he wrote, to "*belong*, to be in and of a community. Well, by the time I left I knew every third person I passed on the street—I sure was a citizen of Cambridge—but it was the most difficult year of my life."[71]

He found it "very gratifying" to receive an honorary doctorate at the Harvard commencement, and agreed to address the Harvard alumni reunion that day—an event, he said, that "many people throng to; they expect 8000 in Harvard Yard. . . . Damn, damn, I can never talk in general matters on America Whither, or our Age of Anxiety, or the Destiny of the New World. Damn. I've been working on it all morning."[72] He titled his address "Thoughts for Our Times," and framed his remarks as a comparison of the "thought-worlds" of students when he himself had been one in 1917–20, and those he had known as a teacher in the thirties at the University of Chicago and at Harvard in 1950–51. Students in the fifties, he observed, were living in stormy times—the

"Age of Upheaval" and the "Age of Anxiety," as the period had been called. He was optimistic about the future because modern young people understood that "the things that separate men from one another are less important than the things that they have in common."[73] Wilder concluded:

> All the languages in the world are but local differentiations of one planetary tongue. These concepts are very full of something frightening, but they are also full of promise. Oh, it is a lonely and alarming business to feel oneself one in the creation of billions and billions, and especially lonely if one's parents seem never to have felt that sensation at all, but it is exciting and inspiriting to be among the first to hail and accept the only fraternal community that finally can be valid—that emerging, painfully emerging, unity of those who live on the one inhabited star.[74]

In that Cold War era, while many writers and artists turned their attention away from the concerns of the world community, Wilder was articulating a bold global view in a cynical and suspicious time. On international stages in South America and in Europe, he had interpreted American characteristics for people from other countries and cultures. During his watershed year at Harvard, Wilder interpreted the American experience for the American audience in a nation seeking to redefine its identity in a postwar world. Masterful teacher and lecturer that he was, Wilder had learned a great deal, he said, from his "young friends in Cambridge" that year, and it gave him hope for the future. He told his audience in Harvard Yard that these young people had shown him "over and over again that to them it is as simple as breathing that all societies are but variants of one another . . . and the human adventure is much the same in all times and all places."[75]

34

KALEIDOSCOPIC VIEWS

No view of life, then, is real to me save that it presents itself as
kaleidoscopic,—which does not mean essentially incoherent. (The very
children's toys of that name show us always a beautifully ordered
though multi-fragmented pattern.)

—THORNTON WILDER,
"Notes Toward the Emporium," February 15, 1954

The United States and Europe (1950s)

Wilder was so exhausted by his Harvard experience that he told Isabel he would never forgive the university for the way he had aged in just that one year. "As far as Harvard is concerned," he said, "the phrase is unjust; it is myself to blame. . . . Now it remains to be seen, not whether I can recuperate to the extent of being an adequate 54, but whether I can enter into the rights and privileges of being a good 60."[1] He promised himself and his lawyer that for at least a year and a half he was going to "withdraw from all that speaking-teaching-bowing-smiling racket—even if I have to dig into capital for it."[2]

He spent most of the summer of 1951 outlining and writing passages for his Norton book. He was expanding his theories of the American sense of time and place, the American transformations of the English language, and the "American Disconnectedness," and he considered developing a section on American religion. He continued to explore the work of Poe, Melville, Dickinson, Whitman, Hawthorne, Emerson, and Henry James with much the same fervor he had given to Joyce and Lope de Vega. He decided that Hawthorne was not truly an American writer. He found Emerson "repugnant," writing to Malcolm Cowley: "Isn't he awful? Yet how that colossus bestrode the world for so long! His ideas basely, soothingly, flattering all that is facile and evasive in the young republic. . . . Melville's copies of [Emerson's] Essays are in the Harvard Library and it's a joy to see how Melville dug his pencil into the page in scornful attention."³ Wilder sketched out a "chapter" on Poe tantalizingly called "How Literature Can Be Made out of Necrophilic Sadism."⁴

He polished an essay titled "Toward An American Language," which was published in the July 1952 issue of the *Atlantic Monthly*, with a photograph of Wilder on the cover. Because the journal would serialize only three of the six Norton lectures, Wilder set to work cutting and "making a sort of cuisine of passages robbed from the other chapters." He worried that there might be a "sort of 'incoherence in application,' " but believed that would be smoothed out in the Norton book he was determined to write.⁵ In August the *Atlantic Monthly* published Wilder's essay "The American Loneliness," with a focus on Thoreau, and in November, "Emily Dickinson," which turned out to be the last publication of any of the Norton material in Wilder's lifetime.

One American characteristic that Wilder especially prized was mobility, which, thanks to his car, meant independence. He was traveling now in a gray Mercury Dynaflow convertible with red leather seats. He loved the freedom of the American road, where he could drive himself to New Hampshire or Rhode Island or Florida, or to Atlantic City or Tucson, or to the Massachusetts coast, where he and Isabel took refuge in the summer, or to Maine, where Amos and Catharine had built a summer cabin at Blue Hill. There was also the freedom of the sea, his escape route to Europe. By mid-September Wilder was on the way to Europe again, hoping to continue his Norton work in Italy and France. He was convinced he could get some rest on the voyage; he told his lawyer, as he told many others, "Baby's best on a boat."⁶ He was back home in Hamden in November but soon headed off again, this time to Florida. More peripatetic than ever, he planned to go to Key West and maybe to Havana, or maybe to Tucson, and then—who knew where?⁷

Wilder was in New York on May 28, 1952, to accept the Gold Medal for Fiction from the American Academy of Arts and Letters. He had been elected to membership in the academy in 1939.⁸ Pearl Buck presented him with the "highest honor for fiction" bestowed by the National Institute of Arts and Letters (the "inner body" of the Academy), observing that it was rare to "find a writer gifted and successful in such different fields as the play and the novel."[9] In his acceptance Wilder identified two "essential requirements" of the novelist: "He must be more interested in human beings than in forming generalized ideas about human beings; and he must believe profoundly in the principle of freedom in the life of the human mind."[10]

The accolades kept coming: On June 9 Wilder was at Oberlin College, where he and his brother would receive honorary degrees. The college conferred an honorary doctorate of divinity on Amos, now Professor of New Testament Interpretation at the Chicago Theological Seminary at the University of Chicago. Thornton received an honorary doctor of letters degree and gave the commencement address. He was "triply happy" that he and his brother would receive honorary degrees at the same time.[11] His commencement address, "Wrestling with Thoreau," was one of his Norton lectures, tailored for the occasion.

———

THE WILDERS were keeping careful watch over Charlotte, who was now living on her own in Greenwich Village. "So I had lunch with Sharlie," Wilder had written to Isabel in the fall of 1951. He was happy to see that his sister was "most definitely better in every way. Hat and dress downright smart. She's now forbidden liquor and smokes only some expensive de-nicotined cigarettes." He noted the irony, however, that although Charlotte seemed "almost completely well," her conversations were less interesting.[12] Had he been privy to some of the prose she was writing at the time, he would have changed his mind on both counts. "My life is a smashed crystal—I don't know any other way to describe it," she wrote.

> It is like the lens of a huge telescope that an explosive bullet has struck; the glass has not fallen out, but the entire surface—even the inside—shows an infinite cross-pattern of a mosaic of cracks without a centre. This situation, of course, started, as it

happens[,] virtually with birth; but the inciting cause of the present situation began in what my notes tell me was 1940— about eleven years ago, or a trifle more. . . . The gist of the centre of it, itself, I think, is the complex of ten years in hospitals and psychiatric institutions, for a *double* reason—one of which, the one that kept me there the full ten years, was "a severe nervous breakdown," which only I, of all the world, evidently, know that I did not have. . . .[13]

The sister and brother summarized their lives with metaphors that were uncannily similar images, yet with enormously different implications: Charlotte's life was a smashed crystal, a mosaic of cracks without a center. Thornton's life was kaleidoscopic—a "beautifully ordered though multi-fragmented pattern."

However, Charlotte had shown so much improvement nearly three years after her lobotomy that her doctors had decided she could try to live independently. With Thornton's financial support, she rented an apartment at 220 Sullivan Street, off Washington Square, and was soon "on a high grade octane work program," she wrote to Isabel. "Writing like dear life." She wanted to resume her writing career, planning, she said, to "write out of the experience of the last ten years. (That will be an exposition of my character that will certainly put me on a guillotine in the public gaze!)"[14] But most of the time she didn't know what to write, and still insisted that she had never had a "nervous breakdown or any other mental or physical trouble."[15]

In the winter of 1951–52, Charlotte stopped taking care of herself, failed to eat properly, filled her apartment to overflowing with newspapers. "Honey, why will you collect old papers?" Thornton wrote to her. "I'm the quickest tearer-upper in the world. Isabel's always afraid that I'm about to throw away some 'treasure.'" He liked rooms "as near to monastic cells as possible," he told Charlotte, and expressed his concern that old papers lying about would "collect dust: asthmatic, choking, wearying, unclean, disorderly dust."[16]

Charlotte began to experience occasional paranoid episodes, usually directing her angry outbursts at Isabel and Thornton, but sometimes at

Amos and Janet as well. She developed bleeding ulcers and eventually had to be hospitalized for a hemorrhaging gastric ulcer. Afterward she recuperated at the Amityville home, but then was allowed to return to Sullivan Street. Ten months later, in a second hospitalization, most of her stomach and part of her colon had to be removed. In June 1953 she returned to the Long Island Home in Amityville for her recuperation from surgery. "Remember: you don't *only* eat to support your body," Wilder wrote to his sister. "You eat to support your soul. . . . Do not read while you eat—do as the Mohammedans do: eat in silent admiration: eating is thanking,—thanking for being."[17]

By now it was clear that physically and emotionally, Charlotte was incapable of living alone. She was officially readmitted to residency at the Long Island Home July 18, 1953, to stay there indefinitely. "Yes, I went to see Charlotte," Thornton wrote from the MacDowell Colony in September 1953. "Amazing. Best she's been since her first illness. Climbs up and downstairs like you or I." He reported that one of the Long Island Home doctors had told him that there had been a "radical change" in her attitude, and that she had finally acknowledged that she did have a nervous breakdown and that her family "was acting for her own good and not merely maliciously restraining her liberty."[18]

It is not clear whether Wilder knew at the time of Charlotte's surgery that another American playwright had a schizophrenic sister who had been lobotomized. In 1943, after six years of futile treatment for her schizophrenia, Tennessee Williams's older sister, Rose, was subjected to the surgery. For Williams, his sister and her tragic illness were subject matter for *Suddenly Last Summer* and *The Glass Menagerie*. (In 1959 Wilder's young friends Montgomery Clift and Elizabeth Taylor played in the movie version of *Suddenly Last Summer*, with its graphic depiction of a lobotomy and of conditions in some psychiatric institutions.) What was public, center-stage subject matter for Williams the dramatist was private business for the Wilders, although Thornton Wilder the novelist would later portray in his fiction two young women who suffer mental or physical breakdowns—Sophia in *The Eighth Day* and Elspeth in *Theophilus North*. As shall be seen, these characters evoke images of Charlotte Wilder and the lessons her family learned from her illness. Like Wilder, Williams was devoted to his sister, financed her lifetime of medical care, and set up a trust to protect her as long as she lived.

———

FOR MOST of the fifties Wilder was, as usual, overwhelmed with work and by "unredeemed pledges of work"—projects ranging from writing a screenplay to leading a diplomatic cultural mission.[19] In 1952 he accepted a five-thousand-dollar payment from the celebrated producer-director Vittorio De Sica to write "story ideas, plot ideas and dialogue" for a screenplay set in Chicago and based on what Wilder soon called a "worthless story" by Ben Hecht, drawn from Hecht's 1943 novel, *Miracle in the Rain*.[20] To be produced by Warner Bros., the film was De Sica's first movie project in the United States. After numerous sessions with De Sica in New York, Wilder withdrew from the project out of concern that "the whole constructions" might "suddenly topple down about our ears as forced, contrived."[21] He also worried that De Sica and his colleagues were bent on depicting Chicago as "a love-less jungle of concrete," and that they were working with "plot and dialogue, of abysmal conventionality," perhaps out of the "problem of picture-making in a new country," where they feared rejection by American studio heads—which, Wilder recalled, had been the fate of Max Reinhardt and other European filmmakers.[22]

Wilder's attention swiftly turned from a film about Chicago to an international gathering in Italy. He was asked to lead the American delegation to the UNESCO International Conference on the Artist in Contemporary Society, to be held in Venice in September 1952, and to prepare the official report. He refused the invitation twice but finally agreed to go, in large part because this was the first time a "truly international company of artists has met together." There were visual artists, writers in various genres, and musicians. Distinguished artists were chosen to report on their individual disciplines: Henry Moore on sculpture; Georges Rouault on painting; Arthur Honegger on music; Marc Connelly on theater—and Thornton

Wilder, the Reporter General, speaking on behalf of them all. The artists who gathered in Venice wished to "re-affirm two principles which the world is in constant danger of forgetting," Wilder wrote in his official summary:

> That the artist through his creation, has been in all times a force that draws men together and reminds them that things which men have in common are greater than the things that separate them; and that the work of the artist is the clearest example of the operation of freedom in the human spirit.[23]

He wrote much of his official report in Venice, chafing to get back to his creative work, but still wondering where to go next, and what to do. At fifty-five he was growing more aware of the exigency of time, and the dilemma of how to use it. "Oh, how badly I run my life," he wrote to Elizabeth Shepley Sergeant. "How I postpone from year to year the establishment of those conditions under which I can work. And I don't mean *work* in the sense of producing volumes, I mean work in the sense of working on and in and with myself."[24]

He was being pursued at that time by a resolute "lioness" in the diminutive form of his friend Ruth Gordon, who was determined to revive and stage *The Merchant of Yonkers* in London. In a flurry of telephone calls from Paris to Venice, she and Garson Kanin urged Wilder to come to Paris to confer with them and Tyrone Guthrie about a potential production, starring Gordon, of course.[25] Despite misgivings, Wilder was tempted. He bargained with himself: If he agreed to the project, he would have to be "stern thereafter—say goodbye to collaborations and go and hide myself."[26] He thought he would finish his play, and then write a movie script, an opera libretto, and a comic novel—all in the spirit of freedom, and in the hope of enjoying the "modest gift" that had been given him.[27] Nevertheless, Wilder acquiesced to Ruth Gordon's wishes and met her in Paris in mid-October to talk about adapting *The Merchant of Yonkers* into the script, slightly revised, which became *The Matchmaker*.

IN HIS January 1953 journal Wilder struggled with doubts about him-self as an artist and a person, analyzing and overanalyzing his earlier work, and regretting the consequences of the "Externalizing Years," as he now called his Harvard experience.[28] He was sick with a "deep-lodged cold and deafness." Alone and ill in his hotel room in Baden-Baden, he worried that the time he had spent on events other than writing had been wasteful, even harmful. Yet he had to believe that he could still create literary work that showed "that during these years I have been watching, listening and feeling, in the . . . presence of multi-faceted life."[29] He promised himself that "the next things I write must have a new theme and form, a new theme in form."[30]

He was not afraid of the literary challenges. Instead, he confessed in his journal, "What I am afraid of is myself—of those tiresome drives toward moralization and over-simplification."[31] He wanted to "rein-troduce lyrical and romantic beauty into the theatre"—elements that would "surprise" an audience with "lyrical feeling"—despite the danger of being didactic and even "bombastic."[32] But whether he wrote a play next or a novel, he resolved never "to be caught up into that 'non-fiction' thought-world again."[33] Later, when the critic, editor, and translator Eric Bentley asked Wilder to provide an introduction to a Spanish play for one volume of his four-volume series, *The Classic The-atre*, Wilder declined because, he said, he wrote nonfiction "badly and with excruciating effort."[34]

He acknowledged in a journal entry that "Even the dear Lope-studies are an albatross about my neck. And the [Norton] book!—[It] is like some greedy improper self-deception that I can adequately write that kind of book."[35] Two of his Lope research papers were published in the early 1950s—"New Aids Toward Dating the Early Plays of Lope de Vega" in *Varia Variorum: Festgabe für Karl Reinhardt* in Germany in 1952; and "Lope, Pinedo, Some Child Actors, and a Lion" in *Romance Philology* in August 1953.[36] He vowed to finish the Norton book as soon as he returned to the United States in May 1953. Despite conscientious efforts over the next several years, this was a promise he would never be able to keep.

ON JANUARY 12, 1953, while Wilder was still in Europe, he made the cover of *Time*. The artist Boris Chaliapin, who created more than four hundred cover portraits for the magazine, painted a striking image of Wilder, with a framed drawing of the American flag in the background. Chaliapin captured a sadness in Wilder's eyes that most artists and photographers missed during the fifties. "The American is the first planetary mind," ran the caption under Wilder's portrait, alluding to his recent lectures. The *Time* cover led many people to conclude that it was Wilder himself who had "the first planetary mind," when he was actually referring to Americans in general. The magazine's biographical portrait of Wilder described him as "a kindly, grey-haired gentleman from the East" and a "loquacious American" who lectured "with much waggling of eyebrows and flourishing of hands." The author of the article also advanced the mistaken premise that "for one of his years and talents, he has written comparatively little."[37]

Wilder frequently heard but paid little heed to this quantitative assessment of his career. However, he was very proud to discover in 1953 that his sister Janet, the one Wilder sibling who had in *fact* written very little and had never been published widely except for scientific articles, was now a magazine columnist. While Janet and Toby Dakin were well known in and around Amherst for their good works and philanthropy and their proactive citizenship, Janet was also recognized for her scientific and equestrian interests. Since falling in love with horses when she was a schoolgirl in England, she had become a skilled equestrienne and a leading figure in equestrian circles, but she had never raised a foal until Lord Jeff was born to her Morgan horse Bonnie. In December 1952 Janet published the first of a series of popular magazine articles about bringing up Lord Jeff. Her background as a scientist informed her work as she researched and devised training methods. Called "Jeffy's Journal," the series ran in the *Morgan Horse* through April 1956, and was later published as a book, *Jeffy's Journal: Raising a Morgan Horse* (1990). Janet wrote about the adventures, good and bad, that she and Jeffy shared over the years, whether he was winning horse shows or bucking her sky-high and tossing her into the snow.[38] She dedicated the book to her mother.

When Thornton read Janet's first magazine column, he wrote her a fan letter: "I never saw a happier illustration of the deepest rule about writing. Be possessed by your subject—know it, live it—and you will write well."[39]

———

ACCORDING TO the noted director Tyrone Guthrie, it was Ruth Gordon's husband, the writer Garson Kanin, who had the brilliant idea for a revival of Wilder's unsuccessful play *The Merchant of Yonkers*. Guthrie, Gordon, and Kanin agreed that the most serious obstacle to a successful revival was that the play "bore the stigma of failure"—something Guthrie suggested was "in present-day America far more damning than a conviction for rape or arson." Therefore Gordon and Kanin proposed that Wilder revise, update, and rename the play; that Ruth Gordon star as Dolly Levi; and that the production be mounted in London rather than New York, knowing that if they "tried and succeeded in London" the play might then open in New York "cleansed of the guilt of failure, redeemed, restored to a state of grace."[40]

Although *Merchant* had failed on Broadway, it had often been revived in professional and amateur productions. In March 1952, early in his discussions with Gordon, Guthrie, and Kanin, Wilder decided to withdraw *The Merchant of Yonkers* from Samuel French representation in England "until further notice."[41] Guthrie easily persuaded the producer Binkie Beaumont, who had successfully produced *The Skin of Our Teeth*, to present the "new" version of the play, now titled *The Matchmaker*. Beaumont wrote to Wilder, "I am enormously optimistic that we may be launching something which will eventually be a wonderful success for London and, who knows?—we might even visit New York."[42] Ruth Gordon was set to star in the show, which was soon scheduled as one of the plays in the spotlight at the Edinburgh Festival in 1954, after a tryout in Newcastle-upon-Tyne. Wilder, who was usually reluctant to attend the opening nights of his own plays, was present in Newcastle and found it "very heady and exciting."[43] From there *The Matchmaker* moved to Edinburgh, to open August 23, 1954. If all went well there would be a ten-week tour, including an appearance at the Berliner Fest-wochen, a drama festival in Berlin, and then an opening in London at the Theatre Royal, Haymarket, on November 4, 1954.

In his memoirs Guthrie recalled that the production of the play went like clockwork, but behind the scenes there were the usual con-volutions and crises inherent in pulling a play from script to stage. At first Wilder revised his original script extensively, only to return to most of the original text, filling the "wastepaper baskets of Europe" with rewritten pages.[44] In the end he produced a retitled script that was, he wrote to his dramatic agent, "merely a cut, trimmed, original, touched up YONKERS."[45]

The Matchmaker—the first American drama to be staged at the Ed-inburgh Festival—was launched to mixed but largely positive reviews. "It does not add up to anything at all in the end except an over-long, over-dressed, over-elaborated bore," wrote Alan Dent in the Edin-burgh *News Chronicle*.[46] For Derek Granger in the *Financial Times*, how-ever, the play was "consistently ebullient and daisy-fresh," and full of "those little saws and scraps of home-spun wisdom with which Mr. Wilder has enriched American comedy."[47]

Behind the scenes of his farce about love and money, Wilder was worrying about his own financial situation. His lawyer had informed him in 1954 that his 1952–53 income was about seven thousand dollars less than the year before, while his expenses were about six thousand dollars more, not counting the now-doubled cost of supporting Char-lotte—more than four thousand dollars from May 1953 through April 1954.[48] To make ends meet, Wilder had to draw about nine thousand dollars from his savings. But, he assured his lawyer cheerfully, the Brit-ish production of *The Matchmaker* was going to make him "very rich."[49]

The Matchmaker went on to great success and a long run in London, not as a retread of an old play but as a fresh, lively new production. This was a different time, a different production, a different director, a slightly different script, and most of all, a different Dolly Levi. Ac-cording to Binkie Beaumont, the acting was impeccable in the London engagement, most of the reviews were "jolly good," and the audience

"burst into rounds of applause on countless occasions out of sheer ecstasy of joy."[50] Furthermore, Beaumont wrote to Wilder, Ruth Gordon
was "very definitely the toast of the town, a pillar of strength, and the
most wonderful actress to work with that one could ever hope to be
lucky enough to meet."[51]

From London *The Matchmaker* moved on to New York under the auspices of the Theatre Guild and the producer David Merrick. It opened
on Broadway on December 5, 1955, and ran for 486 performances—
Wilder's Broadway record. In 1964, transfigured once again, this time
as *Hello, Dolly!* with star turns by Carol Channing, Ginger Rogers,
Betty Grable, Pearl Bailey, Ethel Merman, and others, the musical
played 2,844 Broadway performances.[52]

SOON AFTER *The Matchmaker's* success at the 1954 Edinburgh Festival, Ian Hunter, the director of the festival, asked Wilder to contribute
a play in 1955 for the "problem hall" in Edinburgh—the Assembly
Room of the Presbyterian Church on the Mound, a large auditorium
with pewlike rows of seats rimming three sides of a central platform.
It was absurd even to consider the invitation, Wilder wrote in his journal, because he was facing "so many unfinished projects," as well as his
"increasing inability to carry through a project in a prolonged effort of
concentration."[53] Still he began to think seriously about it. Perhaps he
would write a science-fiction drama in the manner of Aristophanes. He
could see a spaceship heading for another star, and Martians wanting
to immigrate to earth, and people inhabiting caves on earth. He would
call it "The Martians," or perhaps, "Fifty Billion Acres." In the flush
of his initial enthusiasm, he pitched the idea to Binkie Beaumont, who
was "bewitched" by it and immediately saw Helen Hayes in the lead
role of the mother of eleven children, including four sons who went off
to war.[54] By mid-November, however, Wilder abandoned the idea.

That fall, in Aix-en-Provence, he was rereading, in French, Kierkegaard's *Philosophical Scraps* (Wilder's rendition of the title most commonly
translated as *Philosophical Fragments*)—the philosopher's meditations on
the nature of truth. In this book Kierkegaard questioned whether truth

lies within the subconscious or the "true self" of an individual, waiting to be discovered, or whether it is external, waiting to be learned. He raised the possibility that there are universal truths that cannot be fully known or understood, and posed questions about the nature of love and of faith. At the same time that Wilder revisited Kierkegaard, he picked up the manuscript draft of *The Alcestiad*, which he had accidentally brought along to Europe in his baggage. He was almost immediately caught up in the script again, "with full conviction."[55]

The Greek legend of Alcestis has long been a magnet for dramatists, beginning with Euripides and including, in the twentieth century, T. S. Eliot as well as Thornton Wilder. Eliot drew loosely on the legend in *The Cocktail Party*, a play Wilder saw in New York in 1950 and heartily disliked. It made him "angry as a boil," he had written to Laurence Olivier and Vivien Leigh. "No, sir, life is not restricted to two choices only—dreary inconsequentiality *or* absolute sainthoood. No, sir. T.S. Eliot does not like people."[56]

Wilder's drama, set in the mythical time and place, depicts the full saga of Alcestis, the daughter of a king, who was wooed and won by another king, Admetus. When the gods proclaimed that Admetus would be spared death if someone would die in his place, Alcestis willingly stepped in. Wilder made it clear on the title page of the manuscript that his *Alcestiad* is a play of questions. Alcestis does not want to go to her grave "loved and honored," but ignorant. She does not want to reach the end of her life "knowing as little of why we live and why we die—of why the hundred thousand live and die—as the day we were born."[57] In his journal Wilder examined ways of posing the questions to "express the incommensurability of the human and the divine, the ambiguity to which all human reading of a divine would be subject." He wondered if he could "mould the story in such a way that it left in doubt whether the Supernatural had spoken to men or whether Men had sublime promptings which they immediately ascribed to the Supernatural?"[58]

One reason Wilder had put the play aside in 1953 was that he grew bored "with writing a 'beautiful' saint's legend," and wanted to make it all "wider, newer, crazier." He considered introducing a "company of twentieth-century archaeological trippers surveying under a guide the site of the palace at Pherai." They would be invisible to the ancient characters in the play, who would likewise be invisible to them. "Ladies and gentlemen, please stay together in a group," the tour guide would say to the modern tourists. "Here, it is believed, was the palace of Admetus." He abandoned the idea, but wished that he could achieve in the play a tone of "high comedy—lyrical, diaphanous and tender—just because it threatens so to be sententious and didactic."[59] While he was not a *poetic* dramatist, Wilder wrote in his journal, he was a poetic *dramatist*, and he kept his "darks and lights" in "continual juxtaposition."[60]

In 1954, after time away from the play, Wilder could see the problems that had stalled his work, and even better, he saw how to fix them.[61] For one thing, King Admetus had come alive for him, and he could now picture his good friend Montgomery Clift in the part. Wilder wrote to Thew Wright, now one of his lawyers, that *The Alcestiad* would "play to shaken and sobbing audiences for years to come. It's a mixture of religious revival, mother-love-dynamite, and heroic derring-do. You can't beat that combination."[62]

In private, however, Wilder doubted the play, and himself. "What have I got now?" he wrote in his journal. "A play of faith which is not a very good or radiant or convinced play of faith. . . . What I should have written is a play of scepticism which is continually shot through with an almost violent and demanding invocation to interpret the actions in the light of faith."[63] He fell short, he believed, because the "silly life" he had been living since the war had "dulled and dimmed" his "capabilities for intellectual passion" and a "clearer, harder intellectual structure." He had been a lazy artist for the past few years, he wrote, and he feared he could no longer summon his "total concentration" to write an entire, unified play.[64]

In some of his earlier work, especially his fiction, Wilder had confronted the question of *how* we live. In *The Alcestiad* he turned to the question of *why*. In the questions posed and the answers offered, *The Alcestiad* may be read as a sequel to Wilder's novels, especially *The Bridge of San Luis Rey*, and to his depiction of death in *Our Town*. Unlike

Emily, who is granted her wish to revisit one day of her life, Alcestis is brought back from the underworld by Hercules to live again. Although death brings "great grief," she has learned that the bitterness of death is not the parting. Instead, she says, "It is the despair that one has not lived. It is the despair that one's life has been without meaning. That it has been nonsense; happy or unhappy, that it has been senseless." She speaks of the dead in the underworld—"all those millions lie imploring us to show them that their lives were not empty and foolish."[65]

Wilder asks in his early novels if love is sufficient to give life meaning. "But the love will have been enough," the Abbess says in the unforgettable conclusion to *The Bridge of San Luis Rey*; "all those impulses of love return to the love that made them. Even memory is not necessary for love. There is a land of the living and a land of the dead and the bridge is love, the only survival, the only meaning."[66] In the play produced twenty-eight years after *The Bridge* was published, Alcestis says, "Yes, but love is not enough. Love is not the meaning. It is one of the signs that there is a meaning—it is only one of the signs that there is a meaning."[67]

———

LONG BEFORE his play opened, Wilder wrote a dispassionate critique of it—and he anticipated the largely negative responses by theater critics that would follow the play's debut on August 22, 1955, at the Edinburgh Festival. Still, much of the public was quite moved by it. "If the play were written by someone else, what would I have to say about it," he wrote in a journal entry on January 25, 1955. "First, that Wilder has again tried to succeed in a vast undertaking and has fallen conspicuously short."[68]

The great American actress Irene Worth, distinguished in Britain as well as the United States, played Alcestis in the Edinburgh Festival production, and Wilder hoped that Montgomery Clift would take on the role of Admetus. At first Clift agreed and began growing a beard for the role. Guthrie and Beaumont knew that Clift would be "a very tempting plum" for the part, and, happy to meet his demands, leased a private home for the duration of his stay in Scotland.[69] However, Clift changed his mind, apparently on the grounds that the script needed major changes because some of the dialogue was "forced and pedantic."[70] Wilder told the press that Clift had withdrawn from the role because he felt it wasn't the part for him.[71] A second actor, Michael Goodliffe, was cast in the part. He withdrew after a few rehearsals in a dispute with Guthrie, who quickly replaced him with Robert Hardy, fresh from his acclaimed Old Vic performance as Prince Hal in *Henry IV, Parts I and II.*

Concerned that the title of the play might not attract an audience, Guthrie and Beaumont, with Wilder's permission, changed it to *A Life in the Sun.* Irene Worth was "sublime" as Alcestis, according to the critics, and to the actress Rosemary Harris, who was performing at the festival with the Old Vic Company, playing Desdemona to an Othello portrayed on alternate days by Richard Burton and John Neville. She would slip over to the Church of Scotland Assembly Hall between her own performances especially to see Worth in Wilder's play.[72] Reviews of *The Alcestiad* were mixed, with some of them highly critical. Others praised the acting but disliked the play's lack of unity. One critic applauded Wilder's "good honest prose, often with more than a touch of colloquial usage and frequently with a decided stroke of humour."[73]

LIFE ON the road could be lonely, especially for someone getting along in years, and whether he was in company or in solitude, Wilder's affinity for alcohol became more of an issue as he grew older. His usual ability to drink freely without much obvious detriment seemed to wane. From the MacDowell Colony in the summer of 1952 he had written to Thew Wright, "The New Hampshire laws about liquor are perfectly fantastic. You have to sign a pledge never to touch liquor before you're allowed to take a drink. It's worse in Vermont: There you have to get four doctors to swear that you're a vicious alcoholic and that only a drink can save you from DEATH."[74]

His father had coerced Thornton into taking that temperance pledge when he was a boy, but college and travel had introduced him to the pleasures of good wine and whiskey. (While most of his Wilder relatives may have been teetotalers, his Niven ancestors hailed from Bowmere on the Scottish island of Islay, home of some of the best distilleries in the world.) Wilder's incessant travel during the 1950s led to more solitary and social cocktails and bottles of good wine, especially in Italy, Germany, and France. He usually wanted to drink after a hard day's work, or a speech, or some other public obligation. Most of the time he drank a lot with few visible effects. He frequently enjoyed an abundance of alcohol at social hours or leisurely dinners with Olivier and Leigh, or Clift, or Ruth Gordon and Garson Kanin, or other friends and strangers. While Wilder seldom appeared to be drunk, he usually grew more animated and loquacious the more he drank. In 1957, when an interviewer asked him to explain how liquor helped some writers write, Wilder replied, "I drink a good deal, but I do not associate it with writing."[75]

He had met and befriended the young Canadian actor and writer Timothy Findley when Findley played Rudolph in the original production of *The Matchmaker*, and he became Findley's mentor as well as his drinking companion. In his memoir, *Inside Memory*, Findley described the pub crawls he and Wilder enjoyed in the midfifties. "These could take place anywhere," Findley wrote. "You named a street— a district—a town—and you tried to drink in all its pubs and bars. Highfalutin hotel bars were out." Once he and Wilder started on Fleet Street in London, imbibing "many glasses of wine and many tumblers of Scotch." If you started at the Temple Bar (the old gate to London), Wilder told Findley, and ended at Saint Paul's Churchyard, you could "practically touch the whole of English literature." Wilder knew that Daniel Defoe, Samuel Pepys, John Dryden, Henry Fielding, Oliver Goldsmith, William Makepeace Thackeray, and even Charlotte Brontë had been on Fleet Street, not in the pubs but in the buildings lining the street—Child's Bank, Temple Hall—or simply driving down the street. Dr. Johnson lived just up the alley.[76] Wilder drew a verbal picture of how Fleet Street would have been in Shakespeare's day—"the color of it all—the dawning of universal knowledge." As Wilder praised Shakespeare and Johnson and the rest, Findley thought, "Thornton tooted every horn but his own."[77]

Perhaps his drinking accelerated during the fifties as an antidote for loneliness, or as a by-product of it, or perhaps by now as an addiction. But alcohol did not figure in Wilder's exploration of loneliness as an American characteristic. He had explored the American loneliness through the prism of the lives of Dickinson and Thoreau. He chose Melville and Whitman as filters for his reflections on sexuality and the breakdown of love in the American experience. He noted in his journal that many human problems are attributed to the failure to "make 'harmonious sexual adjustments.'" Wilder believed, however, that it had "to do—more deeply and first—with love." There was a risk, he wrote, in failing to recognize that "sheer emotional devotion" is qualitatively different from "the libido element in parental and sibling love."[78] He examined the "sort of vibration of homosexual feeling and intimation" in Melville's *Billy Budd*. Melville's use of "feminine similes for Billy" made him uncomfortable, as did Melville's apparent preoccupation with phallic symbols, and Wilder thought that Melville "almost lost his story through his own infatuation with Billy Budd."

Wilder wrote in his journal that he would leave for later consideration a number of "aspects of this neurotic overturn," such as "the off-center sexuality in a number of these writers to the total American character; even the consideration that extreme ideality may always arise . . . from a strain and tension proceeding not from a serene 'rising above' sexual love but from a fear-laden repudiation of it—a shrinking from it which inevitably constitutes a fretting relation to it." Nevertheless, he wrote, "it is very remarkable finally how little this element though radical and omnipresent harms this work or renders it 'special.' "[79]

In the legally and socially repressive 1950s, new and often opposing theories about sexuality, including homosexuality, were emerging, espoused by researchers such as Alfred Kinsey and psychoanalysts such as Anna Freud, who took issue with some of her deceased father's theories. Wilder knew Freud's views of the repercussions of an infancy and childhood "starved of the environment of love," especially the "demand and command to be loved." Immediately following that observation in his journal, Wilder wrote in parentheses that he was "more and more willing to agree with certain authorities that homosexuality is negative—that it is, even when apparently aggressive, a submission to solicitations. These solicitations are not necessarily those coming from the outside; they come from within also, from an exorbitant need for tenderness, *i.e.*, to be valued by another."[80]

He wrote in his journal that he was now ready to alter his views that "man, such as he is, has no choice but to believe, to insist on believing, that the world is grounded in love—love as affection. Which brings us back to the main premise of Christianity. The human soul must feel that it is loved."[81] And how did this relate to Melville and Whitman and American characteristics in the New World—and perhaps to Wilder himself? He noted that the American's "love-object" is usually and conventionally a person of the opposite sex. "But," he wrote in his journal,

> as we saw that an American does not fix himself upon a concrete sense of place (one place, my own), and submit to one situation in society (that station to which God and the social order have assigned him) and correspondingly does not feel himself enclosed in one moment of time—so his erotic emotion is capable of a wider focus than the European's, not as polyandry, but as sublimation. . . . He has unfocused affection to dispose of and cannot find durably any object. This is combined with his independence to take a certain autoerotic color (as in Thoreau and Melville—not, I think, Poe). . . .
>
> Does the American sublimate easily? Yes. But the term *sublimation* is misleading: it implies only a *higher* transference of the sexual drive. The American sublimates into business, into infatuation with celebrities, into philanthropies.[82]

This was only "a first skirmish with a deeply complicated subject," Wilder concluded.[83] As he neared sixty he was preoccupied with these questions about the nature of love and its manifestations in the

American experience and the universal human experience, including his own family, perhaps trying to put them to rest in his literary life and in his personal life, once and for all.

————

IN THE fifties Wilder roamed, as usual, from Europe to the United States, writing as he moved about, searching for just the right place to work on his new series of "Four-Minute Plays for Four Persons" and his Norton lectures. As challenging as it was, he even tried to work in the house on Deepwood Drive during the spring of 1956. He wrote from Hamden to the noted modernist composer Louise Talma,

> What do all of these long stays abroad mean, but my eternal effort to find a time and a place when I can follow an idea through? . . . I know, in a way (but one part "of oneself" is always refusing to see what one knows) that I shouldn't have tried to return to Deepwood Drive these last months. But I was trying to do an amiable thing for Isabel. Word had reached me (though I needed no word from outside) that rightly or wrongly she felt in a mortifying position—that was my home and she was its chatelaine—why, then, was I never there? What was the matter? Translate this into terms of the set she moves in . . . was she a bad housekeeper . . . was she this or that? Anyway, I've done my duty.[84]

Throughout the fifties Wilder was caught in a tug-of-war between his duty to others and his duty to himself, and between his plays in progress and his stalled nonfiction work. He found comfort, he said, in the fact that the eminent art historian Erwin Panofsky took seven years to ready his Norton lectures for publication. Actually Panofsky took five years, but others took much longer, and Robert Frost, Eric Bentley, and a few other Norton lecturers joined Wilder in never submitting the complete series for publication at all.[85]

He had been so preoccupied with innovations in form for *The Alcestiad* and *The Emporium* that he abandoned his usual strategy of coaxing a play's form from its subject and themes. Instead he sought to impose the form on the subject matter, and this artificial scaffolding ultimately failed rather than supported the life of the drama. His struggle with *The Emporium* involved a shifting of subject and theme as well as a search for form. In Wilder's cosmic G. and S. Emporium, the best department store in the world, his characters "sold" or "shopped for" answers to the questions of the meaning of existence, of identity, faith, love, alienation, the presence or absence of a divine plan—the questions that had long permeated Wilder's work as well as his personal philosophical and spiritual journey. His struggles with the play in part reflected the twists and turns of his own personal search for answers that remained stubbornly elusive. "I hate allegory, and here I am deep in allegory," he had written in his journal in the early years of his work on the play.[86]

Wilder wanted to mask his own investigation of the boundless misery of the human condition in comedy. To that end, during his six years of work on *The Emporium*, he kept hunting for the "right form—the right statement for this cosmological comedy."[87] He worried that his form was not "bold and splendid and revolutionary enough," and that left him "inhibited and tentative and scratchily groping."[88] Ultimately, however, he was defeated by his search for the hero and for the crux of the hero's journey, and he laid the blame at Kafka's door. "I have been too much drawn into the Kafka hero, the frustrated pre-condemned struggler," Wilder wrote. "That's not my bent: I'm not the stuff of which nihilists are made."[89]

He never finished *The Emporium*, putting it away for good in 1954, but saving the manuscript among his papers. He knew before *The Alcestiad* opened in Edinburgh that it would not succeed and, most important, that he had failed to write the play he wanted to write. In his earlier work as a dramatist, he had aspired to achieve innovations in form, and he did so—but those plays were driven by their characters and themes, and the structure emerged organically from the marriage of form and content. In the fifties, try as he might to write about the "misery of the human condition," Wilder could not do it without cloaking his characters and themes in history and myth. Although he had long ago vowed not to repeat *Our Town*, he wanted once again to write "a really original play—original not in the sense that it is filled with novel devices," he said, "but that it makes people see for the first time things that hitherto they had known without being aware that they knew them."[90]

IN 1956 Wilder's mail brought an unexpected invitation: "The Miss America Pageant cordially invites you to serve on our 1956 Panel of eleven Judges to select Miss America 1957." The committee promised to "leave no stone unturned" to provide a "memorable visit" to the Atlantic City resort. Somebody there clearly knew that George Antrobus had been a beauty pageant judge in Atlantic City in *The Skin of Our Teeth*, which had enjoyed a revival in 1955 starring Helen Hayes as Mrs. Antrobus and Mary Martin as Sabina. But, Wilder wrote in response, while he believed that "Thornton George Antrobus Wilder" had inherited Mr. Antrobus's "*expertise*," he also felt that as president of the Albert Schweitzer Hospital Fund, he would have to "restrict the range" of his interests. Therefore he declined.[91]

35

"THE HUMAN ADVENTURE"

*As a child of the Twentieth Century and particularly of America, I grew up
in a world which—as never before—was aware of the vast extents of time
and space that surround the human adventure on one planet, the multiplicity
of souls, and the innumerable repetitions of any typical occasion.*

—THORNTON WILDER,
journal entry 742, June 2, 1957

The United States and Europe (1950s and 1960s)

Wilder's journals throughout the 1950s and early 1960s provide a remarkable road map through the terrain of his interior life and its exterior expression in drama, fiction, and nonfiction. Hundreds of pages are full of ideas, sketches, and drafts—experimental passages of work in progress; reflections on his reading; analyses of his occasional dreams, relying at times on Freud, at times on Jung; ruminations on the masses of Palestrina and Schubert; a detailed account of getting "sick as a dog" from food poisoning in Milan and a subsequent discourse on pain; now and then a stride forward with his Lope work; but most of all documentation of his intentions as a writer, and his prolonged and futile efforts to finish writing the Norton lectures and to write a series of short plays.[1]

For the published Nortons, Wilder searched for an innovation in nonfiction form, inventing a character he first called Tom Everedge, the avatar of the average American, the everyman living his individual version of the human adventure. The name soon modulated to Tom Everage, and then to John Everage—and back to Tom again. By April 3, 1956, Wilder had established a table of contents for the Norton book, which he titled *American Characteristics*. He had arrived at an intricate plan: He would intersperse the lectures with "interludes" narrating the "Amazing Saga of Thomas Everage," illustrating an aspect of his hero's life that would contrast the old world of European letters with the new world of American literature. He would compare Everage's American life with the lives of his contemporaries in "the Old World."[2]

Wilder was fascinated with Tom Everage's infancy and childhood, and his relationship with his parents—especially his fixation on his emotionally distant mother—and wrote lengthy passages about them. He thought he could actually make a whole "astonishing" book about the life of Tom Everage, although he continued to subordinate that story to the Norton chapters. He thought of having the serial essays and the serial Everage story printed on different-colored paper, but was told it would be too expensive. He also envisioned writing "Lay Sermons" for the book to help illuminate his "thick and many-layered rich subject matter."[3] Wilder's plans for the Norton book grew increasingly ambitious and complex until it collapsed under the weight of his extravagant vision and expectations.

He wrote in his journal on April 8, 1956, "I hadn't meant to use this Journal for this kind of 'first draft of the final text'—it is rather for a 'let's look around and see what we've got'—but I keep running away with myself."[4] Then there was a six-month hiatus in the journal in 1956 until Wilder decided to write his series of "Four-Minute Plays for Four Persons as a continuation of the Oberlin-Yale-and later Three-Minute Plays" because he always found the "self-imposition of a schema" helpful, even when it became "an appallingly exacting discipline."[5] Now he decided to create fourteen new one-act plays, two cycles of seven each, intended for the arena stage. In them he would explore the much-traveled territory of the Seven Deadly Sins and the Seven Ages of Man. Once again, as he had often done in the past, he resurrected ideas from his portfolio of unfinished work: "I have salvaged literary ventures which appear to have been discards," he wrote. For instance, two characters in his new one-act play *Bernice* were "salvaged' from his screen treatment for Vittorio De Sica. He would "ransack" his other past projects for ideas and material for new plays, and snatch new ideas out of thin air—or out of his reading. A Henry James short story prompted the idea for Wilder's play *In Shakespeare and the Bible.*[6]

Wilder made a study of the history of the arena stage and embarked enthusiastically on his ambitious project. He originally intended each play to represent "a different mode of playwriting: Grand Guignol, Chekhov, Noh play, etc., etc."[7] By the end of 1956 he had finished six plays, counting *The Drunken Sisters*, the satyr play he wrote to accompany *The Alcestiad*, in keeping with the tradition in Greek theater of following a tragic drama with a short play "in the spirit of diversion— even of the comical."[8]

His enthusiasm soon faded, however, because he simply couldn't "catch fire" on some of the new plays, perhaps because he was "straining so hard" to find a lighter comedic one to accompany the more somber dramas. Nevertheless he persisted. "I grope," he wrote in his journal in January 1957. "In the meantime, I suppose the best thing to do is to write more,----to put them in the oven and to hope that two out of four (my average so far) will come out well-baked; to inform my subconscious that that is what I am doing, and leave the rest to the mysterious operation."[9]

Meanwhile, *The Alcestiad* was "going on journeys," Wilder reported to friends.[10] He revised the script and, translated into German, it would be performed at the Zurich Festival in June 1957, accompanied by Wilder's new satyr play. Then came a tour of German-language countries, from Frankfurt and Munich to Zurich and Salzburg— sixteen venues from June 1957 to September 1959.[11] Wilder took the drafts of his one-act plays with him to Switzerland, where *The Alcestiad*, or *Die Alkestiade*, translated into German by H. E. Herlitschka, would be produced in Zurich's great Schauspielhaus beginning on June 27, 1957. In addition Wilder's friend Louise Talma, whom he had met at the MacDowell Colony in 1953, began composing a twelve-tone opera based on the play, with Wilder contributing the libretto.

In May he received a signal recognition—induction into Germany's Orden Pour le Mérite für Wissenschaften und Künste. He was honored at a luncheon with Chancellor Konrad Adenauer and other distinguished guests, and then was back in St. Moritz preparing for the premiere of *The Alcestiad*. Sadly he no longer believed in the play, he wrote in his journal. "It never found its way into the center of my stresses. . . . The reading of Kierkegaard had not penetrated into me deeply enough. Like an ill-baked cake only portions of it are fitfully touched with heat." He had intended his play to say "that the road on which we tread has been paved by the sufferings of innumerable anonymous souls who have been guided only by their own half-understood ethical intuitions, and those intuitions have been derived from the heart of the universe, which is an ethically oriented source."[12] Although in Wilder's judgment his play did not succeed, he was moving closer to his own answers to the questions about the "heart of the universe"—questions he had examined over a lifetime. He was so disappointed in *The Alcestiad* as a stage play, however, that he decided to withdraw it.

WILDER TOILED away that June in St. Moritz, where he had worked so well in the past. In his journal he sketched tentative drafts to fulfill various writing and speaking commitments. He drafted "First Gropings" for a speech he would make in Frankfurt in the fall, when he would receive the prestigious annual Peace Prize of the Association of German Publishers and Booksellers, given annually to an author whose work advanced the cause of world peace. Since its inception in 1950 the prize had been given to such luminaries as Martin Buber, Albert Schweitzer, and Hermann Hesse; and Wilder, the first American to receive it, was relieved to hear that he did not necessarily have to center the speech on world peace. "What I would wish to do is to redeliver those two or three notions which I have thrown together a number of times as the 'planetary man,'" he wrote in his journal on May 26, already looking ahead to the address he would deliver October 6.[13]

He wrote a "Sketch" in his journal for a preface to his three major plays, to be collected in a new edition in 1957. The journal version differed completely from the ultimately published preface, recapitulating in some detail Wilder's intentions as dramatist and novelist. "I have long felt that to each of us is accorded one, two, or three native notions," he wrote in the journal. "These cannot be acquired from books though later reading may confirm, modify or destroy them. They arise from the deepest well of individuality and are developed by continual counteraction of our self and the things that befall us . . . we should be aware of them as being capable of sufficient exploration and unfoldment to last us for a life time."[14] For him the "notions" took the form of questions about destiny, fate, and chance; about the myriad forms of love, and its power to uplift as well as to harm; about faith and doubt, hope and despair; about "the vast extents of time and space" surrounding the "human adventure on one planet, the multiplicity of souls, and the innumerable repetitions of any typical occasion."[15] Wilder wrote that the central question in his own search had been "how can we justify a validity for any one moment in the homely daily life? Is that more difficult than to justify even a high experience, of passionate love or loss or hate?—in a universe where innumerable beings have claimed a meaningfulness for their ecstasy or anguish, and now are dust."[16] As readers of his plays would see, he wrote, "I stake my wager not on the supreme crises of the soul; I have wanted to say, for dignity, what is humble."[17]

He summarized his evolution as a playwright: Looking back, he wrote, "I entered this school from which one never graduates with determination and circumspection. I wrote one-act plays; I translated plays from foreign languages; I worked in the motion-pictures (all entertainment business is one); I harassed directors for permission to attend rehearsals; later I acted on the stage."[18] *The Skin of Our Teeth*, Wilder continued, "is another extension of my principal preoccupation. It is an attempt to set the situation of the family, that nexus of attraction and repulsion, that arena of dependence and independence, against the dimensions of ten thousand years of human history."[19] The play's last act was indebted, he wrote, to his one-act *Pullman Car Hiawatha*. The whole play was "much indebted to James Joyce's *Finnegans Wake*, as it is to the books [to] which *Finnegans Wake* is in turn indebted." The first part of that acknowledgment of *Finnegans Wake* would make it into the published preface.

In his unpublished preface Wilder wrote, "To those who love literature and who follow it closely as a tradition and a craft, it presents itself in the image of a torch race, rather than as a jealous and airless patent office. I hope that in turn others will find occasion to acknowledge an indebtedness to me."[20] The reference to the debt and the torch race also made it into the published preface, which reads: "The play is deeply indebted to James Joyce's *Finnegans Wake*. I should be very happy if, in the future, some author should feel similarly indebted to any work of mine. Literature has always more resembled a torch race than a furious dispute among heirs."[21]

Wilder also included in his journal a detailed passage on farce as a dramatic form, especially in *The Matchmaker*, wherein he tried "to extract a believability, by sheer surprise, from a form that at first glance was childishly unbelievable."[22] He noted that "parody is the letting of fresh air into stale rooms," adding that he had parodied conventional farce in *The Skin of Our Teeth*.[23] Effective parody of a dramatic form could lead to freedom of expression—for the playwright and his characters, for everyone who wants to escape "society's tiresome tyrannies." He was speaking for the man as well as the writer when he said, "There is no adventure in life equal to that of being and asserting one's self."[24]

He wondered if a writer could effectively parody serious subject matter. "Romantic eloquence and formal tragic elevation are dead as a door-nail in our time," he wrote. "Could they be recovered by a [discreet] use of parody? I have long planned a play or novel which would move against a background imitating the 'Gothic novels' of the mid-Nineteenth Century—'East Lynne and Lady Audley's Secret' and the 'Last of the Dobervilles.' "[25] The published preface to the edition of Wilder's three plays would be almost entirely different from the draft in his journal—much shorter, much more general, devoid of the lively examples and telling reflections. But on that June day in St. Moritz, in the privacy of his journal, Wilder at sixty summarized his intentions as playwright and novelist, and although he could not have known it at the time, his words also foreshadowed one of the major achievements of his writing life. In latent dreams, memories, and imagination, he was already moving toward his epic novel *The*

Eighth Day. Everything Wilder had written and was writing pointed him in the direction of that novel—but he would have to follow an evolving path to get there.

For the time being his focus was on his new one-act plays, especially one that had just come to him—*The Rivers Under the Earth.* In keeping with his habit of recycling characters and ideas from his unfinished work, Wilder imported Tom Everage from the Norton manuscript, re-named him Tom Carter, and planted him firmly in the center of this new one-act play. He noted the connection in his journal: He wondered if he could write the play out of the "train of thought" he was experiment-ing with in the Norton lectures—"that often far-reaching decisions of our life are made on the basis of irrational promptings hidden from us." He believed that "the most powerful of these are in the erotic, and in the magnetic field of the Oedipus complex."[26] The play was developing, he wrote, "along the lines of Tom's relation to his mother; I planned it to arrive at a culmination illustrating—so recurrent in me—the rela-tions between a daughter and a father. After today's work it looks as though the boy's story will be oh! quite sufficient."[27]

BY EARLY September, Wilder was in Germany for a series of special events—first the opening of the new Congress Hall in Berlin, a spa-cious cultural hall and auditorium built for West Berlin by the United States, working with the government of West Germany. For the launch of the new auditorium, seven one-act American plays were performed for an appreciative audience of twelve hundred—plays by Tennessee Williams, Eugene O'Neill, William Saroyan, and Wilder. Lillian Gish, Ethel Waters, Eileen Heckart, and Wilder led the roster of actors for the evening, which marked the world premieres of two of his new one-acts—*Bernice* and *The Wreck on the 5:25.* The finale of the evening was Wilder's *The Happy Journey to Trenton and Camden,* starring Waters as the mother and Wilder as the Stage Manager.[28] "I cannot conceal from you the fact that I was the dear little whammo of Berlin," Wilder wrote to Thew Wright.[29]

Wilder was in Frankfurt on October 6 to deliver an address and to receive the peace prize. His speech, written in English, was translated, and he delivered it in German to the audience of two thousand, including such dignitaries as Albert Schweitzer and Chancellor Adenauer. Titled "Culture in a Democracy," Wilder's remarks were provocative. He noted that in a democracy, the "leadership of elites" was being replaced by the "leadership of majority opinion," and one's perspective depended on one's belief "in the potentialities—the so-to-speak intuitive capabilities—of the average man existing in a democracy."[30] He named T. S. Eliot among other literary critics who believed "that only elites can produce an excellent thing."[31] He reflected on what he termed the "Feudal Fiction"—the confused images and metaphors surrounding the nature of God, and hence of mankind. Wilder suggested that this "inextricable metaphorical confusion of God—King—Father—Above" gave rise to another confusion—the assumption that "we are low, base, subject, childish, common, ordinary and vulgar."[32]

He cited the "thousand-year-old lies that are gradually disappearing" in the democracies in which women now had equal responsibilities in civil life; married women had property rights and rights regarding their children; slavery was abolished; poor children could not be made to work "from dawn to sunset"; no person could be deemed "an inferior creature" because of race, color, or religion; no longer were most men viewed as "God's stepchildren." Wilder concluded: "Democracy is not only an effort to establish a social equality among men; it is an effort to assure them that they are not sons, nor subjects, nor low—that they should be equal in God's grace."[33] Culture in a democracy had dangers, but it also had hope and promise, he said. "Democracy has a large task: to find new imagery, new metaphors, and new myths to describe the new dignity into which man has entered."[34]

"I'VE RAISED a little hornet's nest," Wilder wrote in his journal on October 19. The unorthodox structure of his Frankfurt speech, built on questions and speculations rather than answers, offended some listeners, and some of his linguistic nuances and metaphors and his implied humor apparently suffered in translation. One critic charged that Wilder had a "pernicious effect on the German psyche." Yet Wilder remained widely esteemed in Germany.[35] "My speech in Frankfort raised a veritable stink in certain quarters," he wrote, "but the province of Hesse has ordered 20,000 copies for a distribution in the schools and populace."[36] His enduring popularity in Germany can be explained in part by the fact that he was a man of letters who knew and deeply appreciated European literature, especially the work of Goethe, Nietzsche, and Kafka. Coupled with that was his facility with the German language.

Most of all there was the German appreciation for Wilder's work, especially *The Skin of Our Teeth*, *The Ides of March*, and *The Alcestiad*. The German-born comparative literature professor and author Horst Frenz, writing in the *American-German Review* in the fall of 1957, called Wilder "probably the best known and the most highly regarded living American writer in all of Western Germany," and believed Wilder "helped correct, to clarify, to widen and to deepen the concept of the United States in German minds."[37] He rose to Wilder's defense again in 1961, commenting that after World War II, *Our Town* had given German audiences the "hope of finding a new order in themselves" and that Wilder's "predominately optimistic and hopeful plays" spoke to them in those bleak postwar days.[38] According to Amos Wilder, "both the scholars and the audiences of Germany were well situated to appraise, on the one hand, the new dramaturgy and, on the other, the old moralities in Thornton's plays."[39]

Wilder was awarded an honorary degree from Goethe University in Frankfurt that fall, and received three additional international honors in 1957 and 1958—the Medal of Honor for Science and Fine Arts from Austria, a medal from the government of Peru, and a Polish embassy award in honor of a 1957 production of *The Skin of Our Teeth* in Warsaw. By 1960 he had accepted nine honorary degrees, and counted as his "best three" the degrees from Harvard, Yale, and Goethe University.

His brother, Amos, had also been awarded multiple honorary degrees, including one that beat all of his, Thornton observed—the one from the University of Basel on its five-hundredth anniversary.[40]

"ALMOST A year has gone by," Wilder wrote aboard the SS *Vulcania*, approaching Barcelona on November 24, 1958, as he resumed the journal he had put aside in November 1957. He was not given to looking backward, he said, so he would not "try to give the reasons for the intermittence."[41] He was still struggling with his one-act plays. He was pouring his excitement and energy into "The Melting Pot," a film project with the legendary designer Norman Bel Geddes, who had made his mark on theater and film design, creating sets for more than a hundred movies and plays. After seeing *Our Town* in 1938, Bel Geddes had written to Wilder that it was encouraging for a dramatist to break the theater free visually from some of its "hidebound" traditions so that the audience could participate imaginatively in the production of a play.[42] In January 1958 Wilder and Bel Geddes began talking about collaborating on a motion picture—an American epic that would dramatize the history, ancestry, and events of the national experience. Bel Geddes suggested that they could make significant use of the new wide-screen movie technology—photographing a scene from several directions, yielding a kind of movie "in the round."[43]

By late February 1958 Wilder had written three "episodes" for the movie, building on the theme of "America's responsibility for safe-guarding the values of civilization throughout the whole world, illustrated by the racial mixtures of the American people."[44] He planned to dramatize the lives of the descendants in one family from 1600 to the present day, a coming-to-America saga that would demonstrate "the problems and rewards of the mixed bloods in the Melting Pot."[45] He forged ahead with a script, six "episodes" in all, but gave up the writing after Bel Geddes died on May 8, 1958. Wilder was not involved in writing the treatment or any part of the screenplay for another film made that year—the movie version of *The Matchmaker* starring Shirley Booth, Anthony Perkins, and Shirley MacLaine.

During this time Wilder was once again compulsively absorbed in his study of *Finnegans Wake*. Since June 1951 he had enjoyed a detailed correspondence with a colleague as obsessed with the novel as he was. She was Adaline Glasheen, an independent scholar and part-time librarian who was at work on *A Census of 'Finnegans Wake,'* published in 1956 in the United States. For twenty-five years the two exchanged letters and notes—enough to fill a 732-page book.[46] They were companions on a literary archaeological expedition, the first ones, Wilder wrote to Glasheen, to "sift, sift, sift."[47]

On April 23, 1959, Wilder spoke on Joyce and *Finnegans Wake* to the Yale Romance Language Club, joined by the university's German and Slavic clubs. Wilder called his talk *"Finnegans Wake:* The Polyglot Everyman," and emphasized that in Joyce's novel "each man carries Everyman within himself."[48] In a revision of his talk Wilder wrote of Joyce that "his subject is Man, his instincts, the operation of his mind, the institutions he has created, and, above all, the documents he has made in an effort to give an account of himself."[49] He noted Joyce's allusion to the seven deadly sins in the novel, a device at the crux of Wilder's play cycle.

Wilder took another detour in August 1959 to Williamstown, Massachusetts, to play the Stage Manager in *Our Town* one last time. After this performance Wilder the actor retired from the stage. He was still working on the libretto for the operatic setting of *The Alcestiad* with Louise Talma. He was trying to simplify and focus his life, however, and to that end he made an "immeasurably important decision" in November 1959: He resolved to close *Finnegans Wake* for five years, realizing that "like some will-undermining narcotic, it was sapping not only all interest in any writing I might do myself, but the very springs from which come reflection, observation, and my very attention to the people and events about me."[50] He had enjoyed the satisfaction of being "a pioneer" on an "unfolding journey," he wrote in his journal, and the researches made him happy, but he realized that his new one-act plays were written "from the peripheral areas" of his will and imagination—"the small area left half-alive beside the bewitched devotion to Lope and Joyce."[51] That devotion had to stop, immediately. He was sixty-two, rapidly growing older—and squandering time and energy as if he possessed boundless quantities of both.

He notified Adaline Glasheen about his decision: "I'm writing you with a mixture of sorrow and relief. I'm *giving up* Finnegans Wake."[52] In his journal he wrote:

> It may take a long time to re-fire the center of the mind, and I am old. And with dismay I recognize that it is not merely a matter of finding subjects and presenting them as literature; it is a matter of re-awakening the fields of observation and reflection that alone nourish and give significance to the fictions. I return as one from an illness or from a long journey into a remote territory to make my house and hearth again.[53]

MORE AND more often Wilder received requests to adapt his work, and most of the time he turned them down. For years, he wrote, "I've said no to many requests to make operas, musical plays etc. etc. out of the plays and novels." An opera based on *The Bridge of San Luis Rey* was occasionally performed in German opera houses, but that began during the war, he said, and "I now pretend I don't know about [it]."[54] An opera based on *The Woman of Andros* "got quite a ways," he said.[55] Mary Martin wanted to do a Cleopatra musical based on *The Ides of March*, and Aaron Copland and Richard Rodgers approached him about other properties. Wilder declined to grant them permission, and also disappointed a composer who had already finished twenty songs "for a Musical Matchmaker."[56] Over the years Wilder turned down requests from composers he admired, including Ned Rorem, who would eventually compose the music for an *Our Town* opera, and Leonard Bernstein, who wanted to make an opera of *The Skin of Our Teeth* after the collapse of a proposed musical version.[57]

In 1960 Wilder turned down a request from the State Department that he undertake another cultural relations tour, this time to lecture in conjunction with international performances of *The Skin of Our Teeth* on a multicountry jaunt in 1961 throughout Europe, followed by a tour of fifteen cities in thirteen weeks in eleven Latin American countries. "If your invitation had come a number of years ago I would have accepted it gladly," Wilder wrote to the State Department official who extended the invitation. "I talked often in foreign countries for the Department, as you probably know. . . . But I have given my last lecture and taught my last class. With what time and energy that remains to me, I must devote myself to writing only."[58]

The international tour of *The Skin of Our Teeth* starred June Havoc as Sabina and Helen Hayes as Mrs. Antrobus. Wilder was pleased that his play was part of the tour, and had great confidence in the producer Lawrence Langner and the Theatre Guild American Repertory Company, who would do the play in English. He was surprised that they wished to take abroad such a large cast and all the "specialized machinery" necessary for staging *Skin*. This very successful State Department–sponsored production traveled to theaters in Germany, Italy, Austria, France, the Netherlands, Belgium, Spain, Greece, Sweden, Yugoslavia, Israel, Turkey, and then South America, with Hayes and Havoc joined by Leif Erickson as Mr. Antrobus.[59] The show was a hit almost everywhere, with packed houses and glitzy receptions and parties in one city after another.[60]

Wilder did not go around the world with his play in 1961, but he soon set off on another long journey into a "remote territory"—the desert of Arizona this time—where he could escape, rest, and do his work: as it turned out, some of the best of his life. But it took some time to get there. First he had to take care of other commitments with certain collaborators. There was the actor and playwright Jerome Kilty, who was adapting *The Ides of March* for the stage, with Wilder's approval and assistance. The two men met at Harvard in 1950, and Wilder admired Kilty's successful play *Dear Liar* (1960), based on the correspondence of George Bernard Shaw and Mrs. Patrick Campbell. Wilder was also collaborating with the composer Paul Hindemith—adapting *The Long Christmas Dinner* so that Hindemith could stage it as an opera. "Of all my plays it is the one that has found the widest variety of receptions," Wilder wrote to Gertrude Hindemith, the composer's wife.[61] Hindemith's opera was success, but even with John Gielgud and Irene Worth on board, Kilty's *The Ides of March* was not well received when it opened in London in 1963. "I wrote some new scenes for it," Wilder told his New Haven friend Catherine Coffin; "then my will-power broke down. It's tedious work to rewarm yesterday's porridge."[62]

In addition to these collaborations, Wilder was a mentor to a number of gifted people over many years—former students and new friends and acquaintances alike. He encouraged Timothy Findley when he showed Wilder one of his plays and ask for comments. Findley never forgot the night Wilder summoned him to the Savoy Hotel in London to render his verdict. First he fed the nervous young writer—shrimp cocktail, filet mignon, roast potatoes, and broccoli, accompanied by a bottle of wine—because, Wilder told him, writers had to eat. "*You* are your *body's* servant. Feed it. *Eat!*" Wilder commanded. Then Wilder proceeded to talk to Findley, writer to writer. Pacing, smoking, and drinking Scotch and water, Wilder gave Findley a compressed graduate seminar on writing—and a good deal of encouragement. "He was all great teachers in one," Findley remembered. "In writing—the craft is all," Wilder told him. He encouraged Findley to start something new—and to keep on writing. Put the pages of his play away in a drawer, Wilder said. "Ordinarily, I say the wastepaper basket is a writer's best friend—but keep these pages as a reminder of how intentions go awry."[63]

After the young Edward Albee gave Wilder a sheaf of his poems to read, and then sent Wilder a play, Wilder encouraged Albee to concentrate on drama. He urged Albee not to read "too much contemporary prose and poetry," but to read "some of the great writing of the past" for a short time each day—Baudelaire or Rimbaud or Mallarmé. "And," Wilder wrote, "remember: don't only *write* poetry; *be* a poet."[64] When Albee sent Wilder *The Zoo Story* in 1958, Wilder commended his content and criticized his form. "The trouble is that your content is real, inner, and your own, and your form is tired old grandpa's." He asked Albee the very question he was asking himself during that time:

"Why does your sense of form, your vision of the *how* lag so far behind your vision of the *what*? It's as tho you were frozen very young into the American 'little theatre' movement." At present, Wilder said, Albee had no style, but he had "much to say." Wilder urged him to "write much, write many things. Only that way will your [imagination] teach you to make your mode as original as expressive as your thought."[65]

Wilder stood at the center of an ever-expanding circle of friends, collaborators, and protégés who enriched his life as he did theirs. But beyond the circumference of these personal relationships were the incessant demands of the public—the strangers or friends of friends who wanted him to read manuscripts, give talks, perform, and write prefaces, introductions, or letters of reference; and the stream of supplicants who sought permission to produce, publish, or adapt his work. He knew himself to be too obliging and, as he had been for a lifetime, he was too eager to please. He suffered from a "stern parent-to-child complex," he reflected in the late sixties. "I was obsequious and servile . . . even when I was a Colonel in the Army I had an aim-to-be-adequate tension. I hated it in myself, but that's the way I am."[66] But he had finally recognized that his life was finite—that there were only so many years left; only so much more time for living, for writing; only so many unwritten words left in him; only so much breath and energy left to empower and express them. He wanted peace and privacy to write. He wanted to retire from every other endeavor. He wanted to get away. He decided to be a hermit in Arizona.

But there were rivers to cross, he wrote, before he could drive into the desert, and one of them led to the Circle in the Square, the pioneering off-Broadway theater founded in 1951 by the producer and artistic director Ted Mann and the director José Quintero (later joined by the producing director Paul Libin). First located on Sheridan Square, Circle in the Square moved to Bleecker Street, also in Greenwich Village. By then Mann and Quintero had led the way in establishing off-Broadway theater as a robust force in the theater world, producing a variety of experimental new plays, as well as revivals of classics and standards. A few plays, including some of Wilder's new one-acts, were written expressly for production in Circle in the Square.

One night in 1959 Wilder had slipped into the audience at Circle in the Square to see a production of *Our Town*, directed by Quintero. Ted Mann spotted Wilder in the audience that night, appearing to enjoy the play. Afterward Mann introduced himself to Wilder, who was indeed pleased with what he had seen.[67] The Circle in the Square production of *Our Town* was adapted for a television performance that aired on November 13, 1959, with the Stage Manager played by the popular television actor Art Carney, famous as Jackie Gleason's sidekick on *The Honeymooners* and other formats of Gleason's television shows.[68] Wilder's *Our Town* was such an American icon that there were two television presentations of the play in the fifties. The 1959 production, with its off-Broadway roots, was preceded by a ninety-minute musical *Producers' Showcase* version, broadcast on September 19, 1955. Delbert Mann directed, with Eva Marie Saint as Emily and the young Paul Newman as George Gibbs. Frank Sinatra starred—and, of course, sang—as the Stage Manager. A number of Sinatra's hit songs were written by Sammy Cahn, one of the most successful lyricists in American movies and theater, and it was Sinatra who had connected Cahn with composer James Van Heusen in 1955 and who brought them on board to compose the music for *Our Town*—including the hit song "Love and Marriage."[69] So it was that Wilder found himself, by association, on the national hit parade in 1955, although it was Dinah Shore, not Sinatra, whose cover made the list.

About a year and a half after the *Our Town* production at Circle in the Square, Mann recalled, Wilder wrote to him about his new one-act-play cycles and asked if Mann and Quintero would be interested in seeing them. Wilder sent them *Infancy, Someone from Assisi,* and *Childhood*. They were "honored and thrilled" when Wilder named them "Plays for Bleecker Street," and the three one-acts opened on January 11, 1962, to mixed reviews.[70] Wilder and Mann hoped to stage the remaining eleven plays in Wilder's two cycles, but they were never finished to Wilder's satisfaction. Quintero did go on to direct a well-received production of Wilder's *Pullman Car Hiawatha* in December 1962.[71]

Also in 1962—a year jam-packed with projects—Wilder and Talma finished their opera. He had worked closely with Talma, who for six years had poured herself heart and soul into *The Alcestiad*. He was with her for the opera's premiere in German translation at the Alte Oper in Frankfurt, Germany, on March 2, 1962, with the great soprano Inge Borkh singing the title role. Afterward there was an "unprecedented ovation . . . curtain calls for 19 minutes."[72] Talma's elation gave way to dismay, however, when the reviews came in, many of them attacking her music. "These things don't affect me (an old battered ship)," Wilder wrote, "but it is especially hard for Louise with her first large work and coming after that undoubted appreciation by the audience."[73]

"With our opera we had the damndest experience," Wilder wrote to Irene Worth afterward. They had a full house, wonderful singers, "a noble conductor" (Harry Buckwitz), countless rehearsals of the "devilishly difficult" twelve-tone score, and a superb performance followed by forty curtain calls. Then the negative reviews appeared, partly because the composer was an American, and a woman at that, the director thought. The opera still played to full houses but, "damn it," Wilder wrote, "those reviews have so far prevented other opera houses from picking it up and a Publishing House from adopting it. Damn, damn, double damn. Anyway it *is* beautiful music and in time it *will* be rediscovered."[74]

At the State Department auditorium in Washington on April 30, 1962, a black-tie audience gathered for "An Evening with Thornton Wilder," part of a cultural series sponsored by President John F. Kennedy's cabinet. Wilder appeared onstage that night in a "baggy old suit and a lumpy felt hat," his costume for reading lines as the Stage Manager for *Our Town*.[75] In press interviews for the event, he announced his plans for a two-and-a-half-year sabbatical in the desert of Arizona. He also shared the news with friends. "I shall soon be far away. Farewell, O world. Arizona desert—2 ½ years. A bum. Loaf, read, learn Russian, polish up my Greek . . . and finally start some writing of my own," he wrote Irene Worth on March 18, 1962. "Go for weeks without saying a word (oh blessing) except buying avocado pears and helping to close bars at 2:00 a.m."[76] He wrote to Glenway Wescott that he was going to Arizona to be a "hermit—without shoe-laces necktie or telephone."[77]

On May 11 Wilder was one of 162 guests at a White House dinner, where he stood in line between the Robert Penn Warrens and Tennessee Williams to shake hands with the president, who thanked him for his State Department program. He was seated at Vice President Johnson's table with Anne Morrow Lindbergh and the poet Robert Lowell. The food was perfect, he said, and the first lady was "glorious in a white and pale raspberry Dior." After dinner Isaac Stern, Leonard Rose, and Eugene Istomin played Schubert. "I finished the evening at the Francis Biddles with the Edmund Wilsons, the Saul Bellows, Balanchine, and Lowell," Wilder wrote. The following Friday he visited Charlotte at Amityville, and on Sunday, May 20, 1962, with his Thunderbird convertible packed full of baggage and books, Wilder set out on his way to be a hermit in the desert, "Don Quixote following his mission."[78]

HE WAS driving across the country for the sixth time, loving "the gas stations, the motels—the fried egg sandwich joints"—and the Road itself.[79] (He enjoyed the motels the way he had loved Pullman upper berths when he was a boy, he had written to Charlotte in 1960 when he was driving to New Orleans. When people asked him if he would be lonesome on such a journey, he replied, "I hope so.")[80] He was fed up with "academic and cultured society," with people asking him what he thought of T. S. Eliot, with public demands, with the fettering burden of correspondence and obligations that wore him down.[81] Arizona might not be paradise, but it would be freedom. With each passing mile his weariness diminished. He was a sixty-five-year-old vagabond, adventure bound.

When he and his siblings were children and forbidden to swear, they never said, "Go to hell." Instead, thinking of the region in South America, they said, "Go to Patagonia."[82] Wilder had looked at a map of Arizona and announced that he would go to the town called Patagonia. When that word had gotten out in the press he was inundated with real-estate offers, and soon decided Patagonia would not provide the anonymity he longed for. He would simply head west to Arizona and see what happened. Just as he reached the crest of a hill where a sign welcomed him to Arizona, the T-Bird began to sputter and stall. He made it to the bottom of the hill and saw another sign: Douglas, Arizona.

This was either destiny or as good a place as any—and far more private than Patagonia. He stayed for twenty months. "No phone," he wrote. "Made my own breakfast and lunch. Closed the local bar (midnight in that State)," meaning, he said, that he stayed in the bar till it closed and "had to be cajoled out."[83] Census records of the time counted 11,925 citizens in Douglas in 1960, although Wilder wrote that there were five thousand people in that Arizona border town in 1962—three-quarters of them Mexicans who crossed the border from Agua Prieta and other villages to put their children in Arizona schools.[84] A few ranchers lived in town, as did engineers and other workers at the Phelps Dodge Company's gigantic Copper Queen smelter two miles outside the town limits. Most Douglas citizens had no idea who Wilder was, and didn't care. They started calling him Professor—or, in some cases, "Perfesser"—and treated him as they treated everybody else.

Wilder went to the desert to finish his plays and work on some other projects, staying first in the fading grandeur of the historic Gadsden Hotel. In late summer he rented a three-room apartment on the second floor of an apartment building at 757 12th Street, and settled into one of the happiest, most productive periods of his life. He felt completely free from the push and pull of the life he had left behind. His days were his own—no appointments; no telephone calls, unless he called Isabel from a public telephone; no demands. He walked the wide streets in town to buy a newspaper, pick up his mail, shop for food. At the risk of life, limb, and eyesight, he cooked simple meals in his small kitchen, afraid all the while he'd make the oven explode. "Several times I've almost lost an eye from far-spitting fat," he wrote to Isabel, "and that lifting hot water from one place to another."[85] He washed and dried drinking glasses obsessively because, he said, he had inherited from both the Wilder and the Niven sides of the family "a compulsive perfectionism. I can never *believe* that the glass is clean and dry."[86]

For variety, meals in good restaurants, provisions, nightlife, and bars, he drove to nearby Arizona towns—Nogales, Bisbee, Tombstone—or to Phoenix, and often to Tucson, 118 miles to the northwest, where he could stay at the Arizona Inn and do research in the University of Arizona library. Almost every day he took the T-Bird out for sunset drives in the "glorious desert."[87] He admired the "frontier" qualities of his fellow citizens—"Ready courtesy and much reserve. A real deference for women, immediately recognizable as different from big city politeness. As frontier, very church-going."[88] (There were, in fact, thirty-six churches in Douglas and the immediate area.) He spent his first months in his desert hermitage resting; clearing his mind; walking; driving; listening to people talk in restaurants, shops, and bars; but most of all enjoying the solitude. Sometimes he felt a "pang for friends and conversation and music," but that abated when he took his late-afternoon drives into the desert, where the silhouettes of the Chiricahua Mountains and the fanciful shapes of cactus came to life in the drama of the sunset.[89] Once, when he found himself longing for the sea, he drove all day to Guaymas, Mexico, on the gulf the Mexicans called El Mar de Cortés, and spent two weeks watching the waves come in to the shore.[90]

It took him three months "to blow the cobwebs of self-conscious genteeldom out of my head," he wrote to a friend, but, finally refreshed, he eased gradually into a writing schedule. He focused on *The Seven Ages of Man* and *The Seven Deadly Sins*, the plays he had told a journalist he envisioned as a reflection of "the tendency of the mature artist in all ages to forge a definitive statement of his crystallized philosophy."[91] In addition to the one-act-play cycles, Wilder, as usual, kept a list of ideas and works in progress in his journal. Letters to and from Isabel and their occasional telephone talks kept Wilder as connected as he wanted to be to the outside world. His "Plays for Bleecker Street" were a "sensational success" in Milan.[92] Plans for a "musical *Matchmaker*"— the work in progress that would become *Hello, Dolly!*—were "coming along great."[93]

Wilder was proud to hear from friends that Edward Albee had been telling interviewers that a conversation with Wilder "long ago made him turn playwright." Albee had sent Wilder a copy of the text of *Who's Afraid of Virginia Woolf?* and Wilder thought it was "fine to have a new dramatist who speaks *in his own voice*."[94] Later Wilder would nominate Albee for membership in the National Institute of Arts and Letters, endorsing him as a "dramatist of distinguished quality, high seriousness and notable technical accomplishment" who had "fulfilled his early promise and taken his place in the first rank of American dramatists."[95]

By December 1962 Wilder was still not able to do any sustained work. He spent some time before Christmas reflecting on the past few months. The decision to escape to the desert was not a "light one," he wrote to Louise Talma. Instead, it "sprang from deep sources—and I've discovered that I was more shaken than I thought." He tried to work on his projects, only to find them "powder away" in his hands. He could not finish things. He could not make commitments, especially to any schedule that involved other people. "It is above all a date-line that inhibits me," he wrote. He hoped that "the *turn for the better*—the recovery of the full self" would occur any minute.[96]

He was chronically torn between his need to be with people and his need to be alone. "I'm getting to be a growly-smily grouching-chuckling old humbug curmudgeon," he had written to Charlotte in 1960. "I don't hate people. I merely hate to be in groups of over four."[97] He was a writer with a unique and reverent grasp of the billions and billions of souls who had inhabited the universe, and a man with a growing aversion to seeing his fellow human beings in groups. He wrote to his nephew in December 1962:

> *The sense of the multitude of human souls affects every man in a different way: It renders some cynical; it frightens many; it made Wordsworth sad: me it exhilarates. I must go back and submerge myself in it from time to time or I go spiritually sluggish. What I have fled to the desert from is not the multitude but the coterie.*[98]

In his desert retreat the Professor was alone and lonely that Christmas of 1962 but only because he chose to be. Townsfolk had invited him for Christmas dinner, but he declined. Wilder gave himself a record player for Christmas, and three records—Bach's Magnificat, Mozart's Sinfonia Concertante, and a Lotte Lehmann lieder recital. The music gave him great pleasure and helped him in his work. He spent Christmas in Santa Fe and Taos, wanting to see snow—as well as to see his old friends the poet Witter Bynner and British-born artist Dorothy Brett, who had lived in Taos since 1924, painting landscapes and portraits of Native Americans. There were ghosts in Taos, and Wilder and Brett reminisced about the old days, and old friends, especially Mabel Dodge Luhan, who died in August 1962 after several years of illness and senility. Tony Luhan died a few months later.[99]

AS HE stepped into the new year, Wilder realized he was not "a 100% hermit." He wrote Thew Wright that he now had a "considerable acquaintance," but they were the "type of persons that closes the bars."[100] Whether it was all fact or mostly fancy, Wilder wrote a whimsical newsletter of Douglas "Society Notes" for Ruth Gordon and Garson Kanin, mainly highlighting his own activities. With an engineer named Louie and a highway patrol officer named Pete, Wilder had allegedly crossed the border into Mexico for dinner, dancing, and "smooching" at the Copa, followed by a visit to a "house of ill-fame" from which all concerned emerged with virtue intact. The Professor took flowers to Vera, a waitress, who was in the Douglas hospital for an operation. He danced with a waitress-turned-cook at Dawson's on the Lordsburg Road, helped a traveling salesman write a letter to a lawyer and judge in hopes of reducing his alimony, and listened to the life story of a woman who was wintering at the Hotel Gadsden.[101]

Whether the events were true or imagined, they foreshadowed details that would later emerge in his last book, *Theophilus North*. Theophilus interacted with the populace of Newport just as Thornton did with the inhabitants of Douglas, mingling with people from an intriguing variety of backgrounds, listening to their life stories, dispensing advice. By February 1963, three months short of a year since his arrival in Douglas, the Professor was surrounded by local friends. In a letter to his dear friend Catherine Coffin in New Haven, he identified them with names and significant details—Louie the engineer; Rosie the hotel elevator girl; Gladys the cook at the Palm Grove; his best friend, Harry

Ames, who had been going through a "terrible time," being ousted from his Round-Up Bar and liquor store.[102] Wilder was fascinated with his new town and his new friends, content—even happy—in this unlikely setting.

The new freedom in his personal life released him to work with new zest and energy and new material. His old projects had wilted away, he said, but he threw himself into a new one after Christmas—something entirely unexpected. He thought that his new record player helped to set things in motion—the music of Mozart and some Bach organ works. Nothing he had ever written had "advanced so fast."[103] This was a secret he kept entirely to himself until March 1963, when he wrote Isabel about it:

> *Well, I won't stew about any longer but come right out with it that I've written what must be 90 pages or more of a novel. I can't describe it except by suggesting it's as though* Little Women *were being mulled over by Dostoevsky. It takes place in a mining town in southern Illinois ("Anthracite") around 1902. And there's Hoboken . . . and Tia Bates of Araquipa, Peru, transferred to Chile. . . . . and there's the opera-singer Clare Dux (Swift) . . . and Holy Rollers. . . . and how a Great Love causes havoc (the motto of the book could be "nothing too much") and how gifts descend in family lines, making for good, making for ill, and demanding victims. You'll be astonished at how much I know about how a family, reduced and ostracized, runs a boarding house. But mostly it's about familial ties, and, oh, you'll need a handkerchief as big as a patchwork quilt. The action jumps about in time, though not as schematically as in* The Ides. *The form is just original enough to seem fresh; it's not really like usual novels.*[104]

He added that between the lines there were "lots of Wilders."[105] He was liberated, rejuvenated, exhilarated. "Every new day is so exciting," he wrote to his sister, "because I have no idea beforehand *what will come out of the fountain-pen.*"[106]

By mid-November 1963, still in Douglas, Wilder believed his novel was nearing its final draft. He still cooked most of his meals, still helped close the local bars, sometimes just going down for the last half hour to enjoy two highballs to help him sleep. But soon he had to head north to accept the Presidential Medal of Freedom, awarded by John F. Kennedy but to be conferred after his death by Lyndon B. Johnson in December. Wilder was sorry to leave the desert. "It's done a lot for me," he wrote to his dramatic agent, Harold Freedman. He was not yet ready to resume his life in "urban civilization," but when he did, he told Freedman, he would "go theatre" again.[107]

Wilder was wrong. He would not ever "go theatre" again. He gave up his fading experiments with the one-act-play cycles for the theater-in-the-round. Although he had created Dolly Levi, he had no hand in the stunning musical transformation of *The Matchmaker* into *Hello, Dolly!*—which was a smash hit from its opening on Broadway in January 1964. Wilder was in Europe at the time, and so did not see the production for himself until May 1965. He was so pleased with it, Isabel wrote to Vivien Leigh, that one would have thought he wrote it all himself, not just the play on which the book, lyrics, music, and dances were based.[108] *Dolly* brought Wilder financial security to the end of his life.

Despite the playwright's best intentions and efforts, however, the novelist took over at the end of his career, and the summation of Wilder's work came not in drama but in fiction. His literary career would culminate as it had begun, with the publication of two novels. He had gone to the desert searching for himself, searching for his plays. He found something different from what he expected, something more— not only a renewal of self but an epic novel, teeming with vivid characters, intertwining plots, mystery, romance, tragedy, transcendence, pithy aphorisms, and lofty wisdom.

He called his novel *Anthracite* and *Make Straight in the Desert* before he settled on *The Eighth Day* for a title. The reference to the desert came from Isaiah 40:3: "The voice of him that crieth in the wilderness, Prepare ye the way of the Lord, make straight in the desert a highway for our God." This verse was "the Leit-motif in *The Eighth Day*," Wilder told his brother.[109] The title is explained in the words the town physician speaks on the eve of a new year and a new century: "Nature never sleeps. The process of life never stands still. The creation has not come to an end. . . . Man is not an end but a beginning. We are at the beginning of the second week. We are children of the eighth day."

Like Wilder's earlier novels and his plays, *The Eighth Day* is suffused with questions, yet as he wrote in his desert solitude, he seemed to come closer to some answers. He would be seventy when he finished the novel, and it would prove to be the mature artist's summation of a life's work, and of life itself.

36

"TAPESTRY"

History is one tapestry. No eye can venture to compass a hand's-breadth of it.
—THORNTON WILDER,
The Eighth Day

North America and Europe (1963–1970)

In November 1963, after twenty months in Douglas, Arizona, Wilder packed his bags, his briefcase, and his books and left his desert hermitage reluctantly. He had been happy in Douglas: He worked all day, and when the sun set, he "circulated," he wrote Amy Wertheimer. His acquaintances were "just us bums and bar workers and bar frequenters. It was very good for me."[1] He had gone into the desert intending to finish the one-act-play cycles that he had originally conceived as the summation of his literary life—his examination of the seven deadly sins and the seven ages of man. Despite his determination, however, this vision proved too vast and complex to be contained in the modest framework of the one-act play. Furthermore, in December in the desert, to Wilder's great surprise, the plays had been swept aside by his absorbing idea for a novel.

He had always been a gifted storyteller, and had always done his best work in fiction or in drama when he was completely caught up in the story and the characters. *The Eighth Day* was driven by the powerful central story of a death and its far-reaching repercussions. Wilder gave himself up to the saga of two men and their families and dozens of satellite life stories. Once again he depicted the particular in the general, the general in the particular, the life of the village against the life of the stars. His themes and the novel's structure grew organically out of a complicated story as it unfolded within him. Steeped in the work of such nineteenth-century novelists as Tolstoy, Dostoevsky, Melville, Hawthorne, and Austen, Wilder infused the deceptively familiar form of the nineteenth-century novel with twentieth-century characters who wrestled, sometimes to the death, with questions and themes that transcend time, geography, and circumstance. He transmuted the form of the conventional, old-fashioned novel into something surprisingly new and modern, with twentieth- and twenty-first-century resonance.

He carried a sheaf of handwritten pages in his briefcase that November day when he drove out of Douglas for the last time. "From Arizona I drove 2,500 miles without bumping into anything," he wrote gratefully in a letter to Ruth Gordon and Garson Kanin. "Little Douglas was very good for me (I didn't let it be good *to* me) but I'm not ready to return to urban civilization yet. I'm going to find a Douglas-in-North Italy for a year. I still don't know where."[2] His immediate destination was Washington, D.C., where he received the Presidential Medal of Freedom from President Johnson on December 6. The award for meritorious service to the nation in a variety of fields, including the arts, had been announced by President Kennedy a few months before his assassination. Medals were presented that December day to thirty-one people, among them Edmund Wilson, Marian Anderson, Pablo Casals, Ralph Bunche, E. B. White, Edward Steichen, and Wilder. There were posthumous honors for Pope John XXIII and President Kennedy.

From Washington Wilder went to Hamden, where he prepared for a January journey to Europe, hoping to find his "Douglas-in-North Italy" so that he could finish writing *The Eighth Day*.[3] Before his departure he spent Christmas with his family and attended a dinner honoring Amos's retirement from the Harvard Divinity School.[4] By the time *Hello, Dolly!* opened on Broadway on January 16, 1964, Thornton and Isabel were on their way to Europe. The ocean voyage was always their favorite mode of travel, if time permitted. Otherwise, they opted for the speed of air travel. Isabel flew home in March, but Thornton stayed, anticipating that for the next few months or even for the entire year, he would live and work as he had so often done "on boats and in hotels."[5]

"Am enjoying my late sixties plus my *existence en marge*," Wilder wrote to his brother and sister-in-law from Nice in April 1964.[6] His "life on the edge" was beset with distractions, but somehow they did not vex him as they had done in earlier years. He suffered his customary January-February "head cold virus" that left him, as usual, intermittently deaf. He searched for his Italian Douglas to no avail, but "Nothing makes much difference to me except the hours at my desk," he wrote, and for once in his life he seemed able to write anywhere.[7] *The Eighth Day* was flourishing, growing even longer than he had foreseen. Just as he had written *The Bridge of San Luis Rey* without seeing Peru, he had never been to southern Illinois, one of the settings for the novel. He thought he ought to go to "look at the locale and read their 1902–1905 newspapers," but in the meantime he had "great fun inventing how a coal mine is run, how a murder trial is staged." His sojourn in Douglas had given him some firsthand knowledge of copper mines and copper smelting; consequently, he was "no slouch either at describing copper mining at 13,000 feet in Chile" for one of the episodes of his ambitious novel.[8]

He was homeward bound in May aboard a slow-moving ship out of Genoa, headed to the Netherlands Antilles. He had taken this leisurely two- to three-week-long voyage before because it allowed him to circumvent a landing in New York, but best of all he found the prolonged time at sea ideal for writing. He could unpack, set up a writing space in his cabin, settle in, and concentrate on his work. He planned to fly from Curaçao to Miami, rent a "drive-yourself" car, and "fool around Florida." He would also pay a visit to his aunt Charlotte, now retired in Florida and having health problems, but in transit by sea or by land, he managed to devote regular "daily working hours" to *The Eighth Day*.[9]

By late June he was back in Hamden, catching up with mail and business affairs, and visiting his doctor, who discovered a cancerous mole near Wilder's left eye. He underwent surgery in late June followed by radiation treatments that extended into late October. It was a time of family illness and convalescence: Charlotte Niven was hospitalized in St. Petersburg, Florida, for lung and bronchial problems. Charlotte

Wilder, now severely overweight, was suffering in Amityville with arthritis, kidney disease—and respiratory problems aggravated by her chain-smoking. Thornton was undergoing a long series of radium treatments in New Haven and recuperating at the Hotel Taft, with occasional visits from his nephew, Tappan, who was working in New Haven that summer. They paid such frequent visits to the Anchor Bar and Grill, one of Wilder's favorite hangouts in New Haven, that the proprietors thought Wilder had actually written the entire *Eighth Day* right there on the premises. Isabel, who had been on Martha's Vineyard, came home to Hamden so that her brother could finish his convalescence in the house on Deepwood Drive, where he worked on the novel for hours each day.[10]

He made short trips in New England in August, traveled to Quebec in September, and headed back to Florida in his T-Bird in December, writing wherever he landed. He needed to find another "hermitage," he wrote to Aunt Charlotte, but he still didn't know where. In January 1965, his radiation treatments completed, Wilder was back in Curaçao to board the *Rossini*, another slow boat to Europe. This time he bypassed winter in Italy for the warmth of Cannes and Nice, where he stayed in his hotel room all day, working on the novel. Room service delivered his standing daily order for two sandwiches and two bottles of beer for lunch. (The menu might vary, but Wilder liked to have lunch delivered to the door when he was working, whether he was at the MacDowell Colony or on shipboard or in a hotel.) At the end of the day, his writing quota accomplished, Wilder would "sally out at sunset, healthily hungry and ready for some chance conversations in bars and restaurants." Those conversations fed his imagination and his evolving book. "The Riviera is a magnet to drifters," he wrote to his aunt, who, along with Ruth Gordon and his New Haven friend Catherine Coffin, had succeeded his deceased mother and his deceased friend Sybil Colefax as the recipients of letters about his work in progress. "I don't frequent milieux that are sordid," he wrote to Charlotte Niven,

> but these people like to tell their life-story (editing it to their own advantage)—stories of lost direction, broken homes, disappointment.

Places celebrated for their beauty attract these broken-winged = Capri,
Santa Fe, Tahiti, Taormina (aren't there many in Florence?). All this
is perfect LOOT for a novelist and many a trait or anecdote entered my
work. I wasted a good deal of time but it wasn't all wasted.[11]

He returned to the United States in March aboard another slow
ship, the *Verdi*—a comfortable vessel with "splendid" Italian food. He
consumed gnocchi and lasagna and tagliatelle "like a glutton," and
when he was not eating or writing, he was reading "long books" by
Dostoevsky and Tolstoy.[12] He read *War and Peace* in French on this
crossing, and Murasaki Shikibu's *The Tale of Genji* in English.[13] Because
the ship was bound for Venezuela, Peru, and Chile, most of the passengers were Spanish-speaking, including an ambassador Wilder had met
at the UNESCO conference in Venice. Some of the Chileans helped him
with questions regarding the section of *The Eighth Day* that was set in
their country.[14] Back in Florida, his days were "centered around" his
novel, he wrote Amy Wertheimer. "I think it will be the best thing I
have done—but I wish that *it* did not insist on growing longer than I
had first planned."[15]

He headed back to Washington in May to receive another honor—
the first National Medal for Literature, to be conferred at the White
House May 4. The president attended, and Lady Bird Johnson presented the medal. Wilder was pleased about that, he said, as "my
novel says (I mean: implies) over and over again, Apollo makes art, but
Athene fosters it."[16]

He was back in Connecticut in June for his forty-fifth class reunion at
Yale. "How we senior-citizens will scan one another for signs of general
delapidation!" he wrote to his niece, Dixie. "I entertained the notion of
going to the Beau Brummel Beauty Parlor and taking the 'budget treatment'" to try to repair the permanent damage of the years, he teased.[17]
Afterward he wrote to Ruth Gordon and Garson Kanin:

Harry Luce was there for one day; Bill Whitney and Walter Millis
also. Well, chums, I was a contented little sleepwalker, a narrow-chested

bookworm as an undergraduate (as I told 'em at the Class Banquet Saturday night) . . . but NOW: I'm Stover at Yale in Spades. I'm rah-rah Eli—handshaking, horsing around. . . . Get it? For 20 years I've been the Texas Guinan of reunions.[18]

He spent a few weeks of the summer with Isabel on Martha's Vineyard, and then traveled back to New Haven to do research at the Yale library, staying part of the time at the Taft Hotel near the Yale campus because he and the Deepwood Drive house did not always fare well when he lived there alone. He usually managed to make a mess of the house, especially the kitchen, if he tried to prepare his own meals. At least at the hotel he could count on someone else to cook and keep house. In October 1965 he and Isabel were back in Europe, where he hoped to immerse himself in *The Eighth Day*, vowing not to return to the United States until his manuscript was ready for the printer. By April 1966 he had finished and polished the handwritten manuscript sufficiently to give it to a typist.

Amy wrote to him that April to suggest that *Our Town* was being performed less and less, superseded by Sartre's *No Exit*. The two plays bore a "partial resemblance to one another," Wilder replied. The last act of *Our Town*, he said, "suggests that life—viewed directly—is damned near Hell; [Sartre's] play says that the proximity of other people renders life a Hell." Sartre had told him, Wilder wrote, "that at the time of the first production he received scores of protests—They found that line too cruel, 'You *are* your life'—(i.e. there are no alibis.) It's a savage play." He then contrasted Sartre's perspective to his own view as expressed in *The Eighth Day*: "In the long novel that I've almost finished I assert roundly that life is *not* an image for hell."[19]

In that volatile decade of civil rights struggles, assassinations, and antiwar protests, Wilder firmly asserted in his novel his conviction that there was hope for the future. He believed that mankind was still evolving—that "in this new century we shall be able to see that mankind is entering a new stage of development—the Man of the Eighth Day."[20] Wilder himself was living testimony to his theory—a "Man of the Eighth Day" who had spent a lifetime continuously evolving, as a person and as an artist, never static or satisfied with his writing or himself, always looking inward and outward for the next "stage of development." The title and the symbol he chose for his sixth novel aptly summed up his own life and work.

BY APRIL 1966 Wilder was exhausted, and ready for the long journey of writing the novel to be over. He turned sixty-nine that April, and wrote to the director Cheryl Crawford, "I've put my foot into my 70th year and intend to enjoy it."[21] He indulged in two pleasures: traveling abroad and spending time on Martha's Vineyard, a retreat he and Isabel had enjoyed so much over the years that in 1966 they bought a house there on Katama Point in Edgartown. On September 13, 1966, Wilder wrote that he was sitting at a "table-desk" in their new house, looking at the Atlantic. Because it was after Labor Day, he said, "all those trashy worldlings have left the Island except us."[22]

Soon he was headed for Europe again, writing to his aunt Charlotte from Innsbruck, Austria, on November 24 that he had finished reading the proofs of *The Eighth Day* and had sent them off to New York.[23] Although he had spent forty hours reading them himself, he paid Louise Talma a thousand dollars to go over the galleys with her keen eye for detail.[24] The book was scheduled for publication on March 29, 1967, and Wilder had to forgo his slow voyage home to fly back to New York and sign "a bushel" of books for his publisher. After that, he said again, he was determined to find that other "hideaway—like Douglas, Arizona—though I think that this one will be in the 'piney woods' of North Carolina." This was a matter of urgency, he wrote, because "I've begun on another novel which may take me some time."[25]

WHEN ROBERT PENN WARREN wrote Wilder a "generous warming letter" about *The Eighth Day*, Wilder responded with a revealing analysis of his novel's structure and sources:

Book One: "Little Women" and how they made a boarding house.

Book Two: The exiled wanderer in search of his soul. And after Kierkegaard's study of "the man of faith."

Book Three: Horatio Alger, combined with the Bildungsroman (Merton's Magic Mountain [sic] after Goethe.)

All mixed up with the family under an evil star—
    The doomed children rehabilitated.

And Teilhard de Chardin.

And Jung's theory (though I'm no Jungian) that
        The Greek and Roman pantheons are projections
        of ourselves. The women are passing through
        the phases Artemis to Aphrodite to Hera to Athene (or
        getting stuck en route like poor Beata.)

The overriding notion (no more than a notion) is that men
        make (secrete, project) gods and then the gods
        they have created in turn make civilization (for good
        and ill.) So it's not finally very important whether the
        gods are outside us or inside us.[26]

At 435 pages, this was Wilder's longest work of fiction, and his first novel in nineteen years. He dedicated the book to Isabel. The central idea was simple, Wilder wrote to a reader: The novel is about "evolution—Man evolving and individuals evolving (and backsliding!)."[27] The novel was an immediate bestseller and the winner of the National Book Award in 1968. When the news of that honor reached Wilder in Genoa, he sent a statement of acceptance to Cass Canfield, his editor and publisher at Harper & Row (as Harper & Brothers had become in 1962). Wilder shed more light on the novel's theme: "The principal idea that is expressed in the novel (and in its title) has been present in Western thought for some time—that Man is not a final and arrested creation, but is evolving toward higher mental and spiritual faculties."[28]

Wilder was indebted to Teilhard, the French Jesuit priest who also held a doctorate in geology and was an experienced paleontologist.[29] Science, religion, and metaphysics converged in Teilhard's landmark book, *The Phenomenon of Man*, published in French in 1955 and in English in 1959. According to Teilhard, there were four steps of evolution: the evolution of the galaxy; the evolution of the earth; the evolution of life; and the ongoing evolution of consciousness. He also embraced Nietzsche's idea of the unfinished, still-evolving human being. Wilder's novel featured a cast of unfinished human beings and their still-evolving, unfolding lives. Some of his characters firmly believe that they are living lives that are preordained. Others believe that they possess powers of free will and choice. Others have no opinion at all because they are so absorbed in or overwhelmed by the lives they are living—or the lives that are living *them*, as Dr. Gillies, the Coaltown physician, often observed. (According to Dr. Gillies, "We keep saying that we 'live our lives.' Shucks! Life lives us.")[30]

In the novel's prologue Wilder introduces his readers to a tantalizing murder mystery in the fictional small town in Illinois where the tragedy happened in the summer of 1902, and then to the questions the residents of the town confront as they speculate on the mystery of the shooting death—and by extension the mysteries of life itself. Time is not simply chronological in *The Eighth Day*, but fluid and malleable. The setting frequently shifts from Illinois to Chile, Russia, and various destinations in the United States, with Coaltown, Illinois, the hub.

The novel is a saga of two families, as well as a virtual turn-of-the-twentieth-century travelogue and social history. It is also an exploration of Wilder's belief that "nothing is more interesting than the inquiry as to how creativity operates in anyone, in everyone," as the novel overflows with illustrations of creativity expressed, nurtured, fulfilled—or thwarted, denied, distorted. But foremost *The Eighth Day* is Wilder's summation of the recurring universal questions that infuse his work—many of his early playlets; his major plays; his later experimental plays; every novel from *The Cabala* onward; the profusion of literary and personal reflections in his journals. *The Eighth Day* is also Wilder's culminating treatment of the challenges of family life; the often perilous variations of love, especially married love and familial love; the positive as well as negative manifestations of creativity; the dynamics of memory and imagination; the endless quest to understand the self and the inner life; and the significance of the multiplicity of souls—"the disturbing discovery of the human multitude," as Roger Ashley, the son of the murder suspect, expresses it.[31]

Wilder's themes are dramatized in the parallel lives of two families, the Ashleys and the Lansings. The murder victim, Breckenridge Lansing, has one principal goal in life—to "found that greatest of all institutions—a God-fearing American home." He holds that a husband and a father "should be loved, feared, honored, and obeyed." But as his life and his family disappoint him he asks, "What had gone wrong?"[32] John Ashley, the accused murderer, realizes that "he had formed himself to be the opposite of his father and that his life had been as mistaken as his father's."[33] As noted, Wilder is reflecting on his own life as Ashley wonders,

> Is that what family life is? The growing children are misshapen by those parents who were in various ways warped by the blindness, ignorance, and passions of their own parents; and one's own errors impoverish and cripple one's children? Such is the endless chain of the generations?[34]

In another examination of family dynamics, Wilder echoes the words Freud spoke to him about his sister Charlotte three decades earlier. In *The Eighth Day*, Freud's words are delivered by the Maestro, a singing teacher, who says that family life is

> like that of nations: each member battles for his measure of air and light, of nourishment and territory, and particularly for that measure of admiration and attention which is called "glory." It is like a forest; each tree must fight for its sunlight; under the ground the roots engage in a death struggle for moisture . . . in every healthy family there is one who must pay.[35]

The novel is studded with reflections on marriage and family; the shifting concept of the patriarch and the matriarch, despite social constraints; the relationships of fathers and sons, mothers and daughters, permeated with Wilder's characteristic faith in the wisdom and strength of women.

The boardinghouse is a pervasive symbol in *The Eighth Day*. Young Sophia Ashley transforms the family home into a boardinghouse after her father is accused of murder and then disappears. Ashley the fugitive finds shelter in boardinghouses, particularly at the inn in Manantiales, Chile, run by Mrs. Wickersham, who is based on Anna Bates, whom Wilder met in Peru in 1941 during his South American tour. (She appears in his journal on May 23, 1941, in an entry written in Arequipa about the "famous, kind, roaring, strongwilled, childhearted mistress of the best inn on the west coast of South America.")[36] As adults, the children of *The Eighth Day*'s two protagonists find shelter in boardinghouses in various strange cities.

After a lifetime of "boarding"—living in countless rented houses with his family, in school and college dormitories, in hotels around the world, and aboard ships traversing the oceans—Wilder had a firsthand acquaintance with boardinghouses, and several times chose them as symbols in his work. A boardinghouse could provide temporary shelter, transient company, anonymity. A boardinghouse could be a cheerful and comfortable resting place, or a facade for illicit pleasures, or, most often, a lodging for loneliness and alienation. George Brush, the hero of *Heaven's My Destination*, was a frequent guest in boardinghouses, particularly Queenie Craven's, his "substitute home" in Kansas City, and Ma Crofut's "very fine house" full of "daughters" in that same city.[37] Mrs. Cranston's boardinghouse in Newport, Rhode Island, as will be seen, was "a temporary boardinghouse for many and a permanent residence for a few" in *Theophilus North*.[38] In Wilder's experience as in his imagination, an endless pilgrimage of people traveling through life lodge briefly in boardinghouses and then move on, and most of these travelers are searching for home.

Whether he was writing a novel or a play, endings were always difficult for Wilder, and he struggled with the finale of *The Eighth Day*— not only the denouement, but the precise language of the last passage. He settled on one last homage to James Joyce, who had ruminated for a while before choosing the final word in the concluding passage of

Finnegans Wake, leaving that word suspended in the last sentence of the novel for the reader to continue or complete. There is no period—nothing at all following the article "the," so that the final line reads, "A way a lone a last a loved a long the   "[39]

In the last paragraph of *The Eighth Day*, Wilder offers the same incompletion, a word hanging in air to lead the reader off into the future, or into confusion or into his or her own reverie:

> There is much talk of a design in the arras. Some are certain they see it. Some see what they have been told to see. Some remember that they saw it once but have lost it. Some are strengthened by seeing a pattern wherein the oppressed and exploited of the earth are gradually emerging from their bondage. Some find strength in the conviction that there is nothing to see. Some   [40]

This dangling fill-in-the-blank is in essence a question. Wilder was always reluctant to impose answers on his audience, but it is possible to discern in *The Eighth Day* and its context some of his personal conclusions in his own lifelong search for answers. He was exhilarated by the "sense of the multitude of human souls," he wrote to his nephew.[41] He had high hopes that Teilhard de Chardin and others were right that human beings are still evolving "toward higher mental and spiritual faculties."[42] He saw the characters in his book as people living "storm-tossed lives as stages in a vast unfoldment."[43] He recognized that there was "an awful lot of suffering" in the book, although he had not intended that effect, but he hoped his readers would understand that "most of the characters don't regard themselves as suffering— they're learning and struggling and hoping."[44] They are, in other words, evolving.

Wilder, the grandson and the brother of clergymen, was criticized from time to time as too much of a preacher himself. He acknowledged that he was "more reprehended than commended for introducing many short reflections or even 'essays'" into *The Eighth Day*. He pointed out that he did this in his plays as well; that there were, for instance, "little disquisitions on love and death and money" in *Our Town* and in *The*

Matchmaker. He wrote to Cass Canfield, "I seem to be becoming worse with the years: the works of very young writers and very old writers tend to abound in these moralizing digressions."[45]

Between the lines in Wilder's work, as in his life, there was an enduring appreciation for all that is good and beautiful in a difficult world. Wilder wrote to his friend Timothy Findley, "At my time of life—I'm that old Chinese fool-poet sitting on a verandah watching the moonlight on the pond—I'm at a distance from all emotion except awe."[46]

HE WAS seventy on April 17, 1967. ("You know how it is: you're twenty-one or twenty-two and you make some decision; then whissh! You're seventy," the Stage Manager says in *Our Town*.) Thornton, Isabel, and Janet celebrated what they planned to be a quiet, private birthday in Hamden. He had tried not to draw attention to his upcoming birthday milestone, but the word got out in Germany, and "the telegraph boys of New Haven kept arriving in relays—cables from everybody, from the President of the Republic—through the university presidents, the directors of theatres—down to . . . the former bar maid at the Mimosa Bar in Baden-Baden." He wrote that she was the

> *only bar maid I ever knew who was undergoing a psychoanalysis. She*
> *got it free, I think, because she was so beautiful. She came, as my guest*
> *to the opening of the opera Die Alkestiade in Frankfurt am Main, and*
> *attended all the official junkets that surround such an occasion—much*
> *to the consternation of Louise Talma, Isabel Wilder, Inge Borkh, the*
> *Mayor and the Operdirektor. I don't intend to cause pain in life,—but*
> *things just happen to come out that way.*[47]

Wilder drove to Edgartown the day after his birthday in a rare April snow- and hailstorm, leaving Isabel to cope with the "bedlam" at home on Deepwood Drive—"the phone-calls, visitors, strangers, the enormous mail resulting from the combined novel-publication and birthday (interviewers, photographers, TV proposals, cakes baked by high school students, Vietnam petitions,—bedlam)."[48]

Bestseller, National Book Award winner, Book-of-the-Month Club selection—*The Eighth Day* was a magnet for attention, and a lightning rod for critics, some stridently negative, others effusively positive. The reviews in the United States and England were largely favorable, but Brooks Atkinson at the *New York Times* was disappointed in Wilder and his novel, as were Stanley Kauffmann at the *New Republic*; Benjamin DeMott, also at the *Times*; Edward Weeks at the *Atlantic*; and David J. Gordon at the *Yale Review*. Granville Hicks at the *Saturday Review* praised the book, as did David Galloway at the *Spectator* in London, Warren French at the *Kansas City Star*, Malcolm Cowley in his nationally syndicated Book Week column, Fanny Butcher in the *Chicago Tribune*, and many others in the United States and abroad. Needless to say, Clifton Fadiman, a member of the Book-of-the-Month Club editorial board, reviewed *The Eighth Day* very favorably for the *Book-of-the-Month Club News*, and one of the enthusiastic judges who voted for the novel for the National Book Award was the young novelist John Updike.

OVER THE years Wilder gave astute writing advice to many younger novelists and playwrights—advice that could apply to life as well as art. After he encouraged the young would-be novelist John Knowles, also a Yale graduate, to write about vivid memories and experience, Knowles wrote *A Separate Peace* (1960) and dedicated it to Wilder. In 1970 Wilder wrote a letter of literary advice to novelist, actor, and playwright James Leo Herlihy, who had already published two novels, first the commercially and critically successful *All Fall Down* (1960) and then *Midnight Cowboy* (1965), which would be far more successful as a movie (1969) than as a book. Herlihy was looking for a new fiction project, and Wilder wrote, "James-the-Lion, see to it [that] in every novel you write (NOVEL: a window on Life—and on all life) you touch all bases: death and despair and also the ever-renewing life-force, sex, courage, food, the family. I think you've always done that anyway, but *know that you're doing it.* Touch all bases to make a home run."[49] That was a glimpse of the compass guiding Wilder as he wrote *The Eighth Day*, and it would guide him in his final novel as well.

———

CHARACTERISTICALLY WILDER did not look back for long at the literary work he had completed, for a new book was already stirring in his imagination and in experimental drafts as early as 1967. He wrote to Amy about it in the spring of 1968: "The work I've begun is a story using the background of my boyhood in China. I'm not sure yet if it'll take shape as I would want it to. It may follow a number of other projects into the wastepaper basket."[50]

Wilder had earlier written that "our true life is in the imagination and in the memory."[51] In 1967 he began merging memory and imagination in a manuscript he first viewed as a novel, and then alternately called a novel and an autobiography with a " 'controlled' fictional element." He was every bit as innovative and unorthodox a novelist as he was a dramatist, and by 1968 he was once more experimenting energetically with a new form—this time an intentional hybrid of fiction and autobiography. His concept was to begin and end each separate episode with autobiography, but to insert fiction in the center, fusing memory and imagination. He explained his idea to Ruth Gordon in a letter on August 15, 1968. "I fancy that I'm writing everything!" he said.

> *Not autobiography—but 10 episodes from my life into each of which I introduce one fictional person. Each of these stories begins and ends with extended accounts that really happened—then enters a catalyst who precipitates on a more significant level the essence of the time and place. (An indefensible literary trick, I know.) . . . I've begun one about Gertrude Stein—and I shall do one about the boys' school in Chefoo, China, where Harry Luce and I went. It would bore me to write an autobiography without this "controlled" fictional element.*[52]

By February 1969, he was in Europe again, deep into the work, with two principal characters—Theophilus and his twin brother

Todger—sharing the part-fictional, part-autobiographical adventures. (Todger was one of Thornton's nicknames when he was a boy, and Theophilus was the name given to his stillborn twin.) "The book is shaping up to some very striking material," Wilder wrote to Isabel on February 11, 1969, from St. Moritz. "I now have two WINDOWS on Yale 1917–1920."[53] He was writing for hours each day without getting tired.[54] "I'm astonished at myself—how plenteously I've been writing. . . . I cannot understand why I am so full of beans." Once he was aboard ship again to return to the United States, he predicted, "the light will never go out."[55]

"Writing's been going right smartly," Wilder wrote to Isabel from Pension Spiess in Vienna on January 19, 1970: "Theophilus surely takes to Italy and keeps getting Todger into very hot water. Terrible!"[56] His letters to Isabel that winter gave serial updates on the adventures of Theophilus—and his own adventures as a consequence of the writing. "Theophilus gets into danger with that man who smuggles art objects from the digs in Heraclea and now I've gone crazy in Greek vases," he wrote from St. Moritz in February. Wilder the amateur archaeologist was so fascinated that he was buying books about Greek vase painting wherever he stopped in Austria, Switzerland, Italy, and France. He quickly developed his own "home-cooked theories about the pots."[57] "I'd go crazy, if I weren't pursuing some hobby—absorbing, totally occupying train of inquiry," he wrote to a friend. "At present it's Greek Vase-painting. I've lived 72 and 10/12 years without giving it a thought. For something I'm writing I needed just a small bit of knowledge about it. . . . Just enough to make a bit of literary magic about it. . . . Every hobby is also an exploration, a constructive question-answering journey of my own."[58]

By March 1970, in Cannes, he was absorbed in writing a chapter he called "SS *Independenza*," about his first trip to Italy–that enthralling, life-changing, journey abroad fifty years earlier. He outlined the book's current status for Isabel: It began with a long chapter on Chefoo, which he had written in 1968 and had rewritten in a "whole new draft" in February 1969 in St. Moritz, to strengthen "the underpinnings."[59] ("I think I'm writing a short novel about the China

I knew as a boy," he had told Gordon and Kanin at the outset of his new endeavor. "Clergymen's children are supposed to be rascals,—well you can imagine what *missionaries'* children are!")[60] This chapter on Chefoo would be followed by a long chapter on Oberlin, but he was having a "terrible time" with it.[61]

He had almost finished the "Rome 1920–21" chapter in January 1969, he wrote to his niece, Dixie. "Harrowing subject matter," he said. "I'm beginning to be embarrassed by the discovery that Todger seems to be coming to the rescue of 'Despairful' creatures in episode after episode—anyway that's not true of 'Salzburg.' I do at least three [chapters] in which I am only an onlooker and two in which I'm a downright nuisance."[62] Chapters on Caserta and Salzburg were "well advanced," he reported to Isabel in March 1970.[63] He was bypassing almost every other activity and depriving himself of human company so he could write the wide-ranging stories, part history, part invention, pouring out of his memory and his imagination.

AS HE worked on the new novel, Wilder also had to tend to other business, closing some circles, moving ahead. He gave the editor/anthologist Whit Burnett permission to publish *The Drunken Sisters* in *This Is My Best: In the Third Quarter of the Century*—a 1970 collection of work by America's eighty-five greatest living authors. Wilder was ranked sixth on the list of the fifty top vote getters for inclusion in the book. He had served for years on the MacDowell Colony board; had received the first Edward MacDowell Award in 1960; had found escape, shelter, and companionship at MacDowell; and had written there productively for years. He was invited in 1969 or 1970 to work at MacDowell in an apartment-studio apparently designed for "senior citizens," he wrote to Isabel, but he declined. "Often summers I've fallen a-dreaming about the 'sea-blue hills of Peterborough' (Elinor Wylie), but I think I'm too old to take the table-life—the quasi-happy young composers and painters," he wrote. "But, oh, those hours in the studio, 'the world forgetting; by the world forgot.'"[64]

In 1969 Wilder was trying by long distance from Baden-Baden to arrange a donation of his manuscripts to the Beinecke Library at Yale, with Donald Gallup, its curator of American Literature, in charge of them, and Isabel and Louise Talma assisting with the transfer. Gallup and Wilder's lawyers were pressing him, trying to maximize Wilder's tax advantage for the gift. "I feel terrible imagining you and Louise (and Don) marshaling all that anxious scrupulosity on the job," Wilder wrote from Europe. "As I cabled, throw every damn MS into the hopper: next year is time enough to consider the letters."[65] Fortunately for posterity, the manuscripts were not destroyed.[66]

As he moved into the final years of his life Wilder was holding on to some lifelong friendships—writing weekly letters to Robert Hutchins, who was undergoing treatment for bladder cancer; and hoping to go to the Beinecke Library at Yale to an eightieth-birthday party for Wilmarth "Lefty" Lewis, who had donated to their alma mater his vast collection of eighteenth-century books, papers, art, and artifacts focusing on the life and writings of Horace Walpole. Wilder was also endeavoring to avoid scholars and biographers, trying to discourage those who wanted to write about him—such as an English professor in a Maryland community college, to whom Wilder wrote, "I am about to be 75; I have lost most of the vision in one eye—I can only give only a few hours to reading and writing in order to spare the other eye. . . . It must be damned hard to find a thesis subject about me because I change all the time." He had no philosophy, Wilder went on—"just some contradictory notions," and he changed his religion "every ten years." He had no unified technique as a novelist or as a playwright, because every novel was different from all the others, and the same was true for his plays. Besides, there was always a "veil of irony" over what he wrote, and, consequently, it was difficult to tell when he was "talking seriously" or putting words into the mouths of his characters. "Give it up," he urged the professor, or "wait till I'm dead." Better yet, "Work on another author."[67]

Wilder was particularly unhappy about a biography being written by the English professor Richard H. Goldstone, scheduled to be published by Harper. Instead of writing the critical biography he had originally proposed, Goldstone began to solicit copies of Wilder's letters and to seek interviews with his friends and associates for the book ultimately published in 1975 by E. P. Dutton as *Thornton Wilder: An Intimate Portrait*. Despite the fact that the two men had known each other during World War II, Goldstone did not understand him, Wilder wrote to him in 1968:

> *I'm not tearful, I'm not self-pitying. I don't view myself tragically, I don't spend any time complaining or even looking backward. . . . Struggles? Disappointments? Just out of college I got a good job at Lawrenceville and enjoyed it. I made a resounding success with my second book. The years at Chicago were among the happiest in my life. I got a Pulitzer Prize with my first play. What friendships—Bob Hutchins, Sibyl Colefax (400 letters), Gertrude Stein, Ruth Gordon (hundreds of joyous letters, right up to this week). . . . Of course my work is foreign to you. You can't see or feel the play of irony. You have no faculty for digesting serious matters when treated with that wide range that humor confers. . . . Go pick on Dreiser or Faulkner. Leave me alone. Write about Arthur Miller.*[68]

IN APRIL 1970 Wilder embarked on his last voyage by slow boat—a leisurely, uneventful trek across the ocean. He loved these old-fashioned ships with no telephones in the cabins, and portholes that could actually be opened to the sea air and the sound of the waves "all night—wonderful."[69] He was traveling a long, circuitous path to the final version of his last novel—from the seminal stages in 1967 to the publication of *Theophilus North* in April 1973, when he was seventy-six. As he worked on the novel, he also worked sporadically on two new one-act plays for the "Bleecker Street" series, but did not complete them, concentrating his creative energy once and for all on the novel that had its genesis in 1967 even before *The Eighth Day* was published.[70] As the new book took deep root in his memory and imagination, Wilder explored the tapestry of his whole life, so seamlessly fusing memoir and fiction that it is difficult to discern where one leaves off and the other begins.

37

"LIFE AND DEATH"

God damn it . . . in times of mortal danger (which is also any time in life, if
you're really alive) you must encompass both poles—life and death.

—THORNTON WILDER TO JAMES LEO HERLIHY,
February 12, 1970

The United States and Europe (1970–1975)

You're constantly alluding to your 'last days,'" Wilder wrote to
Amy Wertheimer, trying to lift her spirits after she had under-
gone major surgery. "That's bad for you—as well as ungrateful—
since you're obviously full of lively response and generous energy. Let's
have some more birthdays—some more sun, rain, and snow—and
then 'greet the unseen with a cheer' (Browning), but not mention it
to others."[1]

That was his attitude in the final five years of his life as his physical
energy failed, sabotaged by too much good food and wine, too many
highballs and cigarettes, too little exercise (the inveterate walker who
could cover five, ten, or even twenty miles a day had long since retired), and the onset of ailments that plague the human body as it
wears out. He suffered from hypertension, heart problems, pain in his
right knee, and "general rheumatism" as he termed it. He grew increasingly deaf, and had to limit the daily use of his eyes because of a
circulatory problem and cataracts. He had a hernia operation in 1968.
"I'm very old now," he wrote to a friend in March 1971. "I'll be 74 next
month. I'm having eye-trouble and circulation trouble but inside I'm as
cheerful as a cricket and Lord be praised, there's nothing the matter
with my stomach and my appetite."[2]

A recurrence of the excruciating back pain that had plagued him
in earlier years led to three weeks in the hospital in 1973 for a slipped

disk.[3] In 1974 he wrote to friends, "I have lost most of the vision in my left eye and I have some trouble with respiration, but I am cheerful inside. I have good digestion. I read and read and when the spirit gives me an idea I write."[4] He underwent surgery for prostate cancer in September 1975, when he was seventy-eight. But the intellectual energy and the creative energy flourished as other powers ebbed, and despite encroaching age and failing health, Wilder had an exuberant good time writing what would be his final book. "I got a spurt of energy and have been working quite 'smartly' as New Englanders say," he wrote to a friend in 1971. "Some droll stuff—who said I didn't have a sense of humor!"[5]

By April 1972 he had set aside all but one of the often rollicking, sometimes reflective stories in progress, and that one was set in one of his favorite cities, Newport, Rhode Island. He banished Todger and made Theophilus—the stillborn twin—the living hero of the book. As Wilder thought about his twin—his "identical replica," and his own life as the twinless twin, he reflected:

> Non-identical twins are like other brothers but identical twins are not only several generations of characteristics inherited from their ancestors—as is every one—but are *one man's packet* of characteristics in two editions. If your name (say) is George, there are two Georges. Outwardly you and your brother George resemble one another exactly. . . . Inwardly, too, you are identical, but the ingredients are differently mixed. . . . One's not all saint and the other all sinner, sage or dolt.[6]

As Wilder later explained to journalists, his stillborn twin brother would have been named Theophilus, the traditional name of second sons in earlier generations of the Wilder family, and he called Theophilus his "other self."[7] "North" was an anagram for "Thornton."

Wilder had written to his longtime friends Eileen and Roland Le Grand, "I have been 'poorly' as they say in the American language—eye-doctors, ear-doctors—respiration-doctors. Now at 74 I don't bustle about easily."[8] But he could still sustain the difficult, patient, solitary work of writing a novel, and by October 1972 he had made substantial progress with *Theophilus North*. He had been writing various episodes for five years before he decided to concentrate on Theophilus and Newport, but once that decision was made in 1972, he finished the novel in a year's time. "As my book—I have been working very hard—approaches its end, more and more earnest notes about suffering in life insist on coming to the surface—and I want to 'get them right,'" he wrote "and then the book will end in a blaze of fun and glamor and happy marriages (at the annual 'Servants' Ball' at Newport!)."[9]

Theophilus North is another Don Quixote, this time on a quest to discover what people do with their despair, their "rage, or frustration." From the beginning Wilder the writer and Wilder the man had probed the eschatology of human existence, as had his brother, Amos, poet and theologian. How do we live, knowing that we will die? Wilder grappled with that central question in his last novel, written in the maturity of old age: "What does every different kind of person 'store up' to evade, surmount, transmute, incorporate those aspects of his life which are beyond our power to alter?"[10]

He was having his own adventures as he wrote the adventures of Theophilus North. He was keeping up with the times, with current events, with flower children, hippies, pop culture. "There are two songs in the new Beatles album that are bitter, beautiful and very mature," he had written to Gordon and Kanin: "She's Leaving Home" and "A Day in the Life."[11] There were almost always adventures when Wilder sat at the steering wheel of an automobile. In 1972 he bought a new car—a blue two-door HT 8-cylinder Ford Mustang, which, on July 23 of that year, he drove into the left fender of a parked car near the Whitney Theater on Whitney Avenue in Hamden. He and the driver exchanged addresses and information, and Wilder went home and wrote out a detailed "Description of the Accident," complete with a color-coded diagram of the scene.[12] This was Wilder's last recorded automobile accident. Fortunately, danger-prone as he was, he usually collided with inert vehicles rather than those on the move, and no injuries resulted.

Later in 1972, on the strength of the first eight chapters of

Theophilus North, Harper & Row paid Wilder "a smashing advance," he wrote Irene Worth.[13] The amount was one hundred thousand dollars.[14] "Not bad for one in his 75th year—wot?"[15] He described his novel to Worth:

> *I must break the bounds of modesty to tell you that it's a humdinger. It has all the colors of the rainbow—it ranges from the top of society and gives a large attention to servants—a bevy of beautiful women wrapped in tender language—Two splendid men friends of Theophilus—old man, old woman . . . and a real monster or two. . . . And there's some laughter for dear Irene and every now and then a situation so painful that you'll shake your head and say with Elspeth Skeel [a character in the novel],"Why is life so cruel and yet so beautiful?" The author does not presume to answer the question.[16]*

This is a novel created by an old man with a young and vital spirit, a man with his eyes on the past and the future, imbuing his book with lighthearted vision and deep-hearted wisdom. Autobiography and fiction intertwine, as readers who know Wilder's life will discover. Theophilus is part rascal, part saint, part tutor, part interloper, an outsider looking in the windows at life in Newport—and then barging in the front door and taking matters into his own hands. As the novel opens, Theophilus, twenty-nine, a schoolmaster "in the best of health" but "innerly exhausted," resigns his teaching job, buys a used car, and revisits Newport, where he had been briefly stationed during World War I. Theophilus makes his home in the YMCA and embarks on a summer rife with adventures that take him into the drawing rooms and libraries of Newport's grand mansions, or "cottages," and into Mrs. Cranston's boardinghouse, an establishment run with strict decorum, and home to many of the servants who work in the grand cottages. Thanks to word of mouth and three days of newspaper advertisements, Theophilus is soon employed teaching tennis; tutoring young people in algebra, English, French, German, and Latin; and reading aloud in those languages, plus Italian, to invalids, shut-ins, and people with poor eyesight.

Theophilus has been "afire" at various times with nine "Life Ambitions," cautioning that "it is well to be attentive to successive ambitions that flood a growing boy's and girl's imagination" because they "leave profound traces behind them," and "we are shaped by the promises of the imagination."[17] In one guise or another, to one degree or another over the course of the novel, Theophilus fulfills his nine ambitions: First, at times he appears to be a saint, although that may be more perception than reality. Second, he is an anthropologist, recognizing that "the past and the future are always *present* within us."[18] Third, he is an archaeologist exploring the "Nine Cities" of Newport. Fourth, he is a detective, tracking lives and motives. He is, fifth, sixth, and seventh, an actor; a magician (part mesmerist, part shaman); and a lover—not an "omnivorous" Casanova or a romantic troubadour, but a man with a "Charles Marlow Complex," like Charles Marlow, the hero of Oliver Goldsmith's *She Stoops to Conquer*—inhibited, shy, and tongue-tied in the presence of " 'ladies' and genteel well-brought up girls," but "all boldness and impudence" with "servant girls and barmaids" and "emancipated women."[19] Theophilus is also part rascal, or *picaro*, his eighth ambition—living by his wits, "without plan, without ambition, at the margin of decorous living, delighted to outwit the clods, the prudent, the money-obsessed, the censorious, the complacent." He dreams of "covering the entire world, of looking into a million faces."[20] His ninth and ultimate ambition is to be a free man. Free, at least of his teaching job, Theophilus is ready for adventure—"for risk, for intruding myself into the lives of others, for extracting fun from danger."[21] Intrude he does, sometimes by invitation, sometimes by his own choice, sometimes by chance.

Like *The Eighth Day*, *Theophilus North* may be read on many levels— first as a rousing good story, and then as a richly textured evocation of character and theme. Wilder gives Theophilus free rein to explore a wide range of topics—imagination, memory, friendship, romance, the architecture of family and community. He celebrates the imagination at the beginning and the end of the novel. "Imagination draws on memory," he writes in the final lines of *Theophilus North*. "Memory and imagination combined can stage a Servants' Ball or even write a book, if that's what they want to do."[22] He advances an intriguing formula for friendship, one he had tried to honor for years. "I recalled a theory that I had long held and tested and played with—the theory of the Constellations," Theophilus says:

> A man should have three masculine friends older than himself, three of about his own age, and three younger. And he should have three older women friends, three of his own age, and three younger. These twice-nine friends I call his Constellation. Similarly, a woman should have her Constellation. These friendships have nothing to do with passionate love. Love as a passion is a wonderful thing but it has its own laws and its own histories. Nor do they have anything to do with the relationships within the family which have their own laws and their own histories. . . . But we must remember that we also play a part in the Constellations of others.[23]

Wilder told friends in Newport that his book was "all about Newport! A Newport in large part spun out of my own head." It should be read, he said, as "one of those historical novels—highly romantic and extravagant."[24] It was actually "a dozen novellas which finally 'come together' and justify its being called one novel," he explained. This was a structure akin to those he had used in *The Cabala* and *The Bridge of San Luis Rey* all those years ago.[25]

In a letter to the English professor Dalma H. Brunauer in November 1975, Wilder looked back over his life and work: "I have often been reproached for not having made a more explicit declaration of commitment to the Christian faith," he wrote:

> *If I had had a strict upbringing in the Catholic Church—like Mauriac or Graham Greene—I would certainly have done so. But I was a Protestant and I was thoroughly formed in the Protestant beliefs—my father's, my school's in China; Oberlin!—and the very thoroughness of my exposure to dogmatic Protestant positions made me aware that they were insufficient to encompass the vast picture of history and the burden of suffering in the world.[26]*

He emphasized that his novels are novels of questions: "I took refuge in Chekhov's statement: it is not the business of writers . . . to answer the great questions (let the theologians and philosophers do that if they feel they must) but *'to state the questions correctly.'* "[27]

Why are we on this earth? How do we live? And why? Wilder had asked these questions repeatedly in his published work and in his private life, testing possible answers: We are on this earth to serve, to work, to create, to love and be loved, to struggle and suffer and survive, to constantly evolve—the "Man of the Eighth Day." We live as best we can, "every, every minute," as Emily says in *Our Town*, appreciating the gift of life, aware of the universal in the particular—the multitude—without diminishing the value of the particular, the one. Theophilus, like Thornton, studied archaeology in Rome. In a reprise of his earlier allusions to the experience, Wilder writes in his last novel about learning to dig:

> We dug and dug. After a while we struck what was once a much traveled road over two thousand years ago—ruts, milestones, shrines. A million people must have passed that way . . . laughing . . . worrying . . . planning . . . grieving. I've never been the same since. It freed me from the oppression of vast numbers and vast distances and big philosophical questions beyond my grasp. I'm content to cultivate half an acre at a time.[28]

Wilder had lived a lifetime exploring the questions, groping for the answers, challenging others and himself in his novels, plays, essays, lectures, journals, letters, conversations. He had lived a robust life out in the world, and a constantly thoughtful, sometimes painful inward life, exploring deep within the self, "learning, struggling, hoping."[29] There were enduring mysteries, philosophical questions beyond his grasp. But there were also profound illuminations, consolations, wonders, and, he said, awe.

He was still seeking, he revealed in an unfinished, unpublished preface to *Theophilus North*, the novel that mirrored the theological and poetic writings of his brother, Amos:

Pascal said: "Neither the sun nor death permit themselves to be looked at fixedly." At the margin of every man's consciousness is the knowledge that he must die and that the universe must have an end; i.e. the possibility that all the efforts to achieve an orderly world are doomed—that existence is an absurdity and a farce.

What does a man do with his despair, his rage, his frustration?

There is a wide variety of things he does with it. One or the other of them is pictured in each of the chapters of this book.[30]

According to Theophilus, the fundamental antidote for despair, rage, and frustration is hope: "Hope is a projection of the imagination; so is despair. Despair all too readily embraces the ills it foresees; hope is an energy and arouses the mind to explore every possibility to combat them."[31]

WILDER FINISHED writing the novel a little after midnight on Palm Sunday, April 15, 1973, two days before his seventy-sixth birthday. It was, he said, "a mixture of *Pilgrim's Progress*, *Casanova's Memoir*, and *The Canterbury Tales*."[32] He dedicated the novel to Robert Maynard Hutchins, who was still convalescing from major surgery. Hutchins read an advance copy and was pleased. The book was published in the United States in October 1973, and in England in June 1974, and was translated and published in Germany, Italy, France, Spain, Poland, Bulgaria, Hungary, Russia, Sweden, Brazil, and Japan. A Literary Guild alternate selection, it was also a book club choice in England. The novel stayed on the *New York Times* bestseller list for twenty-six weeks, and was generally the subject of positive reviews. There were many "lemons" as well, however, Wilder said—"unfavorable and even contemptuous reviews," he wrote to his brother, but to his pleasure he did not receive even "one antagonistic letter from acquaintances or strangers in the public."[33]

"SO I finished the plaguéd book," Wilder wrote to Gordon and Kanin April 20, 1973. "I'm accustomed to turn my back on a piece of work once it's finished—but it's something new for me to feel empty-handed and deflated,—to wake up each morning without that sense of the task waiting for me on my desk. Daily writing is a habit—and a crutch and a support; and for the first time I feel cast adrift and roofless without it. I hate this and am going to get back into a harness as soon as I can."[34] He decided that "every aspect of the literary life is tiresome except those moments when the fancy is disporting itself," but his spirits lifted when he was "suddenly stung with an idea for a play." He couldn't wait to get to Martha's Vineyard so he could "get back into a harness" with this new project.[35]

Wilder's last surviving journal entry holds other clues as to how he expected to get back into harness yet again. In January 1969, in St. Moritz, in an entry headed *"Induration: Have you had your drop of arsenic today?"* he had written about "the practice of taming and domesticating the thing one most dreads."[36] Because Wilder habitually chose his words deliberately, the word "induration" resonates, announcing a hardening of an idea or position. He was searching, he wrote, for the "word or condensed image to describe one of the methods we resort to [in order to] deal with "The Falling Tile and The Creeping Dark"— not for escaping but rather for "taming and domesticating" fears or dreads. There was currently, he noted, an open confrontation with "the stalking menace" of cancer because of its recently discovered association with cigarette smoking.[37] He had been a chain-smoker for years, and was already suffering from hypertension and other health problems associated with tobacco use. But it was literature, not his health, that prompted his "induration."

He had believed for years, he wrote, that "detective stories have played the role of accustoming the reader gradually, homeopathically, to horror, evil and sudden death,—as did the Gothic Novel in its day; and the melodrama."[38] In 1931 he had written a partial draft of a one-act play called "The Detective Story Mystery." ("Mystery stories *are* wonderful, though," says one character. "They not only pass the time, but they fill you with the most tremendous shudders.")[39] In addition to his prolonged study of Edgar Allan Poe's dark stories, Wilder analyzed the

> popular literature of evil and violence: these works are written within clearly defined conventions: the Man we admire, the Man who is defending us against the evil thing, will not die nor be castrated (the threat of castration lurks behind the James Bond books and perhaps gave the ultimate horror to the Gothic Novel and to the melodrama); the woman-beset will not be raped (a violence doubly exciting because of its ambiguity). The reader-spectator can approach the edge of the precipice without actually looking down into the abyss. The "School of the Little Shudders."[40]

He recalled in the 1969 journal that he had considered these ideas years earlier, speculating that "the element of fear in any human being could be compared to an atoll—innumerable recurrences of fears, large and small, heaped, superimposed like coral polyps on the fear or fears of earliest infancy,—perhaps derived from the ante-natal fear of escape from a small aperture, the 'trauma of birth.'" He believed that an infant "confronts almost hourly the fear of deprivation, abandonment, and so on," and then must experience "the fear of the dark; the fear of that Interloper (the father that plays so large a part in the Oedipus Complex); perhaps with the increasing consciousness of the loss of gravity, the fear of falling or being dropped." As these infantile fears accrued and intensified, other fears grew from "reflection and observation: The fear of losing the self (of madness, of not being 'master of one's own house,' of losing the self in death . . .)."[41]

"To be continued," he wrote at the end of this final journal entry—but he did not pick it up again.

———

"I HAVEN'T been well these last months—had a lumbago (slipped disc) from sheer fatigue after finishing the book and had two separate 9-day hospitalizations," Wilder wrote to friends in 1973. "Am better now, but limp about cautiously. . . . Had to cancel my trip abroad. I was slow convalescing because I'm so old."[42] Of his siblings, the eldest and the youngest Wilders seemed to hold up best physically as the years went by. "Amos is the only one among us who is really flourishing," Thornton had written to Aunt Charlotte in 1967. "Charlotte (don't mention it) *wants* a considerable operation. Isa's just had new x-rays. I go soon for my radio-therapy inspection and may have cataract troubles next year. Of course JANET'S all right."[43]

Yet despite his age and his infirmities, Wilder did not seem to fear "losing the self in death." From the earliest days death had been a multifaceted reality in his work—violent, accidental death; murder; suicide; deaths caused by nature, by disease, by childbirth, by war, by old age. He had long ago accepted death not as the obvious inevitability, but as an organic progression in the cycle of life. As he grew older and his health began to decline, Wilder responded with forbearance and fortitude. When his rheumatism grew "quite bad" during a visit to Paris when he was sixty-nine, he thought he would have to "limp and flinch before stairs" for the rest of his life—but, he wrote to Isabel, "I walked slowly from place to place,—subdued and resigned—and enjoyed myself." That time the pain disappeared almost completely.[44] In 1970, when he heard that his old friend Gene Tunney had been ill and in pain, Wilder wrote to commiserate:

> *No one lives to my time of life without experience of pain—of body and of spirit. My trials of body have not been as extensive or as racking as yours, but I have known them. Each person meets these demands in a different way. I am not a religious man in the conventional sense and cannot claim that consolation that is conveyed in the word "Trial" . . . nor am I willing to endure pain in that spirit that so many noble men and women have done—merely stoically. . . . Physical pain is the summit of aloneness, of solitude.*[45]

Well acquainted as he was with pain, Wilder had long ago given up any dread of death. As he kept on working, remembering, imagining, he did not give up his interest in the detective novel. Soon after

Theophilus North was published, he set to work on a manuscript he titled "Theophilus North, Zen Detective." (After all, one of Theophilus's nine "Life Ambitions" was to be a detective, and there was a brief mention of "That amazing detective Chief Inspector Theophilus North" in *Theophilus North* itself.)[46] Wilder would not live to finish his detective novel, but pages of handwritten drafts survive among his papers, full of notes; revisions; passages written, edited, and edited again. "In my third year at college," one paragraph reads, "I planned to become an amazing detective. I had read widely in the literature, not only in its fictional treatment, but in technical works dealing with its refined scientific methods. Chief Inspector North would play a leading role among those who shield our lives from the intrusion of evil and madness lurking about the workshop and home."[47]

In June 1974 Thornton wrote thoughtfully about how the novel and the novelist function: Every "imagined story about human beings" could be read as parable or myth—"trashy novels and Horatio Alger and Sherlock Holmes right up to *Don Quixote* and *War and Peace*." Wilder believed that the

> *narrating mind is working in a field of apparently free association—but there is really no such thing as free association. Fabulation opens the trapdoor to the unremitting attempt of the race (through its multiple voices) to render intelligible the movements of the stars, the attractions and repulsions within the family, the behavior of flora and fauna.*
>
> *For the last million years every story is consciously based upon some story already in existence. . . . For me all stories that work are visceral myths—not for edification (which comes later) but for the reconciliation of tensions.*[48]

He had invested a lifetime of creative energy in telling and retelling "visceral myths," working in his own distinctive way to "render intelligible the movements of the stars" and the "attractions and repulsions" within the family—from the smallest domestic family unit to the great human family struggling on the "one inhabited star."

From the first page to the very last page Wilder wrote, his work was studded with questions, and from beginning to end, he offered his audience and himself not answers, not edification, but reconciliation. Hope.

WILDER MOVED through the final years of his life with acceptance, serenity, and—most of the time—good humor. In Edgartown in June 1974, in a letter to Dixie, he wrote a lighthearted description of his daily life: When Isabel was not in residence, he tended to relapse into "bachelor squalor," he said. He made most of his own meals by opening cans and heating up the contents, but he went out to dinner every other night and invited guests to go with him. For years he had enjoyed visiting with friends or strangers in bars around the world. One young woman who found herself talking with him in Edgartown's Harborside Inn bar one summer evening remembered their conversation as the most fascinating of her life.[49] Wilder was enjoying the occasional company of the actor Robert Shaw and his family that summer, for Shaw was starring in *Jaws*, which was "being intermittently shot all over the island." Wilder reported to Dixie that Shaw had honored him with the dedication of his play *Cato Street* (1971), starring Vanessa Redgrave in its short run in London. Each day, Wilder teased, "I take a nap after breakfast and a nap after lunch and three naps between sundown and dawn. But I'm cheerful inside." He thought his vitality would return to him if he cooperated with it.[50]

In December 1974 and January 1975, he and Isabel were at Sanibel Island, Florida, where Wilder was "perishing of boredom and sometimes of the cold."[51] He was "flexing up" to write his New Year's resolutions. "One is to see a lot of you," he wrote to Gordon and Kanin:

> *Another is to obey my doctor's orders almost scrupulously. I can't smoke, I can't drink, I can't rassle alligators. As it is I obey him pretty well. I don't even like cigarettes, but I can't break myself of reaching out for one, especially when I'm trying to "write." As to drinking I*

told him, face to face, that I must have one drink a day when the shades
of night fall. He looked severe and changed the subject, but I do have
one and make it a double.[52]

Wilder once told Paul Horgan that Goethe believed "each of us is
born with some inner resonance that for all our lives tell us what our
ideal age is," no matter what the calendar said. "*I* was an old man
when I was 12," Wilder told Horgan, "and now I *am* an old man, *and
it's splendid!*"[53] One reason it was splendid was because Wilder himself was walking testimony to the adage that creativity, if sustained,
defies time, age, and even infirmity, and that the fruits of creativity
can outlast a human life. Gertrude Stein had spoken years earlier about
the importance of the "spirit of play" in creative work, and he was
playing with his new novel and with other tempting ideas.[54] In April
1974 he traveled to New York for meetings about a "mini-TV-serial"
of *Theophilus North*.[55] He wrote to Sol Lesser in September that he was
collaborating "over a script for *Theophilus North*," but that he was not
permitted to reveal names yet for the project, which did not materialize.[56] Lesser had sent him a reprint of their *Our Town* correspondence,
first published in *Theatre Arts* in 1940, and Wilder wrote of this evidence of their collaboration all those years ago, "It breathes the joy in
concentrated work."[57]

"There is no limit to creativity, but there are two required conditions," Wilder wrote in 1972: "EROS at your right hand, Praise of life
at your left."[58] As a writer and as a man, he knew many incarnations
of love and praise. He wrote after Gertrude Stein and Sibyl Colefax
died that he had "always believed emphatically that all and every
derivation of Eros is the sole fount" of energy.[59] For Wilder, trained
from boyhood in the classics, and acquainted as an adult with Freud
in person and in theory, "eros," or "love," was a complex term with
multiple meanings, ancient and modern, including but also reaching
beyond the sexual. Wilder knew Plato's views of Eros, expressed in
his *Symposium*—love as the universal principle or energy that drives
human life, illustrated by the Scala Amoris—the evolution and ascent
from love and desire for the beauty of the physical body to love and

desire for the beauty of the soul, the beauty of goodness, knowledge, wisdom, and truth. Wilder was acquainted with Freud's conceptions of eros as the life instinct, as opposed to the death instinct; of the variations of love—love between the sexes; self-love; family love; the love in friendship; the love for ideas or objects; the love for mankind. He wrote of *Theophilus North*, "The book is about the humane impulse to be useful, about compassion, and about non-demanding love."[60]

"Is creative work difficult in the mid-70s?" a journalist asked Thornton Wilder when he was seventy-six.[61] Wilder had never forgotten Freud's observation years earlier that Verdi had composed "his most radiant life-affirming work" when he was old.[62] Wilder told the journalist, "If you get a concentrated idea, all your writing blocks disappear. Writing at this age is not hard, not if you have the right idea—an idea deeply relative to yourself." He went on to say:

> Verdi wrote *Otello* at 78 and *Falstaff* at 79. Picasso was a beaver until his death in his 90s . . . Sophocles at 90 was hauled into court by his grandchildren, saying the old man was non compos and might will his estate to somebody else. When he went before the court the judge said, "What do you have to say for yourself?" "I'll tell you something," Sophocles replied. "I wrote this morning the great chorus from *Oedipus at Colonus*. This work is a treasure." "Either I am crazy or you are," the judge said. "Case dismissed."
>
> This is an attractive story for us old men.[63]

———

WILDER ONCE called himself the poet laureate of the family. "As I say *so beautifully* in *Theophilus North*," he wrote to his brother, " 'The bane of family life is advice.'—We were all but strangled with it."[64] In his plays and his novels family was a predominant subject. In Wilder's daily life family was an anchor, usually a comfort and help, sometimes a nuisance, and always a responsibility, generously fulfilled. He supported Charlotte and her medical care from 1941 onward, first with out-of-pocket funds and income from investments, and then from a trust established in 1966, and a second trust "related to the proceeds from *Theophilus North*," set up in 1972.[65] He set up a substantial trust for his other siblings as well.

He had also established two separate trusts for Isabel, his longtime hostess, companion, agent, and assistant. She was an indispensable help to him, even though at times each of them chafed at the bonds that united them. Wilder had written to Garson Kanin that if *The Eighth Day* made any money, he wouldn't get a penny of it because it was in a trust for Isabel, "administered by a New Haven Bank and Donald Gallup (Yale Univ. Library), my literary executor. *By law*, I have no voice in any decisions regarding it. The assumption would be that Isabel and Gallup and the bankers (who couldn't distinguish *Anna Karenina* from *The Girl of the Limberlost* or *The Trail of the Lonesome Pine*) would consult me deferentially on any question of T.V., radio, film, musicalization, etc. But *legally* they shouldn't and I'm going to stick by the law." But, he added, he would reserve the rights to the next novel for himself.[66] From the outset *The Eighth Day* was a robust moneymaker, with more than $391,245.02 in domestic earnings and $115,795.19 in foreign royalties by 1975, and while Wilder apparently kept the rights to his final novel, he steered the royalties from *Theophilus North* to Charlotte's trust.[67]

For the forty years of Charlotte's illness, Thornton, Amos, Isabel, and Janet never wavered in their devotion to their sister. On November 12, 1969, by family decision, Charlotte had moved from the Long Island Home in Amityville, where she lived for more than twenty years, to the Brattleboro Retreat in Brattleboro, Vermont, one of the oldest private psychiatric hospitals in the United States.[68] By that time Charlotte's arthritis and her weight so severely affected her knees and her feet that she could barely walk. Janet had taken over much of the oversight of Charlotte's care as Isabel suffered more frequent health problems of her own. Janet was very much in favor of the move to Brattleboro, believing that Charlotte would have more privacy, her own room, better care, more personal attention, and more freedom. It would be easier for the family to travel back and forth to visit her. As financially and morally supportive of his sister's treatment as he always was, Wilder harbored the concern that her doctors had never gotten to the root of Charlotte's illness. "Incidentally," he had written in 1969, "we Freudians are convinced that no treatment of an out-and-out schizophrenic is worth a bean that does not find the sources in early childhood and report those thoroughly."[69]

Charlotte was grateful for the improved conditions at Brattleboro. She had always dreamed of returning to her Greenwich Village apartment, but, she wrote to Thornton, some of her friends had told her that New York was no longer a pleasant place to live because of crime and congestion. She seemed content in Vermont. She told her brother she needed a Polaroid camera to help her in her writing. In her excursions out of the hospital, she said, she wanted to "find some little known part of the U.S.A." where she could photograph the inhabitants and write about them. He immediately wrote to Brattleboro to approve the idea and the expense.[70]

The family ordered a new Remington typewriter for Charlotte in 1971 because she had her heart and mind set on resuming her writing. "The food here is *impossible*," Charlotte typed in a letter to "Dear Thornt," but otherwise, she said, "I have a private room, the typewriter and beginning draft of a prose book."[71] Meantime, in the attic of the Wilder home in Hamden, there were boxes full of Charlotte's papers—brittle pages of poems and prose gathering dust under the eaves.

ON APRIL 17, 1975, the day he turned seventy-eight, Wilder wrote a letter of regret to his old friend and colleague Sol Lesser, who had approached him on behalf of Martha Scott about doing a new, technicolor film of *Our Town*.[72] He did not want any new film version made, Wilder replied. Besides, he added, "I'm old now and not in the best of health and must limit my activities of every sort for the slow but steady progress I am making on a new work."[73] He tried to cooperate with his publisher's wishes that he continue to promote his work, giving interviews on *Theophilus North* and on the Kennedy Center's American Bicentennial production of *The Skin of Our Teeth*, with Martha Scott as Mrs. Antrobus and Elizabeth Ashley as Sabina. (Later that year, José Quintero directed a production of *Skin* at the Mark Hellinger Theatre on Broadway.) "I always feel slightly soiled by thus ostentatiously selling my baked goods like a market-crier—but that's because I was born and brought up a Wilder-Niven," Wilder wrote to his brother in July 1975. He apologized to his family for some of the "annihilating reviews" that his work had received. "I take and forget them like the weather but it distresses me that my kinfolks are among the readers. Sorry, I'm sorry."[74]

He was following his doctors' orders 90 percent of the time, he said, and that meant that to protect his eyes he could not read as copiously as he had always loved to do. Nevertheless, in the months before his death, he "devoured with joy" Lewis Thomas's *The Lives of a Cell* and James D. Watson's *The Double Helix*. "What sublime reaches," he wrote. He had studied evolution at Yale, had written about it in *The Eighth Day*, and was "glad to have lived long enough to peek into these processes," he wrote Amos. "What would Darwin have thought! And what Goethe!"[75]

"I SUPPOSE you know I go into Mass. Gen. Hospital on the 2nd (best hospital in the country)," Wilder wrote to his nephew on August 22, 1975. "The specialist from there who diagnosed me here (he visits Martha's Vineyard twice a month) indicated that it was the most routine form of the prostate trouble,—no problem." Wilder planned, he said, "to be a cheerfuller and more sociable fellow next year—. One doctor has brought my blood pressure down to normal and shown me how to keep it there; and now another doctor is ready and eager to correct this nuisance. . . . Let's plan to be cheerful together."[76]

In November 1975, seventy-eight and still convalescing from the cancer surgery, Wilder was reading Montaigne, he wrote to his friend Malcolm Cowley—"grand reading for us old men. He lived through woeful times and retained that equilibrium. His mainstay was neither religion nor the (later) reliance on reason and the Enlightenment's belief in progress, but on the wisdom of antiquity—*especially Plutarch*!" He reported to Cowley that he was "guardedly convalescing and cheerful. . . ." [77]

As Isabel looked after Thornton during his recovery from the prostate surgery, she herself was "bravely coping with her handicaps,—respiratory mostly," he wrote to Eileen and Roland Le Grand. He and Isabel were hoping to go South to escape the Connecticut winter, but they thought there were too many "elderly Americans" in Mexico and Florida. Perhaps they would get through the winter in Hamden and then go to Martinique. [78]

In late November 1975, with his doctor's permission, Wilder made plans to go to New York for two weeks. He wanted—needed—another "hideaway." He especially wanted to see two movies which he believed would be "very beautiful"—Satyajit Ray's *Distant Thunder* (*Ashani Sanket*), and Ingmar Bergman's *Magic Flute*—and to enjoy Thanksgiving dinner in the city with Isabel and Ruth Gordon and Garson Kanin. His friend the young actor and director Jim O'Neil gave him a guest card to stay at the Harvard Club on West Forty-fourth Street in New York, where, Wilder said, he would be "presumably cut dead (though I do have a Harvard degree)." He had not yet regained his strength, nor was he confident about walking any distance, so he would not "venture out much except to those movies." However, he said, "I've been housebound and hospital cocooned so long that I can get a grand feeling of adventurous freedom just strolling from 44th Street to the New York Public Library." [79] After Thanksgiving he had dinner with Gordon and Kanin, and then they took a taxi to the Algonquin Hotel for a nightcap. Afterward they strolled along Forty-fourth Street back to the Harvard Club. [80]

On December 6, bone weary from his journey, Wilder returned one last time to the house on Deepwood Drive. On December 7 he and Isabel looked forward to having dinner at the home of Catherine Coffin. Her son, William Sloane Coffin, Jr., Yale's chaplain, would be there as well. Needing to rest before the evening's engagement, Wilder retreated to his room, donned his bathrobe, and lay down to sleep.

Sometime later in the afternoon, he died of a heart attack.

FOUR DAYS before his death Thornton Niven Wilder had written to friends, "I am now old, really old, and these recent set-backs have taken a lot of energy out of me." He had not given up, however. Far from it. He wrote, "I think I'm pulling myself together for another piece of work."[81]

EPILOGUE

There is no adventure in life equal to that of being and asserting one's self.
—THORNTON WILDER
journal entry 742, June 2, 1957

He was buried on December 9, 1975, in the cemetery in Mount Carmel, Connecticut, where Amos Parker Wilder had been buried in 1936, and Isabella Thornton Niven Wilder in 1946. A simple stone marks the site and bears the name of Amos Parker Wilder, followed by "His Wife Isabella Thornton Niven" and the names of three of his children: Thornton Niven Wilder (1975), Charlotte Elizabeth Wilder (1980), and Isabel Wilder (1995). Amos Niven Wilder died on May 1, 1993, and was buried in Mount Carmel Cemetery on May 4, 1993. A separate headstone carries his name, and his wife's. Catharine Kerlin Wilder was buried there in 2006. Janet Wilder Dakin, who died October 7, 1994, was buried near her husband in Wildwood Cemetery in Amherst, Massachusetts.

Thornton Wilder's interment service was led by the Reverend William Sloane Coffin, Jr., and attended by family and a few invited friends. The Reverend Amos Niven Wilder read scripture, and said of his brother, "He realized life while he lived it—and brought incomparable visions to all experiences and relationships, and not only in his writing." Amos gave thanks in the benediction for his brother's work, for his "conviviality and incandescence," and for the "rich annals of friendship, devotion, talent, and praise."[1]

On Sunday afternoon, January 8, 1976, Thornton Wilder's friends and family gathered in Yale's Battell Chapel for a memorial service. Flowers filled the chapel—tributes from the president of the German Federal Republic, the American Academy of Arts and Letters, the officials of Yale University, and the Orden Pour le Mérite für Wissenschaften und Künste—testimony to Wilder's bonds with a global audience. An organist and two violinists played Bach. As in *Our Town*, the hymn "Blest Be the Tie That Binds" was sung. After the service the music of the Yale Memorial Carillon drifted through the winter air.

A few of his multitude of longtime friends spoke at the memorial service—Ruth Gordon, Bob Hutchins, and Lefty Lewis, among others. Tappan Wilder read from his uncle's work, including these words spoken by Julius Caesar in *The Ides of March*: "Where there is an unknowable there is a promise"; and these from the archbishop in *The Eighth Day*: "Life is surrounded by mysteries beyond the comprehension of our limited minds. . . . We transmit (we hope) fairer things than we can fully grasp."[2] These characters spoke for Wilder the writer and Wilder the man who evolved from the boy running alone in China, going his own way, then and always transcending the boundaries.

Through the voice of Chrysis, his Woman of Andros, Wilder reflected that "the most exhausting of all our adventures is that journey down the long corridors of the mind to the last halls where belief is enthroned."[3] He traveled down those corridors all his life. He did not pretend to know the answers to the mysteries, but he knew the questions and was not afraid to ask them, over and over again, in his work and in his personal life.

Wilder's death was duly noted internationally. This quintessential American writer had lived, worked, and traveled as a citizen of the world, connecting globally with his era. He captured the spirit and the promise of his own country, and his planetary themes and questions touched a global audience as well, transcending time and place. Many of his novels and plays are vividly alive and relevant in the twenty-first century. To the end of his life he believed, as he had written in 1952, that "the artist through his creation, has been in all times a force that draws men together and reminds them that things which men have in common are greater than the things that separate them; and that the work of the artist is the clearest example of the operation of freedom in the human spirit."[4]

He was a rare writer: one who worked as intensely hard on the innermost self as he did on the art. He had written to Isabel in 1937,

"We're all People, before we are anything else. People, even before we're artists. The rôle of being a Person is sufficient to have lived and died for."[5] In his unfinished lecture on biography, composed in the early 1930s, Wilder wrote out a premise that described his own life: "By a strange spiritual law positive personalities so far assimilate their lives that they would not wish their very misfortunes otherwise. Their destiny is themselves."[6]

GUIDE TO NOTES AND SOURCES

Through the facts, as scaffolding, we hope to see the SOUL
and we hope thereby to gain light on our own.
—THORNTON WILDER,
notes for a lecture on biography, n.d., TNW Collection, YCAL

Thornton Wilder left a mass of unpublished and published letters, manuscripts, journal pages, and other documents—a substantial scaffolding of facts that shape and support a narrative of his life and work. This biography has grown out of more than a decade of close study of these primary sources. In their magnitude they document and illuminate Wilder's exterior life and much of his interior life, as well as the evolution of his creative work.

The majority of Wilder's papers may be found in the Thornton Wilder Papers and the Thornton Wilder Collection, Yale Collection of American Literature, the Beinecke Rare Book and Manuscript Library, Yale University, New Haven, Connecticut. These papers and resources include correspondence, manuscripts, and other documentation of the lives of the Wilder family, including Amos Parker Wilder, Isabella Thornton Niven Wilder, Amos Niven Wilder, Charlotte Elizabeth Wilder, Isabel Wilder, and Janet Wilder Dakin. Throughout the endnotes, I have referred to the Thornton Wilder Papers and the Thornton Wilder Collection as the Thornton Niven Wilder Collection, or TNW Collection, YCAL. In addition there are numerous uncataloged letters, manuscripts, and other Wilder resources in the Yale Collection of American Literature at the Beinecke. When they are quoted or cited, these documents are designated as uncataloged. Papers quoted or cited from other public collections are so noted. There are significant private collections of Wilder papers, but the holders of these collections are, by request, not identified in the annotations. Other libraries and institutions containing Wilder resources include the following:

Academy of Motion Picture Arts and Sciences Library, Beverly
    Hills, CA
Amherst College, Amherst, MA
Amherst Public Library, Amherst, MA
Berea College, Berea, KY
Berg Collection, New York Public Library, New York, NY
Billy Rose Theatre Collection, New York Public Library,
    Performing Arts Research Center
Boston University, Boston, MA
British Library, London
College of Wooster, Wooster, OH
Columbia University, New York, NY
Cornell University, Ithaca, NY
Federal Bureau of Investigation Files/Freedom of Information Act
Franklin Delano Roosevelt Library, Hyde Park, NY
Houghton Library, Harvard University, Cambridge, MA
Huntington Library, San Marino, CA
John F. Kennedy Library, Boston, MA
Lawrenceville School, Lawrenceville, NJ
Library and Archives of Canada, Ottawa
Library of Congress, Washington, DC
Mount Holyoke College, South Hadley, MA
National Archives and Records Administration, Washington, DC
National Library of Scotland, Edinburgh
Newberry Library, Chicago
New York University, New York
Northfield Mount Hermon School, Mount Hermon, MA
Oberlin College, Oberlin, OH
Österreichisches Theatermuseum, Vienna, Austria
Princeton University, Princeton, NJ
Private Collections

Rice University, Houston, TX

Schlesinger Library, Radcliffe College/Harvard University,
    Cambridge, MA

School of Oriental and African Studies Library, London, repository
    of the archives and records of the China Inland Mission School,
    Chefoo (now Yantai, Shandong, China)

Smith College, Northampton, MA

Syracuse University, Syracuse, NY

Thacher School, Ojai, CA

University of California, Berkeley, CA

University of Chicago Library, Chicago

University of Houston, Houston, TX

University of North Carolina, Chapel Hill

University of Pennsylvania, Philadelphia

University of Southern California, Los Angeles

University of Tennessee, Knoxville

University of Texas, Austin

University of Virginia, Charlottesville

University of Wisconsin, Madison

Wisconsin Historical Society, Madison

In lieu of a separate bibliography, titles and complete publication details are provided in the notes for all works quoted or cited. Titles, sources, and dates of Thornton Wilder's published and unpublished work are given in full in the notes. Throughout, readers are referred to the most readily available editions of Wilder's published works.

Major publications during his lifetime, with copyright information provided by the Wilder Family LLC c/o The Barbara Hogensen Agency, include the following:

Novels

1926: *The Cabala* © 1926 Wilder Family LLC

1927: *The Bridge of San Luis Rey* © 1927 Wilder Family LLC

1930: *The Woman of Andros* © 1930 Wilder Family LLC

1935: *Heaven's My Destination* © 1935 Wilder Family LLC

1948: *The Ides of March* © 1948 Yale University, Fisk University, and Oberlin College

1967: *The Eighth Day* © 1967 Wilder Family LLC

1973: *Theophilus North* © 1973 Wilder Family LLC

Plays

1928: *The Angel That Troubled the Waters and Other Plays* © 1928 Wilder Family LLC

1931: *The Long Christmas Dinner and Other Plays in One Act* [*The Long Christmas Dinner; Pullman Car Hiawatha; The Happy Journey to Trenton and Camden; Queens of France; Love and How to Cure It; and Such Things Happen Only in Books*] © 1931 Wilder Family LLC

1933: *Lucrece* © 1933 Wilder Family LLC

1938: *Our Town* © 1938 Wilder Family LLC

1939: *The Merchant of Yonkers* © 1939 Wilder Family LLC

1942: *The Skin of Our Teeth* © 1942 Wilder Family LLC

1955: *The Matchmaker* © 1955 Wilder Family LLC

1955: *The Alcestiad, with a Satyr Play, The Drunken Sisters* © 1977 Yale University, Fisk University, and Oberlin College

1959: *The Wreck on the 5:25* © 1959 Yale University, Fisk University, and Oberlin College

1960: *Infancy* [*Childhood*] © 1960 Yale University, Fisk University, and Oberlin College

Wilder's selected nonfiction was published posthumously in Donald A. Gallup, ed., *American Characteristics and Other Essays* (New York: Harper & Row, 1979). © 1979 Wilder Family LLC.

Selected entries from Wilder's journals are published in Donald A. Gallup, ed., *The Journals of Thornton Wilder 1939–1961* (New Haven: Yale University Press, 1985). © 1985 Wilder Family LLC.

TNW's surviving early journals (from 1912, 1916–17, and 1922–33) are unpublished, and while the entries in these journals are usually dated, they are not numbered until October 11, 1926. There are a few 1969 journal entries, also unpublished. Quoted or cited journal entries in the later years follow Gallup's designations: "The 1939–1941 Journal" and "The 1948–1961 Journal," but many of these entries are not included in the published volume.

Wilder's selected letters appear in the following editions:

Edward M. Burns with Joshua A. Gaylord, eds., *A Tour of the Darkling Plain: The Finnegans Wake Letters of Thornton Wilder and Adaline Glasheen* (Dublin: University College Dublin Press, 2001).

Ulla Dydo and Edward M. Burns, with William Rice, eds., *The Letters of Gertrude Stein and Thornton Wilder* (New Haven: Yale University Press, 1996).

Robin G. Wilder and Jackson R. Bryer, eds., *The Selected Letters of Thornton Wilder* (New York: HarperCollins, 2009). Copyright © 2008 Wilder Family LLC. (Compilation of the letters and added text copyright © Robin G. Wilder and Jackson R. Bryer, eds.)

Previous full-length biographies of Wilder include:

Richard H. Goldstone, *Thornton Wilder: An Intimate Portrait* (New York: E. P. Dutton, 1975).

Gilbert Harrison, *The Enthusiast: A Life of Thornton Wilder* (Boston: Ticknor & Fields, 1983).

Linda Simon, *Thornton Wilder: His World* (Garden City, NY: Doubleday, 1979).

Book-length Wilder bibliographies include:

Richard H. Goldstone and Gary Anderson, *Thornton Wilder: An
    Annotated Bibliography of Works by and About Thornton Wilder*
    (New York: AMS Press, 1982).
Claudette Walsh, *Thornton Wilder: A Reference Guide, 1926–1990*
    (New York: G.K. Hall, 1993).

Many of the papers of Amos Niven Wilder, Charlotte Wilder, Isabel
Wilder, and Janet Wilder Dakin are deposited with the Thornton
Niven Wilder Collection at Yale. As of this writing, however, mystery surrounds the fate of some of Charlotte's papers. In the year after
Thornton's death, it fell to Isabel to deal with twenty years' accrual
of Charlotte's papers in the "dust-covered, untidy, hastily packed
cartons" stored in the attic of the house on Deepwood Drive. As
Isabel wrestled with the boxes in the attic, pages fell out. Notebooks
opened. In glancing at the pages, Isabel wrote, she came across "startling words," painful words. There were, she estimated, hundreds if
not thousands of pages of prose—fiction and nonfiction—most likely
Charlotte's unfinished memoir and her autobiographical novel. Letters over the next few years trace the movement of Charlotte's manuscripts from Isabel to Amos to Janet and back again. The manuscripts
themselves have not been found. No records have been uncovered to
document their ultimate disposition, nor can family memories shed
light, and the search continues. Among Charlotte's surviving papers,
however, are many pages with poems typed on one side and fragments
of prose on the reverse, as sadly incomplete and incoherent as Charlotte's life itself.

———————

THE THREE earlier biographies listed above were written without
access to all of the resources now housed at the Beinecke Library or
in other collections, public and private. Now that Thornton Wilder's papers are more fully available, rich opportunities for research
await students and scholars who are interested in American literary,

theater, cultural, and social history in general, or in Wilder's plays, novels, lectures, essays, translations, adaptations, and/or journals in particular.

For further exploration of Wilder resources, readers are invited to consult the following Wilder-related Web sites:

www.library.yale.edu/beinecke
www.PenelopeNiven.com
www.ThorntonWilder.com
www.ThorntonWilderSociety.org

Key to Abbreviations Used in the Notes

TNW	Thornton Niven Wilder
ANW	Amos Niven Wilder, TNW's brother
APW	Amos Parker Wilder, TNW's father
AWC	Alexander Woollcott Collection
HLH	Houghton Library, Harvard University
LB	TNW's Letter Book
LC	Library of Congress
LD	TNW's Letter Diary
NARA	National Archive and Records Administration, Washington, DC
PEN	Penelope Ellen Niven
SL	Robin G. Wilder & Jackson R. Bryer, eds., *The Selected Letters of Thornton Wilder*. This designation in the notes indicates that a quoted or cited letter is published in this edition of Wilder's letters.
TS	Typescript
YCAL	Yale Collection of American Literature, Beinecke Rare Book and Manuscript Library, Yale University (TNW Collection, YCAL designates papers of TNW, ANW, APW, and other members of the Wilder family; YCAL alone designates papers held in other collections in the Yale Collection of American Literature in the Beinecke Rare Book and Manuscript Library)

NOTES

PREFACE: "THE HISTORY OF A WRITER"

1. TNW, unpublished semiautobiographical fragment, n.d., TNW Collection, YCAL.
2. TNW, "On Reading the Great Letter Writers," in Donald Gallup, ed., *American Characteristics and Other Essays* (New York: Harper & Row, 1979), 152. This was titled "English Letters and Letter Writers" when it was delivered by TNW on May 4, 1928, as the Daniel S. Lamont Memorial Lecture at Yale University.
3. TNW, unpublished lecture/essay on biography, n.d., TNW Collection, YCAL.
4. TNW, "On Reading the Great Letter Writers," 153.

1: "GODLY FOLK" (1862–1906)

1. The address of TNW's birthplace differs in various accounts. The Madison *City Directory* for 1896–97 gives the address as 14 West Gilman Street. The 1898–99 directory gives a Mendota Court address for the Wilders. The 1900–1901 directory lists the Wilders' address as 211 West Gilman, a duplex apartment they kept until about 1912.
2. TNW, "On Reading the Great Letter Writers," 158.
3. Isabel Wilder, "Thornton Wilder: The Anchor of Midwestern Beginnings," *Wisconsin Academy Review* 26, no. 3 (1980), 8.
4. Amos Parker Wilder, "Sketch Written by Himself for His Children," *History of Dane County, Biographical and Genealogical* (Madison, WI: Western Historical Association, 1906), 960.
5. *Historic Madison: A Journal of the Four Lake Region* 12 (1995).
6. APW, "Sketch written by himself for his children," 957.
7. There were Baptist congregations, often much persecuted, in Massachusetts as early as 1638, and in Maine as early as 1681. See Joshua Millet, *A History of Baptists in Maine* (Portland: C. Day, 1845), 24.
8. "Merry and Some Others: A Family Chronicle," Wilder Family Papers, TNW Collection, YCAL, uncataloged microfilm.
9. APW, "Sketch written by himself for his children," 957. Calais, Maine, in the St. Croix Valley, stands just across the St. Croix River from St. Stephens, New Brunswick, Canada.
10. APW Papers, TNW Collection, YCAL, uncataloged letters.
11. Munsey later went on to found a publishing empire inspired by the mail-order-magazine business in Augusta, which, from 1869 until 1942, was known as the mail-order-magazine capital of the United States.

12. APW to ANW, August 21, 1916, ANW, Wilder Family Record, TNW Collection, YCAL, uncataloged papers.
13. APW, "Sketch written by himself for his children," 958.
14. ANW, 1939, ANW, Wilder Family Record, Private Collection.
15. Isabel Wilder Interview, [1981?], TNW Collection, YCAL, uncataloged tape recording and transcription.
16. Some published accounts indicate that the Reverend Thornton M. Niven was a founder of the school. While he helped the Misses Masters secure the lease on the Dobbs Ferry building that housed the school for its first six years, he was not, so far as is known, a founder of the school, according to Renée Bennett, Director of Communications, Masters School, Renée Bennett to PEN, September 15, 2010.
17. Isabel Wilder Interview, [1981?], TNW Collection, YCAL, uncataloged tape recording and transcription.
18. Quoted in Arthur Channing Downs, Jr., *The Architecture and Life of the Hon. Thornton MacNess Niven (1806–1895)* (Goshen, NY: Orange County Community of Museums & Galleries, 1971), 55.
19. Richard F. Snow, "The Most Beautiful Dry Dock," *American Heritage* 6, no. 1 (Spring/Summer 1990): 4.
20. The seminary was located in Hampden-Sydney, Virginia, before it was moved to Richmond in 1898.
21. Downs, *The Architecture and Life of the Hon. Thornton MacNess Niven*, 13. See also "Bibles with Family Genealogies," "Family Connections," ANW, Wilder Family Record, June 4, 1987. Information about Thornton MacNess Niven's theological training and ordination is recorded in "Tribute to Dr. T. M. Niven," *New York Observer*, February 20, 1908.
22. Charlotte Tappan Niven wrote to her niece, Charlotte Elizabeth Wilder, on August 18, 1969, "My elder brother was the last Archibald Campbell N. He died of TB in Pasadena, Calif. at age of 20 in 1891." TNW Collection, YCAL, uncataloged letters.
23. In 1887–88 Robert Louis Stevenson had spent several months in treatment there, and composed *The Master of Ballantrae* during his residency.
24. Archibald Campbell Niven to his family, May 15, 1891, TNW Collection, YCAL, uncataloged letters.
25. "Amos Wilder, Editor, Hong Kong Consul, Dies," *Wisconsin State Journal*, July 2, 1936.
26. See Bertram Wyatt-Brown, *Lewis Tappan and the Evangelical War Against Slavery*, (Cleveland, OH: Press of Case Western Reserve University, 1969), 100, 127–31.
27. Lewis Tappan, *The Life of Arthur Tappan* (New York: Hurd & Houghton, 1871), 241.
28. For background on the Tappan brothers, see Wyatt-Brown, *Lewis Tappan and the Evangelical War Against Slavery*, 1–16, 41–59, 98–125, 126–48, 185–204, 226–47, 310–27, 328–46.
29. Isabel Wilder to ANW, March 1, 1970, ANW, Wilder Family Record, Private Collection.
30. A handwritten note among the uncataloged Thornton Wilder Family papers, TNW Collection, YCAL, refers to this oration and indicates that it "may be related to the Columbian Exposition."
31. "Club News and Gossip," *New York Times*, March 6, 1892, 19.
32. Caroline W. Olyphant to Isabella Niven Wilder, May 2, 189[3 or 4?], Isabella Niven Wilder's "Commonplace Book," TNW Collection, YCAL, uncataloged album.

33. Isabel Wilder to ANW, March 1, 1970, ANW, Wilder Family Record, Private Collection.

34. Isabella Niven Wilder to ANW, May 18, 1917, ANW, Wilder Family Record. The marriage certificate indicates that the Wilders were married in the Presbyterian Manse rather than in the church. Private Collection.

35. Ibid.

36. APW, "Sketch written by himself for his children," 958.

37. APW to Amos Lincoln Wilder, December 6, 1880, TNW Collection, YCAL, uncataloged letters.

38. APW to Amos Lincoln Wilder, March 29, 1883, TNW Collection, YCAL, uncataloged letters.

39. APW, "Sketch written by himself for his children," 959.

40. Ibid.

41. Edward S. Jordan, "Madison of Yesteryear Had Its Debates . . . and Horseplay, Too," *Wisconsin State Journal*, August 21, 1949.

42. Isabel Wilder to ANW, March 1, 1970, ANW, Wilder Family Record, Private Collection.

43. ANW, April 1932, ANW, Wilder Family Record. In the official affidavit certifying ANW's birth, APW indicated that Margaret Donoghue was the nurse present at his birth on September 18, 1895. ANW's wife, Catharine Kerlin Wilder, wrote that Nurse Donoghue assisted in the births of all five of the Wilder children; the first four were born in Madison, Wisconsin, and Nurse Donoghue was "summoned" from Wisconsin to Berkeley, California, for the birth of the fifth. See Catharine Kerlin Wilder, *Milestones in My Life* (Family Publication, 2000), 21.

44. Isabel Wilder Interview, July 6, 1981, TNW Collection, YCAL, uncataloged transcription.

45. Isabella Niven Wilder to ANW, June 7, 1917, ANW, Wilder Family Record, Private Collection.

46. Jordan, "Madison of Yesteryear Had Its Debates . . . and Horseplay, Too."

47. "Even La Follette Men See Errors. Madison Journal Advises La Follette's Overthrow If He Hinder's [*sic*] Spooner's Re-Election," *Janesville (Wisconsin) Daily Gazette*, June 20, 1902.

48. Ibid.

49. "Wilder on Suffrage," *Oshkosh (Wisconsin) Daily Northwestern*, September 27, 1902. The text was submitted by mail to the *Northwestern* on September 24, 1902, from Dunkirk, New York, where Wilder made an address on the subject.

50. The church was founded in 1840, and in 1873 ground was broken for a new building with a sanctuary capable of seating fifteen hundred people. *First Congregational Church Register*, vol. 2, "Communicants and Baptisms," 141. Courtesy of John B. Toussaint.

51. Isabella Niven Wilder to ANW, May 24, 1917, ANW, Wilder Family Record, Private Collection.

52. *The Seventy-fifth Anniversary of the First Congregational Church of Madison, Wisconsin 1840–1915 and the Quarter Centennial of Eugene Grover Updike*, 33. Also see then-current church membership roster and index in the above publication, 115.

53. Mrs. E. B. Stensland to APW, October 1, 1933, TNW Collection, YCAL, uncataloged letters.

54. Isabel Wilder, "Thornton Wilder: The Anchor of Midwestern Beginnings," 8.

55. Ibid., 9.
56. Isabel Wilder, foreword to *The Alcestiad or A Life in the Sun* (New York: Samuel French, Inc., 1980), 7.
57. ANW, "Practice: A Road the Layperson Can Travel to the Domain of the Arts," *Harvard Divinity Bulletin* 8, no. 3 (February/March 1978): 2.
58. APW to "My dear Children," June 12, 1910, TNW Collection, YCAL, uncataloged letters.
59. TNW to Richard H. Goldstone, "The Art of Fiction XVI," in Jackson R. Bryer, ed., *Conversations with Thornton Wilder* (Jackson: University of Mississippi Press, 1992), 69–70.

2: "A FORETASTE OF HEAVEN" (1906–1909)

1. ANW, *Thornton Wilder and His Public* (Philadelphia: Fortress Press, 1980), 62.
2. "Motto of New York. Wisconsin Man's Comment After Riding City's Cars." *New York Times*, April 29, 1905.
3. "Badger Editor Speaks: Amos P. Wilder Will Address Young Men of Racine," *Racine (Wisconsin) Daily Journal*, February 10, 1906.
4. William Howard Taft to APW, April 14, 1905, TNW Collection, YCAL, uncataloged papers; *Janesville (Wisconsin) Daily Gazette*, June 27, 1905.
5. "Badger Editor Speaks: Amos P. Wilder Will Address Young Men of Racine."
6. "La Follette and Wilder," reprinted from *New York World* in *Oshkosh (Wisconsin) Daily Northwestern*, March 2, 1906.
7. ANW, *Thornton Wilder and His Public*, 62. Research information provided on February 27, 2008, by Katherine Mollan of the Center for Legislative Archives, NARA, indicates that Sen. Robert La Follette objected to Wilder's appointment "on the grounds that Wilder was personally offensive to him." Other than that record, no documents have yet been located to describe a confirmation hearing for APW. Ms. Mollan observes, "It is quite possible that Wilder never testified. Confirmation hearings were still relatively uncommon in the beginning of the 20th century."
8. APW to his mother, May 14, [1906?], TNW Collection, YCAL, uncataloged letters.
9. Ibid.
10. Ibid.
11. Details of the voyage and of life in China are drawn primarily from APW's letters and diary entries of the period, largely contained in the TNW Collection, YCAL, especially the uncataloged papers. In addition there are accounts by Isabella Niven Wilder, TNW, and ANW. There are, furthermore, accounts by Isabel Wilder, published in her foreword to Donald Gallup, ed., *The Journals of Thornton Wilder 1939–1961* (New Haven: Yale University Press, 1985), and other sources, as indicated in the notes, and recollections given in interviews she recorded in the 1980s (TNW Collection, YCAL, uncataloged papers). Isabel Wilder was six years old at the time of the move to China, and some of her memories and interpretations, expressed when she was in her eighties, do not coincide with the letters, diaries, and other documents generated during the China sojourn. Here and throughout this biography, when Isabel Wilder seems to be a reliable eyewitness to events, I have relied on her accounts. When she seems to be reporting events or interpretations by hearsay, I have not relied on her accounts unless they can be verified by other sources. Likewise I have noted in the narrative text the semiautobiographical nature of TNW's

own writings on China, and have incorporated details from those writings into the narrative as fact only when the facts could be corroborated by other sources, especially letters, diaries, and other documents of the period in question.

12. Isabel Wilder, foreword to Gallup, *The Journals of Thornton Wilder 1939–1961*, viii–ix.

13. APW to his mother, May 18, 1906, TNW Collection, YCAL, uncataloged letters.

14. APW to his mother, May 14, [1906?], TNW Collection, YCAL, uncataloged letters.

15. Ibid.

16. Ibid.

17. APW to his mother, May 27, 1906, TNW Collection, YCAL, uncataloged letters.

18. APW to his mother, June 10, 1906, TNW Collection, YCAL, uncataloged letters.

19. APW to his mother, May 27, 1906, TNW Collection, YCAL, uncataloged letters.

20. TNW, "Chefoo, China," unpublished semiautobiographical manuscript, n.d. 1, TNW Collection, YCAL.

21. Ibid., 3.

22. Ibid., 1.

23. APW to his mother, July 24, 1906, TNW Collection, YCAL, uncataloged letters.

24. Ibid.

25. TNW, "Chefoo, China," 5.

26. US Department of State Inspection Report of the American Consulate General, Hongkong, March 8, 1907, General Records of the Department of State 1906–1939, NARA (RG59/250/48/13/2), 28.

27. Ibid., 28–29.

28. Ibid., 1.

29. Ibid., 28–29.

30. Ibid.

31. Isabel Wilder, "A Handfull [*sic*] of Facts," TNW Collection, YCAL.

32. APW to his mother, June 10, 1906, TNW Collection, YCAL, uncataloged letters.

33. Ibid.; Apollinaris is a still or sparkling water first bottled in Germany in 1892.

34. APW to his mother, July 24, 1906, TNW Collection, YCAL, uncataloged letters.

35. APW to his mother, August 28, 1906, TNW Collection, YCAL, uncataloged letters.

36. APW recorded this fact on an application to the Thacher School that he filled out for Thornton in 1910. Thacher School Records.

37. APW to his mother, July 24, 1906, TNW Collection, YCAL, uncataloged letters.

38. APW to Mother Niven, July 1, 1906, TNW Collection, YCAL, uncataloged letters.

39. Ibid.

40. Tappan Wilder Interview with PEN, July 16, 2008.

41. Isabella Niven Wilder to ANW, August 23, 1917, ANW, Wilder Family Record, Private Collection.

42. APW to his mother, July 24, 1906, TNW Collection, YCAL, uncataloged letters.

43. The former Madison friends were Professor O'Connor, who, when the Wilders moved to Berkeley, was a member of the Latin Department at the University of California, and his sisters. APW to his mother, November 4, 1906, TNW Collection, YCAL, uncataloged letters.

44. Ibid.

45. APW to his mother, [November 1906?], TNW Collection, YCAL, uncataloged letters.

46. APW to his mother, December 4, 1906, TNW Collection, YCAL, uncataloged letters.

47. ANW, *Thornton Wilder and His Public*, 62.

48. Isabel Wilder to ANW, March 1, 1970, ANW, Wilder Family Record, Private Collection.

49. ANW, *Thornton Wilder and His Public*, 62.

50. Isabel Wilder, foreword to Gallup, *The Journals of Thornton Wilder*, ix.

51. Isabel Wilder, foreword to *The Alcestiad or A Life in the Sun*, 8.

52. TNW to Papa, n.d., TNW Collection, YCAL.

53. TNW to Mother, June 8, 1912, TNW Collection, YCAL.

54. ANW, *Thornton Wilder and His Public*, 63.

55. Quoted by Isabel Wilder, foreword to Gallup, *American Characteristics*, ix.

56. APW, "Hong Kong Diary," November 3, 1906, 1, TNW Collection, YCAL, uncataloged manuscripts.

57. APW to his mother, December 4, 1906, TNW Collection, YCAL, uncataloged letters.

58. ANW, *Thornton Wilder and His Public*, 53.

59. APW, "A Consul's Busy Day," *Hearst's International: The World Today* (New York: International Magazine Company, 1908), 938–46.

60. W. R. Schery, American Brewing Company, to APW, January 2, 1908, TNW Collection, YCAL, uncataloged letters.

61. APW to the Assistant Secretary of State, February 26, 1908, TNW Collection, YCAL, uncataloged letters.

62. APW to the Assistant Secretary of State, June 2, 1908, with enclosed letter of resignation addressed to President Theodore Roosevelt, June 2, 1908, TNW Collection, YCAL, uncataloged letters.

63. Alvey A. Adee to APW, August 19, 1908, TNW Collection, YCAL, uncataloged letters.

64. APW to F. S. Stratton, February 22, 1909, Bancroft Library, University of California.

65. APW to F. S. Stratton, May 5, 1909, Bancroft Library, University of California.

66. "May Be New President," *La Crosse (Wisconsin) Tribune*, May 1, 1909.

3: "BEING LEFT" (1909–1911)

1. APW to "Dearest Children," March 11, 1910, TNW Collection, YCAL, uncataloged letters.

2. Ibid.

3. APW to "My dear Quartette," [from Shanghai], TNW Collection, YCAL, uncataloged letters.

4. Ibid.

5. APW to "My dear Children," June 12, 1910, TNW Collection, YCAL, uncataloged letters. APW refers to Amos's musical training in APW to "My dear Children," July 3, 1910, TNW Collection, YCAL, uncataloged letters.

6. APW to "My dear Children," June 6, 1910, TNW Collection, YCAL, uncataloged letters.

7. APW to "Dear Children," April 16, 1910, TNW Collection, YCAL, uncataloged letters.

8. APW to "My dear Children," June 12, 1910, TNW Collection, YCAL, uncataloged letters.

9. APW to "My dear Quartette," [from Shanghai], TNW Collection, YCAL, uncataloged letters.

10. APW to "My dear Children," June 12, 1910, TNW Collection, YCAL, uncataloged letters.

11. APW to "My dear Children," July 24, 1910, TNW Collection, YCAL, uncataloged letters.

12. APW to "My dear Children," August 1, 1910, TNW Collection, YCAL, uncataloged letters.

13. APW to "My dear Children," July 24, 1910, TNW Collection, YCAL, uncataloged letters.

14. APW to "My dear Children," August 1, 1910, TNW Collection, YCAL, uncataloged letters.

15. APW to "My dear Children," June 12, 1910, TNW Collection, YCAL, uncataloged letters.

16. APW to "Dear Children," April 16, 1910, TNW Collection, YCAL, uncataloged letters.

17. Ibid.

18. APW to "My dear Children," June 6, 1910, TNW Collection, YCAL, uncataloged letters.

19. APW to "My dear Children," July 3, 1910, TNW Collection, YCAL, uncataloged letters.

20. TNW, "Chefoo, China," 5.

21. Ibid.

22. Ibid.

23. APW, Thacher School application, November 20, 1910, Thacher School Records.

24. Sherman Thacher to APW, August 20, 1910, TNW Collection, YCAL, uncataloged letters.

25. Catharine Kerlin Wilder, *Milestones in My Life* (Family Publication, 2000), 21.

26. APW to ANW, January 28, 1911, TNW Collection, YCAL, uncataloged letters.

27. APW to ANW, February 2, 1911, TNW Collection, YCAL, uncataloged letters.

28. APW to ANW, [March 11, 1911?], TNW Collection, YCAL, uncataloged letters.

29. P. C. Knox, Department of State, to APW, April 10, 1910, TNW Collection, YCAL, uncataloged letters.

30. William Howard Taft to APW, April 14, 1910, TNW Collection, YCAL, uncataloged letters.

31. TNW to Alexander Woollcott, September 17, 1936, copy, TNW Collection, YCAL. "Bones" refers to Yale's Skull and Bones.

32. Ibid.

33. TNW quoted in ANW, *Thornton Wilder and His Public*, 65.

34. Ibid.

35. US Department of State Inspection Report of the American Consulate General, Hongkong 1909, made by Fleming D. Cheshire, American Consul General at Large, General Records of the Department of State 1906–1939, NARA (RG59/250/48/13/2), 9.

36. APW to ANW, March 11, [1911], TNW Collection, YCAL, uncataloged letters.

37. Stanley Houghton, Edith B. Harman, and Margaret Pyle, *Chefoo* (London: China Inland Mission/Religious Tract Society, 1931), 8.

38. APW to ANW, March 28, [1911], TNW Collection, YCAL, uncataloged letters.

39. For background on Chefoo, see Stanley Houghton, Edith B. Harman, and Margaret Pyle above; Gordon Martin below; and Frances Osborne's engaging memoir, *Lilla's Feast* (London: Black Swan, 2004).

40. "Hundreds a Day Dying of Plague . . . ," Associated Press story reprinted in *Waterloo Tribune Times*, February 18, 1911, and many other newspapers.

41. Ibid.

42. TNW, "Chinese Story," undated, unpublished manuscript, 5, 7, TNW Collection, YCAL. There are several fragments in this draft, with many pages unnumbered and some sequences of five to eight pages.

43. Ibid.

44. Gordon Martin, *Chefoo School 1881–1951: A History and Memoir* (Braunton, Devon, UK: Merlin Books Ltd., 1990), 38–39. The late Dr. Morris Martin, brother of Gordon Martin, acquainted me with this book, and shared his impressions of the school and his brother's role in its administration.

45. APW to Sherman D. Thacher, June 10, 1911, [from Shanghai, China], TNW Collection, YCAL.

46. Houghton, Harman, and Pyle, *Chefoo*, 10–11.

47. Ibid., 6–7.

48. TNW, "Chefoo, China," 7.

49. Ibid., 3.

50. Ibid.

51. TNW to Family, n.d., TNW Collection, YCAL.

52. TNW, "Chefoo, China," 15.

53. Ibid., 15–16.

54. Ibid, 16.

55. Ibid.

56. Ibid.

57. TNW, "The Old Days," *Saturday Evening Post: Number of the Thacher School Semicentennial Publications*, September 1919–June 1929, n.p.

58. TNW, "Chefoo, China," 6.

59. APW to "My dear Quartette," [from Shanghai], TNW Collection, YCAL, uncataloged letters.

60. TNW, "Chefoo, China," 8.

61. TNW to APW, n.d., TNW Collection, YCAL.

62. TNW to Family, [April–May 1911?], TNW Collection, YCAL.

63. TNW to APW, [Summer 1915?], TNW Collection, YCAL.

64. TNW, "Chefoo, China," 6.

65. APW to Sherman Thacher, June 10, 1911, Thacher School Records.

66. APW to ANW, July 24, [1911?], TNW Collection, YCAL, uncataloged letters.

67. APW to ANW, July 11, [1911?], TNW Collection, YCAL, uncataloged letters.

68. Ibid.

69. TNW to APW, [1911?], TNW Collection, YCAL.

70. TNW to APW , n.d., TNW Collection, YCAL.

71. TNW to Papa, June 24, [1911?], TNW Collection, YCAL.

72. TNW to Mother, n.d., TNW Collection, YCAL.

73. Charlotte Wilder to ANW, August 28, 1911, ANW, Wilder Family Record, Private Collection.

74. Martin, *Chefoo School*, 86–87.
75. Charlotte Wilder to ANW, July 21, 1911, ANW, Wilder Family Record, Private Collection.
76. TNW, "Chefoo, China," 5.
77. Catharine Kerlin Wilder, *Milestones in My Life*, 21, indicates that the nurse accompanied Isabella and the girls to Florence, Italy.
78. TNW, "Chefoo, China," 4–5.

4: FOREIGN DEVILS (1911–1912)

1. "Safe-guarding the Americans in China," *Waterloo (Iowa) Times-Tribune*, November 23, 1911.
2. APW to Isabella Niven Wilder, October 1, [1911?], TNW Collection, YCAL, uncataloged letters.
3. Ibid.
4. APW to Isabella Niven Wilder, October 11, [1911?], TNW Collection, YCAL, uncataloged letters.
5. Ibid.
6. APW to Isabella Niven Wilder, October 16, [1911?], TNW Collection, YCAL, uncataloged letters.
7. APW to Isabella Niven Wilder, October 11, [1911?], TNW Collection, YCAL, uncataloged letters.
8. APW to Isabella Niven Wilder, October 16, [1911?], TNW Collection, YCAL, uncataloged letters.
9. Ibid.
10. Background on the Revolution of 1911 is drawn from Jonathan D. Spence, *The Search for Modern China* (New York: W. W. Norton, 1990), 244–68.
11. APW to ANW, November 11, [1911?], TNW Collection, YCAL, uncataloged letters.
12. APW to Isabella Niven Wilder, October 1, [1911], TNW Collection, YCAL, uncataloged letters.
13. TNW to APW, [1911?], TNW Collection, YCAL.
14. TNW, unpublished holograph draft of remarks to "Mr. Coleman, Miss MacDowell, Miss Carroll, Mr. President, Dean Matthews, Friends of the [Chicago] University Settlement," n.d., TNW Collection, YCAL.
15. Martin, *Chefoo School*, 51.
16. TNW to APW, June 24, 1911, TNW Collection, YCAL.
17. Quoted in Martin, *Chefoo School*, 52.
18. TNW to APW, n.d., TNW Collection, YCAL.
19. TNW, "The Old Days."
20. TNW, "Chefoo, China," 6.
21. Ibid., 7–8.
22. Ibid., 4.
23. Ibid.
24. APW to ANW, January 8, [1912?], TNW Collection, YCAL, uncataloged letters.
25. APW, Temperance Pledge, holograph manuscript, January 7, 1912, TNW Collection, YCAL, uncataloged manuscripts.

26. APW to Isabella Niven Wilder, December 7, [1911?], TNW Collection, YCAL, uncataloged letters.

27. Ibid.

28. Ibid.

29. APW to Sherman Thacher, October 24, 1911, Thacher School Records.

30. APW to Sherman Thacher, January 17, [1912?], Thacher School Records. In his haste Amos misdated this letter 1911.

31. Ibid.

32. TNW to Isabella Niven Wilder, February 10, 1912, TNW Collection, YCAL.

33. TNW to Isabella Niven Wilder, n.d., TNW Collection, YCAL.

34. APW, 1912–13 "Notes," brown leather journal, TNW Collection, YCAL, uncataloged collection.

35. APW to Sherman Thacher, March 9, 1912, Thacher School Records.

36. Asian or tropical sprue, similar to celiac disease but without the gluten intolerance, appears in the Caribbean, India, and Asia, infecting native populations and newcomers alike. Tropical sprue is caused by bacterial or viral infection, or by parasites, vitamin deficiencies, or food toxins.

37. TNW to APW, March 3, 1912, TNW Collection, YCAL.

38. Ibid.

39. TNW's academic report, China Inland Mission Boys' School, Summer Term, July 1912, TNW Collection, YCAL, uncataloged papers.

40. TNW to Isabella Niven Wilder, July 14, 1912, TNW Collection, YCAL.

41. TNW to Isabella Niven Wilder, June 16, 1912, TNW Collection, YCAL.

42. TNW to Isabella Niven Wilder, [1912?], TNW Collection, YCAL.

43. TNW to APW, May 10, 1911, TNW Collection, YCAL.

44. TNW to APW, [1911?] TNW Collection, YCAL.

45. TNW to APW, May 13, 1911, TNW Collection, YCAL.

46. TNW to APW, September 16, 1911, TNW Collection, YCAL.

47. Headnote on letter from TNW to Father, [pre-September 30, 1911?], TNW Collection, YCAL.

48. TNW to APW, September 30, 1911, TNW Collection, YCAL.

49. APW to ANW, January 8, [1912?], and October 2, [1911?], respectively, TNW Collection, YCAL, uncataloged letters.

50. TNW to APW, n.d., TNW Collection, YCAL.

51. US Department of State Inspection Report, Shanghai, China, June 1911 [covers 1910 and 1911], General Records of the Department of State 1906–1939, NARA (RG59/250/48/13/2). Inspection Report of the American Consulate General, Shanghai, made by Fleming D. Cheshire.

52. US Department of State Inspection Report, Shanghai, China, June 1913 [covers 1912 and 1913], General Records of the Department of State 1906–1939, NARA (RG59/250/48/13/2), "Explanatory Memorandum" to page 2. Inspection Report of the American Consulate General, Shanghai, made by George M. Murphy. This endnote applies to the entire passage.

53. TNW, "Chinese Story: Doremus Tries Again," II. 1, unpublished manuscript, n.d., TNW Collection, YCAL.

54. Ibid.

5: "PARENTAL EXPECTATION" (1912–1913)

1. TNW to Isabella Niven Wilder, [late summer 1912?], TNW Collection, YCAL.
2. TNW to Isabella Niven Wilder, n.d., TNW Collection, YCAL.
3. Ibid.
4. ANW, *Thornton Wilder and His Public*, 52.
5. ANW to APW, May 11, [1913?], TNW Collection, YCAL, uncataloged letters.
6. Sherman Thacher to L. B. Husted, June 12, 1912, Thacher School Records.
7. Spence, *The Search for Modern China*, 283.
8. APW to Sherman Thacher, January 3, 1911, Thacher School Records.
9. Ibid.
10. APW, Thacher School Application Questionnaire, June 12, 1912, Thacher School Records.
11. APW to "Dear Children," June 3, 1910, TNW Collection, YCAL, uncataloged letters.
12. TNW to Isabella Niven Wilder, "Sept. Something," [1912?], TNW Collection, YCAL.
13. Ibid.
14. Background on Thacher and Thacher School is drawn from LeRoy McKim Makepeace, *Sherman Thacher and His School* (New Haven: Yale University Press, 1941; reprint, Ojai, CA: Ojai Printing and Publishing Company, 1989), 70–136; 188–98.
15. Sherman Thacher to APW, March 6, 1911, Thacher School Records.
16. Sherman Thacher to APW, October 11, 1911, Thacher School Records.
17. TNW to APW, Dec. 13 [apparently misdated by TNW; more likely January 13, 1913, or late December 1912?], TNW Collection, YCAL.
18. Makepeace, *Sherman Thacher and His School*, 128–29.
19. Wilmarth Sheldon Lewis, "Thornton Wilder," Typescript, 1947, TNW Collection, YCAL. Wilmarth "Lefty" Lewis knew Amos and Thornton Wilder at Thacher and later at Yale. Lewis wrote his remembrance of TNW in response to an invitation from Clifton Fadiman on November 14, 1947, to contribute a piece on Wilder to *'47: The Magazine of the Year*, in conjunction with the publication of his novel *The Ides of March* in 1948. Lewis wrote and submitted the piece, but it was not published in Fadiman's magazine.
20. Ibid.
21. Ibid.
22. Isabella Niven Wilder to ANW, March 10, 1941, ANW, Wilder Family Record, Private Collection.
23. TNW to APW, "Thatcher [*sic*]. Sick room. Broken Heart. Sunday P.M.," [1912?], TNW Collection, YCAL.
24. Isabel Wilder, "About Charlotte Wilder," [1941 or 1942?], ANW, Wilder Family Record, TNW Collection, YCAL, uncataloged papers.
25. Charlotte Wilder to APW, [June 24?], 1913 [with a headnote in Charlotte's handwriting: "This is a letter that was written & mislaid so I send it on now."], TNW Collection, YCAL, uncataloged letters.
26. Ibid.
27. TNW to APW, March [1913?], TNW Collection, YCAL.
28. TNW to Isabella Niven Wilder, June 11, 1913, TNW Collection, YCAL.
29. TNW to APW, [1912 or 1913?], TNW Collection, YCAL.

30. TNW to Isabella Niven Wilder, "Jan. Sometime ad 20" [most likely January 1913], TNW Collection, YCAL.

31. Ibid.

32. Sherman Thacher to APW, May 15, 1913, TNW Collection, YCAL, uncataloged letters.

33. APW to Sherman Thacher, September 27, [1922?], TNW Collection, YCAL.

34. TNW to Isabella Niven Wilder, June 11, 1913, TNW Collection, YCAL.

35. Ibid.

36. Ibid.

37. TNW to APW, [June 1913?], TNW Collection, YCAL.

38. US Department of State Inspection Report, Shanghai, China, June 1913 [covers 1912 and 1913], General Records of the Department of State 1906–1939, NARA (RG59/250/48/13/2), Inspection Report of the American Consulate General, Shanghai, made by George M. Murphy.

39. Ibid.

40. TNW to APW, [September 1913?], TNW Collection, YCAL.

41. US Department of State Inspection Report, Shanghai, China, June 1913 [covers 1912 and 1913], General Records of the Department of State 1906–1939, NARA (RG59/250/48/13/2), Inspection Report of the American Consulate General, Shanghai, made by George M. Murphy.

42. Ibid.

43. Ibid.

6: "ALL ASPIRATION" (1913–1915)

1. *Olla Podrida*, December 1913, 46. Private Collection.

2. TNW to APW, September 21, [19]13, TNW Collection, YCAL.

3. Ibid.

4. Ibid.

5. Ibid.

6. TNW to APW, [1914?], TNW Collection, YCAL.

7. TNW to APW, [July 1913?], TNW Collection, YCAL. Also see *Galveston County (Texas) Daily News*, August 5, 1913.

8. APW, 1914 Shanghai Diary, TNW Collection, YCAL, uncataloged papers.

9. TNW to APW, December 14, 1913, TNW Collection, YCAL.

10. TNW to APW, [late 1913 or early 1914?], TNW Collection, YCAL.

11. Ibid.

12. APW, 1914 Shanghai Diary, TNW Collection, YCAL, uncataloged papers.

13. "Dr. A. P. Wilder. Farewell Receptions. Brilliant Speech to Young China." Unidentified, undated news clipping, Wilder Family Record, TNW Collection, YCAL.

14. *Olla Podrida*, June 1914, 75. Private Collection. A printed program for TNW's 1914 playlet, "Successful Failure," is contained in the TNW, YCAL, uncataloged papers.

15. APW to ANW, [March 21?], 1914, TNW Collection, YCAL, uncataloged letters.

16. APW to ANW, April 12, [1914?], TNW Collection, YCAL, uncataloged letters.

17. APW to ANW, May 25, [1914?], TNW Collection, YCAL, uncataloged letters.

18. Ibid.

19. APW to ANW, April 27, [1914?], TNW Collection, YCAL, uncataloged letters.

20. APW to ANW, [Summer 1914?], TNW Collection, YCAL, uncataloged letters.

21. TNW to "Familie," [p.m. June 15, 1914?], TNW Collection, YCAL.

22. Ibid.

23. ANW, "1914 Summer," ANW, Wilder Family Record, Private Collection.

24. APW to ANW, May 18, [1914?], TNW Collection, YCAL, uncataloged letters.

25. APW to ANW, July 31, [1914?], TNW Collection, YCAL, uncataloged letters.

26. APW to ANW, June 30, [1914?], TNW Collection, YCAL, uncataloged letters.

27. For detailed background on Yale-in-China, see Nancy E. Chapman with Jessica C. Plumb, *The Yale-China Association: A Centennial History* (Chinese University Press, 2001), and Reuben Holden, *Yale in China: The Mainland/1907–1951* (New Haven: Yale-in-China Association, 1964).

28. APW to ANW, June 3, 1915, TNW Collection, YCAL uncataloged letters.

29. TNW to APW, June 27 and 28, [19]14, TNW Collection, YCAL.

30. TNW to APW, n.d., TNW Collection, YCAL.

31. TNW to APW, [Fall 1914?], TNW Collection, YCAL.

32. TNW to APW, October 1, [1914?], TNW Collection, YCAL.

33. Isabel Wilder to APW, n.d., TNW Collection, YCAL.

34. TNW to ANW, November 18, [19]14, TNW Collection, YCAL.

35. TNW to APW, n.d., TNW Collection, YCAL.

36. TNW to ANW, November 18, [19]14, TNW Collection, YCAL.

37. TNW to APW, [May 1915?], TNW Collection, YCAL.

38. TNW to Percy MacKaye, n.d., TNW Collection, YCAL. In this undated letter, written when TNW was an adult, he confessed to MacKaye that as pleased as he had been as a boy to receive MacKaye's letter, he was "too shy" to respond but had always dreamed of writing "scenarios for Percy MacKaye."

39. TNW to ANW, April 7, [19]15, TNW Collection, YCAL.

40. TNW to APW, [1915?], TNW Collection, YCAL.

41. Ibid.

42. The painting was later sold—at a fine profit—to the art collectors Louise and Walter Arensberg, and eventually wound up in the Philadelphia Museum of Art. See also Daniella Thompson, "East Bay Then and Now: Berkeleyan Torrey Owned Duchamp's Most Famous Painting," *Berkeley Daily Planet*, February 4, 2009.

43. TNW to APW, [1914?], TNW Collection, YCAL. Actually, Robert Louis Stevenson dedicated the 1879 edition of his *The Silverado Squatters* to his cousin, Robert Alan Mowbray Stevenson, known as Bob. Mrs. Williams's memory may have been faulty, or TNW may not have gotten the correct title from their conversations, but it is a fact that Dora Norton Williams and her husband were close friends of Robert Louis Stevenson and his wife. See, for instance, Frank McLynn, *Robert Louis Stevenson: A Biography* (London: Hutchinson, 1993); and Ernest Mehew, ed., *Selected Letters of Robert Louis Stevenson* (New Haven: Yale University Press, 1997).

44. Talcott Williamson, Interview, "Biography in Sound," NBC Radio, March 27, 1956.

45. TNW to ANW, November 18, [19]14, TNW Collection, YCAL.

46. TNW to APW, [April 16, 1915?], TNW Collection, YCAL.

47. APW to Isabella Niven Wilder, January 2, [1915?], TNW Collection, YCAL, uncataloged letters.

48. Ibid.

49. TNW to APW, [April 16, 1915?], TNW Collection, YCAL.

50. APW to ANW, [Summer 1915?], TNW Collection, YCAL, uncataloged letters.

51. TNW to APW, [May 1915?], TNW Collection, YCAL.

52. TNW to Elizabeth Lewis Niven, January 7, [19]15, TNW Collection, YCAL.

53. TNW to APW, April 16, [19]15, TNW Collection, YCAL.

54. TNW to APW, May 9, [1915?], TNW Collection, YCAL.
55. TNW describes this table of contents in the foreword to the collection of his three-minute playlets, *The Angel That Troubled the Waters and Other Plays* (New York: Coward-McCann, Inc., 1928). Page references for the three-minute playlets in this collection are to A. Tappan Wilder, ed. *The Collected Short Plays of Thornton Wilder* (New York: Theatre Communications Group, 1998), vol. 2.
56. TNW, foreword to *The Angel That Troubled the Waters and Other Plays.*
57. TNW to ANW, April 7, [19]15, TNW Collection, YCAL.
58. TNW to APW, n.d. [May ? 1915], TNW Collection, YCAL.
59. TNW to APW, May 30, 1915, TNW Collection, YCAL.
60. APW to ANW, June 3, 1915, TNW Collection, YCAL, uncataloged letters. The "Seven Sisters," prestigious colleges for women, originally included Barnard, Bryn Mawr, Mount Holyoke, Radcliffe, Smith, Vassar, and Wellesley. Vassar is now co-educational, and Radcliffe merged with Harvard.
61. Ibid.
62. TNW to APW, [May 1915?], TNW Collection, YCAL.
63. TNW to APW, [1915?], TNW Collection, YCAL.
64. TNW to APW, May 25, [1915?], TNW Collection, YCAL.
65. TNW to APW, June 20, [19]15, TNW Collection, YCAL.
66. TNW to APW, [Summer 1915?], TNW Collection, YCAL.
67. APW to ANW and TNW, August 2, 1915, TNW Collection, YCAL, uncataloged letters.
68. TNW to APW, July [13?], [1915?], TNW Collection, YCAL.
69. TNW to APW, July [13?], [1915?], TNW Collection, YCAL, and TNW to APW, [Summer 1915?], TNW Collection, YCAL.

7: "LITERARY DEVELOPMENT" (1915–1916)

1. APW to President Henry C. King, April 11, 1913, Oberlin College Archives.
2. Quoted in Wyatt-Brown, *Lewis Tappan and the Evangelical War Against Slavery*, 129–30.
3. TNW to APW, [Fall 1915?], TNW Collection, YCAL.
4. Ibid. The Psychology Department was officially established at Oberlin in 1909, and by 1915, psychology courses were so popular that Professor Raymond Herbert Stetson, chairman of the department, appealed for additional teachers and better facilities and equipment to keep up with the demand. Dr. Stetson was an Oberlin graduate with a doctorate from Harvard, and would teach at Oberlin for thirty years.
5. ANW, quoted by Krister Stendahl, "'Imagining the Real,' a 'Memorial Minute,'" *Harvard Divinity Bulletin* 23, no. 1 (1994): 13.
6. TNW to Mother, [1915?], TNW Collection, YCAL.
7. TNW to Family, [Fall 1915?], TNW Collection, YCAL. (Letter begins ". . . have not called?"; pages 1 and 2 are missing.)
8. Isabel Wilder, untitled typescript, n.d., TNW Collection, YCAL, uncataloged manuscript.
9. TNW to Family, [1915?], TNW Collection, YCAL.

10. 1915–1916 Annual Report of the President and Treasurer, Oberlin College. In the nineteenth century this house had been the home of Oberlin's first physician, James Dascomb, a science professor at the college, whose wife, Marianne, was head of the Oberlin Women's Department.

11. TNW to Mother, [1915?], TNW Collection, YCAL.

12. TNW to Family, [1915?], TNW Collection, YCAL.

13. APW to Isabella Niven Wilder, January 2, [1915?], TNW Collection, YCAL, uncataloged letters.

14. Charlotte Wilder to APW, May 30, 1915, TNW Collection, YCAL, uncataloged letters.

15. APW to ANW, December 8, [1914?], TNW Collection, YCAL, uncataloged letters.

16. ANW, quoted by Stendahl, " 'Imagining the Real,' a 'Memorial Minute,' " 13.

17. TNW to Family, [Fall 1915?], TNW Collection, YCAL.

18. Hubert Jay Stowitts to TNW, November 16, 1915, TNW Collection, YCAL.

19. Ibid.

20. TNW to Family, [Fall 1915?], TNW Collection, YCAL.

21. Ibid.

22. TNW to Papa, December 20, [1915?], TNW Collection, YCAL.

23. TNW to Charlotte Wilder, [March 1916?], TNW Collection, YCAL. Printed program, May 9, 1916, TNW Collection, YCAL.

24. Ibid.

25. TNW to Papa, February 6, 1916, TNW Collection, YCAL.

26. Ibid.

27. TNW, foreword to *The Angel That Troubled the Waters*. This volume is also published in A. Tappan Wilder, ed., *The Collected Short Plays of Thornton Wilder*, vol. 2, 1–86; and J. D. McClatchy, ed., *Thornton Wilder: Collected Plays & Writings on Theater* (New York: Library of America, 2007), 5–60.

28. Ibid.

29. TNW to ANW, April 8, 1916, TNW Collection, YCAL.

30. TNW, "The Language of Emotion in Shakespeare," *Oberlin Literary Magazine*, March 1916, 140–41.

31. TNW to Family, [Fall or Winter 1915?], TNW Collection, YCAL.

32. TNW to Mother, [1916?], TNW Collection, YCAL. (Letter is headed "Family," which is crossed out and supplanted by "Mother only—.")

33. Robin G. Wilder to PEN, August 3, 2008.

34. TNW to Charlotte Wilder, [March 1916?], TNW Collection, YCAL.

35. TNW to Family, May 6, [1916?], TNW Collection, YCAL.

36. TNW to Family, [Fall or Winter 1915?], TNW Collection, YCAL.

37. TNW, "The Last Word About Burglars: A Disordered Fancy in One Act," unpublished holograph manuscript, TNW Collection, YCAL. (In addition to the eight-page script, there is a three-page draft of the final pages, apparently an earlier draft.)

38. TNW to Papa, April 4, [1916?], TNW Collection, YCAL.

39. Ibid.

40. Ibid.

41. Ibid.

42. TNW to Mother, [1916?], TNW Collection, YCAL. (Letter begins, "I hope your splendid long letter . . .")
43. TNW to Papa, May 8, 1916, TNW Collection, YCAL.
44. Isabel Wilder, transcript of taped interview, n.d., TNW Collection, YCAL, uncataloged manuscript.
45. TNW to Isabel Wilder, May 18, [19]16, TNW Collection, YCAL.
46. ANW, 1916, Wilder Family Record.
47. TNW to Papa, May 14, [19]16, TNW Collection, YCAL.
48. TNW to Papa, July 12, 1916, TNW Collection, YCAL.
49. TNW to Mother, July 2, [1916?], TNW Collection, YCAL. The Northfield Seminary was located in Northfield, Massachusetts. The Mount Hermon School for Boys is located nearby in Gill, Massachusetts. The two schools became a single corporation in 1912 and were consolidated in 1971. In September 2005, the Northfield program was moved to the Mount Hermon campus in Gill. The Northfield Mount Hermon School's official address is Mount Hermon, Massachusetts.

8: "THE ART OF WRITING" (1916)

1. *Catalogue of Mount Hermon School, 1915–16* (Brattleboro, VT: Press of E. L. Hildreth & Co., 1916), 24.
2. Ibid.
3. Ibid., 24–25.
4. TNW to Family, Monday Night, [July 1916?], TNW Collection, YCAL.
5. TNW to Mother, July 2, [19]16, TNW Collection, YCAL.
6. TNW to Papa, June 23, [1916?], TNW Collection, YCAL.
7. TNW to ANW, July 11, [1916?], TNW Collection, YCAL.
8. TNW to ANW, October 16, 1916, TNW Collection, YCAL, uncataloged letters.
9. TNW to Papa, [Spring 1916?], TNW Collection, YCAL.
10. Sir Thomas Browne, Knt, *Religio Medici, Hydriotaphia, and the Letter to a Friend*, rev. ed. (Middlesex, England: Echo Library, 2007), part 1: 1, 9.
11. Browne, *Religio Medici*, 10. The text transcription of this passage is incomplete in the source above; I have consulted other sources to determine the complete sentence in question. See, for instance, M. H. Abrams, ed., *The Norton Anthology of English Literature* (New York: W. W. Norton & Company, 1986), vol. 1, 1718.
12. Ibid., 12.
13. Ibid., 14.
14. Ibid., 18.
15. Browne, in *Hydriotaphia*, 98.
16. TNW to Mother, [1916?], TNW Collection, YCAL.
17. Ibid.
18. TNW, "Brother Fire," in *The Angel That Troubled the Waters*, 21–24. This playlet was first published as "Brother Fire: A Comedy for Saints" in the *Oberlin Literary Magazine*, May 1916, 200–202.
19. TNW to Ross Parmenter, "Novelist into Playwright," *Saturday Review of Literature*, June 11, 1938, 10–11; reprinted in Bryer, *Conversations with Thornton Wilder*, 24.
20. TNW to Papa, June 23, [1916?], TNW Collection, YCAL.
21. APW to ANW, July 25, [1916?], TNW Collection, YCAL, uncataloged letters.

22. Ibid.

23. TNW to Mother, July 12, [1916?], TNW Collection, YCAL.

24. Charles A. Wager to TNW, June 27, [1916?], TNW Collection, YCAL.

25. TNW to ANW, July 11, [1916?], TNW Collection, YCAL.

26. APW to TNW, March 18, [1917?], TNW Collection, YCAL.

27. TNW to Papa, [July 11 or 12, 1916?], TNW Collection, YCAL.

28. TNW to Papa, [August 1916?], TNW Collection, YCAL.

29. Ibid.

30. Vacation details are to be found in ANW, Wilder Family Record for 1916, Private Collection.

31. TNW to Papa, September 1, [19]16, TNW Collection, YCAL.

32. TNW to Mother, August 28, [19]16, TNW Collection, YCAL.

33. Ibid.

34. Ibid.

35. TNW to Papa, September 1, [19]16, TNW Collection, YCAL.

36. Ibid.

37. Ibid.

38. TNW to Rudolf Kommer, September 15, [19]16, TNW Collection, YCAL.

39. Vacation details are to be found in ANW, Wilder Family Record, 1916, Private Collection.

40. Ibid.

41. TNW to Rudolf Kommer, September 15, [19]16, TNW Collection, YCAL.

42. TNW to Papa, September 26, [19]16, TNW Collection, YCAL.

43. TNW to Charlotte Wilder, October 16, [19]16, TNW Collection, YCAL.

44. ANW, *Armageddon Revisited : A World War I Journal* (New Haven: Yale University Press, 1994), 6.

45. Ibid.

46. ANW, September 1916, ANW, Wilder Family Record, TNW Collection, YCAL.

47. Ibid.

48. ANW, *Armageddon Revisited*, 2–3.

49. ANW, November 1926, 5, ANW, Wilder Family Record, TNW Collection, YCAL.

50. APW to ANW, November 26, [1916?], TNW Collection, YCAL.

51. Ralph Wentworth to APW, May 24, 1917, Mount Hermon School Archives.

52. Isabel Wilder's Application for Admission to Northfield Seminary, completed by APW, October 16, 1916, Mount Hermon School Archives.

53. APW to Mr. Dickerson, June 30, 1919. Mount Hermon School Archives.

54. TNW to Mother, October 22, [19]16, TNW Collection, YCAL.

55. TNW to ANW, October 16, 1916, ANW, Wilder Family Record, TNW Collection, YCAL.

56. TNW to ANW, December 8, 1916, ANW, Wilder Family Record, TNW Collection, YCAL.

57. TNW to ANW, September 23, [19]16, TNW Collection, YCAL.

58. TNW to Mother, [1915?], TNW Collection, YCAL.

59. Geoffrey Blodgett, *Oberlin Architecture, College and Town: A Guide to Its Social History* (Kent, OH: Kent State University Press, 1985), 93.

60. TNW to Mother, September 4, [19]16, TNW Collection, YCAL.

61. TNW to ANW, September 23, [19]16, TNW Collection, YCAL.

62. TNW to Mother, October 22, [19]16, TNW Collection, YCAL.

63. TNW to Papa, [Fall 1916?], TNW Collection, YCAL.
64. TNW to Mother, September 4, [19]16, TNW Collection, YCAL.
65. TNW to Mama, November 13, [19]16, TNW Collection, YCAL.
66. TNW to Mother, [Fall 1916?], TNW Collection, YCAL.
67. Ibid. The play was published in the *Oberlin Literary Magazine* in December 1916.
68. TNW to Mother, November 23, [19]16, TNW Collection, YCAL. When he was thirteen, TNW had seen the American playwright and poet Percy MacKaye's dramas performed in the Greek Theatre at the University of California, Berkeley. MacKaye's translation of Sophocles' *Antigone* was performed there in June 1910.
69. TNW to Mother, November 23, [19]16, TNW Collection, YCAL.
70. TNW to Mother, [Fall 1916], TNW Collection, YCAL.
71. TNW to Papa, November 14, [19]16, TNW Collection, YCAL.
72. Ibid.
73. Isabella Niven Wilder to TNW, December 1, 1916, TNW Collection, YCAL.
74. Verhaeren was sixty-one that November of 1916 when he fell at Rouen Station in Paris and was crushed to death by a train. "Today suddenly—cruelly it seemed—/ Your long road turned the road long dreamed . . . ," Isabella wrote. Her poem was not published.
75. TNW to Mother, [December 1916?], TNW Collection, YCAL.
76. TNW to ANW, September 7, [1917?], TNW Collection, YCAL.
77. Isabella Niven Wilder to ANW, November 30, 1916, ANW, Wilder Family Record, TNW Collection, YCAL.
78. TNW to ANW, December 8, 1916, ANW, Wilder Family Record, TNW Collection, YCAL.
79. APW to Isabella Niven Wilder, December 1916, ANW, Wilder Family Record, TNW Collection, YCAL.

9: DISTANT SONS (1917)

1. TNW to Mother, October 22, [19]16, TNW Collection, YCAL.
2. TNW to Family, Monday Night, [1916 or 1917?], TNW Collection, YCAL.
3. TNW to Papa, January 11, [19]17, TNW Collection, YCAL.
4. TNW to Papa, February 14, [19]17, TNW Collection, YCAL.
5. Ibid.
6. TNW to Sherman Thacher, March 4, 1917, TNW Collection, YCAL, uncataloged letters.
7. Ibid.
8. APW to TNW, March 18, [1917?], TNW Collection, YCAL.
9. Ibid.
10. TNW to Mother, March 14 [1917?], TNW Collection, YCAL. TNW's pleas to do wartime farmwork may be found in his two postcards to his father, April 21, 1917, TNW Collection, YCAL.
11. TNW refers to the three spiritual stories in TNW to Papa, "Second Sunday in March," [1917?], TNW Collection, YCAL.
12. Ibid.
13. TNW to Papa, "The First Day of Spring / The Third Year of the War," [March 1917?], TNW Collection, YCAL.

14. Ibid.
15. Isabella Niven Wilder to ANW, March 15, 1917, TNW Collection, YCAL, uncataloged letters.
16. ANW, *Armageddon Revisited*, 9.
17. TNW to Family, [April 6, 1917?], TNW Collection, YCAL.
18. TNW to APW, [1917?], TNW Collection, YCAL.
19. TNW to Family, "The day War was declared / Good Friday . . . ," [April 6, 1917?], TNW Collection, YCAL.
20. Isabella Niven Wilder to ANW, April 13, 1917, TNW Collection, YCAL, uncataloged letters.
21. TNW to APW, Isabella Niven Wilder, Isabel, and Janet, April 10, [19]17, TNW Collection, YCAL.
22. TNW to ANW, April 11, 1917, TNW Collection, YCAL, uncataloged letters.
23. TNW to Elizabeth Lewis Niven, April 19, 1917, TNW Collection, YCAL.
24. TNW to Mother, April 20, 1917, TNW Collection, YCAL.
25. Isabella Niven Wilder to ANW, April 27, 1917, TNW Collection, YCAL uncataloged letters.
26. TNW to Family, April 22, [1917?], TNW Collection, YCAL.
27. TNW to Family, Monday Night, n.d., TNW Collection, YCAL.
28. TNW to Family, April 22, [1917?], TNW Collection, YCAL.
29. TNW to Mother, [Fall 1916?], TNW Collection, YCAL.
30. TNW to Family, April 22, [1917?], TNW Collection, YCAL.
31. TNW to Papa, April 21, 1917, TNW Collection, YCAL.
32. TNW to APW, May 1, 1917, TNW Collection, YCAL.
33. TNW to Family, April 10, [1917?], TNW Collection, YCAL.
34. TNW, "Journal. Commencing April 25, 1917," April 25, [1917?], TNW Collection, YCAL.
35. TNW to APW, Monday Morning, [June 4, 1917?], TNW Collection, YCAL.
36. TNW, "Journal. Commencing April 25, 1917," April 25, [1917?], TNW Collection, YCAL.
37. TNW, "Journal. Commencing April 25, 1917," May 14, 1917, TNW Collection, YCAL. After a long career in theater and motion pictures, Gareth Hughes became Brother David in the early 1940s, and in 1944 began working with the Paiute Indians in Nevada (not as a priest, but as a layperson). He died at the age of seventy on October 1, 1965, at the Motion Picture House and Country Home, Woodland Hills, California, according to his official biographer, Stephen Lyons.
38. TNW, "Journal. Commencing April 25, 1917," May 17, [1917?], TNW Collection, YCAL.
39. Ibid.
40. Ibid.
41. TNW, "Journal. Commencing April 25, 1917," April 29, 1917, TNW Collection, YCAL.
42. APW to TNW, April 30, [1917?], TNW Collection, YCAL.
43. TNW, "Journal. Commencing April 25, 1917," April 28, 1917, TNW Collection, YCAL.
44. TNW, "Journal. Commencing April 25, 1917," April 30, 1917, TNW Collection, YCAL.

45. TNW, "Journal. Commencing April 25, 1917," May 3, 1917, TNW Collection, YCAL.
46. TNW to Papa, May 10, [1917?], TNW Collection, YCAL.
47. Ibid.
48. Isabella Niven Wilder to ANW, May 10, 1917, TNW Collection, YCAL, uncataloged letters.
49. Isabella Niven Wilder to ANW, May 18, 1917, TNW Collection, YCAL, uncataloged letters.
50. TNW to ANW, May 26, [19]17, TNW Collection, YCAL.
51. TNW to Papa, [May 1917?], TNW Collection, YCAL.
52. Ibid.
53. TNW to Papa, [1917?], TNW Collection, YCAL.
54. TNW to Papa, [May 1917?], TNW Collection, YCAL.
55. TNW, "Journal. Commencing April 25, 1917," May 26, 1917, TNW Collection, YCAL.
56. TNW to ANW, May 26, [19]17, TNW Collection, YCAL.
57. Ibid.
58. ANW, *Thornton Wilder and His Public*, 10.
59. TNW to ANW, May 26, [19]17, TNW Collection, YCAL.

10: "FLOWERING INTO LITERATURE" (1917–1918)

1. Isabella Niven Wilder to ANW, March 1, 1917, TNW Collection, YCAL, uncataloged letters.
2. Isabella Niven Wilder to ANW, May 31, 1917, TNW Collection, YCAL, uncataloged letters.
3. TNW to ANW, October 18, 1917, TNW Collection, YCAL, uncataloged letters.
4. TNW, *The Eighth Day* (New York: HarperPerennial, 2006), 10.
5. TNW to Papa & Family, June 13, [1917?], TNW Collection, YCAL.
6. APW to "My Darling Son," [June 1917?], TNW Collection, YCAL.
7. Ibid.
8. APW to TNW, June 30, [1917?], TNW Collection, YCAL.
9. Isabella Niven Wilder to ANW, June 28, 1917, TNW Collection, YCAL, uncataloged letters.
10. Isabella Niven Wilder to ANW, July 5, 1917, TNW Collection, YCAL, uncataloged letters.
11. Charlotte Wilder, "Hollows," 1918–19, LD 7096.6 1919, courtesy of Mount Holyoke College Archives and Special Collections. Robert Frost's message was conveyed in a letter from Clara F. Stevens to Charlotte, June 6, 1919, also courtesy of Mount Holyoke.
12. APW to ANW, June 30, [1914?], TNW Collection, YCAL, uncataloged letters.
13. Ibid.
14. APW to TNW, [1917?], TNW Collection, YCAL. (One page of typed letter is missing.)
15. TNW to ANW, August 1, 1917, TNW Collection, YCAL.
16. TNW to Mother, July 26, [1917?], TNW Collection, YCAL.
17. TNW to Papa & Family, June 13, [1917?], TNW Collection, YCAL.
18. TNW to Mother, July 26, [1917?], TNW Collection, YCAL.
19. TNW to Mother, July 20, [1917?], TNW Collection, YCAL.
20. Ibid.

21. TNW to Mother, [1917?], TNW Collection, YCAL.

22. Charles Wager to TNW, June 26, 1917, TNW Collection, YCAL.

23. TNW to Charles Wager, [June 1917?], TNW Collection, YCAL.

24. APW to TNW, June 30, [1917?], TNW Collection, YCAL.

25. Quoted in Shannon H. Wilson, *Berea College: An Illustrated History* (Louisville: University of Kentucky Press, 2006), synopsis.

26. TNW to APW, [Summer 1917?], TNW Collection, YCAL.

27. Isabella Niven Wilder to ANW, January 18, 1917, TNW Collection, YCAL uncataloged letters.

28. TNW to ANW, August 1, 1917, TNW Collection, YCAL.

29. TNW to Charles Wager, September 2, [1917?], Oberlin College Archives, Oberlin, OH.

30. Isabella Niven Wilder to ANW, August 9, 1917, TNW Collection, YCAL, uncataloged letters.

31. TNW to Papa, n.d. [August 1917], TNW Collection, YCAL.

32. Isabella Niven Wilder to ANW, August 9, 1917, TNW Collection, YCAL, uncataloged letters.

33. Isabella Niven Wilder to ANW, September 7, 1917, TNW Collection, YCAL, uncataloged letters.

34. TNW to ANW, September 7, [1917?], TNW Collection, YCAL.

35. Ibid.

36. TNW to Charles Wager, September 25, [1917?], TNW Collection, YCAL.

37. TNW to ANW, September 13, 1917, TNW Collection, YCAL, uncataloged letters.

38. TNW to Charles Wager, September [1917?], *SL*, 113–14.

39. Leonard M. Daggett, ed., *The Record of the Class of Eighty-Four, Yale College, 1914–1936* (New Haven, 1936), 187.

40. Isabel Wilder to ANW, September 7, 1917, TNW Collection, YCAL, uncataloged letters.

41. APW to ANW, September 12, [1917?], TNW Collection, YCAL.

42. TNW to ANW, October 18, 1917, TNW Collection, YCAL, uncataloged letters.

43. Ibid.

44. TNW to Charles Wager, October 16, [1917?], TNW Collection, YCAL.

45. Ibid.

46. Wilmarth "Lefty" Lewis, "Thornton Wilder," unpublished typescript. TNW Collection, YCAL.

47. Morehead Patterson, ed., *History of the Class of Nineteen Hundred Twenty* (New Haven: Tuttle, Morehouse & Taylor Company, 1920), 433.

48. TNW to Charles Wager, October 4, [1917?], TNW Collection, YCAL.

49. Ibid.

50. Ibid.

51. TNW to Charles Wager, October 16, [1917], TNW Collection, YCAL. Lingering questions about conventional versus unconventional religious faith and practice emerge from the compressed intensity of this playlet.

52. TNW's published playlets included *The Message and Jehanne* in November 1917; *The Walled City* (later revised, renamed, and published as *Nascuntur Poetae . . .*) and *That Other Fanny Otcott* in April 1918; *The Penny That Beauty Spent* in March 1919; *Not for Leviathan* in April 1919; and *Childe Roland to the Dark Tower Came* in June 1919. He reviewed W. B. Yeats's "Per Amica Silentia Lunae" in the March 1918 issue.

53. TNW, "Measure for Measure," [1917?], manuscript, TNW Collection, YCAL. TNW's sonnet, worked on in his spare time for a week at Berea, reads in part:

> *Then Love in dark aspect Lord Shakespeare brings,*
> *Now in the highest reason of his Thought;*
> *And shows all Beauty trembling as she sings,*
> *And all the ruin that the God hath wrought.*
> *Wherefore to give this dire conception tongue*
> *An Eros-ridden world moves to his call*
> *The agéd villainous and the piteous young;*
> *And see! That chain, or wreath, is worn by all.*

54. Charles A. Wager to TNW, January 15, 1918, TNW Collection, YCAL.
55. *The Book of the Yale Elizabethan Club* (New Haven: Yale University Press, 1913), 43.
56. TNW to Charles Wager, "Dialogue in the Elizabethan Club," [December 11, 1917?], TNW Collection, YCAL.
57. Isabella Niven Wilder to ANW, January 17, 1918, TNW Collection, YCAL uncataloged letters.
58. TNW, "The Walled City," holograph manuscript, n.d., TNW Collection, YCAL.
59. APW to ANW, September 12, [1917?], TNW Collection, YCAL.
60. TNW, *Nascuntur Poetae . . .* , in *The Angel That Troubled the Waters*, 9–12.

11: "HEROES" (1918)

1. TNW to ANW, May 27, 1917, ANW, Wilder Family Record, TNW Collection, YCAL.
2. TNW to Theodore Wilder, February, [19]18, TNW Collection, YCAL.
3. Charles Wager to TNW, January 15, 1918, TNW Collection, YCAL.
4. TNW to Charles Wager, January [day illegible], [19]18, TNW Collection, YCAL.
5. Ibid.
6. Ibid.
7. Ibid.
8. Ibid.
9. Ibid.
10. TNW quoting the letter from Gareth Hughes, in TNW to Charles Wager, January [day illegible], [19]18, TNW Collection, YCAL.
11. TNW to Theodore Wilder, February [19]18, TNW Collection, YCAL.
12. TNW to Charles Wager, January [day illegible], [19]18, TNW Collection, YCAL.
13. ANW, *Armageddon Revisited*, 57.
14. "7,873 Yale Men in War," *New York Times*, March 9, 1919.
15. The John Hubbard Curtis Prize was endowed by Mrs. Virginia Curtis in memory of her son, John, (Yale 1887), who had committed suicide. At her request Professor William Lyon Phelps was one of the permanent members of the prize committee.
16. TNW, "Spiritus Valet," John Hubbard Curtis Prize story, *Yale Courant*, May 1918, 230, 232–34, 246, 251.
17. Ibid.
18. TNW to ANW, n.d., TNW Collection, YCAL, uncataloged letters.
19. Ibid.
20. "7,873 Yale Men in War."
21. Andrew Mangino, "Yalies in the Military," *New York Times*, December 1, 2006.

22. Walter Millis, "The War," in Patterson, *History of the Class of Nineteen Hundred Twenty*, 63–76.

23. Tappan Wilder to PEN, July 2008.

24. "7,873 Yale Men in War."

25. Millis, "The War," 63–76.

26. Stephen Vincent Benét to John Farrar, December 14, 1918, in Charles A. Fenton, ed., *Selected Letters of Stephen Vincent Benét* (New Haven: Yale University Press, 1960), 19.

27. Charles A. Fenton, *Stephen Vincent Benét: The Life and Times of an American Man of Letters 1898–1943* (New Haven: Yale University Press, 1958), 73.

28. Stephen Vincent Benét to John Farrar, December 14, 1918, in Fenton, *Selected Letters of Stephen Vincent Benét*, 19.

29. APW to ANW, May 25, 1918, TNW Collection, YCAL uncataloged letters.

30. TNW to Bruce T. Simonds, July 19, 1918, TNW Collection, YCAL.

31. Ibid.

32. Ibid. *Vecy-Segal*, a comedy, was not completed but survives in typescript in the TNW Collection, YCAL. A segment of it, "Sea Chanty: 'Vecy-Segal,' Scene IV," appeared in December 1919 in *S4N*, a journal published by TNW's Yale friend Norman Fitts, class of 1919.

33. TNW to Papa, June 29, [1918?], TNW Collection, YCAL.

34. TNW to Papa, [Summer 1918?], TNW Collection, YCAL.

35. TNW, *Centaurs*, in *The Angel That Troubled the Waters and Other Plays*, 40–43. As shall be seen, this playlet was first published in *S4N* in April 1920, as *The Death of the Centaur: A Footnote to Ibsen*.

36. TNW to Mother, [Summer 1918?], TNW Collection, YCAL. Holograph notes, a typescript, and a carbon typescript of *The Breaking of Exile* are among TNW's papers in the TNW Collection, YCAL.

37. TNW to Mother, August 9, 1918, TNW Collection, YCAL.

38. "Almost boisterously": TNW to Papa, June 29, [1918?], TNW Collection, YCAL. "More genial and approachable": TNW to Papa, [Summer 1918?], TNW Collection, YCAL.

39. APW to ANW, September 7, 1918, ANW, Wilder Family Record, Private Collection.

40. APW to ANW, June 14, 1918, TNW Collection, YCAL, uncataloged letters.

41. APW to ANW, July 3, 1918, TNW Collection, YCAL, uncataloged letters.

42. ANW, *Armageddon Revisited*, 110.

43. ANW to TNW, July 14, [1918?] TNW Collection, YCAL.

44. APW to TNW, July 5, [1918?], TNW Collection, YCAL.

45. Ibid.

46. TNW to "Pops," August 14, 1918, TNW Collection, YCAL.

47. Ibid.

48. APW to ANW, August 29, [1918?], and September 21, [1918?], ANW, Wilder Family Record, TNW Collection, YCAL.

49. ANW, *Armageddon Revisited*, 125.

50. Ibid., 126–50.

51. Ibid., 128–29.

52. Ibid., 129.

53. Ibid., 138–39.

54. The Panthéon tribute to Guynemer read in part, "A legendary hero, fallen from the

very zenith of victory after three years' hard and continuous fighting, he will be considered the most perfect embodiment of the national qualities for his indomitable energy and perseverance and his exalted gallantry."

55. TNW, "Guynemer," holograph manuscript, n.d., TNW Collection, YCAL.

56. TNW, "In Praise of Guynemer," December 1918, TNW Collection, YCAL. Published in the *Yale Literary Magazine* 84, no. 1 (December 1918): 27–29.

57. TNW, "From a Dialogue 'In Praise of Guynemer,'" in Patterson, *History of the Class of Nineteen Hundred Twenty*, 441.

58. APW to ANW, August 2, [1918?], TNW Collection, YCAL, uncataloged letters.

59. APW to ANW, August 29 [1918?], ANW, Wilder Family Record, Private Collection.

60. ANW to TNW, [June 1918?], TNW Collection, YCAL.

61. APW to TNW, July 5, [1918?], TNW Collection, YCAL.

62. APW to TNW, August 11, [1918?], TNW Collection, YCAL.

63. Trench mouth: Dr. Austin Temple provided the information that trench mouth was so named because of the epidemic of severe gingivitis among the men in the trenches during World War I.

64. APW to TNW, August 11, [1918?], TNW Collection, YCAL.

65. TNW to Papa, August 1, [1918?], TNW Collection, YCAL.

66. TNW to Mother, [September 1918?], TNW Collection, YCAL.

67. TNW to Mother, October 16, [1918?], TNW Collection, YCAL.

68. Ibid. That fall Thornton helped set up a weekly newspaper at Fort Adams. He contributed a poem, which quickly became popular and was circulated widely. Arguably, it may have been the best verse he ever wrote:

> *Beans*
> *The bean, the bean's the only thing!*
> *Lima, castor, jelly, string*
> *In our porridge, in our hash,*
> *Stirred up in our succotash;*
> *Soldiers, sailors and marines*
> *Live and die on army beans;*
> *Officers must face them too,*
> *Boiled or baked or in a stew.*
> *In the pod or in the pot,*
> *Red or green or cold or hot,*
> *I'll break away from this routine,*
> *Desert the army—and the bean.*

69. TNW to Mother, November 30, 1918, TNW Collection, YCAL.

70. TNW to Mother, December 16, [19]18, TNW Collection, YCAL.

71. TNW to Papa, December 4, 1918, TNW Collection, YCAL.

72. APW to ANW, November 29, [1918?], ANW, Wilder Family Record, Private Collection.

73. Ibid.

74. The George F. Kaufman–Marc Connelly script was a satire of Hollywood, featuring a very serious actor who was so seriously bad that he was funny. Studio executives let Merton believe he had gotten a very serious part in a tragic drama, but, unknown to him, they filmed it as a comedy. A remake of the film in 1947 starred the comedian Red Skelton.

75. Glenn Hunter to TNW, [postmarked December 8, 1918], TNW Collection, YCAL.

76. Glenn Hunter to TNW, December 23 and 26, 1918, TNW Collection, YCAL.
77. Glenn Hunter to TNW, [postmarked December 8, 1918], TNW Collection, YCAL.
78. Glenn Hunter to TNW, December 12, 1918, TNW Collection, YCAL.
79. Glenn Hunter to TNW, December 23 and 26, 1918, TNW Collection, YCAL.
80. *History of Hamden Men in the World War from Information Collected and Compiled by the Hamden War Bureau* (New Haven: Tuttle, Morehouse & Taylor Company, n.d.), ix–x.

12: "HIS OWN TUNE" (1919–1921)

1. TNW, "Student-Life at Yale Since the War," [1919?] TNW Collection, YCAL.
2. TNW to Charlotte Wilder, [Spring 1919?], TNW Collection, YCAL.
3. A story about Charlotte Niven's plans for YWCA work in Italy was carried nationally, as in the *Clearfield (Pennsylvania) Progress*, February 27, 1919.
4. Charlotte Wilder to APW and Isabella Niven Wilder, August 15, 1920, TNW Collection, YCAL, uncataloged letters.
5. ANW, 1919, ANW, Wilder Family Record, TNW Collection, YCAL.
6. William Lyon Phelps, *Autobiography with Letters* (New York: Oxford University Press, 1939), 661. Phelps had been a freshman at Yale when APW was a senior and "even then known outside of academic walls for his brilliance as an orator."
7. APW to ANW, April 25, 1919, TNW Collection, YCAL, uncataloged letters.
8. TNW, foreword to *The Angel That Troubled the Waters*, 3–7. Again, page references are to A. Tappan Wilder, *The Collected Short Plays of Thornton Wilder*, vol. 2.
9. Ibid.
10. TNW, "New Haven," unpublished semiautobiographical manuscript, n.d., TNW Collection, YCAL.
11. Ibid.
12. Fenton, *Stephen Vincent Benét*, 83–85.
13. Memories differ about what TNW worked on in this class. Wilmarth "Lefty" Lewis conjectured that it may have been the beginning of his novel *The Cabala*, which would be published in 1926, but Lewis apparently telescoped time and events, for TNW had not yet journeyed to Rome. See Wilmarth Sheldon Lewis, "Thornton Wilder," unpublished manuscript, 1947, written at the request of Clifton Fadiman, ed., *'47: The Magazine of the Year*, November 14, 1947, TNW Collection, YCAL. Lewis, who had known TNW and ANW at the Thacher School, adapted this article as a tribute to TNW and read it at his memorial service. Lewis also referred to the Canby class in his autobiography, *One Man's Education* (New York: Alfred A. Knopf, 1967), 143.
14. Donald Haberman to Isabel Wilder, August 17, 1961, TNW Collection, YCAL.
15. Fenton, *Stephen Vincent Benét*, 85.
16. Norman Fitts, *S4N* 21 (Summer 1922): 24.
17. Patterson, *History of the Class of Nineteen Hundred Twenty*, 49.
18. TNW, "SS *Independenza*," unpublished semiautobiographical manuscript, n.d., TNW Collection, YCAL.
19. APW to TNW, [Summer 1918 or 1919?], TNW Collection, YCAL
20. ANW, "Vita Notes with Special Reference to Literary Interests," November 1971, ANW, Wilder Family Record, TNW Collection, YCAL.
21. Ibid.
22. Ibid.

23. TNW to Charlotte Wilder, [Spring 1919?], TNW Collection, YCAL.
24. Ibid.
25. Isabella Niven Wilder to Bruce Simonds, August 15, 1920, TNW Collection, YCAL.
26. TNW, "SS *Independenza*," unpublished semiautobiographical manuscript, n.d., TNW Collection, YCAL.
27. Ibid.
28. Isabella Niven Wilder to Bruce Simonds, August 15, 1920, TNW Collection, YCAL. In this letter Isabella Wilder identified the SS *Providence* as the ship that took TNW to Italy. In his semiautobiographical manuscript, he called the ship the SS *Independenza*.
29. Ibid.
30. APW to ANW, April 25, 1919, TNW Collection, YCAL, uncataloged letters.
31. TNW, "SS *Independenza*," unpublished semiautobiographical manuscript, n.d., TNW Collection, YCAL.
32. Ibid.
33. Ibid.
34. Certain passages narrating the Rome experience also appear in my foreword to TNW, *The Cabala and The Woman of Andros* (New York: HarperPerennial, 2006), xi–xxv.
35. TNW, "SS *Independenza*," unpublished semiautobiographical manuscript, n.d., TNW Collection, YCAL.
36. TNW to Family from the Hotel Cocumella in Sorrento, September 25, 1920, TNW Collection, YCAL.
37. TNW, "SS *Independenza*," unpublished semiautobiographical manuscript, n.d., TNW Collection, YCAL.
38. Ibid.
39. TNW to Amos P., Isabella N., Isabel, and Janet F. Wilder, October 14, [1920?], TNW Collection, YCAL.
40. TNW to Family, September 25, 1920, [from Sorrento], TNW Collection, YCAL.
41. TNW to Family, October 4, 1920, TNW Collection, YCAL.
42. TNW to Amos P., Isabella N., Isabel, and Janet F. Wilder, October 14, [1920], TNW Collection, YCAL.
43. TNW to ANW from Sorrento, October 14, [1920?], TNW Collection, YCAL.
44. TNW to Family, October 4, 1920, TNW Collection, YCAL.
45. TNW, *Villa Rhabani: Play in Four Acts*, unpublished manuscript, TNW Collection, YCAL.
46. TNW to Family, September 25, 1920, TNW Collection, YCAL.
47. TNW to Amos P., Isabella N., Isabel, and Janet F. Wilder, October 14, [1920?], TNW Collection, YCAL.
48. TNW to Family, October 21, 1920, TNW Collection, YCAL.
49. Ibid.
50. TNW, "James Joyce and the Modern Novel," in Gallup, *American Characteristics*, 174–75.
51. TNW to Family, October 21, 1920, TNW Collection, YCAL.
52. TNW to Family, November 16, 1920, TNW Collection, YCAL.
53. TNW to Family, November 20, 1920, TNW Collection, YCAL.
54. TNW to Family, [October 15, 1920?], TNW Collection, YCAL.
55. TNW to Family, October 21, 1920, TNW Collection, YCAL.
56. TNW to Family, October 14, [1920?], TNW Collection, YCAL. (In a typescript

copy of this letter, it is noted that TNW's self-description seemed to be a postscript added to the October 14 letter. TNW Collection, YCAL, uncataloged letters.)

57. APW to TNW, [Fall 1920?], TNW Collection, YCAL.
58. Ibid.
59. Daggett, *The Record of the Class of Eighty-Four, Yale College, 1914–1936*, 146.
60. APW to TNW, [Fall 1920?], TNW Collection, YCAL.
61. Ibid.
62. Ibid.
63. Charlotte Wilder to Isabella Niven Wilder, [1920?], TNW Collection, YCAL. There are several undated letters from Charlotte in Italy to her mother and father, TNW Collection, YCAL, uncataloged letters.
64. TNW to ANW, December 13, 1920, TNW Collection, YCAL.
65. TNW to Isabel Wilder, April 4, 1921, TNW Collection, YCAL.
66. TNW to Family, October 21, 1920, TNW Collection, YCAL.
67. TNW to Isabella Niven Wilder, "Aprile" 13, 1921, TNW Collection, YCAL.
68. TNW to ANW, December 13, 1920, TNW Collection, YCAL.
69. TNW to APW, February 24, 1921, TNW Collection, YCAL.
70. TNW to APW, February 1, 1921, TNW Collection, YCAL.
71. Ibid.
72. TNW to Isabella Niven Wilder, March 10, 1921, TNW Collection, YCAL.
73. Ibid.
74. Ibid.
75. TNW to Family, March 3, 1921, TNW Collection, YCAL.
76. Ibid.
77. TNW to ANW, December 13, 1920, TNW Collection, YCAL.
78. TNW to Isabella Niven Wilder, April 13, 1921, TNW Collection, YCAL.
79. See, for instance, *SL*, 126.
80. TNW to Isabella Niven Wilder, April 13, 1921, TNW Collection, YCAL.

13: "CHOICE SOULS" (1921–1922)

1. TNW to APW, February 1, 1921, TNW Collection, YCAL.
2. Ibid.
3. APW to TNW, [March 16 or 26, 1921?], TNW Collection, YCAL.
4. Ibid.
5. TNW to APW, March 21, 1921, TNW Collection, YCAL.
6. TNW to APW, February 25, 1921, TNW Collection, YCAL.
7. APW to TNW, March 26, 1921, TNW Collection, YCAL.
8. APW to TNW, [March 16 or 26, 1921?], TNW Collection, YCAL.
9. APW to TNW, March 26, [1921?], TNW Collection, YCAL.
10. Ibid.
11. APW to TNW, April 15, 1921, TNW Collection, YCAL.
12. TNW to APW, July 30, 1921, TNW Collection, YCAL.
13. TNW to APW, June 27, [1921?], TNW Collection, YCAL. (TNW mistakenly wrote 1920.)
14. Ibid.
15. Ibid.
16. Tappan Wilder, "Afterword and Readings," in *The Cabala and The Woman of Andros*,

219. In a letter to his mother April 16, 1925, TNW confirms that in Paris in 1921, he began working on his Roman memoirs, which would evolve into his first novel, *The Cabala* (1926). See TNW to Isabella Niven Wilder, April 16, 1925, LD, TNW Collection, YCAL. (During 1924–25, TNW occasionally copied outgoing letters by hand into a letter diary.)

17. TNW, "The Memoirs of Charles Mallison: The Year in Rome," holograph manuscript, n.d., TNW Collection, YCAL.

18. TNW to APW, June 27, [1921?], TNW Collection, YCAL. TNW mistakenly wrote 1920. Whereas many people may write the number of the previous year in January, TNW seemed to make that error in June or July in several different years.

19. Ibid.

20. TNW to Isabella Niven Wilder, [August 1921?], TNW Collection, YCAL.

21. Quoted in Noel Riley Fitch, *Sylvia Beach and the Lost Generation: A History of Literary Paris in the Twenties and Thirties* (New York: W. W. Norton & Company, 1983), 81–82. Sylvia Beach recalled erroneously that Isabel Wilder also came into her shop with TNW in 1921. Isabel's visits must have come at a later time.

22. See Richard Ellmann, *James Joyce: New and Revised Edition* (Oxford and New York: Oxford University Press, 1983) 502–8, for background on the trial and the eventual publication of *Ulysses*.

23. Meeting James Joyce: TNW to Bill Bissell, August 20, 1923, TNW Collection, YCAL. "Self-imposed exile," TNW, "James Joyce, 1882–1941," in Gallup, *American Characteristics*, 167.

24. TNW, "Joyce and the Modern Novel," ibid., 172.

25. Edmund Wilson (Leon Edel, ed), *The Twenties* (New York: Farrar, Straus & Giroux, 1975), 94.

26. See Edmund Wilson, "Thornton Wilder," *The Shores of Light: A Literary Chronicle of the Twenties and Thirties* (New York: Farrar, Straus & Young, 1952; reprint, Boston, Northeastern University Press, 1985), 384–91, for a discussion of Proust's influence on Wilder's fiction.

27. TNW, Journal, September 28, 1922, TNW Collection, YCAL.

28. Ibid.

29. TNW, "Some Thoughts on Playwrighting," in Augusto Centeno, ed., *The Intent of the Artist* (Princeton: Princeton University Press, 1941); reprinted in Gallup, *American Characteristics*, 115, 120, 122.

30. TNW to APW, June 8, 1921, TNW Collection, YCAL.

31. APW to TNW, June 22, [1921?], TNW Collection, YCAL.

32. APW to TNW, June 27, [1921?], TNW Collection, YCAL.

33. Ibid.

34. APW to TNW, July 12, [1921?], TNW Collection, YCAL. Blair Academy was founded in 1848 by John Insley Blair, a railroad tycoon who endowed the school with money and hilltop land—435 acres just outside Blairstown, New Jersey. The academy educated boys and girls until 1915, when it became a boys' school only (a situation that would be reversed in 1970).

35. TNW to APW, July 30, 1921, TNW Collection, YCAL.

36. Ibid.

37. APW to TNW, August 5, 1921, TNW Collection, YCAL.

38. Ibid.

39. TWN to Isabella Niven Wilder, [August 1921?], TNW Collection, YCAL.

40. TNW to APW, July 30, 1921, TNW Collection, YCAL.

41. TNW to Charles Wager, November 4, 1921, TNW Collection, YCAL.

42. TNW to APW, October 3, 1921, TNW Collection, YCAL.

43. TNW to APW, November 11, 1921, TNW Collection, YCAL.

44. TNW to Charles Wager, November 4, 1921, *SL*, 151–52.

45. TNW to APW, March 4, [1922?], TNW Collection, YCAL.

46. TNW to E. C. Foresman, June 28, 1922, TNW Collection, YCAL.

47. TNW to Isabella Niven Wilder, September 19, 1922, TNW Collection, YCAL.

48. ANW, "Vita Notes with Special Reference to Literary Interests, November 1971," typescript, ANW Family Record, Private Collection. Also see ANW, "Albert Schweitzer and the New Testament in the Perspective of Today," in Abraham Aaron Roback, ed., *In Albert Schweitzer's Realms: A Symposium* (Cambridge, MA: Sci-Art, 1962), 361–62.

49. TNW to APW, July 20, 1922, TNW Collection, YCAL.

50. TNW to Isabella Niven Wilder, July 20, 1922, TNW Collection, YCAL.

51. TNW to Charlotte Wilder, July 21, 1922, TNW Collection, YCAL.

52. "Mists": TNW to APW, July 20, 1922, TNW Collection, YCAL; "wild and up-thrusting": TNW to APW, July 31, 1922, TNW Collection, YCAL.

53. TNW to APW, July 31, 1922, TNW Collection, YCAL.

54. TNW, "A House in the Country," 1922 typescript, TNW Collection, YCAL.

55. TNW to Isabella Niven Wilder, March 10, 1922, TNW Collection, YCAL. TNW may also have been working on *Précautions Inutiles*, another short story, during this time. This story is published in J. D. McClatchy, ed., *Thornton Wilder: The Bridge of San Luis Rey and Other Novels 1926–1948* (New York: Library of America, 2009), 631–34.

56. TNW to APW, July 20, 1922, TNW Collection, YCAL.

57. TNW to Isabella Niven Wilder, July 20, 1922, TNW Collection, YCAL.

58. TNW to APW, July 20, 1922, TNW Collection, YCAL.

59. The Italian artist Properzia (born in 1495) had been greatly admired for her carvings, the best-known of which was a *Gloria of Saints* with more than sixty minuscule heads carved with precision on a single cherrystone. Elizabeth Barrett Browning, in her *Essays on the English Poets and the Greek Christian Poets* (1889), praised the writing of Alexander Pope for its "exquisite balancing of sounds and phrases" and its "glorifying of commonplaces by antithetic processes," summarizing his style as "this Indian jugglery and Indian carving upon—cherry-stones!" Samuel Johnson addressed his comment to Hannah More (1745–1833), a British author, critic, educator, and philanthropist, who opposed slavery and wrote evangelical tracts and good-conduct manuals.

60. TNW, "Sentences," *Double Dealer*, September 1922, 110. The literary magazine was established, according to the *New York Times Book Review* in July 1921, to be "a national magazine from the South," designed to offset "a certain disquietude" in the region "over the lack of its intellectual outlets."

61. TNW to "The Editors of The Dial," August 3, 1922, TNW Collection, YCAL. A French writer and diplomat born in Russia, Morand (1888–1976) wrote novels, short stories, poetry, screenplays, biography, and travel narratives.

62. TNW to Isabella Niven Wilder, August 22, 1922, TNW Collection, YCAL.

63. TNW, Journal, September 8, 1922, TNW Collection, YCAL. As noted above,

TNW's surviving early journals are unpublished, and while the journal entries are usually dated, he did not begin numbering them until October 11, 1926.

64. TNW to Isabella Niven Wilder, November 5, 1922, TNW Collection, YCAL.
65. TNW to Isabella Niven Wilder, September 19, 1922, TNW Collection, YCAL.
66. TNW to APW, February 17, 19[22?], TNW Collection, YCAL. (Letter is headed "Davis House, Lawrenceville, Feb. 17, 1921," but TNW was in Paris then.)
67. TNW to Isabella Niven Wilder, November 5, 1922, TNW Collection, YCAL.
68. Ibid. This is the "first sighting" of TNW's plans to write the story of Julius Caesar, documenting the earliest recorded date of his concept for a novel he would bring to fruition twenty-six years later as *The Ides of March*. This is notable in and of itself, and also because, as will be seen, this date refutes and disproves an accusation that TNW stole the idea from a young novelist in the late 1930s or 1940s.
69. Ibid.

14: "ALL MY FAULTS AND VIRTUES" (1922–1923)

1. TNW to APW, February 7, 1923, TNW Collection, YCAL.
2. APW to TNW, February 13 [1922?], TNW Collection, YCAL.
3. TWN, Journal, September 12, 1922, TNW Collection, YCAL.
4. TNW, Journal, September 15, 1922, TNW Collection, YCAL.
5. TNW, Journal, September 5, 1922, TNW Collection, YCAL.
6. Ibid.
7. TNW, Journal, September 11, 1922, TNW Collection, YCAL.
8. TNW, Journal, September 12, 1922, TNW Collection, YCAL.
9. TNW, Journal, September 11, 1922, TNW Collection, YCAL.
10. TNW, Journal, September 29, 1922, TNW Collection, YCAL.
11. Ibid.
12. TNW, Journal, September 9, 1922, TNW Collection, YCAL.
13. TNW to Isabella Niven Wilder, May 16, 1923, TNW Collection, YCAL.
14. TNW, Journal, September 4, 1922, TNW Collection, YCAL.
15. TNW, Journal, September 22, 1922, TNW Collection, YCAL.
16. Charlotte Wilder to Isabella Niven Wilder, [January 1921?], TNW Collection, YCAL, uncataloged letters.
17. TNW to Isabella Niven Wilder, March 26, 1923, TNW Collection, YCAL.
18. APW to TNW, n.d., TNW Collection, YCAL.
19. TNW to APW, May 5, 1923, TNW Collection, YCAL.
20. TNW, "James Joyce, 1882–1941," in Gallup, *American Characteristics*, 168.
21. TNW to Isabella Niven Wilder, November 19, 1922, TNW Collection, YCAL.
22. APW to Charlotte Wilder, May 19, 1923, TNW Collection, YCAL, uncataloged letters.
23. TNW to Isabella Niven Wilder, March 10, 1922, TNW Collection, YCAL.
24. TNW to Gwynne [Mrs. Mather] Abbott, May 4, 1923, LB, TNW Collection, YCAL. From May 1 to December 30, 1923, TNW copied most of his outgoing letters by hand into a letter book.
25. Isabel Wilder, "A Handfull [*sic*] of Facts," n.d., TNW Collection, YCAL.
26. Isabel Wilder to TNW, [June 1923?], TNW Collection, YCAL. Isabel writes in the

letter that she is twenty-three and a half. She would have turned twenty-three in January 1923.

27. Ibid.

28. TNW to Mame Gammon, May 10, 1923, LB, TNW Collection, YCAL.

29. TNW to Barbara Leighton, July 9, 1923, LB, TNW Collection, YCAL.

30. ANW was an outstanding tennis player for most of his life. In 1920, at Yale, as has been noted, he and Lee Wiley won the National Intercollegiate Doubles Championship in lawn tennis. In June 1922 Amos and his Oxford partner, Charles Kingsley, played Centre Court at Wimbledon, losing to the Australian team who went on to win the doubles championship. In 1977, when Wimbledon celebrated its one-hundredth anniversary, Dr. Amos Niven Wilder, at the age of ninety, was recognized as the oldest living person to have played Wimbledon's Centre Court.

31. TNW to Isabella Niven Wilder, March 10, 1922, TNW Collection.

32. Ibid.

33. TNW to Isabella Niven Wilder, February 10, 1923, TNW Collection, YCAL.

34. TNW to Charlotte Wilder, n.d., TNW Collection, YCAL.

35. Ibid.

36. TNW to Isabella Niven Wilder, February 10, 1923, TNW Collection, YCAL.

37. Ibid.

38. Ibid.

39. TNW to Isabella Niven Wilder, April 21, 1923, TNW Collection, YCAL.

40. Ibid.

41. TNW to APW, April 18, 1923, TNW Collection, YCAL.

42. TNW to Norman Fitts, May 1, 1923, LB, TNW Collection, YCAL.

43. Ibid.

44. TNW to Norman Fitts, June 7, 1923, LB, TNW Collection, YCAL.

45. TNW to Edith Isaacs, May 3, 1923, LB, TNW Collection, YCAL.

46. Ibid.

47. Ibid.

48. TNW to ANW, June 12, 1923, LB, TNW Collection, YCAL.

49. TNW to Isabella Niven Wilder, June 5, 1923, LB, TNW Collection, YCAL.

50. Ibid.

51. Charlotte Wilder to ANW, July 5, 1923, TNW Collection, YCAL, uncataloged letters.

52. TNW to APW, July 9, 1923, LB, TNW Collection, YCAL.

53. TNW to Jim Lane, [June 24, 1923?], LB, TNW Collection, YCAL.

54. TNW to Isabella Niven Wilder, July 2, 1923, LB, TNW Collection, YCAL.

55. TNW to Isabella Niven Wilder, August 15, 1923, LB, TNW Collection, YCAL.

56. TNW to Isabella Niven Wilder, July 2, 1923, LB, TNW Collection, YCAL.

57. TNW to Gilbert McCoy Troxell, July 10, 1923, LB, TNW Collection, YCAL.

58. TNW to William I. Nichols, July 27, 1923, LB, TNW Collection, YCAL.

59. TNW to Bill Bissell, August 20, 1923, LB, TNW Collection, YCAL.

60. TNW to Gwynne [Mrs. Mather] Abbott, August 28, 1923, LB, TNW Collection, YCAL.

61. TNW to Bill Bissell, August 20, 1923, LB, TNW Collection, YCAL.

62. TNW to Gwynne [Mrs. Mather] Abbott, August 28, 1923, LB, TNW Collection, YCAL.

63. TNW to Edith Isaacs, August 4, 1923, LB, TNW Collection, YCAL.

64. TNW to Gwynne Abbott, August 27, 1923, LB, TNW Collection, YCAL. Gwynne Abbott was the daughter of Mrs. Mather Abbott, above.
65. "Professional theatre-goer": TNW to William I. "Bill" Nichols, September 19, 1923, LB, TNW Collection, YCAL. "My dear School": TNW to Isabella Niven Wilder, August 15, 1923, LB, TNW Collection, YCAL.
66. TNW to Barbara Leighton, July 9, 1923, LB, TNW Collection, YCAL.
67. TNW to APW, July 21, 1923, LB, TNW Collection, YCAL.
68. TNW to APW, August 5, 1923, LB, TNW Collection, YCAL.
69. TNW to Isabella Niven Wilder, May 15, 1923, LB, TNW Collection, YCAL.
70. TNW to Bill Bissell, August 20, 1923, LB, TNW Collection, YCAL.
71. Ibid.

15: "MILLSTONES" (1923–1925)

1. APW to TNW, September 25, 1923, LB, TNW Collection, YCAL.
2. Ibid.
3. TNW to ANW, October 2, 1925, TNW Collection, YCAL.
4. ANW to Charlotte Wilder, June 29, [1923?], TNW Collection, YCAL, uncataloged letters.
5. Ibid.
6. Isabella Niven Wilder to TNW, October 26, 1923, LB, TNW Collection, YCAL.
7. Jeanne-Françoise de Récamier (1777–1849) was the vivacious hostess of a literary and artistic salon in early nineteenth-century French society.
8. TNW to Isabella Niven Wilder, October 29, 1923, LB, TNW Collection, YCAL.
9. Ibid.
10. Isabella Niven Wilder to TNW, November 1, 1923, LB, TNW Collection, YCAL.
11. TNW to Mrs. Hildegarde Donaldson, December 3, 1923, LB, TNW Collection, YCAL.
12. TNW to Leslie Glenn, October 9, 1923, LB, TNW Collection, YCAL.
13. TNW to Isabella Niven Wilder, November 19, 1923, LB, TNW Collection, YCAL.
14. TNW to Isabella Niven Wilder, October 23, 1923, LB, TNW Collection, YCAL.
15. Ibid.
16. TNW to Isabella Niven Wilder, November 6, 1923, LB, TNW Collection, YCAL.
17. TNW to Family, December 2, 1923, LB, TNW Collection, YCAL.
18. TNW to G. M. Troxell, November 27, 1923, LB, TNW Collection, YCAL.
19. TNW to Stark Young, November 2, 1923, LB, TNW Collection, YCAL.
20. TNW to Isabella Niven Wilder, December 18, 1923, LB, TNW Collection, YCAL.
21. TNW to Stark Young, December 18, 1923, LB, TNW Collection, YCAL.
22. TNW to Bill Bissell, Christmas 1923, LB, TNW Collection, YCAL.
23. TNW, "Notes," LD, February 5, 1924, TNW Collection, YCAL.
24. TNW to Isabella Niven Wilder, March 16, 1924, TNW Collection, YCAL.
25. APW to TNW, February 13, [1924?], TNW Collection, YCAL.
26. Isabel Wilder to Ted [Wilder?], May 24, 1924, TNW Collection, YCAL. Despite every effort to establish the last name of this correspondent, we are left with the conjecture that it was Theodore Wilder, TNW's friend from Chefoo and Oberlin days. Ted Wilder was not a relative.
27. APW to TNW, February 13, [1924?], TNW Collection, YCAL.
28. Ibid.

29. Isabel Wilder to Ted [Wilder?], [September 1925?], TNW Collection, YCAL.

30. APW to unidentified member of his family, most likely TNW; handwritten note on reverse of a letter from Dr. George Blumer to APW, April 16, 1924, Private Collection.

31. Dr. George Blumer to APW, April 16, 1924, Private Collection.

32. APW to TNW, February 13, [1924?], TNW Collection, YCAL.

33. Ibid.

34. Ibid.

35. TNW to Isabella Niven Wilder, May 6, 1924, TNW Collection, YCAL.

36. TNW to Isabella Niven Wilder, May 25, 1924, TNW Collection, YCAL.

37. TNW to Phil Thomas, May 10, 1925, LB, TNW Collection, YCAL.

38. Ibid.

39. TNW to J. P. Monod, January 22, 1925, LD, TNW Collection, YCAL.

40. TNW to Ethel Andrews Murphy, January 20 [TNW wrote "December" by mistake], 1925, LD, TNW Collection, YCAL.

41. TNW to Margaret Whitney, March 16, 1925, LD, TNW Collection, YCAL.

42. TNW to Isabella Niven Wilder, August 14, 1924, TNW Collection, YCAL.

43. TNW to Isabella Niven Wilder, December 2, 1924, TNW Collection, YCAL.

44. For background see Judith Ann Schiff, "Old Yale: Before He Came to Dinner," *Yale Alumni* magazine, April 1999; and "Yale Workshop," *Time*, Monday, December 8, 1924.

45. TNW to Ethel Andrews Murphy, January 20, 1925 [TNW wrote "December" by mistake in his Letter Diary], LD, TNW Collection, YCAL.

46. TNW to APW, February 4, 1925, LD, TNW Collection, YCAL.

47. TNW to Edith Isaacs, January 30, 1925, LD, TNW Collection, YCAL.

48. TNW to Edwin Arlington Robinson, March 31, 1925, LD, TNW Collection, YCAL.

49. TNW's record, Princeton University, March 2, 1925, Seeley G. Mudd Manuscript Library, Princeton University.

50. TNW to Isabel Wilder, February 13, 1925, LD, TNW Collection, YCAL.

51. TNW to Edith Isaacs, January 18, 1925, LD, TNW Collection, YCAL.

52. Ibid.

53. Edith Isaacs to TNW, January 26 [1925], LD, TNW Collection, YCAL.

54. TNW, "The Turn of the Year," *Theatre Arts Monthly* 9, no. 3 (March 1925): 143–44.

55. Ibid., 151.

56. Baer was heir to the Stix-Baer Department Store fortune in St. Louis, Missouri, and most likely secured his job with the Boni brothers by investing in their firm.

57. TNW to Lewis Baer, Feburary 14, 1925, LD, TNW Collection, YCAL.

58. Lewis Baer to TNW, March 3, 1925, LD, TNW Collection, YCAL.

59. TNW to Edith Isaacs, March 11, 1925, LD, TNW Collection, YCAL.

60. TNW, "Bibliography," LD, [1927?], TNW Collection, YCAL.

61. TNW to Bill Bissell, March 16, 1925, LD, TNW Collection, YCAL.

62. TNW to Helen M. Allen, April 13, 1925, LD, TNW Collection, YCAL.

63. TNW to Isabella Niven Wilder, April 16, 1925, LD, TNW Collection, YCAL.

64. Proust's seven volumes: *Swann's Way, In the Shadow of Young Girls in Flower, The Guermantes Way, Sodom and Gomorrah, The Prisoner, The Fugitive,* and *Finding Time Again*.

65. TNW to Lewis Baer, April 21, 1925, LD, TNW Collection, YCAL.

66. Ibid.

67. TNW to Lewis Baer, April 1925, LD, TNW Collection, YCAL.

68. TNW to Lewis Baer, May 7, 1925, LD, TNW Collection, YCAL.
69. TNW to Phil Thomas, May 10, 1925, LD, TNW Collection, YCAL.
70. Dr. James Semans to PEN, 2002. Dr. Semans was a student at the Lawrenceville School when TNW was teaching there.
71. TNW to Isabella Niven Wilder, June 12, 1925, LD, TNW Collection, YCAL.
72. TNW to Isabella Niven Wilder, May 21, 1925, LD, TNW Collection, YCAL.

16: "THE 'WAY WITHIN'" (1925–1926)

1. TNW to Bruce Simonds, June 15, 1925, LD, TNW Collection, YCAL.
2. Ibid.
3. TNW to Family, April 11, 1922, TNW Collection, YCAL.
4. TNW to Bruce Simonds, June 15, 1925, LD, TNW Collection, YCAL.
5. TNW to Miss Whitney, [Summer 1925?], LD, TNW Collection, YCAL.
6. TNW to Isabella Niven Wilder, [Summer 1925?], TNW Collection, YCAL.
7. Ibid.
8. Ibid.
9. TNW to Amy Wertheimer, October 8, 1925, TNW Collection, YCAL.
10. Ibid.
11. Ibid.
12. Ames was the star fullback of the Princeton University football team during the 1890s and became a successful businessman and publisher in Chicago. He committed suicide during the Depression.
13. TNW to Rosemary Ames, January 6, 1925, LD, TNW Collection, YCAL.
14. TNW to Miss Whitney, [Summer 1925?], LD, TNW Collection, YCAL.
15. TNW to Isabella Niven Wilder, [Summer 1925?], TNW Collection, YCAL.
16. Ibid.
17. TNW to Amy Wertheimer, October 20, [1925?], TNW Collection, YCAL. (TNW wrote 1924 by mistake.)
18. Isabel Wilder to Ted [Wilder?], [September 26, 1925?], TNW Collection, YCAL.
19. ANW, Oberlin College Biographical Form, Oberlin College Records.
20. TNW to ANW, October 2, 1925, TNW Collection, YCAL.
21. Isabel Wilder to Ted [Wilder?], [September 26, 1925?], TNW Collection, YCAL.
22. Ibid.
23. ANW, "Vita Notes with Special Reference to Literary Interests," n.d., ANW, Wilder Family Record, TNW Collection, YCAL.
24. Isabel Wilder to Ted [Wilder?], [September 26, 1925?], TNW Collection, YCAL.
25. TNW to Warren Dolben, October 3, 1925, LD, TNW Collection, YCAL.
26. TNW to Ann Harding, October 16, 1925, LD, TNW Collection, YCAL.
27. TNW to Amy Wertheimer, October 28, 1925, TNW Collection, YCAL.
28. TNW to Amy Wertheimer, November 23, 1925, TNW Collection, YCAL.
29. TNW to Amy Wertheimer, October 28, 1925, TNW Collection, YCAL.
30. TNW to Amy Wertheimer, October 13, 1925, TNW Collection, YCAL.
31. Ibid.
32. TNW to Isabella Niven Wilder ["Dearest of Mothers"], November 2, 1925, TNW Collection, YCAL.
33. TNW to Amy Wertheimer, November 23, 1925, TNW Collection, YCAL.

34. TNW to Richard Boleslavsky, November 16, 1925, LD, TNW Collection, YCAL.

35. TNW to Amy Wertheimer, October 13, 1925, TNW Collection, YCAL.

36. TNW to Amy Wertheimer, December 20, 1925, TNW Collection, YCAL.

37. TNW to Amy Wertheimer, October 28, 1925, TNW Collection, YCAL.

38. TNW to Isabella Niven Wilder, November 2, 1925, TNW Collection, YCAL.

39. TNW to Rosemary Ames, [November 19, 1925?], TNW Collection, YCAL.

40. Ibid.

41. TNW to ANW, December 20, 1925, TNW Collection, YCAL.

42. TNW to Isabella Niven Wilder, February 10, 1923, TNW Collection, YCAL.

43. Charlotte Wilder to ANW, [January 6, 1925?], Private Collection.

44. TNW to Amy Wertheimer, January 5, 1926, TNW Collection, YCAL.

45. TNW to Amy Wertheimer, January 8, 1926, TNW Collection, YCAL.

46. TNW to Amy Wertheimer, January 12, 1926, TNW Collection, YCAL.

47. TNW, Journal, [between November 20 and December 2, 1926?], TNW Collection, YCAL.

48. TNW to Amy Wertheimer, February 7, 1926, TNW Collection, YCAL.

49. TNW to Amy Wertheimer, November 4, 1925, TNW Collection, YCAL.

50. TNW to Amy Wertheimer, January 20, 1926, TNW Collection, YCAL.

51. TNW's choice of pronunciation and spelling was noted in *Bookman*, March 1928, 78.

52. TNW to Amy Wertheimer, January 5, 1926, TNW Collection, YCAL.

53. TNW to Amy Wertheimer, February 7, 1926, TNW Collection, YCAL.

54. TNW to Amy Wertheimer, January 8, 1926, TNW Collection, YCAL.

55. TNW to Amy Wertheimer, February 7, 1926, TNW Collection, YCAL.

56. Ibid.

57. TNW to Amy Wertheimer, January 31, 1926, TNW Collection, YCAL.

58. TNW to Amy Wertheimer, February 14, 1926, TNW Collection, YCAL.

59. Ibid.

60. TNW to Amy Wertheimer, February 21, 1926, TNW Collection, YCAL.

61. TNW to Amy Wertheimer, January 20, 1926, TNW Collection, YCAL.

62. Ibid.

63. TNW to Amy Wertheimer, February 25, 1926, TNW Collection, YCAL.

64. Ibid.

65. TNW to Amy Wertheimer, February 28, 1926, TNW Collection, YCAL.

66. TNW to Rosemary Ames, May 9, 1926, TNW Collection, YCAL.

67. Ibid.

68. TNW to Rosemary Ames, July 4, 1925, TNW Collection, YCAL.

69. TNW to Isabella Niven Wilder, March 23, 1926, TNW Collection, YCAL.

70. TNW listed the following plays: *Cecilia*, a three-act play he wrote at Berkeley High School and destroyed; *The Skyrocket*, a four-act comedy-drama written at Oberlin and, he wrote, "destroyed," although *The Rocket*, a four-act play from his Oberlin days, survives among his papers; *The Dreamers*, a "Ballad play," written at Yale, which survives; *The Exiles*, the three-act play set in China, written at Yale; *The Trumpet Shall Sound*; *The Wedding Breakfast*, a three-act comedy written at Yale, where it won a prize, although the manuscript was lost by William Lyon Phelps, who was one of the judges; *Villa Rhabani*, set in Capri, a full-length play that according to TNW was best forgotten; and *Geraldine de Gray*.

71. TNW to Isabella Niven Wilder, March 23, 1926, TNW Collection, YCAL.

72. TNW to Charles A. Wager, May 25, 1926, TNW Collection, YCAL.
73. TNW, "The Memoirs of Charles Mallison: The Year in Rome," undated manuscript, TNW Collection, YCAL. A portion of this manuscript is published in the Afterword in TNW, *The Cabala and The Woman of Andros*, 219–22.
74. TNW to Isabella Niven Wilder, February 10, 1923, TNW Collection, YCAL.
75. TNW, *The Cabala and The Woman of Andros*, 61–62.
76. TNW to Claus Clüver, May 29, 1961, copy of letter enclosed in Jürgen Wolter to Jackson R. Bryer, March 3, 1989, Private Collection.
77. TNW, *The Cabala*, 4.
78. Ibid., 72.
79. Ibid., 76.
80. Ibid., 70–94.
81. Ibid., 133.
82. Ibid., 133–34.
83. Ibid., 134.
84. "Mordant": TNW to Isabella Niven Wilder, February 10, 1923, TNW Collection, YCAL.
85. TNW, *The Cabala*, 107.

17: "MY REAL VOCATION" (1926–1927)

1. TNW to ANW, April 25, 1926, TNW Collection, YCAL.
2. Ibid.
3. Ibid.
4. Ibid.
5. Theodore Purdy, Jr., "Mr. Wilder's *Cabala*," *Saturday Review of Literature*, May 8, 1926, 771.
6. John Farrar, as JF, "Brilliant, Bitter, Imaginative," *Bookman* 63, June, 1926, 478.
7. Agnes Repplier, "The Cabala," *Commonweal* 4 (August 25, 1926): 391–92.
8. TNW to Marie Townson, September 15, 1926, TNW Collection, YCAL.
9. William Lyon Phelps, "As I Like It," *Scribner's Magazine* 80 (August 1926): 224–31.
10. Charles A. Wager to TNW, May 23, 1926, TNW Collection, YCAL.
11. TNW to Charles A. Wager, May 25, 1926, TNW Collection, YCAL.
12. Ibid.
13. TNW to Amy Wertheimer, June 21, 1926, TNW Collection, YCAL.
14. TNW to Amy Wertheimer, March 29, 1926, TNW Collection, YCAL.
15. TNW to Amy Wertheimer, April 5, 1926, TNW Collection, YCAL.
16. TNW to Amy Wertheimer, April 22, 1926, TNW Collection, YCAL.
17. TNW to Amy Wertheimer, April 25, 1926, TNW Collection, YCAL.
18. TNW to Amy Wertheimer, August 15, 1926, TNW Collection, YCAL.
19. TNW to Amy Wertheimer, May 23, 1926, TNW Collection, YCAL. "Fox Film Company . . .": TNW to Amy Wertheimer, June 6, 1926, TNW Collection, YCAL.
20. TNW to Isabella Niven Wilder, June 10, 1926, TNW Collection, YCAL.
21. TNW to Amy Wertheimer, June 21, 1926, TNW Collection, YCAL.
22. Ibid.
23. TNW to Amy Wertheimer, July 5, 1926, TNW Collection, YCAL.
24. TNW to Marie Townson, August 12, 1926, TNW Collection, YCAL.

25. TNW to Amy Wertheimer, July 8, 1926, TNW Collection, YCAL.

26. Ibid.

27. TNW to Marie Townson, August 12, 1926, TNW Collection, YCAL.

28. Ibid.

29. TNW to Isabella Niven Wilder, August 19, 1926, TNW Collection, YCAL.

30. Charlotte Wilder, "In a Corner of France," August 16, 1926, TNW Collection, YCAL, uncataloged manuscript.

31. TNW to Marie Townson, September 15, 1926, TNW Collection, YCAL.

32. TNW to Amy Wertheimer, April 11, 1926, TNW Collection, YCAL.

33. TNW to Isabella Niven Wilder, June 19, 1926, TNW Collection, YCAL.

34. TNW to Douglas Townson, August 28, 1926, TNW Collection, YCAL.

35. TNW to Amy Wertheimer, July 8, 1926, TNW Collection, YCAL.

36. TNW to APW, July 14, 1926, TNW Collection, YCAL.

37. TNW to Family, October 25, 1926, TNW Collection, YCAL.

38. Ibid.

39. TNW, Journal, October 11, 1926, TNW Collection, YCAL.

40. TNW to William I. "Bill" Nichols, October 18, 1926, Nichols Papers, LC.

41. TNW to Family, October 25, 1926, TNW Collection, YCAL.

42. TNW, Journal, October 11, 1926, TNW Collection, YCAL.

43. TNW, Journal, October 14, 1926, TNW Collection, YCAL.

44. TNW to APW, November 12, 1926, TNW Collection, YCAL.

45. TNW, Journal, [October 1926?], TNW Collection, YCAL.

46. TNW to Bill Nichols, October 13, 1926, Nichols Papers, LC.

47. TNW to Isabella Niven Wilder, [October 22, 1926?], TNW Collection, YCAL.

48. TNW to Amy Wertheimer, October 25, 1926, TNW Collection, YCAL.

49. TNW to Douglas C. Townson, [October/November 1926?], TNW Collection, YCAL.

50. TNW to Family, October 25, 1926, TNW Collection, YCAL.

51. TNW to Bill Nichols, October 13, 1926, Nichols Papers, LC.

52. TNW to Henry R. Luce, September 9, 1926, TNW Collection, YCAL.

53. TNW, *The Bridge of San Luis Rey* (New York: HarperPerennial, 2003), 16.

54. TNW to Doug and Marie Townson, November 4, 1926, TNW Collection, YCAL.

55. TNW to APW, November 12, 1926, TNW Collection, YCAL.

56. TNW to APW, October 25, 1926, TNW Collection, YCAL.

57. TNW to Douglas and Marie Townson, November 4, 1926, TNW Collection, YCAL.

58. TNW to Amy Wertheimer, November 2, 1926, TNW Collection, YCAL.

59. TNW to Isabella Niven Wilder, November 6, 1926, TNW Collection, YCAL.

60. TNW to Bill Nichols, November 3, 1926, Nichols Papers, LC.

61. Ibid.

62. TNW to Bill Nichols, [December 1926?], Nichols Papers, LC.

63. TNW to Family, October 25, 1926, TNW Collection, YCAL.

64. Ibid.

65. TNW to Family, November 28, 1926, TNW Collection, YCAL.

66. Hemingway took his novel's epigraph from his good friend in Paris, Gertrude Stein, whom TNW would not meet and befriend until years later, in Chicago rather than Paris.

67. TNW to Isabella Niven Wilder and daughters, November 28, 1926, TNW Collection, YCAL.

68. TNW to Isabella Niven Wilder, [December 1926?], TNW Collection, YCAL. The Hemingways had separated because of his affair with Pauline Pfeiffer. The Hemingways were divorced on January 17, 1927, after six months of separation, and Hemingway married Pauline Pfeiffer on May 10, 1927.

69. TNW to Isabella Niven Wilder and daughters, November 28, 1926, TNW Collection, YCAL.

70. TNW to Isabella Niven Wilder, [December 9, 1926?], TNW Collection, YCAL.

71. Ibid.

72. TNW to Isabella Niven Wilder, [December 9, 1926?], TNW Collection, YCAL.

73. TNW to Ernest Hemingway, November 9, 1926 [dated in holograph that may not be TNW's handwriting], *SL*, 193–94. It is unclear whether TNW read the play, or Hemingway sent it to Boleslavsky.

74. TNW to Amy Wertheimer, November 30, 1926, TNW Collection, YCAL.

75. TNW to Amy Wertheimer, December 13, 1926, TNW Collection, YCAL.

76. Ibid.

77. TNW to Ernest Hemingway, November 9, 1926, *SL*, 193–94.

78. TNW to Isabella Niven Wilder and daughters, November 28, 1926, TNW Collection, YCAL.

79. Ibid.

80. TNW to Isabella Niven Wilder, [December 9, 1926?], TNW Collection, YCAL. "Pack of Rhodes Scholars . . .": TNW to Marie and Doug Townson, March 12, 1927, TNW Collection, YCAL.

81. TNW to Marie and Doug Townson, March 12, 1927, TNW Collection, YCAL.

82. TNW to Isabella Niven Wilder, [December 9, 1926?], TNW Collection, YCAL.

83. Ibid.

84. Richard Boleslavsky to HKS [Herbert K. Stockton], June 6, 1926, quoted by Ronald Arthur Willis, "The American Laboratory Theatre, 1923–1930" (Ph.D. thesis, University of Iowa, June 1968), 146. Herbert K. Stockton was treasurer of the Trustees of the American Laboratory Theatre, according to the ALT program for 1926–27.

85. TNW to Isabella Niven Wilder and daughters, November 28, 1926, TNW Collection, YCAL.

86. The other plays were *The Sea Woman's Cloak* by Amelie Rives, Princess Troubetzkoy; and *The Straw Hat*, a "Farce Comedy with Music" adapted by Paul Tulane and Agnes Hamilton James from the French play by Eugène Labiche.

87. "New American Play Is Quite Fantastic," *New York Times*, December 11, 1926, 15.

88. TNW, *Theophilus North* (New York: HarperPerennial, 2003), 56.

89. "New American Play Is Quite Fantastic," *New York Times*, December 11, 1926, 15.

90. TNW to Marie and Doug Townson, March 12, 1927, TNW Collection, YCAL.

91. TNW to Madam Kelly Wilder, December 30, 1926, TNW Collection, YCAL.

92. TNW to Bill Nichols, February 4, 1927, *SL*, 202–5.

93. TNW to Marie and Doug Townson, March 12, 1927, TNW Collection, YCAL.

18: DR. JEKYLL AND MR. HYDE (1927)

1. TNW to Bill Nichols, February 4, 1927, *SL*, 202–5.

2. TNW to Amy Wertheimer, February 15, 1927, TNW Collection, YCAL.

3. TNW to Bill Nichols, February 4, 1927, *SL*, 202–5.

4. Ibid.

5. TNW, Journal, November 11, 1926, TNW Collection, YCAL.

6. TNW, Journal, October 11, 1926, TNW Collection, YCAL.

7. TNW, Journal, Entry 33, [between November 20 and December 2, 1926?], TNW Collection, YCAL.

8. TNW to Bill Nichols, [Spring 1927?], Nichols Papers, LC.

9. TNW to Bill Nichols, [1927?], Nichols Papers, LC.

10. TNW to Bill Nichols, February 16, 1927, *SL*, 205–7.

11. TNW to Amy Wertheimer, March 14, 1927, TNW Collection, YCAL.

12. TNW to ANW, [March 1927?], TNW Collection, YCAL.

13. TNW to Bill Nichols, July 3, 1927, Nichols Papers, LC.

14. TNW to Bill Nichols, April 16, 1927, Nichols Papers, LC.

15. TNW to Bill Nichols, March 15, 1927, Nichols Papers, LC.

16. Ibid.

17. TNW to Bill Nichols, March 23, 1927, Nichols Papers, LC. Jouve's first novel was the story, set in Italy, of the illicit love affair between Count Michele Cantarini and the woman reputed to be the most beautiful in Milan.

18. TNW to Bill Nichols, February 16, 1927, *SL*, 205–7.

19. TNW to Bill Nichols, February 27, 1927, Nichols Papers, LC.

20. Ibid.

21. TNW to Bill Nichols, March 15, 1927, Nichols Papers, LC.

22. TNW to Bill Nichols, February 27, 1927, Nichols Papers, LC.

23. TNW to Bill Nichols, March 23, 1927, Nichols Papers, LC.

24. TNW to ANW, March 7, 1927, TNW Collection, YCAL.

25. Lewis Baer to TNW, March 21, 1927, TNW Collection, YCAL.

26. Lewis Baer to TNW, March 30, 1927, TNW Collection, YCAL.

27. Quoted phrases from TNW to Isabella Niven Wilder, January 10, 1927, TNW Collection, YCAL.

28. Edward Weeks to Ruth Gordon and Garson Kanin, July 20, 1977, enclosing the typescript of a proposed Chautauqua lecture on TNW, to be given in August 1977. TNW Collection, YCAL.

29. TNW to Edward Weeks, June 3, 1927, TS, TNW Collection, YCAL.

30. Ibid.

31. TNW to Isabella Niven Wilder, March 29, 1927, TNW Collection, YCAL. TNW often referred to the older firm, Boni & Liveright, when he meant Albert & Charles Boni.

32. Lewis Baer to TNW, April 7, 1927, TNW Collection, YCAL.

33. TNW to Marie and Doug Townson, June 7, 1927, TNW Collection, YCAL.

34. TNW to Grace Foresman, May 25, 1927, TNW Collection, YCAL.

35. TNW to Lewis Baer, July 25, 1927, *SL*, 215–16.

36. TNW to Grace Foresman, July 25, 1927, TNW Collection, YCAL.

37. TNW to Isabel Wilder, July 21, 1927, TNW Collection, YCAL.

38. TNW to Bill Nichols, July 3, 1927, Nichols Papers, LC.

39. TNW to Lewis Baer, July 25, 1927, *SL*, 215–16.

40. TNW to C. Leslie Glenn, June 14, 1927, TNW Collection, YCAL.

41. TNW to Grace Foresman, July 25, 1927, TNW Collection, YCAL.

42. TNW to Isabel Wilder, July 21, 1927, TNW Collection, YCAL.

43. TNW to Marie Townson, August 28, 1927, TNW Collection, YCAL.

44. In later years Elizabeth Shepley Sergeant would write memoirs of Willa Cather and Robert Frost, and correspond with TNW about the nature and methodology of biography.
45. TNW to Marie Townson, August 28, 1927, TNW Collection, YCAL.
46. TNW to Isabel Wilder, August 22, 1927, TNW Collection, YCAL.
47. Ibid.
48. Ibid.
49. Ibid.
50. Lewis Baer to TNW, August 18, 1927, TNW Collection, YCAL.
51. Ibid.
52. TNW to Isabel Wilder, August 22, 1927, TNW Collection, YCAL.
53. Albert Boni to TNW, August 30, 1927, TNW Collection, YCAL.
54. According to *Time*, March 28, 1938, the Little Leather Library, between 1923 and 1925, sold 40 million inexpensive leatherbound books through Woolworth's stores and the Whitman Candy Company.
55. TNW to Marie Townson, August 28, 1927, TNW Collection, YCAL.
56. TNW to Marie Townson, December 39, 1927, TNW Collection, YCAL.
57. Clark Andrews, "To Us He Was Always 'T.W.,'" *Yankee*, September 1978, 120–25, 152–68.
58. Ibid.
59. Ibid.
60. TNW to Marie Townson, [postmarked November 9, 1927], TNW Collection, YCAL.
61. Lewis Baer to TNW, January 6, 1928, TNW Collection, YCAL.
62. TNW to Marie Townson, December 30, 1927, TNW Collection, YCAL.
63. TNW to Isabella Niven Wilder, December 28, 1927, TNW Collection, YCAL.
64. TNW to Marie Townson, December 30, 1927, TNW Collection, YCAL.
65. TNW to Chauncey B. Tinker, December 6, 1927, *SL*, 219–20.
66. Ibid.
67. Ibid.
68. Ibid.

19: "THE FINEST BRIDGE IN ALL PERU" (1928)

1. During an argument, it is said, the viceroy called the actress "Perra Chola"—in translation, "dog-bitch," or "native or half-breed bitch." Mérimée annotated his play to assert it as historical fact that Ribera called the actress "Perra-chola"— which, because of his Castilian accent and his loss of teeth, became "Perichole."
2. TNW, *The Bridge of San Luis Rey*, 18. As noted in a previous chapter, TNW had written to Henry Luce about this. TNW to Henry R. Luce, September 9, 1926, TNW Collection, YCAL.
3. TNW to John Townley, March 6, 1928, YCAL.
4. TNW, *The Bridge of San Luis Rey*, 7–8.
5. Ibid., 8–9.
6. Ibid., 100.
7. Ibid.
8. Ibid., 72.

9. TNW, Journal, Entry 51, December 22, 1926. TNW Collection, YCAL. TNW did not number the entries in his earlier journals. When I have quoted or cited a numbered entry, I have provided the number.

10. Captain Alvarado: TNW, *The Bridge of San Luis Rey*, 58; Valéry's Captain: Paul Valéry, *Eupalinos, or The Architect, Dialogues*, William McCausland Stewart, trans. (Princeton: Princeton University Press, 1956), 135.

11. TNW, *The Bridge of San Luis Rey*, 82.

12. TNW, 1926 Journal, Entry 22, October 11, 1926, TNW Collection, YCAL.

13. TNW, *The Bridge of San Luis Rey*, 7.

14. Ibid., 101.

15. Ibid., 32.

16. Ibid., 35.

17. Ibid., 49.

18. "All onlooker . . .": TNW to Mabel Dodge Luhan, [1934?], TNW Collection, YCAL; "inhabitants of the world . . .": TNW, *The Bridge of San Luis Rey*, 112.

19. TNW, *The Bridge of San Luis Rey*, 83.

20. Ibid., 18.

21. Malcolm Goldstein, *The Art of Thornton Wilder* (Lincoln: University of Nebraska Press, 1965), 56.

22. TNW, *The Bridge of San Luis Rey*, 45–46.

23. Ibid., 89.

24. Ibid., 38.

25. Ibid., 103.

26. Ibid., 102–3.

27. Ibid., 27–28.

28. Ibid., 107.

29. See Tappan Wilder, afterword to *The Bridge of San Luis Rey* (New York: Harper-Perennial, 2004), 109–31, for a comprehensive discussion of the novel's sales and reviews, as well as sources.

30. Clifton P. Fadiman, "The Quality of Grace," *Nation*, December 14, 1927.

31. Arnold Bennett, "A Strange Work on Art and a 'Dazzling' Novel," *Evening Standard* (London), November 14, 1927, 5.

32. Vita Sackville-West, "New Novels: Realists and Romantics," *Observer* (London), November 20, 1927, 8.

33. Edwin Muir, "Fiction," *Nation and Athenaeum* (London), December 10, 1927, 404.

34. Edmund Wilson, "Thornton Wilder," *New Republic*, August 8, 1928, 303–5.

35. Louis Untermeyer, "A London Letter," *Saturday Review of Literature*, May 12, 1928, 867.

36. Hugh Walpole, "Geniuses Are Rare in A.D. 1928," *Daily Express* (London), August 22, 1928, 8.

37. TNW to Isabella Niven Wilder, [January 1928?], TNW Collection, YCAL.

38. Ibid.

39. Harry Salpeter, "Thornton Wilder: One Young Author Not Yet Bored with His Double-Barrelled Success," unidentified clipping, 1928, Wilder Clipping File, TNW Collection, YCAL. This article differs from another Salpeter column on Wilder, "Why Is a Best Seller?" *Outlook*, April 18, 1928.

40. TNW to Isabella Niven Wilder, [February 1928?], TNW Collection, YCAL. (Handwritten on the letter, most likely by Isabella: "Written 23 Feb.")

41. TNW to ANW, [early 1928?], TNW Collection, YCAL.

42. TNW to Isabella Niven Wilder, [February 1928?]. TNW Collection, YCAL.

43. Ibid.

44. Ibid.

45. Ibid.

46. TNW to Cass Canfield, January 16, 1928, [carbon copy], TNW Collection, YCAL.

47. TNW to Doug and Marie Townson, February 15, 1928, TNW Collection, YCAL.

48. TNW to Marie Townson, June 27, 1928, TNW Collection, YCAL.

49. Ibid.

50. Lee Keedick to TNW, February 4, 1928, TNW Collection, YCAL.

51. TNW to Lee Keedick, February 9, 1928, TNW Collection, YCAL.

52. TNW to Dr. ——Bridges, June 31, 1929, TNW Collection, YCAL.

53. Lee Keedick to TNW, February 21, 1928, TNW Collection, YCAL.

54. TNW to Lee Keedick, February 23, 1928, TNW Collection, YCAL.

55. Ibid.

56. Daniel Scott Lamont (1851–1905) was secretary of war during President Grover
    Cleveland's second term. After he left the post, Lamont became vice president of
    the Northern Pacific Railroad. The Lamont lecture was endowed by an anonymous
    donor in 1905. Lamont was not a Yale graduate; he attended Union College in Sche-
    nectady, New York.

57. TNW to Lee Keedick, [1928?], TNW Collection, YCAL.

58. TNW, "English Letters and Letter Writers," in *American Characteristics*, 152–53. In
    this volume Donald Gallup titled the lecture "On Reading the Great Letter Writers."

59. Ibid., 157.

60. TNW to ANW, n.d. [ca January or February 1928], TNW Collection, YCAL.

61. Gene Tunney to TNW, January 17, 1928, TNW Collection, YCAL.

62. Gene Tunney to TNW, January 30, 1928, TNW Collection, YCAL.

63. Gene Tunney to TNW, March 6, 1928, TNW Collection, YCAL.

64. TNW to F. Scott Fitzgerald, January 12, 1928, *SL*, 220–21.

65. TNW to F. Scott Fitzgerald [February 1928?], in Matthew J. Bruccoli and Margaret
    M. Duggan, eds., *Correspondence of F. Scott Fitzgerald* (New York: Random House,
    1979), 217.

66. Wilson, *Shores of Light*, 376–77.

67. Gilbert Harrison, *The Enthusiast: A Life of Thornton Wilder* (New Haven and New
    York: Ticknor & Fields, 1983), 109–10.

68. Wilson, *Shores of Light*, 380–81.

69. F Scott Fitzgerald to TNW, [March 23, 1928?], TNW Collection, YCAL.

70. Zelda Fitzgerald to TNW, [March or April 1928?], TNW Collection, YCAL.

71. Carl C. Lohman, Secretary, Yale University, to TNW, March 14, 1928, TNW Col-
    lection, YCAL.

72. TNW to Carl C. Lohman, [March 1928?], TNW Collection, YCAL. Incomplete
    rough draft of a letter, with strikeovers and revisions.

73. William Lyon Phelps, *Autobiography with Letters* (New York and London: Oxford Uni-
    versity Press, 1939), 793. Among other topics, Tunney explained how Shakespeare's
    plays helped him relax and even helped him train and plan strategy for his fights.

74. Gene Tunney to TNW, holograph letter to "Dear Thornt.," [June 11?], 1928, TNW
    Collection, YCAL.

75. "Tunney and Wilder Plunge into River as Canoe Upsets," *New York Times*, June 29, 1928, 18.

76. Quoted in Jay R. Tunney, *The Prizefighter and the Playwright: Gene Tunney and Bernard Shaw* (Richmond Hill, ONT, and Buffalo, NY: Firefly Books, Ltd, 2010), 128. TNW recounted this incident to a reporter from the *Glasgow* (*New Hampshire*) *Bulletin*.

77. TNW to Gene Tunney, December 4, 1970, Private Collection. Tunney was quoting a line from Shakespeare's *Measure for Measure*, act 3, scene 1: "And the poor beetle, that we tread upon, in corporal sufferance finds a pang as great / As when a giant dies."

78. Gene Tunney, telegram to TNW, [July 1928?], TNW Collection, YCAL.

79. Charlotte Wilder record, Appointment Bureau of Mount Holyoke College, January 21, 1930, Mount Holyoke College Library/Archives.

80. TNW to Ernest Hemingway, June 20, 1928, *SL*, 227–28.

81. TNW to F. Scott Fitzgerald, [February 1928], in Bruccoli and Duggan, *Correspondence of F. Scott Fitzgerald*, 217.

20: PREPARATION AND CIRCUMSTANCE (1930S)

1. TNW to Lewis Baer, August 7, 1926, TNW Collection, YCAL.

2. TNW, foreword to *The Angel That Troubled the Waters*, xv. This book is reprinted in its entirety in Tappan Wilder, *The Collected Short Plays of Thornton Wilder*, vol. 2, 3–7, as well as in McClatchy, *Thornton Wilder: Collected Plays & Writings on Theater*, 651–54.

3. The two plays printed in *Harper's Magazine* in October 1928 were *The Angel on the Ship* and *Mozart and the Gray Steward*, 564–67.

4. "Thornton Wilder's Three-Minute Plays," *New York Times Book Review*, November 18, 1928.

5. TNW to Bill Nichols, August 17, 1928, Nichols Papers, LC.

6. TNW to Isabel Wilder, September 24, 1928, TNW Collection, YCAL.

7. Tunney, *The Prizefighter and the Playwright*, 129.

8. Isabel Wilder, Interview, "1928," unpublished transcript, TNW Collection, YCAL, uncataloged papers.

9. See Tappan Wilder, afterword to *The Cabala and The Woman of Andros*, 229.

10. Isabel Wilder Interview, November 9,1982, unpublished transcript, TNW Collection, YCAL, uncataloged transcript.

11. Ibid.

12. TNW to Isabella Niven Wilder, [1928?], TNW Collection, YCAL, quoted in Tappan Wilder, afterword to *The Cabala and the Woman of Andros*, 228.

13. TNW, notations on manuscript of *The Woman of Andros*, TNW Collection, YCAL.

14. TNW to ANW, [August 1929?], TNW Collection, YCAL.

15. Ibid.

16. TNW, Income Tax Summary, Private Collection.

17. TNW to Sarah Frantz, October 13, 1934 *SL*, 287–88.

18. TNW to T. E. Lawrence, January 20, 1930, *SL*, 244–45.

19. TNW to Isabel and Isabella Niven Wilder, date illegible [May 1930?], TNW Collection, YCAL.

20. TNW to Lee Keedick, [June 1928?], TNW Collection, YCAL.

21. TNW, 1929 Appointment Book, TNW Collection, YCAL.

22. John E. Pember, "Thornton Wilder No Slave to His Work; Drops Everything and Takes a Rest Whenever He Feels Like It," *Boston Herald Magazine*, March 31, 1929, 2; reprinted in Bryer, *Conversatioins with Thornton Wilder*, 3–8.

23. TNW to Lee Keedick, April 11, 1929, TNW Collection, YCAL.

24. TNW to Lee Keedick, April 19, 1929, TNW Collection, YCAL.

25. Ibid.

26. TNW to Lee Keedick, December 19, 1929, TNW Collection, YCAL.

27. Some passages about *The Woman of Andros* were first published in my foreword to TNW's *The Cabala and The Woman of Andros*, xi–xxv. All citations of *The Woman of Andros* refer to this edition.

28. TNW to Isabel Wilder, September 27, 1929, TNW Collection, YCAL.

29. TNW to Lee Keedick, November 23, 1930, TNW Collection, YCAL.

30. TNW to Isabel Wilder, September 27, 1929, TNW Collection, YCAL.

31. Ibid.

32. TNW to Isabel Wilder, October 7, 1929, TNW Collection, YCAL.

33. TNW to Isabel Wilder, September 27, 1929, TNW Collection, YCAL.

34. TNW to Sybil Colefax, November 24, 1929, New York University.

35. Ibid.

36. TNW to Albert Boni, January 23, 1930, TNW Collection, YCAL.

37. Frederick James Smith, "Wilder and Wilder: Mlle. Damita Torches Up the Bridge of San Luis Rey," *Liberty*, April 27, 1929, TNW Collection, YCAL. *Liberty*, a weekly magazine with a circulation of three million, was one of the most popular magazines in the United States during the twenties and thirties.

38. TNW to Mrs. Coker, c/o the X.X.M.D. Study Club, St. Joseph, Missouri, December 15, 1947, Private Collection.

39. TNW, 1929 Journal, Entries 71–72, TNW Collection, YCAL.

40. Other playwrights who adapted Terence's comedy were Richard Steele, *The Conscious Lovers*, in 1722; and Daniel Bellamy, *The Perjured Devotee*, in 1739.

41. This passage is adapted from my foreword to *The Woman of Andros*, xxi–xxii.

42. TNW, 1929 Journal, Entry 73, TNW Collection, YCAL. TNW to Norman Fitts, *SL*, 240–41.

43. TNW, 1929 Journal, Entry 73.

44. TNW to Sibyl Colefax, July 24, 1929, *SL*, 237–40.

45. TNW, *The Cabala and The Woman of Andros*, 137.

46. Ibid., 184.

47. Ibid., 150–51.

48. Ibid., 179.

49. Ibid., 176.

50. Ibid., 197.

51. Ibid., 148–50.

52. Ibid., 197.

53. TNW, 1929 Journal, Entry 77, TNW Collection, YCAL.

54. Ibid.

55. TNW to Sibyl Colefax, February 20, 1930, *SL*, 246–47.

56. Ibid.

57. TNW to Lee Keedick, December 19, 1929, TNW Collection, YCAL.

58. Lee Keedick to TNW, telegram, January 7, 1930, TNW Collection, YCAL.

59. TNW to Lee Keedick, telegram, January 9, 1930, TNW Collection, YCAL.

60. "The Future of American Literature," University of Iowa brochure, 1930, Private Collection.

61. TNW to Sibyl Colefax, February 20, 1930, *SL*, 246–47.

21: "VARIETY, VARIETY" (1930s)

1. TNW, "CHRONOLOGY," n.d., TNW Collection, YCAL. (The list ends at 1952.)

2. Ibid.

3. Advertisement, *Saturday Review of Literature*, March 15, 1930.

4. Wilson, "The Critic Who Does Not Exist," *Shores of Light*, 369. For reference to Gold's intelligence, see Wilson, "Dos Passos and the Social Revolution," *Shores of Light*, 433.

5. TNW was just one target of what the critic Joan Acocella calls "the politicizing of criticism in the thirties," along with Willa Cather, William Faulkner, James Joyce, T. S. Eliot, and others. Joan Acocella, *Willa Cather and the Politics of Criticism* (New York: Vintage Books/Random House, 2002), 24–29.

6. Michael Gold, "Wilder: Prophet of the Genteel Christ," *New Republic*, October 22, 1930.

7. "I kept to one issue with Mike," Carl Sandburg wrote Archibald MacLeish October 6, 1933. "I had to hold in because I have Mike's number from so many directions." Sandburg had written for left-wing publications, and for a time lent his name to the masthead of Gold's *New Masses*.

8. Edmund Wilson, "The Literary Class War," *New Republic*, May 4, 1932; reprinted in *Shores of Light*, 534–39.

9. TNW to Lee Keedick, November 23, 1930, TNW Collection, YCAL.

10. TNW to Sybil Colefax, November 24, 1929, New York University.

11. TNW to William Prohme, "Wilder vs. His Critics," *Honolulu Advertiser*, November 5, 1933. See also, for Hawaii lecture coverage, "Author Finds Hawaii to His Liking," *Honolulu Star-Bulletin*, November 2, 1933; TNW to Clifford Gessler, "Wilder Talks on the Novel: Novelist Tells How Literature Gives Coherence to Chaotic World," November 10, 1933 [one of Wilder's lecture topics in Hawaii was "Some Thoughts on the Novel"]; TNW to Edna B. Lawson, "Wilder Predicts Drama as Form of American Literary Expression," *Honolulu Advertiser*, November 17, 1933; "Wilder Talks on the Drama: Theater May Be on the Eve of Great Era, Says Author in Closing Lecture," *Honolulu Star-Bulletin*, November 17, 1933.

12. TNW to Sybil Colefax, November 2, 1932, *SL*, 255–59.

13. TNW to Sibyl Colefax, July 24, 1929, *SL*, 237–40.

14. TNW to Dr. ——Bridges, July 31, 1929, TNW Collection, YCAL.

15. For background on Robert Maynard Hutchins, see Mary Ann Dzuback, *Robert M. Hutchins: Portrait of an Educator* (Chicago: University of Chicago Press, 1991); and Harry S. Ashmore, *Unseasonable Truths: The Life of Robert Maynard Hutchins* (Boston: Little, Brown, 1989).

16. TNW to Isabella Niven Wilder, (Spring 1930?), TNW Collection, YCAL.

17. TNW to Isabella Niven and APW, February 2, 1932, TNW Collection, YCAL.

18. Isabella Niven Wilder to Dwight Dana, May 7, 1931, TNW Collection, YCAL.

19. Dwight Dana to TNW, September 10, 1931, carbon copy, Private Collection.
20. Dwight Dana to TNW, October 13, 1931, carbon copy, Private Collection.
21. TNW to Dwight Dana, November 2, 1931, TNW Collection, YCAL.
22. Ibid.
23. TNW to Family, May 5, 1931, TNW Collection, YCAL.
24. TNW to Edward Sheldon, August 7, 1933, *SL*, 262–66.
25. TNW, preface to *Three Plays* (New York: HarperPerennial, 2006), xxv. This volume contains the texts of *Our Town*, *The Skin of Our Teeth*, and *The Matchmaker*.
26. Ibid.
27. *The Long Christmas Dinner* was produced in November 1931 in New Haven by the Yale Dramatic Association and the Vassar College Philalethesis, for instance, and *Pullman Car Hiawatha* was staged at Antioch College in Yellow Springs, Ohio, in March 1932. That same month *Queens of France* graced the stage at Wilder's mother's alma mater, the Misses Masters School in Dobbs Ferry, New York, and the Hill School, Pottstown, Pennsylvania. For additional production and publishing details for these one-act plays, see Donald Gallup and A. Tappan Wilder, eds., *The Collected Short Plays of Thornton Wilder* (New York: Theatre Communications Group, 1997), vol. 1, 321–22.
28. TNW, preface to *Three Plays*, xxx.
29. TNW to Bob McCoy, "Thornton Wilder in Our Town," *San Juan Star*, January 2, 1974; reprinted in Bryer, *Conversations with Thornton Wilder*, 110–15.
30. TNW, Journal, Entry 80, June 27, 1930, TNW Collection, YCAL.
31. Isabel Wilder, TS, n.d., TNW Collection, YCAL, uncataloged manuscripts.
32. TNW, *The Cabala and The Woman of Andros*, 134.
33. TNW to Bill Nichols, [Summer 1932?], Nichols Papers, LC.
34. TNW to Mabel Dodge Luhan, [1934?], YCAL.
35. TNW to Isabel Wilder, May 1, 1933, TNW Collection, YCAL. Texas Guinan wrote to TNW on her distinctive letterhead, emblazoned with a map of Texas on the palm of a hand supporting the word "TEXAS" in bold black letters, with the "Guinan" arranged under the hand like a jewel-encrusted bracelet. She invited Wilder to visit her and offered to give a party for him, promising to do her best to entertain him. See Texas Guinan to TNW, June 25, 1930, TNW Collection, YCAL.
36. TNW to Dwight Dana, January 18, 1932, TNW Collection, YCAL.
37. Also among TNW's Chicago friends was the former University of Chicago student Martha Dodd (later Martha Dodd Stern), assistant literary editor of the *Chicago Tribune*. TNW exchanged a few flirtatious letters with Martha Dodd. She left Chicago in 1933 to accompany her father, William Dodd, to Germany, where he took up his post as U.S. ambassador in Berlin. Martha Dodd also wrote flirtatious letters to Chicagoan Carl Sandburg (thirty years older than she, and a friend of her father's), and a number of other men over the years, sometimes giving the false impression, deliberately or otherwise, that there had been a full-fledged love affair.
38. TNW to Sibyl Colefax, November 2, 1932, *SL*, 255–59.
39. TNW to Edward Sheldon, August 7, 1933, *SL*, 262–66.
40. Ibid.
41. TNW to Ruth Gordon, June 18, 1933, Private Collection.
42. TNW to Family, June 26, 1933, TNW Collection, YCAL.
43. Dzuback, *Robert M. Hutchins: Portrait of an Educator*, 100.
44. TNW to Mabel Dodge Luhan, [1934?], YCAL.
45. Fanny Butcher, *Many Lives—One Love* (New York: Harper & Row, 1972), 79.

46. TNW to Isabel Wilder, May 1, 1933, TNW Collection, YCAL.
47. TNW to Ruth Gordon, June 18, 1933, Private Collection.
48. TNW to Edward Sheldon, August 7, 1933, *SL*, 262–66.
49. Ibid. Sadly, after her run at the fair, Guinan took her show on a Western tour and fell gravely ill. She died that November in Vancouver. She was forty-nine years old.
50. TNW to Edward Sheldon, August 7, 1933, *SL*, 262–66.
51. TNW to Sibyl Colefax, August 30, 1933, New York University.
52. Ibid.
53. Here, as elsewhere, I quote from or cite my foreword to *The Cabala and The Woman of Andros*, in this instance, from p. xxi.
54. TNW to Sibyl Colefax, November 2, 1932, *SL*, 255–59.
55. Ibid.
56. TNW to Katharine Cornell, April 8, 1932 *SL*, 254–55.
57. TNW to Sibyl Colefax, November 2, 1932, *SL*, 255–59.
58. Katharine Cornell, *I Wanted to Be an Actress: The Autobiography of Katharine Cornell* (New York: Random House, 1938), 117–18.
59. TNW to Sibyl Colefax, August 30, 1933, New York University.
60. TNW to Ruth Gordon, June 18, 1933, Private Collection.
61. TNW to Sibyl Colefax, August 30, 1933, New York University.

22: "HOME" (1930s)

1. TNW to Family, October 21, 1920. TNW Collection, YCAL.
2. TNW, "A PREFACE FOR OUR TOWN," *New York Times*, February 13, 1938. The preface is reprinted in TNW, *Our Town* (New York: HarperPerennial, 2003), as well as in TNW, *American Characteristics*; Tappan Wilder, *The Collected Short Plays of Thornton Wilder*, vol. 2; and McClatchy, *Thornton Wilder: Collected Plays & Writings on Theater*.
3. TNW to Mabel Dodge Luhan, December 11, 1933, YCAL.
4. APW to L. N. Flint, June 17, 1935, TNW Collection, YCAL, uncataloged letters.
5. TNW to Isabel Wilder, [May 1931?], TNW Collection, YCAL.
6. TNW to Leslie Glenn, July 15, 1932, TNW Collection, YCAL.
7. TNW to Amy Wertheimer, [no day], 1933, TNW Collection, YCAL.
8. Dr. John Beebe to APW, March 30, 1935, TNW Collection, YCAL, uncataloged letters.
9. Charlotte Wilder to APW, n.d., TNW Collection, YCAL, uncataloged letters. ("December 1930" is written in another hand at the top of the letter.)
10. Ibid.
11. Charlotte Wilder to APW, [Summer 1933 or 1934, judging by return address: Christodora House, 147 Avenue B, New York], TNW Collection, YCAL, uncataloged letters.
12. Janet Wilder Dakin, "Light and Shadow: An Autobiographical Sketch of My Childhood (1910–1923)," TS, headed, in JWD's handwriting, "A talk I am giving today," and dated February 22, 1982, TNW Collection, YCAL, uncataloged manuscripts. Janet apparently sent her fifteen-page typescript to Isabel Wilder. In notes on the manuscript, Isabel not only corrected her sister's memory of certain events, but challenged some of Janet's personal reflections.
13. Ibid.

14. Ibid.

15. Janet Wilder Dakin to Tappan Wilder, March 13, 1978, Private Collection.

16. Janet Wilder Dakin, "Light and Shadow: An Autobiographical Sketch of My Childhood."

17. TNW to Ruth Gordon, June 18, 1933, Private Collection.

18. Janet Wilder to Family, February 6, 1938, TNW Collection, YCAL, uncataloged letters. There is no record of her family's response to Janet's diet.

19. Janet Wilder Dakin to Tappan Wilder, March 13, 1978, Private Collection.

20. "A thoroughly American story": Isabel Wilder to Charlotte Wilder, March 28, [1934?], TNW Collection, uncataloged papers. "Had a modest success": ANW, "Isabel's Writings," June 4, 1987, ANW, Wilder Family Record, TNW Collection, YCAL.

21. Isabel Wilder to Charlotte Wilder, [1933 or 1934?], TNW Collection, YCAL, uncataloged letters.

22. Charlotte Wilder to Isabel Wilder, [1940?; as Charlotte refers to her Guggenheim application, which was submitted on March 3 of that year], TNW Collection, YCAL, uncataloged letters.

23. Charlotte Wilder to Isabella Niven Wilder, n.d., TNW Collection, YCAL, uncataloged letters. ("March 1933" in Isabella's hand.)

24. Charlotte Wilder to APW, [from Yaddo, Summer 1933?], TNW Collection, uncataloged letters. During the summers of 1928 and 1929 Charlotte taught English and literature in the Barnard Summer School for Women Workers in Industry at Barnard College in New York City.

25. APW to Charlotte Wilder, September 7, 1932, TNW Collection, YCAL, uncataloged letters.

26. TNW to Charlotte Wilder, [September 3, 1933?], TNW Collection, YCAL. ANW received his Ph.D. at Yale in 1933. Isabel's first novel was published in 1933. Charlotte Wilder went to Yaddo in 1933. She resigned her teaching post at Smith College in 1933 so that she could write full-time.

27. See Robert Pollock to Charlotte Wilder, August 3, 1925, TNW Collection, YCAL, uncataloged letters.

28. Charlotte Wilder to Ernestine Friedmann, n.d. and September 8, 1928, TNW Collection, YCAL, uncataloged letters. Ernestine Friedmann to Charlotte Wilder, n.d., TNW Collection, YCAL, uncataloged letters.

29. Charlotte Wilder to ANW, n.d., TNW Collection, YCAL, uncataloged letters. ("1932," written in ANW's hand.)

30. Charlotte Wilder, untitled manuscript, April 2, [1932?], TNW Collection, YCAL, uncataloged manuscript.

31. Ibid.

32. APW to Charlotte Wilder, February 8, [1930?], TNW Collection, YCAL, uncataloged letters.

33. Charlotte Wilder to ANW, [1932?], TNW Collection, YCAL, uncataloged letters.

34. ANW to Catharine Kerlin, January 17, 1935, Private Collection.

35. ANW to Catharine Kerlin, [postmarked November 17, 1934], Private Collection.

36. ANW to Catharine Kerlin, December 13, 1934, Private Collection.

37. ANW, quoted by Tappan Wilder, "Amos Niven Wilder: The Memorial Service," June 21, 1993.

38. ANW to Catharine Kerlin, December 25, [1934?], Private Collection.

39. ANW to Catharine Kerlin, January 17, 1935, Private Collection.

40. ANW to Catharine Kerlin, February 11, [1935?], Private Collection.

41. TNW to Leslie Glenn, [March 1935?], TNW Collection, YCAL.

42. ANW to Catharine Kerlin, February 15, [1935?], Private Collection.

43. "Amos Niven Wilder: The Memorial Service," June 21, 1993, Private Collection.

44. APW to Charlotte Wilder, January 29, 1935, TNW Collection, YCAL, uncataloged letters.

45. TNW to Grace Foresman, October 6, 1934, TNW Collection, YCAL.

46. TNW to Sarah Frantz, October 13, 1934, *SL*, 287–88.

47. TNW to Grace Foresman, December 21, 1934, TNW Collection, YCAL.

48. ANW to Catharine Kerlin, January 9, [1935?], Private Collection. The name was Marian Truby.

49. TNW to Amos Niven and Catharine Kerlin Wilder, September 22, 1935, TNW Collection, YCAL.

50. TNW, *Heaven's My Destination*, 22–23.

51. Ibid., 27.

52. Ibid., 170.

53. Ibid., 177.

54. Ibid., 176.

55. Ibid., 180.

23: "STRANDS AND THREADS" (1930S)

1. TNW, "James Joyce, 1882–1941," *American Characteristics*, 168.

2. TNW to Dwight Dana, December 9, 1934, Private Collection.

3. TNW to Dwight Dana, May 16, 1934, Private Collection.

4. TNW, *Joan of Arc: Treatment for Motion Pictures*, March 1934, TNW Collection, YCAL.

5. Ibid. TNW took a proprietary interest in his rejected scenario for *Joan of Arc*, and approached Cass Canfield at Harper about publishing it. TNW argued that it would be the first movie scenario to be published in English, and publication would preserve the work from alteration. Nothing came of that proposal, however, and TNW's treatment rested among his papers after his death, until it was published in the *Yale Review* in 2003.

6. TNW to Mabel Dodge Luhan, August 29, [1934?]; YCAL. (TNW misdated this letter 1933.)

7. Mollie Herrick, "Hollywood Sidelights," September 14, 1934, quoted in A. Tappan Wilder, "Movie Treatment for Joan of Arc," *Yale Review* 91, no. 4 (October 2003): 1–34.

8. TNW to Mabel Dodge Luhan, October 7, 1934, YCAL.

9. TNW to Family, [1933?], TNW Collection, YCAL. Hughes wrote a three-volume biography of George Washington.

10. TNW to Charles Laughton, September 2, 1934, *SL*, 280–82.

11. TNW to Alexander Woollcott, August 31, 1934, AWC, MS Am 1449 (1770), HLH. While we do not know why TNW chose this pseudonym in 1934, an actor who changed his name to James Craven played movie and television villains, beginning in 1940.

12. TNW to Isabella Niven Wilder, September 8, 1934, TNW Collection, YCAL.

13. TNW to Grace Foresman, October 6, 1934, TNW Collection, YCAL.

14. TNW to Mabel Dodge Luhan, December 6, 1934, YCAL.

15. TNW to Isabella Niven Wilder and Isabel Wilder, August 25, 1934, TNW Collection, YCAL.

16. Tappan Wilder, introduction to "Joan of Arc: Treatment for Motion Pictures," 4–5. This article provides background on TNW's sojourns in Hollywood.

17. Lee Keedick to TNW, March 1, 1933, TNW Collection, YCAL.

18. TNW to Lee Keedick, January 14, 1935, TNW Collection, YCAL.

19. TNW to Sarah M. Frantz, October 13, 1934, *SL*, 287–88.

20. TNW to Lee Keedick, January 9, 1936, TNW Collection, YCAL. The Keedick letters are drawn from either the TNW Collection, YCAL, or a private collection, as noted in each instance. The Keedick correspondence at YCAL can be found in Call #162, Box 5, Folder 102.

21. TNW to Dwight Dana, August 18, 1938, Private Collection. TNW's name was not listed among the writing credits for *Golden Boy* and *Union Pacific* when they were released in 1939.

22. TNW to Mabel Dodge Luhan, August 29, [1934], *SL*, 266–67. (TNW misdated this letter 1933.)

23. TNW to Dwight Dana, August 18, 1938, Private Collection.

24. TNW to Alexander Woollcott, January 27, 1938, *SL*, 333–37.

25. TNW to J. Dwight Dana, January 18, [1934?], Private Collection. (Wilder mistakenly wrote 1933.)

26. Cass Canfield for Harper & Brothers to Albert and Charles Boni, August 29, 1934, carbon copy, Private Collection.

27. TNW to Harper & Brothers, September 29, 1924, carbon copy, Private Collection.

28. Charles Bloch, A & C Boni, Inc., to J. Dwight Dana, November 21, 1934, carbon copy, TNW Collection, YCAL.

29. TNW to Mabel Dodge Luhan, August 29, [1934?], *SL*, 266–67. (TNW misdated this letter 1933.)

30. Mabel Dodge Luhan to TNW, April 6, [1929?], TNW Collection, YCAL.

31. TNW to Mabel Dodge Luhan, May 19, 1934, YCAL.

32. TNW, "Taos," holograph manuscript, 1934, YCAL.

33. TNW to Mabel Dodge Luhan, May 19, 1924, YCAL.

34. TNW to Sibyl Colefax, November 2, 1932, *SL*, 255–59.

35. Ibid. Lines from Nietzsche's *The Wanderer and His Shadow* are quoted from Walter Kaufmann, ed., *Basic Writings of Nietzsche* (New York: Modern Library, 2000), 165. Edward M. Burns, Ulla E. Dydo, and William Rice point out that Wilder may have drawn from Nietzsche's *Thus Spoke Zarathustra* for the moment when Brush says, "If you do pure good to a man that's harmed you that shames him too much. No man is so bad that you ought to shame him that way. . . . You ought to do just a little bit of bad in return so he can keep his self-respect." As Nietzsche expresses it, "But if you have an enemy, do not requite him evil with good, for that would put him to shame." Burns, Dydo, and Rice, eds., *The Letters of Gertrude Stein & Thornton Wilder* (New Haven & London: Yale University Press, 1996), 11n8.

36. TNW to Creighton Barker, M.D., February 3, 1935, TNW Collection, YCAL.

37. Ibid.

38. TNW to William Frazier, July 5, 1935, *SL*, 295–96.

39. Ibid.

40. TNW to Les Glenn, [March 1935?], *SL*, 291–93.

41. Gertude Stein, *Everybody's Autobiography* (New York: Random House, 1937; reprint, Cambridge, MA: Exact Change, 1991), 173.

42. For detailed background on the production of *Xerxes*, see Burns, Dydo, and Rice, *The Letters of Gertrude Stein & Thornton Wilder*, 356–60.

43. TNW to Dwight Dana, June 10, 1935, Private Collection.

44. ANW, "Don Quixote in the American Scene," *Anglican Theological Review* 25, no. 3 (July 1943), 272–80.

45. TNW to Alexander Woollcott, [August 1933?], *SL*, 268–71.

46. According to Simon Callow, Welles "was always delighted to admit" that he "stole" the idea from Wilder and *The Long Christmas Dinner*. See Simon Callow, *Orson Welles: The Road to Xanadu* (New York: Viking Penguin, 1996), 504.

47. TNW to Mabel Dodge Luhan, December 6, 1934, YCAL.

48. See Lois Palken Rudnick, *Mabel Dodge Luhan: New Woman, New Worlds* (Albuquerque: University of New Mexico Press, 1984), 49–51.

49. TNW to Gertrude Stein, [February 16, 1935?], YCAL.

50. TNW, "Gertrude Stein's NARRATION," introduction to *Narration: Four Lectures by Gertrude Stein* (Chicago: University of Chicago Press, 1935); reprinted in Gallup, *American Characteristics*, 183.

51. Stein, *Everybody's Autobiography*, 270. For other accounts of Stein's lectures in the United States in 1934–35, see Mortimer J. Adler, *Philosopher at Large: An Intellectual Biography* (New York: Macmillan, 1977); Ashmore, *Unseasonable Truths*; Burns, Dydo, and Rice, *The Letters of Gertrude Stein & Thornton Wilder*; Butcher, *Many Lives, One Love*; and James R. Mellow, *Charmed Circle: Gertrude Stein & Company* (New York: Praeger, 1974).

52. TNW to Les Glenn, [March 1935?], TNW Collection, YCAL.

53. Butcher, *Many Lives, One Love*, 422–23.

54. Stein, *Everybody's Autobiography*, 269.

55. TNW to Gertrude Stein, April 2, 1935, YCAL.

56. TNW to Sarah Frantz, October 13, 1934, *SL*, 287–88.

57. TNW to Les Glenn, [March 1935?] *SL*, 291–93.

58. TNW to Amy Wertheimer, May 1, 1935, TNW Collection, YCAL.

59. TNW to Gertrude Stein, January 15, [1935?]; YCAL. (TNW misdated this letter 1934.) See also TNW to Gertrude Stein, December 14, 1935.

60. J. Dwight Dana to Albert Boni, April 13, 1935, TNW Collection, YCAL.

61. TNW to Gertrude Stein and Alice B. Toklas, May 26, 1935, YCAL.

62. Ibid.

63. Ibid.

64. TNW to Mabel Dodge Luhan, June 28, [1935?], attached to letter written June 16, 1935, Huntington Library, San Marino, CA. TNW mistakenly dated this letter July 28, but it was written aboard ship en route to Europe. The two letters were connected and mailed as one.

65. Ibid.

66. TNW, "M Marries N," July 2, 1935, TNW Collection, YCAL.

67. TNW to Gertrude Stein, [February 16, 1935?], YCAL.

68. TNW to Amy Wertheimer, May 1, 1935, TNW Collection, YCAL.

69. TNW to Gertrude Stein, April 6, 1935, YCAL.

70. TNW to Dwight Dana, April 9, 1935, Private Collection.

71. TNW to Mabel Dodge Luhan, September 13, [1935?], *SL*, 297–98.

72. TNW to Hilda Doolittle [H.D.], October 2, 1935, *SL*, 300–301.

73. TNW to Mabel Dodge Luhan, June 28, [1935?], Huntington Library. (TNW mistakenly dated this letter July 28.)

24: OUR LIVING AND OUR DYING (1930S)

1. TNW to Gertrude Stein and Alice B. Toklas, May 26, 1935, YCAL.

2. TNW to Gertrude Stein and Alice B. Toklas, August 30, 1935, YCAL.

3. Ibid.

4. Ibid.

5. TNW to Gertrude Stein and Alice B. Toklas, August 20, 1935, YCAL.

6. TNW to Gertrude Stein and Alice B. Toklas, August 6, 1935, YCAL.

7. TNW to Gertrude Stein, August 10, 1935, YCAL.

8. TNW to Gertrude Stein and Alice B. Toklas, [September 27, 1935?], YCAL.

9. TNW to Gertrude Stein and Alice B. Toklas, August 10, 1935, YCAL.

10. TNW to Amos Niven and Catharine Wilder, September 22, 1935, TNW Collection, YCAL.

11. TNW to Gertrude Stein and Alice B. Toklas, August 10, 1935, YCAL.

12. TNW to Amos Niven and Catharine Wilder, September 22, 1935, TNW Collection, YCAL.

13. TNW to Gertrude Stein and Alice B. Toklas, [September 1935?], YCAL. Stein speculated about what would have happened if Grant had been a religious leader who became a saint, or if the Wrights had been painters, or if James had been a general and Washington a novelist.

14. TNW to Gertrude Stein and Alice B. Toklas, September 23, 1935, YCAL.

15. TNW, introduction to Gertrude Stein, *The Geographical History of America or The Relation of Human Nature to the Human Mind* (New York: Random House, Inc., 1936); reprinted in Gallup, *American Characteristics*, 187–92.

16. See Howard Teichmann, *Smart Aleck: The Wit, World, and Life of Alexander Woollcott* (New York: William Morrow, 1976), 10–14.

17. TNW to Alexander Woollcott, December 1, 1935, *SL*, 304–6.

18. TNW, introduction to Gertrude Stein, *Four in America* (New Haven: Yale University Press, 1947), xi. TNW, "James Joyce, 1882–1941," *Poetry*, March 1941; reprinted in Gallup, *American Characteristics*, 168.

19. TNW to Mabel Dodge Luhan, December 31, 1936, YCAL.

20. TNW to Gertrude Stein and Alice B. Toklas, October 14, 1935, *SL*, 302–4.

21. TNW to Alexander Woollcott, October 23, 1935, AWC, MS Am 1449 (1772), HLH.

22. Ibid.

23. TNW to Gertrude Stein and Alice B. Toklas, October 14, 1935, *SL*, 302–4.

24. Ibid.

25. Ibid.

26. Ibid.

27. For background on Anna Freud, see www.annafreudcentre.org. and the extensive writings of Anna Freud. I appreciate the research of my former editor at Scribner's, Robert Stewart (*Carl Sandburg: A Biography* and *James Earl Jones: Voices and Silences*), an authority on Anna Freud, who kindly checked the archives of Anna Freud and Sigmund Freud for letters or other documents pertaining to TNW.

28. TNW to Alexander Woollcott, October 23, 1935, AWC, MS Am 1449 (1772), HLH.

TNW wrote to Woollcott on this date, "I come back with tons to tell you. Specially about my calls on Prof. Freud. Splendid matter. He's 79. I see him again tonight."

29. TNW recalled this meeting and conversation with Freud in marginal notes written in a copy of *The Eighth Day* that he presented to Otto Klemperer in August 1967; quoted in Tappan Wilder, afterword to TNW, *The Eighth Day*, 469.

30. Stein, *Everybody's Autobiography*, 18–19,

31. TNW to Gertrude Stein and Alice B. Toklas, October 7, [1935?], YCAL.

32. TNW to Alexander Woollcott, October 23, 1935, AWC MS Am 1449 (1772), HLH.

33. TNW to Gertrude Stein and Alice B. Toklas, October 14, 1935, *SL*, 302–4.

34. TNW to Alexander Woollcott, December 1, 1935, *SL*, 304–6.

35. TNW to Gertrude Stein and Alice B. Toklas, November 22, 1935, YCAL.

36. TNW to Charlotte Wilder, March 23, 1936, TNW Collection, YCAL.

37. Charlotte Wilder, *Phases of the Moon* (New York: Coward-McCann, Inc., 1936), 87. "do [*sic*] you love me? Let me hear it . . . if I could feel it," she wrote in "Monologue of Repression." "am [*sic*] I loved? O what—is it nothing?—will pierce through/the ice-benumbed texture of an inward-bound psyche. . . ."

38. TNW to Alexander Woollcott, December 1, 1935, *SL*, 304–6.

39. TNW to Gertrude Stein and Alice B. Toklas, December 14, 1935, YCAL.

40. TNW to Sibyl Colefax, January 23, 1936, *SL*, 307–10.

41. TNW to Gertrude Stein and Alice B. Toklas, March 6, 1936, YCAL.

42. Lee Keedick was responsive over the years to TNW's requests for adjustments in his contract, reducing the number of originally stipulated required lectures, and on occasion counting two lectures as one, according to Lee Keedick to J. Dwight Dana, September 12, 1930, and Lee Keedick to J. Dwight Dana, May 6, 1935, Private Collection.

43. TNW to Mabel Dodge Luhan, April 8, 1936, YCAL.

44. TNW to Leslie Glenn, April 7, 1936, TNW Collection, YCAL.

45. TNW to Isabella Niven Wilder, May 25, 1936, TNW Collection, YCAL.

46. Ibid.

47. Kirsty McLeod, *A Passion for Friendship: Sibyl Colefax & Her Circle* (London: Michael Joseph, 1991), 153–55.

48. TNW to Mabel Dodge Luhan, July 1, 1936, YCAL.

49. *Wisconsin State Journal*, July 2, 1936.

50. TNW to Gertrude Stein and Alice B. Toklas, August 14, 1936, YCAL.

51. TNW to Grace Foresman, October 6, 1935, TNW Collection, YCAL.

52. TNW to John K. Tibby, Jr., May 5, 1967, TNW Collection, YCAL.

53. TNW, *The Eighth Day*, 148.

54. TNW to Mabel Dodge Luhan, November 24, 1935, YCAL.

55. TNW to Janet Wilder, November 16, 1936, TNW Collection, YCAL.

56. Ibid.

57. TNW to Alexander Woollcott, October 2, 1936, AWC, MS Am 1449 (1774), HLH.

58. TNW to Alexander Woollcott, November 17, 1936, AWC, MS Am 1449 (1774), HLH.

59. TNW to Gertrude Stein and Alice B. Toklas, December 20, 1936, YCAL.

60. TNW to Alexander Woollcott, November 17, 1936, AWC, MS Am 1449 (1774), HLH.

61. TNW to Gertrude Stein and Alice B. Toklas, December 20, 1936, YCAL.

62. Ibid.

63. TNW to Bobsy Goodspeed, [December 25?] 1936, TNW Collection, YCAL.

64. TNW to Grace Foresman, [December 20, 1937?], *SL*, 326–27.

65. TNW to Sibyl Colefax, January 23, 1936, *SL*, 307–10.

66. TNW to Gertrude Stein and Alice B. Toklas, January 25, 1936, YCAL.

67. TNW to Gertrude Stein and Alice B. Toklas, February 20, 1936, YCAL.

68. Ibid.

69. Jones Harris, among others, thought that TNW was in love with Ruth Gordon, Jones's mother.

70. TNW to Sibyl Colefax, January 23, 1936, *SL*, 307–10.

71. TNW to Mabel Dodge Luhan, January 17, 1937, YCAL. Samuel French published an acting edition of the play in England in 1932—its only acting edition to date.

72. TNW, preface to *Three Plays: Our Town, The Skin of Our Teeth, The Matchmaker* (New York: Harper & Brothers, 1957), vii.

73. TNW to Leslie Glenn, April 7, 1936, TNW Collection, YCAL.

74. TNW to Gertrude Stein and Alice B. Toklas, March 14, 1936, YCAL.

75. TNW to Mabel Dodge Luhan, January 17, 1937, YCAL.

76. TNW to ANW, April 9, 1937, TNW Collection, YCAL.

77. Ibid.

78. TNW to ANW, [April or May 1937?], TNW Collection, YCAL.

79. TNW to Amy Wertheimer, May 5, 1937, TNW Collection, YCAL.

80. TNW to ANW, n.d. [April or May 1937], TNW Collection, YCAL.

81. He wrote to his family September 15 or 16, 1937, that *The Prince of Baghdad* was "the best of em all." TNW to Isabella Niven Wilder and Isabel Wilder, "Sept 15th or 16th, 1937," TNW Collection, YCAL. An incomplete manuscript draft of *The Hell of the Vizier Kabäar* (one of the variations TNW used when spelling the title) survives among his papers at the Beinecke Library.

82. TNW to ANW, [April or May 1937?], TNW Collection, YCAL.

83. TNW to Amy Wertheimer, May 5, 1937, TNW Collection, YCAL.

84. TNW interview with Lucius Beebe, *New York Herald Tribune*, May 29, 1938; reprinted in Bryer, *Conversations with Thornton Wilder*, 18–21.

85. TNW, dedication to *The Ides of March* (New York: Harper & Brothers, 1948.)

86. TNW to Alexander Woollcott, [April 30, 1937], AWC, MS Am 1449 (1775), HLH.

87. TNW to Alexander Woollcott, Memorial Day 1937 [May 31], AWC, MS Am 1449 (1775), HLH.

25: THE VILLAGE AND THE STARS (1930S)

1. TNW, preface to *Three Plays*, xxviii.

2. TNW, "A PREFACE FOR OUR TOWN," 100–103

3. Ibid.

4. TNW to Family, October 21, 1920, TNW Collection, YCAL.

5. TNW, "Aphorisms," manuscript fragment, [1920s?], TNW Collection, YCAL.

6. TNW, *Our Town*, act 1.

7. TNW, manuscript fragment, n.d., TNW Collection, YCAL.

8. TNW to Gertrude Stein and Alice B. Toklas, May 30, 1937, YCAL.

9. TNW to Mabel Dodge Luhan, June 24, 1937, YCAL.

10. TNW to Alexander Woollcott, June 24, 1937, AWC, MS Am 1449 (1776), HLH.

11. Ibid.

12. TNW to Mabel Dodge Luhan, June 24, 1937, YCAL.

13. TNW to Dorothy Ulrich (Troubetzkoy), November 21, 1936, Private Collection.

14. TNW to Sibyl Colefax, September 25, 1937, New York University.

15. Ibid.

16. TNW to Mabel Dodge Luhan, March 22, 1937, YCAL. While TNW does not name *Swing Time* in this letter, he went to see the film in question for the second time in March 1937. *Swing Time*, directed by George Stevens, was released in 1936, and the plot centers around the need to raise money. The only Astaire-Rogers film in 1937 was *Shall We Dance*, which was not released until May of that year.

17. Ibid.

18. TNW to Mabel Dodge Luhan, June 24, 1937, YCAL.

19. TNW to Gertrude Stein and Alice B. Toklas, March 26, 1937, YCAL.

20. Ibid.

21. See TNW to Gertrude Stein and Alice B. Toklas, September 9, 1937, YCAL, for instance.

22. TNW to Alexander Woollcott, Memorial Day 1937 [May 31, 1937], AWC, MS Am 1449 (1775), HLH.

23. TNW to Mabel Dodge Luhan, June 24, 1937, YCAL.

24. TNW to Gertrude Stein and Alice B. Toklas, March 26, 1937, YCAL.

25. TNW to Alexander Woollcott, June 24, 1937, AWC, MS Am 1449 (1776), HLH.

26. With his appointment as the American delegate, TNW decided he should become a more active voice in the community of American writers. In 1937 he attended the Congress of American Writers meeting in New York, where he saw Hemingway, MacLeish, and Van Wyck Brooks and gathered ideas to take to the conference. He also became a more outspoken advocate for the work of other writers: In June, for instance, he heard Robert Frost read and encouraged Woollcott to include some of Frost's poems in his forthcoming new reader.

27. TNW to Gertrude Stein and Alice B. Toklas, June 22, 1937, YCAL.

28. TNW to Gertrude Stein and Alice B. Toklas, [July 1937?], YCAL.

29. TNW to Isabella Niven Wilder and Isabel Wilder ["Dear Children"], August 9, 1937, TNW Collection, YCAL.

30. Gertrude Stein to TNW, [July 18, 1937?], TNW's transcription of Stein's letter, YCAL.

31. TNW to Alexander Woollcott, October 29, 1937, AWC, MS Am 1449 (1776), HLH. This is a continuation of a letter begun on October 24, 1937.

32. TNW to Isabella Niven Wilder and Isabel Wilder, ["Dear Children"], August 9, 1937, TNW Collection, YCAL. In *Everybody's Autobiography* Stein wrote briefly of meeting TNW, and of their time together in Chicago, Paris, and Belignin. She praised their conversations, and wrote of making TNW her literary executor, but had second thoughts about whether he would make firm, clear decisions about her papers. She wrote about her concerns in *Everybody's Autobiography*, 310. Stein later made Carl Van Vechten her literary executor.

33. TNW to Isabella Niven Wilder and Isabel Wilder, ["Dear Children"], August 9, 1937, TNW Collection, YCAL.

34. TNW to Alexander Woollcott, August 29, 1937, AWC, MS Am 1449 (1776), HLH.

35. TNW to Alexander Woollcott, October 24, 1937, AWC, MS Am 1449 (1776), HLH. Sibyl Colefax's papers, records, diaries, and drawings may be found, for the most part, in the Bodleian Library, Oxford University. Her letters to TNW are, for the most part, housed at New York University, as Richard Goldstone bought the letters for use in his biography of Wilder, and later deposited them there. He was an English professor at the College of the City of New York, and the author of *Thornton Wilder: An Intimate Portrait*.

36. TNW to Isabel Wilder, August 25, 1937, TNW Collection, YCAL.

37. Isabel Wilder to Janet Wilder [Dakin], May 3, 1937, TNW Collection, YCAL, uncataloged letters.

38. Ibid.

39. TNW to Isabel Wilder, August 25, 1937, TNW Collection, YCAL.

40. TNW to Gertrude Stein and Alice B. Toklas, August 26, 1937, *SL*, 319–20. Years later TNW would use this scenario, with slight changes, in his semiautobiographical, semifictional early manuscript drafts for *Theophilus North*.

41. TNW to Gertrude Stein and Alice B. Toklas, September 3, 1937, YCAL.

42. TNW to Gertrude Stein and Alice B. Toklas, September 9, 1937, YCAL.

43. TNW to Samuel Steward, [September 9, 1937?], TNW Collection, YCAL.

44. Samuel Steward, *Chapters from an Autobiography* (San Francisco: Grey Fox Press, 1981), 75.

45. Ibid.

46. Ibid., 45.

47. Ibid., 46.

48. Ibid., 73.

49. TNW to Gertrude Stein and Alice B. Toklas, September 13, 1937, YCAL.

50. Steward to Gertrude Stein and Alice B. Toklas, September 15, 1937, YCAL.

51. Steward, *Chapters from an Autobiography*, 74.

52. Ibid., 75.

53. Ibid.

54. Owen Keehnen, "A Very Magical Life: Talking with Samuel Steward," Summer 1993, http://www.queerculturalcenter.org/Pages/Keehnen/Steward.html.

55. Samuel Steward, *Dear Sammy: Letters from Gertrude Stein & Alice B. Toklas* (Boston: Houghton Mifflin, 1977), 32.

56. TNW to Alexander Woollcott, June 24, 1937, AWC, MS Am 1449 (1776), HLH, quoted in part above, and TNW to Sibyl Colefax, January 2, 1938, *SL*, 328–31.

57. TNW to Isabella Niven Wilder and Isabel Wilder, September "16 or 17," 1937, YCAL. Steward gives this account in *Chapters from an Autobiography*, 74, in the section titled "Thornton and the Touch of Eros," 70–77. In a slightly different, third-hand account in his earlier book, *Dear Sammy: Letters from Gertrude Stein and Alice B. Toklas*, 32, Steward quotes Alice B. Toklas, repeating what she said that Gertrude Stein said to her: "And Sammy, do you know he [Wilder] liked you? He was writing *Our Town* in Zurich and was stuck at the end of the second act, and you walked all night in the rain with him and he struck a match on you, he said, and wrote the whole third act the next day while you were sleeping."

58. TNW to Georg Wagner, "A 'European in the New World': A Conversation with Thornton Wilder," *Freude an Beuchem* (Vienna) 4 (June 1953): 126–28; reprinted in Bryer, *Conversations with Thornton Wilder*, 59.

59. TNW to Isabella Niven Wilder, November 5, 1922, TNW Collection, YCAL.

60. TNW to Edward Howard Marsh, [June 1, 1931?], Berg Collection, New York Public Library.

61. TNW, Journal, February 9, 1939, TNW Collection, YCAL.

62. Steward, *Chapters from an Autobiography*, 76–77. Steward's recollections about Wilder were first published in a slightly different version as "The Secret Citizen of 'Our Town': Thornton Wilder: Sam Steward Remembers the Man," *The Advocate*,

May 29, 1980, 24–27, 59. Steward later wrote pornographic novels under a pseud-onym—Phil Andros, one of many pseudonyms he used as a writer. He also had a long, colorful career as a tattoo artist under the name Phil Sparrow. He was inter-viewed and filmed as part of the studies of homosexuality conducted by Dr. Alfred Kinsey of the Institute for Sex Research in Bloomington, Indiana. Late in his life, using his real name, Steward wrote two mystery novels starring Gertrude Stein and Alice B. Toklas as detectives. He died in 1993. For a full-length biography of Stew-ard, see Justin Spring, *Secret Historian: The Life and Times of Samuel Steward, Professor, Tattoo Artist, and Sexual Renegade* (New York: Farrar, Straus & Giroux, 2010).

63. Quoted in Jerry Rosco, *Glenway Wescott Personally: A Biography* (Madison: Univer-sity of Wisconsin Press, 2002), 143.

64. PEN conversation with Arthur Laurents, University of North Carolina School of the Arts, Winston-Salem, May 2007; Paul Gregory to PEN, November 19, 2010. Jerome Kilty is quoted as saying, "I would have heard rumors and I heard none; he was a most fastidious man." See Harrison, *The Enthusiast*, 168–69.

    See Acocella, *Willa Cather and the Politics of Criticism*, for a relevant and astute discussion of the literary implications of sex and gender and the critical perspec-tives thereof.

65. TNW, Journal, Entry 649, July 20, 1953, TNW Collection, YCAL.

66. TNW, Journal, Entry 33, October 29, 1940, TNW Collection, YCAL.

67. TNW to Gertrude Stein and Alice B. Toklas, September 13, 1937, YCAL.

68. Quoted in TNW, introduction to Stein, *Four in America.*

69. TNW, *The Woman of Andros,* 197.

70. TNW to Gertrude Stein and Alice B. Toklas, September 22, 1937, YCAL.

71. Gilles Deleuze, "Commentary," in Kaufmann, *Basic Writings of Nietzsche*, 858.

72. Gertrude Stein, *The Making of Americans* (London: Dalkey Archive Press, 1995), 743.

73. TNW, *The Woman of Andros,* 148–49.

74. TNW to Isabella Niven Wilder and Isabel Wilder, "September 15th or 16th 1937," TNW Collection, YCAL.

75. TNW to Sibyl Colefax, September 25, 1937, New York University.

76. TNW to Alexander Woollcott, October 24, 1937, AWC, MS Am 1449 (1776), HLH.

26: "CHALK . . . OR FIRE" (LATE 1930S)

1. TNW to Isabella Niven Wilder and Isabel Wilder, October 28, 1937, TNW Collec-tion, YCAL.

2. Ruth Gordon to TNW, August 18, [1937?], TNW Collection, YCAL.

3. Bibi Gaston, *The Loveliest Woman in America* (New York: William Morrow, 2008). Bibi Gaston is the granddaughter of Rosamund Pinchot (Gaston).

4. TNW to Max Reinhardt, December 9, 1937, *SL*, 323–24.

5. TNW to Amy Wertheimer, November 24, 1937, TNW Collection, YCAL.

6. TNW to J. Dwight Dana, December 20, 1937, *SL*, 324–26.

7. Ruth Gordon to TNW, August 18, [1937?], TNW Collection, YCAL.

8. TNW to J. Dwight Dana, December 20, 1937, *SL*, 324–26.

9. TNW to Sibyl Colefax, January 2, 1938, *SL*, 328–31.

10. Ibid.

11. TNW to J. Dwight Dana, December 20, 1937, *SL*, 324–26.

12. TNW to Sibyl Colefax, January 2, 1938, *SL*, 328–31.

13. Ibid.

14. Ibid.

15. Readers interested in seeing these variations can read the entire letter from TNW to Sibyl Colefax, January 2, 1938, in *SL*, 328–31, and compare it with the text of the play in TNW, *Our Town* (New York: HarperPerennial, 2003), 47–48.

16. TNW to Gertrude Stein and Alice B. Toklas, January 12, 1938, YCAL.

17. TNW to Alexander Woollcott, January 27, 1938, *SL*, 333–37.

18. TNW to Edward Sheldon, quoted in Eric Wollencott Barnes, *The Man Who Lived Twice: The Biography of Edward Sheldon* (New York: Charles Scribner's Sons, 1956), 219.

19. Ibid.

20. TNW, 1926 Journal, TNW Collection, YCAL.

21. Edward Sheldon to TNW, quoted in Barnes, *The Man Who Lived Twice: The Biography of Edward Sheldon*, 220.

22. Ibid.

23. Ibid.

24. TNW to Jed Harris, [January 1938?], *SL*, 332.

25. TNW, Note on "Elements in the Production of 'Our Town,'" January 22, 1938, TNW Collection, YCAL.

26. TNW to Dwight Dana, January 23, 1938, Private Collection.

27. [———] Rosen, "Plays Out of Town: *Our Town*," *Variety*, January 26, 1938, 58.

28. For detailed accounts of the Harris-Pinchot relationship, see Martin Gottfried, *Jed Harris: The Curse of Genius* (Boston: Little, Brown, 1984); and Gaston, *The Loveliest Woman in America*.

29. Gaston, *The Loveliest Woman in America*, 240–43.

30. TNW to Alexander Woollcott, January 27, 1938, *SL*, 333–37.

31. "Miss Pinchot's Suicide Follows New Play Theme," *New York Daily News*, January 25, 1938, 1.

32. For various accounts of Rosamund Pinchot's death, see Gaston, *The Loveliest Woman in America*, 200–58; Gottfried, *Jed Harris: The Curse of Genius*, 163–74; Marc Connelly, *Voices Offstage: A Book of Memoirs* (Chicago, New York, and San Francisco: Holt, Rinehart & Winston, 1968), 232–33; Donald Haberman, *Our Town: An American Play* (Boston: Twayne Publishers, 1989), 99; Tappan Wilder, afterword to *Our Town*, 122–24.

33. TNW to Alexander Woollcott, January 27, 1938, *SL*, 333–37.

34. Alexander Woollcott to TNW, January 26, 1938, TNW Collection, YCAL.

35. TNW to Alexander Woollcott, January 27, 1938, *SL*, 333–37.

36. Alexander Woollcott to TNW, January 28, 1938, TNW Collection, YCAL.

37. Ibid.

38. "Thornton Wilder Presented with a Gavel," *Boston Evening Transcript*, January 26, 1938.

39. TNW to Alexander Woollcott, January 27, 1938, *SL*, 333–37. The *Boston Evening Transcript* report on the gavel presentation on January 26, 1938, indicated that there were fifty members rather than the forty-one cited by TNW in his letter.

40. TNW to Dwight Dana, January 29, 1938, *SL*, 337–38.
41. Ibid.
42. Ibid.
43. Ibid.
44. Connelly, *Voices Offstage: A Book of Memoirs*, 233–34.
45. Ibid., 234–35.
46. TNW to Isabella Niven Wilder, Feb. 2, [1938?], YCAL.
47. TNW to Dwight Dana, [February 6, 1938?], *SL*, 339.
48. Tappan Wilder to PEN, May 6, 2010.
49. Eleanor Roosevelt, "My Day," *New York World-Telegram*, March 2, 1938.
50. Brooks Atkinson, "Standards in Drama Criticism: Mrs. Roosevelt's Dissatisfaction with the Comments on the Stage in This Newspaper and One Other," *New York Times*, March 13, 1938, p. 1, sec. 9.
51. TNW to Harry Luce, February 14, 1938, Henry Luce Papers, LC.
52. TNW to Gertrude Stein and Alice B. Toklas, [late February 1938?], YCAL.
53. TNW to Gertrude Stein and Alice B. Toklas, February 1, 1938, YCAL.
54. TNW to Ernest Hemingway, March 1, 1938, *SL*, 340–41.
55. Quoted by TNW in a letter to his family, [March 10, 1938?], TNW Collection, YCAL.
56. Charlotte Wilder to ANW, [1938?], TNW Collection, YCAL, uncataloged papers.
57. Isabella Niven Wilder to Isabel Wilder, April 29, [1938?], TNW Collection, YCAL, uncataloged papers. Net income tax figures provided by Tappan Wilder and used by permission.
58. TNW to Sibyl Colefax, January 2, 1938, *SL*, 328–38.
59. TNW to Gertrude Stein and Alice B. Toklas, March 27, 1938, YCAL.
60. TNW to Family, March 11, 1938, TNW Collection, YCAL.
61. TNW to Gertrude Stein and Alice B. Toklas, March 27, 1938, YCAL.
62. Ibid.
63. TNW to Gertrude Stein and Alice B. Toklas, April 23, 1938, YCAL.
64. TNW to Family, March 16, 1938, TNW Collection, YCAL.
65. TNW to Gertrude Stein and Alice B. Toklas, April 23, 1938, YCAL.
66. TNW to Family, March 21, 1938, TNW Collection, YCAL.
67. TNW to Christina Hopkinson Baker, March 27, 1938, YCAL.
68. Ibid.
69. TNW to Elizabeth Shepley Sergeant, April 27, 1938, University of Virginia, Charlottesville.
70. TNW to Christina Hopkinson Baker, March 27, 1938, *SL*, 341–42.
71. Isabella Niven Wilder to Isabel Wilder, April 29, [1938?], TNW Collection, YCAL, uncataloged letters.
72. Isabella Niven Wilder to Charlotte Wilder, [1938?], TNW Collection, YCAL, uncataloged letters.
73. Isabella Niven Wilder to Isabel Wilder, April 29, [1938?], TNW Collection, YCAL, uncataloged letters.
74. TNW to Sam Steward, May 18, 1938, TNW Collection, YCAL.
75. TNW to Sam Steward, March 28, [1938], TNW Collection, YCAL.
76. TNW to Elizabeth Shepley Sergeant, April 27, 1938, University of Virginia, Charlottesville.

77. TNW to Family, March 21, 1938, TNW Collection, YCAL.
78. Ibid.
79. TNW to Alexander Woollcott, May 17, 1938, AWC, MS Am 1449 (1777), HLH.
80. TNW to Ruth Gordon, [no day] 1938, Private Collection.
81. TNW to Alexander Woollcott, June 17, 1938, AWC, MS Am 1449 (1777), HLH.
82. For background on Max Reinhardt, see Gottfried Reinhardt, *The Genius: A Memoir of Max Reinhardt* (New York: Alfred A. Knopf, 1979).
83. TNW to Max Reinhardt, May 12, 1938, Österreichisches Theatermuseum, Vienna.
84. TNW to Ruth Gordon, June 21, 1938, *SL*, 345–47.
85. Ibid.
86. Ibid.
87. The Pilgrimage Theatre in Hollywood is now known as the John Anson Ford Amphitheatre. It was built in 1920, destroyed by fire in 1929, and rebuilt in 1931. It was constructed to resemble the gates of Jerusalem because it was used for an annual pilgrimage play.
88. TNW to Alexander Woollcott, July 20, 1938, AWC, MS Am (1777), HLH.
89. Ibid.
90. TNW to Alexander Woollcott, [September 1938?], *SL*, 347–48. I have dated this letter September because Jed Harris asked TNW to step into the Stage Manager's role on September 6, 1938, according to TNW's September 20, [1938?], letter to his mother.
91. TNW to Isabella Niven Wilder, September 20, [1938?], TNW Collection, YCAL.
92. TNW to Gertrude Stein and Alice B. Toklas, September 23, 1938, YCAL.
93. "'Mice and Men' Gets Award of Drama Critics," *New York Herald Tribune*, April 17, 1938.
94. TNW to Alexander Woollcott, [September 1938?], *SL*, 347–48.

27: "PERSEVERANCE" (1938–1940)

1. TNW to Alexander Woollcott, March 28, 1938, AWC, MS Am 1449 (1777), HLH.
2. Ibid.
3. Tappan Wilder to PEN, June 4, 2010.
4. TNW to Albert Einstein, September 19, 1938, *SL*, 351–52.
5. TNW to John Hobart, "Thoughts from a Novelist in the Throes of Stage Fever," *San Francisco Chronicle*, September 11, 1938, 17, 21; reprinted in Bryer, *Conversations with Thornton Wilder*, 27–20.
6. TNW to Alexander Woollcott, [September 1938?], *SL*, 347–48; and TNW to Alexander Woollcott, September 30, 1938, AWC, MS Am 1449 (1778), HLH.
7. TNW to Alexander Woollcott, September 30, 1938, AWC, MS Am 1449 (1778), HLH.
8. TNW to Alexander Woollcott, October 22, 1938, AWC, MS Am 1449 (1778), HLH.
9. TNW to Alexander Woollcott, November 9, 1938, AWC, MS Am 1449 (1779), HLH.
10. TNW to Alexander Woollcott, November 2, [1938?], AWC, MS Am 1449 (1778), HLH.
11. TNW to Bobsy Goodspeed [later Mrs. Gilbert Chapman], November 4, 1938, YCAL.
12. TNW to Dr. Sergei Bertensson, October 24, 1938, Österreichisches Theatermuseum, Vienna.

13. TNW to Bobsy Goodspeed, November 4, 1938, YCAL.

14. Ibid.

15. TNW to Alexander Woollcott, November 2, [1938?], AWC, MS Am 1449 (1778), HLH.

16. TNW to Dr. Sergei Bertensson, October 24, 1938, Österreichisches Theatermuseum, Vienna.

17. Ibid.

18. TNW to Alexander Woollcott, November 2, [1938?], AWC, MS Am 1449 (1778), HLH.

19. TNW to Helene Thimig Reinhardt, November 20, 1938, *SL*, 352–54.

20. TNW to Helene Thimig Reinhardt, November 15, 1938, Österreichisches Theatermuseum, Vienna.

21. Alexander Woollcott to Robert Maynard Hutchins, December 19, 1938, published in Beatrice Kaufman and Joseph Hennessey, eds., *The Letters of Alexander Woollcott* (New York: Viking Press, 1944), 215.

22. TNW to Alexander Woollcott, December 6, [1938?], AWC, MS Am 1449 (1779), HLH.

23. TNW to Gertrude Stein and Alice B. Toklas, March 2, 1939, YCAL.

24. TNW to Sibyl Colefax, February 7, 1939, *SL*, 363–66.

25. TNW to Elizabeth Shepley Sergeant, January 9, 1939, University of Virginia, Charlottesville.

26. TNW to Max and Helene Thimig Reinhardt, January 13, 1939, Österreichisches Theatermuseum, Vienna.

27. Talcott B. Clapp, "Thornton Wilder Writing New Play," *Waterbury (Connecticut) Republican*, June 19, 1949; reprinted in Bryer, *Conversations with Thornton Wilder*, 49.

28. TNW to Gertrude Stein and Alice B. Toklas, March 28, 1939, YCAL.

29. TNW to Max and Helene Thimig Reinhardt, February 11, 1939, Österreichisches Theatermuseum, Vienna. By "both my plays," TNW was referring to *Our Town* and *The Merchant of Yonkers*.

30. Ibid.

31. TNW to Max Reinhardt, August 2, 1938, Österreichisches Theatermuseum, Vienna.

32. TNW to Max and Helene Thimig Reinhardt, January 13, 1939, Österreichisches Theatermuseum, Vienna.

33. TNW to Sibyl Colefax, February 7, 1939, *SL*, 363–66.

34. TNW to Max and Helene Thimig Reinhardt, February 11, 1939, Österreichisches Theatermuseum, Vienna.

35. TNW to Sibyl Colefax, February 7, 1939, NYU [*SL*, 364].

36. Ibid.

37. Ibid.

38. TNW to Alexander Woollcott, February 8, 1939, AWC, MS Am 1449 (1779), HLH.

39. TNW to Alexander Woollcott, February 25, 1939, AWC, MS Am 1449 (1779), HLH.

40. TNW to Gertrude Stein and Alice B. Toklas, March 2, 1939, YCAL.

41. TNW to Sibyl Colefax, February 7, 1939, *SL*, 363–66.

42. TNW to Alexander Woollcott, March 21, 1939, AWC, MS Am 1449 (1780), HLH.

43. Ibid.

44. TNW to Max Reinhardt, April 26, 1939, Österreichisches Theatermuseum, Vienna.

45. Ibid.

46. TNW, "Sophocles's [*sic*] *Oedipus Rex*," introduction to Francis Storr, ed., *Oedipus the King* (New York: Heritage Press, 1955); reprinted in Gallup, *American Characteristics*, 77–87, and McClatchy, ed. *Thornton Wilder: Collected Plays & Writings on Theater*, 710–19.

47. TNW to Max Reinhardt, April 26, 1939, Österreichisches Theatermuseum, Vienna.

48. TNW to Professor and Mrs. Max Reinhardt, July 28, 1939, Österreichisches Theatermuseum, Vienna.

49. TNW to Dwight Dana, April 26, 1939, Private Collection.

50. TNW to Professor and Mrs. Max Reinhardt, July 28, 1939, Österreichisches Theatermuseum, Vienna.

51. TNW to Gertrude Stein and Alice B. Toklas, [June 24, 1939?], YCAL.

52. Isabel Wilder to Dwight Dana, August 15, 1939, Private Collection.

53. TNW to Gertrude Stein and Alice B. Toklas, [August 20, 1939?], YCAL.

54. Ibid.

55. TNW to Gertrude Stein and Alice B. Toklas, September 11, 1939, YCAL.

56. Ibid.

57. Gertrude Stein to TNW, [postmarked October 1, 1939], TNW Collection, YCAL.

58. TNW to Dwight Dana, September 23, 1939, Private Collection.

59. TNW to Wilson Lehr, September 29, 1939, YCAL. Wilson Lehr was a 1939 graduate of the drama program at Yale. Cheryl Crawford was an organizing founder with Lee Strasberg and Howard Clurman of the Group Theatre on Broadway.

60. As noted, Wilder never finished the adaptation of *The Beaux' Stratagem*. After his literary executor, Tappan Wilder, discovered the unfinished manuscript among his papers at the Beinecke Library, he persuaded the playwright Ken Ludwig to complete the adaptation. The Shakespeare Theatre Company in Washington, D.C., gave the world premiere performance of the Farquhar-Wilder-Ludwig script on November 7, 2006. "Practical entertainment": TNW to Wilson Lehr, November 26, 1939, *SL*, 370–71.

61. TNW to Huntington T. Day [Dwight Dana's law partner], September 8, 1939, Private Collection.

62. Ibid.

63. TNW to Wilson Lehr, September 29, 1939, TNW Collection, YCAL.

64. Readers interested in the making of the script and the film may read much of the Wilder-Lesser correspondence in "Our Town—From Stage to Screen: A Correspondence Between Thornton Wilder and Sol Lesser," in McClatchy, *Thornton Wilder: Collected Plays & Writings on Theater*, 663–81.

65. TNW to Sol Lesser, October 7, 1939, in McClatchy, *Thornton Wilder: Collected Plays & Writings on Theater*, 663–65.

66. TNW to Sol Lesser, October 9, 1939, *SL*, 368–70.

67. TNW to Gertrude Stein and Alice B. Toklas, October 20, 1939, YCAL.

68. "In solitary confinement": TNW to Gertrude Stein and Alice B. Toklas, September 11, 1939, YCAL; "Hope and dread": TNW to Gertrude Stein and Alice B. Toklas, October 29, 1939, YCAL.

69. TNW to Wilson Lehr, November 26, 1939, *SL*, 370–71.

70. TNW to Gertrude Stein and Alice B. Toklas, [November 18, 1939?], YCAL.

71. Charlotte Wilder to ANW, [March 11, 1940?], TNW collection, YCAL, uncataloged letters.

72. TNW to Edmund Wilson, January 13, 1940, YCAL.

73. TNW to Gertrude Stein and Alice B. Toklas, January 28, 1940, YCAL.

74. TNW to Edmund Wilson, February 23, 1940, YCAL.

75. TNW to Gertrude Stein and Alice B. Toklas, January 28, 1940, YCAL.

76. TNW to Sol Lesser, November 12, 1939, in McClatchy, *Thornton Wilder: Collected Plays & Writings on Theater*, 671–72.

77. Sol Lesser to TNW, March 21, 1940, TNW Collection, YCAL.

78. TNW to Sol Lesser, [Easter Night 1940?], *SL*, 374–76.

79. Sol Lesser to Isabel Wilder, December 4, 1939, TNW Collection, YCAL; Isabel Wilder to Sol Lesser, December 5, 1939, in McClatchy, *Thornton Wilder: Collected Plays & Writings on Theater*, 672.

80. TNW to Sol Lesser, December 26, 1939, in McClatchy, *Thornton Wilder: Collected Plays & Writings on Theater*, 672.

81. TNW to Gertrude Stein and Alice B. Toklas, January 28, 1940, *SL*, 371–74.

82. TNW to Gertrude Stein and Alice B. Toklas, "Middle of March" [1940?], YCAL.

83. Charlotte Wilder's share of the 1936 Shelley Memorial Award was $425. P. A. Scott, Trust Officer, Mary P. Sears Trust, to Charlotte Wilder, January 5, 1937, Private Collection.

84. In his later books e. e. cummings became E. E. Cummings. Hugh Van Dusen to PEN, May 19, 2010.

85. TNW to Gertrude Stein and Alice B. Toklas, January 28, 1940, YCAL.

86. TNW, February 21, 1939, 1939–1941 Journal, TNW Collection, YCAL. Many passages from this journal and other TNW journals are published in Donald Gallup, ed., *The Journals of Thornton Wilder 1939–1961* (New Haven: Yale University Press, 1985), but many key passages, especially from 1940 onward, remain unpublished as of this writing.

87. TNW, February 21, 1939, 1939–1941 Journal, TNW Collection, YCAL.

88. Ibid.

89. TNW to Gertrude Stein and Alice B. Toklas, "Middle of March" 1940, YCAL.

90. Ibid.

91. Ibid.

92. Isabel Wilder to Dwight Dana, June 16, 1931, private collection.

93. TNW to Alexander Woollcott, March 29, [1940], AWC, MS Am 1449 (1781), HLH.

94. Ibid.

95. TNW, 1939–1941 Journal, May 2, 1940, TNW Collection, YCAL.

96. TNW to Gertrude Stein and Alice B. Toklas, May 3, 1940, YCAL.

97. "Boston Welcomes *Our Town* After All Nation Has," *New Haven Register*, May 24, 1940.

98. Bosley Crowther, "The Screen: 'Our Town' a Beautiful and Tender Picture, at the Music Hall . . . ," *New York Times*, June 14, 1940, 25. Frank Craven played the Stage Manager on-screen as he had onstage. Martha Scott was Emily, receiving an Academy Award nomination as best actress. (Ginger Rogers won for *Kitty Foyle*, one of her few movies that didn't involve dancing.) The young William Holden, at the beginning of his film career, played George Gibbs, and the cast included Beulah Bondi, Fay Bainter, and Thomas Mitchell. Aaron Copland was nominated for an Academy Award for Best Score (which went to the music for Walt Disney's *Pinocchio*).

99. "Vast and terrible events": TNW to Richard Beer-Hofmann, August 6, 1940, *SL*, 377–78; "More in crisis than the last": TNW to Sibyl Colefax, June 14, 1940, *SL*, 376–77.

28: "SEEING, KNOWING AND TELLING" (1940S)

1. TNW to Edmund Wilson, June 3, 1940, YCAL. Wilson wrote several articles on Joyce, including a two-part article on *Finnegans Wake* that appeared in the *New Republic* in 1939.
2. TNW to Edmund Wilson, June 15, 1940, YCAL.
3. Ibid. "The Figure in the Carpet" is the title of a short story by Henry James in which a novelist observes that literary critics often miss his themes and intentions because they must be detected and deciphered like a subtle "figure" in a Persian carpet.
4. Edmund Wilson to TNW, June 20, 1940, TNW Collection, YCAL.
5. TNW to Edmund Wilson, June 26, 1940, YCAL.
6. Edmund Wilson to TNW, June 20, 1940, TNW Collection, YCAL.
7. TNW, 1939–41 Journal, July 6, 1940, TNW Collection, YCAL.
8. TNW to Gertrude Stein and Alice B. Toklas, July 31, 1940, YCAL.
9. TNW, 1939–41 Journal, May 23, 1940, TNW Collection, YCAL. As previously noted, while many entries from TNW's journals are published in Gallup, *The Journals of Thornton Wilder, 1939–1961*, many other entries, including this one, are unpublished at this writing.
10. Ibid.
11. TNW to Richard Beer-Hofmann, August 6, 1940, *SL*, 377–78.
12. TNW, 1939–41 Journal, October 26, 1940, TNW Collection, YCAL. Later, in the final text of the play, Wilder changed the length of the Antrobus marriage to five thousand years.
13. TNW to Max Reinhardt, December 17, 1940, Österreichisches Theatermuseum, Vienna.
14. TNW, 1939–41 Journal, October 26, 1940, TNW Collection, YCAL.
15. Ibid.
16. Ibid.
17. Ibid.
18. TNW, 1939–41 Journal, November 1, 1940, TNW Collection, YCAL.
19. TNW to Richard Beer-Hofmann, August 6, 1940, *SL*, 377–78.
20. TNW to Rosemary Ames, December 6, 1940, YCAL.
21. TNW to Alexander Woollcott, October 1940, AWC, MS Am 1449 (1781B), HLH.
22. Ibid.
23. Ibid.
24. TNW to Rosemary Ames, December 6, 1940, YCAL.
25. TNW to Gertrude Stein and Alice B. Toklas, July 31, 1940, YCAL.
26. "Unknown Subjects: Austrian Refugee Camp," Federal Bureau of Investigation File 65–1146, September 25, 1940, regarding July 19, 1940, Period. Obtained under the Freedom of Information Act.
27. "Thornton Niven Wilder, Unknown Subjects: Austrian Refugee Camp [Redacted] Estate Near Keene, New Hampshire," Federal Bureau of Investigation File 65–265,

January 9, 1941, regarding November 25, 26, 1940, to December 8, 1940/January 7, 1941, Period. Obtained under the Freedom of Information Act.

28. Ibid.

29. "Re: Thornton Wilder," Federal Bureau of Investigation File 65–1146, December 15, 1949. Obtained under the Freedom of Information Act.

30. These associations are listed in Wilder's FBI file. By 1954 all of these organizations had been declared suspect and/or subversive by the attorney general of the United States.

31. TNW to Gertrude Stein and Alice B. Toklas, January 28, 1940, *SL*, 371–74. TNW also helped the Austrian author Hermann Broch; the Austrian dramatist and poet Richard Beer-Hofmann (writing the introduction of an English translation of Beer-Hofmann's play, *Jakobs Traum*, in 1946); and the Austrian critic and teacher Frederick (Friedrich) Lehner and his wife, among others.

32. Eleanor Roosevelt's remarks and TNW remarks, "Prominent Writers' Statements of Why They Are for Franklin D. Roosevelt, Made on the Radio Program Presented Under the Auspices of The Women's Division of the Democratic National Committee, Friday, September 27, 1940," Franklin D. Roosevelt Library, 2.

33. TNW, 1939–41 Journal, October 2, 1940, TNW Collection, YCAL.

34. TNW to Sibyl Colefax, September 26, 1940, New York University.

35. TNW, 1939–41 Journal, October 26, 1940, TNW Collection, YCAL.

36. Ibid.

37. TNW, 1939–41 Journal, October 29, 1940, TNW Collection, YCAL.

38. Ibid.

39. TNW, *Theophilus North*, 4.

40. An allusion to Gaetano Donizetti's comic opera, *The Daughter of the Regiment* (1840).

41. TNW, *The Skin of Our Teeth* (New York: HarperPerennial, 2003), 14–15. Page references for *The Skin of Our Teeth* are from this edition. The reference to the rape in the Sabine Hills alludes to the legend that Roman soldiers kidnapped and raped Sabine women in order to increase the population of Rome. George Antrobus's alleged participation in these transgressions occurred in his youth, thousands of years in the distant past; of course, that is no excuse, as far as Maggie Antrobus is concerned.

42. Ibid., 81–83.

43. Ibid., 54.

44. Ibid., 102–3.

45. TNW, 1939–41 Journal, October 26, 1940, YCAL.

46. Ibid.

47. TNW, 1939–41 Journal, October 2, 1940, YCAL.

48. TNW, 1939–41 Journal, November 3, 1940, YCAL.

49. Ibid.

50. Ibid.

51. Ibid.

52. TNW to Amy Wertheimer, November 13, 1940, TNW Collection, YCAL.

53. TNW, 1939–41 Journal, November 3, 1940, YCAL.

54. TNW to Isabella Niven Wilder and Isabel Wilder, November 6, 1940, TNW Collection, YCAL.

55. Ibid.

56. Ibid.

57. TNW to Alexander Woollcott, November 8, 1940, AWC, MS Am 1449 (1781B), HLH.
58. TNW to Alexander Woollcott, December 27, 1940, AWC, MS Am 1449 (1781B), HLH.
59. Ibid.
60. Alexander Woollcott to Lynn Fontanne, February 21, 1941, in Kaufman and Hennessey, *The Letters of Alexander Woollcott*, 271.
61. "Protracted conversations": TNW to "Agatha" [Elizabeth Artzybasheff], January 26, [1941?], YCAL; "Brotherhood of Man": TNW to Isabella Niven Wilder, January 21, [1941?], TNW Collection, YCAL.
62. TNW to Sibyl Colefax, February 20, 1941, New York University.
63. TNW to "Agatha" [Elizabeth Artzybasheff], January 26, [1941?], YCAL.
64. TNW to Alexander Woollcott, November 8, 1940, AWC, MS Am 1449 (1781B), HLH.
65. TNW to Charlotte Wilder, calling card, [February 1941?], Private Collection.
66. TNW to Charlotte Wilder, [February 27, 1941?], TNW Collection, YCAL.
67. TNW to Robert Hutchins, February [no day] 1941, University of Chicago Library.

29: "THE ETERNAL FAMILY" (1940s)

1. The *Santa Lucia* was one of the Grace Line ships regularly making the voyage from New York to South America. In 1942 the U.S. Navy took over the ship and renamed it the USS *Leedstown*. The ship was sunk in the North African invasion.
2. Isabella Niven Wilder to ANW, March 1, 1941, ANW, Wilder Family Record, TNW Collection, YCAL, uncataloged papers.
3. Ibid. "Frightened and exhausted": ANW handwritten notes on Charlotte's illness, n.d., Private Collection. The details of Charlotte's breakdown are drawn from letters, documents, and medical records of the period. Many years after the 1941 event Isabel Wilder gave interviews about it, but her later accounts diverge in some matters from the accounts she, her mother, and others gave in 1941.
4. The Payne Whitney Psychiatric Clinic of New York–Presbyterian Hospital and the Cornell University Medical College (now known as Weill Cornell Medical College) were founded in 1932.
5. During his tenure at the New York Hospital and Departments of Medicine, Cornell University Medical College, New York, Dr. Lincoln Rahman (1904–56) was already publishing his research. He moved from New York to Los Angeles, where he worked until his death in 1956 in an automobile accident. He was associate professor of psychiatry at the University of Southern California Medical School, director of the Clinic of the Los Angeles Institute for Psychoanalysis, and an officer of the Southern California Psychiatric Society.
6. Isabella Niven Wilder to Dwight Dana, March 3, 1941, Private Collection.
7. Ibid.
8. Dwight Dana to Isabella Niven Wilder, March 5, 1941, carbon copy, Private Collection.
9. Isabel Wilder to Dwight Dana, March 31, 1941, Private Collection.
10. TNW to Toby Dakin, March 21, 1941, TNW Collection, YCAL.

11. Isabel Wilder to Dwight Dana, March 5, 1941, Private Collection.

12. Isabel Wilder to Dwight Dana, March 8, 1941, Private Collection.

13. Isabel Wilder to Dwight Dana, March 13, 1941, Private Collection.

14. TNW, *The Skin of Our Teeth*, 45.

15. Ibid., 45–46.

16. Ibid., 25.

17. Charlotte Wilder to Isabella Niven Wilder, n.d. [from 102 Greenwich Avenue, New York], TNW Collection, YCAL, uncataloged letters.

18. Charlotte Wilder to ANW, October 11, 1939, TNW Collection, YCAL, uncataloged letters.

19. Charlotte Wilder to Rollo Brown, October 15, [1939?], TNW Collection, YCAL, uncataloged letters.

20. Charlotte Wilder to ANW, [1938 or 1939?], ANW, Wilder Family Record, Private Collection.

21. ANW, *The Spiritual Aspects of the New Poetry* (New York: Harper & Brothers, 1940), 90–94.

22. Charlotte Wilder, "(For the Two)," *Phases of the Moon*, 90.

23. Charlotte Wilder, "Monologue of Repression, ii. The Virginal Inference, iv," *Phases of the Moon*, 88.

24. Isabel Wilder to Dwight Dana, March 5, 1941, Private Collection.

25. Isabella Niven Wilder to ANW, March 23, 1941, discussed by ANW, Wilder Family Record, n.d., TNW Collection, YCAL, uncataloged papers.

26. Isabel Wilder to Dwight Dana, March 13, 1941, Private Collection.

27. Dwight Dana to Isabel Wilder, March 14, 1941, Private Collection.

28. Isabel Wilder to Dwight Dana, April 10, 1941, Private Collection.

29. Ibid.

30. TNW to Gertrude Stein and Alice B. Toklas, April 1, 1941, YCAL.

31. TNW to Gertrude Stein and Alice B. Toklas, May 8, 1941, YCAL.

32. Isabel Wilder to Dwight Dana, April 3, 1941, Private Collection.

33. TNW to Alexander Woollcott, [April 6?] 1941, *SL*, 385–86.

34. TNW to Ruth Gordon, May 26, 1941, Private Collection.

35. TNW to Gertrude Stein and Alice B. Toklas, April 1, 1941, YCAL.

36. Ibid.

37. TNW to Gertrude Stein and Alice B. Toklas, May 8, 1941, YCAL. The novel by Fernando González Ochoa was *El maestro de escuela*. Erico Verissimo's book was *Préto em Campo de Neve*, about the United States, and included a chapter headed "Os Wilders de New Haven."

38. TNW to Sibyl Colefax, February 20, 1941, New York University.

39. TNW to Ruth Gordon, May 26, 1941, *SL*, 387. A copy of TNW's unofficial report on his South American trip may be found among his YCAL papers, a holograph "Memorandum" regarding "Some suggestions derived from a trip to Colombia, Ecuador, and Peru. . . ," May 1941.

40. TNW to Gertrude Stein and Alice B. Toklas, July 28, 1941, YCAL.

41. See, for instance, TNW, 1939–41 Journal, October 2, 1940, TNW Collection, YCAL.

42. TNW, 1939–41 Journal, May 23, 1941, TNW Collection, YCAL.

43. TNW, 1939–41 Journal, November 27, 1940, TNW Collection, YCAL.

44. TNW, 1939–41 Journal, December 17, 1942, TNW Collection, YCAL.
45. Isabella Niven Wilder to ANW, in a footnote to a copy of a letter to Isabel Wilder from the Medical Director of the New York Hospital, Westchester Division, June 28, 1941, discussed by ANW, Wilder Family Record, n.d., TNW Collection, YCAL, uncataloged papers.
46. Isabel Wilder to Dwight Dana, June 26, 1941, Private Collection.
47. Isabel Wilder to Dwight Dana, July 3, 1951, Private Collection.
48. Isabel Wilder, "About Charlotte Wilder," TS, October 15, 1961, Private Collection.
49. Charlotte Wilder to Isabella Niven Wilder, [June or July 1941?], discussed by ANW, Wilder Family Record, n.d., TNW Collection, YCAL, uncataloged papers.
50. Isabella Niven Wilder to ANW, in a footnote to a copy of a letter to Isabel Wilder from the Medical Director of the New York Hospital, Westchester Division, June 28, 1941, TNW Collection, YCAL, uncataloged papers.
51. TNW to Gertrude Stein and Alice B. Toklas, July 28, 1941, YCAL.
52. Ibid.
53. Ibid.
54. TNW to Robert Hutchins, February [no day], 1941, University of Chicago Library.
55. Ibid.
56. TNW to Gertrude Stein and Alice B. Toklas, November 12, 1941, YCAL.
57. TNW to Gertrude Stein and Alice B. Toklas, January 28, 1940, *SL*, 373.
58. TNW to Isabella Niven Wilder and Isabel Wilder, July 14, 1941, YCAL.
59. Hermon Ould, ed., *Writers in Freedom: A Symposium Based on the XVII International Congress of P.E.N. Club Held in London, September 1941* (London: Hutchinson, 1942), 6.
60. TNW to Gertrude Stein and Alice B. Toklas, [September 7, 1941], YCAL.
61. TNW to Robert and Maude Hutchins, October 28, 1941, University of Chicago Library.
62. TNW to Alexander Woollcott, October 13, 1941, AWC, MS Am 1449 (1781D), HLH. The Baths of Caracalla were grand thermal baths built in Rome by the emperor Caracalla (Marcus Aurelius Antoninus) in A.D. 217.
63. TNW to Isabella Niven Wilder, August 26, [1941?], TNW Collection, YCAL.
64. TNW, "The Strength of a Democracy Under Siege," transcription of "Speaking of Liberty," NBC Radio broadcast, October 30, 1941; reprinted in Bryer, *Conversations with Thornton Wilder*, 34–40.
65. TNW, "After a Visit to England," *Yale Review*, December 1941.
66. TNW to Gertrude Stein and Alice B. Toklas, March 25, 1942, YCAL.
67. Dr. —— Cheney to the Wilder Family, January 13, 1942, ANW, Wilder Family Record, Private Collection.

30: "THE CLOSING OF THE DOOR" (1940S)

1. TNW to Alexander Woollcott, January 9, 1942, AWC, MS Am 1449 (1781E), HLH.
2. TNW to Sibyl Colefax, October 9, 1942, *SL*, 405–7.
3. TNW to Gertrude Stein and Alice B. Toklas, March 25, 1942, YCAL.
4. Ibid.
5. TNW to Alexander Woollcott, February 18, 1942, AWC, MS Am 1449 (1781E), HLH.
6. TNW to Gertrude Stein and Alice B. Toklas, March 25, 1942, YCAL.
7. TNW to Alexander Woollcott, February 2, 1942, AWC, MS Am 1449 (1781E), HLH.

8. TNW to Harold Freedman, February 20, 1942, *SL*, 392–95.

9. TNW to Lynn Fontanne and Alfred Lunt, February 5, 1942, *SL*, 391–93.

10. Ibid.

11. TNW to Dwight Dana, January 29, 1942, *SL*, 389–90.

12. Ibid.

13. TNW to Harold Freedman, February 20, 1942, *SL*, 391–95.

14. Ibid.

15. Ibid.

16. TNW to Ruth Gordon, June 11, [1942?], *SL*, 398–99.

17. Tallulah Bankhead, *Tallulah: My Autobiography* (New York: Harper & Brothers, 1952), 251.

18. TNW to Alexander Woollcott, August 12, 1942, AWC, MS Am 1449 (1781I), HLH.

19. TNW to Michael Kahn, November 8, 1973, *SL*, 691–92.

20. TNW to Alexander Woollcott, May 6, 1942, AWC, MS Am 1449 (1781G), HLH. TNW wrote to Isabel as he was preparing the text of *The Skin of Our Teeth* for publication that the published text would not "vary from the acted text as much as 'Our Town's' does; but I shall go on making 'a' version without regard to what's being acted. And I want to write in more stage directions to aid the reader's imagination." He hoped the published text would be ready for the Christmas trade. TNW to Isabel Wilder, October 26, 1942, TNW Collection, YCAL.

21. TNW to Harold Freedman, February 20, 1942, *SL*, 393–94.

22. TNW to Alexander Woollcott, May 12, 1942, AWC, MS Am 1449 (1781G), HLH.

23. "Hitchcock Technique Prevails Even in the Birth of a Script," *New York Herald Tribune*, December 13, 1942.

24. TNW to Alexander Woollcott, May 12, 1942, AWC, MS Am 1449 (1781G), HLH.

25. Ibid.

26. TNW to Alexander Woollcott, May 17, 1942, AWC, MS Am 1449 (1781G), HLH.

27. TNW to Alexander Woollcott, May 23, 1942, AWC, MS Am 1449 (1781G), HLH.

28. Skirball was an ordained rabbi who had become a movie producer in 1938, and worked as an independent producer as well as a studio producer, an officer at Grand National Pictures, and later a president of Arcadia Pictures. Skirball was interested in Broadway as well, and produced S. N. Behrman's *Jacobowsky and the Colonel* on Broadway with Jed Harris in 1944.

29. TNW to Isabella Niven Wilder and Isabel Wilder, [May 1942?], TNW Collection, YCAL.

30. TNW to Isabella Niven Wilder and Isabel Wilder, [May 1942?], TNW Collection, YCAL; George Cukor dinner details: TNW to Ruth Gordon, June 11, [1942?], *SL*, 398–99.

31. TNW to Isabel Wilder, May 26, [1942?], *SL*, 395–97.

32. TNW to Alexander Woollcott, May 23, 1942, AWC, MS Am 1449 (1781G), HLH.

33. TNW, *Shadow of a Doubt*, in McClatchy, *Thornton Wilder: Collected Plays & Writings on Theater*, 747. The script for *Shadow of a Doubt* is published in full in this volume, with background notes by Geoffrey O'Brien.

34. TNW to Robert Hutchins, June 16, 1942, *SL*, 400–402.

35. TNW to Sibyl Colefax, January 30, 1940, New York University.

36. TNW to Isabel Wilder, May 26, [1942?], *SL*, 395–97.

37. Ibid.

38. TNW to Alexander Woollcott, June 10, 1942, AWC, MS Am 1449 (1781H), HLH.

39. Ibid.

40. TNW to Ruth Gordon, June 11, [1942?], *SL*, 398–99.

41. John Russell Taylor, *Hitch: The Life and Times of Alfred Hitchcock* (New York: Pantheon Books, 1978), 185–86. For additional commentary on the film, see Martin Blank, "Wilder, Hitchcock, and Shadow of a Doubt," in Martin Blank, Dalma Hunyadi Brunauer, and David Garrett Izzo, eds., *Thornton Wilder: New Essays* (West Cornwall, CT: Locust Hill Press, 1999), 409–16.

42. TNW to Sol Lesser, February 14, 1943, UCLA, Los Angeles. Their collaboration on the motion picture version of *Our Town* remained the only time the two men worked together.

43. Isabella Niven Wilder to ANW, May 13, 1942, ANW Papers, TNW Collection, YCAL, uncataloged letters.

44. TNW to Robert Hutchins, June 16, 1942, *SL*, 400–402.

45. Paul Horgan, "Captain Wilder, T. N.," [June 16, 1987?], TS, TNW Collection, YCAL, uncataloged papers. Paul Horgan's twenty-page manuscript concentrates on his first meeting with TNW in Miami in July 1942, and recounts their ensuing friendship. Quotations herein come from the unpublished typescript, which varies slightly from the essay published in Paul Horgan, *Tracings: A Book of Partial Portraits* (New York: Farrar, Straus & Giroux, 1993), 121–34.

46. TNW to Alexander Woollcott, February 2, 1942, AWC, MS Am 1449 (1781E), HLH.

47. Paul Horgan, "Captain Wilder, T. N.," TS, TNW Collection, YCAL, uncataloged papers.

48. TNW to Family, July 5, 1942, TNW Collection, YCAL.

49. TNW to Alexander Woollcott, August 16, 1942, AWC, MS Am 1449 (1781I), HLH.

50. TNW to Alexander Woollcott, [July 1942?], AWC, MS Am 1449 (1781H), HLH.

51. TNW to Alexander Woollcott, August 16, 1942, AWC, MS Am 1449 (1781I), HLH.

52. TNW to Robert Maynard Hutchins, June 16, 1942, *SL*, 400–402.

53. Ibid.

54. TNW to Amos Wilder, [Summer 1942?], TNW Collection, YCAL.

55. TNW to Amos Wilder, [July 20 or 28, 1942?], TNW Collection, YCAL.

56. TNW to Isabel Wilder, August 24, 1942, TNW Collection, YCAL.

57. TNW to Isabel Wilder, [September 13, 1942?], TNW Collection, YCAL.

58. TNW, "Notes Toward a History and Historical Records of the 328th Fighter Group," First Draft, holograph manuscript, n.d., TNW Collection, YCAL.

59. TNW to Alexander Woollcott, September 28, 1942, AWC, MS Am 1449 (1781I), HLH.

60. TNW to Sibyl Colefax, October 9, 1942, *SL*, 405–7.

61. TNW to Isabella Niven Wilder, October 7, 1942, *SL*, 403–5.

62. TNW to Sibyl Colefax, October 9, 1942, *SL*, 405–7.

63. TNW to Jed Harris, "Sketch of Letter Sent," January 29, 1942, TNW Collection, YCAL.

64. TNW, *The Skin of Our Teeth*, act 3, 103–12.

65. TNW to Amy Wertheimer, April 11, [1943?], TNW Collection, YCAL.

66. Richard Maney, *Fanfare: The Confessions of a Press Agent* (New York: Harper & Brothers, 1957), 330–31.

67. "Wilder (Adjective, Not Noun) Reaction Grows to 'Skin of Our Teeth,'" *Variety*, February 24, 1943, 1.

68. Maney, *Fanfare*, 329–30.

69. TNW to Michael Myerberg, copy of letter sent to Isabel Wilder, [October 21, 1942?], TNW Collection, YCAL.

70. TNW to Michael Myerberg, October 27, 1942, *SL*, 409–10.

71. Alexander Woollcott to Sibyl Colefax, September 1, 1942, in Kaufman and Hennessey, *The Letters of Alexander Woollcott*, 357.

72. Alexander Woollcott to TNW, November 4, 1942, TNW Collection, YCAL.

73. Ibid.

74. Tappan Wilder, afterword to *The Skin of Our Teeth*, 127.

75. TNW to Harold Freedman, November 24, 1942, Private Collection.

76. Joseph Campbell and Henry Morton Robinson, "The Skin of Whose Teeth?—The Strange Case of Mr. Wilder's New Play and *Finnegans Wake*," *Saturday Review of Literature*, December 19, 1942, 3–4.

77. TNW to Benjamin W. Huebsch, June 28, 1940, Library of Congress.

78. Benjamin W. Huebsch to TNW, July 12, 1940, TNW Collection, YCAL.

79. "Fourth Estate: Finnegan Reawakened," *Newsweek*, December 28, 1942, 41. This article noted that Wilder would "answer his critics later."

80. Bennett Cerf, "Trade Winds," *Saturday Review of Literature*, January 9, 1943, 12.

81. Draft of letter to the editor, *Saturday Review of Literature*, enclosed in TNW to Isabel Wilder, December 17, 1942, Private Collection. TNW enclosed his letter to the editor of the *Saturday Review* in this letter to Isabel, telling her to "erase this note." The letter was never mailed, and, fortunately, never "erased." The entire letter may be found in *SL*, 412–15. In May 1943, before going overseas, TNW prepared a list of possible defenses for his attorneys, should there be litigation in the matter, but that did not occur. His detailed analysis of the Campbell-Robinson charges was headed "MATERIALS To use in my absence if stupidity, malice, envy or avarice should institute a plagiarism suit against The Skin of Our Teeth." TNW, May 13, 1943, Private Collection.

82. Draft of a letter to the editor, the *Saturday Review of Literature*, enclosed in TNW to Isabel Wilder, December 17, 1942, Private Collection.

83. Ibid.

84. Bankhead, *Tallulah: My Autobiography*, 257.

85. TNW, preface to *Three Plays*, xxxii.

86. TNW to Zoë Akins Rumbold, November 18, 1940, *SL*, 382.

31: "WARTIME" (1940s)

1. TNW to Isabella Niven Wilder, November 2, 1942, TNW Collection, YCAL.

2. TNW to Amy Wertheimer, October [no day], 1942, TNW Collection, YCAL.

3. TNW to Alexander Woollcott, December 8, 1942, AWC, MS Am 1449 (1781J), HLH.

4. Ibid.

5. TNW to Alexander Woollcott, September 17, [1942?], AWC, MS Am 1449 (1781J), HLH.

6. TNW to Isabella Niven Wilder, November 2, 1942, TNW Collection, YCAL.

7. TNW to Isabella Niven Wilder, January 1, [1943?], TNW Collection, YCAL. TNW wrote 1942 on this letter, but its contents clearly place it in 1943.

8. Woollcott's *As You Were: A Portable Library of American Prose and Poetry Assembled for Members of The Armed Forces and The Merchant Marine* was published by Viking Press in 1943. It was 657 pages long and measured 4.24 inches by 6.5—sturdy and convenient packaging for people who, Woollcott said, were on the move and had

to travel light. TNW's play was not included in the final publication, apparently because the decision was made to publish only poetry and fiction. Woollcott's idea and his anthology launched Viking's series of "portable" books, including, during World War II, a portable Bible, a portable Shakespeare, and portable editions of authors such as Dorothy Parker and Ernest Hemingway.

9. Alexander Woollcott to TNW, November 13, 1942, TNW Collection, YCAL.

10. Alexander Woollcott to TNW, December 29, 1942, TNW Collection, YCAL.

11. TNW, "Five Thousand Letters to Alexander Woollcott," 1951, edited by Donald Gallup and first printed in the *Harvard Library Bulletin* 32, no. 4 (Fall 1984): 401–7.

12. TNW to Alexander Woollcott, [1933?], *SL*, 268–71.

13. TNW to ANW, April [no day], 1943, TNW Collection, YCAL.

14. TNW to Dwight Dana, Easter [April 25?], 1943, Private Collection.

15. TNW to ANW, April [no day], 1943, TNW Collection, YCAL.

16. TNW to Michael Myerberg, May 21, 1943, *SL*, 416–18.

17. TNW, "MATERIALS To use in my absence if stupidity, malice, envy or avarice should institute a plagiarism suit against The Skin of Our Teeth," May 13, 1942, Private Collection.

18. For a detailed discussion of TNW's letter and legal memorandum, as well as publication of the complete texts of these documents, see Tappan Wilder, "A Footnote to *The Skin of Our Teeth*," *Yale Review*, no. 4 (October 1999): 66–76.

19. TNW, "MATERIALS To use in my absence if stupidity, malice, envy or avarice should institute a plagiarism suit against The Skin of Our Teeth," May 13, 1942, Private Collection.

20. Ibid.

21. Dwight Dana to TNW, telegram, December 18, 1942, Private Collection.

22. TNW, "MATERIALS To use in my absence if stupidity, malice, envy or avarice should institute a plagiarism suit against The Skin of Our Teeth," May 13, 1942, Private Collection.

23. TNW to Dwight Dana, April 6, 1944, Private Collection.

24. TNW to Isabella Niven Wilder, July 15, 1943, TNW Collection, YCAL.

25. TNW to Isabella Niven Wilder, September 15, 1943, TNW Collection, YCAL; TNW to Family, December 20, [1943?], TNW Collection, YCAL.

26. TNW to Family, June 1943, TNW Collection, YCAL.

27. TNW to Isabella Niven Wilder, September 26, 1943, TNW Collection, YCAL.

28. TNW to ANW, September 1, 1942, TNW Collection, YCAL.

29. TNW to Alexander Woollcott, November 24, 1942, AWC, MS Am 1449 (1781J), HLH.

30. Isabel Wilder, "About Charlotte Wilder," October 15, 1961, Private Collection.

31. TNW to Evelyn Scott Metcalfe, July 28, 1944, *SL*, 422–23.

32. TNW to William Layton, April 9, 1944, TNW Collection, YCAL.

33. TNW to Charlotte Niven, April 25, 1944, TNW Collection, YCAL.

34. TNW to William Layton, April 9, 1944, TNW Collection, YCAL.

35. TNW to Charlotte Niven, April 25, 1944, TNW Collection, YCAL.

36. TNW to William Layton, April 9, 1944, TNW Collection, YCAL. This three-week run at New York's City Center began on January 19, 1944, also starring Martha Scott. Montgomery Clift played George Gibbs. After the war, in May 1946, Harris took the revival production to London, with Marc Connelly as the Stage Manager. According to TNW, all those in the New York production donated their services

except Frank Craven, who "asked 1200 a week and 10% of the gross"; that was why Connelly was asked to step in.

37. TNW to Dwight Dana, April 6, 1944, Private Collection. TNW intentionally differentiated between the terms "WAAC [Women's Army Auxiliary Corps]" and "WAC [Women's Army Corps]." The WAACs dated from World War I when women could work *with* the army but not as personnel *in* the army. In 1943 the Women's Army Corps was established by an act of Congress so that women could serve as members of the armed forces, with equitable pay and benefits, including disability benefits.

38. TNW to Isabella Niven Wilder, June 7, 1944, TNW Collection, YCAL.

39. TNW to Isabella Niven Wilder and Isabel Wilder, October 17, 1944, *SL*, 423–25.

40. TNW to Family, October 29, 1944, TNW Collection, YCAL.

41. John Hobart, "Grover's Corners, Italy," *Theatre Arts* 29 (April 1945): 234–39.

42. TNW to Isabella Niven Wilder and Isabel Wilder, November 19, 1944, TNW Collection, YCAL.

43. TNW to Joseph Still, November 13, [1944?], YCAL.

44. TNW to Family, October 29, 1944, TNW Collection, YCAL. TNW noted in this letter that he was free, a year and a half after the fact, to give details of his movements in North Africa.

45. TNW to Family, December 15, 1944, TNW Collection, YCAL.

46. TNW to Charlotte Niven, April 5, 1945, TNW Collection, YCAL.

47. Ibid.

48. TNW to Family, December 15, 1944, TNW Collection, YCAL. Isabella Niven Wilder translated Carducci's poems, including, we can speculate, his sonnet beginning "T'amo Pio Bove," his ode to an ox grazing in a field in Italy.

49. TNW to Laurence Olivier, February 18, 1945, TS carbon copy, *SL*, 429–31.

50. Hugh "Binkie" Beaumont to Harold Freedman, March 22, 1945, TNW Collection, YCAL.

51. TNW to Isabella Niven Wilder and Isabel Wilder, February 19, 1945, TNW Collection, YCAL, regarding this donation in Italy. See also TNW to Philip G. Hodge, December 10, 1945, TS carbon copy, TNW Collection, regarding this donation in Yugoslavia.

52. TNW to Amos and Catharine Wilder, February 1, 1945, TNW Collection, YCAL.

53. TNW to Charlotte Niven, April 5, 1945, TNW Collection, YCAL.

54. TNW to Amy Wertheimer, March 29, 1945, TNW Collection, YCAL.

55. Ibid.

56. TNW to Family, April 14, 1945, TNW Collection, YCAL.

57. TNW to Harry J. Traugott, May 20, 1945, Private Collection.

58. "Citation: Lieutenant-Colonel Thornton H. [*sic*] Wilder, U.S. Army Air Forces, Honorary Member of the Military Division of the Most Excellent Order of the British Empire," n.d. [1946 written on document], TNW Collection, YCAL.

59. TNW to William Layton, August 16, 1945, TNW Collection, YCAL.

60. Adjutant General Owen Elliot, U. S. War Department, to TNW, August 28, 1947, TNW Collection, YCAL.

61. TNW to Sibyl Colefax, August 20, 1945, *SL*, 433–36.

62. TNW to Charlotte Niven, April 5, 1945, TNW Collection, YCAL.

63. TNW to Gertrude Stein and Alice B. Toklas, July 20, 1945, YCAL.

64. TNW to Alice B. Toklas, October 8, 1946, *SL*, 446–48.

65. Isabel Wilder to Sol Lesser, October 1, 1945, TNW Collection, YCAL.

66. Isabel Wilder to Sibyl Colefax, TS carbon, July 23, 1945, TNW Collection, YCAL.

67. Ibid.

68. Ibid.

69. Patricia Bosworth, *Montgomery Clift: A Biography* (New York: Harcourt Brace Jova-novich, 1978), 99–100.

70. Quoted ibid., 99.

71. Isabel Wilder to Sibyl Colefax, TS carbon, July 23, 1945, TNW Collection, YCAL

72. Ibid.

73. Isabel Wilder, foreword to TNW, *The Alcestiad or A Life in the Sun with a Satyr Play, The Drunken Sisters* (New York: Harper & Row, 1977), 10.

74. TNW, *The Alcestiad*, holograph manuscript, TNW Collection, YCAL. TNW's note ends after "Dec" and gives no day or year.

75. Isabel Wilder to Sibyl Colefax, TS carbon, July 23, 1945, TNW Collection, YCAL.

76. Ibid.

77. TNW to Eliza [Elizabeth (Mrs. Boris) Artzybasheff], June 26, [1945?], TNW Col-lection, YCAL.

78. TNW to Eliza [Elizabeth (Mrs. Boris) Artzybasheff], August 5, 1945, TNW Col-lection, YCAL.

79. TNW to William Layton, August 16, 1945, TNW Collection, YCAL. TNW wrote: "Night before last was having dinner here with my married sister and the news broke."

80. Ibid.

81. TNW to Sibyl Colefax, August 20, 1945, *SL*, 433–36. "Numinous": Sprititual belief based on ancient Roman animism.

82. Ibid.

83. Ibid.

84. Ibid.

85. Isabella Niven Wilder to TNW, May 15, 1945, TNW Collection, YCAL.

86. Army of the United States Certificate of Service for Lt. Col. Thornton N. Wilder, issued at the Separation Center, Fort Devens, Massachusetts, September 19, 1945, Private Collection.

32: "POST-WAR ADJUSTMENT EXERCISE" (1940S)

1. TNW to Eileen and Roland Le Grand, March 9, 1946, *SL*, 439–40.

2. Ibid.

3. TNW to June and Leonard Trolley, February 23, 1947, *SL*, 451–54. TNW had helped to make it possible for the Trolleys to marry during the war years in Caserta, where Leonard Trolley was one of TNW's clerks. As it happened, the bride was an officer and the groom was an enlisted man, complicating their plans to marry.

4. TNW to Eileen and Roland Le Grand, March 9, 1946, *SL*, 439–40.

5. TNW to Glenway Wescott, April 7, 1948, *SL*, 459–61.

6. TNW's work on Lope de Vega would earn him election to the Hispanic Society of America, an honor that meant a great deal to him.

7. TNW to Eileen and Roland Le Grand, March 9, 1946, *SL*, 439–40.

8. TNW to Ruth Gordon and Garson Kanin, [March 30, 1946?], *SL*, 441–42. See also TNW to Jean-Paul Sartre, March 16, 1946, TNW Collection, YCAL.

9. TNW to Eileen and Roland Le Grand, March 9, 1946, *SL*, 439–40.

10. "About how Alcestis": TNW to ANW [February 10, 1946?], TNW Collection, YCAL. "Grounded transparently in": Walter Lowrie, trans., Søren Kierkegaard, *The Sickness unto Death by Anti-Climacus*, in Robert Bretall, ed., *A Kierkegaard Anthology* (Princeton: Princeton University Press, 1946), 351. Kierkegaard writes of "the Despair which is Conscious of being Despair, as also it is Conscious of being a Self wherein there is there after all something Eternal, and then is either in despair at not willing to be itself, or in despair at willing to be itself," ibid., 349. This passage evokes the Stage Manager's words in act 3 of *Our Town*: "There's something way down deep that's eternal about every human being."

11. TNW to ANW, [February 10, 1946], TNW Collection, YCAL.

12. TNW to Eileen and Roland Le Grand, March 9, 1946, *SL*, 439–40.

13. TNW to ANW, [February 10, 1946?], TNW Collection, YCAL.

14. Isabel Wilder to ANW, January 24, 1946, TNW Collection, YCAL.

15. Ibid.

16. Tappan Wilder to PEN, July 8, 2010.

17. TNW to Robert Van Gelder, "Interview with a Best-Selling Author: Thornton Wilder," *Cosmopolitan*, April 1948, 18, 120–23; reprinted in Bryer, *Conversations with Thornton Wilder*, 41–45.

18. Thomas Coward, Coward-McCann, Inc., to Isabel Wilder, March 11, 1940, TNW Collection, YCAL. See also Isabel Wilder to Thew Wright, January 28, 1959, Private Collection. In the 1959 letter Isabel Wilder is in error about the dates, writing 1939 instead of 1940.

19. Thomas Coward, Coward-McCann, Inc., to Isabel Wilder, April 28, 1939, TNW Collection, YCAL.

20. Isabel Wilder to Family, April 14, 1944, TNW Collection, YCAL, uncataloged papers. Throughout this book, background on Charlotte Wilder's illness is drawn from her medical records and from numerous letters, as well as her correspondence to and from her family and friends contained in the uncataloged papers in the TNW Collection, YCAL, or in private collections.

21. Charlotte Wilder to Evelyn Scott, October 20, 1945, quoted by ANW, "Concerning Charlotte Wilder running from 1932 to 1961," Wilder Records, August 1969, Private Collection.

22. Charlotte Wilder to Evelyn Scott, November 9, 1945, quoted by ANW, "Concerning Charlotte Wilder running from 1932 to 1961," Wilder Records, August 1969. Private Collection.

23. Charlotte Wilder to Isabella Niven Wilder, April 15, 1946, TNW Collection, YCAL, uncataloged letters.

24. Charlotte Wilder to ANW, February 23, 1946, quoted by ANW, "Concerning Charlotte Wilder running from 1932 to 1961," Wilder Records, August 1969, Private Collection.

25. Charlotte Wilder to ANW, March 9, 1946, quoted by ANW, "Concerning Charlotte Wilder running from 1932 to 1961," Wilder Records, August 1969. Private Collection.

26. TNW to ANW, May 31, [1946?], TNW Collection, YCAL.

27. TNW to Sibyl Colefax, January 7, 1947, *SL*, 449–50. The Dioscuri were Castor and Pollux or Polydeuces, the twin sons of Leda and Zeus. The Dioscuri were sometimes called the Heavenly Twins, part of the constellation of Gemini.

28. TNW to Amy Wertheimer, July 4, 1946, TNW Collection, YCAL.

29. TNW to William Rose Benét, July 17, 1946, YCAL.

30. Isabella Niven Wilder's poem was quoted by Tappan Wilder at Isabel Wilder's Memorial Service, March 25, 1995. Private Collection.

31. TNW to Ruth Gordon and Garson Kanin, July 23, 1946, *SL*, 443–46.

32. TNW to Alice B. Toklas, October 8, 1946, *SL*, 446–48.

33. Ibid.

34. TNW, introduction, "Gertrude Stein's *Four in America*," in *Four in America* (New Haven: Yale University Press, 1947), vii; reprinted in Gallup, *American Characteristics*, 193–222.

   In this book Stein created portraits of four national figures, speculating on what each would have done if he had chosen a different profession, picturing Ulysses S. Grant as a religious leader who became a saint; the Wright brothers as painters; Henry James as a general; and George Washington as a novelist.

35. Ibid., x, 200.

36. TNW, *The Eighth Day*, 10.

37. TNW to Isabel Wilder [January 30, 1947, postmarked Biloxi, Mississippi], TNW Collection, YCAL.

38. TNW to Isabel Wilder, [March?] 5, 1947, TNW Collection, YCAL. TNW dated this letter February 5, 1947, from Mérida, Yucatán. He must have meant March, judging by his travel schedule.

39. TNW to Isabel Wilder, [January 30, 1947], TNW Collection, YCAL.

40. TNW to Isabel Wilder, March 11, 1947, TNW Collection, YCAL.

41. TNW to Leonard Bacon, March 11, 1947, YCAL.

42. TNW to Isabel Wilder, March 24, 1947, TNW Collection, YCAL.

43. TNW to Leonard Bacon, July 22, 1947, YCAL.

44. TNW to June and Leonard Trolley, February 23, 1947, *SL*, 451–54.

45. TNW to Isabella Niven Wilder, November 5, 1922, TNW Collection, YCAL.

46. TNW, 1939–41 Journal, February 8, 1939, TNW Collection, YCAL.

47. TNW to Gertrude Stein and Alice B. Toklas, September 4, 1937, YCAL.

48. TNW to Gertrude Stein and Alice B. Toklas, March 25, 1942, YCAL.

49. TNW to Maxwell Anderson, November 13, 1956, *SL*, 543–44.

50. TNW to Ruth Gordon and Garson Kanin, July 23, 1946, *SL*, 443–46.

51. TNW to Sibyl Colefax, January 7, [19]47, *SL*, 449–50.

52. TNW, in Whit Burnett, ed., *105 Greatest Living Authors Present the World's Best Stories, Humor, Drama, Biography, History, Essays, Poetry* (New York: Dial Press, 1950), 104–5. Wilder ranked nineteenth in the voting for the 105 greatest living authors. George Bernard Shaw was at the top of the list.

53. TNW to Maxwell Anderson, November 13, 1956, *SL*, 543–44.

54. Priscilla Booth Behnken, RN, and Elizabeth Good Merrill, RN, "Nursing Care Following Prefrontal Lobotomy," *American Journal of Nursing* 49, no. 7 (July 1949): 418–19.

55. Janet Wilder Dakin, "Biographical Notes on Charlotte Wilder," October 15, 1969, Private Collection.

56. Isabel Wilder, "About Charlotte Wilder," TS, October 15, 1969, TNW Collection, YCAL, uncataloged papers; and ANW, "Concerning Charlotte Wilder running from 1932 to 1961," Wilder Records, August 1969, Private Collection.

57. Isabel Wilder, "About Charlotte Wilder," TS, October 15, 1969, TNW Collection, YCAL, uncataloged papers. Zelda Fitzgerald was a patient of Dr. Mildred

Squires, then a resident at the Phipps Clinic at Johns Hopkins Hospital. As part of her therapy, Dr. Squires encouraged Zelda to write *Save Me a Waltz*, which was published in 1932. Dr. Squires also encouraged Charlotte Wilder to continue writing.

58. Ibid.

59. TNW to Brooks Atkinson, December 20, 1947, Billy Rose Theatre Collection, New York Public Library for the Performing Arts; TNW, *The Ides of March*, 25.

60. TNW, dedication to *The Ides of March*. All citations of *The Ides of March* throughout are to TNW, *The Ides of March* (New York: HarperPerennial, 2003), with a foreword by Kurt Vonnegut, Jr., and an afterword by Tappan Wilder.

61. For a detailed account of De Bosis's flight over Rome see Dorothy Warren, ed., *The Letters of Ruth Draper: Self-Portrait of an Actress 1920–1956* (Carbondale: Southern Illinois University Press, 1999). Giovanni Bassanesi flew to Milan from Paris July 11, 1930, dropped his 150,000 pamphlets, and crashed his plane on the St. Gotthard Pass after he fled Milan. He survived the crash, however.

   De Bosis and/or Ruth Draper and TNW had several friends in common, including Edward Sheldon, Sibyl Colefax, and Sir John Gielgud. Ruth Draper and TNW corresponded occasionally over the years, and in one of her letters Draper enclosed a four-page typed copy of a letter De Bosis wrote to an unidentified English friend on December 28, 1930, about his plans. Ruth Draper to TNW, n.d., TNW Collection, YCAL.

62. TNW, *The Ides of March*, 212.

63. TNW, dedication to *The Ides of March*.

64. Ruth Draper to TNW, n.d. [March 18, 1948], TNW Collection, YCAL. In *The Poet and the Dictator: Lauro de* [sic] *Bosis Resists Facism in Italy and America* (Westport, CT: Praeger Publishers, 2002), the biographer Jean McClure Mudge suggests that Wilder may have been infatuated or in love with De Bosis, and that he may have been jealous of Ruth Draper. My study of the Draper-Wilder correspondence, the Wilder–De Bosis correspondence, and other sources has not to date yielded documentation of the theory.

65. TNW to Maxwell Anderson, November 13, 1956, *SL*, 543–44.

66. TNW to Brooks Atkinson, December 20, 1947, Billy Rose Theatre Collection, New York Public Library for the Performing Arts.

67. TNW, *The Ides of March*, 32.

68. Ibid., 80

69. TNW to Brooks Atkinson, December 20, 1947, Billy Rose Theatre Collection, New York Public Library for the Performing Arts.

70. TNW to Rosemary Benét, [December 19?], 1947, YCAL.

71. Ibid.

72. TNW, *The Ides of March*, 89.

73. Ibid., epigraph.

74. TNW to Robert Van Gelder, "Interview with a Best-Selling Author: Thornton Wilder," *Cosmopolitan*, April 1948, 1, 120–23; reprinted in Bryer, *Conversations with Thornton Wilder*, 41–45.

75. TNW, *The Ides of March*, 108.

76. TNW to Amy Wertheimer, February 25, 1948, TNW Collection, YCAL.

77. Henry Seidel Canby, Dorothy Canfield, John P. Marquand, and Christopher Morley, "Addenda From the Other Judges," *Book-of-the-Month Club News*, February 1948, 5.

78. TNW to Amy Wertheimer, February 25, 1948, TNW Collection, YCAL.
79. TNW to Alice B. Toklas, March 19, 1949, *SL*, 462–65.
80. TNW, *The Ides of March*, 153.
81. TNW to William Rose Benét, February 7, [1948?], YCAL.
82. TNW to Glenway Wescott, April 7, 1948, *SL*, 459–61.
83. Ibid.
84. TNW to Lillian Gish, April 1, 1947, *SL*, 454–56.
85. Century Association Program for April 26, 1947, published April 11, 1948, by the Century Association, TNW Collection, YCAL. There was a presentation of TNW's work written just for the occasion and titled "Our Century." The Century Association is an organization of writers, artists, and "amateurs" of letters and the fine arts.
86. *The Unerring Instinct* is published in McClatchy, *Thornton Wilder: Collected Plays & Writings on Theater*, 453–61. The play tells the story of a woman who plays a trick on her sister in order to demonstrate how susceptible unthinking people can be to falsehoods that are built on prejudice.
87. Glenway Wescott, *Images of Truth: Remembrances and Criticism* (New York: Harper & Row, 1962), 305–6.
88. Ibid., 256, 306.
89. TNW to Sam Steward, September 14, 1948, TNW Collection, YCAL; TNW to Eliza ——, August 7, [1948?], YCAL.
90. TNW, 1948–61 Journal, Entry 420, December 27, 1948, TNW Collection, YCAL.

33: SEARCHING FOR THE RIGHT WAY (1948–1950S)

1. TNW, Application for Military Permit to Enter Germany, 1948, TNW Collection, YCAL.
2. TNW to Maxwell Anderson, July 5, 1948, *SL*, 461–62.
3. TNW, 1948–61 Journal, Entry 441, May 4, 1950, TNW Collection, YCAL. Approximately 60 percent of Wilder's journal entries are published in Donald Gallup, ed., *The Journals of Thornton Wilder, 1939–1961* (New Haven: Yale University Press, 1985). Some of these entries are published only in part. TNW's journals prior to 1939 are unpublished at this writing.
4. Gallup, *The Journals of Thornton Wilder, 1939–1961*, xxv–xxvi.
5. TNW, "Toward an American Language," *Atlantic Monthly*, July 1952. This was TNW's first Charles Eliot Norton Lecture, delivered at Harvard in 1950, and reprinted with some of Wilder's later insertions, in Gallup, *American Characteristics*, 24. The *Atlantic Monthly* also published a second Norton Lecture, "The American Loneliness," in August 1952; and a third, "Emily Dickinson," in November 1952.
6. TNW, 1948–61 Journal, Entry 407, September 21, 1948, TNW Collection, YCAL.
7. Ibid.
8. TNW, 1948–61 Journal, Entry 408, also September 21, 1948, TNW Collection, YCAL.
9. TNW, 1948–61 Journal, Entry 409, September 22, 1948, TNW Collection, YCAL.
10. Ibid.; TNW to Leonard Bacon, October 23, 1948, YCAL.
11. TNW, 1948–61 Journal, Entry 410, September 23, 1948, TNW Collection, YCAL.
12. Ibid.
13. TNW, 1948–61 Journal, Entry 412, September 24, 1948, TNW Collection, YCAL.
14. TNW, 1948–61 Journal, Entry 413, September 25, 1948, TNW Collection, YCAL.

15. TNW, 1948–61 Journal, Entry 414, September 26, 1948, TNW Collection, YCAL.

16. TNW, 1948–61 Journal, Entry 415, September 30, 1948, TNW Collection, YCAL.

17. TNW, 1948–61 Journal, Entry 417, October 1948, TNW Collection, YCAL. In the original Journal, TNW labels the points of discussion a, b, c, and d. In the published version, the numbers 1, 2, 3, and 4 are used.

18. Ibid.

19. "Some Thoughts on Playwriting" was published first in Centeno, *The Intent of the Artist*, and then in Gallup, *American Characteristics*.

20. TNW, 1948–61 Journal, Entry 418, [1948?], TNW Collection, YCAL.

21. Ibid.

22. TNW, 1948–61 Journal, Entry 423, January 15, 1949, TNW Collection, YCAL.

23. TNW, 1948–61 Journal, Entry 421, December 27, 1948, TNW Collection, YCAL.

24. TNW, 1948–61 Journal, Entry 424, May 7, 1949, TNW Collection, YCAL.

25. Ibid.

26. Quoted in Ashmore, *Unseasonable Truths*, 282.

27. TNW to ANW, July 7, 1949, *SL*, 468–71.

28. TNW, "Goethe and World Literature," Goethe Convocation, Aspen Colorado, July 1949. This lecture was first published in the proceedings of the convocation in 1949 as "World Literature and the Modern Mind," *Goethe and the Modern Age: The International Convocation at Aspen, Colorada, 1949*. It was published as "Goethe and World Literature" in Arnold Bergstraesser, ed., *Perspectives USA for Fall 1952* (Chicago: Henry Regnery Company, [1950?]). In that form it was reprinted in Gallup, *American Characteristics*, 137–48, from which quotations are taken.

29. TNW to ANW, July 7, 1949, *SL*, 468–71.

30. Ibid.

31. TNW, "Goethe and World Literature," in Gallup, *American Characteristics and Other Essays*, 140.

32. Ibid., 142.

33. Ibid., 147.

34. Ibid., 147–48.

35. Ibid., 148.

36. TNW, 1948–61 Journal, Entry 426-A, July 23, 1949, TNW Collection, YCAL.

37. Ibid.

38. TNW, 1948–61 Journal, Entry 649, July 20, 1953, TNW Collection, YCAL.

39. TNW, 1948–61 Journal, Entry 428, August 25, 1949, TNW Collection, YCAL.

40. TNW to Cary Grant, August 23, 1948, *SL*, 473–75.

41. TNW, 1948–61 Journal, Entry 429, September 28, [1949?], TNW Collection, YCAL.

42. TNW, 1948–61 Journal, Entry 436, March 26, [1950?], TNW Collection, YCAL.

43. TNW to Ava Bodley, Lady Anderson, March 19, 1950, *SL*, 486–88.

44. Ibid.

45. The professorship honored Harvard art professor, author, social critic, and man of letters Charles Eliot Norton (1827–1908), and the term "poetry" attached to the professorship embraced all the written arts, as well as music and the visual arts. Wilder was immediately preceded by the composer Paul Hindemith, with whom he would later collaborate on an opera based on *The Long Christmas Dinner*.

46. TNW, 1948–61 Journal, Entry 436, March 26, [1950/], TNW Collection, YCAL.

47. Ibid.

48. Ibid.
49. TNW, 1948–61 Journal, Entry 441, May 3, 1950, TNW Collection, YCAL.
50. TNW to Laurence Olivier and Vivien Leigh, July 19, 1950, *SL*, 489–91.
51. TNW, 1948–61 Journal, Entry 445, July 8, [1950?], TNW Collection, YCAL.
52. TNW, 1948–61 Journal, Entry 624, October 11, 1952, TNW Collection, YCAL.
53. TNW, 1948–61 Journal, Entry 542, April, [no day], 1951, TNW Collection, YCAL.
54. TNW to Howard Lowry, November 4, 1951, 493–96. TNW received an honorary degree from the College of Wooster, Wooster, OH, in 1950, and played the Stage Manager in a college production of *Our Town* there. Dr. Lowry was president of the college.
55. TNW, 1948–61 Journal, Entries 471, 478, and 487, November 4 and 15, and December 4, 1950, TNW Collection, YCAL.
56. TNW, 1948–61 Journal, Entry 543, May [no day], 1951, TNW Collection, YCAL.
57. TNW, "Toward an American Language," in Gallup, *American Characteristics*, 9.
58. Ibid., 12.
59. Ibid., 14–15.
60. Ibid., 35.
61. Ibid., 63.
62. Ibid., 52.
63. Ibid., 52–53.
64. TNW, 1948–61 Journal, Entry 518, March 19, 1951, TNW Collection, YCAL.
65. Ibid.
66. TNW, 1948–61 Journal, Entry 520, March 22, 1951, TNW Collection, YCAL.
67. TNW, 1948–61 Journal, Entry 518, March 19, 1951, TNW Collection, YCAL.
68. TNW, 1948–61 Journal, Entry 528, April 1, 1951, TNW Collection, YCAL.
69. TNW to Howard Lowry, November 4, 1951, *SL*, 493–96.
70. TNW, 1948–61 Journal, Entry 542, April, [no day], 1951, TNW Collection, YCAL.
71. TNW to Howard Lowry, November 4, 1951, *SL*, 493–96.
72. TNW to Ruth Gordon and Garson Kanin, June 15, [1951?], Private Collection.
73. TNW, "Thoughts for Our Times," *Harvard Alumni Bulletin*, July 7, 1951, 779–81. This address has been widely republished as a whole or in part.
74. Ibid.
75. Ibid., 781.

34: KALEIDOSCOPIC VIEWS (1950s)

1. TNW, 1948–61 Journal, Entry 551, July [no day], 1951, TNW Collection, YCAL.
2. TNW to Thew Wright, January 5, 1952, Private Collection.
3. "Repugnant": TNW to Dr. Hans Sahl, August 22, [1950?], Marbach; "Isn't he awful": TNW to Malcolm Cowley, March [1952?], *SL*, 501–3.
4. TNW, 1948–61 Journal, Entry 556, August 5 and 7, 1951, TNW Collection, YCAL.
5. TNW 1948–61 Journal, Entry 608, May 9, 1952, TNW Collection, YCAL.
6. TNW to Thew Wright, October 10, 1951, Private Collection.
7. TNW to Thew Wright, January 5 and 23, 1952, Private Collection.
8. TNW to the President and Chancellor, American Academy of Arts and Letters, February 17, 1939, Copy, TNW Collection, YCAL. At this ceremony Carl Sandburg received the Gold Medal for History and Biography for his Lincoln work. TNW had been elected to the National Institute of Arts and Letters in 1929 and to the American Academy of Arts and Letters in 1939. See Louis Auchincloss, Jack

Beeson, Hortense Calisher, et al., *A Century of Arts & Letters* (New York: Columbia University Press, 1998), vii–xii.

9. Pearl S. Buck, "Presentation to Thornton Wilder of the Gold Medal for Fiction," *Proceedings of the American Academy of Arts and Letters and the National Institute of Arts and Letters*, 2nd series, no. 3, New York: 1953.

10. TNW, "Acceptance by Thornton Wilder," ibid.

11. TNW to T. E. Harris, November 27, [1951?], copy, Private Collection. The invitations to TNW and ANW were extended by William E. Stevenson, President, Oberlin College, November 14, 1951, TNW Collection, YCAL.

12. TNW to Isabel Wilder, [Fall 1951?], TNW Collection, YCAL.

13. Charlotte Wilder, undated, unpublished manuscript fragment, [1951?], TNW Collection, uncataloged manuscripts.

14. Charlotte Wilder to Isabel Wilder, September 29, 1950, TNW Collection, YCAL.

15. Charlotte Wilder to Catharine and ANW, September 6, 1950, TNW Collection, YCAL.

16. TNW to Charlotte Wilder, [June 6, 1953?], TNW Collection, YCAL.

17. Ibid.

18. TNW to Catharine and ANW, [September 10, 1953?], TNW Collection, YCAL.

19. TNW, 1948–61 Journal, Entry 608, May 9, [1952?], TNW Collection, YCAL.

20. "Worthless story": ibid. "Story ideas": Charles Feldman Group Productions Contract and Certificate of Authorship, signed by TNW June 20, 1952, Private Collection.

21. TNW, 1948–61 Journal, Entry 608, May 9, [1952?], TNW Collection, YCAL.

22. Ibid. De Sica did not complete the project. The 1956 film *Miracle in the Rain* was written by Hecht and directed by Rudolph Maté.

23. TNW, "Report of the Rapporteur General," International Conference of Artists, Venice, September 28, 1952, UNESCO document, UNESCO/ART/DIV/7.

24. TNW to Elizabeth Shepley Sergeant, October 11, [1952?], *SL*, 503–5.

25. TNW, 1948–61 Journal, Entry 624, October 11, [1952?], TNW Collection, YCAL.

26. Ibid.

27. Ibid.

28. TNW, 1948–61 Journal, Entry 636, January 28, 1953, TNW Collection, YCAL.

29. Ibid.

30. Ibid.

31. Ibid.

32. Ibid.

33. Ibid.

34. TNW to Eric Bentley, January 5, 1956, *SL*, 539–41.

35. TNW, 1948–61 Journal, Entry 606, March 6, 1952, TNW Collection, YCAL.

36. The Lope papers are reprinted in Gallup, *American Characteristics*, 257–77.

37. "An Obliging Man," *Time*, January 12, 1953, 44–49.

38. See Janet Wilder Dakin, *Jeffy's Journal: Raising a Morgan Horse*, Sheila Rainford, ed. (London: Stephen Greene Press/Pelham Books, 1990; distributed by Penguin Books USA).

39. TNW to Janet Wilder Dakin, May 8, 1953, TNW Collection, YCAL. TNW addressed his sister fondly as Janetberry, one of the family nicknames.

40. Tyrone Guthrie, *A Life in the Theatre* (New York: McGraw-Hill Book Company, Inc., 1959), 233.

41. TNW to M. Abbot Van Nostrand, Samuel French, March 11, 1952, Private Collection.

42. Hugh "Binkie" Beaumont to TNW, December 31, 1953, TNW Collection, YCAL.

43. TNW to Ruth Gordon and Garson Kanin, "All Souls Day" [November 2, 1954?], *SL*, 522–24.

44. TNW to Harold Freedman, October 7, 1954, Private Collection.

45. Ibid.

46. Alan Dent, *News Chronicle*, August 24, 1954, courtesy of the National Library of Scotland.

47. Derek Granger, "The Matchmaker," *Financial Times*, August 24, 1954, courtesy of the National Library of Scotland.

48. Thew Wright to TNW, May 19, 1954, Private Collection.

49. TNW to Thew Wright, January 14, [1954?], Private Collection.

50. Hugh "Binkie" Beaumont to Isabel Wilder, November 6, 1954, TNW Collection, YCAL.

51. Hugh "Binkie" Beaumont to TNW, December 14, 1954, TNW Collection, YCAL.

52. For more production details on *The Merchant of Yonkers* and *The Matchmaker*, see TNW, *Three Plays*.

53. TNW, 1948–61 Journal, Entry 698, September 6, [1954?], TNW Collection, YCAL.

54. TNW, 1948–61 Journal, Entry 699, September 30, [1954?], TNW Collection, YCAL.

55. TNW, 1948–61 Journal, Entry 702, December 7, [1954?], TNW Collection, YCAL.

56. TNW to Laurence Olivier and Vivien Leigh, July 19, 1950, *SL*, 489–91.

57. TNW, *The Alcestiad*, in McClatchy, *Thornton Wilder: Collected Plays & Writings on Theater*, 376–77.

58. TNW, 1948–61 Journal, Entry 658, September 18, 1953, TNW Collection, YCAL.

59. TNW, Journal, Entry 662, November 17, 1953, TNW Collection, YCAL.

60. TNW, Journal, Entry 704, January 6, 1955, TNW Collection, YCAL.

61. TNW, Journal, Entry 702, December 7, [1954?], TNW Collection, YCAL.

62. TNW to Thew Wright, November 19, 1954, Private Collection.

63. TNW, Journal, Entry 704, January 25, 1955, TNW Collection, YCAL.

64. Ibid.

65. TNW, *The Alcestiad*, in McClatchy, *Thornton Wilder: Collected Plays & Writings on Theater*, 429.

66. TNW, *The Bridge of San Luis Rey*, 107.

67. TNW, *The Alcestiad*, in McClatchy, *Thornton Wilder: Collected Plays & Writings on Theater*, 428.

68. TNW, Journal, Entry 704, January 25, 1955.

69. Hugh "Binkie" Beaumont to TNW, February 18, 1955; March 4, 1955; and April 29, 1955, TNW Collection, YCAL.

70. Bosworth, *Montgomery Clift: A Biography*, 257–58.

71. "Comedy or Tragedy? Mr. Wilder Discusses 'A Life in the Sun,' " *The Scotsman*, August 12, 1955, courtesy of the National Library of Scotland.

72. Rosemary Harris to PEN, March 27, 2010.

73. " 'A Life in the Sun': Thornton Wilder's Classic Morality," *The Scotsman*, August 16, 1955, courtesy of the National Library of Scotland.

74. TNW to Thew Wright, August 18, 1952, Private Collection.

75. TNW to Richard H. Goldstone, "The Art of Fiction XVI: Thornton Wilder," *Writers at Work: The Paris Review Interviews*, Malcolm Cowley, ed. (New York: Viking

Press, 1958), 101–18; reprinted in Bryer, *Conversations with Thornton Wilder*, 64–79.

76. Timothy Findley, *Inside Memory: Pages from a Writer's Notebook* (Toronto: Harper-Collins, 1990), 32–33.

77. Ibid., 33.

78. TNW, Journal, Entry 649, July 20, 1953, TNW Collection, YCAL.

79. TNW, Journal, Entry 472, November 4, 1950, TNW Collection, YCAL.

80. TNW, Journal, Entry 649, July 20, 1953, TNW Collection, YCAL.

81. Ibid.

82. Ibid.

83. Ibid.

84. TNW to Louise Talma, May 14, 1956, YCAL.

85. According to the records of the Harvard University English Department, TNW was not alone in leaving his Norton lectures unpublished. The art historian Erwin Panofsky's lectures were published in 1953, after his appointment for 1947–48.

86. TNW, Journal, Entry 425, May 7, 1949, TNW Collection, YCAL.

87. TNW, "Notes Toward 'The Emporium,'" February 23, 1954, TNW Collection, YCAL.

88. Ibid.

89. TNW, "Notes Toward 'The Emporium,'" June 17, 1954, TNW Collection, YCAL.

90. TNW, "Notes Toward 'The Emporium,'" February 9, 1954, TNW Collection, YCAL.

91. J. Howard Buzby and Arthur G. Broll, Co-Chairmen, 1956 Judges Committee, Miss America Pageant, to TNW, April 20, 1956, TNW Collection, YCAL. TNW's holograph note at the end of the letter, May 12, 1956, explained his response. *The Skin of Our Teeth* had also been presented in an hour-long television version on ABC in August 1952, with Thomas Mitchell as Mr. Antrobus, Peggy Wood as Mrs. Antrobus, and Nina Foch as Sabina.

35: "THE HUMAN ADVENTURE" (1950s AND 1960s)

1. "Sick as a dog": TNW, Journal, Entry 747, June 11, 1957, TNW Collection, YCAL.

2. TNW, 1948–61 Journal, Entry 724, April 3, 1956, TNW Collection, YCAL. This entry is published in large part in Gallup, *The Journals of Thornton Wilder*, and gives the name as Tom Everage, although Wilder actually writes John Everage in his journal.

3. Ibid.

4. TNW, 1948–61 Journal, Entry 728, April 8, 1956, TNW Collection, YCAL.

5. TNW, 1948–61 Journal, Entry 736, December 2, 1956, TNW Collection, YCAL.

6. Ibid.

7. TNW, 1948–61 Journal, Entry 771, December 25, 1960, TNW Collection, YCAL. "Grand Guignol" referred to the popular theater in Paris known from 1897 to 1962 for its repertory of macabre, often violent short plays.

8. TNW, "Transition from *The Alcestiad* to *The Drunken Sisters*," *The Alcestiad* or *A Life in the Sun, A Play in Three Acts with a Satyr Play, The Drunken Sisters*, 107–9. The German translation of the play was published in 1960 by S. Fischer Verlag, but *The Alcestiad* was not published in the United States until 1977. *The Drunken Sisters* was published in the November 1957 edition of the *Atlantic*. See also McClatchy, *Thornton Wilder: Collected Plays & Writings on Theater*, 431–32; and Gallup and Tappan

Wilder, *The Collected Short Plays of Thornton Wilder*, vol. 2, 115–24.

9. TNW, 1948–61 Journal, Entry 736, January 31, 1957, TNW Collection, YCAL.

10. TNW to Eileen, Roland, and Julian Le Grand, December 19, 1956, *SL*, 545–47.

11. Deutschsprächige Aufführungen der ALKESTIADE, TNW Collection, YCAL.

12. TNW, 1948–61 Journal, Entry 745, June 8, 1957, TNW Collection, YCAL.

13. TNW, 1948–61 Journal, Entry 739, May 26, 1957, TNW Collection, YCAL.

14. TNW, 1948–61 Journal, Entry 742, June 2, 1957, TNW Collection, YCAL.

15. Ibid.

16. Ibid.

17. Ibid.

18. Ibid.

19. Ibid.

20. Ibid.

21. TNW, preface to *Three Plays*, xxxii.

22. TNW, 1948–61 Journal, Entry 742, June 2, 1957, TNW Collection, YCAL.

23. Ibid.

24. Ibid.

25. Ibid. TNW referred here to Ellen Wood's 1861 bestseller, *East Lynne*, and to Mary Elizabeth Braddon's sensational *Lady Audley's Secret*, published in serial form in 1862. He may have meant to cite Thomas Hardy's *Tess of the d'Urbervilles* (1891).

26. TNW, 1948–61 Journal, Entry 749, June 15, 1957, TNW Collection, YCAL.

27. Ibid.

28. "American Plays Given in Berlin," *New York Times*, September 21, 1957.

29. TNW to Thew Wright, September 29, [1957?], Private Collection.

30. TNW, "Culture in a Democracy," in Gallup, *American Characteristics*, 68–69.

31. Ibid., 70. See also Cynthia Ozick, "T. S. Eliot at 101," *New Yorker*, November 20, 1989, 119.

32. TNW, "Culture in a Democracy," in Gallup, *American Characteristics*, 72.

33. Ibid.

34. Ibid., 73.

35. Paul Fussell quoted in Horst Frenz, "American Playwrights and the German Psyche," *South-Central Bulletin* 21(February 1961): 1, 6–9.

36. TNW to Thew Wright, [Fall 1957?], Private Collection.

37. Horst Frenz, "Thornton Wilder's Visits to Postwar Germany," *American-German Review* 24 (October–November): 8–10.

38. Frenz, "American Playwrights and the German Psyche."

39. ANW, *Thornton Wilder and His Public*, 13.

40. TNW to Laurence Olivier, December 10, [1960?], *SL*, 575–77.

41. TNW, 1948–61 Journal, Entry 755, November 24, 1958, TNW Collection, YCAL.

42. Norman Bel Geddes to TNW, February 10, 1938, TNW Collection, YCAL. Bel Geddes had produced extravagant sets for Max Reinhardt's *The Miracle* in 1924. He was also known for his architectural, industrial, and civic designs, and for his futuristic prototypes for automobiles.

43. Norman Bel Geddes to TNW, January 6, 1958, TNW Collection, YCAL.

44. TNW, Treatment for "A Film on the Role of America as Returning to Share What It Received from Europe," February 1958, TNW Collection, YCAL.

45. TNW to Norman Bel Geddes, January 19, 1950, copy, Private Collection.

46. See Edward M. Burns with Joshua A. Gaylord, eds., *A Tour of the Darkling Plain: The*

Finnegans Wake Letters of Thornton Wilder and Adaline Glasheen (Dublin: University College Dublin Press, 2001).

47. TNW to Adaline Glasheen, [October 1962?], Burns with Gaylord, *A Tour of the Darkling Plain*, 393.

48. TNW, "*Finnegans Wake*: The Polyglot Everyman," TNW Collection, YCAL. This piece and the alternative draft are published in Burns with Gaylord, *A Tour of the Darkling Plain*, 595–611.

49. TNW, "*Finnegans Wake*: The Polyglot Everyman," alternative draft, TNW Collection, YCAL.

50. TNW, 1948–61 Journal, Entry 759, November 10, 1959, TNW Collection, YCAL.

51. Ibid.

52. TNW to Adaline Glasheen, October 11, 1959, in Burns with Gaylord, *A Tour of the Darkling Plain*, 242–43.

53. TNW, 1948–61 Journal, Entry 750, November 10, 1959, TNW Collection, YCAL.

54. TNW to Ludi Clair, December 28, [1958?], Private Collection.

55. Ibid.

56. Ibid.

57. Rorem apparently wanted to set some of Wilder's three-minute playlets to music in 1961, but Wilder asked him to "wait a year" because of the then-current "glut" of operas based on his work. [TNW to Ned Rorem, June 25, (1961), Private Collection]. The *Our Town* opera project, conceived many years after Wilder's death, had its premiere in 2006, with music by Rorem and libretto by J. D. McClatchy. Wilder had granted Bernstein, along with his colleagues Jerome Robbins, Betty Comden, and Adolph Green, permission to create a musical version of *The Skin of Our Teeth* in 1964, but the collaboration fell apart. Bernstein apparently wanted to go in a different direction with an opera of *The Skin of Our Teeth*, but Wilder declined permission for that project.

58. TNW to Robert H. Thayer, Special Assistant to the Secretary of State and Coordinator of International Educational and Cultural Relations, October 16, 1960, TS copy, TNW Collection, YCAL.

59. The Theatre Guild American Repertory Company performed *The Skin of Our Teeth*, Tennessee Williams's *The Glass Menagerie*, and William Gibson's *The Miracle Worker*. The tour concluded in October 1961. From July 18 through July 30, 1955, Alan Schneider had directed a production of *The Skin of Our Teeth* starring Hayes, with Mary Martin as Sabina, George Abbott as Mr. Antrobus, and Florence Reed as the fortune-teller.

60. The actress Nancy Nutter da Silva and the artist and designer Arthur "Pete" Ballard provided vivid eyewitness accounts of the European productions to PEN, October 2010.

61. TNW to Gertrude Hindemith, April 11, 1960, *SL*, 569–70.

62. TNW to Catherine Coffin, February 7, 1963, *SL*, 621–23. TNW knew Kilty's work with the Brattle Street Theatre in Cambridge, Massachusetts, and admired his play *Dear Liar*. He and Kilty had worked together on the *Ides* script for nearly three weeks in Atlantic City. The adaptation of *The Ides of March* was moderately successful in Berlin in 1962, and in 1963 was approved for production by the Moscow Ministry of Culture. It had performance dates in Warsaw, Turin, Milan, Rome, and Paris, in addition to London, where the reviews were largely negative.

63. Findley, *Inside Memory*, 27–32.

64. TNW to Edward Albee, November 22, [1953?], *SL*, 516–17.

65. TNW to Edward Albee, August 17, [1958?], *SL*, 554–55.

66. TNW to Everett Gibbs, May 22, 1967, Charles Von der Ahe Library, Loyola Marymount University, Los Angeles, CA.

67. Ted Mann Interview with Ken Witty, n.d., TNW Collection, YCAL.

68. Art Carney was also an experienced stage actor. He left *The Honeymooners* in 1957 (he would later rejoin Gleason) to take on dramatic television roles on *Playhouse 90* and *Kraft Television Theater.*

69. Sammy Cahn (1913–93) was nominated for twenty-six Academy Awards for his songs, and won four for Best Song, including "Three Coins in a Fountain" and "Call Me Irresponsible."

70. Ted Mann Interview with Ken Witty, n.d., TNW Collection, YCAL.

71. Ibid. In his *Paris Review* interview in 1957, TNW said that he still regarded the theater "as the greatest of all art forms, the most immediate way in which a human being can share with another the sense of what it is to be a human being." His growing disappointment with the quality and cost of Broadway productions led to his increased support of off-Broadway theater.

   TNW's one-act plays are published in Gallup and A. Tappan Wilder, *The Collected Short Plays of Thornton Wilder*, vol. 1, and in McClatchy, *Thornton Wilder: Collected Plays & Writings on Theater.*

72. TNW to Cass Canfield, March 13, 1962, *SL*, 595–96.

73. Ibid.

74. TNW to Irene Worth, March 18, 1962, *SL*, 597–99. The opera was published by Carl Fisher in 1978, as *The Alcestiad: An Opera in Three Acts.*

75. Don Irwin, "*Our Town* Costume for a Cabinet Soiree," *New York Herald Tribune*, May 1, 1962, 1, 10.

76. TNW to Irene Worth, March 18, 1962, *SL*, 597–99.

77. TNW to Glenway Wescott, March 30, 1962, *SL* 599–601.

78. TNW to Louise Talma, May 17, 1962, *SL*, 601–4. On January 19, 1957, Isabel Wilder wrote to Janet Wilder Dakin, "Thorny has a dark gray, red-lined Thunderbird! Oh, oh, fabulous!!" Private Collection.

79. TNW to James Leo Herlihy, July 25, [1969?], *SL* 666–69.

80. TNW to Charlotte Wilder, November 30, [1960?], Private Collection.

81. TNW to James Leo Herlihy, July 25, [1969?], *SL*, 666–69.

82. Ibid.

83. Ibid.

84. Decennial Census Population of Arizona, Counties, Cities, Places, 1860–2000, U.S. Bureau of Census.

85. TNW to Isabel Wilder, August 26, 1962, TNW Collection, YCAL.

86. Ibid.

87. TNW to Charlotte Tappan Niven, September 8, 1962, TNW Collection, YCAL.

88. Ibid.

89. TNW to Elizabeth Shepley Sergeant, September 12, 1962, *SL*, 608–9. For additional information on TNW's sojourn in Douglas, see Tom Miller, "Thornton Wilder's Desert Oasis," *Smithsonian Magazine*, July 2009, 80: 82–86.

90. TNW to Eileen and Roland Le Grand, December 10, 1962, *SL*, 610–12.

91. TNW to Arthur Gelb, "Thornton Wilder, 63, Sums Up Life and Art in New Play Cycle," *New York Times*, November 5, 1961, 1.

92. TNW to Tappan Wilder, December 19, 1962, Private Collection.

93. TNW to Thew Wright, January 11, 1963, *SL*, 617–18.

94. Ibid.

95. TNW, Nomination of Edward Albee, [1965?], TNW Collection, YCAL.

96. TNW to Louise Talma, December 6, 1962, YCAL.

97. TNW to Charlotte Wilder, November 30, [1960?], Private Collection.

98. TNW to Tappan Wilder, December 19, 1962, Private Collection.

99. Tony Luhan died in January 1963.

100. TNW to Thew Wright, January 11, 1963, *SL*, 617–18.

101. TNW to Ruth Gordon and Garson Kanin, January 14, 1963, *SL*, 619–621; TNW to Thew Wright, January 11, 1963, *SL*, 617–18.

102. TNW to Catherine Coffin, February 7, 1963, *SL*, 621–23.

103. TNW to Isabel Wilder, March 17, 1963, *SL*, 624–26.

104. Ibid.

105. Ibid.

106. Ibid.

107. TNW to Harold Freedman, November 18, 1963, *SL*, 626–28.

108. Isabel Wilder to Vivien Leigh, November 12, 1965, copy, TNW Collection, YCAL.

109. TNW to ANW, October 22, 1975, TNW Collection, YCAL, uncataloged letters.

36: "tapestry" (1963–1970)

1. TNW to Amy Wertheimer, "May 20 or 27," 1964, TNW Collection, YCAL.

2. TNW to Ruth Gordon and Garson Kanin, January 11, 1964, Private Collection.

3. TNW to Catharine and ANW, April 21, 1964, *SL*, 630–32.

4. TNW to Charlotte Niven, December 19, 1963, TNW Collection, YCAL.

5. TNW to Tappan Wilder, December 19, 1963, *SL*, 628–30.

6. TNW to Catharine and ANW, April 21, 1964, *SL*, 630–32.

7. Ibid.

8. Ibid.

9. Ibid.

10. TNW to Charlotte Niven, June 15, 1964, TNW Collection, YCAL; Isabel Wilder to Carol Brandt, June 25 and June 26, 1964, TNW Collection, YCAL. Also see Isabel Wilder to Bill Layton, July 30, 1964, copy, TNW Collection, YCAL.

11. TNW to Charlotte Niven, March 26, 1965, TNW Collection, YCAL.

12. Ibid.

13. TNW to Phyllis McGinley, April 2, 1965, *SL*, 633–35.

14. TNW to Charlotte Niven, March 26, 1965, TNW Collection, YCAL.

15. TNW to Amy Wertheimer, May 1, 1965, TNW Collection, YCAL.

16. TNW to Charlotte Niven, May 1, 1965, TNW Collection, YCAL.

17. TNW to Catharine Dix "Dixie" Wilder, June 3, 1965, *SL*, 636–37. As Robin Wilder and Bryer point out in *The Selected Letters of Thornton Wilder*, TNW quoted Jean Racine's *Athalie* in French in the reference in this letter.

18. TNW to Ruth Gordon and Garson Kanin, June 21, 1965, Private Collection. *Stover at Yale* was a novel by Owen Johnson, published in 1911, wherein Stover goes to Yale from the Lawrenceville School and makes a name for himself.

19. TNW to Amy Wertheimer, April 7, 1966, *SL*, 638–39.

20. TNW, *The Eighth Day*, 17.

21. TNW to Cheryl Crawford, "Maundy Thursday," [April 7?], 1966, *SL*, 639–41.

22. TNW to ANW, September 13, 1966, TNW Collection, YCAL, uncataloged letters.

23. TNW to Charlotte Niven, November 24, 1966, TNW Collection, YCAL.

24. TNW to Isabel Wilder, November 28, 1966, TNW Collection, YCAL.

25. TNW to Charlotte Niven, February 23, [1967?], TNW Collection, YCAL.

26. TNW to Robert Penn Warren, September 14, 1968, YCAL. "Merton's Magic Mountain": Thomas Merton (1915–68), a Trappist monk, was an American writer and the author of more than seventy books, including an autobiography, *The Seven Storey Mountain* (1948). TNW was thinking of Thomas Mann's *Magic Mountain* (1924).

27. TNW to unidentified reader, March 16, 1968, typed copy, YCAL.

28. TNW to Cass Canfield, March 1, 1968, *SL*, 653–54.

29. Marie-Joseph-Pierre Teilhard de Chardin (1885–1955) was, by preference, customarily referred to as "Teilhard."

30. TNW, *The Eighth Day*, 309, 318, 367.

31. Ibid., 217.

32. Ibid., 351.

33. Ibid., 148.

34. Ibid., 148.

35. Ibid., 407.

36. TNW, 1948–61 Journal, Entry 40 [titled "Sketch for a Portrait of Tia Bates"], May 23, 1941, TNW Collection, YCAL.

37. TNW, *Heaven's My Destination*, 62, 75.

38. TNW, *Theophilus North*, 26.

39. Quoted in Richard Ellmann, *James Joyce, New and Revised Edition* (Oxford and New York: Oxford University Press, 1983), 711–12.

40. TNW, *The Eighth Day*, 435.

41. TNW to Amos Tappan Wilder, December 19, 1962, *SL*, 615–16.

42. TNW to Cass Canfield, March 1, 1968, *SL*, 653–54.

43. TNW to Grace Christy Foresman, April 21, 1967, *SL*, 643–44.

44. TNW to Isabel Wilder, March 19, 1965, TNW Collection, YCAL.

45. TNW to Cass Canfield, February 28, 1968, TNW Collection, YCAL.

46. TNW to Timothy Findley, May 5, 1967, National Archives of Canada.

47. TNW to Ruth Gordon and Garson Kanin, April 24, 1967, Private Collection.

48. Ibid.

49. TNW to James Leo Herlihy, February 12, 1970, *SL*, 671–74.

50. TNW to Amy Wertheimer, "Easter 1968" [April 14, 1968], TNW Collection, YCAL.

51. TNW, holograph note, [1960s?], TNW Collection, YCAL.

52. TNW to Ruth Gordon, August 15, 1968, Private Collection.

53. TNW to Isabel Wilder, February 11, 1969, TNW Collection, YCAL.

54. TNW to Isabel Wilder, February 16, 1969, TNW Collection, YCAL.

55. TNW to Isabel Wilder, February 23, 1969, TNW Collection, YCAL.

56. TNW to Isabel Wilder, January 29, 1970, TNW Collection, YCAL.

57. TNW to Isabel Wilder, February 3, 1970, TNW Collection, YCAL.

58. TNW to James Leo Herlihy, February 12, 1970, *SL*, 671–74.

59. TNW to Isabel Wilder, February 4, 1969, TNW Collection, YCAL.

60. TNW to Ruth Gordon and Garson Kanin, February 27, 1968, Private Collection.

61. TNW to Isabel Wilder, April 11 and June 12, 1969, TNW Collection, YCAL.

62. TNW to Dixie Wilder [January 7, 1969?], TNW Collection, YCAL.

63. TNW to Isabel Wilder, March 7, [1970?], TNW Collection, YCAL.

64. TNW to Isabel Wilder, October 27, [1969 or 1970?], TNW Collection, YCAL. TNW was quoting lines from Alexander Pope's "Eloisa to Abelard" (1717): "How happy is the blameless vestal's lot! / The world forgetting, by the world forgot. / Eternal sunshine of the spotless mind!"
65. TNW to Isabel Wilder, November 6, 1969, TNW Collection, YCAL.
66. Isabel Wilder to Miss Camargo, May 28, 1967, TNW Collection, YCAL.
67. TNW to George F. Edmonds, April 14, 1972, typed copy, TNW Collection, YCAL.
68. TNW to Richard H. Goldstone, November 19, 1968, *SL*, 661–63. In 1969 Goldstone purchased 117 letters written by TNW to Sibyl Colefax. See Gloria Emerson, "Wilder's Letters to London Hostess Are Disclosed," *New York Times*, September 3, 1969. Goldstone's biography of TNW was at that time scheduled to be published by Harper, TNW's publisher. Sibyl Colefax's letters to Wilder are housed in the TNW Collection, YCAL.
69. TNW to Isabel Wilder, April 10, [1970?], TNW Collection, YCAL.
70. TNW to Ruth Gordon and Garson Kanin, March 15, 1970, Private Collection.

37: "LIFE AND DEATH" (1970–1975)

1. TNW to Amy Wertheimer, April 17, 1967, TNW Collection, YCAL.
2. TNW to Gertrude Abercrombie, March 2, 1971, Archives of American Art.
    In our series of interviews, Catharine "Dixie" Wilder Guiles furnished details and context for the last years of TNW's life, as well as invaluable general background on Wilder family life, especially in the later years.
3. TNW to Sol Lesser, October 29, 1973, TNW Collection, YCAL. Context and many details of the later years of TNW's life are drawn in part from Isabel Wilder's letters to Professor Guelfo Frulla, a professor at Yale for eleven years, from 1947 to 1958, and a Wilder family friend. These letters, from 1958 to 1976, record copious details about Isabel's life with TNW, particularly during the last decade of his life. Dr. Frulla's nephew Dr. Tommaso Munari kindly provided copies of the letters, as well as of TNW's letters to Dr. Frulla.
4. TNW to C. M. and Pani ——[April 23, 1974?], TNW Collection, YCAL.
5. TNW to Charles Abramson, September 2, 1971, Bancroft Library, University of California, Berkeley.
6. TNW, "Twinhood," manuscript fragment, 1969, TNW Collection, YCAL. "Identical replica": "Chapter Three: First Sketches Toward a Characterization of Theophilus," n.d., TNW Collection, YCAL.
7. TNW to Simon Blow, "Arts Guardian: 'I was Born an Identical Twin . . . ,'" *Manchester Guardian*, June 29, 1974.
8. TNW to Eileen and Roland Le Grand, April 25, 1971, *SL*, 678–79.
9. TNW to Mia Farrow, October 4, 1972, *SL*, 682–85.
10. TNW to Catherine Coffin, November 1, 1968, *SL*, 656–58.
11. TNW to Ruth Gordon and Garson Kanin, n.d., Private Collection. The songs TNW refers to appear on the Beatles' 1967 album, *Sgt. Pepper's Lonely Hearts Club Band*.
12. TNW, "Description of the Accident," July 23, 1972, TNW Collection, YCAL.
13. TNW to Irene Worth, February 5, 1973, YCAL.
14. Record of the Harper & Row advance for *Theophilus North*, Private Collection.
15. TNW to Irene Worth, February 5, 1973, YCAL.
16. Ibid.

17. TNW, *Theophilus North*, 2.
18. Ibid., 3.
19. Ibid., 4. In this scene Theophilus North and Sigmund Freud discuss the oedipal implications of this aversion to "respectable women," citing Charles Marlow in Oliver Goldsmith's *She Stoops to Conquer*.
20. TNW, *Theophilus North*, 5.
21. Ibid., 6.
22. Ibid., 374.
23. Ibid., 310.
24. TNW to Peggy and Roy Anderson, October 11, 1973, *SL*, 688–89.
25. Ibid.
26. TNW to Dalma H. Brunauer, November 11, 1975, *SL*, 700–701.
27. Ibid.
28. TNW, *Theophilus North*, 372–73.
29. TNW to Isabel Wilder, March 19, 1965, TNW Collection, YCAL.
30. TNW, "Preface," incomplete manuscript draft of preface to *Theophilus North*, TNW Collection, YCAL.
31. TNW, *Theophilus North*, 291–92.
32. TNW to Gladys Campbell, April 20, 1973, University of Chicago Library.
33. TNW to ANW, April 8, 1974, TNW Collection, YCAL, uncataloged letters.
34. TNW to Ruth Gordon and Garson Kanin, April 20, 1973, *SL*, 685–86.
35. "Every aspect": TNW to Catharine and ANW, June 9–11, 1973, TNW Collection, YCAL, uncataloged letters. "Suddenly stung": TNW to Ruth Gordon and Garson Kanin, April 29, 1973, *SL*, 685–86. This April 29 passage is a continuaton of the letter TNW began writing to Gordon and Kanin on April 20, 1973.
36. TNW, 1948–61 Journal, Entry 502 [January 1969?], TNW Collection, YCAL. From his vantage point in Europe, away from his earlier journals, Wilder apparently began the numbering from memory and so mistakenly assigned the 1969 entries numbers he had already used in his 1951 journal.
37. Ibid.
38. Ibid.
39. TNW, "The Detective Story Mystery," April 27 and May 3 and 4, 1931, TNW Collection, YCAL. This five-page, unfinished holograph draft was written in Munich.
40. TNW, 1948–61 Journal, Entry 502 [January 1969?], TNW Collection, YCAL.
41. Ibid.
42. TNW to Peggy and Roy Anderson, October 11, 1973, *SL*, 688–89.
43. TNW to Charlotte Niven, June 22, 1967, TNW Collection, YCAL.
44. TNW to Isabel Wilder, November 17, 1966, TNW Collection, YCAL.
45. TNW to Gene Tunney, December 4, 1970, *SL*, 675–77.
46. TNW, *Theophilus North*, 151.
47. TNW, "Theophilus North, Zen Detective," n.d., holograph manuscript, TNW Collection, YCAL.
48. TNW to ANW, June 9, 1974, TNW Collection, YCAL, uncataloged letters.
49. Susan H. Llewellyn's telling of Barbara Effron's anecdote to PEN, April 1, 2011.
50. TNW to Catharine "Dixie" Wilder, June 30, 1974, *SL*, 693–94.
51. TNW to Ruth Gordon and Garson Kanin, January 17, 1975, Private Collection.
52. TNW to Ruth Gordon and Garson Kanin, December 31, 1974, Private Collection.

53. TNW to Paul Horgan, "Thornton Wilder: A Little Drawing in Line," *Book-of-the-Month Club News*, March 1967, 6, 16.

54. TNW to ANW, [June 18, 1974?], TNW Collection, YCAL, uncataloged letters.

55. TNW to ANW, April 3, 1974, TNW Collection, YCAL, uncataloged letters.

56. TNW to Sol Lesser, September 23, 1974, UCLA.

57. Ibid.

58. TNW to Enid Bagnold, paraphrasing Goethe, June 29, 1972, *SL*, 679–82. TNW may have been paraphrasing or at least alluding to Goethe's 1814 poem, "Phänomen," which says, in part,

> *Though the brow is white,*
> *it is still heaven's.*
> *So you, lively old man, do not be sad.*
> *Though your hair is white, still you will love.*

59. TNW, 1948–1961 Journal, Entry 542, April [no day], 1951, TNW Collection, YCAL.

60. TNW to Helen and Jacob Bleibtreu, November 3, 1973, *SL*, 689–90.

61. TNW to Robert J. Donovan, "Thornton Wilder on Life Today: 'It's an Age of Transition—and It's Exciting,'" *Los Angeles Times*, October 15, 1973, reprinted in Bryer, *Conversations with Thornton Wilder*, 107.

62. TNW to Ellen Gates Starr, February 23, 1939, Private Collection.

63. TNW to Robert J. Donovan, "Thornton Wilder on Life Today: 'It's an Age of Transition—and It's Exciting.'"

64. TNW to ANW, [June 18, 1974?], TNW Collection, YCAL, uncataloged letters.

65. Janet Wilder Dakin to Winthrop "Toby" Dakin, [January 1979?], Private Collection.

66. TNW To Garson Kanin, March 7, 1967, TNW Collection, YCAL. See also Edmund W. Pavenstedt, White and Case, to TNW, September 2, 1966, and to John W. Barnett, Wiggin & Dana, October 20, 1966, TNW Collection, YCAL.

67. "*The Eighth Day* Royalty Earnings," [1975?], Private Collection.

68. "Charlotte Elizabeth Wilder," Admissions Report, November 12, 1969, Private Collection.

69. TNW to Ruth Gordon, January [no day], 1969, Private Collection.

70. TNW to Isabel Wilder, January 29, 1970, TNW Collection, YCAL.

71. Charlotte Wilder to TNW, June 30, 1971, TNW Collection, YCAL.

72. Sol Lesser to TNW, April 3, 1975, TNW Collection, YCAL.

73. TNW to Sol Lesser, April 17, 1975, holograph drafts and a typescript copy, TNW Collection, YCAL.

74. TNW to ANW, July 28, 1975, TNW Collection, YCAL, uncataloged letters. Wilder would most likely have appreciated the work that would be done in the future by scholars cited in this biography, as well as others, including Martin Blank, ed., *Critical Essays on Thornton Wilder* (New York: G. K. Hall & Company, 1996); Lincoln Konkle, *Thornton Wilder and the Puritan Narrative Tradition* (Columbia, MO: The University of Missouri Press, 2006); Paul Lifton, *The Theatre of Thornton Wilder: Contributions in Drama and Theatre Studies* (Westport, CT: Greenwood Press, 1995); and Christopher J. Wheatley, *Thornton Wilder & Amos Wilder: Writing Religion in Twentieth-Century America* (Notre Dame, IN: University of Notre Dame Press, 2011).

75. TNW to ANW, July 28, 1975, TNW Collection, YCAL, uncataloged letters.

76. TNW to Amos Tappan Wilder, August 22, 1975, Private Collection.

77. TNW to Malcolm Cowley, November 18, 1975, *SL*, 701–2.
78. TNW to Eileen and Roland Le Grand, December 3, 1975, *SL*, 704–5.
79. TNW to Carol Brandt, November 18, 1975, *SL*, 703.
80. Ruth Gordon, Remarks at TNW's Memorial Service, January 18, 1976, TNW Collection, YCAL.
81. TNW to Eileen and Roland Le Grand, December 3, 1975, *SL*, 704–5.

EPILOGUE

1. ANW, Interment Service for TNW, December 9, 1975, TNW Collection, YCAL.
2. Tappan Wilder, Memorial Service for TNW, January 8, 1976, TNW Collection, YCAL.
3. TNW, *The Woman of Andros*, 176.
4. TNW, "Report of the Rapporteur General," International Conference of Artists, Venice, September 28, 1952, UNESCO document, UNESCO/ART/DIV/7.
5. TNW to Isabel Wilder, August 25, 1937, TNW Collection, YCAL.
6. TNW, unpublished lecture on biography, n.d., TNW Collection, YCAL.

ACKNOWLEDGMENTS

The art of biography is more difficult than is generally supposed.
—THORNTON WILDER,
The Bridge of San Luis Rey

Several years ago, after I spoke to some elementary school children about my adventures as a writer, a little girl said, "I've just decided I'm going to be a writer when I grow up. It sounds like so much more fun than working!" Researching and writing biography can be fun, but it is most often difficult, complicated, painstaking work. Providentially, I love doing it, and fortunately, my work has been facilitated and encouraged by countless individuals who have performed innumerable acts of kindness and assistance.

I could not have finished this book without miracles. Some of them were worked by the following: First Jennifer, my wise and beautiful daughter, a gifted writer, and a person of extraordinary grace, strength, and wit. She gives me boundless love, inspiration, encouragement, and joy. Without her I could not have surmounted the challenges in my own life while I was writing this book about Wilder's life.

Next, Tappan Wilder, a remarkable literary executor. He has given me unflagging encouragement and support, all the while respecting and protecting my total independence. He has generously shared papers and documents, questions and ideas, and enlightening memories and conversations, holding nothing back. He always stands by to help but never stands in the way. His mantra has been "This is *your* book. Tell the story as *you* see it." Like his uncle Thornton, he has a consummate gift for friendship.

Next I owe an enduring debt to Dr. William Rice III, my friend and physician, whose perceptive, farseeing care has prolonged and enhanced my life. Words cannot adequately express my gratitude to him, or to the following people who have helped me keep on writing: Dr. Samuel Lentz; Dr. Daniel W. Dubovsky; my cousin-in-law Dr. John Moore; Dr. Austin Temple; Dr. Dale Browne; Linda Mock, who helps me hear; and Rick Robinson, who helps me see.

I am grateful to the Wilder scholars with whom I have worked on various projects: again, the foremost Wilder scholar and archivist, Tappan Wilder; Dr. Jackson R. Bryer; J. D. McClatchy; and especially, Dr. Robin Gibbs Wilder, who has generously and meticulously shared her knowledge of Wilder and his family and of American history and culture. Invaluable contributions to the biography have been made by Catharine "Dixie" Wilder Guiles, and the late Catharine Kerlin Wilder, whose memories, letters, and support I deeply appreciate.

I am grateful to the following for their contributions to the book in the form of interviews, or letters and documents, or consultation, or questions answered, or research assistance, or photographs, or hospitality, or a combination of those: Oscar Ardila, Arthur "Pete" Ballard, Sally Begley, Dr. Scott Bennett, Susan Bianconi, the late Dr. John Broderick, Harlan Blynn, Francesca Calderone-Steichen, Rowe Carenen, Carol Channing, Vicki Crouser, Dr. Louie Eargle, Mia Farrow, David Finkle, Paul Green, Jr., Paul Gregory, the late Philip Guiles, Rosemary Harris, Lisa Hartjens, William Henderson, Archie Hobson, Dr. John Hutton, Louis Kapeleris, Dr. Lincoln Konkle, Matt Lutz, the late Dr. Morris Martin, Christopher Morss, Betsy Green Moyers, Tom Munroe, Dr. Tommaso Murani, Dr. Edyta Oczkowicz, the late Dr. Elizabeth Phillips, Dr. Tim Redman, Ray Roberts, Dr. Eva Rodtwit, the late Dr. James Semans, Cindy Shirley, Nancy Nutter da Silva, Justin Spring, Ariana Rodina Calderone Stahmer, Robert Stewart, Rosey Strub, Harold Tedford, Tazewell Thompson, Anna Livia Plurabelle ("Liffey") Thorpe, Jay Tunney, the late Kurt Vonnegut, Jr., Scott Warhoven, Jenney Wilder, Michael Williams, Nita Kendrick Williamson, Dr. Edwin Wilson, Emily Herring Wilson, Ken Witty, and Don Wolfe.

I have spent productive hours over many years engrossed in the Thornton Wilder papers at the Beinecke Rare Book & Manuscript Library at Yale University, and before Wilder, in the papers of Edward and Clara Smith Steichen in the Beinecke's Alfred Stieglitz Collection. The quality of the Beinecke collections is matched by the quality of the outstanding people who work there. I have been the grateful beneficiary of the professionalism and generosity of the Beinecke staff. I owe special appreciation to Stephen Jones. My thanks go to Dr. Patricia Willis, former curator of American Literature; Dr. Nancy Kuhl, current curator of American Literature; Dr. Louise Bernard, curator of American Literature: Prose and Drama; Anne Marie Menta, Timothy Young, Diane Ducharme, Eva Wrightson, Moira Fitzgerald, and all the people at the Beinecke who help by retrieving materials, copying papers and photographs, and protecting books and papers with courteous care. Gratitude goes out as well to Judith Ann Schiff, chief research archivist of Manuscripts and Archives; and Diane E. Kaplan, head of public Services, Manuscripts, and Archives, Yale University Library. I also thank Amy Boratko and Anna Chen for their excellent research assistance. I learned a great deal in conversation with the late Donald Gallup, curator of the Yale Collection of American Literature from 1947 until 1980, and editor of Wilder's journals and his selected nonfiction.

I appreciate the assistance of the following additional institutions and individuals: Renée Bennett, director of communications, The Masters School, as it is known today; Heather Cole, assistant curator of Modern Books & Manuscripts, Houghton Library, Harvard University; Margaret R. Dakin, Archives and Special Collections, Amherst College; Mollie Gathro, archives assistant, Mount Holyoke College; Ken Grossi, acting college archivist, Oberlin College Archives; David Kessler, The Bancroft Library, University of California at Berkeley; Nancy R. Miller, University of Pennsylvania Archives; Katherine Mollen, Center for Legislative Archives, National Archives and Records Administration; Megan O'Shea, manuscripts specialist, Manuscripts and Archives Division, New York Public Library; Mark Renovitch, Franklin Delano Roosevelt Presidential Library and Museum; Peter Weis, archivist; Dr. Rose Simon and her colleagues in the Salem College Library; the Mount Hermon School; the Thacher School; The Library and Archives of Canada; and the National Library of Scotland.

I will always be thankful for the affirmation and support of a

Fellowship in American Literature from the National Endowment for the Humanities, and the Thornton Wilder Fellowship at the Beinecke Library at Yale.

It has been a great pleasure to work with my venerable editor, Hugh Van Dusen. For more than two years he read the manuscript chapter by chapter as I finished each draft, and he sent me immediate feedback, comments, and questions that greatly helped to shape and refine the book at a crucial time. His consideration of the person as well as the writer helped to sustain me on this extended journey, and I am deeply grateful. I received vital help, guidance, and support from the remarkable Maya Ziv, who has my enduring thanks. When Maya moved on to another role at HarperCollins, Barry Harbaugh capably took over the reins as Hugh Van Dusen's assistant, and I appreciate his attentive help as we moved toward the finish line.

It is always exciting and gratifying when a manuscript is at last delivered to the publisher and embarks on the production process. Many skilled people work together to transform a manuscript into a book, and I have been fortunate to have as colleagues at HarperCollins Peter London of the Permissions Department; Eric Levy, the production manager; Emily Walters, the production editor; Susan Llewellyn, the copy editor; Richard Ljoenes, designer of the book's jacket; Fritz Metsch, the designer of the book's interior; Nancy Wolff, the indexer; and Kate Blum and Martin Wilson in publicity.

For taking care of countless matters over many years, daily thanks go to my friend and longtime agent, Barbara Hogenson, of The Barbara Hogenson Agency, and to her assistants Nicole Verity and Lori Styler. It was Barbara who first suggested Thornton Wilder as my next subject, and introduced me to Tappan Wilder, and she has been a wonderful guide, companion, and cheerleader from the beginning.

Always I appreciate my family and friends. I give thanks for them and to them: My sisters, Lynn Niven Duval Clark and Doris Niven Knapp, and my brother, William Olin "Bill" Niven; my aunt, Frances Niven Gamble; my nieces and nephews, especially Lisa, Bob, Nathaniel, Learyn, and Annalise von Sprecken; all the Niven cousins, especially Patsy McGee, Gay Diller, Glo Hope, Jan Moore, and Angela and Dominic Moresco; Joe Kraemer, Claire Christopher, Francesca Calderone-Steichen, Joel Stahmer, Ariana Stahmer, Jeffrey Couchman, Coddy Granum, Jenney Wilder, Blanton and Betty Belk, Carol Edwards, Sophia Cody, Sue Wall, Ed and Emily Wilson, Nick Bragg, the late Mary Louise Davis, Melanie and Michael Kraemer, Ceci and James Earl Jones, Majie Failey, Connie Backlund, Caywood Hendricks, Mary Ausley, Denise Franklin, Robert Hamilton, Bruce Monks, Carroll Leggett, Leslie Pocchiari, David Solomon, Guy Blynn, William "Chan" Chandler, Judy Kessler, Angelo Surmelis, Ed Baran, Eileen Wilson-Oyelaran, Olasope Oyelaran, and Julianne Still Thrift. I extend thanks to my Salem College creative writing students for their company over the years. My life and my work have been enriched for more than a decade by the creativity and friendship of the talented women in my writers' group—Joy Beshears, Ginger Hendricks, and Sheryl Monks.

A biographer has to be something of a gypsy, and my research travels have been enhanced on occasion by wonderful traveling companions: Jennifer and I have consolidated our research trips as often as possible, and have shared unforgettable adventures in Canada, Wales, Scotland, England, France, Switzerland, and many locations in the United States; Francesca Calderone-Steichen and I have worked side by side in Switzerland, New Jersey, and New Haven; Edyta Oczkowicz and I have shared discoveries at the Beinecke Library; I explored Wilder's Zurich with Jennifer, Francesca, and her daughter, Ariana; and with the encouragement and help of my sister Lynn, I retraced Wilder's steps through ancient Rome. We also spent an inspiring afternoon in the Keats house near the Spanish Steps, especially in the room where Keats died. I came away with a much deeper understanding of what Rome meant to Wilder, and, therefore, of his first novel, *The Cabala*.

I have often been asked if I am related to Thornton Niven Wilder. As I embarked on the journey of this book, I had never looked into the matter. I was drawn to Wilder not because we share a name but because of his extraordinary work. It was only after I moved deeper into the exploration of his life that I began to study his ancestry and, simultaneously, my own. More than a decade ago, on a Wilder research trip to Scotland, I investigated my personal Niven heritage in the genealogical archives in Edinburgh, taking along a copy of the family history prepared by my aunts and cousins over the years. I did not then have names or dates for the Nivens from whom Wilder was descended. Later, Tappan Wilder found a copy of the Niven genealogy among the papers of his father, Amos Niven Wilder. With that information and my own expanding research, I could confirm that Thornton Wilder's Niven family and my Niven family came from the same Scottish village: Bowmore on Islay in the Inner Hebrides. Curious now, and believing that there might actually be some distant family connection, I continued the search.

Finally, on January 5, 2012, the vital piece of the puzzle came: His name was Malcolm MacNiven. He was born about 1715 on Islay. He fathered four sons: Daniel, Duncan, Archibald, and Neil. Malcolm's son Daniel emigrated to the United States in 1765, settling in New York State. Duncan's son Daniel—Malcolm's grandson—emigrated in 1791 and also settled in New York; he dropped the "Mac" from his surname. Archibald's son Duncan—Malcolm's grandson—emigrated in 1819, settling in North Carolina. Isabella Thornton Niven Wilder and her children are descendants of Malcolm's son Duncan. My Niven family and I are descendants of Malcolm's son Archibald, brother of Duncan. To our surprise, Tappan Wilder, Catharine "Dixie" Wilder Guiles, and I now know that we share this grandfather many generations back. In a salute to Malcolm MacNiven of Islay, I am tempted to believe that perhaps it was destiny that led me to write this book—or as Malcolm might have called it in Scottish Gaelic, *Cinneamhainn*.

In the years since I began exploring Thornton Wilder's life and work, many people dear to me have died. As I think of them I remember the words Wilder gave to the poet Catullus in *The Ides of March*: "Love *is* its own eternity. Love is in every moment of its being: all time. It is the only glimpse we are permitted of what eternity is." I have worked in loving memory of Olin and Eleanor Marsh Hearon Niven, my parents, and of family members Dr. Harry Y. Gamble, Sr., Jack Fain McJunkin, Jr., Richard Knapp, Philip Clark, Charles Kelly, Charles McGee, and William McLaughlin. Finally, I pay special memorial tribute to Amos Todd Wilder.

PERMISSIONS

The author and the publisher acknowledge with appreciation the following individuals and institutions that granted permission and consent for the use, quotation, and citation of sources in this biography:

The published and unpublished writings of Janet Wilder Dakin are published by consent of the Wilder Family LLC c/o The Barbara Hogenson Agency.

The published and unpublished writings of Amos Niven Wilder are published by consent of the Wilder Family LLC c/o The Barbara Hogenson Agency.

The published and unpublished writings of Amos Parker Wilder are published by consent of the Wilder Family LLC c/o The Barbara Hogenson Agency.

The published and unpublished writings of Catharine Kerlin Wilder are published by consent of the Wilder Family LLC c/o The Barbara Hogenson Agency.

The published and unpublished writings of Charlotte Elizabeth Wilder are published by consent of the Wilder Family LLC c/o The Barbara Hogenson Agency.

The published and unpublished writings of Isabel Wilder are published by consent of the Wilder Family LLC c/o The Barbara Hogenson Agency.

The published and unpublished writings of Isabella Thornton Niven Wilder are published by consent of the Wilder Family LLC c/o The Barbara Hogenson Agency.

The published and unpublished writings of Thornton Niven Wilder are published by consent of the Wilder Family LLC c/o The Barbara Hogenson Agency. Copyright information for Wilder's published works may be found in the Guide to Notes and Sources.

F. Scott Fitzgerald's letter to Thornton Wilder is published by permission of Harold Ober Associates Incorporated.

Zelda Fitzgerald's letter to Thornton Wilder is published by permission of Harold Ober Associates Incorporated.

Access to the correspondence of Dr. Guelfo Frulla and Thornton and Isabel Wilder was kindly provided by Dr. Tommaso Munari, along with his permission to quote and/or cite Dr. Frulla's letters.

Excerpts from the writings and interviews of Samuel Steward are reprinted by permission of Michael Williams, executor, Samuel Steward Estate.

Excerpts from "A Very Magical Life: Talking with Samuel Steward," Owen Keehnen's 1993 interview with Samuel Steward, are reprinted by permission of Owen Keehnen.

Excerpts from the writings of Gene Tunney and Jay Tunney are reprinted by permission of the Estate of Gene Tunney.

Excerpts from *The Selected Letters of Thornton Wilder* (New York: HarperCollins, 2008) are reprinted with permission of Robin G. Wilder and Jackson R. Bryer, editors, and the Wilder Family LLC c/o The Barbara Hogenson Agency.

For the courtesy of access to Thornton Wilder's letters to Alexander Woollcott in the Houghton Library, Harvard University, the author appreciates the assistance of Heather Cole, assistant curator of Modern Books & Manuscripts.

For the courtesy of access to and use of letters by Thornton Niven Wilder and Wilder family members, the author gratefully acknowledges the Yale Collection of American Literature, Beinecke Rare Book and Manuscript Library, Yale University, and the kind assistance of Dr. Louise Bernard, curator of Prose and Drama, curator of American Literature. Appreciation is also extended for the courtesy of access to and use of the collections of Mabel Dodge Luhan, Gertrude Stein and Alice B. Toklas, Glenway Wescott, and Edmund Wilson in the Yale Collection of American Literature at the Beinecke Library; William Nichols at the Library of Congress; and Robert Hutchins at the University of Chicago Library. Permission to quote from Wilder's letters and papers has in all instances, including four unpublished letters to Sibyl Colefax, been granted by the Wilder Family LLC c/o The Barbara Hogenson Agency.

Unless otherwise noted, the photographs of Thornton Wilder and the Wilder family, as well as of Thornton Wilder's manuscript, are published with the consent of the Wilder Family LLC, and with the courtesy of the Yale Collection of American Literature, Beinecke Rare Book and Manuscript Library.

Invaluable assistance in clearing permissions was provided by Hugh Van Dusen of HarperCollins, especially his guidance in the matter of fair use; Peter London of the Permissions Department at HarperCollins; Maya Ziv of HarperCollins; Tappan Wilder; and Barbara Hogenson and Lori Styler of The Barbara Hogenson Agency, on behalf of the Wilder Family LLC.

INDEX

Note: TNW refers to Thornton Niven Wilder. ANW refers to Amos Niven Wilder (brother). APW refers to Amos Parker Wilder (father).